סדר התפלות

FORMS OF PRAYER

FOR

JEWISH WORSHIP

EDITED BY
THE ASSEMBLY OF RABBIS
OF THE REFORM SYNAGOGUES
OF GREAT BRITAIN

I

DAILY, SABBATH, AND
OCCASIONAL PRAYERS

SEVENTH EDITION
5737–1977
תשל״ז

THE REFORM SYNAGOGUES OF
GREAT BRITAIN

Published by
The Reform Synagogues of Great Britain
The Manor House
80 East End Road
Finchley, London N3 2SY

© *Copyright 1977*
Reform Synagogues of Great Britain
Reprinted 1990

ISBN 0 9505920 0 5 *cloth bound*
ISBN 0 9505920 1 3 *leather bound*

Printed in Great Britain by
Richard Clay Ltd, Bungay, Suffolk

TABLE OF CONTENTS

PREFACE

SINCE the sixth edition of the Daily and Sabbath Prayer Book in 1930 two generations have lived through both history-shattering and history-making periods in Jewish existence. We are still the same people: the descendants of Abraham whose response to God's call, 'Here am I!', remains our response. We are heirs of the family of Israel who left Egypt in haste and stood at the foothills of Sinai, who listened to the prophets and wept in Babylon. We are among the disciples of the rabbis of the Talmud and the poetry and philosophy of the middle ages form part of our spiritual treasury. Our forebears lived and worked, studied and prayed in *Sepharad* and *Ashkenaz*; they built Golden Ages and marched along the roads of expulsions, they knew prosperity and pogrom. They greeted the dawn of the modern era with hope and instituted reforms in Judaism to keep the Jew in harmony with God and with the highest social ideals of the wider society. We are still the same people.

We are also not the same people and the Prayer Book reflects our experience and our aspirations. We are living under the still impenetrable cloud of the holocaust and in the century of the refugee. We have witnessed the rebirth of a sovereign State of Israel and the spiritual horizons of Zion fill us with high expectations. We have the feeling that our generation is participating in the shaping of Jewish destiny itself. The pace is swift and the responsibilities very great.

In the pages of this Prayer Book we affirm our faith in God, the creator of a universe whose vastness and complexity is continually revealed to us and who guides the destiny of His creation. We affirm our unity with the family of Israel and our sense of kinship with all mankind. We pray for peace and harmony among all people and nations and seek that vision and inspiration which can make us conscious partners of God in perfecting the building of His kingdom here on earth.

Our Prayer Book is no longer that of the West London Synagogue but is to serve the Reform Synagogues of Great Britain, happily a growing movement of like-minded congregations, and indeed

all such communities and individuals who may find its approach spiritually congenial. This volume goes out with the fervent hope and prayer that it will deepen the faith of our people, strengthen ties of affection and concern amongst us, and keep the spark of holiness alive in our synagogues, our homes, and ourselves.

HUGO GRYN
Chairman
Prayer Book Committee

Altneushul, Prague

INTRODUCTION

THE difference between the last edition of the Forms of Prayer in 1930 and the present one is a measure of the tragedies and triumphs of the years between, and of the religious needs which came from the terrifying changes. This version has tried to join the piety of the world which died in the holocaust to the spirit which has arisen from its ashes; to bring the fullness of Jewish tradition to our communities, and let the Voice that speaks in it sound loud and clear to our needs.

Since the destruction a greater religious responsibility has fallen on us, therefore this edition is richer than previous ones in new and old material. Sectarian labels in Judaism have been ignored, and whatever helps us to integrity and faithfulness has been sought. A great joy is experienced as a holy unity appears which underlies all the diversities of the Jewish world, and a Truth emerges so great that legalists and mystics, orthodox, conservative and progressives, pious and secular Jews alike witness to it. This quality and consistency testify to a revelation which has not ended, and progresses both in our history and in us.

Until recently piety flowed from the home to the synagogue. Today the reverse is often true. It is hoped that much in the Prayer Book after becoming familiar in the synagogue will return to the home with the worshipper. This is especially important with the songs, hymns and *zemirot* which are included for the first time. Just as the study passages deepen the devotion of the mind, so may these songs intensify the devotion of the heart.

By new prayers, and new use of old ones, we tried to bring the circumstances of modern life into the orbit of Jewish devotion. Their purpose is to strengthen us against the special dangers of our time, the secularism that is within us, the necessary but dangerous compromises we make, and the subtle but definite changes in the priorities and purposes of life today. The problems of the universe and our society have not been seen as external to us, but we have tried to find their roots within ourselves and our experience of the world.

We have also tried to bridge the gulf between past belief and present doubt by strengthening the old bond between prayer and

study and between synagogue and *shul*. The anthologies should help the worshipper not only in his synagogue but also in his private meditations and prayers, accompany him in his home as well as in his synagogue, and find a place in his bookcase and beside his bed, uniting his religious and his daily life.

A richness of tradition has been preferred to a simplified uniformity. Our movement is a broad one in which all who take part in the holy debate can find their religious home. This gives future generations as well as the present greater freedom. The turmoil has not yet settled, and who can foresee the paths and the needs of those who come after?

The Hebrew text shows the influence of the many rites and *minhagim* which have been used in our synagogues, reflecting the richness and variety of our traditions, and the diverse origins of our members. In the course of time Sephardi, Ashkenazi and other elements have come together. Traditional formulations have been retained wherever possible. Occasionally our modern understanding of them has been expressed by a freer translation rather than by a change in the original. It is a characteristic of such time-defeating statements that though their words are fixed their message deepens and develops. This has always been implicit in the growth of the Jewish liturgy.

The translation is in the English of our time because of its directness and lucidity. Our first loyalty has been to the message of the original, and that aspect of it which is most relevant to our lives. Occasionally it has been necessary to depart from a misleading literalism especially as many words in English express one in Hebrew. Roughnesses in the original have occasionally been matched by roughnesses in the translation. We have tried to keep the connection between the Hebrew and the English while trying to avoid the danger of pedantry. Other modern translations have been used and consulted freely. We have kept in mind the primacy of the Masoretic text and traditional interpretations, but the form and choice have been guided by the liturgical use.

This book is one stage in a complete revision of the liturgy in use in our synagogues. It is hoped that other volumes will follow, including a handbook and a guide. Alone of all the holy books of the Jewish people the Prayer Book can change and grow. It is therefore our most sensitive and faithful companion and in our time the only

religious book which comes into the hands of every Jew. On it rests the burden and the hope of our survival and purpose. May it come to life in the prayers and deeds of those who use it.

LIONEL BLUE
JONATHAN MAGONET

The Prayer Book Committee of the Assembly of Rabbis consisted of Rabbis Lionel Blue, Michael Goulston ל״ז, L. G. Graf, Hugo Gryn, Arthur Katz, Michael Leigh and Jonathan Magonet. Until his retirement Rabbi W. Van der Zyl served as its chairman and much of the early work was co-ordinated by the Revd. Stanley Solomons ל״ז. The translations into Hebrew were made by Rabbi N. Ginsbury, Dr. Ellen Littmann ל״ז and Naomi Nimrod. The preliminary work on the glossary was done by Rabbi J. Newman. The manuscript was prepared by Rabbis Michael Boyden and Michael Heilbron assisted by Teresa Gribbon, C. R. Holman, Mary Kelly and Marrianne Vogel, and proof-read by Rabbi M. Marcus and the Revd. S. Pereira. The Committee wish to express their thanks to Joy Goldman for her assistance and to Robin Hyman and Anthony Rudolf for their technical advice, and to Raymond Goldman and the staff of the R.S.G.B. office for their administrative and secretarial help. Our thanks are also due to all the rabbis and congregations whose constructive suggestions and advice were most valuable and helpful, and to all those, too numerous to list, who gave their assistance at the various stages of production of this volume.

The Old Manchester Reform Synagogue

FROM THE INTRODUCTION TO
THE FIRST EDITION
1841

No monuments above the earth proclaim the once lauded greatness of Zion; catacombs usurp the place of cities once replete with glorious life, and solitary tombs alone speak to the antiquarian of the birth-place of those heaven-directed minds, by whose instrumentality the face of the whole moral world has been so wonderfully changed. Mount Zion, the pomp of whose temple inspired the beholder with reverence and awe, has been furrowed by the plough; and the words of the seer have long since been literally fulfilled, 'The mount Zion, the desolate, the jackal haunts it' (Lam. v. 18). But a monument there is, at once commemorative of the true glory and the astounding destinies of the 'house of Jacob'—a monument whose foundation is in our hearts, and whose summit penetrates into the heaven of heavens— a monument clear to the view of all mankind, and in whose shadow all the children of the earth shall find repose—it is the sacred volume of our Scriptures. Again then do the words of Jeremiah attest the truth of Him that spoke them, 'The jackal haunts the hill of Zion; but the Lord endureth for ever, and his throne throughout all generations' (ibid. v. 18, 19).

It being thus evident that time has exerted its influence on these prayers, it is but meet that the exigencies of the time should again be consulted, when we have arrived at the conviction that the house of prayer does not exercise that salutary influence over the minds and hearts of the congregants which it is intended and capable to exert. History bears us out in the assumption, that it becomes a congregation of Israelites to adapt the ritual to the wants of its members; and it must be universally admitted that the present mode of worship fails to call forth the devotion, so essential to the religious improvement of the people.

Two indispensable requisites of a petition with which man may approach his God, are, first,—That the prayer should be perfectly intelligible to the mind of the humble supplicant; and, secondly, That the sentiments which it expresses should be of a pure and elevating

character. In our collection we have, with all solicitude, retained only those portions of the common rituals in which these essentials are to be found. We have removed those parts of the service which are deficient in devotional tendency; and have expunged the few expressions which are known to be the offspring of feelings produced by oppression, and are universally admitted to be foreign to the heart of every true Israelite of our day.

The differences which formerly existed between the Portuguese and German Jewish congregations, and which caused them to consider each other as half aliens in religious matters, have happily, by the progress of liberal sentiments, been removed, in as far as they obstructed that brotherly feeling which the unity of our religious system requires; and the efforts of our newly established Congregation have been directed, we hope successfully, to the obliteration of every vestige of that useless and hurtful separation. We have discarded the names indicating a connection between us, natives of Great Britain professing the Jewish religion, and the countries from which our ancestors immigrated, and we have adopted for our place of worship the sufficiently explicit designation of 'West London Synagogue of British Jews.' In making this statement, it is expedient to notice that the term 'British Jews' has been chosen only with a view to efface the distinction now existing between the German and Portuguese Jews, and not in any way to constitute a new distinction, in a religious point of view, between the Jews of Great Britain and those of any other country.

Such then are the motives which have influenced the execution of the present task. And if, by promulgating this improved form of the Jewish Ritual, we contribute to the glorious end of endearing our holy institutions, and the pure fountain from which they flow, to the heart of every member of Israel; if, by the measures we have adopted after mature deliberation and with all the seriousness befitting our great cause, we become instrumental in attaching our rising generation to a mode of worship as impressive in its form as it is holy in its essence, we shall have ample cause for unbounded gratitude to our Heavenly Guide, for the glorification of whose name this work is wrought, and by whose omnipotent hand we humbly hope that it will be made to prosper for the peace, happiness, and salvation of Israel.

London, Ab, 5601—August, 1841.

MEDITATIONS BEFORE PRAYER

When you call Me and come and pray to Me, I will hear you. When you seek Me, you will find Me, if you search for Me with all your heart. I shall let you find Me, says the Lord.

Jeremiah 29: 12–14

PREPARATION FOR PRAYER

A man must purify his heart before he prays.

Exodus Rabbah

None may stand up to say the *Tefillah* (the statutory prayer, the *Amidah*) save in a sober mood. The pious men of old used to wait an hour before they said the *Tefillah*, that they might direct their heart toward God.

Mishnah

Our Rabbis taught: one should not stand up to say the *Tefillah* while immersed in sorrow, or idleness, or laughter, or frivolity, or chatter, or idle talk, but only while rejoicing in the performance of some religious act.

Berachot

R. Meir said: A man's words should always be few towards God. 'Be not rash with your mouth and let not your heart be hasty to utter a word before God; for God is in heaven, and you upon earth; therefore let your words be few. For a dream comes through a multitude of business; and a fool's voice through a multitude of words' (*Ecclesiastes 5: 1–2*).

Berachot

When you cannot pray with the proper concentration, try your utmost to speak the words in a spirit of belief in their truth.

Nachman of Bratzlav

The Tzanzer was asked by a Chasid: 'What does the Rabbi do before praying?' 'I pray,' was the reply, 'that I may be able to pray properly.'

Chasidic

When you pray do not make your prayer a fixed formal thing, but an appeal for mercy, a supplication before God.

Sayings of the Fathers

He who is about to pray should learn from a common labourer, who sometimes takes a whole day to prepare for a job. A wood-cutter, who spends most of the day sharpening the saw and only the last hour cutting the wood, has earned his day's wage.

Mendel of Kotzk

Forget everybody and everything during your worship. Forget yourself and your needs. Forget the people of whom you have need. Then in truth you may worship the Lord.

When you offer prayer, imagine yourself as one who is newly born; without achievements of which to be proud; without high family descent to make you arrogant. Forget all dignity and self-esteem. Remember only your maker.

Before the prayers, remember any good qualities you have, or any good deeds which you have performed. This will put life into you and enable you to pray from the heart.

Nachman of Bratzlav

Let everyone cry out to God and lift his heart up to Him, as if he were hanging by a hair, and a tempest were raging to the very heart of heaven, and he were at a loss for what to do, and there were hardly time to cry out. It is a time when no counsel, indeed, can help a man and he has no refuge save to remain in his loneliness and lift his eyes and his heart up to God, and cry out to Him. And this should be done at all times, for in the world a man is in great danger.

Chasidic

THE NATURE OF PRAYER

He prays for the sake of his soul as he takes food for the sake of his body.

Judah Halevi

However, it is essential that you know how to be careful when you make supplication for man's needs. God forbid that your intention should be for the gratification of your own desires, for this is self-worship, of which God has no desire, indeed it is abhorrent in His eyes . . . Therefore, when a man asks of God his material needs, such as health, riches, peace, and other material perfections, his intention should be that these will help him to serve his Creator, seeing that a man cannot properly serve God if he lacks the material goods of life, which are God-given aids for the aim he really desires—the improvement of the soul.

Jacob Emden

As the flame clothes the black, sooty clod in a garment of fire, and releases the heat imprisoned therein, even so does prayer clothe a man in a garment of holiness, evoke the light and fire implanted within him by his Maker, illumine his whole being, and unify the Lower and the Higher Worlds.

Zohar

The aim of our worship is the purification, enlightenment and uplifting of our inner selves . . . Its aim is not simply to stir up the emotions, or to produce fleeting moments of devotion, empty sentimentalism and idle tears, but the cleansing of heart and mind. Life robs us of the correct judgment concerning God, the world, man, and Israel, and concerning our own relationship to them all. Leaving the disturbing influences of life, and turning to God, you can find it again through the contemplation that is part of *tefillah* . . . Contemplate afresh our prayers, our divine service as a whole, and see if you do not find it more dignified, meaningful and important than you had ever before imagined.

Samson Raphael Hirsch

What then is devotion? One must free his heart from all other thoughts and regard himself as standing in the presence of God. Therefore, before engaging in prayer, a man ought to go aside for a little in order to bring himself into a devotional attitude, and then he should pray quietly and with feeling, not like one who carries a weight and goes away. Then after prayer the worshipper ought to sit quiet for a little and then depart.

Maimonides

Prayer is a brazen act. For it is impossible to stand before God, blessed be He, but brazenly. Every man imagines—in one way or another—the greatness of the Creator: How then can one stand in prayer before Him? For prayer is a wonder; (its task is) chiefly the assault upon, and the despoiling of, the heavenly order . . . Man comes wishing to despoil the order and do marvels. Therefore man must be shameless in prayer.

Nachman of Bratzlav

Not all tears come before the King. Sullen tears, and tears accompanying the petition for vengeance do not ascend on high. But tears of entreaty and penitence, and tears beseeching relief, cleave the very heavens, open the portals and ascend to the King of kings.

Zohar

Prayer is our humble answer to the inconceivable surprise of living.

Abraham Joshua Heschel

We must bear in mind that all such religious acts as reading the *Torah*, praying, and the performance of other precepts, serve exclusively as the means of causing us to occupy and fill our minds with the precepts of God, and free it from worldly business; for we are thus, as it were, in communication with God, and undisturbed by any other thing. If we, however, pray with the motion of our lips, and our face toward the wall, but at the same time think of our business; if we read with our tongue, whilst our heart is occupied with the building of our house, and we do not think of what we are reading; if we perform the commandments only with our limbs, we are like those who are engaged in digging in the ground, or hewing wood in the forest, without reflecting on the nature of these acts, or by whom they are commanded, or what is their object. We must not imagine that in this way we attain the highest perfection; on the contrary, we are then like those in reference to whom Scripture says 'Thou art near in their mouth, and far from their inner life' (*Jeremiah 12: 2*).

Maimonides

To serve the Lord your God with all your heart (*Deuteronomy 11: 13*). What is a service with the heart? It is prayer.

Sifre

We do not even know how we are supposed to pray. All we do is call for help because of the need of the moment. But what the soul intends is spiritual need, only we are not able to express what the soul means. That is why we do not merely ask God to hear our call for help, but also beg Him who knows what is hidden, to hear the silent cry of the soul.

Chasidic

So long as the world moves along accustomed paths, so long as there are no wild catastrophes, man can find sufficient substance for his life by contemplating surface events, theories and movements of society. He can acquire his inner richnesses from this external kind of 'property'. But this is not the case when life encounters fiery forces of evil and chaos. Then the 'revealed' world begins to totter. Then the man who tries to sustain himself only from the surface aspects of

existence will suffer terrible impoverishment, begin to stagger . . .
then he will feel welling up within himself a burning thirst for that
inner substance and vision which transcends the obvious surfaces of
existence and remains unaffected by the world's catastrophes. From
such inner sources he will seek the waters of joy which can quicken
the dry outer skeleton of existence.

Rav Kook

'You are My witnesses,' the Eternal says, 'and I am God.' Rabbi
Simeon ben Yochai said: 'If you give witness unto Me, then I am the
Eternal. If you are not My witnesses, then I am not the Eternal, as it
were.'

Pesikta d'Rav Kahana

THE PRAYER OF THE COMMUNITY

What are our places of prayer . . . but schools of prudence,
courage, temperance and justice, of piety, holiness and virtue?

Philo

R. Jose ben Chalafta taught: There are proper times for prayer, as
it says: 'As for me, let my prayer come before You at the proper
time' (*Psalm 69: 14*). What is a 'proper time'? When the community
is at prayer.

Tanchuma

Community prayer is preferable for many reasons. Firstly, the
community does not pray for what is hurtful to an individual, whilst
the individual sometimes prays for something to the hurt of other
individuals, and these pray for something that hurts him; a prayer,
however, can be heard only if its object is profitable to the world and
in no ways hurtful.

An individual rarely accomplishes his prayer without digression
of mind and negligence; we are therefore commanded that the individual recite the prayers of a community, and if possible in a community of not less than ten persons, so that one makes up for the
digression or negligence of the other, in order that a perfect prayer,
recited with unalloyed devotion, may be made, and its blessing
bestowed on the community, each individual receiving his portion.

Judah Halevi

Rav said: Whoever has it in his power to pray on behalf of his
neighbour, and fails to do so, is called a sinner.

Berachot

The Baal Shem Tov once refused to enter a certain synagogue because he said it was too full of prayer. Noting his followers' astonishment at his attitude, he explained that so many routine insincere prayers were uttered there that they could not rise to the heavenly throne and stayed on earth, cramming the synagogue full.

Baal Shem Tov

Feel the tribulations of the individual and of the multitude, and implore God to ease their burden.

Nachman of Bratzlav

If a man is accustomed to attend synagogue and one day he does not go, the Holy One, blessed be He, makes enquiry about him.

Berachot

SOME INDIVIDUAL PRAYERS

And if I say: 'I will not make mention of Him, nor speak any more in His name,' then there is in my heart as it were a burning fire, shut up in my bones, and I weary myself to hold it in, but cannot.

Jeremiah 20: 9

I gave orders for my horse to be brought round from the stable. The servant did not understand me. I myself went to the stable, saddled my horse and mounted. In the distance I heard a bugle call, I asked him what this meant. He knew nothing and had heard nothing. At the gate he stopped me, asking: 'Where are you riding to, master?' 'I don't know,' I said, 'only away from here, away from here. Always away from here, only by doing so can I reach my destination.' 'And so you know your destination?' he asked. 'Yes,' I answered, 'didn't I say so? Away-From-Here, that is my destination.' 'You have no provisions with you,' he said. 'I need none,' I said, 'the journey is so long that I must die of hunger if I don't get anything on the way. No provisions can save me. For it is, fortunately, a truly immense journey.'

Franz Kafka

Inscription on the walls of a cellar in Cologne, Germany, where Jews hid from the Nazis:

I believe in the sun even when it is not shining.
I believe in love even when feeling it not.
I believe in God even when He is silent.

I pray to You O Lord
From all my heart,
O Lord! I pray to You
With fervour and zeal,
For the sufferings of the humiliated,
For the uncertainty of those who wait;
For the non-return of the dead;
For the helplessness of the dying;
For the sadness of the misunderstood,
For those who request in vain;
For all those abused, scorned and disdained;
For the silly, the wicked, the miserable;
For those who hurry in pain
To the nearest physician;
Those who return from work
With trembling and anguished hearts to their homes;
For those who are roughly treated and pushed aside,
For those who are hissed on the stage;
For all who are clumsy, ugly, tiresome and dull,
For the weak, the beaten, the oppressed,
For those who cannot find rest
During long sleepless nights;
For those who are afraid of Death,
For those who wait in pharmacies;
For those who have missed the train;
—For all the inhabitants of our earth
And all their pains and troubles,
Their worries, sufferings, disappointments,
All their griefs, afflictions, sorrows,
Longings, failures, defeats;
For everything which is not joy,
Comfort, happiness, bliss . . .
Let these shine for ever upon them
With tender love and brightness,
I pray to You O Lord most fervently—
I pray to You O Lord from the depths of my heart.

Juljan Tuwim

The prayer of a shepherd who 'did not know how to pray':

Lord of the Universe! It is apparent and known unto You, that if You had cattle and gave them to me to tend, though I take wages for tending from all others, from You I would take nothing, because I love You.

Sefer Chasidim

A favourite saying of the Rabbis of Yavneh was:

I am God's creature and my fellow is God's creature.
My work is in the town and his work is in the country.
I rise early for my work and he rises early for his work.
Just as he does not presume to do my work, so I do not
    presume to do his work.
Will you say, I do much and he does little?
We have learnt: One may do much or one may do little;
It is all one, provided he directs his heart to heaven.

Berachot

Lord, where shall I find You?
High and hidden is Your place.
And where shall I not find You?
The world is full of Your glory.

I have sought Your nearness,
With all my heart I called You
and going out to meet You
I found You coming to meet me.

Judah Halevi

Blessed are You Lord, my God, spirit of the universe, who brought me across the (Yabok) bridge of life. When the dim light of my own self will sink and merge within the light which illumines the world and eternity, I shall conclude the order of my days.

In this twilight glow of my life, I stand before the dawn of my new sun with tense consciousness, a man about to die and to live, who feels at one with the universe and eternity, as in the ancient words: 'Hear, Israel, the Lord our God, the Lord is One.' Blessed is the God of life and death, of light and love.

Nachman Syrkin

Lord of the universe, You are doing much to make me desert my faith, but I assure You that, even against the will of the dwellers in heaven, a Jew I am and a Jew I shall remain, and neither the

sufferings that You have brought upon me nor that which You will
yet bring upon me will be of any avail.

Solomon Ibn Verga

God on high, divine King, enlighten my soul at all times. Give me,
God, true faith, and perfect humility against the world's vanities.
Do not give me riches, God, that may make me proud; nor poverty,
that may deject me. Give me, God, some help that I may serve You,
and life that I may praise You and death that I may find salvation.

Marrano

When all within is dark,
and former friends misprise;
From them I turn to You,
and find love in Your eyes.

When all within is dark,
and I my soul despise;
From me I turn to You,
And find love in Your eyes.

When all Your face is dark,
and Your just angers rise;
From You I turn to You,
And find love in Your eyes.

Israel Abrahams based on Ibn Gabirol

Where I wander—You!
Where I ponder—You!
Only You, You again, always You!
You! You! You!
When I am gladdened—You!
When I am saddened—You!
Only You, You again, always You!
You! You! You!
Sky is You, earth is You!
You above! You below!
In every trend, at every end,
Only You, You again, always You!
You! You! You!

Levi Yitzchak of Berditchev

Good morning, to You, Almighty God,
I, Levi Yitzchak son of Sarah of Berditchev,
Have come for a judgment against You,
On behalf of Your people Israel.
What do You want of Your people Israel?
Why do You afflict Your people Israel?
The slightest thing and You say,
    'Speak to the children of Israel,'
The slightest thing and You turn to the children of Israel,
The slightest thing and You say,
    'Tell the children of Israel.'
Our father! There are so many nations in the world,
Persians, Babylonians, Edomites.
The Russians, what do they say?
That their Emperor is the Emperor.
The Germans, what do they say?
That their Empire is the Empire.
And the English, what do they say?
That their Empire is the Empire.
And I, Levi Yitzchak son of Sarah of Berditchev, say,
'From this spot I shall not stir,
I shall not stir from this spot,
There must be an end of this,
The exile must end!
Magnified and sanctified be His great name!'

Levi Yitzchak of Berditchev

The needs of Your people Israel are many, but their knowledge
is small. May it be Your will, Lord our God and God of our fathers,
to give to every creature what it needs and to every body what it lacks.
Blessed is the Lord, for You heard the voice of my supplication.
Blessed are You Lord, who hears prayer.

Yerushalmi

May it be Your will, O Lord, that no man foster hatred against us
in his heart, and that we foster no hatred in our hearts against any
man; that no man foster envy of us in his heart, and that we foster
no envy in our hearts of any man.

Talmud

Your eternal providence has appointed me to watch over the life and health of Your creatures. May the love for my art actuate me at all times; may neither avarice nor miserliness, nor the thirst for glory or for a great reputation engage my mind, for the enemies of truth and philanthropy could easily deceive me and make me forgetful of my lofty aim of doing good to Your children. May I never see in a patient anything but a fellow creature in pain. Grant me strength, time and opportunity always to correct what I have acquired, always to extend its domain, for knowledge is immense and the spirit of man can extend indefinitely to enrich itself daily with new requirements.

Today he can discover his errors of yesterday and tomorrow he may obtain new light on what he thinks himself sure of today.

O God, You have appointed me to watch over the life and death of Your creatures. Here I am, ready for my vocation.

Maimonides (The Medical Oath)

Lord, let Your light be only for the day,
And the darkness for the night.
And let my dress, my poor humble dress
Lie quietly over my chair at night.

Let the church-bells be silent,
My neighbour Ivan not ring them at night.
Let the wind not waken the children
Out of their sleep at night.

Let the hen sleep on its roost, the horse in the stable
All through the night.
Remove the stone from the middle of the road
That the thief may not stumble at night.

Let heaven be quiet during the night.
Restrain the lightning, silence the thunder,
They should not frighten mothers giving birth
To their babies at night.

And me too protect against fire and water,
Protect my poor roof at night.
Let my dress, my poor humble dress
Lie quietly over my chair at night.

Nachum Bomze

My Lord and God, I do not desire Your paradise; I do not desire the bliss of the world to come; I desire only You Yourself.

Shneur Zalman of Ladi

When I travel in my coach to teach Torah, give me thought for the mare that carries me, and guard her from my impatience; when I walk through Your woods, may my right foot and my left foot be harmless to the little creatures that move in the grasses; as it is said by the mouth of Your prophet, They shall not hurt nor destroy in all My holy mountain. Amen.

Rabbi Moshe Hakotun

You were my death;
You I could hold
when all fell away from me.

Paul Celan

And yet I pray, for I do not desire to lose the blessed feeling of unity, of communication with You.

Arnold Schoenberg

I do not beg You to reveal to me the secret of Your ways—I could not bear it. But show me one thing; show it to me more clearly and more deeply: show me what this, which is happening at this very moment, means to me, what it demands of me, what You, Lord of the world, are telling me by way of it. Ah, it is not why I suffer, that I wish to know, but only whether I suffer for Your sake.

Levi Yitzchak of Berditchev

Anyway, can I pretend I have much choice? I look at myself and see chest, thighs, feet—a head. This strange organization, I know it will die. And inside—something, something, happiness . . . 'Thou movest me.' That leaves no choice. Something produces intensity, a holy feeling, as oranges produce orange, as grass green, as birds heat. Some hearts put out more love and some less of it, presumably. Does it signify anything? There are those who say this product of hearts is knowledge . . . I couldn't say that, for sure. My face too blind, my mind too limited, my instincts too narrow. But this intensity, doesn't it mean anything? Is it an idiot joy that makes this animal, the most peculiar animal of all, exclaim something? And he thinks this reaction a sign, a proof, of eternity? And he has it in his breast? But I have no arguments to make about it. 'Thou movest me.' 'But what do you want . . .?' 'But that's just it—not a solitary thing. I am pretty well satisfied to be, to be just as it is willed, and for as long as I may remain in occupancy.'

Saul Bellow

West London Synagogue, 1870

תפלת ערבית לשבת

מַה־טֹּבוּ אֹהָלֶיךָ יַעֲקֹב מִשְׁכְּנֹתֶיךָ יִשְׂרָאֵל:
וַאֲנִי בְּרֹב חַסְדְּךָ אָבוֹא בֵיתֶךָ
אֶשְׁתַּחֲוֶה אֶל־הֵיכַל־קָדְשְׁךָ בְּיִרְאָתֶךָ:
יְהֹוָה אָהַבְתִּי מְעוֹן בֵּיתֶךָ וּמְקוֹם מִשְׁכַּן כְּבוֹדֶךָ:
וַאֲנִי אֶשְׁתַּחֲוֶה וְאֶכְרָעָה אֶבְרְכָה לִפְנֵי־יְהֹוָה עֹשִׂי:
וַאֲנִי תְפִלָּתִי־לְךָ יְהֹוָה עֵת רָצוֹן
אֱלֹהִים בְּרָב־חַסְדֶּךָ עֲנֵנִי בֶּאֱמֶת יִשְׁעֶךָ:

I   אֱלֹהֵינוּ וֵאלֹהֵי־אֲבוֹתֵינוּ כֻּלָּנוּ יִשְׂרָאֵל · בַּעֲבוֹדָתְךָ הִתְנַסָּה
לִבֵּנוּ כְּלֵב־יְשִׁישִׁים וְנִתְחַדֵּשׁ חֶזְיוֹנֵנוּ כְּחֶזְיוֹן־עֲלוּמִים וְכֵן
הוּא תּוֹךְ־תּוֹכֵי־נַפְשֵׁנוּ · בְּיוֹם־שַׁבָּת זֶה אֵלֶיךָ נִפְנֶה בְּעֵינַיִם
מְיֻחָלוֹת בְּהִתְנַעֲרוּת תִּקְוָתֵנוּ מִקְּלִיפּוֹת הַדְּאָגָה וְהַסָּפֵק
שֶׁסּוֹבְבוּ אֶת־לְבָבֵנוּ:
כֻּלָּנוּ יִשְׂרָאֵל בְּרוּאִים בִּבְרִית־שְׁבוּעָתְךָ· גְּדֵלִים בְּבִרְכָתְךָ·
שְׂבֵעֵי־רָצוֹן בַּעֲבוֹדָתְךָ· נוֹפְשִׁים בְּשַׁבַּת־אַהֲבָתֶךָ:
כֻּלָּנוּ יִשְׂרָאֵל קְדוֹשִׁים בְּאִמְרָתְךָ· מְחֻכָּמִים בְּתוֹרָתְךָ·
מְצֻדָּקִים בְּמִצְוֹתֶיךָ· מְחֻדָּשִׁים בְּשַׁבַּת־מְנוּחָתֶךָ:
בְּיוֹם־שַׁבָּת זֶה שְׁמַרְנוּ· בְּיוֹם־שַׁבָּת זֶה זָכַרְנוּ· וּלְקַדְּשׁוֹ
שָׁמוֹר וְזָכוֹר כְּאֶחָד נָקַיֵּם· אָמֵן:

II   רִבּוֹן־הָרַחֲמִים וּמְקוֹר־הַבְּרָכוֹת· שְׁעֵה־נָא לִתְפִלּוֹתֵינוּ
בְּלֵיל־שַׁבָּת זֶה: עֹנֶג־הַשַּׁבָּת בָּא לְאַחַר שֵׁשֶׁת־יְמֵי־הַמַּעֲשֶׂה
וְלִבּוֹתֵינוּ הַמְטֹרָדִים מַגִּיעִים אֶל־שַׁלְוָתָם וְאֶל־מְנוּחָתָם:
בִּתְפִלּוֹת וּבְהוֹדָיוֹת נְבַקֵּשְׁךָ לְקַדֵּשׁ עָלֵינוּ אֶת־הַיּוֹם הַזֶּה:
מְחֵה פְּשָׁעֵינוּ בְּרַחֲמֶיךָ וְחַזֵּק מַעֲשֵׂינוּ לְטוֹבָה: טַהֵר לִבֵּנוּ
מֵהָאַנְכִיּוּת וְתֵן בְּלִבֵּנוּ לִשְׁאוֹף לַיָּפֶה וְלָאֱמֶת: הָאֵר אֶת־הַחֹשֶׁךְ
הַשָּׁרוּי בְּתוֹכֵנוּ וּבָרֵךְ אֶת־בָּתֵּינוּ וְאֶת־כָּל־אוֹהֲבֵינוּ: אָז נִבְטַח
בְּעֶזְרָתְךָ וְנִשְׁמוֹר בְּרִיתְךָ לְעוֹלָם:

SABBATH EVENING SERVICE

How good are your tents, O Jacob, and your homes, O Israel. Through the greatness of Your love I enter Your house. In awe I worship before the ark of Your holiness.

Lord, as I loved the courts of Your temple, and the place where Your glory dwelt, so I still worship and bend low, humble before the Lord my maker.

As for me, let my prayer come before You at the proper time. Answer me God, in the greatness of Your love, for Your deliverance is sure.

I   Our God and God of our fathers, we are all Israel; in Your service we have become old in experience and young in hope. We carry both in the deepest places of our hearts and minds. On this Sabbath day we turn to You with eyes newly open, with hope re-awakened, shrugging off the layers of worry and doubt that have closed about us.

We are all Israel, created by Your promise, raised in Your blessing, fulfilled by Your task, refreshed by the Sabbath of Your love.

We are all Israel, holy by Your word, wise through Your Torah, righteous through Your commands, renewed by the Sabbath of Your rest.

On this Sabbath day keep us; on this Sabbath day remember us; as we keep and remember the Sabbath day, to make it holy. Amen.

II   Creator of mercy and of blessings, be present in our prayers this Sabbath eve. Sabbath joy follows the working week, and our troubled minds find their comfort and rest. With prayers and thanks we turn to You to make this day holy. Wipe away our sins in Your mercy, and strengthen our work for good. Cleanse us from selfishness, and give us new longing for all that is good and true. Enlighten the darkness that lies within us, and bring a blessing to our homes and to those we love. So may we keep Your covenant forever, for Your help is sure.

לֹא עָלֵינוּ לְבַד תָּבוֹא בְּרִכַּת־שַׁבָּת זוֹ כִּי־אִם עַל־כָּל־
בְּרוּאֵי־עוֹלָם כִּי בְּנָתְנֶנוּ יִשְׁבַּע רְצוֹנֶנוּ בְּשָׁרְתֵנוּ נִשְׁתַּחְרֵר
חֵרוּת־אֱמֶת. וּבְבָרְכֵנוּ אֲחֵרִים נִתְבָּרֵךְ. בָּנוּ תִּתְקַיֵּם אִמְרָתְךָ
וְנִבְרְכוּ בְךָ כָּל־מִשְׁפְּחוֹת־הָאֲדָמָה. אָמֵן:

III רִבּוֹן־כָּל־הַמַּעֲשִׂים הִמְשַׁלְתָּנוּ בְּעוֹלָמְךָ לְעָבְדוֹ לְשָׁמְרוֹ
וְלֵיהָנוֹת מִמֶּנּוּ. בְּשֵׁשֶׁת־יְמֵי־הַמַּעֲשֶׂה אָנוּ אוֹמְדִים וּבוֹנִים.
מְחַבְּרִים אֶת־חֶשְׁבּוֹן־עֲמָלֵנוּ הָאֲמִיתִי וְהַמְדֻמֶּה. מַעֲבִירִים
אֶת־יִתְרַת־הַצְלָחָתֵנוּ וְאֶת־מְחִירָה:
אַךְ בְּזֶה יוֹם־הַשַּׁבָּת הַמַּצִיא לָנוּ מְנוּחָה:
בְּשֵׁשֶׁת־יְמֵי־הַמַּעֲשֶׂה אִם אָנוּ יְגֵעִים אוֹ רְצוּצִים תַּחַת־נֵטֶל־
הַחַיִּים. אִם נִתְחַזֶּה כַּעֲנָקִים אוֹ נַכְאִיב לַאֲחֵרִים. אֵין לָנוּ רֶגַע
לְהַרְהֵר וְלֹא פְנַאי לְהַכִּיר בַּמֶּה שֶׁצְּרִיכִים אָנוּ לִהְיוֹת בֶּאֱמֶת:
אַךְ בְּזֶה יוֹם־הַשַּׁבָּת הַמַּצִיא לָנוּ הֲפוּגָה:
בְּשֵׁשֶׁת־יְמֵי־הַמַּעֲשֶׂה אָנוּ קְרוּעִים בֵּין־תַּאֲוָתֵנוּ אָנוּ וּבֵין־
צָרְכֵיהֶם הַדְּחוּפִים שֶׁל־אֲחֵרִים. בֵּין־הַטְּפִלוּת הַנִּשְׁמַעַת
בְּאָזְנֵינוּ וּבֵין־תְּפִלַּת־נַפְשֵׁנוּ שֶׁבִּדְמָמָה דַקָּה:
אַךְ בְּזֶה יוֹם־הַשַּׁבָּת הַמַּצִיא לָנוּ הֲבָנָה וְשָׁלוֹם:
עֲזֹר לָנוּ יְיָ לְהוֹסִיף לְקְחֵי־הַמְּנוּחָה וְהַהֲפוּגָה הַהֲבָנָה
וְהַשָּׁלוֹם לְשֵׁשֶׁת־יְמֵי־הַמַּעֲשֶׂה הַבָּאִים וּלְכָל־יְמֵי־מַעֲשֵׂה־
יָדֵינוּ לְמַעַן נִתְבָּרֵךְ בְּכָל־חַיֵּינוּ. אָמֵן:

IV בָּרוּךְ יְיָ הַכּוֹבֵשׁ מְרִיבָה. הַמַּעֲבִיר שִׂנְאָה וְהַמֵּבִיא אַחֲוָה
בְּמַעֲשֵׂה־בְרֵאשִׁית: בָּרוּךְ הָאֵל הַנִּגְלָם מֵעֵינֵינוּ הַמְקַשֵּׁר
כָּל־בְּרִיּוֹתָיו בְּקִשְׁרֵי־שֵׁרוּת וְאַהֲבָה: בָּרוּךְ שְׁמוֹ הַנִּכְבָּד
הַמַּסִירֵנוּ מִדַּרְכֵי־אַכְזְרִיּוּת וּמְלַמְּדֵנוּ דַּרְכֵי־חֲסִידוּת: בָּרוּךְ
הַמּוֹרֵינוּ צְנִיעוּת וְיִרְאַת־כָּבוֹד לְקָטֹן בִּקְטַנֵּי־הַבְּרוּאִים
לְפְנֵי־הוֹדוֹ נִשְׁתַּחֲוֶה: בָּרוּךְ מְקוֹר־הַשָּׁלוֹם. מְשֻׁבָּח וּמְפֹאָר
שְׁמוֹ. כִּי הַשָּׁלוֹם הוּא שַׁעַר לִשְׁלֵימוּתֵנוּ וְהִיא מְנוּחָתֵנוּ:

May the blessing of this Sabbath come not for ourselves alone but for all. For it is in giving that we find contentment, in serving that we find our true freedom, and in blessing others that we ourselves are blessed. Through us may the promise be fulfilled 'and all the families of the world shall bless themselves by You'. Amen.

III   Lord of all creation, You have made us the masters of Your world, to tend it, to serve it, and to enjoy it. For six days we measure and we build, we count and carry the real and the imagined burdens of our task, the success we earn and the price we pay.

On this, the Sabbath day, give us rest.

For six days, if we are weary or bruised by the world, if we think ourselves giants or cause others pain, there is never a moment to pause, and know what we should really be.

On this, the Sabbath day, give us time.

For six days we are torn between our private greed and the urgent needs of others, between the foolish noises in our ears and the silent prayer of our soul.

On this, the Sabbath day, give us understanding and peace.

Help us, Lord, to carry these lessons, of rest and time, of understanding and peace, into the six days that lie ahead, to bless us in the working days of our lives. Amen.

IV   We bless the Lord who conquers strife, who removes all hatred, and brings harmony to His creation. We praise the God we cannot see, who binds together all His creatures with unseen threads of service and of love. We honour the master who has brought us from ways of cruelty and shown us the ways of kindness. We bend low before the majesty which teaches us humility and respect for the smallest things in creation. We glorify the source of peace, for peace is the gate to our perfection, and in perfection is our rest.

יְיָ פְּקַח עֵינֵינוּ לְיִפִּי־הָעוֹלָם וּלְטוּבוֹ. נִהְיֶה־נָא מְפִיצֵי־
שְׁלוֹמְךָ הַמְקָרֵב כָּל־חָי. הָאֵם וּבָנֶיהָ בְּאַהֲבָתָם· יְדִידִים
בְּנֶאֱמָנוּתָם· אָדָם וּבַעֲלֵי־חַיִּים בְּחַבְרוּתָם. וְעַתָּה יְיָ אֱלֹהֵינוּ
בְּשַׁבַּת־מְנוּחָה זוֹ שׁוּב מַכִּירִים אָנוּ בִשְׁכִינָתְךָ הַשְּׁרוּיָה
בְּאַחֲוַת־הָעוֹלָם. בָּרוּךְ אַתָּה יְיָ שֶׁהַכֹּל מְשַׁבְּחִים וּמְיַחֲדִים
אֶת־שְׁמוֹ. אָמֵן.

I **יוֹם זֶה לְיִשְׂרָאֵל** אוֹרָה וְשִׂמְחָה. שַׁבַּת מְנוּחָה:

צִוִּיתָ פִּקּוּדִים בְּמַעֲמַד סִינַי. שַׁבָּת וּמוֹעֲדִים לִשְׁמֹר בְּכָל־
שָׁנַי. לַעֲרוֹךְ לְפָנַי מַשְׂאֵת וַאֲרוּחָה. שַׁבַּת מְנוּחָה:
יוֹם זֶה לְיִשְׂרָאֵל אוֹרָה וְשִׂמְחָה. שַׁבַּת מְנוּחָה:

חֶמְדַּת הַלְּבָבוֹת לְאֻמָּה שְׁבוּרָה. לִנְפָשׁוֹת נִכְאָבוֹת נְשָׁמָה
יְתֵרָה. לְנֶפֶשׁ מְצֵרָה יָסִיר אֲנָחָה. שַׁבַּת מְנוּחָה:
יוֹם זֶה לְיִשְׂרָאֵל אוֹרָה וְשִׂמְחָה. שַׁבַּת מְנוּחָה:

קִדַּשְׁתָּ בֵּרַכְתָּ אוֹתוֹ מִכָּל־יָמִים. בְּשֵׁשֶׁת כִּלִּיתָ מְלֶאכֶת
עוֹלָמִים. בּוֹ מָצְאוּ עֲגוּמִים הַשְׁקֵט וּבִטְחָה. שַׁבַּת מְנוּחָה:
יוֹם זֶה לְיִשְׂרָאֵל אוֹרָה וְשִׂמְחָה. שַׁבַּת מְנוּחָה:

II **יָהּ רִבּוֹן** עָלַם וְעָלְמַיָּא. אַנְתְּ הוּא מַלְכָּא מֶלֶךְ
מַלְכַיָּא:
עוֹבַד גְּבוּרְתֵּךְ וְתִמְהַיָּא. שַׁפִּיר קֳדָמָךְ לְהַחֲוָיָה:
יָהּ רִבּוֹן עָלַם וְעָלְמַיָּא. אַנְתְּ הוּא מַלְכָּא מֶלֶךְ מַלְכַיָּא:

Lord, open our eyes to the beauty of the world and its goodness. Let us be the servants of Your peace which brings all life together: the love of mother and child, the loyalty of friends, and the companionship of animal and man. On this Sabbath day of rest, we know this harmony again and Your presence in it. With all creation we reply in praise, and unify Your name. Amen.

SONGS FOR
THE
SABBATH

I   This day for Israel is light and is joy
a Sabbath of rest.

You commanded our fathers who stood at Mount Sinai
to keep Sabbath and seasons for all of our years,
to share at our table the choicest of foods,
a Sabbath of rest.
This day for Israel is light and is joy
a Sabbath of rest.

Treasure for the hearts of a wounded people,
for souls that have suffered, a soul that is new,
to soothe away sighs from a soul that is bound,
a Sabbath of rest.
This day for Israel is light and is joy
a Sabbath of rest.

You have made this the holy, most blessed of days.
In six days You finished the work of the worlds,
this day the saddest find safety and peace,
a Sabbath of rest.
This day for Israel is light and is joy
a Sabbath of rest.

Isaac Luria

II   God, Lord of the world, and timeless master,
You are King above all kings that men obey.
Many deeds of Your might, and Your wonders,
it delights You to display.
God, Lord of the world, and timeless master,
You are King above all kings that men obey.

שְׁבָחִין אֲסַדֵּר צַפְרָא וְרַמְשָׁא ׃ לָךְ אֱלָהָא קַדִּישָׁא דִּי בְרָא כָל־נַפְשָׁא ׃ עִירִין קַדִּישִׁין וּבְנֵי אֱנָשָׁא ׃ חֵיוַת בָּרָא וְעוֹפֵי שְׁמַיָּא ׃

יָהּ רִבּוֹן עָלַם וְעָלְמַיָּא ׃ אַנְתְּ הוּא מַלְכָּא מֶלֶךְ מַלְכַיָּא ׃

רַבְרְבִין עוֹבְדָיךְ וְתַקִּיפִין ׃ מָכֵךְ רָמַיָּא זַקֵּף כְּפִיפִין ׃ לוּ יְחֵא גְבַר שְׁנִין אַלְפִין ׃ לָא יֵעֹל גְּבוּרְתֵּךְ בְּחֻשְׁבְּנַיָּא ׃

יָהּ רִבּוֹן עָלַם וְעָלְמַיָּא ׃ אַנְתְּ הוּא מַלְכָּא מֶלֶךְ מַלְכַיָּא ׃

III **שָׁלוֹם עֲלֵיכֶם** מַלְאֲכֵי הַשָּׁרֵת מַלְאֲכֵי עֶלְיוֹן מֶלֶךְ מַלְכֵי הַמְּלָכִים הַקָּדוֹשׁ בָּרוּךְ הוּא ׃

בּוֹאֲכֶם לְשָׁלוֹם מַלְאֲכֵי הַשָּׁלוֹם מַלְאֲכֵי עֶלְיוֹן מֶלֶךְ מַלְכֵי הַמְּלָכִים הַקָּדוֹשׁ בָּרוּךְ הוּא ׃

בָּרְכוּנִי לְשָׁלוֹם מַלְאֲכֵי הַשָּׁלוֹם מַלְאֲכֵי עֶלְיוֹן מֶלֶךְ מַלְכֵי הַמְּלָכִים הַקָּדוֹשׁ בָּרוּךְ הוּא ׃

צֵאתְכֶם לְשָׁלוֹם מַלְאֲכֵי הַשָּׁלוֹם מַלְאֲכֵי עֶלְיוֹן מֶלֶךְ מַלְכֵי הַמְּלָכִים הַקָּדוֹשׁ בָּרוּךְ הוּא ׃

IV   הַחַמָּה מֵרֹאשׁ הָאִילָנוֹת נִסְתַּלְּקָה ׃
בֹּאוּ וְנֵצֵא לִקְרַאת שַׁבָּת הַמַּלְכָּה ׃
הִנֵּה הִיא יוֹרֶדֶת ׃ הַקְּדוֹשָׁה הַבְּרוּכָה ׃
וְעִמָּהּ מַלְאָכִים ׃ צְבָא שָׁלוֹם וּמְנוּחָה ׃
בֹּאִי ׃ בֹּאִי הַמַּלְכָּה ׃
בֹּאִי ׃ בֹּאִי הַכַּלָּה ׃
שָׁלוֹם עֲלֵיכֶם מַלְאֲכֵי הַשָּׁלוֹם ׃

My praise I bring You, morning and evening,
God who makes all of His creation live;
holy messengers, each human being,
beasts and birds their form You give.
   God, Lord of the world, and timeless master,
   You are King above all kings that men obey.

Numberless and powerful are Your actions.
The proud You teach humility, the weak You raise.
If a man's years would be a thousand
he could not express Your praise.
   God, Lord of the world, and timeless master,
   You are King above all kings that men obey.

Israel Najara

III   Peace and welcome to you, servants of the Lord, messengers of the Most High, of the King above the kings of kings, the Holy One, blessed be He.

Enter in peace you servants of peace, messengers of the Most High, of the King above the kings of kings, the Holy One, blessed be He.

Bless me with peace, you servants of peace, messengers of the Most High, of the King above the kings of kings, the Holy One, blessed be He.

Go forth in peace, you servants of peace, messengers of the Most High, of the King above the kings of kings, the Holy One, blessed be He.

IV   The sun on the treetops no longer is seen.

Come out, let us greet the Sabbath, the queen.

See! she descends, the holy, the blessed,

her messengers with her, of peace and of rest.

   Welcome! welcome the queen!

   Welcome! welcome the bride!

Peace be with you, messengers of peace!

קִבַּלְנוּ פְּנֵי שַׁבָּת בְּרִנְּנָה וּתְפִלָּה׃
הַבַּיְתָה נָשׁוּבָה בְּלֵב מָלֵא גִילָה׃
שָׁם עָרוּךְ הַשֻּׁלְחָן הַנֵּרוֹת יָאִירוּ׃
כָּל־פִּנּוֹת הַבַּיִת יִזְרְחוּ יַזְהִירוּ׃
שַׁבַּת שָׁלוֹם וּבְרָכָה׃
שַׁבַּת שָׁלוֹם וּמְנוּחָה׃
בֹּאֲכֶם לְשָׁלוֹם מַלְאֲכֵי הַשָּׁלוֹם׃

צה I

לְכוּ נְרַנְּנָה לַיהֹוָה נָרִיעָה לְצוּר יִשְׁעֵנוּ׃
נְקַדְּמָה פָנָיו בְּתוֹדָה בִּזְמִרוֹת נָרִיעַ לוֹ׃
כִּי אֵל גָּדוֹל יְהֹוָה וּמֶלֶךְ גָּדוֹל עַל־כָּל־אֱלֹהִים׃
אֲשֶׁר בְּיָדוֹ מֶחְקְרֵי־אָרֶץ וְתוֹעֲפוֹת הָרִים לוֹ׃
אֲשֶׁר־לוֹ הַיָּם וְהוּא עָשָׂהוּ וְיַבֶּשֶׁת יָדָיו יָצָרוּ׃
בֹּאוּ נִשְׁתַּחֲוֶה וְנִכְרָעָה נִבְרְכָה לִפְנֵי־יְהֹוָה עֹשֵׂנוּ׃
כִּי הוּא אֱלֹהֵינוּ וַאֲנַחְנוּ עַם מַרְעִיתוֹ וְצֹאן יָדוֹ
הַיּוֹם אִם־בְּקֹלוֹ תִשְׁמָעוּ׃

צו II

שִׁירוּ לַיהֹוָה שִׁיר חָדָשׁ שִׁירוּ לַיהֹוָה כָּל־הָאָרֶץ׃
שִׁירוּ לַיהֹוָה בָּרְכוּ שְׁמוֹ בַּשְּׂרוּ מִיּוֹם לְיוֹם יְשׁוּעָתוֹ׃
סַפְּרוּ בַגּוֹיִם כְּבוֹדוֹ בְּכָל־הָעַמִּים נִפְלְאוֹתָיו׃
כִּי גָדוֹל יְהֹוָה וּמְהֻלָּל מְאֹד נוֹרָא הוּא עַל־כָּל־אֱלֹהִים׃
כִּי כָּל־אֱלֹהֵי הָעַמִּים אֱלִילִים וַיהֹוָה שָׁמַיִם עָשָׂה׃

We received the Sabbath with song and with prayer,
to our homes we bring hearts filled with gladness to share.
The table is set there, the candles are bright,
each corner is shining, the house spreads its light.
   Sabbath of peace and blessing,
   Sabbath of peace and rest.
Enter in peace, messengers of peace!

Bialik

I   Psalm 95

Come let us sing out to the Lord
   call out to the rock of our safety.
Let us come before Him with thanks
   call out to Him with psalms.
For the Lord is almighty God
   mighty ruler beyond all gods.
The depths of the earth are in His hand
   and His are the mountain peaks.
The sea is His, it is He who made it
   the land His hands have shaped.
Come in, let us worship and bend low
   humble before the Lord who made us.
For He is our God
   and we are a people He pastures,
   a flock in His hand.
Today, if you would only hear His voice!

II   Psalm 96

Sing to the Lord a new song
   sing to the Lord all the earth
   sing to the Lord, bless His name.
Proclaim His salvation day after day
   describe His glory among the nations
   and His wonders among all peoples.
For great is the Lord and praised aloud
   He is awesome beyond all gods
   for all the peoples' gods are false gods,
but the Lord has made the heavens.

הוֹד־וְהָדָר לְפָנָיו עֹז וְתִפְאֶרֶת בְּמִקְדָּשׁוֹ:

הָבוּ לַיהוָה מִשְׁפְּחוֹת עַמִּים הָבוּ לַיהוָה כָּבוֹד וָעֹז:

הָבוּ לַיהוָה כְּבוֹד שְׁמוֹ שְׂאוּ מִנְחָה וּבֹאוּ לְחַצְרוֹתָיו:

הִשְׁתַּחֲווּ לַיהוָה בְּהַדְרַת־קֹדֶשׁ חִילוּ מִפָּנָיו כָּל־הָאָרֶץ:

אִמְרוּ בַגּוֹיִם יְהוָה מָלָךְ אַף־תִּכּוֹן תֵּבֵל בַּל־תִּמּוֹט
יָדִין עַמִּים בְּמֵישָׁרִים:

יִשְׂמְחוּ הַשָּׁמַיִם וְתָגֵל הָאָרֶץ יִרְעַם הַיָּם וּמְלֹאוֹ:

יַעֲלֹז שָׂדַי וְכָל־אֲשֶׁר־בּוֹ אָז יְרַנְּנוּ כָּל־עֲצֵי־יָעַר:

לִפְנֵי יְהוָה כִּי בָא כִּי בָא לִשְׁפֹּט הָאָרֶץ יִשְׁפֹּט־תֵּבֵל בְּצֶדֶק
וְעַמִּים בֶּאֱמוּנָתוֹ:

III   צז

יְהוָה מָלָךְ תָּגֵל הָאָרֶץ יִשְׂמְחוּ אִיִּים רַבִּים:

עָנָן וַעֲרָפֶל סְבִיבָיו צֶדֶק וּמִשְׁפָּט מְכוֹן כִּסְאוֹ:

אֵשׁ לְפָנָיו תֵּלֵךְ וּתְלַהֵט סָבִיב צָרָיו:

הֵאִירוּ בְרָקָיו תֵּבֵל רָאֲתָה וַתָּחֵל הָאָרֶץ:

הָרִים כַּדּוֹנַג נָמַסּוּ מִלִּפְנֵי יְהוָה מִלִּפְנֵי אֲדוֹן כָּל־הָאָרֶץ:

הִגִּידוּ הַשָּׁמַיִם צִדְקוֹ וְרָאוּ כָל־הָעַמִּים כְּבוֹדוֹ:

יֵבֹשׁוּ כָּל־עֹבְדֵי פֶסֶל הַמִּתְהַלְלִים בָּאֱלִילִים
הִשְׁתַּחֲווּ־לוֹ כָּל־אֱלֹהִים:

Splendour and radiance are in His presence
strength and beauty in His holy place.
Give to the Lord, you races and peoples,
give the Lord glory and strength,
give the Lord the glory due to His name.
Bear an offering and enter His courts
worship the Lord in the radiance of holiness
tremble before Him all the earth.
Say among the nations: 'The Lord rules!'
The world too is set firm and cannot be shaken
He will judge the peoples with justice.
Let the heavens rejoice and the earth delight
let the sea thunder in its fullness.
Let the field be glad and all within it
let all trees of the forest sing out
at the presence of the Lord who comes,
for He comes to judge the earth.
He will judge the world with righteousness
and the peoples with His truth.

III   Psalm 97

The Lord is king, let the earth be glad
let the many isles rejoice!
A cloud and darkness surround Him
but righteousness and justice
are the foundations of His throne.
Fire strides before Him
blazing round His foes.
His lightning lights up the world,
the earth sees and trembles.
Mountains melt like wax before the Lord
before the master of all the earth.
The heavens declare His righteousness,
all peoples see His glory.
Shame on all those who are slaves to an image,
who puff up their pride with hollow gods.
False gods, bow down before Him!

שָׁמְעָה וַתִּשְׂמַח צִיּוֹן וַתָּגֵלְנָה בְּנוֹת יְהוּדָה
לְמַעַן מִשְׁפָּטֶיךָ יְהֹוָה:

כִּי־אַתָּה יְהֹוָה עֶלְיוֹן עַל־כָּל־הָאָרֶץ
מְאֹד נַעֲלֵיתָ עַל־כָּל־אֱלֹהִים:

אֹהֲבֵי יְהֹוָה שִׂנְאוּ רָע שֹׁמֵר נַפְשׁוֹת חֲסִידָיו
מִיַּד רְשָׁעִים יַצִּילֵם:

אוֹר־זָרֻעַ לַצַּדִּיק וּלְיִשְׁרֵי־לֵב שִׂמְחָה:

שִׂמְחוּ צַדִּיקִים בַּיהֹוָה וְהוֹדוּ לְזֵכֶר קָדְשׁוֹ:

צח מִזְמוֹר   IV

שִׁירוּ לַיהֹוָה שִׁיר חָדָשׁ כִּי־נִפְלָאוֹת עָשָׂה
הוֹשִׁיעָה־לּוֹ יְמִינוֹ וּזְרוֹעַ קָדְשׁוֹ:

הוֹדִיעַ יְהֹוָה יְשׁוּעָתוֹ לְעֵינֵי הַגּוֹיִם גִּלָּה צִדְקָתוֹ:

זָכַר חַסְדּוֹ וֶאֱמוּנָתוֹ לְבֵית יִשְׂרָאֵל
רָאוּ כָל־אַפְסֵי־אָרֶץ אֵת יְשׁוּעַת אֱלֹהֵינוּ:

הָרִיעוּ לַיהֹוָה כָּל־הָאָרֶץ פִּצְחוּ וְרַנְּנוּ וְזַמֵּרוּ:

זַמְּרוּ לַיהֹוָה בְּכִנּוֹר בְּכִנּוֹר וְקוֹל זִמְרָה:

בַּחֲצֹצְרוֹת וְקוֹל שׁוֹפָר הָרִיעוּ לִפְנֵי הַמֶּלֶךְ יְהֹוָה:

יִרְעַם הַיָּם וּמְלֹאוֹ תֵּבֵל וְיֹשְׁבֵי בָהּ:

נְהָרוֹת יִמְחֲאוּ־כָף יַחַד הָרִים יְרַנֵּנוּ:

לִפְנֵי יְהֹוָה כִּי בָא לִשְׁפֹּט הָאָרֶץ
יִשְׁפֹּט־תֵּבֵל בְּצֶדֶק וְעַמִּים בְּמֵישָׁרִים:

Zion heard and rejoiced, the daughters of Judah were glad
  because of Your judgments, O Lord.
Because You are the Lord, supreme over all the earth.
  You are supreme beyond all gods.
Those who love the Lord, hate evil.
  He guards the souls devoted to Him.
  He saves them from the hand of the wicked.
A harvest of light is sown for the righteous,
  and joy for the constant heart.
You who are righteous, rejoice in the Lord,
  call His holiness to mind and praise Him!

IV   Psalm 98

Sing to the Lord a new song
  for the wonders He has done.
He has saved through His right hand
  and the power of His holiness.
The Lord has made known His power to save
  shown His righteousness in the sight of the nations.
He remembers His love
  keeping faith with the family of Israel.
All the ends of the earth have seen
  the power of our God to save.
Call out to the Lord all the earth
  cheer and sing and play!
Play to the Lord with the harp
  with the harp and the voice of music.
With trumpets and the sound of the horn
  call out before the king, the Lord.
Let the sea thunder in its fullness
  the world and all who live in it.
Let the rivers clap their hands
    let the mountains sing out as one
    at the presence of the Lord
    for He comes to judge the earth.
He will judge the world with righteousness
  and the peoples with justice.

לְכָה דוֹדִי לִקְרַאת כַּלָּה . פְּנֵי שַׁבָּת נְקַבְּלָה:

שָׁמוֹר וְזָכוֹר בְּדִבּוּר אֶחָד . הִשְׁמִיעָנוּ אֵל הַמְּיֻחָד .
יְיָ אֶחָד וּשְׁמוֹ אֶחָד . לְשֵׁם וּלְתִפְאֶרֶת וְלִתְהִלָּה:
לְכָה דוֹדִי לִקְרַאת כַּלָּה · פְּנֵי שַׁבָּת נְקַבְּלָה:

לִקְרַאת שַׁבָּת לְכוּ וְנֵלְכָה · כִּי הִיא מְקוֹר הַבְּרָכָה ·
מֵרֹאשׁ מִקֶּדֶם נְסוּכָה · סוֹף מַעֲשֶׂה בְּמַחֲשָׁבָה תְּחִלָּה:
לְכָה דוֹדִי לִקְרַאת כַּלָּה · פְּנֵי שַׁבָּת נְקַבְּלָה:

הִתְעוֹרְרִי הִתְעוֹרְרִי · כִּי בָא אוֹרֵךְ קוּמִי אוֹרִי ·
עוּרִי עוּרִי שִׁיר דַּבֵּרִי · כְּבוֹד יְיָ עָלַיִךְ נִגְלָה:
לְכָה דוֹדִי לִקְרַאת כַּלָּה · פְּנֵי שַׁבָּת נְקַבְּלָה:

בּוֹאִי בְשָׁלוֹם עֲטֶרֶת בַּעְלָהּ · גַּם בְּשִׂמְחָה וּבְצָהֳלָה ·
תּוֹךְ אֱמוּנֵי עַם סְגֻלָּה · בּוֹאִי כַלָּה · בּוֹאִי כַלָּה:
לְכָה דוֹדִי לִקְרַאת כַּלָּה · פְּנֵי שַׁבָּת נְקַבְּלָה:

A passage from the Study Anthology (pages 352–356) is read.

> Come, my friend, to greet the bride,
> to welcome in the Sabbath eve.

'Observe!', 'Remember!'—one command,
God made us hear a single phrase.
For He is one, His name is one,
in fame, in glory and in praise.
> Come, my friend, to greet the bride,
> to welcome in the Sabbath eve.

To greet the Sabbath let us join
for from her endless blessings pour.
First of all creation willed,
the final act, thought long before.
> Come, my friend, to greet the bride,
> to welcome in the Sabbath eve.

Arouse yourself, arouse yourself,
your light is come, arise and shine!
Awake, awake and pour out song,
God's glory greets us at this time.
> Come, my friend, to greet the bride,
> to welcome in the Sabbath eve.

Come in peace and come in joy,
God, your husband; you, His pride;
among the faithful chosen people,
come my bride, come my bride!
> Come, my friend, to greet the bride,
> to welcome in the Sabbath eve.

Alkabetz

צב

מִזְמוֹר שִׁיר לְיוֹם הַשַּׁבָּת׃

טוֹב לְהֹדוֹת לַיהוָה וּלְזַמֵּר לְשִׁמְךָ עֶלְיוֹן׃

לְהַגִּיד בַּבֹּקֶר חַסְדֶּךָ וֶאֱמוּנָתְךָ בַּלֵּילוֹת׃

עֲלֵי־עָשׂוֹר וַעֲלֵי־נָבֶל עֲלֵי הִגָּיוֹן בְּכִנּוֹר׃

כִּי שִׂמַּחְתַּנִי יְהוָה בְּפָעֳלֶךָ בְּמַעֲשֵׂי יָדֶיךָ אֲרַנֵּן׃

מַה־גָּדְלוּ מַעֲשֶׂיךָ יְהוָה מְאֹד עָמְקוּ מַחְשְׁבֹתֶיךָ׃

אִישׁ־בַּעַר לֹא יֵדָע וּכְסִיל לֹא־יָבִין אֶת־זֹאת׃

בִּפְרֹחַ רְשָׁעִים כְּמוֹ־עֵשֶׂב וַיָּצִיצוּ כָּל־פֹּעֲלֵי אָוֶן לְהִשָּׁמְדָם עֲדֵי־עַד׃

וְאַתָּה מָרוֹם לְעֹלָם יְהוָה׃

כִּי הִנֵּה אֹיְבֶיךָ יְהוָה כִּי־הִנֵּה אֹיְבֶיךָ יֹאבֵדוּ יִתְפָּרְדוּ כָּל־פֹּעֲלֵי אָוֶן׃

וַתָּרֶם כִּרְאֵים קַרְנִי בַּלֹּתִי בְּשֶׁמֶן רַעֲנָן׃

וַתַּבֵּט עֵינִי בְּשׁוּרָי בַּקָּמִים עָלַי מְרֵעִים תִּשְׁמַעְנָה אָזְנָי׃

צַדִּיק כַּתָּמָר יִפְרָח כְּאֶרֶז בַּלְּבָנוֹן יִשְׂגֶּה׃

שְׁתוּלִים בְּבֵית יְהוָה בְּחַצְרוֹת אֱלֹהֵינוּ יַפְרִיחוּ׃

עוֹד יְנוּבוּן בְּשֵׂיבָה דְּשֵׁנִים וְרַעֲנַנִּים יִהְיוּ׃

לְהַגִּיד כִּי־יָשָׁר יְהוָה צוּרִי וְלֹא־עַוְלָתָה בּוֹ׃

Psalm 92

A psalm to sing for the Sabbath day.

It is good to give thanks to the Lord
    to praise Your name, O God beyond all,
to tell of Your love in the morning
    and Your faithfulness every night.
With the ten-stringed lute, with the lyre
    with the gentle sound of the harp.
For You made me rejoice in Your deeds, O Lord,
    at the works of Your hand I sing out.
Lord, how great are Your works,
    Your thoughts are so very deep.
A stupid man does not know this
    nor can a foolish man understand
that when the wicked flourish
    they are only like grass
and when all who do evil spring up
    their end is always destruction,
    and only You, Lord, are exalted forever.
For see Your enemies, Lord!
    see how Your enemies shall perish,
    all who do evil shall scatter.
But You exalted my strength like an ox,
    anointed me with fresh oil.
My eyes saw the fate of my enemies;
    and those who rose up to harm me,
    my ears have heard their end.
The righteous shall flourish like the palm tree
    grow tall like a cedar in Lebanon.
Planted in the house of the Lord
    they shall flourish in the courts of our God,
bearing new fruit in old age
    still full of sap and still green,
to declare that the Lord is upright
    my rock in whom there is no wrong.

צג

יְהֹוָה מָלָךְ גֵּאוּת לָבֵשׁ לָבֵשׁ יְהֹוָה עֹז הִתְאַזָּר אַף־תִּכּוֹן תֵּבֵל בַּל־תִּמּוֹט:

נָכוֹן כִּסְאֲךָ מֵאָז מֵעוֹלָם אָתָּה:

נָשְׂאוּ נְהָרוֹת יְהֹוָה נָשְׂאוּ נְהָרוֹת קוֹלָם יִשְׂאוּ נְהָרוֹת דָּכְיָם:

מִקֹּלוֹת מַיִם רַבִּים אַדִּירִים מִשְׁבְּרֵי־יָם אַדִּיר בַּמָּרוֹם יְהֹוָה:

עֵדֹתֶיךָ נֶאֶמְנוּ מְאֹד לְבֵיתְךָ נַאֲוָה־קֹדֶשׁ יְהֹוָה לְאֹרֶךְ יָמִים:

בָּרְכוּ אֶת־יְיָ הַמְבֹרָךְ:

בָּרוּךְ יְיָ הַמְבֹרָךְ לְעוֹלָם וָעֶד:

בָּרוּךְ אַתָּה יְיָ אֱלֹהֵינוּ מֶלֶךְ הָעוֹלָם ∙ אֲשֶׁר בִּדְבָרוֹ מַעֲרִיב עֲרָבִים ∙ בְּחָכְמָה פּוֹתֵחַ שְׁעָרִים ∙ וּבִתְבוּנָה מְשַׁנֶּה עִתִּים ∙ וּמַחֲלִיף אֶת־הַזְּמַנִּים ∙ וּמְסַדֵּר אֶת־הַכּוֹכָבִים בְּמִשְׁמְרוֹתֵיהֶם בָּרָקִיעַ כִּרְצוֹנוֹ: בּוֹרֵא יוֹם וָלָיְלָה ∙ גּוֹלֵל אוֹר מִפְּנֵי חֹשֶׁךְ וְחֹשֶׁךְ מִפְּנֵי אוֹר: הַמַּעֲבִיר יוֹם וּמֵבִיא לָיְלָה ∙ וּמַבְדִּיל בֵּין יוֹם וּבֵין לָיְלָה ∙ יְיָ צְבָאוֹת שְׁמוֹ: בָּרוּךְ אַתָּה יְיָ ∙ הַמַּעֲרִיב עֲרָבִים:

אַהֲבַת עוֹלָם בֵּית יִשְׂרָאֵל עַמְּךָ אָהַבְתָּ ∙ תּוֹרָה וּמִצְוֹת חֻקִּים וּמִשְׁפָּטִים אוֹתָנוּ לִמַּדְתָּ: עַל־כֵּן יְיָ אֱלֹהֵינוּ ∙ בְּשָׁכְבֵנוּ וּבְקוּמֵנוּ נָשִׂיחַ בְּחֻקֶּיךָ ∙ וְנִשְׂמַח וְנַעֲלוֹז בְּדִבְרֵי תוֹרָתֶךָ וּמִצְוֹתֶיךָ וְחֻקוֹתֶיךָ לְעוֹלָם וָעֶד ∙ כִּי הֵם חַיֵּינוּ וְאֹרֶךְ יָמֵינוּ ∙ וּבָהֶם נֶהְגֶּה יוֹמָם וָלָיְלָה ∙ וְאַהֲבָתְךָ אַל־תָּסִיר מִמֶּנּוּ לְעוֹלָמִים: בָּרוּךְ אַתָּה יְיָ ∙ אוֹהֵב אֶת־עַמּוֹ יִשְׂרָאֵל:

Psalm 93

The Lord is king
He puts on the robes of pride
He puts on the robes of power
strength surrounds Him.

So the world was set firm
and cannot be shaken,
Your throne was set firm long ago
from eternity You are.

Lord, the floods may storm
the floods may storm aloud
the floods may storm and thunder.

But even above the roar of great waves
mighty breakers of the ocean
the might of the Lord is supreme.

The proofs You give are very sure,
holiness is the mark of Your house,
Lord, as long as time endures.

THE CALL TO COM-MUNITY PRAYER

Bless the Lord whom we are called to bless.

Blessed be the Lord whom we are called to bless forever and ever.

THE CREATOR OF THE UNIVERSE

Blessed are You, Lord our God, king of the universe. By His word He brings on the evening twilight; in wisdom He opens the gates of dawn, and with foresight makes times pass and seasons change. He sets the stars in their courses in the sky according to His plan. He creates day and night, turning light into darkness and darkness into light. He makes the day fade away and brings on the night, and separates day and night, for He is the Lord of the hosts of heaven. Blessed are You Lord, who brings on the evening twilight.

HIS LOVE FOR ISRAEL

With everlasting love have You loved Your people the family of Israel. Teaching and practice, duty and justice—these You have taught us. Therefore, Lord our God, we think upon all this before we sleep and when we wake, and rejoice and delight in Your teaching and its practice forever and ever, for they are our life and the measure of our days. We keep them in mind both day and night. Never take Your love away from us. Blessed are You Lord, who loves His people Israel.

שְׁמַ**ע** יִשְׂרָאֵל · יְהוָֹה אֱלֹהֵינוּ יְהוָֹה אֶחָֽ**ד** :

בָּרוּךְ שֵׁם כְּבוֹד מַלְכוּתוֹ לְעוֹלָם וָעֶֽד :

וְאָהַבְתָּ אֵת יְהוָֹה אֱלֹהֶֽיךָ · בְּכָל־לְבָבְךָ וּבְכָל־נַפְשְׁךָ
וּבְכָל־מְאֹדֶֽךָ : וְהָיוּ הַדְּבָרִים הָאֵֽלֶּה אֲשֶׁר אָנֹכִי מְצַוְּךָ הַיּוֹם
עַל־לְבָבֶֽךָ : וְשִׁנַּנְתָּם לְבָנֶֽיךָ וְדִבַּרְתָּ בָּם · בְּשִׁבְתְּךָ בְּבֵיתֶֽךָ
וּבְלֶכְתְּךָ בַדֶּֽרֶךְ וּבְשָׁכְבְּךָ וּבְקוּמֶֽךָ : וּקְשַׁרְתָּם לְאוֹת עַל־יָדֶֽךָ ·
וְהָיוּ לְטֹטָפֹת בֵּין עֵינֶֽיךָ : וּכְתַבְתָּם עַל־מְזֻזוֹת בֵּיתֶֽךָ
וּבִשְׁעָרֶֽיךָ :

אֱ**מֶת וֶאֱמוּנָה** כָּל־זֹאת וְקַיָּם עָלֵֽינוּ כִּי הוּא יְיָ
אֱלֹהֵֽינוּ וְאֵין זוּלָתוֹ וַאֲנַֽחְנוּ יִשְׂרָאֵל
עַמּוֹ · הָעֹשֶׂה גְדֹלוֹת עַד־אֵין חֵֽקֶר וְנִפְלָאוֹת עַד־אֵין מִסְפָּר ·
וְרָאוּ בָנָיו גְּבוּרָתוֹ שִׁבְּחוּ וְהוֹדוּ לִשְׁמוֹ וּמַלְכוּתוֹ בְּרָצוֹן קִבְּלוּ
עֲלֵיהֶם · מֹשֶׁה וּבְנֵי יִשְׂרָאֵל לְךָ עָנוּ שִׁירָה בְּשִׂמְחָה רַבָּה ·
וְאָמְרוּ כֻלָּם ·

מִי־כָמֹֽכָה בָּאֵלִם יְהוָֹה מִי כָּמֹֽכָה נֶאְדָּר בַּקֹּֽדֶשׁ נוֹרָא
תְהִלֹּת עֹֽשֵׂה פֶֽלֶא :

מַלְכוּתְךָ יְיָ אֱלֹהֵֽינוּ רָאוּ בָנֶֽיךָ עַל הַיָּם · יַֽחַד כֻּלָּם הוֹדוּ
וְהִמְלִֽיכוּ וְאָמְרוּ · יְהוָֹה יִמְלֹךְ לְעֹלָם וָעֶד :

וְנֶאֱמַר כִּי־פָדָה יְיָ אֶת־יַעֲקֹב וּגְאָלוֹ מִיַּד חָזָק מִמֶּֽנּוּ ·
בָּרוּךְ אַתָּה יְיָ · גָּאַל יִשְׂרָאֵל :

THE GOD
OF ISRAEL   Hear O Israel, the Lord is our God, the Lord is One.

Blessed is His name, whose glorious kingdom is forever and ever.

Love the Lord your God with all your heart, and all your soul, and all your might. These words that I command you today shall be upon your heart. Repeat them to your children, and talk about them when you sit in your home, and when you walk in the street; when you lie down, and when you rise up. Hold fast to them as a sign upon your hand, and let them be as reminders before your eyes. Write them on the doorposts of your home and at your gates.

Deuteronomy 6: 4–9

The second and third paragraphs of the Shema are on pages 60–62. Other Sabbath prayers on pages 344–349.

OUR
REDEEMER   All this is true and firmly held by us, that He is the Lord our God, for no other exists, and that we are Israel, His people. He performs great deeds beyond research, too wonderful to tell. His children saw His power, praised and thanked His name, and willingly accepted His rule over them. With great joy Moses and the children of Israel answered You in song, all of them saying:

'Who is like You, Lord, among the gods men worship!

Who is like You, majestic in holiness,

awesome in praise, working wonders!'

Lord our God, Your children saw Your rule over the Red Sea. All of them as one honoured You as king, saying:

'The Lord shall rule forever and ever!'

And it is prophesied:

'For the Lord has set Jacob free and rescued him

from a hand stronger than his own.'

Blessed are You Lord, who rescues Israel.

הַשְׁכִּיבֵנוּ אָבִינוּ לְשָׁלוֹם וְהַעֲמִידֵנוּ מַלְכֵּנוּ לְחַיִּים · וּפְרוֹשׂ
עָלֵינוּ סֻכַּת שְׁלוֹמֶךָ וְתַקְּנֵנוּ בְּעֵצָה טוֹבָה מִלְּפָנֶיךָ וְהוֹשִׁיעֵנוּ
לְמַעַן שְׁמֶךָ · וְהָגֵן בַּעֲדֵנוּ וְהָסֵר מֵעָלֵינוּ אוֹיֵב דֶּבֶר וְחֶרֶב
וְרָעָב וְיָגוֹן · וּבְצֵל כְּנָפֶיךָ תַּסְתִּירֵנוּ כִּי אֵל שׁוֹמְרֵנוּ וּמַצִּילֵנוּ
אָתָּה כִּי אֵל מֶלֶךְ חַנּוּן וְרַחוּם אָתָּה · וּשְׁמוֹר צֵאתֵנוּ וּבוֹאֵנוּ
לְחַיִּים וּלְשָׁלוֹם מֵעַתָּה וְעַד עוֹלָם · וּפְרוֹשׂ עָלֵינוּ סֻכַּת
שְׁלוֹמֶךָ · בָּרוּךְ אַתָּה יְיָ · הַפּוֹרֵשׂ סֻכַּת שָׁלוֹם עָלֵינוּ וְעַל־עַמּוֹ
יִשְׂרָאֵל וְעַל־כָּל־הָעוֹלָם :

וְשָׁמְרוּ בְנֵי־יִשְׂרָאֵל אֶת־הַשַּׁבָּת לַעֲשׂוֹת אֶת־הַשַּׁבָּת לְדֹרֹתָם
בְּרִית עוֹלָם : בֵּינִי וּבֵין בְּנֵי יִשְׂרָאֵל אוֹת הִוא לְעֹלָם כִּי־
שֵׁשֶׁת יָמִים עָשָׂה יְהוָֹה אֶת־הַשָּׁמַיִם וְאֶת־הָאָרֶץ וּבַיּוֹם הַשְּׁבִיעִי
שָׁבַת וַיִּנָּפַשׁ :

אֲדֹנָי שְׂפָתַי תִּפְתָּח · וּפִי יַגִּיד תְּהִלָּתֶךָ :

בָּרוּךְ אַתָּה יְיָ אֱלֹהֵינוּ וֵאלֹהֵי אֲבוֹתֵינוּ · אֱלֹהֵי אַבְרָהָם ·
אֱלֹהֵי יִצְחָק · וֵאלֹהֵי יַעֲקֹב · הָאֵל הַגָּדוֹל הַגִּבּוֹר
וְהַנּוֹרָא · אֵל עֶלְיוֹן · גּוֹמֵל חֲסָדִים טוֹבִים קוֹנֵה הַכֹּל וְזוֹכֵר
חַסְדֵי אָבוֹת וּמֵבִיא גוֹאֵל לִבְנֵי בְנֵיהֶם לְמַעַן שְׁמוֹ בְּאַהֲבָה :
מֶלֶךְ עוֹזֵר וּמוֹשִׁיעַ וּמָגֵן · בָּרוּךְ אַתָּה יְיָ · מָגֵן אַבְרָהָם :

אַתָּה גִּבּוֹר לְעוֹלָם יְיָ · מְחַיֶּה מֵתִים אַתָּה רַב לְהוֹשִׁיעַ ·
מְכַלְכֵּל חַיִּים בְּחֶסֶד · מְחַיֶּה מֵתִים בְּרַחֲמִים רַבִּים ·
סוֹמֵךְ נוֹפְלִים · וְרוֹפֵא חוֹלִים · וּמַתִּיר אֲסוּרִים · וּמְקַיֵּם אֱמוּנָתוֹ
לִישֵׁנֵי עָפָר : מִי כָמוֹךָ בַּעַל גְּבוּרוֹת וּמִי דוֹמֶה לָּךְ · מֶלֶךְ
מֵמִית וּמְחַיֶּה · וּמַצְמִיחַ יְשׁוּעָה : וְנֶאֱמָן אַתָּה לְהַחֲיוֹת מֵתִים ·
בָּרוּךְ אַתָּה יְיָ · מְחַיֶּה הַמֵּתִים :

HIS GIFT
PEACE, JOY
AND REST
Cause us, our father, to lie down in peace, and rise again to enjoy life. Spread over us the covering of Your peace, guide us with Your good counsel and save us for the sake of Your name. Be a shield about us, turning away every enemy, disease, violence, hunger and sorrow. Shelter us in the shadow of Your wings, for You are a God who guards and protects us, a ruler of mercy and compassion. Guard us when we go out and when we come in, to enjoy life and peace both now and forever, and spread over us the shelter of Your peace. Blessed are You Lord, who spreads the shelter of peace over us, over His people Israel, and over all the world.

The children of Israel shall keep the Sabbath, observing the Sabbath as a timeless covenant for all generations. It is a sign between Me and the children of Israel forever. For in six days the Lord made heaven and earth and on the seventh day He ceased from work and was at rest.

Exodus 31: 16–17

The half Kaddish on page 168 may be included here.

THE
AMIDAH
Lord, open my lips and my mouth shall declare Your praise.

GOD OF
HISTORY
Blessed are You, Lord our God, and God of our fathers, God of Abraham, God of Isaac, and God of Jacob, the great, the mighty, and the awesome God, God beyond, generous in love and kindness, and possessing all. He remembers the good deeds of our fathers, and therefore in love brings rescue to the generations, for such is His being. The king who helps and saves and shields. Blessed are You Lord, the shield of Abraham.

GOD OF
MIGHT
You, O Lord, are the endless power that renews life beyond death; You are the greatness that saves. You care for the living with love. You renew life beyond death with unending mercy. You support the falling, and heal the sick. You free prisoners, and keep faith with those who sleep in the dust. Who can perform such mighty deeds, and who can compare with You, a king who brings death and life, and renews salvation. You are faithful to renew life beyond death. Blessed are You Lord, who renews life beyond death.

וְאַתָּה קָדוֹשׁ · יוֹשֵׁב תְּהִלּוֹת יִשְׂרָאֵל :

אַתָּה קָדוֹשׁ וְשִׁמְךָ קָדוֹשׁ וּקְדוֹשִׁים בְּכָל־יוֹם יְהַלְלוּךָ סֶּלָה · בָּרוּךְ אַתָּה יְיָ · הָאֵל הַקָּדוֹשׁ :

קָדוֹשׁ קָדוֹשׁ קָדוֹשׁ יְהֹוָה צְבָאוֹת · מְלֹא כָל־הָאָרֶץ כְּבוֹדוֹ :

בָּרוּךְ כְּבוֹד־יְהֹוָה מִמְּקוֹמוֹ :

יִמְלֹךְ יְהֹוָה לְעוֹלָם · אֱלֹהַיִךְ צִיּוֹן לְדֹר וָדֹר הַלְלוּיָהּ :

בָּרוּךְ אַתָּה יְיָ · הָאֵל הַקָּדוֹשׁ :

וַיְכֻלּוּ הַשָּׁמַיִם וְהָאָרֶץ וְכָל־צְבָאָם : וַיְכַל אֱלֹהִים בַּיּוֹם הַשְּׁבִיעִי מְלַאכְתּוֹ אֲשֶׁר עָשָׂה · וַיִּשְׁבֹּת בַּיּוֹם הַשְּׁבִיעִי מִכָּל־ מְלַאכְתּוֹ אֲשֶׁר עָשָׂה : וַיְבָרֶךְ אֱלֹהִים אֶת־יוֹם הַשְּׁבִיעִי וַיְקַדֵּשׁ אֹתוֹ · כִּי בוֹ שָׁבַת מִכָּל־מְלַאכְתּוֹ אֲשֶׁר בָּרָא אֱלֹהִים לַעֲשׂוֹת :

אֱלֹהֵינוּ וֵאלֹהֵי אֲבוֹתֵינוּ · רְצֵה־נָא בִמְנוּחָתֵנוּ · קַדְּשֵׁנוּ בְּמִצְוֹתֶיךָ · שִׂים חֶלְקֵנוּ בְּתוֹרָתֶךָ · שַׂבְּעֵנוּ מִטּוּבֶךָ · שַׂמַּח נַפְשֵׁנוּ בִּישׁוּעָתֶךָ · וְטַהֵר לִבֵּנוּ לְעָבְדְּךָ בֶּאֱמֶת · וְהַנְחִילֵנוּ יְיָ אֱלֹהֵינוּ בְּאַהֲבָה וּבְרָצוֹן שַׁבַּת קָדְשֶׁךָ · וְיָנוּחוּ בָהּ כָּל־יִשְׂרָאֵל מְקַדְּשֵׁי שְׁמֶךָ : בָּרוּךְ אַתָּה יְיָ · מְקַדֵּשׁ הַשַּׁבָּת :

רְצֵה יְיָ אֱלֹהֵינוּ בְּעַמְּךָ יִשְׂרָאֵל · וְלִתְפִלָּתָם שְׁעֵה · וּבְרַחֲמֶיךָ הָרַבִּים תַּחְפֹּץ בָּנוּ וְתַשְׁרֶה שְׁכִינָתְךָ עַל צִיּוֹן · וְתֶחֱזֶינָה עֵינֵינוּ בְּשׁוּבְךָ לְצִיּוֹן בְּרַחֲמִים · בָּרוּךְ אַתָּה יְיָ · הַמַּחֲזִיר שְׁכִינָתוֹ לְצִיּוֹן :

מוֹדִים אֲנַחְנוּ לָךְ שָׁאַתָּה הוּא יְיָ אֱלֹהֵינוּ וֵאלֹהֵי אֲבוֹתֵינוּ לְעוֹלָם וָעֶד · צוּרֵנוּ צוּר חַיֵּינוּ וּמָגֵן יִשְׁעֵנוּ אַתָּה הוּא לְדוֹר וָדוֹר · נוֹדֶה לְּךָ וּנְסַפֵּר תְּהִלָּתֶךָ עַל חַיֵּינוּ הַמְּסוּרִים בְּיָדֶךָ · וְעַל נִשְׁמוֹתֵינוּ הַפְּקוּדוֹת לָךְ · וְעַל נִסֶּיךָ שֶׁבְּכָל־יוֹם עִמָּנוּ ·

GOD OF HOLINESS You are holy, dwelling in the prayers of Israel.

Holy, holy, holy is the Lord of all creation, the whole earth is full of His glory.

Blessed is His glory revealed in every place.

The Lord shall rule forever! Zion, He is your God for all generations! Praise the Lord!

Blessed are You Lord, the holy God.

You are holy and Your name is holy, and those who seek holiness praise You day by day.

Blessed are You Lord, the holy God.

THE HOLINESS OF THE SABBATH Heaven and earth were finished and all their host. On the seventh day God finished the work that He had done, and He ceased on the seventh day from all the work that He had done. God blessed the seventh day, and made it holy, because on it God ceased from all the work of creation that He had done.

Genesis 2: 1–3

Our God and God of our fathers, may our rest be pleasing to You. Make us holy by doing Your commands and let us share in the work of Your Torah. Make us content with Your goodness and let our souls know the joy of Your salvation. Purify our hearts to serve You in truth. In Your love and goodwill let us inherit Your holy Sabbath and may all Israel who seek holiness find in it their rest. Blessed are You Lord, who makes the Sabbath holy.

THANKS-GIVING AND PEACE Lord our God, be pleased with Your people Israel and listen to their prayers. In Your great mercy delight in us so that Your presence may rest upon Zion. Our eyes look forward to Your return to Zion in mercy! Blessed are You Lord, who restores His presence to Zion.

We declare with gratitude that You are our God and the God of our fathers forever. You are our rock, the rock of our life and the shield that saves us. In every generation we thank You and recount Your praise for our lives held in Your hand, for our souls that are in Your care, and for the signs of Your presence that are with us every

וְעַל נִפְלְאוֹתֶיךָ וְטוֹבוֹתֶיךָ שֶׁבְּכָל־עֵת עֶרֶב וָבֹקֶר וְצָהֳרָיִם: הַטּוֹב כִּי לֹא כָלוּ רַחֲמֶיךָ · הַמְרַחֵם כִּי לֹא תַמּוּ חֲסָדֶיךָ · כִּי מֵעוֹלָם קִוִּינוּ לָךְ:

וְעַל כֻּלָּם יִתְבָּרַךְ וְיִתְרוֹמֵם וְיִתְנַשֵּׂא תָּמִיד שִׁמְךָ מַלְכֵּנוּ לְעוֹלָם וָעֶד: וְכָל־הַחַיִּים יוֹדוּךָ סֶּלָה · וִיהַלְלוּ וִיבָרְכוּ אֶת־שִׁמְךָ הַגָּדוֹל בֶּאֱמֶת · הָאֵל יְשׁוּעָתֵנוּ וְעֶזְרָתֵנוּ סֶלָה: בָּרוּךְ אַתָּה יְיָ · הַטּוֹב שִׁמְךָ וּלְךָ נָאֶה לְהוֹדוֹת:

שָׁלוֹם רָב עַל יִשְׂרָאֵל עַמְּךָ תָּשִׂים לְעוֹלָם · כִּי אַתָּה הוּא מֶלֶךְ אָדוֹן לְכָל־הַשָּׁלוֹם · וְטוֹב בְּעֵינֶיךָ לְבָרֵךְ אֶת־עַמְּךָ יִשְׂרָאֵל בְּכָל־עֵת וּבְכָל־שָׁעָה בִּשְׁלוֹמֶךָ: בָּרוּךְ אַתָּה יְיָ · הַמְבָרֵךְ אֶת־עַמּוֹ יִשְׂרָאֵל בַּשָּׁלוֹם:

אֱלֹהַי נְצוֹר לְשׁוֹנִי מֵרָע · וּשְׂפָתוֹתַי מִדַּבֵּר מִרְמָה · וְלִמְקַלְלַי נַפְשִׁי תִדּוֹם · וְנַפְשִׁי כֶּעָפָר לַכֹּל תִּהְיֶה: פְּתַח לִבִּי בְּתוֹרָתֶךָ · וְאַחֲרֵי מִצְוֹתֶיךָ תִּרְדּוֹף נַפְשִׁי · וְכָל־הַקָּמִים עָלַי לְרָעָה מְהֵרָה הָפֵר עֲצָתָם וְקַלְקֵל מַחֲשַׁבוֹתָם: יִהְיוּ לְרָצוֹן אִמְרֵי־פִי · וְהֶגְיוֹן לִבִּי לְפָנֶיךָ · יְהֹוָה צוּרִי וְגֹאֲלִי:

עֹשֶׂה שָׁלוֹם בִּמְרוֹמָיו   הוּא יַעֲשֶׂה שָׁלוֹם עָלֵינוּ וְעַל־כָּל־יִשְׂרָאֵל · וְאִמְרוּ אָמֵן:

עָלֵינוּ לְשַׁבֵּחַ לַאֲדוֹן הַכֹּל לָתֵת גְּדֻלָּה לְיוֹצֵר בְּרֵאשִׁית · אֲשֶׁר בָּחַר־בָּנוּ מִכָּל־הָעַמִּים · וְנָתַן־לָנוּ אֶת־תּוֹרָתוֹ · וַאֲנַחְנוּ כֹּרְעִים וּמִשְׁתַּחֲוִים וּמוֹדִים לִפְנֵי מֶלֶךְ מַלְכֵי הַמְּלָכִים הַקָּדוֹשׁ בָּרוּךְ הוּא · שֶׁהוּא נוֹטֶה שָׁמַיִם וְיוֹסֵד אָרֶץ · וּמוֹשַׁב יְקָרוֹ בַּשָּׁמַיִם מִמַּעַל וּשְׁכִינַת עֻזּוֹ בְּגָבְהֵי מְרוֹמִים: הוּא אֱלֹהֵינוּ · אֵין עוֹד · אֱמֶת מַלְכֵּנוּ · אֶפֶס זוּלָתוֹ · כַּכָּתוּב בְּתוֹרָתוֹ · וְיָדַעְתָּ הַיּוֹם וַהֲשֵׁבֹתָ אֶל־לְבָבֶךָ כִּי יְיָ הוּא הָאֱלֹהִים בַּשָּׁמַיִם מִמַּעַל וְעַל־הָאָרֶץ מִתָּחַת אֵין עוֹד:

day. At every moment, at evening, morning and noon, we experience Your wonders and Your goodness. You are goodness itself, for Your mercy has no end. You are mercy itself, for Your love has no limit. Forever have we put our hope in You. And for all these things may Your name, our king, be blessed, exalted and honoured forever and ever. May every living being thank You; may they praise and bless Your great name in truth for You are the God who saves and helps us. Blessed are You Lord, known as goodness, whom it is right to praise.

Set true peace upon Your people Israel forever. For You are the king, the Lord of all peace, and in Your eyes it is good to bless Your people Israel at every time and in every hour with Your peace. Blessed are You Lord, who blesses His people Israel with peace.

MEDI-TATION My God, keep my tongue from causing harm and my lips from telling lies. Let me be silent if people curse me, my soul still humble and at peace with all. Open my heart to Your teaching, and give me the will to practise it. May the plans and schemes of those who seek my harm come to nothing. May the words of my mouth and the meditation of my heart be acceptable to You, O Lord, my rock and my redeemer.

May He who makes peace in the highest bring this peace upon us and upon all Israel. Amen.

Kiddush is on pages 316–318.

BUILDING THE KINGDOM OF GOD: THE DUTY OF ISRAEL It is our duty to praise the Lord of all, to recognise the greatness of the creator of first things, who has chosen us from all peoples by giving us His Torah. Therefore we bend low and submit, and give thanks before the King above the kings of kings, the Holy One, blessed be He. He extends the limits of space and makes the world firm. His glory extends through the universe beyond, and the presence of His strength into farthest space. He is our God; no other exists. Our king is truth; the rest is nothing. It is written in His Torah: 'Realise this today and take it to heart—it is the Lord who is God in the heavens above and on the earth beneath; no other exists.'

עַל־כֵּן נְקַוֶּה לְּךָ יְיָ אֱלֹהֵינוּ לִרְאוֹת מְהֵרָה בְּתִפְאֶרֶת עֻזֶּךָ ·
לְהַעֲבִיר גִּלּוּלִים מִן הָאָרֶץ וְהָאֱלִילִים כָּרוֹת יִכָּרֵתוּן · לְתַקֵּן
עוֹלָם בְּמַלְכוּת שַׁדַּי וְכָל־בְּנֵי בָשָׂר יִקְרְאוּ בִשְׁמֶךָ · לְהַפְנוֹת
אֵלֶיךָ כָּל־רִשְׁעֵי אָרֶץ : יַכִּירוּ וְיֵדְעוּ כָּל־יוֹשְׁבֵי תֵבֵל כִּי לְךָ
תִּכְרַע כָּל־בֶּרֶךְ תִּשָּׁבַע כָּל־לָשׁוֹן : לְפָנֶיךָ יְיָ אֱלֹהֵינוּ יִכְרְעוּ
וְיִפּוֹלוּ · וְלִכְבוֹד שִׁמְךָ יְקָר יִתֵּנוּ · וִיקַבְּלוּ כֻלָּם אֶת־עֹל
מַלְכוּתֶךָ · וְתִמְלוֹךְ עֲלֵיהֶם מְהֵרָה לְעוֹלָם וָעֶד · כִּי הַמַּלְכוּת
שֶׁלְּךָ הִיא וּלְעוֹלְמֵי עַד תִּמְלוֹךְ בְּכָבוֹד · כַּכָּתוּב בְּתוֹרָתֶךָ ·
יְהֹוָה יִמְלֹךְ לְעֹלָם וָעֶד : וְנֶאֱמַר · וְהָיָה יְהֹוָה לְמֶלֶךְ עַל־
כָּל־הָאָרֶץ בַּיּוֹם הַהוּא יִהְיֶה יְהֹוָה אֶחָד וּשְׁמוֹ אֶחָד :

יִתְגַּדַּל וְיִתְקַדַּשׁ שְׁמֵהּ רַבָּא בְּעָלְמָא דִּי־בְרָא כִרְעוּתֵהּ ·
וְיַמְלִיךְ מַלְכוּתֵהּ בְּחַיֵּיכוֹן וּבְיוֹמֵיכוֹן וּבְחַיֵּי
דִי־כָל־בֵּית יִשְׂרָאֵל בַּעֲגָלָא וּבִזְמַן קָרִיב · וְאִמְרוּ אָמֵן :
יְהֵא שְׁמֵהּ רַבָּא מְבָרַךְ לְעָלַם וּלְעָלְמֵי עָלְמַיָּא ·
יִתְבָּרַךְ וְיִשְׁתַּבַּח וְיִתְפָּאַר וְיִתְרוֹמַם וְיִתְנַשֵּׂא וְיִתְהַדָּר וְיִתְעַלֶּה
וְיִתְהַלָּל שְׁמֵהּ דִּי־קֻדְשָׁא · בְּרִיךְ הוּא · לְעֵלָּא מִן־כָּל־בִּרְכָתָא
וְשִׁירָתָא תֻּשְׁבְּחָתָא וְנֶחֱמָתָא דִּי־אֲמִירָן בְּעָלְמָא · וְאִמְרוּ אָמֵן :
יְהֵא שְׁלָמָא רַבָּא מִן־שְׁמַיָּא וְחַיִּים עָלֵינוּ וְעַל־כָּל־
יִשְׂרָאֵל · וְאִמְרוּ אָמֵן :
עֹשֶׂה שָׁלוֹם בִּמְרוֹמָיו הוּא יַעֲשֶׂה שָׁלוֹם עָלֵינוּ וְעַל־כָּל־
יִשְׂרָאֵל · וְאִמְרוּ אָמֵן :

THE HOPE FOR MANKIND   Therefore, Lord our God, we put our hope in You. Soon let us witness the glory of Your power; when the worship of material things shall pass away from the earth, and prejudice and superstition shall at last be cut off; when the world will be set right by the rule of God, and all mankind shall speak out in Your name, and all the wicked of the earth shall turn to You. Then all who inhabit this world shall meet in understanding, and shall know that to You alone each one shall submit, and pledge himself in every tongue. In Your presence, Lord our God, they shall bow down and be humble, honouring the glory of Your being. All shall accept the duty of building Your kingdom, so that Your reign of goodness shall come soon and last forever. For Yours alone is the true kingdom, and only the glory of Your rule endures forever. So it is written in Your Torah:

'The Lord shall rule forever and ever.'

So it is prophesied:

'The Lord shall be as a king over all the earth.

On that day the Lord shall be One, and known as One.'

Let us magnify and let us sanctify the great name of God in the world which He created according to His will. May His kingdom come in your lifetime, and in your days, and in the lifetime of the family of Israel—quickly and speedily may it come. Amen.

May the greatness of His being be blessed from eternity to eternity.

Let us bless and let us extol, let us tell aloud and let us raise aloft, let us set on high and let us honour, let us exalt and let us praise the Holy One—blessed be He!—though He is far beyond any blessing or song, any honour or any consolation that can be spoken of in this world. Amen.

May great peace from heaven and the gift of life be granted to us and to all the family of Israel. Amen.

May He who makes peace in the highest bring this peace upon us and upon all Israel. Amen.

יִגְדַּל אֱלֹהִים חַי וְיִשְׁתַּבַּח · נִמְצָא וְאֵין עֵת אֶל־מְצִיאוּתוֹ :

אֶחָד וְאֵין יָחִיד כְּיִחוּדוֹ ··נֶעְלָם וְגַם אֵין סוֹף לְאַחְדוּתוֹ :

אֵין לוֹ דְמוּת הַגּוּף וְאֵינוֹ גוּף · לֹא נַעֲרוֹךְ אֵלָיו קְדֻשָּׁתוֹ :

קַדְמוֹן לְכָל־דָּבָר אֲשֶׁר נִבְרָא · רִאשׁוֹן וְאֵין רֵאשִׁית לְרֵאשִׁיתוֹ :

הִנּוֹ אֲדוֹן עוֹלָם · לְכָל־נוֹצָר יוֹרֶה גְדֻלָּתוֹ וּמַלְכוּתוֹ :

שֶׁפַע נְבוּאָתוֹ נְתָנוֹ אֶל־אַנְשֵׁי סְגֻלָּתוֹ וְתִפְאַרְתּוֹ :

לֹא קָם בְּיִשְׂרָאֵל כְּמֹשֶׁה עוֹד נָבִיא · וּמַבִּיט אֶל־תְּמוּנָתוֹ :

תּוֹרַת אֱמֶת נָתַן לְעַמּוֹ אֵל · עַל יַד נְבִיאוֹ נֶאֱמַן בֵּיתוֹ :

לֹא יַחֲלִיף הָאֵל וְלֹא יָמִיר־דָּתוֹ לְעוֹלָמִים לְזוּלָתוֹ :

צוֹפֶה וְיוֹדֵעַ סְתָרֵינוּ · מַבִּיט לְסוֹף דָּבָר בְּקַדְמוּתוֹ :

גּוֹמֵל לְאִישׁ חָסִיד כְּמִפְעָלוֹ · נוֹתֵן לְרָשָׁע רָע כְּרִשְׁעָתוֹ :

יִשְׁלַח לְקֵץ יָמִים מְשִׁיחֵנוּ · לִפְדּוֹת מְחַכֵּי קֵץ יְשׁוּעָתוֹ :

מֵתִים יְחַיֶּה אֵל בְּרֹב חַסְדּוֹ · בָּרוּךְ עֲדֵי עַד שֵׁם תְּהִלָּתוֹ :

יְבָרֶכְךָ יְיָ וְיִשְׁמְרֶךָ ·
יָאֵר יְיָ פָּנָיו אֵלֶיךָ וִיחֻנֶּךָּ ·
יִשָּׂא יְיָ פָּנָיו אֵלֶיךָ וְיָשֵׂם לְךָ שָׁלוֹם :

We praise the living God and Him do we adore
who is outside the bounds of space and time.

Unique is He, and none like Him can ever be
beyond all limitations men define.

He has no human form, no likeness to a man;
more wonderful than any holiness we know.

Before He had begun creation of our world,
He was the first, with no beginning of His own.

Behold He is the Lord of all the universe
who teaches every creature He is king.

And to the world He speaks, and freely gives His word
through prophets that He chooses to proclaim His will.

Another man like Moses, Israel has not known,
a prophet who to God could be so close.

God gave His people truth by which to lead their life
taught by the faithful prophet of His house.

God will never change the teaching that He gave
and He will put no other in its place.

He watches and He knows the secrets in our hearts,
before each deed, its ending He can trace.

The man of loving deeds rejoices in His love,
but evil leads to evil which destroys.

And at the end of days, an anointed He will send
redeeming those who wait for when He saves.

Life beyond all death, He gives through His great love.
We bless for evermore His glorious name.

May the Lord bless you and keep you.

May the face of the Lord enlighten you and be gracious to you.

May the Lord turn His face towards you and give you peace.

It is a tree of life to all who grasp it and those who hold fast to it are happy. Its ways are ways of pleasantness and all its paths are peace.

Siddur

תפלת שחרית לשבת

מַה־טֹּבוּ אֹהָלֶיךָ יַעֲקֹב מִשְׁכְּנֹתֶיךָ יִשְׂרָאֵל׃

וַאֲנִי בְּרֹב חַסְדְּךָ אָבוֹא בֵיתֶךָ

אֶשְׁתַּחֲוֶה אֶל־הֵיכַל־קָדְשְׁךָ בְּיִרְאָתֶךָ׃

יְהֹוָה אָהַבְתִּי מְעוֹן בֵּיתֶךָ וּמְקוֹם מִשְׁכַּן כְּבוֹדֶךָ׃

וַאֲנִי אֶשְׁתַּחֲוֶה וְאֶכְרָעָה אֶבְרְכָה לִפְנֵי־יְהֹוָה עֹשִׂי׃

וַאֲנִי תְפִלָּתִי־לְךָ יְהֹוָה עֵת רָצוֹן

אֱלֹהִים בְּרָב־חַסְדֶּךָ עֲנֵנִי בֶּאֱמֶת יִשְׁעֶךָ׃

יִהְיוּ־נָא חַיֵּי חוּלְיָה אַחַת בְּשַׁרְשֶׁרֶת־הַטּוֹב׃ בְּאָמְרִי אֶת־
תְּפִלּוֹת־אֲבוֹתַי· עֶזְר־נָא לִי לְהִזָּכֵר בִּמְסִירוּת־נַפְשָׁם
וּבֶאֱמָנוּתָם· בְּשִׂמְחָתָם וּבְסִבְלָם· הַטְּבוּעִים בְּכָל־מִלָּה וּמִלָּה
הַקְּדֻשָׁה הִיא יְרֻשָׁתִי· בָּה זַכֵּנִי׃
תִּחְיֶה בִּי מָסָרְתָּם זֹאת· וְיִוָּסְפוּ עָלֶיהָ הָאֱמִיתוֹת שֶׁאֲנִי
מְגַלֶּה וְהַמַּעֲשִׂים שֶׁאֲנִי עוֹשֶׂה וּמִמֶּנִּי תִּמָּסֵר לְדוֹרוֹת לֹא
אִיכָּרֵם· כָּךְ יִתְמַלֵּא תַפְקִידִי בָּעוֹלָם וַאֲקַבֵּל שְׂכָרִי׃
וּכְתֹם הַתְּפִלּוֹת· עָזְרֵנִי לְהָפִיץ רוּחָן בָּעוֹלָם בּוֹ אֲנִי חַי·
מֵעַל־הַכֹּל אֶת־הָאֱלֹהִים אֹהַב וְכֵן לְרֵעַי כָּמוֹנִי וְאֶהְיֶה־נָא
עֵד חַי לָאֱמֶת שֶׁלְּעוֹלָם קַיֶּמֶת· אָמֵן׃

קכא שִׁיר לַמַּעֲלוֹת

אֶשָּׂא עֵינַי אֶל־הֶהָרִים מֵאַיִן יָבֹא עֶזְרִי׃

עֶזְרִי מֵעִם יְהֹוָה עֹשֵׂה שָׁמַיִם וָאָרֶץ׃

I

SABBATH MORNING SERVICE

DIRECTING THE HEART TO GOD

How good are your tents, O Jacob, and your homes, O Israel.

Through the greatness of Your love I enter Your house. In awe I worship before the ark of Your holiness.

Lord, as I loved the courts of Your temple, and the place where Your glory dwelt, so I still worship and bend low, humble before the Lord my maker.

As for me, let my prayer come before You at the proper time.

Answer me God, in the greatness of Your love, for Your deliverance is sure.

TRADITION

May my life be one link in a chain of goodness. As I say the prayers of my fathers, help me to remember their devotion and faithfulness, their joy and suffering, which are in every word. Holiness is my heritage, may I be worthy of it.

May this tradition live in me and pass from me to generations I shall never know, enriched by the truth that I have found and the good deeds I have done. So may I fulfil my task on earth and receive my blessing.

And when the service ends and the prayers have ceased, help me to bring their spirit into the world in which I live. May I love God above all, and my neighbour as myself, and be a living witness to the truth that never changes. Amen.

Psalm 121

A Pilgrim Song

SONGS OF PRAISE

I lift up my eyes to the hills;
where shall I find my help?
My help is from the Lord alone,
maker of heaven and earth.

אַל־יִתֵּן לַמּוֹט רַגְלֶךָ אַל־יָנוּם שֹׁמְרֶךָ׃

הִנֵּה לֹא־יָנוּם וְלֹא יִישָׁן שׁוֹמֵר יִשְׂרָאֵל׃

יְהוָֹה שֹׁמְרֶךָ יְהוָֹה צִלְּךָ עַל־יַד יְמִינֶךָ׃

יוֹמָם הַשֶּׁמֶשׁ לֹא־יַכֶּכָּה וְיָרֵחַ בַּלָּיְלָה׃

יְהוָֹה יִשְׁמָרְךָ מִכָּל־רָע יִשְׁמֹר אֶת־נַפְשֶׁךָ׃

יְהוָֹה יִשְׁמָר־צֵאתְךָ וּבוֹאֶךָ מֵעַתָּה וְעַד־עוֹלָם׃

אֱלֹהַי ׀ נְשָׁמָה שֶׁנָּתַתָּ־בִּי טְהוֹרָה ׀ אַתָּה בְרָאתָהּ ׀ אַתָּה יְצַרְתָּהּ ׀ אַתָּה נְפַחְתָּהּ בִּי ׀ וְאַתָּה מְשַׁמְּרָהּ בְּקִרְבִּי ׀ וְאַתָּה עָתִיד לִטְּלָהּ מִמֶּנִּי לְחַיֵּי עוֹלָם׃ כָּל־זְמַן שֶׁהַנְּשָׁמָה בְקִרְבִּי מוֹדֶה אֲנִי לְפָנֶיךָ יְיָ אֱלֹהַי וֵאלֹהֵי אֲבוֹתַי ׀ שֶׁאַתָּה הוּא רִבּוֹן כָּל־הַמַּעֲשִׂים ׀ מוֹשֵׁל בְּכָל־הַבְּרִיּוֹת ׀ אֲדוֹן כָּל־הַנְּשָׁמוֹת׃ בָּרוּךְ אַתָּה יְיָ ׀ הַמַּחֲזִיר נְשָׁמוֹת לַמֵּתִים׃

לְעוֹלָם יְהֵא אָדָם יְרֵא שָׁמַיִם בַּסֵּתֶר כְּבַגָּלוּי ׀ וּמוֹדֶה עַל־הָאֱמֶת וְדוֹבֵר אֱמֶת בִּלְבָבוֹ׃

יְהִי רָצוֹן מִלְּפָנֶיךָ יְיָ אֱלֹהֵינוּ וֵאלֹהֵי אֲבוֹתֵינוּ ׀ שֶׁתַּרְגִּילֵנוּ בְּתוֹרָתֶךָ וְדַבְּקֵנוּ בְּמִצְוֹתֶיךָ ׀ וְאַל תְּבִיאֵנוּ לֹא לִידֵי חֵטְא וְלֹא לִידֵי עֲבֵרָה וְלֹא לִידֵי נִסָּיוֹן וְלֹא לִידֵי בִזָּיוֹן ׀ וְאַל תַּשְׁלֶט־בָּנוּ יֵצֶר הָרָע ׀ וְהַרְחִיקֵנוּ מֵאָדָם רַע וּמֵחָבֵר רַע ׀ וְדַבְּקֵנוּ בְּיֵצֶר הַטּוֹב וּבְמַעֲשִׂים טוֹבִים ׀ וְכֹף אֶת־יִצְרֵנוּ לְהִשְׁתַּעְבֶּד־לָךְ ׀ וּתְנֵנוּ הַיּוֹם וּבְכָל־יוֹם לְחֵן וּלְחֶסֶד וּלְרַחֲמִים בְּעֵינֶיךָ וּבְעֵינֵי כָל־רוֹאֵינוּ ׀ וְתִגְמְלֵנוּ חֲסָדִים טוֹבִים׃ בָּרוּךְ אַתָּה יְיָ ׀ גּוֹמֵל חֲסָדִים טוֹבִים לְעַמּוֹ יִשְׂרָאֵל׃

He will not allow your foot to slip,
for your guardian does not slumber.
Know that the guardian of Israel
never slumbers and never sleeps.
The Lord is your guardian,
the Lord is your shade at your right hand.
The sun will not strike you by day
nor the moon by night.
The Lord will guard you from all evil,
He will guard your soul.
The Lord will guard your going out and your coming in
now and for evermore.

Alternative Songs of Praise, pages 571–609.

THE GOODNESS OF MAN   My God, the soul You have given me is pure, for You created it, You formed it and You made it live within me. You watch over it within me, but one day You will take it from me to everlasting life. My God and God of my fathers, as long as the soul is within me, I will declare that You are the master of all deeds, the ruler of all creatures and the Lord of every soul. Blessed are You Lord, who brings the dead into everlasting life.

Man should always be in awe of heaven in private as well as in public. He should tell the truth and speak it in his heart.

Lord our God and God of our fathers, help us to live according to Your teaching and to hold fast to Your commands. Let us not come into the power of sin or wrong-doing, temptation or disgrace. Let no evil within us control us, and keep us far from bad people and bad company. Help us hold fast to the good within us and to good deeds, and bend our will and our desires to serve You. Give us today, and every day, grace, kindness and mercy in Your sight and in the sight of all who regard us, and grant us Your love and kindness. Blessed are You Lord, who grants love and kindness to His people Israel.

רִבּוֹן הָעוֹלָמִים וַאֲדֹנֵי הָאֲדֹנִים · לֹא עַל־צִדְקוֹתֵינוּ אֲנַחְנוּ
מַפִּילִים תַּחֲנוּנֵינוּ לְפָנֶיךָ · כִּי עַל־רַחֲמֶיךָ הָרַבִּים: אֲדֹנָי
שְׁמָעָה · אֲדֹנָי סְלָחָה · אֲדֹנָי הַקְשִׁיבָה וַעֲשֵׂה · מָה־אָנוּ · מֶה־
חַיֵּינוּ · מֶה־חַסְדֵּנוּ · מַה־צִּדְקוֹתֵינוּ · מַה־יְשׁוּעָתֵנוּ · מַה־
כֹּחֵנוּ · מַה־גְּבוּרָתֵנוּ · מַה־נֹּאמַר לְפָנֶיךָ יְיָ אֱלֹהֵינוּ וֵאלֹהֵי
אֲבוֹתֵינוּ · הֲלֹא הַגִּבּוֹרִים כְּאַיִן לְפָנֶיךָ · וְאַנְשֵׁי הַשֵּׁם כְּלֹא הָיוּ ·
וַחֲכָמִים כִּבְלִי מַדָּע · וּנְבוֹנִים כִּבְלִי הַשְׂכֵּל · כִּי רֹב מַעֲשֵׂינוּ
תֹהוּ · וִימֵי חַיֵּינוּ הֶבֶל לְפָנֶיךָ · וּמוֹתַר הָאָדָם מִן הַבְּהֵמָה אָיִן ·
כִּי הַכֹּל הָבֶל לְבַד הַנְּשָׁמָה הַטְּהוֹרָה · שֶׁהִיא עֲתִידָה לִתֵּן
דִּין וְחֶשְׁבּוֹן לִפְנֵי כִסֵּא כְבוֹדֶךָ:

יְיָ מֶלֶךְ · יְיָ מָלָךְ · יְיָ יִמְלֹךְ לְעוֹלָם וָעֶד:

וְהָיָה יְיָ לְמֶלֶךְ עַל־כָּל־הָאָרֶץ · בַּיּוֹם הַהוּא יִהְיֶה יְיָ אֶחָד
וּשְׁמוֹ אֶחָד: הוֹשִׁיעֵנוּ יְיָ אֱלֹהֵינוּ · לְהוֹדוֹת לְשֵׁם קָדְשֶׁךָ
לְהִשְׁתַּבֵּחַ בִּתְהִלָּתֶךָ · בָּרוּךְ יְהֹוָה אֱלֹהֵי יִשְׂרָאֵל מִן־הָעוֹלָם
וְעַד הָעוֹלָם · וְאָמַר כָּל־הָעָם אָמֵן · הַלְלוּיָהּ: כֹּל הַנְּשָׁמָה
תְּהַלֵּל יָהּ · הַלְלוּיָהּ:

בָּרוּךְ שֶׁאָמַר וְהָיָה הָעוֹלָם · בָּרוּךְ אוֹמֵר וְעֹשֶׂה · בָּרוּךְ
גּוֹזֵר וּמְקַיֵּם · בָּרוּךְ עֹשֶׂה בְרֵאשִׁית · בָּרוּךְ מְרַחֵם עַל
הָאָרֶץ · בָּרוּךְ מְרַחֵם עַל הַבְּרִיּוֹת · בָּרוּךְ מְשַׁלֵּם שָׂכָר טוֹב
לִירֵאָיו · בָּרוּךְ מַעֲבִיר אֲפֵלָה וּמֵבִיא אוֹרָה · בָּרוּךְ אֵל חַי
לָעַד וְקַיָּם לָנֶצַח · בָּרוּךְ שֶׁאֵין לְפָנָיו עַוְלָה וְלֹא שִׁכְחָה וְלֹא
מַשּׂוֹא פָנִים וְלֹא מִקַּח שֹׁחַד · צַדִּיק הוּא בְּכָל־דְּרָכָיו וְחָסִיד
בְּכָל־מַעֲשָׂיו: בָּרוּךְ פּוֹדֶה וּמַצִּיל · בָּרוּךְ הַמַּנְחִיל מְנוּחָה

THE
WEAKNESS
OF MAN
Master of existence, and Lord of lords, we do not rely on our own good deeds but on Your great mercy as we lay our needs before You. Lord, hear! Lord, pardon! Lord, listen and act! What are we? What is our life? What is our love? What is our justice? What is our success? What is our endurance? What is our power? Lord our God, and God of our fathers, what can we say before You, for in Your presence are not the powerful as nothing, the famous as if they had never existed, the learned as if without knowledge, and the intelligent as if without insight. To You most of our actions are pointless and our daily life is shallow. Even the superiority of man over the beasts is nothing. For everything is trivial except the pure soul which must one day give its account and reckoning before the judgment seat of Your glory.

THE POWER
OF GOD
The Lord does rule, the Lord has ruled, the Lord shall rule forever and ever.

The Lord shall be as a king over the whole earth. On that day the Lord shall be One, and known as One.

Save us, Lord our God, to proclaim Your holy name and be honoured in praising You.

Blessed is the Lord God of Israel from everlasting to everlasting. Let all the people say: Amen! Praise the Lord!

May all who live praise the Lord. Hallelujah!

One of the two following paragraphs.

Blessed be He, at whose word the world existed.

Blessed be He, whose word is deed.

Blessed be He, whose command stands firm.

Blessed be He, who makes creation.

Blessed be He, who has mercy on the earth.

Blessed be He, who has mercy on His creatures.

Blessed be He, who gives a good reward to those in awe of Him.

Blessed be He, who takes away darkness and brings on light.

Blessed be He, who lives forever and exists for eternity.

Blessed be He, who has no fault and no forgetfulness, who shows no favour and takes no bribe. Righteous is He in all His ways and loving in all His deeds.

Blessed be He, who redeems and rescues.

לְעַמּוֹ יִשְׂרָאֵל בְּיוֹם שַׁבַּת קֹדֶשׁ: בָּרוּךְ הוּא וּבָרוּךְ שְׁמוֹ ·
וּבָרוּךְ זִכְרוֹ לְעוֹלְמֵי עַד: בָּרוּךְ אַתָּה יְיָ אֱלֹהֵינוּ מֶלֶךְ
הָעוֹלָם · הַמֶּלֶךְ הַגָּדוֹל וְהַקָּדוֹשׁ · אָב הָרַחֲמָן · מְהֻלָּל בְּפִי
עַמּוֹ · מְשֻׁבָּח וּמְפֹאָר בִּלְשׁוֹן כָּל־חֲסִידָיו וַעֲבָדָיו · וּבְשִׁירֵי
דָוִד עַבְדֶּךָ נְהַלֶּלְךָ יְיָ אֱלֹהֵינוּ · בִּשְׁבָחוֹת וּבִזְמִירוֹת נְהוֹדֶךָ
נְגַדֶּלְךָ נְפָאֶרְךָ וְנַמְלִיכְךָ וְנַזְכִּיר שִׁמְךָ מַלְכֵּנוּ אֱלֹהֵינוּ · יָחִיד
חֵי הָעוֹלָמִים · מְשֻׁבָּח וּמְפֹאָר שְׁמוֹ עֲדֵי־עַד: בָּרוּךְ אַתָּה יְיָ ·
מֶלֶךְ מְהֻלָּל בַּתִּשְׁבָּחוֹת:

וַיְבָרֶךְ דָּוִיד אֶת־יְהוָה לְעֵינֵי כָּל־הַקָּהָל · וַיֹּאמֶר דָּוִיד ·
בָּרוּךְ אַתָּה יְהוָה אֱלֹהֵי יִשְׂרָאֵל אָבִינוּ מֵעוֹלָם וְעַד־עוֹלָם:
לְךָ יְהוָה הַגְּדֻלָּה וְהַגְּבוּרָה וְהַתִּפְאֶרֶת וְהַנֵּצַח וְהַהוֹד · כִּי־
כֹל בַּשָּׁמַיִם וּבָאָרֶץ לְךָ יְהוָה הַמַּמְלָכָה וְהַמִּתְנַשֵּׂא לְכֹל
לְרֹאשׁ: וְהָעֹשֶׁר וְהַכָּבוֹד מִלְּפָנֶיךָ · וְאַתָּה מוֹשֵׁל בַּכֹּל ·
וּבְיָדְךָ כֹּחַ וּגְבוּרָה · וּבְיָדְךָ לְגַדֵּל וּלְחַזֵּק לַכֹּל: וְעַתָּה
אֱלֹהֵינוּ מוֹדִים אֲנַחְנוּ לָךְ · וּמְהַלְלִים לְשֵׁם תִּפְאַרְתֶּךָ:
וִיבָרְכוּ שֵׁם כְּבֹדֶךָ · וּמְרוֹמַם עַל־כָּל־בְּרָכָה וּתְהִלָּה:
אַתָּה־הוּא יְהוָה לְבַדֶּךָ · אַתָּה עָשִׂיתָ אֶת־הַשָּׁמַיִם שְׁמֵי
הַשָּׁמַיִם וְכָל־צְבָאָם · הָאָרֶץ וְכָל־אֲשֶׁר עָלֶיהָ · הַיַּמִּים
וְכָל־אֲשֶׁר בָּהֶם · וְאַתָּה מְחַיֶּה אֶת־כֻּלָּם · וּצְבָא הַשָּׁמַיִם
לְךָ מִשְׁתַּחֲוִים:

בָּרוּךְ יְהוָה לְעוֹלָם · אָמֵן וְאָמֵן:
בָּרוּךְ יְהוָה אֱלֹהִים אֱלֹהֵי יִשְׂרָאֵל · עֹשֵׂה נִפְלָאוֹת לְבַדּוֹ:
וּבָרוּךְ שֵׁם כְּבוֹדוֹ לְעוֹלָם · וְיִמָּלֵא כְבוֹדוֹ אֶת־כָּל־הָאָרֶץ ·
אָמֵן וְאָמֵן:

Blessed be He, who gives rest to His people Israel on the holy Sabbath day.

Blessed be He, and blessed be His name.

Blessed be the knowledge of Him for all eternity.

Blessed are You, Lord our God, king of the universe, the king, great and holy; merciful father, praised by His people; worshipped and glorified by the tongue of all who love and serve Him. Therefore we praise You, Lord our God, with the psalms of Your servant David; with prayers and songs we declare Your glory, Your greatness, Your splendour, and Your majesty. We proclaim Your name, our king, our God, who alone is the life of all existence, and whose name is worshipped and glorified forever and ever. Blessed are You Lord, the king praised in all worship.

Then David blessed the Lord in the sight of all the congregation, and David said: 'Blessed are You Lord, the God of our father Israel from everlasting to everlasting. Yours is the greatness, the power, the splendour, the glory and the majesty, for everything in heaven and earth is Yours. Yours is the kingdom and You are exalted supreme over all. Wealth and honour come from You, for You rule over all. In Your hand are strength and might. It is in Your power to give greatness and strength to all. And now, our God, we give You thanks and praise Your glorious name.' (*1 Chronicles 29: 10-13*) May the people bless Your glorious name, though it is beyond all blessing and praise. You are the Lord alone; You made the sky, the reaches of space and its countless lights, the earth and everything on it, the seas and everything in them; You give life to them all, and the universe worships You (*Nehemiah 9: 5-6*).

Blessed be the Lord forever. Amen and amen.

Blessed be the Lord God, the God of Israel, who alone works wonders.

Blessed be His glorious name forever. All the earth is full of His glory. Amen and amen.

נִשְׁמַת כָּל־חַי תְּבָרֵךְ אֶת־שִׁמְךָ יְיָ אֱלֹהֵינוּ . וְרוּחַ כָּל־
בָּשָׂר תְּפָאֵר וּתְרוֹמֵם זִכְרְךָ מַלְכֵּנוּ תָּמִיד : מִן
הָעוֹלָם וְעַד הָעוֹלָם אַתָּה אֵל . וּמִבַּלְעָדֶיךָ אֵין לָנוּ מֶלֶךְ
גּוֹאֵל וּמוֹשִׁיעַ פּוֹדֶה וּמַצִּיל וְעוֹנֶה וּמְרַחֵם . בְּכָל־עֵת צָרָה
וְצוּקָה אֵין לָנוּ מֶלֶךְ עוֹזֵר וְסוֹמֵךְ זוּלָתֶךָ : אֱלֹהֵי הָרִאשׁוֹנִים
וְהָאַחֲרוֹנִים . אֱלוֹהַּ כָּל־בְּרִיּוֹת . אֲדוֹן כָּל־תּוֹלָדוֹת הַמְהֻלָּל
בְּכָל־הַתִּשְׁבָּחוֹת . הַמְנַהֵג עוֹלָמוֹ בְּחֶסֶד וּבְרִיּוֹתָיו בְּרַחֲמִים :
וַייָ לֹא יָנוּם וְלֹא יִישָׁן . הַמְעוֹרֵר יְשֵׁנִים וְהַמֵּקִיץ נִרְדָּמִים .
מְחַיֶּה מֵתִים וְרוֹפֵא חוֹלִים . פּוֹקֵחַ עִוְרִים וְזוֹקֵף כְּפוּפִים .
לְךָ לְבַדְּךָ אֲנַחְנוּ מוֹדִים :

וְאִלּוּ פִינוּ מָלֵא שִׁירָה כַיָּם .
וּלְשׁוֹנֵנוּ רִנָּה כַּהֲמוֹן גַּלָּיו .
וְשִׂפְתוֹתֵינוּ שֶׁבַח כְּמֶרְחֲבֵי רָקִיעַ .
וְעֵינֵינוּ מְאִירוֹת כַּשֶּׁמֶשׁ וְכַיָּרֵחַ .
וְיָדֵינוּ פְרוּשׂוֹת כְּנִשְׁרֵי שָׁמָיִם .
וְרַגְלֵינוּ קַלּוֹת כָּאַיָּלוֹת .
אֵין אָנוּ מַסְפִּיקִים לְהוֹדוֹת לְךָ יְיָ אֱלֹהֵינוּ .
וּלְבָרֵךְ אֶת־שִׁמְךָ מַלְכֵּנוּ .
עַל אַחַת מֵאֶלֶף אַלְפֵי אֲלָפִים .
וְרִבֵּי רְבָבוֹת פְּעָמִים הַטּוֹבוֹת .
שֶׁעָשִׂיתָ עִם־אֲבוֹתֵינוּ וְעִמָּנוּ :
מִמִּצְרַיִם גְּאַלְתָּנוּ יְיָ אֱלֹהֵינוּ .
מִבֵּית עֲבָדִים פְּדִיתָנוּ .
בְּרָעָב זַנְתָּנוּ .
וּבְשָׂבָע כִּלְכַּלְתָּנוּ .
מֵחֶרֶב הִצַּלְתָּנוּ .
מִדֶּבֶר מִלַּטְתָּנוּ .
וּמֵחֳלָיִם רָעִים וְרַבִּים דִּלִּיתָנוּ :

The breath of life in every creature shall bless You, Lord our God, and the spirit of all flesh ever recalls Your beauty and Your greatness. From everlasting to everlasting You are God. Besides You we have no king who rescues and saves us, frees and delivers us, and answers and cares for us. At all times of trouble and distress there is no king who can help and support us but You.

God of the first and of the last ages, God of all creatures, Lord of history, adored in all worship—He guides His universe with love, and His creatures with mercy. The Lord neither slumbers nor sleeps. He wakes the sleepers, and rouses the uncaring. He gives life beyond death, He heals the sick, He gives sight to the blind and raises up those bent low. To You alone we declare our gratitude.

If our mouths were full of song as the sea,

our tongues with joyful sounds like the roar of its waves,

our lips with praise as the outspread sky,

our eyes shining like the sun and the moon,

our hands stretched out like eagles' wings in the air,

our feet as swift as the wild deer;

we still could not thank You enough, Lord our God,

or bless Your name, our king,

for even one of the thousands upon thousands

of the countless good deeds

You did for our fathers and for us.

Lord our God, You rescued us from Egypt,

freed us from the camp of slavery.

In times of famine You fed us,

in times of plenty You supported us.

From violence You delivered us,

from plagues You saved us,

and from many terrible diseases You rescued us.

עַד־הֵנָּה עֲזָרוּנוּ רַחֲמֶיךָ · וְלֹא עֲזָבוּנוּ חֲסָדֶיךָ · עַל־כֵּן
אֵבָרִים שֶׁפִּלַּגְתָּ בָּנוּ · וְרוּחַ וּנְשָׁמָה שֶׁנָּפַחְתָּ בְּאַפֵּינוּ · וְלָשׁוֹן
אֲשֶׁר שַׂמְתָּ בְּפִינוּ · הֵן הֵם יוֹדוּ וִיבָרְכוּ · וִישַׁבְּחוּ · וִיפָאֲרוּ ·
וִישׁוֹרְרוּ אֶת־שִׁמְךָ מַלְכֵּנוּ תָמִיד: כִּי כָל־פֶּה לְךָ יוֹדֶה ·
וְכָל־לָשׁוֹן לְךָ תְשַׁבֵּחַ · וְכָל־עַיִן לְךָ תְצַפֶּה · וְכָל־בֶּרֶךְ לְךָ
תִכְרַע · וְכָל־קוֹמָה לְפָנֶיךָ תִשְׁתַּחֲוֶה · וְכָל־הַלְּבָבוֹת
יִירָאוּךָ · וְכָל־קֶרֶב וּכְלָיוֹת יְזַמְּרוּ לִשְׁמֶךָ · כַּדָּבָר שֶׁנֶּאֱמַר ·
כָּל־עַצְמוֹתַי תֹּאמַרְנָה · יְיָ מִי כָמוֹךָ: מַצִּיל עָנִי מֵחָזָק מִמֶּנּוּ ·
וְעָנִי וְאֶבְיוֹן מִגֹּזְלוֹ: מִי יִדְמֶה־לָּךְ · וּמִי יִשְׁוֶה־לָּךְ · וּמִי
יַעֲרָךְ־לָךְ · הָאֵל הַגָּדוֹל הַגִּבּוֹר וְהַנּוֹרָא אֵל עֶלְיוֹן קוֹנֵה שָׁמַיִם
וָאָרֶץ: בְּפִי יְשָׁרִים תִּתְהַלָּל · וּבְדִבְרֵי צַדִּיקִים תִּתְבָּרַךְ ·
וּבִלְשׁוֹן חֲסִידִים תִּתְרוֹמָם · וּבְקֶרֶב קְדוֹשִׁים תִּתְקַדָּשׁ:

בָּרוּךְ אַתָּה יְיָ אֱלֹהֵינוּ מֶלֶךְ הָעוֹלָם · אֲשֶׁר קִדְּשָׁנוּ
בְּמִצְוֹתָיו וְצִוָּנוּ לַעֲסוֹק בְּדִבְרֵי תוֹרָה:

To the Book of Deuteronomy, Torah is the life and good which is
set before man as an alternative to death and evil; at the same time it
is Israel's wisdom and understanding in the eyes of the nations.

To the Prophet it is the water for which all men thirst, the bread
for which they starve—which is yet dispensed without silver or price.

To the Psalmist it is the light in which he sees light, or alternatively
the spiritual sustenance whose taste is sweeter than honey and the
drippings of the honeycomb.

To a Rabbi of ancient days it is something to be delved into further
and further, since all things are in it; something over which a man
may grow grey and old, never stirring from its contemplation,
knowing that he can have no better pursuit or rule.

To mediaeval Jews in their ghettos it is, by the testimony of
a folk-song, a treasure better than all worldly goods.

To the modern Hebrew poet, Bialik, it is a great flame kindled on
high altars in olden days.

And to all generations of Jews from Isaiah on, it is the word of
the Lord destined in the end to regenerate man and society.

Milton Steinberg

Until now Your love has been our help and Your kindness has not left us. Therefore the limbs You formed in us, the spirit and soul You breathed into us and the tongue You set in our mouth, ever shall they thank, bless, praise, glorify and sing to Your name, our king. For every mouth shall thank You, every tongue praise You, every eye look to You, every knee bend to You and the height of man shall bow low before You. All hearts shall fear You and our innermost being sing praises to Your name, as it is said: 'All my bones shall say, Lord who is like You, who frees the poor man from those too strong for him, the poor and needy man from his exploiter.' Who is like You, who is equal to You, who can be compared to You, the great, mighty and awesome God, transcendent God, creator of heaven and earth. By the mouth of the upright You are praised, by the words of the righteous You are blessed, by the tongue of the pious You are honoured, and among the holy You are sanctified.

THE DUTY
TO STUDY
Blessed are You, Lord our God, king of the universe, who makes us holy through doing His commands, and who commands us to devote ourselves to the study of His teaching.

One of the following passages or one selected from the Anthology, pages 356–366.

Moses received Torah on Sinai, and handed it on to Joshua, and Joshua to the elders, and the elders to the prophets, and the prophets handed it on to the men of the Great Assembly. They said three things: Be patient and careful in judgment, raise up many disciples, and make a fence to protect the Torah.

Rabban Gamliel, the son of Rabbi Judah the Prince, says, It is an excellent thing to combine the study of Torah with a trade or profession, for the labour necessary for both together puts sin out of mind. Study of Torah, however, which is not combined with work, ends in futility, and becomes the cause of sin. Let all who work for the congregation do it for the sake of heaven. Then the merit of their fathers will come to their aid and their righteousness will last forever. (And God will say,) 'And as for you, I credit you with a great reward, as though you had done it all yourselves.'

Rabbi Yochanan ben Zakkai received tradition from Hillel and Shammai. He used to say: If you have learnt much Torah, do not congratulate yourself, for that is why you were created.

Sayings of the Fathers

יִשְׁתַּבַּח שִׁמְךָ לָעַד מַלְכֵּנוּ · הָאֵל הַמֶּלֶךְ הַגָּדוֹל וְהַקָּדוֹשׁ בַּשָּׁמַיִם וּבָאָרֶץ · כִּי לְךָ נָאֶה יְיָ אֱלֹהֵינוּ וֵאלֹהֵי אֲבוֹתֵינוּ לְעוֹלָם וָעֶד שִׁיר וּשְׁבָחָה · קְדֻשָּׁה וּמַלְכוּת · בְּרָכוֹת וְהוֹדָאוֹת לְשִׁמְךָ הַגָּדוֹל וְהַקָּדוֹשׁ · וּמֵעוֹלָם וְעַד־עוֹלָם אַתָּה אֵל · בָּרוּךְ אַתָּה יְיָ · בּוֹרֵא כָּל־הַנְּשָׁמוֹת · רִבּוֹן כָּל־הַמַּעֲשִׂים · מֶלֶךְ חֵי הָעוֹלָמִים :

The half Kaddish on page 168 may be included here.

בָּרְכוּ אֶת־יְיָ הַמְבֹרָךְ :

בָּרוּךְ יְיָ הַמְבֹרָךְ לְעוֹלָם וָעֶד :

בָּרוּךְ אַתָּה יְיָ אֱלֹהֵינוּ מֶלֶךְ הָעוֹלָם · יוֹצֵר אוֹר וּבוֹרֵא חֹשֶׁךְ · עֹשֶׂה שָׁלוֹם וּבוֹרֵא אֶת־הַכֹּל : הַכֹּל יוֹדוּךָ · וְהַכֹּל יְשַׁבְּחוּךָ · וְהַכֹּל יֹאמְרוּ אֵין קָדוֹשׁ כַּיְיָ : הַמֵּאִיר לָעוֹלָם כֻּלּוֹ וּלְיוֹשְׁבָיו וּבְטוּבוֹ מְחַדֵּשׁ בְּכָל־יוֹם תָּמִיד מַעֲשֵׂה בְרֵאשִׁית : מָה רַבּוּ מַעֲשֶׂיךָ יְיָ · כֻּלָּם בְּחָכְמָה עָשִׂיתָ · מָלְאָה הָאָרֶץ קִנְיָנֶךָ : הַמֶּלֶךְ הַמְרוֹמָם לְבַדּוֹ מֵאָז · הַמְשֻׁבָּח וְהַמְפֹאָר וְהַמִּתְנַשֵּׂא מִימוֹת עוֹלָם : אֱלֹהֵי עוֹלָם · בְּרַחֲמֶיךָ הָרַבִּים רַחֵם עָלֵינוּ · אֲדוֹן עֻזֵּנוּ · צוּר מִשְׂגַּבֵּנוּ · מָגֵן יִשְׁעֵנוּ · מִשְׂגָּב בַּעֲדֵנוּ : בָּרוּךְ אַתָּה יְיָ · יוֹצֵר הַמְּאוֹרוֹת :

אַהֲבָה רַבָּה אֲהַבְתָּנוּ יְיָ אֱלֹהֵינוּ חֶמְלָה גְדוֹלָה וִיתֵרָה חָמַלְתָּ עָלֵינוּ · אָבִינוּ מַלְכֵּנוּ · בַּעֲבוּר שִׁמְךָ הַגָּדוֹל וּבַעֲבוּר אֲבוֹתֵינוּ שֶׁבָּטְחוּ בָךְ · וַתְּלַמְּדֵם חֻקֵּי חַיִּים לַעֲשׂוֹת רְצוֹנְךָ בְּלֵבָב שָׁלֵם · כֵּן תְּחָנֵּנוּ · הָאֵר עֵינֵינוּ בְּתוֹרָתֶךָ · וְדַבֵּק לִבֵּנוּ בְּמִצְוֹתֶיךָ · וְיַחֵד לְבָבֵנוּ לְאַהֲבָה וּלְיִרְאָה אֶת־שְׁמֶךָ · לְמַעַן לֹא נֵבוֹשׁ וְלֹא נִכָּלֵם · כִּי אֵל פּוֹעֵל יְשׁוּעוֹת אָתָּה. וּבָנוּ בָחַרְתָּ מִכָּל־עַם וְלָשׁוֹן. וְקֵרַבְתָּנוּ מַלְכֵּנוּ לְשִׁמְךָ הַגָּדוֹל בְּאַהֲבָה · לְהוֹדוֹת לְךָ וּלְיַחֶדְךָ וּלְאַהֲבָה אֶת־שְׁמֶךָ : בָּרוּךְ אַתָּה יְיָ · הַבּוֹחֵר בְּעַמּוֹ יִשְׂרָאֵל בְּאַהֲבָה :

THE DUTY
OF PRAISE

Praised be Your name forever, for You are the God who is the great and holy king in heaven and on earth. Therefore, Lord our God, and God of our fathers, song and praise, holiness and majesty, blessing and gratitude belong to Your great and holy name forever and ever. From age to age You are God. Blessed are You Lord, creator of every living being, master of all deeds, the king, the life of all existence.

The half Kaddish on page 168 may be included here.

THE CALL
TO COM-
MUNITY
PRAYER

Bless the Lord whom we are called to bless.

Blessed be the Lord whom we are called to bless forever and ever.

THE
CREATOR
OF THE
UNIVERSE

Blessed are You, Lord our God, king of the universe, who forms light yet creates darkness, who makes peace yet creates all. All things proclaim You, all things honour You, and all say: 'None is holy like the Lord.' He gives light to all the world and those who live in it. In His goodness He renews the work of the creation day by day. Lord, how great are Your works; You made them all in wisdom; the earth is full of Your creatures. You are the only king exalted from the beginning of time, who has been worshipped, praised and glorified since days of old.

Everlasting God, in Your great mercy have mercy upon us; Lord of our strength, rock of our protection, shield of our safety, our true protector. Blessed are You Lord, who creates the lights of the universe.

HIS LOVE
FOR ISRAEL

With deep love You have loved us, and with great and over-flowing tenderness You have taken pity on us. Our father, our king, show us compassion because of Your own greatness, and because of our fathers who trusted in You, for You taught them rules to live by, to do Your will with their whole heart. Let our eyes see the light of Your teaching and our hearts embrace Your commands. Give us integrity to love You and fear You. So shall we never lose our self-respect, nor be put to shame, for You are the power which works to save us. You chose us from all peoples and tongues, and in love drew us near to Your own greatness—to honour You, to declare Your unity, and to love You. Blessed are You Lord, who chooses His people Israel in love.

שְׁמַ**ע** יִשְׂרָאֵל · יְהֹוָה אֱלֹהֵינוּ יְהֹוָה אֶחָ**ד** :

בָּרוּךְ שֵׁם כְּבוֹד מַלְכוּתוֹ לְעוֹלָם וָעֶד :

וְאָהַבְתָּ אֵת יְהֹוָה אֱלֹהֶיךָ · בְּכָל־לְבָבְךָ וּבְכָל־נַפְשְׁךָ וּבְכָל־מְאֹדֶךָ : וְהָיוּ הַדְּבָרִים הָאֵלֶּה אֲשֶׁר אָנֹכִי מְצַוְּךָ הַיּוֹם עַל־לְבָבֶךָ : וְשִׁנַּנְתָּם לְבָנֶיךָ וְדִבַּרְתָּ בָּם · בְּשִׁבְתְּךָ בְּבֵיתֶךָ וּבְלֶכְתְּךָ בַדֶּרֶךְ וּבְשָׁכְבְּךָ וּבְקוּמֶךָ : וּקְשַׁרְתָּם לְאוֹת עַל־יָדֶךָ · וְהָיוּ לְטֹטָפֹת בֵּין עֵינֶיךָ : וּכְתַבְתָּם עַל־מְזֻזוֹת בֵּיתֶךָ וּבִשְׁעָרֶיךָ :

וְהָיָה אִם־שָׁמֹעַ תִּשְׁמְעוּ אֶל־מִצְוֹתַי אֲשֶׁר אָנֹכִי מְצַוֶּה אֶתְכֶם הַיּוֹם · לְאַהֲבָה אֶת־יְהֹוָה אֱלֹהֵיכֶם וּלְעָבְדוֹ בְּכָל־לְבַבְכֶם וּבְכָל־נַפְשְׁכֶם : וְנָתַתִּי מְטַר־אַרְצְכֶם בְּעִתּוֹ יוֹרֶה וּמַלְקוֹשׁ וְאָסַפְתָּ דְגָנֶךָ וְתִירֹשְׁךָ וְיִצְהָרֶךָ : וְנָתַתִּי עֵשֶׂב בְּשָׂדְךָ לִבְהֶמְתֶּךָ וְאָכַלְתָּ וְשָׂבָעְתָּ : הִשָּׁמְרוּ לָכֶם פֶּן־יִפְתֶּה לְבַבְכֶם · וְסַרְתֶּם וַעֲבַדְתֶּם אֱלֹהִים אֲחֵרִים וְהִשְׁתַּחֲוִיתֶם לָהֶם : וְחָרָה אַף־יְהֹוָה בָּכֶם וְעָצַר אֶת־הַשָּׁמַיִם וְלֹא־יִהְיֶה מָטָר וְהָאֲדָמָה לֹא תִתֵּן אֶת־יְבוּלָהּ · וַאֲבַדְתֶּם מְהֵרָה מֵעַל הָאָרֶץ הַטֹּבָה אֲשֶׁר יְהֹוָה נֹתֵן לָכֶם : וְשַׂמְתֶּם אֶת־דְּבָרַי אֵלֶּה עַל־לְבַבְכֶם וְעַל־נַפְשְׁכֶם · וּקְשַׁרְתֶּם אֹתָם לְאוֹת עַל־יֶדְכֶם וְהָיוּ לְטוֹטָפֹת בֵּין עֵינֵיכֶם : וְלִמַּדְתֶּם אֹתָם אֶת־בְּנֵיכֶם לְדַבֵּר בָּם · בְּשִׁבְתְּךָ בְּבֵיתֶךָ וּבְלֶכְתְּךָ בַדֶּרֶךְ וּבְשָׁכְבְּךָ וּבְקוּמֶךָ : וּכְתַבְתָּם עַל־מְזוּזוֹת בֵּיתֶךָ וּבִשְׁעָרֶיךָ : לְמַעַן יִרְבּוּ יְמֵיכֶם וִימֵי בְנֵיכֶם עַל הָאֲדָמָה אֲשֶׁר נִשְׁבַּע יְהֹוָה לַאֲבֹתֵיכֶם לָתֵת לָהֶם · כִּימֵי הַשָּׁמַיִם עַל־הָאָרֶץ :

וַיֹּאמֶר יְהֹוָה אֶל־מֹשֶׁה לֵּאמֹר : דַּבֵּר אֶל־בְּנֵי יִשְׂרָאֵל וְאָמַרְתָּ אֲלֵהֶם וְעָשׂוּ לָהֶם צִיצִת עַל־כַּנְפֵי בִגְדֵיהֶם לְדֹרֹתָם · וְנָתְנוּ עַל־צִיצִת הַכָּנָף פְּתִיל תְּכֵלֶת : וְהָיָה לָכֶם לְצִיצִת וּרְאִיתֶם אֹתוֹ וּזְכַרְתֶּם אֶת־כָּל־מִצְוֹת יְהֹוָה וַעֲשִׂיתֶם אֹתָם ·

THE GOD
OF ISRAEL

Hear O Israel, the Lord is our God, the Lord is One.

Blessed is His name, whose glorious kingdom is forever and ever.

Love the Lord your God with all your heart, and all your soul, and all your might. These words that I command you today shall be upon your heart. Repeat them to your children, and talk about them when you sit in your home, and when you walk in the street; when you lie down, and when you rise up. Hold fast to them as a sign upon your hand, and let them be as reminders before your eyes. Write them on the doorposts of your home and at your gates.

Deuteronomy 6: 4–9

During the silence the following two paragraphs, or the prayers on pages 344–349, may be read.

This will happen if you listen carefully to My commands which I give you today, to love the Lord your God and to serve Him with all your heart and all your soul. I shall then give your land rain at the right time, the autumn rain and the spring rain, so that you can harvest your corn, your wine and your oil. I shall also give grass in your fields to your cattle, and you will eat and be full. Take care that your heart is not deceived into straying, obeying other gods and worshipping them. The anger of God will then blaze out against you. He will shut up the sky. There will be no rain. The land will not produce, and you will quickly be destroyed from the good land which the Lord gives you. So put these words of Mine in your heart and in your soul, and hold fast to them as a sign upon your hand and as reminders before your eyes. Repeat them to your children, and talk about them when you sit in your home, and when you walk in the street, when you lie down and when you rise up. Write them on the doorposts of your home and at your gates. Then you and your children may live long on the good land that God promised to give your fathers as long as there is a sky over the earth.

Deuteronomy 11: 13–21

The Lord said to Moses: 'Speak to the children of Israel and tell them that each generation shall put tassels on the corner of their clothes, and put a blue thread on the corner tassel. Then when this tassel catches your eye, you will remember all the Lord's commands and do them. Then you will no longer wander after the desires of

וְלֹא־תָתֻ֫רוּ אַחֲרֵי לְבַבְכֶם וְאַחֲרֵי עֵינֵיכֶם אֲשֶׁר־אַתֶּם זֹנִים אַחֲרֵיהֶם : לְמַ֫עַן תִּזְכְּרוּ וַעֲשִׂיתֶם אֶת־כָּל־מִצְוֹתָי · וִהְיִיתֶם קְדֹשִׁים לֵאלֹהֵיכֶם : אֲנִי יְהֹוָה אֱלֹהֵיכֶם אֲשֶׁר הוֹצֵאתִי אֶתְכֶם מֵאֶ֫רֶץ מִצְרַ֫יִם לִהְיוֹת לָכֶם לֵאלֹהִים · אֲנִי יְהֹוָה אֱלֹהֵיכֶם :

Florence

your heart and your eyes which led you to lust. Then you will remember all My commands and do them and you will be set apart for your God. I am the Lord your God, who brought you out of the land of Egypt, to be your own God. I, the Lord, am your God.'

Numbers 15: 37–41

After the silence the service continues on page 142.

Pesht

תפלת שחרית לשבת

יְהֹוָה מִי־יָגוּר בְּאָהֳלֶךָ מִי־יִשְׁכֹּן בְּהַר קָדְשֶׁךָ׃

הוֹלֵךְ תָּמִים וּפֹעֵל צֶדֶק וְדֹבֵר אֱמֶת בִּלְבָבוֹ׃

מַה־טֹּבוּ אֹהָלֶיךָ יַעֲקֹב מִשְׁכְּנֹתֶיךָ יִשְׂרָאֵל׃

וַאֲנִי בְּרֹב חַסְדְּךָ אָבוֹא בֵיתֶךָ

אֶשְׁתַּחֲוֶה אֶל־הֵיכַל־קָדְשְׁךָ בְּיִרְאָתֶךָ׃

יְהֹוָה אָהַבְתִּי מְעוֹן בֵּיתֶךָ וּמְקוֹם מִשְׁכַּן כְּבוֹדֶךָ׃

וַאֲנִי אֶשְׁתַּחֲוֶה וְאֶכְרָעָה אֶבְרְכָה לִפְנֵי־יְהֹוָה עֹשִׂי׃

וַאֲנִי תְפִלָּתִי־לְךָ יְהֹוָה עֵת רָצוֹן

אֱלֹהִים בְּרָב־חַסְדֶּךָ עֲנֵנִי בֶּאֱמֶת יִשְׁעֶךָ׃

יָי חַיַּי לוֹטִים בְּסֵתֶר · לֹא אֵדַע מַה־לִּפְנֵיהֶם וּמַה־
אַחֲרֵיהֶם · חַיַּי קְצָרִים וּלְעוֹלָמְךָ אֵין סוֹף · אַךְ הֵן בְּחֹשֶׁךְ
אַתָּה וּבְמִסְתָּרִים אַהֲבָתֶךָ · אֲבוֹתַי בָּטְחוּ בְךָ וְהִדְרַכְתָּם
בְּחֻקֵּי־חֶסֶד וְשָׁלוֹם · אֶהְיֶה־נָא כָמוֹתָם וְכִשְׂכָרָם כֵּן יִהְיֶה
שְׂכָרִי׃

בְּכָל־מָקוֹם וּבְכָל־עֵת קוֹלְךָ מְדַבֵּר בְּקִרְבִּי. מוֹבִילֵנִי
בְּמַעְגְּלֵי־כֵנוּת וּצְדָקָה. מַרְאֵנִי אֱמֶת וָטוֹב׃ לְעִתִּים קָשֶׁה
לְשָׁמְעֶךָ. לְעִתִּים קָשֶׁה לָלֶכֶת בִּדְרָכֶיךָ וַהֲרֵינִי הַמַּפְסִיד׃
בְּשַׁלְוַת־שַׁבָּת זוֹ אֶפְנֶה מַחְשְׁבוֹתַי אֵלֶיךָ׃ עָזְרֵנִי לִשְׁמוֹעַ
קוֹלְךָ. לְגַלּוֹת חוֹתָמְךָ בְּנִשְׁמָתִי. וְאֶהְיֶה שָׁלוֹם · אָמֵן׃

II

SABBATH MORNING SERVICE

Lord, who may live in Your tent,
who may dwell on the mountain of Your holiness?

He who follows integrity
and does what is right
and speaks the truth in his heart.

Psalm 15: 1-2

DIRECTING THE HEART TO GOD How good are your tents, O Jacob, and your homes, O Israel. Through the greatness of Your love I enter Your house. In awe I worship before the ark of Your holiness.

Lord, as I loved the courts of Your temple, and the place where Your glory dwelt, so I still worship and bend low, humble before the Lord my maker.

As for me, let my prayer come before You at the proper time. Answer me God, in the greatness of Your love, for Your deliverance is sure.

LIFE AND DEATH Lord, a mystery surrounds my life. What comes before it and what lies after it are hidden from me. My life is very short, and Your universe is vast. But in the darkness is Your presence, and in the mystery, Your love. My fathers put their trust in You, and You put goodness in their hearts and peace within their minds. May I be like them and may my reward be like theirs.

In every place, at every time, Your voice speaks within me. It leads me in the way of honesty and charity. It shows me truth and goodness. There are times when it is hard to hear You, and times when it is hard to follow You; and I know this is my loss.

In the quietness of this Sabbath I turn my thoughts to You. Help me to hear Your voice, to find Your image in my soul, and to be at peace. Amen.

שַׁחַר אֲבַקֶּשְׁךָ. צוּרִי וּמִשְׂגַּבִּי.

אֶעֱרֹךְ לְפָנֶיךָ שַׁחְרִי וְגַם עַרְבִּי:

לִפְנֵי גְדוּלָתְךָ אֶעֱמֹד וְאֶבָּהֵל.

כִּי עֵינְךָ תִרְאֶה כָּל־מַחְשְׁבוֹת לִבִּי:

מַה־זֶּה אֲשֶׁר יוּכַל הַלֵּב וְהַלָּשׁוֹן לַעֲשׂוֹת·

וּמַה כְּחַ־רוּחִי בְּתוֹךְ קִרְבִּי:

הִנֵּה לְךָ תִיטַב זִמְרַת אֱנוֹשׁ· עַל כֵּן

אוֹדְךָ בְּעוֹד תִּהְיֶה נִשְׁמַת אֱלֹהַּ בִּי:

וְאֵרַשְׂתִּיךְ לִי לְעוֹלָם·

וְאֵרַשְׂתִּיךְ לִי בְּצֶדֶק וּבְמִשְׁפָּט וּבְחֶסֶד וּבְרַחֲמִים·

וְאֵרַשְׂתִּיךְ לִי בֶּאֱמוּנָה וְיָדַעַתְּ אֶת־יְיָ:

בָּרוּךְ אַתָּה יְיָ אֱלֹהֵינוּ מֶלֶךְ הָעוֹלָם אֲשֶׁר נָתַן לָנוּ אֶת־
הַשַּׁבָּת לִקְדֻשָּׁה וְלִמְנוּחָה:

בָּרוּךְ אַתָּה יְיָ אֱלֹהֵינוּ מֶלֶךְ הָעוֹלָם· מַתִּיר אֲסוּרִים:

בָּרוּךְ אַתָּה יְיָ אֱלֹהֵינוּ מֶלֶךְ הָעוֹלָם· זוֹקֵף כְּפוּפִים:

בָּרוּךְ אַתָּה יְיָ אֱלֹהֵינוּ מֶלֶךְ הָעוֹלָם· שֶׁעָשָׂה־לִי כָּל־
צָרְכִּי:

בָּרוּךְ אַתָּה יְיָ אֱלֹהֵינוּ מֶלֶךְ הָעוֹלָם· אֲשֶׁר הֵכִין מִצְעֲדֵי־
גָבֶר:

בָּרוּךְ אַתָּה יְיָ אֱלֹהֵינוּ מֶלֶךְ הָעוֹלָם· עוֹטֵר יִשְׂרָאֵל
בְּתִפְאָרָה:

Every dawn I seek You
my refuge and might,
set my prayer before You
each morning and night.

Here before Your greatness
I stand so afraid
for my innermost thoughts
to You are displayed.

Whatever can tongue say
or heart hope to be!
What is even the strength
of life within me!

But since each man's singing
is pleasing to You,
while You give me Your breath
I thank You anew.

Ibn Gabirol

Alternative Songs of Praise, pages 571–609.

I betroth you to Me forever.
I betroth you to Me with integrity and justice,
with tenderness and love.
I betroth you to Me with faithfulness
and you will know the Lord.

Hosea 2: 21–22

Blessed are You, Lord our God, king of the universe, who gives us the Sabbath for holiness and rest.

Blessed are You, Lord our God, king of the universe, who frees those who are bound.

Blessed are You, Lord our God, king of the universe, who lifts up those bent low.

Blessed are You, Lord our God, king of the universe, who provides for my every need.

Blessed are You, Lord our God, king of the universe, who strengthens the steps of man.

Blessed are You, Lord our God, king of the universe, who crowns Israel with glory.

בָּרוּךְ אַתָּה יְיָ אֱלֹהֵינוּ מֶלֶךְ הָעוֹלָם · הַנּוֹתֵן לַיָּעֵף כֹּחַ:

בָּרוּךְ אַתָּה יְיָ אֱלֹהֵינוּ מֶלֶךְ הָעוֹלָם · הַמַּעֲבִיר שֵׁנָה מֵעֵינַי וּתְנוּמָה מֵעַפְעַפָּי:

יְהִי רָצוֹן מִלְּפָנֶיךָ יְיָ אֱלֹהֵינוּ וֵאלֹהֵי אֲבוֹתֵינוּ · שֶׁתַּרְגִּילֵנוּ בְּתוֹרָתֶךָ וְדַבְּקֵנוּ בְּמִצְוֹתֶיךָ · וְאַל תְּבִיאֵנוּ לֹא לִידֵי חֵטְא וְלֹא לִידֵי עֲבֵרָה וְלֹא לִידֵי נִסָּיוֹן וְלֹא לִידֵי בִזָּיוֹן · וְאַל תַּשְׁלֶט־בָּנוּ יֵצֶר הָרַע · וְהַרְחִיקֵנוּ מֵאָדָם רַע וּמֵחָבֵר רַע · וְדַבְּקֵנוּ בְּיֵצֶר הַטּוֹב וּבְמַעֲשִׂים טוֹבִים · וְכֹף אֶת־יִצְרֵנוּ לְהִשְׁתַּעְבֶּד־לָךְ · וּתְנֵנוּ הַיּוֹם וּבְכָל־יוֹם לְחֵן וּלְחֶסֶד וּלְרַחֲמִים בְּעֵינֶיךָ וּבְעֵינֵי כָל־רוֹאֵינוּ · וְתִגְמְלֵנוּ חֲסָדִים טוֹבִים: בָּרוּךְ אַתָּה יְיָ · גּוֹמֵל חֲסָדִים טוֹבִים לְעַמּוֹ יִשְׂרָאֵל:

רִבּוֹן הָעוֹלָמִים וַאֲדֹנֵי הָאֲדֹנִים · לֹא עַל־צִדְקֹתֵינוּ אֲנַחְנוּ מַפִּילִים תַּחֲנוּנֵינוּ לְפָנֶיךָ · כִּי עַל־רַחֲמֶיךָ הָרַבִּים: אֲדֹנָי שְׁמָעָה · אֲדֹנָי סְלָחָה · אֲדֹנָי הַקְשִׁיבָה וַעֲשֵׂה · מָה־אָנוּ · מֶה־חַיֵּינוּ · מֶה־חַסְדֵּנוּ · מַה־צִּדְקוֹתֵינוּ · מַה־יְּשׁוּעָתֵנוּ · מַה־כֹּחֵנוּ · מַה־גְּבוּרָתֵנוּ · מַה־נֹּאמַר לְפָנֶיךָ יְיָ אֱלֹהֵינוּ וֵאלֹהֵי אֲבוֹתֵינוּ · הֲלֹא הַגִּבּוֹרִים כְּאַיִן לְפָנֶיךָ · וְאַנְשֵׁי הַשֵּׁם כְּלֹא הָיוּ · וַחֲכָמִים כִּבְלִי מַדָּע · וּנְבוֹנִים כִּבְלִי הַשְׂכֵּל · כִּי רֹב מַעֲשֵׂינוּ תֹּהוּ · וִימֵי חַיֵּינוּ הֶבֶל לְפָנֶיךָ · וּמוֹתַר הָאָדָם מִן הַבְּהֵמָה אָיִן · כִּי הַכֹּל הָבֶל לְבַד הַנְּשָׁמָה הַטְּהוֹרָה · שֶׁהִיא עֲתִידָה לִתֵּן דִּין וְחֶשְׁבּוֹן לִפְנֵי כִסֵּא כְבוֹדֶךָ:

יְיָ מֶלֶךְ · יְיָ מָלָךְ · יְיָ יִמְלֹךְ לְעוֹלָם וָעֶד:

וְהָיָה יְיָ לְמֶלֶךְ עַל־כָּל־הָאָרֶץ · בַּיּוֹם הַהוּא יִהְיֶה יְיָ אֶחָד וּשְׁמוֹ אֶחָד: הוֹשִׁיעֵנוּ יְיָ אֱלֹהֵינוּ · לְהוֹדוֹת לְשֵׁם קָדְשֶׁךָ לְהִשְׁתַּבֵּחַ בִּתְהִלָּתֶךָ: בָּרוּךְ יְהֹוָה אֱלֹהֵי יִשְׂרָאֵל מִן־הָעוֹלָם וְעַד הָעוֹלָם · וְאָמַר כָּל־הָעָם אָמֵן: הַלְלוּיָהּ: כֹּל הַנְּשָׁמָה תְּהַלֵּל יָהּ · הַלְלוּיָהּ:

Blessed are You, Lord our God, king of the universe, who gives strength to the weary.

Blessed are You, Lord our God, king of the universe, who takes away sleep from my eyes and slumber from my eyelids.

THE GOODNESS OF MAN   Lord our God and God of our fathers, help us to live according to Your teaching and to hold fast to Your commands. Let us not come into the power of sin or wrong-doing, temptation or disgrace. Let no evil within us control us, and keep us far from bad people and bad company. Help us hold fast to the good within us and to good deeds, and bend our will and our desires to serve You. Give us today, and every day, grace, kindness and mercy in Your sight and in the sight of all who regard us, and grant us Your love and kindness. Blessed are You Lord, who grants love and kindness to His people Israel.

THE WEAKNESS OF MAN   Master of existence, and Lord of lords, we do not rely on our own good deeds but on Your great mercy as we lay our needs before You. Lord, hear! Lord, pardon! Lord, listen and act! What are we? What is our life? What is our love? What is our justice? What is our success? What is our endurance? What is our power? Lord our God, and God of our fathers, what can we say before You, for in Your presence are not the powerful as nothing, the famous as if they had never existed, the learned as if without knowledge, and the intelligent as if without insight. To You most of our actions are pointless and our daily life is shallow. Even the superiority of man over the beasts is nothing. For everything is trivial except the pure soul which must one day give its account and reckoning before the judgment seat of Your glory.

THE POWER OF GOD   The Lord does rule, the Lord has ruled, the Lord shall rule for-ever and ever.

The Lord shall be as a king over the whole earth. On that day the Lord shall be One, and known as One.

Save us, Lord our God, to proclaim Your holy name and be honoured in praising You.

Blessed is the Lord God of Israel from everlasting to everlasting. Let all the people say: Amen! Praise the Lord!

May all who live praise the Lord. Hallelujah!

I

Teach us, Lord, the laws of life and the ways of peace.

O man, He has told you what is good and what the Lord asks of you. Is it not to do justice, to love mercy, and to walk humbly with your God!

Micah 6: 8

Teach us, Lord, that the more we give, the more we have.

Giving changes a man's impulse to cruelty into kindness of heart. This is the chief service of giving.

Nachman of Bratzlav

Teach us, Lord, that in order to change the world, we must also change ourselves.

The man whom you strengthen in his service to God will love you. The way to strengthen him is to love him.

Nachman of Bratzlav

Teach us, Lord, to accept the limitations of man.

It is of great advantage that man shall know his place, and not imagine that the whole universe exists for him alone.

Maimonides

Teach us, Lord, to accept the responsibility of man.

Every person in Israel should know and consider that he is unique in the world . . . and that he is called upon to fulfil his particular task.

Chasidic

Teach us, Lord, that within each problem we meet, You have set an answer.

There is no stumbling block one cannot push aside, for the stumbling-block is only there for the sake of the will, and there actually are no stumbling-blocks save in the spirit.

Chasidic

Teach us, Lord, that love is a giving and not a taking.

If love depends on some selfish cause, when the cause disappears, love disappears; but if love does not depend on a selfish cause, it will never disappear.

Sayings of the Fathers

II

Teach us, Lord, to see more than outward things, and to trust Your voice within us.

Prefer the truth and right by which you seem to lose, to the falsehood and wrong by which you seem to gain.

Maimonides

Teach us, Lord, to have the courage to stand alone and walk before You.

Let a man do good deeds and then ask Torah from God. Let a man do righteous and fitting deeds, and then ask wisdom from God. Let a man take the way of humility, and then ask understanding from God.

Seder Eliyahu Rabbah

Teach us, Lord, that we have the right to do the work, but the results are in Your hand.

One may do much or one may do little; it is all one, provided he directs his heart to heaven.

Berachot

Teach us, Lord, that it is not for us to complete the work, but neither may we desist from it.

Do His will as if it were your will so that He may do your will as if it were His will.

Sayings of the Fathers

Teach us, Lord, that this world is not the measure of all things.

Plan for this world as if you were to live forever; plan for the world to come as if you were to die tomorrow.

Ibn Gabirol

Teach us, Lord, to see in every ending a new beginning.

The world is like a corridor to the world to come. Prepare yourself in the corridor so that you may enter the inner chamber.

Sayings of the Fathers

Teach us, Lord, to consider the mystery of life and death.

One hour of repentance and good deeds in this world is better than all the life of the world to come; and one hour of calmness of spirit in the world to come is better than all the life of this world.

Sayings of the Fathers

בָּרוּךְ יְהֹוָה לְעוֹלָם · אָמֵן וְאָמֵן :
בָּרוּךְ יְהֹוָה אֱלֹהִים אֱלֹהֵי יִשְׂרָאֵל · עֹשֵׂה נִפְלָאוֹת לְבַדּוֹ :
וּבָרוּךְ שֵׁם כְּבוֹדוֹ לְעוֹלָם · וְיִמָּלֵא כְבוֹדוֹ אֶת־כָּל־הָאָרֶץ ·
אָמֵן וְאָמֵן :

נִשְׁמַת כָּל־חַי תְּבָרֵךְ אֶת־שִׁמְךָ יְיָ אֱלֹהֵינוּ · וְרוּחַ כָּל־
בָּשָׂר תְּפָאֵר וּתְרוֹמֵם זִכְרְךָ מַלְכֵּנוּ תָּמִיד : מִן
הָעוֹלָם וְעַד הָעוֹלָם אַתָּה אֵל · וּמִבַּלְעָדֶיךָ אֵין לָנוּ מֶלֶךְ
גּוֹאֵל וּמוֹשִׁיעַ פּוֹדֶה וּמַצִּיל וְעוֹנֶה וּמְרַחֵם · בְּכָל־עֵת צָרָה
וְצוּקָה אֵין לָנוּ מֶלֶךְ עוֹזֵר וְסוֹמֵךְ זוּלָתֶךָ : אֱלֹהֵי הָרִאשׁוֹנִים
וְהָאַחֲרוֹנִים · אֱלוֹהַּ כָּל־בְּרִיּוֹת · אֲדוֹן כָּל־תּוֹלָדוֹת הַמְהֻלָּל
בְּכָל־הַתִּשְׁבָּחוֹת · הַמְנַהֵג עוֹלָמוֹ בְּחֶסֶד וּבְרִיּוֹתָיו בְּרַחֲמִים :
וַיְיָ לֹא יָנוּם וְלֹא יִישָׁן · הַמְעוֹרֵר יְשֵׁנִים וְהַמֵּקִיץ נִרְדָּמִים ·
מְחַיֶּה מֵתִים וְרוֹפֵא חוֹלִים · פּוֹקֵחַ עִוְרִים וְזוֹקֵף כְּפוּפִים ·
לְךָ לְבַדְּךָ אֲנַחְנוּ מוֹדִים :

בָּרוּךְ אַתָּה יְיָ אֱלֹהֵינוּ מֶלֶךְ הָעוֹלָם · אֲשֶׁר קִדְּשָׁנוּ
בְּמִצְוֹתָיו וְצִוָּנוּ לַעֲסוֹק בְּדִבְרֵי תוֹרָה :

A king once owned a large, beautiful, pure diamond of which
he was justly proud, for it had no equal anywhere. One day, the
diamond accidentally sustained a deep scratch. The king called in the
most skilled diamond cutters and offered them a great reward if they
could remove the imperfection from his treasured jewel. But none
could repair the blemish. The king was sorely distressed.

After some time a gifted jeweller came to the king and promised to
make the rare diamond even more beautiful than it had been before
the mishap. The king was impressed by his confidence and entrusted
his precious stone to his care. And the man kept his word.

With superb artistry he engraved a lovely rosebud around the
imperfection and he used the scratch to make the stem.

The Dubner Maggid

Blessed be the Lord forever. Amen and amen.

Blessed be the Lord God, the God of Israel, who alone works wonders.

Blessed be His glorious name forever. All the earth is full of His glory. Amen and amen.

ALL CREATION PRAISES GOD The breath of life in every creature shall bless You, Lord our God, and the spirit of all flesh ever recalls Your beauty and Your greatness. From everlasting to everlasting You are God. Besides You we have no king who rescues and saves us, frees and delivers us, and answers and cares for us. At all times of trouble and distress there is no king who can help and support us but You.

God of the first and of the last ages, God of all creatures, Lord of history, adored in all worship—He guides His universe with love, and His creatures with mercy. The Lord neither slumbers nor sleeps. He wakes the sleepers, and rouses the uncaring. He gives life beyond death, He heals the sick, He gives sight to the blind and raises up those bent low. To You alone we declare our gratitude.

THE DUTY TO STUDY Blessed are You, Lord our God, king of the universe, who makes us holy through doing His commands, and who commands us to devote ourselves to the study of His teaching.

One of the following passages or one selected from the Anthology, pages 366–375.

Do not look for the City of God on earth, for it is not built of wood or stone; but look for it in the soul of the man who is at peace with himself and is a lover of true wisdom.

If a man only practises ritual cleansing of his body, but defiles his mind; if he offers public donations, founds a synagogue, adorns the building, but does nothing for making his soul beautiful—let him not be called religious. He has wandered far from real religion, mistaking ritual for holiness; attempting, as it were, to bribe the Incorruptible and so flatter Him whom none can flatter. God welcomes the genuine service of the soul, the sacrifice of truth; but from mere display of wealth He turns away.

Will any man with impure soul and with no intention to repent dare to approach the Most High God? The grateful soul of the wise man is the true altar of God.

Philo

יִשְׁתַּבַּח שִׁמְךָ לָעַד מַלְכֵּנוּ · הָאֵל הַמֶּלֶךְ הַגָּדוֹל וְהַקָּדוֹשׁ בַּשָּׁמַיִם וּבָאָרֶץ · כִּי לְךָ נָאֶה יְיָ אֱלֹהֵינוּ וֵאלֹהֵי אֲבוֹתֵינוּ לְעוֹלָם וָעֶד שִׁיר וּשְׁבָחָה · קְדֻשָּׁה וּמַלְכוּת · בְּרָכוֹת וְהוֹדָאוֹת לְשִׁמְךָ הַגָּדוֹל וְהַקָּדוֹשׁ · וּמֵעוֹלָם וְעַד־עוֹלָם אַתָּה אֵל : בָּרוּךְ אַתָּה יְיָ · בּוֹרֵא כָּל־הַנְּשָׁמוֹת · רִבּוֹן כָּל־הַמַּעֲשִׂים · מֶלֶךְ חֵי הָעוֹלָמִים :

The half Kaddish on page 168 may be included here.

בָּרְכוּ אֶת־יְיָ הַמְבֹרָךְ :

בָּרוּךְ יְיָ הַמְבֹרָךְ לְעוֹלָם וָעֶד :

בָּרוּךְ אַתָּה יְיָ אֱלֹהֵינוּ מֶלֶךְ הָעוֹלָם · יוֹצֵר אוֹר וּבוֹרֵא חֹשֶׁךְ · עֹשֶׂה שָׁלוֹם וּבוֹרֵא אֶת־הַכֹּל : הַכֹּל יוֹדוּךָ · וְהַכֹּל יְשַׁבְּחוּךָ · וְהַכֹּל יֹאמְרוּ אֵין קָדוֹשׁ כַּיְיָ : הַמֵּאִיר לָעוֹלָם כֻּלּוֹ וּלְיוֹשְׁבָיו וּבְטוּבוֹ מְחַדֵּשׁ בְּכָל־יוֹם תָּמִיד מַעֲשֵׂה בְרֵאשִׁית : מָה רַבּוּ מַעֲשֶׂיךָ יְיָ · כֻּלָּם בְּחָכְמָה עָשִׂיתָ · מָלְאָה הָאָרֶץ קִנְיָנֶךָ : הַמֶּלֶךְ הַמְרוֹמָם לְבַדּוֹ מֵאָז · הַמְשֻׁבָּח וְהַמְפֹאָר וְהַמִּתְנַשֵּׂא מִימוֹת עוֹלָם · אֱלֹהֵי עוֹלָם · בְּרַחֲמֶיךָ הָרַבִּים רַחֵם עָלֵינוּ · אֲדוֹן עֻזֵּנוּ · צוּר מִשְׂגַּבֵּנוּ · מָגֵן יִשְׁעֵנוּ · מִשְׂגָּב בַּעֲדֵנוּ : בָּרוּךְ אַתָּה יְיָ · יוֹצֵר הַמְּאוֹרוֹת :

אַהֲבָה רַבָּה אֲהַבְתָּנוּ יְיָ אֱלֹהֵינוּ · חֶמְלָה גְדוֹלָה וִיתֵרָה חָמַלְתָּ עָלֵינוּ · אָבִינוּ מַלְכֵּנוּ · בַּעֲבוּר שִׁמְךָ הַגָּדוֹל וּבַעֲבוּר אֲבוֹתֵינוּ שֶׁבָּטְחוּ בָךְ · וַתְּלַמְּדֵם חֻקֵּי חַיִּים לַעֲשׂוֹת רְצוֹנְךָ בְּלֵבָב שָׁלֵם · כֵּן תְּחָנֵּנוּ : הָאֵר עֵינֵינוּ בְּתוֹרָתֶךָ · וְדַבֵּק לִבֵּנוּ בְּמִצְוֹתֶיךָ · וְיַחֵד לְבָבֵנוּ לְאַהֲבָה וּלְיִרְאָה אֶת־שְׁמֶךָ · לְמַעַן לֹא נֵבוֹשׁ וְלֹא נִכָּלֵם כִּי אֵל פּוֹעֵל יְשׁוּעוֹת אָתָּה · וּבָנוּ בָחַרְתָּ מִכָּל־עַם וְלָשׁוֹן · וְקֵרַבְתָּנוּ מַלְכֵּנוּ לְשִׁמְךָ הַגָּדוֹל בְּאַהֲבָה · לְהוֹדוֹת לְךָ וּלְיַחֶדְךָ וּלְאַהֲבָה אֶת־שְׁמֶךָ : בָּרוּךְ אַתָּה יְיָ · הַבּוֹחֵר בְּעַמּוֹ יִשְׂרָאֵל בְּאַהֲבָה :

THE DUTY OF PRAISE   Praised be Your name forever, for You are the God who is the great and holy king in heaven and on earth. Therefore, Lord our God, and God of our fathers, song and praise, holiness and majesty, blessing and gratitude belong to Your great and holy name forever and ever. From age to age You are God. Blessed are You Lord, creator of every living being, master of all deeds, the king, the life of all existence.

The half Kaddish on page 168 may be included here.

THE CALL TO COMMUNITY PRAYER   Bless the Lord whom we are called to bless.

Blessed be the Lord whom we are called to bless forever and ever.

THE CREATOR OF THE UNIVERSE   Blessed are You, Lord our God, king of the universe, who forms light yet creates darkness, who makes peace yet creates all. All things proclaim You, all things honour You, and all say: 'None is holy like the Lord.' He gives light to all the world and those who live in it. In His goodness He renews the work of the creation day by day. Lord, how great are Your works; You made them all in wisdom; the earth is full of Your creatures. You are the only king exalted from the beginning of time, who has been worshipped, praised and glorified since days of old.

Everlasting God, in Your great mercy have mercy upon us; Lord of our strength, rock of our protection, shield of our safety, our true protector. Blessed are You Lord, who creates the lights of the universe.

HIS LOVE FOR ISRAEL   With deep love You have loved us, and with great and overflowing tenderness You have taken pity on us. Our father, our king, show us compassion because of Your own greatness, and because of our fathers who trusted in You, for You taught them rules to live by, to do Your will with their whole heart. Let our eyes see the light of Your teaching and our hearts embrace Your commands. Give us integrity to love You and fear You. So shall we never lose our self-respect, nor be put to shame, for You are the power which works to save us. You chose us from all peoples and tongues, and in love drew us near to Your own greatness—to honour You, to declare Your unity, and to love You. Blessed are You Lord, who chooses His people Israel in love.

שְׁמַ**ע** יִשְׂרָאֵל · יְהֹוָה אֱלֹהֵינוּ יְהֹוָה אֶחָ**ד** :

בָּרוּךְ שֵׁם כְּבוֹד מַלְכוּתוֹ לְעוֹלָם וָעֶד :

וְאָהַבְתָּ אֵת יְהֹוָה אֱלֹהֶיךָ · בְּכָל־לְבָבְךָ וּבְכָל־נַפְשְׁךָ
וּבְכָל־מְאֹדֶךָ : וְהָיוּ הַדְּבָרִים הָאֵלֶּה אֲשֶׁר אָנֹכִי מְצַוְּךָ הַיּוֹם
עַל־לְבָבֶךָ : וְשִׁנַּנְתָּם לְבָנֶיךָ וְדִבַּרְתָּ בָּם · בְּשִׁבְתְּךָ בְּבֵיתֶךָ
וּבְלֶכְתְּךָ בַדֶּרֶךְ וּבְשָׁכְבְּךָ וּבְקוּמֶךָ : וּקְשַׁרְתָּם לְאוֹת עַל־
יָדֶךָ · וְהָיוּ לְטֹטָפֹת בֵּין עֵינֶיךָ : וּכְתַבְתָּם עַל־מְזֻזוֹת בֵּיתֶךָ
וּבִשְׁעָרֶיךָ :

אִם־תִּקַּח אֲמָרָי

וּמִצְוֺתַי תִּצְפֹּן אִתָּךְ :

לְהַקְשִׁיב לַחָכְמָה אָזְנֶךָ

תַּטֶּה לִבְּךָ לַתְּבוּנָה :

כִּי אִם לַבִּינָה תִקְרָא

לַתְּבוּנָה תִּתֵּן קוֹלֶךָ :

אִם־תְּבַקְשֶׁנָּה כַכָּסֶף

וְכַמַּטְמוֹנִים תַּחְפְּשֶׂנָּה :

אָז תָּבִין צֶדֶק וּמִשְׁפָּט

וּמֵישָׁרִים כָּל־מַעְגַּל־טוֹב :

כִּי־תָבוֹא חָכְמָה בְלִבֶּךָ

וְדַעַת לְנַפְשְׁךָ יִנְעָם :

מְזִמָּה תִּשְׁמֹר עָלֶיךָ

תְּבוּנָה תִּנְצְרֶכָּה :

לְהַצִּילְךָ מִדֶּרֶךְ רָע

לְמַעַן תֵּלֵךְ בְּדֶרֶךְ טוֹבִים

וְאָרְחוֹת צַדִּיקִים תִּשְׁמֹר :

Hear O Israel, the Lord is our God, the Lord is One.

Blessed is His name, whose glorious kingdom is forever and ever.

Love the Lord your God with all your heart, and all your soul, and all your might. These words that I command you today shall be upon your heart. Repeat them to your children, and talk about them when you sit in your home, and when you walk in the street; when you lie down, and when you rise up. Hold fast to them as a sign upon your hand, and let them be as reminders before your eyes. Write them on the doorposts of your home and at your gates.

Deuteronomy 6: 4–9

During the silence the second and third paragraphs of the Shema (pages 60–62) may be read, or the following:

If you accept My sayings,

and set store by My commands,

turning your ear to wisdom

and applying your heart to reason;

if you appeal to understanding

and speak out for reason;

if you seek these like silver

and search for them like hidden treasure;

then you will understand what is right and just,

integrity, and every path to good.

When wisdom comes into your heart

and knowledge is a pleasure to you,

discretion will watch over you

and reason will guard you,

keeping you from bad ways.

Then you will follow the way of good men,

and keep the paths of the righteous.

From Proverbs, ch. 2

לֹא לַקַּלִּים הַמֵּרוֹץ
וְלֹא לַגִּבּוֹרִים הַמִּלְחָמָה
וְגַם לֹא לַחֲכָמִים לֶחֶם
וְגַם לֹא לַנְּבֹנִים עֹשֶׁר
וְגַם לֹא לַיֹּדְעִים חֵן
כִּי־עֵת וָפֶגַע יִקְרֶה אֶת־כֻּלָּם:
וְיָשֹׁב הֶעָפָר עַל־הָאָרֶץ כְּשֶׁהָיָה
וְהָרוּחַ תָּשׁוּב אֶל־הָאֱלֹהִים אֲשֶׁר נְתָנָהּ:
סוֹף דָּבָר הַכֹּל נִשְׁמָע
אֶת־הָאֱלֹהִים יְרָא וְאֶת־מִצְוֹתָיו שְׁמוֹר
כִּי־זֶה כָּל־הָאָדָם:

Fasanenstrasse Community House, Berlin

The swift do not win the race,
nor the strong the battle;
bread does not belong to the wise,
nor wealth to the shrewd,
nor success to the skilful;
for time and chance govern all.
The dust returns to earth as it was,
but the spirit returns to God who gave it.
This is the end of the matter,
you have heard it all:
Fear God and obey His commands,
there is no more to man than this.

From Ecclesiastes, chs. 9 and 12

After the silence the service continues on page 142.

Fasanenstrasse Temple

תפלת שחרית לשבת

בַּמָּה אֲקַדֵּם יְהֹוָה אִכַּף לֵאלֹהֵי־מָרוֹם:

הִגִּיד לְךָ אָדָם מַה־טּוֹב וּמָה־יְהֹוָה דּוֹרֵשׁ מִמְּךָ כִּי
אִם־עֲשׂוֹת מִשְׁפָּט וְאַהֲבַת חֶסֶד וְהַצְנֵעַ לֶכֶת עִם־אֱלֹהֶיךָ:

מַה־טֹּבוּ אֹהָלֶיךָ יַעֲקֹב מִשְׁכְּנֹתֶיךָ יִשְׂרָאֵל:
וַאֲנִי בְּרֹב חַסְדְּךָ אָבוֹא בֵיתֶךָ
אֶשְׁתַּחֲוֶה אֶל־הֵיכַל־קָדְשְׁךָ בְּיִרְאָתֶךָ:
יְהֹוָה אָהַבְתִּי מְעוֹן בֵּיתֶךָ וּמְקוֹם מִשְׁכַּן כְּבוֹדֶךָ:
וַאֲנִי אֶשְׁתַּחֲוֶה וְאֶכְרָעָה אֶבְרְכָה לִפְנֵי־יְהֹוָה עֹשִׂי:
וַאֲנִי תְפִלָּתִי־לְךָ יְהֹוָה עֵת רָצוֹן
אֱלֹהִים בְּרָב־חַסְדֶּךָ עֲנֵנִי בֶּאֱמֶת יִשְׁעֶךָ:

יְיָ מוֹדִים אֲנַחְנוּ לָךְ עַל שֶׁטִּפַּחְתָּ בָּנוּ תִקְוָה · עֻזֵּנוּ הִיא
בְּעֵת־צָרָה: לַמְרוֹת־הָעָוֶל שֶׁבִּזְמַנֵּנוּ · הָאַכְזָרִיּוּת וְהַמִּלְחָמוֹת ·
נְצַפֶּה לְעוֹלָם שֶׁכֻּלוֹ שָׁלוֹם וְשָׁבוּ יִגְמְלוּ חֲסָדִים וְאֵין מַחֲרִיד:
כָּל־עֲבֵרָה מְעַכַּבְתּוֹ וְכָל־מִצְוָה מְקָרַבְתּוֹ · נִהְיֶה־נָא עֵדֶיךָ
וִיבָרְכוּנוּ דּוֹרוֹת עֲתִידִים לָבוֹא:
תֵּן בְּלִבֵּנוּ לְהִתְפַּלֵּל וּלְקוֹת לַעֲבוֹד וְלִזְכּוֹת לָבוֹא הַיּוֹם
הַנִּרְמַז עַל־יַד־נְבִיאֶךָ וְזָרְחָה שֶׁמֶשׁ צְדָקָה וּמַרְפֵּא בִּכְנָפֶיהָ
לְכָל־בְּרִיּוֹתֶיךָ · בָּרוּךְ אַתָּה יְיָ מִקְוֵה־יִשְׂרָאֵל · אָמֵן:

שַׂחֲקִי שַׂחֲקִי עַל הַחֲלוֹמוֹת ·
זוּ אֲנִי הַחוֹלֵם שָׂח ·
שַׂחֲקִי כִּי בָאָדָם אַאֲמִין ·
כִּי עוֹדֶנִּי מַאֲמִין בָּךְ:

III

SABBATH MORNING SERVICE

How shall I come into the presence of the Lord, and bend low before God on high?

O man, He has told you what is good and what the Lord asks of you! Is it not to do justice, to love mercy, and to walk humbly with your God!

Micah 6: 6, 8

DIRECTING THE HEART TO GOD How good are your tents, O Jacob, and your homes, O Israel. Through the greatness of Your love I enter Your house. In awe I worship before the ark of Your holiness.

Lord, as I loved the courts of Your temple, and the place where Your glory dwelt, so I still worship and bend low, humble before the Lord my maker.

As for me, let my prayer come before You at the proper time.

Answer me God, in the greatness of Your love, for Your deliverance is sure.

THE FUTURE Lord, we thank You for Your gift of hope, our strength in times of trouble. Beyond the injustice of our time, its cruelty and its wars, we look forward to a world at peace when men deal kindly with each other, and no-one is afraid. Every bad deed delays its coming, every good one brings it nearer. May our lives be Your witness, so that future generations bless us. May the day come, as the prophet taught, when 'the sun of righteousness will rise with healing in its wings'. Help us to pray for it, to wait for it, to work for it and to be worthy of it. Blessed are You Lord, the hope of Israel. Amen.

SONGS OF PRAISE
You may laugh, laugh at all the dreams
which I, the dreamer, can weave,
laugh because I believe in man;
for in you I still believe.

כִּי עוֹד נַפְשִׁי דְּרוֹר שׁוֹאֶפֶת׃

לֹא מְכַרְתִּיהָ לְעֵגֶל־פָּז׃

כִּי עוֹד אַאֲמִין גַּם בָּאָדָם׃

גַּם בְּרוּחוֹ ׃ רוּחַ עָז ׃

שַׂחֲקִי כִּי גַם בְּרֵעוּת אַאֲמִין׃

אַאֲמִין כִּי עוֹד אֶמְצָא לֵב׃

לֵב תִּקְווֹתַי גַּם תִּקְווֹתָיו׃

יָחוּשׁ אֲשֶׁר יָבִין כְּאָב ׃

אַאֲמִינָה גַּם בֶּעָתִיד׃

אַף אִם יִרְחַק זֶה הַיּוֹם׃

אַךְ בֹּא יָבֹא — יִשְׂאוּ שָׁלוֹם

אָז וּבְרָכָה לְאֹם מִלְאֹם ׃

יָשׁוּב יִפְרַח אָז גַּם עַמִּי׃

וּבָאָרֶץ יָקוּם דּוֹר׃

בַּרְזֶל־כְּבָלָיו יוּסַר מֶנּוּ׃

עַיִן־בְּעַיִן יִרְאֶה אוֹר ׃

אֱלֹהַי ׃ נְשָׁמָה שֶׁנָּתַתָּ־בִּי טְהוֹרָה׃ אַתָּה בְרָאתָהּ׃ אַתָּה יְצַרְתָּהּ׃ אַתָּה נְפַחְתָּהּ בִּי ׃ וְאַתָּה מְשַׁמְּרָהּ בְּקִרְבִּי׃ וְאַתָּה עָתִיד לִטְּלָהּ מִמֶּנִּי לְחַיֵּי עוֹלָם ׃ כָּל־זְמַן שֶׁהַנְּשָׁמָה בְּקִרְבִּי מוֹדֶה אֲנִי לְפָנֶיךָ יְיָ אֱלֹהַי וֵאלֹהֵי אֲבוֹתַי ׃ שֶׁאַתָּה הוּא רִבּוֹן כָּל־הַמַּעֲשִׂים׃ מוֹשֵׁל בְּכָל־הַבְּרִיּוֹת׃ אֲדוֹן כָּל־הַנְּשָׁמוֹת ׃ בָּרוּךְ אַתָּה יְיָ׃ הַמַּחֲזִיר נְשָׁמוֹת לִפְגָרִים מֵתִים ׃

יְיָ מֶלֶךְ ׃ יְיָ מָלָךְ ׃ יְיָ יִמְלֹךְ לְעוֹלָם וָעֶד ׃

וְהָיָה יְיָ לְמֶלֶךְ עַל־כָּל־הָאָרֶץ׃ בַּיּוֹם הַהוּא יִהְיֶה יְיָ אֶחָד וּשְׁמוֹ אֶחָד ׃ הוֹשִׁיעֵנוּ יְיָ אֱלֹהֵינוּ׃ לְהוֹדוֹת לְשֵׁם קָדְשֶׁךָ לְהִשְׁתַּבֵּחַ בִּתְהִלָּתֶךָ ׃ בָּרוּךְ יְהוָה אֱלֹהֵי יִשְׂרָאֵל מִן־הָעוֹלָם וְעַד הָעוֹלָם׃ וְאָמַר כָּל־הָעָם אָמֵן אַמֵן הַלְלוּיָהּ ׃ כֹּל הַנְּשָׁמָה תְּהַלֵּל יָהּ ׃ הַלְלוּיָהּ ׃

Yet my soul still yearns for freedom
to no golden calf betrayed,
because I still believe in man,
so strong is his spirit made.

Laugh that I still believe in friends
and I yet will find a heart
to share my hope as his own hope,
in my joy and pain take part.

And I believe in the future,
however distant the day,
when nation shall bless each nation
and in peace shall make their way.

My people, too, shall flower again;
generations shall arise,
their fetters of iron cast away,
a new light before their eyes.

Tchernikowsky

Alternative Songs of Praise, pages 571–609.

THE
GOODNESS
OF MAN

My God, the soul You have given me is pure, for You created it, You formed it and You made it live within me. You watch over it within me, but one day You will take it from me to everlasting life. My God and God of my fathers, as long as the soul is within me, I will declare that You are the master of all deeds, the ruler of all creatures and the Lord of every soul. Blessed are You Lord, who brings the dead into everlasting life.

THE POWER
OF GOD

The Lord does rule, the Lord has ruled, the Lord shall rule forever and ever.

The Lord shall be as a king over the whole earth. On that day the Lord shall be One, and known as One.

Save us, Lord our God, to proclaim Your holy name and be honoured in praising You.

Blessed is the Lord God of Israel from everlasting to everlasting. Let all the people say: Amen! Praise the Lord!

May all who live praise the Lord. Hallelujah!

I

These are the promises of God and the duties He lays on man for the building of His kingdom.

I am God of might, walk before Me and be perfect.

Genesis 17: 1

Do not think meanly of yourself and do not despair of perfection.

Maimonides

I will restore honest language to the nations, so that all may speak in the Lord's name, and serve Him together with one mind.

Zephaniah 3: 9

I call heaven and earth to witness that whether it be Jew or non-Jew, man or woman, free or enslaved—only according to their deeds does the spirit of God rest upon them.

Seder Eliyahu Rabbah

No longer will a man teach his neighbour, or a man his brother saying: 'Know the Lord'. All of them will know Me.

Jeremiah 31: 34

Take care of your own soul and of another man's body but not of your own body and of another man's soul.

Mendel of Kotzk

At that time I will bring you in, and at that time I will gather you. I will give you praise and renown among all the peoples of the earth, when I turn your captivity before your eyes.

Zephaniah 3: 20

The world will be freer by our liberty, richer by our wealth, greater by our greatness.

Theodor Herzl

Nation shall not lift up sword against nation, never again shall they train for war.

Micah 4: 3

In God's eyes the man stands high who makes peace between men—between husband and wife, between parents and children, between management and labour, between neighbour and neighbour. But he stands highest who establishes peace among the nations.

Talmud

II

These are the promises of God and the duties He lays on man for the building of His kingdom.

The wolf shall live with the lamb, the leopard lie down with the kid, the calf and young lion shall feed together, and a little child shall lead them.

Isaiah 11: 6

See My works, how fine and excellent they are. All that I created, I created for you. Think upon this, and do not desolate and corrupt My world, for if you corrupt it, there is no one to set it right after you.

Ecclesiastes Rabbah

A shoot shall grow from the broken tree of Jesse, and a branch shall spring from its roots. The spirit of the Lord shall rest upon him, the spirit of wisdom and understanding.

Isaiah 11: 1-2

No duty is more sacred than for man to cherish that spark of the Messiah in his soul and save it from extinction.

Nachman of Bratzlav

Who can endure the day of his coming? Who can stand firm when he appears? He shall sit as a refiner and purifier of silver, and he shall purify the sons of Levi, and purge them as gold and silver.

Malachi 3: 2-3

The world is judged by the majority of its people, and an individual is judged by the majority of his deeds. Happy the man who performs a good deed: that may tip the scales for him and the world.

Kiddushin

It shall be said in that day: This is our God for whom we waited that He might save us; this is the Lord for whom we waited, we will be glad and rejoice in His salvation.

Isaiah 25: 9

May His kingdom come in your lifetime, and in your days, and in the lifetime of all the family of Israel—quickly and speedily may it come.

Kaddish

בָּרוּךְ יְהֹוָה לְעוֹלָם· אָמֵן וְאָמֵן:

בָּרוּךְ יְהֹוָה אֱלֹהִים אֱלֹהֵי יִשְׂרָאֵל· עֹשֵׂה נִפְלָאוֹת לְבַדּוֹ:

וּבָרוּךְ שֵׁם כְּבוֹדוֹ לְעוֹלָם· וְיִמָּלֵא כְבוֹדוֹ אֶת־כָּל־הָאָרֶץ·

אָמֵן וְאָמֵן:

נִשְׁמַת כָּל־חַי תְּבָרֵךְ אֶת־שִׁמְךָ יְיָ אֱלֹהֵינוּ· וְרוּחַ כָּל־

בָּשָׂר תְּפָאֵר וּתְרוֹמֵם זִכְרְךָ מַלְכֵּנוּ תָּמִיד: מִן

הָעוֹלָם וְעַד הָעוֹלָם אַתָּה אֵל· וּמִבַּלְעָדֶיךָ אֵין לָנוּ מֶלֶךְ

גּוֹאֵל וּמוֹשִׁיעַ פּוֹדֶה וּמַצִּיל וְעוֹנֶה וּמְרַחֵם· בְּכָל־עֵת צָרָה

וְצוּקָה אֵין לָנוּ מֶלֶךְ עוֹזֵר וְסוֹמֵךְ זוּלָתֶךָ: אֱלֹהֵי הָרִאשׁוֹנִים

וְהָאַחֲרוֹנִים· אֱלוֹהַּ כָּל־בְּרִיּוֹת· אֲדוֹן כָּל־תּוֹלָדוֹת הַמְהֻלָּל

בְּכָל־הַתִּשְׁבָּחוֹת· הַמְנַהֵג עוֹלָמוֹ בְּחֶסֶד וּבְרִיּוֹתָיו בְּרַחֲמִים:

וַיְיָ לֹא יָנוּם וְלֹא יִישָׁן· הַמְעוֹרֵר יְשֵׁנִים וְהַמֵּקִיץ נִרְדָּמִים·

מְחַיֶּה מֵתִים וְרוֹפֵא חוֹלִים· פּוֹקֵחַ עִוְרִים וְזוֹקֵף כְּפוּפִים·

לְךָ לְבַדְּךָ אֲנַחְנוּ מוֹדִים:

עַד־הֵנָּה עֲזָרוּנוּ רַחֲמֶיךָ· וְלֹא עֲזָבוּנוּ חֲסָדֶיךָ· עַל־כֵּן

אֵבָרִים שֶׁפִּלַּגְתָּ בָּנוּ· וְרוּחַ וּנְשָׁמָה שֶׁנָּפַחְתָּ בְּאַפֵּינוּ· וְלָשׁוֹן

אֲשֶׁר שַׂמְתָּ בְּפִינוּ· הֵן הֵם יוֹדוּ וִיבָרְכוּ· וִישַׁבְּחוּ וִיפָאֲרוּ·

וִישׁוֹרְרוּ אֶת־שִׁמְךָ מַלְכֵּנוּ תָּמִיד: כִּי כָל־פֶּה לְךָ יוֹדֶה·

וְכָל־לָשׁוֹן לְךָ תְשַׁבֵּחַ· וְכָל־עַיִן לְךָ תְצַפֶּה· וְכָל־בֶּרֶךְ לְךָ

תִכְרַע· וְכָל־קוֹמָה לְפָנֶיךָ תִשְׁתַּחֲוֶה· וְכָל־הַלְּבָבוֹת יִירָאוּךָ·

וְכָל־קֶרֶב וּכְלָיוֹת יְזַמְּרוּ לִשְׁמֶךָ· כַּדָּבָר שֶׁנֶּאֱמַר· כָּל־

עַצְמוֹתַי תֹּאמַרְנָה· יְיָ מִי כָמוֹךָ· מַצִּיל עָנִי מֵחָזָק מִמֶּנּוּ·

וְעָנִי וְאֶבְיוֹן מִגֹּזְלוֹ· מִי יִדְמֶה־לָּךְ· וּמִי יִשְׁוֶה־לָּךְ וּמִי יַעֲרָךְ־

לָךְ· הָאֵל הַגָּדוֹל הַגִּבּוֹר וְהַנּוֹרָא אֵל עֶלְיוֹן קוֹנֵה שָׁמַיִם

וָאָרֶץ: בְּפִי יְשָׁרִים תִּתְהַלָּל· וּבְדִבְרֵי צַדִּיקִים תִּתְבָּרַךְ·

וּבִלְשׁוֹן חֲסִידִים תִּתְרוֹמָם· וּבְקֶרֶב קְדוֹשִׁים תִּתְקַדָּשׁ:

Blessed be the Lord forever. Amen and amen.

Blessed be the Lord God, the God of Israel, who alone works wonders.

Blessed be His glorious name forever. All the earth is full of His glory. Amen and amen.

ALL CREATION PRAISES GOD The breath of life in every creature shall bless You, Lord our God, and the spirit of all flesh ever recalls Your beauty and Your greatness. From everlasting to everlasting You are God. Besides You we have no king who rescues and saves us, frees and delivers us, and answers and cares for us. At all times of trouble and distress there is no king who can help and support us but You.

God of the first and of the last ages, God of all creatures, Lord of history, adored in all worship—He guides His universe with love, and His creatures with mercy. The Lord neither slumbers nor sleeps. He wakes the sleepers, and rouses the uncaring. He gives life beyond death, He heals the sick, He gives sight to the blind and raises up those bent low. To You alone we declare our gratitude.

Until now Your love has been our help and Your kindness has not left us. Therefore the limbs You formed in us, the spirit and soul You breathed into us and the tongue You set in our mouth, ever shall they thank, bless, praise, glorify and sing to Your name, our king. For every mouth shall thank You, every tongue praise You, every eye look to You, every knee bend to You and the height of man shall bow low before You. All hearts shall fear You and our innermost being sing praises to Your name, as it is said: 'All my bones shall say, Lord who is like You, who frees the poor man from those too strong for him, the poor and needy man from his exploiter.' Who is like You, who is equal to You, who can be compared to You, the great, mighty and awesome God, transcendent God, creator of heaven and earth. By the mouth of the upright You are praised, by the words of the righteous You are blessed, by the tongue of the pious You are honoured, and among the holy You are sanctified.

בָּרוּךְ אַתָּה יְיָ אֱלֹהֵינוּ מֶלֶךְ הָעוֹלָם · אֲשֶׁר קִדְּשָׁנוּ
בְּמִצְוֹתָיו וְצִוָּנוּ לַעֲסוֹק בְּדִבְרֵי תוֹרָה :

The great aim made holy by time and by Judaism is that all men
be free, all know God, all use their spiritual and material powers
freely and generously so that truth and justice be enthroned on this
earth, a throne which will adorn the lowliest hut as well as the most
glorious palace. Therefore no symbol should be accepted as Jewish
which prevents the Jew from participating in and working towards
the fulfilment of this object with all his powers. He is not permitted
to be a mere spectator of the work of the modern age but must give
himself heart and soul to it, for this is the command of the God of his
fathers who only wishes to have right and love realized on earth, and
therefore called Abraham from the other side of the river and desired
to make him and his descendants a blessing for the world through
their deeds and their suffering.

Samuel Hirsch

יִשְׁתַּבַּח שִׁמְךָ לָעַד מַלְכֵּנוּ · הָאֵל הַמֶּלֶךְ הַגָּדוֹל וְהַקָּדוֹשׁ
בַּשָּׁמַיִם וּבָאָרֶץ · כִּי לְךָ נָאֶה יְיָ אֱלֹהֵינוּ וֵאלֹהֵי
אֲבוֹתֵינוּ לְעוֹלָם וָעֶד שִׁיר וּשְׁבָחָה · הַלֵּל וְזִמְרָה עֹז וּמֶמְשָׁלָה
נֶצַח גְּדֻלָּה וּגְבוּרָה תְּהִלָּה וְתִפְאֶרֶת קְדֻשָּׁה וּמַלְכוּת · בְּרָכוֹת
וְהוֹדָאוֹת לְשִׁמְךָ הַגָּדוֹל וְהַקָּדוֹשׁ · וּמֵעוֹלָם וְעַד־עוֹלָם אַתָּה
אֵל : בָּרוּךְ אַתָּה יְיָ · בּוֹרֵא כָּל־הַנְּשָׁמוֹת · רִבּוֹן כָּל־הַמַּעֲשִׂים ·
מֶלֶךְ חֵי הָעוֹלָמִים :

The half Kaddish on page 168 may be included here.

בָּרְכוּ אֶת־יְיָ הַמְבֹרָךְ :

בָּרוּךְ יְיָ הַמְבֹרָךְ לְעוֹלָם וָעֶד :

THE DUTY TO STUDY   Blessed are You, Lord our God, king of the universe, who makes us holy through doing His commands, and who commands us to devote ourselves to the study of His teaching.

One of the following passages or one selected from the Anthology, pages 376–384.

The wise men and the prophets did not long for the days of the Messiah to seize upon the world, nor to rule over other faiths, nor to be glorified by nations, nor to eat, drink and have a good time, but to be free for Torah and its wisdom, free from oppression and distraction so that they might be fit for the life of the world to come. When that time is here, no-one will go hungry; there will be no war, no fanaticism and no conflict, for goodness will flow abundantly and all delights will be as plentiful as the countless specks of dust, and the whole world will be only concerned with the knowledge of the Lord. Then the people of Israel will be truly wise for they will know what is hidden from us and they will attain that knowledge of their creator that it is humanly possible to attain, as it is written in the prophets: 'For the earth shall be full of the knowledge of the Lord as the waters cover the sea.'

Maimonides

THE DUTY OF PRAISE   Praised be Your name forever, for You are the God who is the great and holy king in heaven and on earth. Therefore, Lord our God, and God of our fathers, song and praise, holiness and majesty, blessing and gratitude belong to Your great and holy name forever and ever. From age to age You are God. Blessed are You Lord, creator of every living being, master of all deeds, the king, the life of all existence.

The half Kaddish on page 168 may be included here.

THE CALL TO COM-MUNITY PRAYER   Bless the Lord whom we are called to bless.

Blessed be the Lord whom we are called to bless forever and ever.

בָּרוּךְ אַתָּה יְיָ אֱלֹהֵינוּ מֶלֶךְ הָעוֹלָם · יוֹצֵר אוֹר וּבוֹרֵא חֹשֶׁךְ · עֹשֶׂה שָׁלוֹם וּבוֹרֵא אֶת־הַכֹּל : הַכֹּל יוֹדוּךָ · וְהַכֹּל יְשַׁבְּחוּךָ · וְהַכֹּל יֹאמְרוּ אֵין קָדוֹשׁ כַּיְיָ : הַמֵּאִיר לָעוֹלָם כֻּלוֹ וּלְיוֹשְׁבָיו וּבְטוּבוֹ מְחַדֵּשׁ בְּכָל־יוֹם תָּמִיד מַעֲשֵׂה בְרֵאשִׁית : מָה רַבּוּ מַעֲשֶׂיךָ יְיָ · כֻּלָּם בְּחָכְמָה עָשִׂיתָ · מָלְאָה הָאָרֶץ קִנְיָנֶךָ : הַמֶּלֶךְ הַמְּרוֹמָם לְבַדּוֹ מֵאָז · הַמְשֻׁבָּח וְהַמְפֹאָר וְהַמִּתְנַשֵּׂא מִימוֹת עוֹלָם : אֱלֹהֵי עוֹלָם · בְּרַחֲמֶיךָ הָרַבִּים רַחֵם עָלֵינוּ · אֲדוֹן עֻזֵּנוּ · צוּר מִשְׂגַּבֵּנוּ · מָגֵן יִשְׁעֵנוּ · מִשְׂגָּב בַּעֲדֵנוּ : בָּרוּךְ אַתָּה יְיָ · יוֹצֵר הַמְּאוֹרוֹת :

אַהֲבָה רַבָּה אֲהַבְתָּנוּ יְיָ אֱלֹהֵינוּ · חֶמְלָה גְדוֹלָה וִיתֵרָה חָמַלְתָּ עָלֵינוּ : אָבִינוּ מַלְכֵּנוּ · בַּעֲבוּר שִׁמְךָ הַגָּדוֹל וּבַעֲבוּר אֲבוֹתֵינוּ שֶׁבָּטְחוּ בְךָ · וַתְּלַמְּדֵם חֻקֵּי חַיִּים לַעֲשׂוֹת רְצוֹנְךָ בְּלֵבָב שָׁלֵם · כֵּן תְּחָנֵּנוּ : הָאֵר עֵינֵינוּ בְּתוֹרָתֶךָ וְדַבֵּק לִבֵּנוּ בְּמִצְוֹתֶיךָ · וְיַחֵד לְבָבֵנוּ לְאַהֲבָה וּלְיִרְאָה אֶת־שְׁמֶךָ · לְמַעַן לֹא נֵבוֹשׁ וְלֹא נִכָּלֵם כִּי אֵל פּוֹעֵל יְשׁוּעוֹת אָתָּה · וּבָנוּ בָחַרְתָּ מִכָּל־עַם וְלָשׁוֹן · וְקֵרַבְתָּנוּ מַלְכֵּנוּ לְשִׁמְךָ הַגָּדוֹל בְּאַהֲבָה · לְהוֹדוֹת לְךָ וּלְיַחֶדְךָ וּלְאַהֲבָה אֶת־שְׁמֶךָ : בָּרוּךְ אַתָּה יְיָ · הַבּוֹחֵר בְּעַמּוֹ יִשְׂרָאֵל בְּאַהֲבָה :

שְׁמַ**ע** יִשְׂרָאֵל · יְהֹוָה אֱלֹהֵינוּ יְהֹוָה אֶחָ**ד** :

בָּרוּךְ שֵׁם כְּבוֹד מַלְכוּתוֹ לְעוֹלָם וָעֶד :

וְאָהַבְתָּ אֵת יְהֹוָה אֱלֹהֶיךָ · בְּכָל־לְבָבְךָ וּבְכָל־נַפְשְׁךָ וּבְכָל־מְאֹדֶךָ : וְהָיוּ הַדְּבָרִים הָאֵלֶּה אֲשֶׁר אָנֹכִי מְצַוְּךָ הַיּוֹם עַל־לְבָבֶךָ : וְשִׁנַּנְתָּם לְבָנֶיךָ וְדִבַּרְתָּ בָּם · בְּשִׁבְתְּךָ בְּבֵיתֶךָ וּבְלֶכְתְּךָ בַדֶּרֶךְ וּבְשָׁכְבְּךָ וּבְקוּמֶךָ : וּקְשַׁרְתָּם לְאוֹת עַל־יָדֶךָ · וְהָיוּ לְטֹטָפֹת בֵּין עֵינֶיךָ : וּכְתַבְתָּם עַל־מְזֻזוֹת בֵּיתֶךָ וּבִשְׁעָרֶיךָ :

THE CREATOR OF THE UNIVERSE   Blessed are You, Lord our God, king of the universe, who forms light yet creates darkness, who makes peace yet creates all. All things proclaim You, all things honour You, and all say: 'None is holy like the Lord.' He gives light to all the world and those who live in it. In His goodness He renews the work of the creation day by day. Lord, how great are Your works; You made them all in wisdom; the earth is full of Your creatures. You are the only king exalted from the beginning of time, who has been worshipped, praised and glorified since days of old.

Everlasting God, in Your great mercy have mercy upon us; Lord of our strength, rock of our protection, shield of our safety, our true protector. Blessed are You Lord, who creates the lights of the universe.

HIS LOVE FOR ISRAEL   With deep love You have loved us, and with great and overflowing tenderness You have taken pity on us. Our father, our king, show us compassion because of Your own greatness, and because of our fathers who trusted in You, for You taught them rules to live by, to do Your will with their whole heart. Let our eyes see the light of Your teaching and our hearts embrace Your commands. Give us integrity to love You and fear You. So shall we never lose our self-respect, nor be put to shame, for You are the power which works to save us. You chose us from all peoples and tongues, and in love drew us near to Your own greatness—to honour You, to declare Your unity, and to love You. Blessed are You Lord, who chooses His people Israel in love.

THE GOD OF ISRAEL   Hear O Israel, the Lord is our God, the Lord is One.

Blessed is His name, whose glorious kingdom is forever and ever.

Love the Lord your God with all your heart, and all your soul, and all your might. These words that I command you today shall be upon your heart. Repeat them to your children, and talk about them when you sit in your home, and when you walk in the street; when you lie down, and when you rise up. Hold fast to them as a sign upon your hand, and let them be as reminders before your eyes. Write them on the doorposts of your home and at your gates.

Deuteronomy 6: 4–9

הוֹי כָּל־צָמֵא לְכוּ לַמַּיִם

וַאֲשֶׁר אֵין־לוֹ כָּסֶף לְכוּ שִׁבְרוּ וֶאֱכֹלוּ

וּלְכוּ שִׁבְרוּ בְּלוֹא־כֶסֶף וּבְלוֹא מְחִיר יַיִן וְחָלָב׃

לָמָּה תִשְׁקְלוּ־כֶסֶף בְּלוֹא־לֶחֶם

וִיגִיעֲכֶם בְּלוֹא לְשָׂבְעָה

הַטּוּ אָזְנְכֶם וּלְכוּ אֵלַי

שִׁמְעוּ וּתְחִי נַפְשְׁכֶם׃

דִּרְשׁוּ יְהֹוָה בְּהִמָּצְאוֹ

קְרָאֻהוּ בִּהְיוֹתוֹ קָרוֹב׃

יַעֲזֹב רָשָׁע דַּרְכּוֹ

וְאִישׁ אָוֶן מַחְשְׁבֹתָיו

וְיָשֹׁב אֶל־יְהֹוָה וִירַחֲמֵהוּ

וְאֶל־אֱלֹהֵינוּ כִּי־יַרְבֶּה לִסְלוֹחַ׃

כֹּה אָמַר יְהֹוָה

שִׁמְרוּ מִשְׁפָּט וַעֲשׂוּ צְדָקָה

כִּי־קְרוֹבָה יְשׁוּעָתִי לָבוֹא

וְצִדְקָתִי לְהִגָּלוֹת׃

אַשְׁרֵי אֱנוֹשׁ יַעֲשֶׂה־זֹּאת

וּבֶן־אָדָם יַחֲזִיק בָּהּ

שֹׁמֵר שַׁבָּת מֵחַלְּלוֹ

וְשֹׁמֵר יָדוֹ מֵעֲשׂוֹת כָּל־רָע׃

וּבְנֵי הַנֵּכָר הַנִּלְוִים עַל־יְהֹוָה

לְשָׁרְתוֹ וּלְאַהֲבָה אֶת־שֵׁם יְהֹוָה

לִהְיוֹת לוֹ לַעֲבָדִים

כָּל־שֹׁמֵר שַׁבָּת מֵחַלְּלוֹ

וּמַחֲזִיקִים בִּבְרִיתִי׃

וַהֲבִיאוֹתִים אֶל־הַר קָדְשִׁי

וְשִׂמַּחְתִּים בְּבֵית תְּפִלָּתִי

כִּי בֵיתִי בֵּית־תְּפִלָּה יִקָּרֵא

לְכָל־הָעַמִּים׃

*During the silence the second and third paragraphs of the Shema (pages 60–62)
may be read, or the following:*

Come all who are thirsty, come to the water,

and he who has no money, come and buy and eat;

buy wine and milk with no money, with no price.

Why spend money for what is not bread

and your labour without satisfaction?

Listen and come to Me,

hear and your soul shall live.

Seek the Lord while He may be found,

call to Him while He is near.

Let the wicked forsake his way

and the evil man his thoughts,

let him turn back to the Lord who will take pity on him,

to our God who is generous to forgive.

So the Lord has said:

Care for justice and do what is right,

for My salvation is about to come

and My righteousness to appear.

Happy is the person who does this

and any man who grasps it,

caring for the Sabbath without dishonouring it,

and keeping his hand from doing evil.

Also the strangers who join themselves to the Lord

to serve Him and love His name

and to be His workers;

and who care for the Sabbath, not dishonouring it,

holding fast to My covenant.

I shall bring them to My holy hill

and give them joy in My house of prayer,

for My house shall be called

a house of prayer for all peoples.

From Isaiah, chs. 55 and 56

הִנֵּה יָמִים בָּאִים נְאֻם־יְהֹוָה וְכָרַתִּי אֶת־בֵּית יִשְׂרָאֵל
וְאֶת־בֵּית יְהוּדָה בְּרִית חֲדָשָׁה: לֹא כַבְּרִית אֲשֶׁר כָּרַתִּי
אֶת־אֲבוֹתָם בְּיוֹם הֶחֱזִיקִי בְיָדָם לְהוֹצִיאָם מֵאֶרֶץ מִצְרַיִם
אֲשֶׁר־הֵמָּה הֵפֵרוּ אֶת־בְּרִיתִי וְאָנֹכִי בָּעַלְתִּי בָם נְאֻם־יְהֹוָה:
כִּי זֹאת הַבְּרִית אֲשֶׁר אֶכְרֹת אֶת־בֵּית יִשְׂרָאֵל אַחֲרֵי הַיָּמִים
הָהֵם נְאֻם־יְהֹוָה נָתַתִּי אֶת־תּוֹרָתִי בְּקִרְבָּם וְעַל־לִבָּם
אֶכְתֲּבֶנָּה וְהָיִיתִי לָהֶם לֵאלֹהִים וְהֵמָּה יִהְיוּ־לִי לְעָם: וְלֹא
יְלַמְּדוּ עוֹד אִישׁ אֶת־רֵעֵהוּ וְאִישׁ אֶת־אָחִיו לֵאמֹר דְּעוּ
אֶת־יְהֹוָה כִּי כוּלָם יֵדְעוּ אוֹתִי לְמִקְטַנָּם וְעַד־גְּדוֹלָם
נְאֻם־יְהֹוָה:

Liberal Synagogue, Amsterdam

The time is coming, says the Lord, when I will make a new covenant with Israel and Judah. It will not be like the covenant I made with their fathers when I took them by the hand and led them out of Egypt. This covenant they broke though I was wedded to them, says the Lord. But this is the covenant which I will make with Israel after those days, says the Lord: I will set My Torah within them and write it on their hearts; I shall be their God and they will be My people. No longer will a man teach his neighbour, or a man his brother saying, 'Know the Lord!' All of them will know Me, from the smallest of them to the greatest of them, says the Lord.

Jeremiah 31: 30–33

After the silence the service continues on page 142.

Middlesex New Synagogue, London

תפלת שחרית לשבת

מִי־יַעֲלֶה בְהַר־יְהֹוָה וּמִי־יָקוּם בִּמְקוֹם קָדְשׁוֹ:

נְקִי כַפַּיִם וּבַר־לֵבָב אֲשֶׁר לֹא־נָשָׂא לַשָּׁוְא נַפְשׁוֹ וְלֹא

נִשְׁבַּע לְמִרְמָה:

מַה־טֹּבוּ אֹהָלֶיךָ יַעֲקֹב מִשְׁכְּנֹתֶיךָ יִשְׂרָאֵל:

וַאֲנִי בְּרֹב חַסְדְּךָ אָבוֹא בֵיתֶךָ

אֶשְׁתַּחֲוֶה אֶל־הֵיכַל־קָדְשְׁךָ בְּיִרְאָתֶךָ:

יְהֹוָה אָהַבְתִּי מְעוֹן בֵּיתֶךָ וּמְקוֹם מִשְׁכַּן כְּבוֹדֶךָ:

וַאֲנִי אֶשְׁתַּחֲוֶה וְאֶכְרָעָה אֶבְרְכָה לִפְנֵי־יְהֹוָה עֹשִׂי:

וַאֲנִי תְפִלָּתִי־לְךָ יְהֹוָה עֵת רָצוֹן

אֱלֹהִים בְּרָב־חַסְדֶּךָ עֲנֵנִי בֶּאֱמֶת יִשְׁעֶךָ:

אֱלֹהֵינוּ וֵאלֹהֵי־אֲבוֹתֵינוּ מוֹדִים אֲנַחְנוּ לָךְ עַל שֶׁהוֹרֵיתָנוּ
לְהַצִּיל אִישׁ אֶת־רֵעֵהוּ וְאֶת־עַצְמוֹ • לָתֵת וּלְקַבֵּל • וְלִתְמוֹךְ
זֶה בָּזֶה בִּימֵי־שְׁנוֹת־חַיֵּינוּ: אֵין סוֹף לְהִתְעַלּוֹתֵנוּ כִּי אֵין
גְּבוּל לִיכָלְתֵּנוּ לְהֵיטִיב: אֵין שִׂמְחָה שֶׁלֹּא נוּכַל לְהַשִּׂיג כִּי
אֵין קֵץ לְנִדְבַת־לִבֵּנוּ: אֵין שִׂיא אֵלָיו לֹא נוּכַל לְהַגִּיעַ כִּי
נִבְרֵאנוּ לְהִזָּקֵק לְאַהֲבָה וְלַהֲבָנָה אִישׁ מֵרֵעֵהוּ:

שַׁעֲרֵי שָׁמַיִם פְּתוּחִים לְכָל־בְּנֵי־אָדָם • וּבְכֵן הָבָה נִתְחַלֵּק
בְּבִרְכוֹתֵינוּ וְנָבוֹא בָם: בַּשָּׁבוּעַ שֶׁעָבַר אוּלַי מָנַעְנוּ אֲשֶׁר
מֵאֲחֵרִים וּמֵעַצְמֵנוּ כִּי חֵטְא הָאֱנוֹכִיּוּת רוֹבֵץ עַל־כָּל־פֶּתַח •
יוֹדְעִים אָנוּ לִהְיוֹת אוֹיְבִים לְשַׁלְוַת־נַפְשֵׁנוּ: שַׁבָּתְךָ מְשִׁיבָה

IV

SABBATH MORNING SERVICE

Who may ascend the mountain of the Lord, and who may stand in the place of His holiness?

He whose hands are clean, whose heart is pure, who has not given up his soul to worthless things nor committed himself to deception.

Psalm 24: 3-4

DIRECTING THE HEART TO GOD

How good are your tents, O Jacob, and your homes, O Israel. Through the greatness of Your love I enter Your house. In awe I worship before the ark of Your holiness.

Lord, as I loved the courts of Your temple, and the place where Your glory dwelt, so I still worship and bend low, humble before the Lord my maker.

As for me, let my prayer come before You at the proper time.

Answer me God, in the greatness of Your love, for Your deliverance is sure.

THE JUST SOCIETY

Our God and God of our fathers, we thank You for teaching us how to save each other and ourselves, to give and to receive, and to support each other on life's journey. There is no limit to our ascent, for there is no limit to the goodness we can do. There is no joy we cannot have, for there is no end to giving. There is no height we cannot attain, for we were created to need each other's love and understanding.

The doors of heaven are open to all mankind. So let us share our blessings and enter in. In the past week we may have denied happiness to others and to ourselves, for selfishness lies in the way, and we can be enemies to our own happiness. Your Sabbath calls us back

אוֹתָנוּ לָאֱמֶת · שׁוּב נִלְמַד לְהָבִיא אַהֲבָה תַּחַת שִׂנְאָה
וּלְהָסִיר מְרִירוּת מִלִּבֵּנוּ · שׁוּב נַכִּיר יִצְרֵנוּ הַטּוֹב: שׁוּב
נִרְאֶה טַהֵר־נַפְשֵׁנוּ וְאֶת־חוֹתָמְךָ הַזּוֹהֵר בָּנוּ: בָּרוּךְ אַתָּה יְיָ
הַמְלַמְּדֵנוּ לִהְיוֹת מְסוּרִים אִישׁ לְרֵעֵהוּ · אָמֵן:

אָנָּא בְּכֹחַ גְּדֻלַּת יְמִינְךָ תַּתִּיר צְרוּרָה:

קַבֵּל רִנַּת עַמְּךָ שַׂגְּבֵנוּ טַהֲרֵנוּ נוֹרָא:

נָא גִבּוֹר דּוֹרְשֵׁי יִחוּדְךָ כְּבָבַת שָׁמְרֵם:

בָּרְכֵם טַהֲרֵם רַחֲמֵם צִדְקָתְךָ תָּמִיד גָּמְלֵם:

חֲסִין קָדוֹשׁ בְּרוֹב טוּבְךָ נַהֵל עֲדָתֶךָ:

יָחִיד גֵּאֶה לְעַמְּךָ פְּנֵה זוֹכְרֵי קְדֻשָּׁתֶךָ:

שַׁוְעָתֵנוּ קַבֵּל וּשְׁמַע צַעֲקָתֵנוּ יוֹדֵעַ תַּעֲלוּמוֹת:

בָּרוּךְ שֵׁם כְּבוֹד מַלְכוּתוֹ לְעוֹלָם וָעֶד:

אֱלֹהַי · נְשָׁמָה שֶׁנָּתַתָּ־בִּי טְהוֹרָה · אַתָּה בְרָאתָהּ · אַתָּה
יְצַרְתָּהּ · אַתָּה נְפַחְתָּהּ בִּי · וְאַתָּה מְשַׁמְּרָהּ בְּקִרְבִּי · וְאַתָּה
עָתִיד לִטְּלָהּ מִמֶּנִּי לְחַיֵּי עוֹלָם: כָּל־זְמַן שֶׁהַנְּשָׁמָה בְּקִרְבִּי
מוֹדֶה אֲנִי לְפָנֶיךָ יְיָ אֱלֹהַי וֵאלֹהֵי אֲבוֹתַי · שֶׁאַתָּה הוּא רִבּוֹן
כָּל־הַמַּעֲשִׂים · מוֹשֵׁל בְּכָל־הַבְּרִיּוֹת: אֲדוֹן כָּל־הַנְּשָׁמוֹת:
בָּרוּךְ אַתָּה יְיָ · הַמַּחֲזִיר נְשָׁמוֹת לַמֵּתִים:

לְעוֹלָם יְהֵא אָדָם יְרֵא שָׁמַיִם בַּסֵּתֶר כְּבַגָּלוּי · וּמוֹדֶה
עַל־הָאֱמֶת וְדוֹבֵר אֱמֶת בִּלְבָבוֹ:

to the truth. We learn again the way to change hatred into love, and banish bitterness. We know again the strength for good that is in our grasp. We see again the purity of our souls, and Your image shining in us. Blessed are You Lord, who teaches us to serve each other. Amen.

SONGS OF PRAISE

Release all captives, we beseech You,
Lord whose mighty hand does set man free;
And hear the glad acclaim of all Your people
    Who praise and glorify You alone.

Preserve the righteous ones who seek You,
And proclaim Your unity in love;
O guard and bless with Your abundant goodness
    Your people who revere Your name.

You Lord, who are alone exalted,
Turn to us and hear our prayers.
We bless You—You who know all things hidden.
    Your kingdom is for eternity.

Attributed to Nechanya ben Hakkana

Alternative Songs of Praise, pages 571–609.

THE GOODNESS OF MAN

My God, the soul You have given me is pure, for You created it, You formed it and You made it live within me. You watch over it within me, but one day You will take it from me to everlasting life. My God and God of my fathers, as long as the soul is within me, I will declare that You are the master of all deeds, the ruler of all creatures and the Lord of every soul. Blessed are You Lord, who brings the dead into everlasting life.

Man should always be in awe of heaven in private as well as in public. He should tell the truth and speak it in his heart.

I

Lord our God, and the God of our fathers, help us to live according to Your teaching, and to hold fast to Your commands.

He asks us to befriend and honour the old, for we too shall grow old.

You shall rise in the presence of grey hairs, give honour to the aged, and fear your God. I am the Lord.

Leviticus 19: 32

He asks us to help the poor because our fathers ate the bread of poverty.

Happy is the man who cares for the poor. The Lord will help him in his time of need.

Psalm 41: 2

He asks us to welcome the stranger, for we have been homeless many times.

Share your food with the hungry, bring the homeless into your home.

Isaiah 58: 7

He asks us to rule other creatures as we would have Him rule over us.

It is forbidden to harm any living creature. It is one's duty to save any living creature from pain.

Kitzur Shulchan Aruch

He asks us to protect the weak, for we, too, are weak and pray for His protection.

Rob not the poor because he is poor, nor use the law to crush the weak.

Proverbs 22: 22

He asks us to share the anxieties of others, for He Himself hears them.

When in my distress I called to the Lord. His answer was to set me free.

Psalm 118: 5

He commands us to love all men whether they be Jew or non-Jew.

Love your neighbour as you love yourself. I am the Lord.

Leviticus 19: 18

II

Lord our God, and the God of our fathers, help us to live according to Your teaching and to hold fast to Your commands.

He asks us to overcome our prejudice, for we have been, and are, the victim of prejudice.

Are not you and the Ethiopians all the same to Me, children of Israel?—It is the Lord who speaks.

Amos 9: 7

He asks us to visit the sick, for our bodies too are frail.

We should pay attention to the needs of the sick, to care for them, give them pleasure and pray for mercy for them.

Kitzur Shulchan Aruch

He asks us to transform enmity, for are we not our own enemies?

Who is mighty among the mighty? He who controls his passion and makes his enemy his friend.

Avot d'Rabbi Natan

He asks us to support the disabled, for some are disabled in body and some in spirit.

You shall not treat the deaf with contempt, nor make the blind stumble.

Leviticus 19: 14

He asks us to understand those who are sick in mind, for who among us knows all reality?

Hold no man insignificant and nothing improbable, for there is no man that has not his hour and no thing that has not its place.

Sayings of the Fathers

He asks us to seek out the lonely, for this is the meaning of community.

You stand this day all of you before the Lord, all of you are pledges one for the other.

Tanchuma

He asks us to strengthen ourselves, for the task He has given us needs all the strength we possess.

Love the Lord your God with all your heart and all your soul and all your might.

Deuteronomy 6: 5

יְיָ מֶלֶךְ · יְיָ מָלָךְ · יְיָ יִמְלֹךְ לְעוֹלָם וָעֶד:

וְהָיָה יְיָ לְמֶלֶךְ עַל־כָּל־הָאָרֶץ · בַּיּוֹם הַהוּא יִהְיֶה יְיָ
אֶחָד וּשְׁמוֹ אֶחָד: הוֹשִׁיעֵנוּ יְיָ אֱלֹהֵינוּ · לְהוֹדוֹת לְשֵׁם קָדְשֶׁךָ
לְהִשְׁתַּבֵּחַ בִּתְהִלָּתֶךָ: בָּרוּךְ יְהֹוָה אֱלֹהֵי יִשְׂרָאֵל מִן־הָעוֹלָם
וְעַד הָעוֹלָם · וְאָמַר כָּל־הָעָם אָמֵן · הַלְלוּיָהּ: כֹּל הַנְּשָׁמָה
תְּהַלֵּל יָהּ · הַלְלוּיָהּ:

בָּרוּךְ שֶׁאָמַר וְהָיָה הָעוֹלָם · בָּרוּךְ אוֹמֵר וְעוֹשֶׂה · בָּרוּךְ
גּוֹזֵר וּמְקַיֵּם · בָּרוּךְ עוֹשֶׂה בְרֵאשִׁית · בָּרוּךְ מְרַחֵם עַל
הָאָרֶץ · בָּרוּךְ מְרַחֵם עַל הַבְּרִיּוֹת · בָּרוּךְ מְשַׁלֵּם שָׂכָר טוֹב
לִירֵאָיו · בָּרוּךְ מַעֲבִיר אֲפֵלָה וּמֵבִיא אוֹרָה · בָּרוּךְ אֵל חַי
לָעַד וְקַיָּם לָנֶצַח · בָּרוּךְ שֶׁאֵין לְפָנָיו עַוְלָה וְלֹא שִׁכְחָה
וְלֹא מַשּׂוֹא פָנִים וְלֹא מִקַּח שֹׁחַד · צַדִּיק הוּא בְּכָל־דְּרָכָיו
וְחָסִיד בְּכָל־מַעֲשָׂיו · בָּרוּךְ פּוֹדֶה וּמַצִּיל · בָּרוּךְ הַמַּנְחִיל
מְנוּחָה לְעַמּוֹ יִשְׂרָאֵל בְּיוֹם שַׁבַּת קֹדֶשׁ: בָּרוּךְ הוּא וּבָרוּךְ
שְׁמוֹ · וּבָרוּךְ זִכְרוֹ לְעוֹלְמֵי עַד : בָּרוּךְ אַתָּה יְיָ אֱלֹהֵינוּ
מֶלֶךְ הָעוֹלָם · הַמֶּלֶךְ הַגָּדוֹל וְהַקָּדוֹשׁ · אָב הָרַחֲמָן · מְהֻלָּל
בְּפִי עַמּוֹ · מְשֻׁבָּח וּמְפֹאָר בִּלְשׁוֹן כָּל־חֲסִידָיו וַעֲבָדָיו:
וּבְשִׁירֵי דָוִד עַבְדֶּךָ נְהַלֶּלְךָ יְיָ אֱלֹהֵינוּ · בִּשְׁבָחוֹת וּבִזְמִירוֹת
נְהוֹדְךָ נְגַדֶּלְךָ נְפָאֶרְךָ וְנַמְלִיכְךָ וְנַזְכִּיר שִׁמְךָ מַלְכֵּנוּ אֱלֹהֵינוּ
יָחִיד חֵי הָעוֹלָמִים · מְשֻׁבָּח וּמְפֹאָר שְׁמוֹ עֲדֵי־עַד : בָּרוּךְ
אַתָּה יְיָ · מֶלֶךְ מְהֻלָּל בַּתִּשְׁבָּחוֹת:

THE POWER OF GOD The Lord does rule, the Lord has ruled, the Lord shall rule forever and ever.

The Lord shall be as a king over the whole earth. On that day the Lord shall be One, and known as One.

Save us, Lord our God, to proclaim Your holy name and be honoured in praising You.

Blessed is the Lord God of Israel from everlasting to everlasting. Let all the people say: Amen! Praise the Lord!

May all who live praise the Lord. Hallelujah!

Blessed be He, at whose word the world existed.

Blessed be He, whose word is deed.

Blessed be He, whose command stands firm.

Blessed be He, who makes creation.

Blessed be He, who has mercy on the earth.

Blessed be He, who has mercy on His creatures.

Blessed be He, who gives a good reward to those in awe of Him.

Blessed be He, who takes away darkness and brings on light.

Blessed be He, who lives forever and exists for eternity.

Blessed be He, who has no fault and no forgetfulness, who shows no favour and takes no bribe. Righteous is He in all His ways and loving in all His deeds.

Blessed be He, who redeems and rescues.

Blessed be He, who gives rest to His people Israel on the holy Sabbath day.

Blessed be He, and blessed be His name.

Blessed be the knowledge of Him for all eternity.

Blessed are You, Lord our God, king of the universe, the king, great and holy; merciful father, praised by His people; worshipped and glorified by the tongue of all who love and serve Him. Therefore we praise You, Lord our God, with the psalms of Your servant David; with prayers and songs we declare Your glory, Your greatness, Your splendour, and Your majesty. We proclaim Your name, our king, our God, who alone is the life of all existence, and whose name is worshipped and glorified forever and ever. Blessed are You Lord, the king praised in all worship.

בָּרוּךְ יְהֹוָה לְעוֹלָם · אָמֵן וְאָמֵן:

בָּרוּךְ יְהֹוָה אֱלֹהִים אֱלֹהֵי יִשְׂרָאֵל · עֹשֵׂה נִפְלָאוֹת לְבַדּוֹ:

וּבָרוּךְ שֵׁם כְּבוֹדוֹ לְעוֹלָם · וְיִמָּלֵא כְבוֹדוֹ אֶת־כָּל־הָאָרֶץ · אָמֵן וְאָמֵן:

נִשְׁמַת כָּל־חַי תְּבָרֵךְ אֶת־שִׁמְךָ יְיָ אֱלֹהֵינוּ · וְרוּחַ כָּל־בָּשָׂר תְּפָאֵר וּתְרוֹמֵם זִכְרְךָ מַלְכֵּנוּ תָּמִיד: מִן הָעוֹלָם וְעַד הָעוֹלָם אַתָּה אֵל · וּמִבַּלְעָדֶיךָ אֵין לָנוּ מֶלֶךְ גּוֹאֵל וּמוֹשִׁיעַ פּוֹדֶה וּמַצִּיל וְעוֹנֶה וּמְרַחֵם · בְּכָל־עֵת צָרָה וְצוּקָה אֵין לָנוּ מֶלֶךְ עוֹזֵר וְסוֹמֵךְ זוּלָתֶךָ: אֱלֹהֵי הָרִאשׁוֹנִים וְהָאַחֲרוֹנִים · אֱלוֹהַּ כָּל־בְּרִיּוֹת · אֲדוֹן כָּל־תּוֹלָדוֹת הַמְהֻלָּל בְּכָל־הַתִּשְׁבָּחוֹת · הַמְנַהֵג עוֹלָמוֹ בְּחֶסֶד וּבְרִיּוֹתָיו בְּרַחֲמִים: וַיְיָ לֹא יָנוּם וְלֹא יִישָׁן · הַמְעוֹרֵר יְשֵׁנִים וְהַמֵּקִיץ נִרְדָּמִים · מְחַיֶּה מֵתִים וְרוֹפֵא חוֹלִים · פּוֹקֵחַ עִוְרִים וְזוֹקֵף כְּפוּפִים · לְךָ לְבַדְּךָ אֲנַחְנוּ מוֹדִים:

בָּרוּךְ אַתָּה יְיָ אֱלֹהֵינוּ מֶלֶךְ הָעוֹלָם · אֲשֶׁר קִדְּשָׁנוּ בְּמִצְוֹתָיו וְצִוָּנוּ לַעֲסוֹק בְּדִבְרֵי תוֹרָה:

The title fellow-man applies to every man . . . and he is our fellow-man by God's appointment. It is not our goodwill nor our kindness, nor is it any social convention or legal enactment, that makes him so. He is so by the appointment of the One God, and therefore no one must deprive him of his standing or reduce its meaning. Every human right means a claim that our fellow-man has upon us as his birthright given to him by God. The commandment to 'do justly and love mercy', which is announced to man and demanded from him, is to govern all behaviour toward our fellow-man. What we owe to God is to be paid first and chiefly to His children. In our relationship to them we find the sum of the duties which God has laid upon us; in our relationship to them we can manifest our love to God and our delight in His service. The Talmud says: 'Love God in the men whom He has created'.

Leo Baeck

Blessed be the Lord forever. Amen and amen.

Blessed be the Lord God, the God of Israel, who alone works wonders.

Blessed be His glorious name forever. All the earth is full of His glory. Amen and amen.

ALL CREATION PRAISES GOD   The breath of life in every creature shall bless You, Lord our God, and the spirit of all flesh ever recalls Your beauty and Your greatness. From everlasting to everlasting You are God. Besides You we have no king who rescues and saves us, frees and delivers us, and answers and cares for us. At all times of trouble and distress there is no king who can help and support us but You.

God of the first and of the last ages, God of all creatures, Lord of history, adored in all worship—He guides His universe with love, and His creatures with mercy. The Lord neither slumbers nor sleeps. He wakes the sleepers, and rouses the uncaring. He gives life beyond death, He heals the sick, He gives sight to the blind and raises up those bent low. To You alone we declare our gratitude.

THE DUTY TO STUDY   Blessed are You, Lord our God, king of the universe, who makes us holy through doing His commands, and who commands us to devote ourselves to the study of His teaching.

One of the following passages or one selected from the Anthology, pages 385–391.

Your first aim here on earth should be to be at peace with all men, Jew and non-Jew alike. Contend with no-one. Your home should be a place of quietness and happiness, where no harsh word is ever heard, but love, friendship, modesty, and a spirit of gentleness and reverence rules all the time. But this spirit must not end with the home. In your dealings with the world you must allow neither money nor ambition to disturb you. Forgo your rights in matters of honour, if need be, and above all envy no man. For the main thing is peace, peace with the whole world.

Rabbi Joel ben Abraham Shemariah

יִשְׁתַּבַּח שִׁמְךָ לָעַד מַלְכֵּנוּ · הָאֵל הַמֶּלֶךְ הַגָּדוֹל וְהַקָּדוֹשׁ בַּשָּׁמַיִם וּבָאָרֶץ · כִּי לְךָ נָאֶה יְיָ אֱלֹהֵינוּ וֵאלֹהֵי אֲבוֹתֵינוּ לְעוֹלָם וָעֶד שִׁיר וּשְׁבָחָה · קְדֻשָּׁה וּמַלְכוּת · בְּרָכוֹת וְהוֹדָאוֹת לְשִׁמְךָ הַגָּדוֹל וְהַקָּדוֹשׁ · וּמֵעוֹלָם וְעַד־עוֹלָם אַתָּה אֵל : בָּרוּךְ אַתָּה יְיָ · בּוֹרֵא כָּל־הַנְּשָׁמוֹת · רִבּוֹן כָּל־הַמַּעֲשִׂים · מֶלֶךְ חֵי הָעוֹלָמִים :

The half Kaddish on page 168 may be included here.

בָּרְכוּ אֶת־יְיָ הַמְּבֹרָךְ :

בָּרוּךְ יְיָ הַמְּבֹרָךְ לְעוֹלָם וָעֶד :

בָּרוּךְ אַתָּה יְיָ אֱלֹהֵינוּ מֶלֶךְ הָעוֹלָם · יוֹצֵר אוֹר וּבוֹרֵא חֹשֶׁךְ · עֹשֶׂה שָׁלוֹם וּבוֹרֵא אֶת־הַכֹּל : הַכֹּל יוֹדוּךָ · וְהַכֹּל יְשַׁבְּחוּךָ · וְהַכֹּל יֹאמְרוּ אֵין קָדוֹשׁ כַּיְיָ : הַמֵּאִיר לָעוֹלָם כֻּלּוֹ וּלְיוֹשְׁבָיו וּבְטוּבוֹ מְחַדֵּשׁ בְּכָל־יוֹם תָּמִיד מַעֲשֵׂה בְרֵאשִׁית : מָה רַבּוּ מַעֲשֶׂיךָ יְיָ · כֻּלָּם בְּחָכְמָה עָשִׂיתָ · מָלְאָה הָאָרֶץ קִנְיָנֶךָ : הַמֶּלֶךְ הַמְרוֹמָם לְבַדּוֹ מֵאָז · הַמְשֻׁבָּח וְהַמְפֹאָר וְהַמִּתְנַשֵּׂא מִימוֹת עוֹלָם : אֱלֹהֵי עוֹלָם · בְּרַחֲמֶיךָ הָרַבִּים רַחֵם עָלֵינוּ · אֲדוֹן עֻזֵּנוּ · צוּר מִשְׂגַּבֵּנוּ · מָגֵן יִשְׁעֵנוּ · מִשְׂגָּב בַּעֲדֵנוּ : בָּרוּךְ אַתָּה יְיָ · יוֹצֵר הַמְּאוֹרוֹת :

אַהֲבָה רַבָּה אֲהַבְתָּנוּ יְיָ אֱלֹהֵינוּ · חֶמְלָה גְדוֹלָה וִיתֵרָה חָמַלְתָּ עָלֵינוּ : אָבִינוּ מַלְכֵּנוּ · בַּעֲבוּר שִׁמְךָ הַגָּדוֹל וּבַעֲבוּר אֲבוֹתֵינוּ שֶׁבָּטְחוּ בָךְ · וַתְּלַמְּדֵם חֻקֵּי חַיִּים לַעֲשׂוֹת רְצוֹנְךָ בְּלֵבָב שָׁלֵם · כֵּן תְּחָנֵּנוּ : הָאֵר עֵינֵינוּ בְּתוֹרָתֶךָ · וְדַבֵּק לִבֵּנוּ בְּמִצְוֹתֶיךָ · וְיַחֵד לְבָבֵנוּ לְאַהֲבָה וּלְיִרְאָה אֶת־שְׁמֶךָ · לְמַעַן לֹא נֵבוֹשׁ וְלֹא נִכָּלֵם כִּי אֵל פּוֹעֵל יְשׁוּעוֹת אָתָּה · וּבָנוּ בָחַרְתָּ מִכָּל־עַם וְלָשׁוֹן · וְקֵרַבְתָּנוּ מַלְכֵּנוּ לְשִׁמְךָ הַגָּדוֹל בְּאַהֲבָה · לְהוֹדוֹת לְךָ וּלְיַחֶדְךָ וּלְאַהֲבָה אֶת־שְׁמֶךָ : בָּרוּךְ אַתָּה יְיָ · הַבּוֹחֵר בְּעַמּוֹ יִשְׂרָאֵל בְּאַהֲבָה :

THE DUTY OF PRAISE   Praised be Your name forever, for You are the God who is the great and holy king in heaven and on earth. Therefore, Lord our God, and God of our fathers, song and praise, holiness and majesty, blessing and gratitude belong to Your great and holy name forever and ever. From age to age You are God. Blessed are You Lord, creator of every living being, master of all deeds, the king, the life of all existence.

The half Kaddish on page 168 may be included here.

THE CALL TO COMMUNITY PRAYER   Bless the Lord whom we are called to bless.

Blessed be the Lord whom we are called to bless forever and ever.

THE CREATOR OF THE UNIVERSE   Blessed are You, Lord our God, king of the universe, who forms light yet creates darkness, who makes peace yet creates all. All things proclaim You, all things honour You, and all say: 'None is holy like the Lord.' He gives light to all the world and those who live in it. In His goodness He renews the work of the creation day by day. Lord, how great are Your works; You made them all in wisdom; the earth is full of Your creatures. You are the only king exalted from the beginning of time, who has been worshipped, praised and glorified since days of old.

Everlasting God, in Your great mercy have mercy upon us; Lord of our strength, rock of our protection, shield of our safety, our true protector. Blessed are You Lord, who creates the lights of the universe.

HIS LOVE FOR ISRAEL   With deep love You have loved us, and with great and overflowing tenderness You have taken pity on us. Our father, our king, show us compassion because of Your own greatness, and because of our fathers who trusted in You, for You taught them rules to live by, to do Your will with their whole heart. Let our eyes see the light of Your teaching and our hearts embrace Your commands. Give us integrity to love You and fear You. So shall we never lose our self-respect, nor be put to shame, for You are the power which works to save us. You chose us from all peoples and tongues, and in love drew us near to Your own greatness—to honour You, to declare Your unity, and to love You. Blessed are You Lord, who chooses His people Israel in love.

שְׁמַ֥ע יִשְׂרָאֵל · יְהֹוָה אֱלֹהֵ֥ינוּ יְהֹוָה אֶחָֽד:

בָּרוּךְ שֵׁם כְּבוֹד מַלְכוּתוֹ לְעוֹלָם וָעֶד:

וְאָהַבְתָּ אֵת יְהֹוָה אֱלֹהֶיךָ · בְּכָל־לְבָבְךָ וּבְכָל־נַפְשְׁךָ
וּבְכָל־מְאֹדֶךָ: וְהָיוּ הַדְּבָרִים הָאֵלֶּה אֲשֶׁר אָנֹכִי מְצַוְּךָ הַיּוֹם
עַל־לְבָבֶךָ: וְשִׁנַּנְתָּם לְבָנֶיךָ וְדִבַּרְתָּ בָּם · בְּשִׁבְתְּךָ בְּבֵיתֶךָ
וּבְלֶכְתְּךָ בַדֶּרֶךְ וּבְשָׁכְבְּךָ וּבְקוּמֶךָ: וּקְשַׁרְתָּם לְאוֹת עַל־
יָדֶךָ · וְהָיוּ לְטֹטָפֹת בֵּין עֵינֶיךָ: וּכְתַבְתָּם עַל־מְזֻזוֹת בֵּיתֶךָ
וּבִשְׁעָרֶיךָ:

יִשְׁאָלוּנִי מִשְׁפְּטֵי־צֶדֶק
קִרְבַת אֱלֹהִים יֶחְפָּצוּן:
הֲלוֹא פָרֹס לָרָעֵב לַחְמֶךָ
וַעֲנִיִּים מְרוּדִים תָּבִיא בָיִת
כִּי־תִרְאֶה עָרֹם וְכִסִּיתוֹ
וּמִבְּשָׂרְךָ לֹא תִתְעַלָּם:
אָז תִּקְרָא וַיהֹוָה יַעֲנֶה
תְּשַׁוַּע וְיֹאמַר הִנֵּנִי
אִם־תָּסִיר מִתּוֹכְךָ מוֹטָה
שְׁלַח אֶצְבַּע וְדַבֶּר־אָוֶן:
וְתָפֵק לָרָעֵב נַפְשֶׁךָ
וְנֶפֶשׁ נַעֲנָה תַּשְׂבִּיעַ
וְזָרַח בַּחֹשֶׁךְ אוֹרֶךָ
וַאֲפֵלָתְךָ כַּצָּהֳרָיִם:
וְנָחֲךָ יְהֹוָה תָּמִיד
אִם־תָּשִׁיב מִשַּׁבָּת רַגְלֶךָ
עֲשׂוֹת חֲפָצֶיךָ בְּיוֹם קָדְשִׁי
וְקָרָאתָ לַשַּׁבָּת עֹנֶג
אָז תִּתְעַנַּג עַל־יְהֹוָה:

THE GOD
OF ISRAEL
Hear O Israel, the Lord is our God, the Lord is One.

Blessed is His name, whose glorious kingdom is forever and ever.

Love the Lord your God with all your heart, and all your soul, and all your might. These words that I command you today shall be upon your heart. Repeat them to your children, and talk about them when you sit in your home, and when you walk in the street; when you lie down, and when you rise up. Hold fast to them as a sign upon your hand, and let them be as reminders before your eyes. Write them on the doorposts of your home and at your gates.

Deuteronomy 6: 4–9

During the silence the second and third paragraphs of the Shema (pages 60–62) may be read, or the following:

They ask Me for laws of justice
for they delight in approaching God.
Is it not sharing your food with the hungry
and bringing the homeless into your home,
clothing the destitute when you meet them
and not evading your duty to your own flesh and blood.
Then if you call, the Lord will answer;
if you cry to Him, He will say: 'Here I am!'
If you do away with the yoke,
the clenched fist, and the wicked word;
if you share what you have with the hungry
and satisfy the needs of the wretched,
then your light will rise like dawn out of darkness,
and your shade be like the noon,
and the Lord will always guide you.
If you stop your foot from doing what it wants
because of the Sabbath, My holy day;
if you call the Sabbath a day of joy,
then you shall find your joy in the Lord.

From Isaiah, ch. 58

שְׂפַת־אֱמֶת תִּכּוֹן לָעַד
וְעַד־אַרְגִּיעָה לְשׁוֹן שָׁקֶר :
מִרְמָה בְּלֶב־חֹרְשֵׁי רָע
וּלְיֹעֲצֵי שָׁלוֹם שִׂמְחָה :
עֹשֵׁק דָּל חֵרֵף עֹשֵׂהוּ
וּמְכַבְּדוֹ חֹנֵן אֶבְיוֹן :
צְדָקָה תְרוֹמֵם־גּוֹי
וְחֶסֶד לְאֻמִּים חַטָּאת :

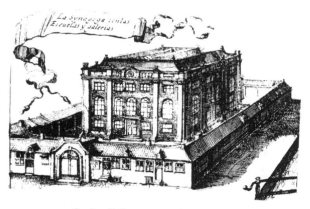

Sephardi Synagogue, Amsterdam

Truth spoken stands firm forever,
but lies live only for a moment.
Those who plot evil deceive themselves,
but there is joy for those who seek the common good.
He who oppresses the poor insults his maker,
he who is generous to the needy honours Him.
Righteousness raises a people to honour,
to do wrong is a disgrace to any nation.

From Proverbs, chs. 12 and 14

After the silence the service continues on page 142.

Liberal Synagogue, The Hague

תפלת שחרית לשבת

וְעַתָּה יִשְׂרָאֵל מָה יְהֹוָה אֱלֹהֶיךָ שֹׁאֵל מֵעִמָּךְ :

כִּי אִם־לְיִרְאָה אֶת־יְהֹוָה אֱלֹהֶיךָ לָלֶכֶת בְּכָל־דְּרָכָיו
וּלְאַהֲבָה אֹתוֹ וְלַעֲבֹד אֶת־יְהֹוָה אֱלֹהֶיךָ בְּכָל־לְבָבְךָ וּבְכָל־
נַפְשֶׁךָ : לִשְׁמֹר אֶת־מִצְוֹת יְהֹוָה וְאֶת־חֻקֹּתָיו לְטוֹב לָךְ :

מַה־טֹּבוּ אֹהָלֶיךָ יַעֲקֹב מִשְׁכְּנֹתֶיךָ יִשְׂרָאֵל :
וַאֲנִי בְּרֹב חַסְדְּךָ אָבוֹא בֵיתֶךָ
אֶשְׁתַּחֲוֶה אֶל־הֵיכַל־קָדְשְׁךָ בְּיִרְאָתֶךָ :
יְהֹוָה אָהַבְתִּי מְעוֹן בֵּיתֶךָ וּמְקוֹם מִשְׁכַּן כְּבוֹדֶךָ :
וַאֲנִי אֶשְׁתַּחֲוֶה וְאֶכְרָעָה אֶבְרְכָה לִפְנֵי־יְהֹוָה עֹשִׂי :
וַאֲנִי תְפִלָּתִי־לְךָ יְהֹוָה עֵת רָצוֹן
אֱלֹהִים בְּרָב־חַסְדֶּךָ עֲנֵנִי בֶּאֱמֶת יִשְׁעֶךָ :

יְיָ הִנְנִי בָא לְפָנֶיךָ מוּקָף חַבְרֵי־הָעֵדָה בָּהּ אֲנִי חַי :
אֲחַלְּקָה שִׂמְחָתִי אִתָּם וְתִגְדַּל : אֲשַׁתְּפֵם בְּצַעֲרִי וְיִקְטַן :
אַל־נָא אֶהְיֶה צַר־עַיִן מִלָּתֵת וְלֹא גֵאֶה מִלְּקַבֵּל כִּי בָתַתִּי
וּבְקַבְּלִי אֲגַלֶּךָ וְאָחֵל לְהָבִין מַשְׁמָעוּת חַיָּי :

V

SABBATH MORNING SERVICE

And now, Israel, what does the Lord your God ask of you?

To fear the Lord your God, to walk in all His ways, to love Him and to serve the Lord your God with all your heart and with all your soul. To keep the commandments of the Lord, and His laws, for your own good.

Deuteronomy 10: 12–13

DIRECTING THE HEART TO GOD How good are your tents, O Jacob, and your homes, O Israel. Through the greatness of Your love I enter Your house. In awe I worship before the ark of Your holiness.

Lord, as I loved the courts of Your temple, and the place where Your glory dwelt, so I still worship and bend low, humble before the Lord my maker.

As for me, let my prayer come before You at the proper time. Answer me God, in the greatness of Your love, for Your deliverance is sure.

THE COM- MUNITY Lord, I come before You surrounded by the members of the community in which I live. I share my happiness with them and it becomes greater. I share my troubles with them and they seem smaller. May I never be too mean to give, nor too proud to receive, for in giving and receiving I discover You, and begin to understand the meaning of life.

אֵל־נָא אֲפָרֵשׁ מֵעֻזּוֹ הָאֲמִתִּי מֵעֻזּוֹ שֶׁל־הַצִּבּוּר · מֵחָכְמַת־
זְקֵנָיו וְנְסִיוֹנוֹתֵיהֶם · מִתְּקָנַת־עֲלָמֶיהָ וּמִדֻּגְמָאוֹת־הָאַהֲבָה
וְאֹמֶץ־הַלֵּב הַמְצוּיִּים בּוֹ כִּי בָהֶם נִתְמַכְתִּי · תֶּן לִי לֵב
פָּתוּחַ וְדֵעָה צְלוּלָה לְהֵעָנוֹת לַנִּזְקָקִים לִי לְמַעַן תִּשְׁרֶה
עָלַי שְׁכִינָתְךָ יוֹם־יוֹם :
חוֹשֵׁב אֲנִי עַל־מַה־שֶּׁהָיִינוּ יְכוֹלִים לִהְיוֹת וְעַל־הָאַחֲדָה
וְהַיְדִידוּת שֶׁהָיוּ יְכוֹלוֹת לְאַחְדֵנוּ · חוֹשֵׁב אֲנִי עַל־בְּדִידוּתֵנוּ
וְעַל־הַחֲבֵרוּת שֶׁהָיְתָה יְכוֹלָה לְמַלֵּא אֶת־חַיֵּינוּ · חוֹשֵׁב אֲנִי
עַל־הַטּוֹב שֶׁהָיִינוּ יְכוֹלִים לַעֲשׂוֹת אִלּוּ הָיִינוּ מְאֻחָדִים
בְּרוּחֵנוּ : יוֹדֵעַ אֲנִי כִּי רְצוֹנְךָ שֶׁאוֹצִיא כָּל־זֶה מִן־הַכֹּחַ
אֶל־הַפֹּעַל לָכֵן לְעֶזְרָתְךָ אֲנִי תִפִלָּה : אַחֵד אוֹתִי וְאוֹתָם
שֶׁמִּסְּבִיבִי בְּשִׂמְחַת־רֵעִים וּנְבָרֶכְךָ עַל־שֶׁהֶאֱלִיתָ בְּיָדֵינוּ
לַעֲזֹר אִישׁ וְרֵעֵהוּ · אָמֵן :

אַנְעִים זְמִירוֹת וְשִׁירִים אֶאֱרוֹג · כִּי אֵלֶיךָ נַפְשִׁי תַעֲרוֹג :

נַפְשִׁי חִמְּדָה בְּצֵל יָדֶךָ · לָדַעַת כָּל־רָז סוֹדֶךָ :

מִדֵּי דַבְּרִי בִּכְבוֹדֶךָ · הוֹמֶה לִבִּי אֶל דּוֹדֶיךָ :

עַל כֵּן אֲדַבֵּר בְּךָ נִכְבָּדוֹת · וְשִׁמְךָ אֲכַבֵּד בְּשִׁירֵי יְדִידוֹת :

אֲסַפְּרָה כְבוֹדְךָ וְלֹא רְאִיתִיךָ · אֲדַמְּךָ אֲכַנְּךָ וְלֹא יְדַעְתִּיךָ :

בְּיַד נְבִיאֶיךָ בְּסוֹד עֲבָדֶיךָ · דִּמִּיתָ הֲדַר כְּבוֹד הוֹדֶךָ :

גְּדֻלָּתְךָ וּגְבוּרָתֶךָ · כִּנּוּ לְתֹקֶף פְּעֻלָּתֶךָ :

רֹאשׁ דְּבָרְךָ אֱמֶת · קוֹרֵא מֵרֹאשׁ דּוֹר וָדוֹר עַם דּוֹרֶשְׁךָ
דְּרוֹשׁ :

מִי יְמַלֵּל גְּבוּרוֹת יְיָ יַשְׁמִיעַ כָּל־תְּהִלָּתוֹ :

Let me not separate myself from the true strength of my community: the experience and wisdom of old people, the hopes of the young, and the examples of care and courage which sustain me. Give me an open heart and an open mind to welcome those who need me, and to receive Your presence in my daily life.

I think of what we could be and the harmony and friendship that could unite us. I think of our loneliness and the friendship that could fill our lives. I think of the good that we could do if we were one in spirit. I know that this is Your will and pray for Your help. May I and those around me find our joy together, and bless You for the power You gave us to help each other. Amen.

The Song of Glory

SONGS OF
PRAISE

I play sweet psalms and weave my songs
because for You my spirit longs.

In Your hand's shade my senses yearn
Your secret mysteries to learn.

Your glory, even as I speak
disturbs my heart, Your love to seek.

And so I tell Your glorious fame,
with songs of love I praise Your name.

I tell Your glory, never shown,
describing You though still unknown.

Yet through Your prophets that You taught
a glimpse of majesty is brought.

Your greatness and Your force they told
and showed the power that You hold.

Each age You call, Your word is true.
Seek us, the people seeking You!

Yet who can tell God's mighty ways
and who can make known all His praise!

Judah HeChasid

Alternative Songs of Praise, pages 571–609.

אֵלוּ דְבָרִים שֶׁאָדָם אוֹכֵל פֵּרוֹתֵיהֶם בָּעוֹלָם הַזֶּה וְהַקֶּרֶן
קַיֶּמֶת לוֹ לָעוֹלָם הַבָּא · וְאֵלוּ הֵן · כִּבּוּד אָב וָאֵם וּגְמִילוּת
חֲסָדִים וְהַשְׁכָּמַת בֵּית הַמִּדְרָשׁ שַׁחֲרִית וְעַרְבִית וְהַכְנָסַת
אוֹרְחִים וּבִקּוּר חוֹלִים וְהַכְנָסַת כַּלָּה וּלְוָיַת הַמֵּת וְעִיּוּן
תְּפִלָּה וַהֲבָאַת שָׁלוֹם בֵּין אָדָם לַחֲבֵרוֹ · וְתַלְמוּד תּוֹרָה
כְּנֶגֶד כֻּלָּם:

רִבּוֹן הָעוֹלָמִים וַאֲדֹנֵי הָאֲדֹנִים · לֹא עַל־צִדְקֹתֵינוּ אֲנַחְנוּ
מַפִּילִים תַּחֲנוּגֵינוּ לְפָנֶיךָ · כִּי עַל־רַחֲמֶיךָ הָרַבִּים: אֲדֹנָי
שְׁמָעָה · אֲדֹנָי סְלָחָה · אֲדֹנָי הַקְשִׁיבָה וַעֲשֵׂה · מָה־אָנוּ ·
מֶה־חַיֵּינוּ · מֶה־חַסְדֵּנוּ · מַה־צִּדְקוֹתֵינוּ · מַה־יְּשׁוּעָתֵנוּ · מַה־
כֹּחֵנוּ · מַה־גְּבוּרָתֵנוּ: מַה־נֹּאמַר לְפָנֶיךָ יְיָ אֱלֹהֵינוּ וֵאלֹהֵי
אֲבוֹתֵינוּ · הֲלֹא הַגִּבּוֹרִים כְּאַיִן לְפָנֶיךָ · וְאַנְשֵׁי הַשֵּׁם כְּלֹא
הָיוּ · וַחֲכָמִים כִּבְלִי מַדָּע · וּנְבוֹנִים כִּבְלִי הַשְׂכֵּל · כִּי רֹב
מַעֲשֵׂינוּ תֹהוּ · וִימֵי חַיֵּינוּ הֶבֶל לְפָנֶיךָ · וּמוֹתַר הָאָדָם מִן
הַבְּהֵמָה אָיִן · כִּי הַכֹּל הָבֶל לְבַד הַנְּשָׁמָה הַטְּהוֹרָה · שֶׁהִיא
עֲתִידָה לִתֵּן דִּין וְחֶשְׁבּוֹן לִפְנֵי כִסֵּא כְבוֹדֶךָ:

יְיָ מֶלֶךְ · יְיָ מָלָךְ · יְיָ יִמְלֹךְ לְעוֹלָם וָעֶד:

וְהָיָה יְיָ לְמֶלֶךְ עַל־כָּל־הָאָרֶץ · בַּיּוֹם הַהוּא יִהְיֶה יְיָ
אֶחָד וּשְׁמוֹ אֶחָד: הוֹשִׁיעֵנוּ יְיָ אֱלֹהֵינוּ · לְהוֹדוֹת לְשֵׁם קָדְשֶׁךָ
לְהִשְׁתַּבֵּחַ בִּתְהִלָּתֶךָ: בָּרוּךְ יְהֹוָה אֱלֹהֵי יִשְׂרָאֵל מִן־הָעוֹלָם
וְעַד הָעוֹלָם · וְאָמַר כָּל־הָעָם אָמֵן: הַלְלוּיָהּ: כֹּל הַנְּשָׁמָה
תְּהַלֵּל יָהּ · הַלְלוּיָהּ:

These are the things whose interest a man enjoys in this world, while the capital remains for him in the world to come—this is what they are:
Respecting one's father and mother,
Acts of generosity and love,
Coming early to the Synagogue for morning and evening study,
Giving hospitality to strangers,
Visiting the sick,
Assisting the bride,
Attending the dead,
Devotion in prayer,
Making peace between a man and his companion.
And the study of Torah leads to them all.

Mishnah

THE WEAKNESS OF MAN   Master of existence, and Lord of lords, we do not rely on our own good deeds but on Your great mercy as we lay our needs before You. Lord, hear! Lord, pardon! Lord, listen and act! What are we? What is our life? What is our love? What is our justice? What is our success? What is our endurance? What is our power? Lord our God, and God of our fathers, what can we say before You, for in Your presence are not the powerful as nothing, the famous as if they had never existed, the learned as if without knowledge, and the intelligent as if without insight. To You most of our actions are pointless and our daily life is shallow. Even the superiority of man over the beasts is nothing. For everything is trivial except the pure soul which must one day give its account and reckoning before the judgment seat of Your glory.

THE POWER OF GOD   The Lord does rule, the Lord has ruled, the Lord shall rule forever and ever.
The Lord shall be as a king over the whole earth. On that day the Lord shall be One, and known as One.
Save us, Lord our God, to proclaim Your holy name and be honoured in praising You.
Blessed is the Lord God of Israel from everlasting to everlasting. Let all the people say: Amen! Praise the Lord!
May all who live praise the Lord. Hallelujah!

I

They are free who serve God by serving man.

Others gain authority over you if you possess a will distinct from God's will.

Nachman of Bratzlav

They are happy who are at peace with themselves.

To begin with oneself, but not to end with oneself;
to start from oneself, but not to aim at oneself;
to comprehend oneself, but not to be preoccupied with oneself.

Martin Buber

They are strong who build their home with patience and with love.

Everyone has in his life a beautiful day when he finds love without care and trouble. But when this day is past, you earn love, as you earn bread, by the sweat of the brow.

Ludwig Boerne

They are worthy who respect their parents.

What is the honour due to parents? To provide them with food, drink, with clothing and cover, to bring them home and take them out, to provide for their needs and to do so with a cheerful face.

Kitzur Shulchan Aruch

They are content who bring up their children with care.

He who brings up a righteous child is like one who never dies.

Rashi

They are blessed who bring peace wherever they are.

Work for peace within your household, then in your street, then in your town.

Bershider Rebbe

They are honoured who bring hope into the society in which they live.

Seek the peace of the city to which I have carried you, and pray to the Lord for it. For on its peace your own peace depends.

Jeremiah 29: 7

II

They are beloved who give and accept friendship.

A faithful friend is a life-giving medicine, and those who fear the Lord will find one. Whoever fears the Lord makes true friends, for as a man is, so is his friend.

Ecclesiasticus

They are generous who rejoice in the fortune of their neighbour.

It is only right that a man desire his neighbour's wellbeing, that he look with goodwill on the fortune of his neighbour and that his neighbour's honour be as dear to him as his own; for he and his neighbour are one.

Moses Cordovero

They are righteous who accept the duties of power.

A person is held responsible for the sins of his family, or of his community, or even of all mankind, when he fails to use his influence for the correction of wrongs.

Shabbat

They are humble who serve the community in which they pray.

Prayers for the community come before those for ourselves, and he who sets its claims above his private interests is especially acceptable to God.

Josephus

They are strengthened who accept their place in the family of Israel.

Accept upon yourself the yoke of the kingdom of heaven, and correct one another in the fear of heaven, and deal with one another in charity.

Sifre

They are wise who take their full responsibility in the world.

What should a man do to be of use in the world . . .? He should devote time to public affairs and to the public welfare.

Leviticus Rabbah

They are holy who share their blessings with the whole of creation.

You shall be a blessing . . . and in you shall all the families of the earth be blessed.

Genesis 12: 2–3

וַיְבָרֶךְ דָּוִיד אֶת־יְהֹוָה לְעֵינֵי כָּל־הַקָּהָל · וַיֹּאמֶר דָּוִיד ·
בָּרוּךְ אַתָּה יְהֹוָה אֱלֹהֵי יִשְׂרָאֵל אָבִינוּ מֵעוֹלָם וְעַד־עוֹלָם :
לְךָ יְהֹוָה הַגְּדֻלָּה וְהַגְּבוּרָה וְהַתִּפְאֶרֶת וְהַנֵּצַח וְהַהוֹד · כִּי־
כֹל בַּשָּׁמַיִם וּבָאָרֶץ לְךָ יְהֹוָה הַמַּמְלָכָה וְהַמִּתְנַשֵּׂא לְכֹל
לְרֹאשׁ : וְהָעֹשֶׁר וְהַכָּבוֹד מִלְּפָנֶיךָ · וְאַתָּה מוֹשֵׁל בַּכֹּל
וּבְיָדְךָ כֹּחַ וּגְבוּרָה · וּבְיָדְךָ לְגַדֵּל וּלְחַזֵּק לַכֹּל : וְעַתָּה
אֱלֹהֵינוּ מוֹדִים אֲנַחְנוּ לָךְ · וּמְהַלְלִים לְשֵׁם תִּפְאַרְתֶּךָ :
וִיבָרְכוּ שֵׁם כְּבֹדֶךָ וּמְרוֹמַם עַל־כָּל־בְּרָכָה וּתְהִלָּה :
אַתָּה־הוּא יְהֹוָה לְבַדֶּךָ · אַתָּה עָשִׂיתָ אֶת־הַשָּׁמַיִם שְׁמֵי
הַשָּׁמַיִם וְכָל־צְבָאָם · הָאָרֶץ וְכָל־אֲשֶׁר עָלֶיהָ · הַיַּמִּים
וְכָל־אֲשֶׁר בָּהֶם · וְאַתָּה מְחַיֶּה אֶת־כֻּלָּם · וּצְבָא הַשָּׁמַיִם
לְךָ מִשְׁתַּחֲוִים :

בָּרוּךְ יְהֹוָה לְעוֹלָם · אָמֵן וְאָמֵן :
בָּרוּךְ יְהֹוָה אֱלֹהִים אֱלֹהֵי יִשְׂרָאֵל · עֹשֵׂה נִפְלָאוֹת לְבַדּוֹ :
וּבָרוּךְ שֵׁם כְּבוֹדוֹ לְעוֹלָם · וְיִמָּלֵא כְבוֹדוֹ אֶת־כָּל־הָאָרֶץ
אָמֵן וְאָמֵן :

נִשְׁמַת כָּל־חַי תְּבָרֵךְ אֶת־שִׁמְךָ יְיָ אֱלֹהֵינוּ · וְרוּחַ כָּל־
בָּשָׂר תְּפָאֵר וּתְרוֹמֵם זִכְרְךָ מַלְכֵּנוּ תָּמִיד : מִן
הָעוֹלָם וְעַד הָעוֹלָם אַתָּה אֵל · וּמִבַּלְעָדֶיךָ אֵין לָנוּ מֶלֶךְ
גּוֹאֵל וּמוֹשִׁיעַ פּוֹדֶה וּמַצִּיל וְעוֹנֶה וּמְרַחֵם · בְּכָל־עֵת צָרָה
וְצוּקָה אֵין לָנוּ מֶלֶךְ עוֹזֵר וְסוֹמֵךְ זוּלָתֶךָ : אֱלֹהֵי הָרִאשׁוֹנִים
וְהָאַחֲרוֹנִים · אֱלוֹהַּ כָּל־בְּרִיּוֹת · אֲדוֹן כָּל־תּוֹלָדוֹת הַמְהֻלָּל
בְּכָל־הַתִּשְׁבָּחוֹת · הַמְנַהֵג עוֹלָמוֹ בְּחֶסֶד וּבְרִיּוֹתָיו בְּרַחֲמִים :
וַיְיָ לֹא יָנוּם וְלֹא יִישָׁן · הַמְעוֹרֵר יְשֵׁנִים וְהַמֵּקִיץ נִרְדָּמִים ·
מְחַיֶּה מֵתִים וְרוֹפֵא חוֹלִים · פּוֹקֵחַ עִוְרִים וְזוֹקֵף כְּפוּפִים ·
לְךָ לְבַדְּךָ אֲנַחְנוּ מוֹדִים :

בָּרוּךְ אַתָּה יְיָ אֱלֹהֵינוּ מֶלֶךְ הָעוֹלָם · אֲשֶׁר קִדְּשָׁנוּ
בְּמִצְוֹתָיו וְצִוָּנוּ לַעֲסוֹק בְּדִבְרֵי תוֹרָה :

Then David blessed the Lord in the sight of all the congregation, and David said: 'Blessed are You Lord, the God of our father Israel from everlasting to everlasting. Yours is the greatness, the power, the splendour, the glory and the majesty, for everything in heaven and earth is Yours. Yours is the kingdom and You are exalted supreme over all. Wealth and honour come from You, for You rule over all. In Your hand are strength and might. It is in Your power to give greatness and strength to all. And now, our God, we give You thanks and praise Your glorious name' (*1 Chronicles 29: 10-13*). May the people bless Your glorious name, though it is beyond all blessing and praise. You are the Lord alone; You made the sky, the reaches of space and its countless lights, the earth and everything on it, the seas and everything in them; You give life to them all, and the universe worships You (*Nehemiah 9: 5-6*).

Blessed be the Lord forever. Amen and amen.

Blessed be the Lord God, the God of Israel, who alone works wonders.

Blessed be His glorious name forever. All the earth is full of His glory. Amen and amen.

ALL CREATION PRAISES GOD   The breath of life in every creature shall bless You, Lord our God, and the spirit of all flesh ever recalls Your beauty and Your greatness. From everlasting to everlasting You are God. Besides You we have no king who rescues and saves us, frees and delivers us, and answers and cares for us. At all times of trouble and distress there is no king who can help and support us but You.

God of the first and of the last ages, God of all creatures, Lord of history, adored in all worship—He guides His universe with love, and His creatures with mercy. The Lord neither slumbers nor sleeps. He wakes the sleepers, and rouses the uncaring. He gives life beyond death, He heals the sick, He gives sight to the blind and raises up those bent low. To You alone we declare our gratitude.

THE DUTY TO STUDY   Blessed are You, Lord our God, king of the universe, who makes us holy through doing His commands, and who commands us to devote ourselves to the study of His teaching.

The Torah demands that we seek what is best for our fellow man:
not by repressing our hatred or rejection of him, nor by loving him
out of a sense of duty, for this is no genuine love. We should simply
love our neighbour as we love ourselves. We do not love ourselves
because we are human beings, but our self-love comes to us naturally without any calculations, or limits, or aims. It would never
occur to someone to say: "I have already fulfilled my obligation
towards myself!"—The same way we should love our fellow man
naturally and spontaneously, with joy and pleasure, without limits,
purposes or rationalisations.

Israel Salanter

יִשְׁתַּבַּח שִׁמְךָ לָעַד מַלְכֵּנוּ · הָאֵל הַמֶּלֶךְ הַגָּדוֹל וְהַקָּדוֹשׁ
בַּשָּׁמַיִם וּבָאָרֶץ · כִּי לְךָ נָאֶה יְיָ אֱלֹהֵינוּ וֵאלֹהֵי
אֲבוֹתֵינוּ לְעוֹלָם וָעֶד שִׁיר וּשְׁבָחָה · קְדֻשָּׁה וּמַלְכוּת · בְּרָכוֹת
וְהוֹדָאוֹת לְשִׁמְךָ הַגָּדוֹל וְהַקָּדוֹשׁ · וּמֵעוֹלָם וְעַד־עוֹלָם אַתָּה
אֵל : בָּרוּךְ אַתָּה יְיָ · בּוֹרֵא כָּל־הַנְּשָׁמוֹת · רִבּוֹן כָּל־
הַמַּעֲשִׂים · מֶלֶךְ חֵי הָעוֹלָמִים :

The half Kaddish on page 168 may be included here.

בָּרְכוּ אֶת־יְיָ הַמְבֹרָךְ :

בָּרוּךְ יְיָ הַמְבֹרָךְ לְעוֹלָם וָעֶד :

בָּרוּךְ אַתָּה יְיָ אֱלֹהֵינוּ מֶלֶךְ הָעוֹלָם · יוֹצֵר אוֹר וּבוֹרֵא
חֹשֶׁךְ · עֹשֶׂה שָׁלוֹם וּבוֹרֵא אֶת־הַכֹּל : הַכֹּל יוֹדוּךָ · וְהַכֹּל
יְשַׁבְּחוּךָ · וְהַכֹּל יֹאמְרוּ אֵין קָדוֹשׁ כַּיְיָ : הַמֵּאִיר לָעוֹלָם כֻּלּוֹ
וּלְיוֹשְׁבָיו וּבְטוּבוֹ מְחַדֵּשׁ בְּכָל־יוֹם תָּמִיד מַעֲשֵׂה בְרֵאשִׁית :
מָה רַבּוּ מַעֲשֶׂיךָ יְיָ · כֻּלָּם בְּחָכְמָה עָשִׂיתָ · מָלְאָה הָאָרֶץ
קִנְיָנֶיךָ : הַמֶּלֶךְ הַמְרוֹמָם לְבַדּוֹ מֵאָז · הַמְשֻׁבָּח וְהַמְפֹאָר
וְהַמִּתְנַשֵּׂא מִימוֹת עוֹלָם : אֱלֹהֵי עוֹלָם · בְּרַחֲמֶיךָ הָרַבִּים
רַחֵם עָלֵינוּ · אֲדוֹן עֻזֵּנוּ · צוּר מִשְׂגַּבֵּנוּ · מָגֵן יִשְׁעֵנוּ · מִשְׂגָּב
בַּעֲדֵנוּ : בָּרוּךְ אַתָּה יְיָ · יוֹצֵר הַמְּאוֹרוֹת :

One of the following passages or one selected from the Anthology, pages 392–400.

There is one who sings the song of his own soul, and in his soul he finds everything, full spiritual satisfaction.

And there is one who sings the song of the people. For he does not find the circle of his private soul wide enough, and so goes beyond it, reaching for more powerful heights. And he unites himself with the soul of the community of Israel, sings its songs, suffers with its sorrows and is delighted by its hopes . . .

And there is one whose soul lifts beyond the limitations of Israel, to sing the song of mankind. His spirit expands to include the glory of the human image and its dreams . . .

And there is one who lifts beyond this level, until he becomes one with all creation and all creatures, and all the worlds. And with all of them he sings a song . . .

And there is one who rises together with the bundle of all these songs. All of them sing out, each gives meaning and life to the other.

And this completeness is the song of holiness, the song of God, the song of Israel . . .

Rav Kook

THE DUTY
OF PRAISE
Praised be Your name forever, for You are the God who is the great and holy king in heaven and on earth. Therefore, Lord our God, and God of our fathers, song and praise, holiness and majesty, blessing and gratitude belong to Your great and holy name forever and ever. From age to age You are God. Blessed are You Lord, creator of every living being, master of all deeds, the king, the life of all existence.

The half Kaddish on page 168 may be included here.

THE CALL
TO COM-
MUNITY
PRAYER
Bless the Lord whom we are called to bless.

Blessed be the Lord whom we are called to bless forever and ever.

THE
CREATOR
OF THE
UNIVERSE
Blessed are You, Lord our God, king of the universe, who forms light yet creates darkness, who makes peace yet creates all. All things proclaim You, all things honour You, and all say: 'None is holy like the Lord.' He gives light to all the world and those who live in it. In His goodness He renews the work of the creation day by day. Lord, how great are Your works; You made them all in wisdom; the earth is full of Your creatures. You are the only king exalted from the beginning of time, who has been worshipped, praised and glorified since days of old.

Everlasting God, in Your great mercy have mercy upon us; Lord of our strength, rock of our protection, shield of our safety, our true protector. Blessed are You Lord, who creates the lights of the universe.

אַהֲבָה רַבָּה אֲהַבְתָּנוּ יְיָ אֱלֹהֵינוּ · חֶמְלָה גְדוֹלָה וִיתֵרָה
חָמַלְתָּ עָלֵינוּ · אָבִינוּ מַלְכֵּנוּ · בַּעֲבוּר שִׁמְךָ הַגָּדוֹל וּבַעֲבוּר
אֲבוֹתֵינוּ שֶׁבָּטְחוּ בָךְ · וַתְּלַמְּדֵם חֻקֵּי חַיִּים לַעֲשׂוֹת רְצוֹנְךָ
בְּלֵבָב שָׁלֵם· כֵּן תְּחָנֵּנוּ · הָאֵר עֵינֵינוּ בְּתוֹרָתֶךָ · וְדַבֵּק לִבֵּנוּ
בְּמִצְוֹתֶיךָ · וְיַחֵד לְבָבֵנוּ לְאַהֲבָה וּלְיִרְאָה אֶת־שְׁמֶךָ · לְמַעַן
לֹא נֵבוֹשׁ וְלֹא נִכָּלֵם כִּי אֵל פּוֹעֵל יְשׁוּעוֹת אָתָּה · וּבָנוּ בָחַרְתָּ
מִכָּל־עַם וְלָשׁוֹן · וְקֵרַבְתָּנוּ מַלְכֵּנוּ לְשִׁמְךָ הַגָּדוֹל בְּאַהֲבָה ·
לְהוֹדוֹת לְךָ וּלְיַחֶדְךָ וּלְאַהֲבָה אֶת־שְׁמֶךָ : בָּרוּךְ אַתָּה יְיָ ·
הַבּוֹחֵר בְּעַמּוֹ יִשְׂרָאֵל בְּאַהֲבָה :

שְׁמַ**ע** יִשְׂרָאֵל · יְהֹוָה אֱלֹהֵינוּ יְהֹוָה אֶחָ**ד** :

בָּרוּךְ שֵׁם כְּבוֹד מַלְכוּתוֹ לְעוֹלָם וָעֶד :

וְאָהַבְתָּ אֵת יְהֹוָה אֱלֹהֶיךָ · בְּכָל־לְבָבְךָ וּבְכָל־נַפְשְׁךָ
וּבְכָל־מְאֹדֶךָ : וְהָיוּ הַדְּבָרִים הָאֵלֶּה אֲשֶׁר אָנֹכִי מְצַוְּךָ הַיּוֹם
עַל־לְבָבֶךָ : וְשִׁנַּנְתָּם לְבָנֶיךָ וְדִבַּרְתָּ בָּם · בְּשִׁבְתְּךָ בְּבֵיתֶךָ
וּבְלֶכְתְּךָ בַדֶּרֶךְ וּבְשָׁכְבְּךָ וּבְקוּמֶךָ : וּקְשַׁרְתָּם לְאוֹת עַל־
יָדֶךָ · וְהָיוּ לְטֹטָפֹת בֵּין עֵינֶיךָ : וּכְתַבְתָּם עַל־מְזוּזוֹת בֵּיתֶךָ
וּבִשְׁעָרֶיךָ :

וַיְדַבֵּר יְהֹוָה אֶל־מֹשֶׁה לֵּאמֹר : דַּבֵּר אֶל־כָּל־עֲדַת בְּנֵי־
יִשְׂרָאֵל וְאָמַרְתָּ אֲלֵהֶם קְדֹשִׁים תִּהְיוּ כִּי קָדוֹשׁ אֲנִי יְהֹוָה
אֱלֹהֵיכֶם : אִישׁ אִמּוֹ וְאָבִיו תִּירָאוּ וְאֶת־שַׁבְּתֹתַי תִּשְׁמֹרוּ אֲנִי
יְהֹוָה אֱלֹהֵיכֶם : לֹא תִּגְנֹבוּ וְלֹא־תְכַחֲשׁוּ וְלֹא־תְשַׁקְּרוּ אִישׁ
בַּעֲמִיתוֹ : וְלֹא־תִשָּׁבְעוּ בִשְׁמִי לַשָּׁקֶר וְחִלַּלְתָּ אֶת־שֵׁם אֱלֹהֶיךָ

HIS LOVE
FOR ISRAEL

With deep love You have loved us, and with great and overflowing tenderness You have taken pity on us. Our father, our king, show us compassion because of Your own greatness, and because of our fathers who trusted in You, for You taught them rules to live by, to do Your will with their whole heart. Let our eyes see the light of Your teaching and our hearts embrace Your commands. Give us integrity to love You and fear You. So shall we never lose our self-respect, nor be put to shame, for You are the power which works to save us. You chose us from all peoples and tongues, and in love drew us near to Your own greatness—to honour You, to declare Your unity, and to love You. Blessed are You Lord, who chooses His people Israel in love.

THE GOD
OF ISRAEL

Hear O Israel, the Lord is our God, the Lord is One.

Blessed is His name, whose glorious kingdom is forever and ever.

Love the Lord your God with all your heart, and all your soul, and all your might. These words that I command you today shall be upon your heart. Repeat them to your children, and talk about them when you sit in your home, and when you walk in the street; when you lie down, and when you rise up. Hold fast to them as a sign upon your hand, and let them be as reminders before your eyes. Write them on the doorposts of your home and at your gates.

Deuteronomy 6: 4–9

During the silence the second and third paragraphs of the Shema (pages 60–62) may be read, or the following:

The Lord spoke to Moses and said:
Speak to all the community of the children of Israel and say to them:
Be holy, for I the Lord your God am holy!
You shall respect, each one of you, his mother and his father.
You shall keep My sabbaths. I am the Lord your God.
You shall not steal, you shall not cheat, and you shall not deceive —any man, his neighbour.
You shall not swear by My name to deceive, and so dishonour the name of your God. I am the Lord.

אֲנִי יְהֹוָה: לֹא־תַעֲשֹׁק אֶת־רֵעֲךָ וְלֹא תִגְזֹל לֹא־תָלִין פְּעֻלַּת שָׂכִיר אִתְּךָ עַד־בֹּקֶר: לֹא־תַעֲשׂוּ עָוֶל בַּמִּשְׁפָּט לֹא־תִשָּׂא פְנֵי־דָל וְלֹא תֶהְדַּר פְּנֵי גָדוֹל בְּצֶדֶק תִּשְׁפֹּט עֲמִיתֶךָ: לֹא־תֵלֵךְ רָכִיל בְּעַמֶּיךָ לֹא תַעֲמֹד עַל־דַּם רֵעֶךָ אֲנִי יְהֹוָה: לֹא־תִשְׂנָא אֶת־אָחִיךָ בִּלְבָבֶךָ הוֹכֵחַ תּוֹכִיחַ אֶת־עֲמִיתֶךָ וְלֹא־תִשָּׂא עָלָיו חֵטְא: לֹא־תִקֹּם וְלֹא־תִטֹּר אֶת־בְּנֵי עַמֶּךָ וְאָהַבְתָּ לְרֵעֲךָ כָּמוֹךָ אֲנִי יְהֹוָה: מִפְּנֵי שֵׂיבָה תָּקוּם וְהָדַרְתָּ פְּנֵי זָקֵן וְיָרֵאתָ מֵּאֱלֹהֶיךָ אֲנִי יְהֹוָה: וְכִי־יָגוּר אִתְּךָ גֵּר בְּאַרְצְכֶם לֹא תוֹנוּ אֹתוֹ: כְּאֶזְרָח מִכֶּם יִהְיֶה לָכֶם הַגֵּר הַגָּר אִתְּכֶם וְאָהַבְתָּ לוֹ כָּמוֹךָ כִּי־גֵרִים הֱיִיתֶם בְּאֶרֶץ מִצְרָיִם אֲנִי יְהֹוָה אֱלֹהֵיכֶם: לֹא־תַעֲשׂוּ עָוֶל בַּמִּשְׁפָּט בַּמִּדָּה בַּמִּשְׁקָל וּבַמְּשׂוּרָה: מֹאזְנֵי צֶדֶק אַבְנֵי־צֶדֶק אֵיפַת צֶדֶק וְהִין צֶדֶק יִהְיֶה לָכֶם אֲנִי יְהֹוָה אֱלֹהֵיכֶם אֲשֶׁר־הוֹצֵאתִי אֶתְכֶם מֵאֶרֶץ מִצְרָיִם: וּשְׁמַרְתֶּם אֶת־כָּל־חֻקֹּתַי וְאֶת־כָּל־מִשְׁפָּטַי וַעֲשִׂיתֶם אֹתָם אֲנִי יְהֹוָה:

אַל־תִּמְנַע־טוֹב מִבְּעָלָיו בִּהְיוֹת לְאֵל יָדְךָ לַעֲשׂוֹת:
אַל־תֹּאמַר לְרֵעֲךָ לֵךְ וָשׁוּב וּמָחָר אֶתֵּן וְיֵשׁ אִתָּךְ:
אַל־תַּחֲרֹשׁ עַל־רֵעֲךָ רָעָה וְהוּא־יוֹשֵׁב לָבֶטַח אִתָּךְ:
אַל־תָּרִיב עִם־אָדָם חִנָּם אִם־לֹא גְמָלְךָ רָעָה:
אַל־תְּקַנֵּא בְּאִישׁ חָמָס וְאַל־תִּבְחַר בְּכָל־דְּרָכָיו:
כִּי תוֹעֲבַת יְהֹוָה נָלוֹז וְאֶת־יְשָׁרִים סוֹדוֹ:

You shall not exploit your neighbour nor rob him.

You shall not keep back a hired-man's wages till the next morning.

You shall not pervert justice, neither by favouring the poor, nor by honouring the great.

You shall judge your neighbour with justice.

You shall not go about slandering your people.

You shall not stand by when your neighbour's blood is shed. I am the Lord.

You shall not hate your brother in your heart, but you shall frankly warn him of his fault and so you will not share his guilt.

You shall not seek revenge nor bear a grudge against any of your people.

You shall love your neighbour as you love yourself. I am the Lord.

In the presence of old age you shall stand up, honour the presence of an old person, and fear your God. I am the Lord.

When a stranger settles with you in your land you shall not oppress him.

The stranger who settles with you shall be treated as one born among you, and you shall love him as you love yourself, for you were strangers in the land of Egypt. I am the Lord your God.

You shall not pervert justice in measurements of length, weight or quantity. You shall have true scales, true weights, true measures.

I am the Lord your God who brought you out of the land of Egypt. You shall keep all My laws and judgments and carry them out. I am the Lord.

From Leviticus 19

Do not refuse any man a kindness that you owe him if it is in your power to do it.

Do not say to your neighbour, 'Go away and come back again and I will give it to you tomorrow'—when you have it already.

Do not plot harm against your neighbour while he lives near you, trusting you.

Do not pick a quarrel with a man for no reason, when he has done you no harm.

Do not envy a violent man and do not model your conduct on his, for one who is not straight is detestable to the Lord, but the upright have His confidence.

Proverbs 3: 27–32

After the silence the service continues on page 142.

תפלת שחרית לשבת

כֹּה תֹאמַר לְבֵית יַעֲקֹב וְתַגֵּיד לִבְנֵי יִשְׂרָאֵל:

וְעַתָּה אִם־שָׁמוֹעַ תִּשְׁמְעוּ בְּקֹלִי וּשְׁמַרְתֶּם אֶת־בְּרִיתִי
וִהְיִיתֶם לִי סְגֻלָּה מִכָּל־הָעַמִּים כִּי־לִי כָּל־הָאָרֶץ: וְאַתֶּם
תִּהְיוּ־לִי מַמְלֶכֶת כֹּהֲנִים וְגוֹי קָדוֹשׁ:

מַה־טֹּבוּ אֹהָלֶיךָ יַעֲקֹב מִשְׁכְּנֹתֶיךָ יִשְׂרָאֵל:
וַאֲנִי בְּרֹב חַסְדְּךָ אָבוֹא בֵיתֶךָ
אֶשְׁתַּחֲוֶה אֶל־הֵיכַל־קָדְשְׁךָ בְּיִרְאָתֶךָ:
יְהוָה אָהַבְתִּי מְעוֹן בֵּיתֶךָ וּמְקוֹם מִשְׁכַּן כְּבוֹדֶךָ:
וַאֲנִי אֶשְׁתַּחֲוֶה וְאֶכְרָעָה אֶבְרְכָה לִפְנֵי־יְהוָה עֹשִׂי:
וַאֲנִי תְפִלָּתִי־לְךָ יְהוָה עֵת רָצוֹן
אֱלֹהִים בְּרָב־חַסְדֶּךָ עֲנֵנִי בֶּאֱמֶת יִשְׁעֶךָ:

אֵין אָנוּ אֶלָּא קְהִלָּה קְטַנָּה בִּכְלַל־מִשְׁפַּחַת־יִשְׂרָאֵל וְיַחַד
עִם כָּל־קְהִלּוֹתֵינוּ הַקְּדוֹשׁוֹת פּוֹנִים אָנוּ אֶל־אֱלֹהֵי־מִבְטָחֵינוּ·
הוּא צִדְקַת־נְבִיאֵינוּ וְחָכְמַת־מוֹרֵינוּ: אֱמֶת וּתְהִלַּת־תּוֹלְדוֹתֵינוּ
וּבְכָל־שִׁנּוּיֵי־הָעוֹלָם הוּא עֻזֵּנוּ וּגְבוּרָתֵנוּ: כַּאֲשֶׁר הִנְחָה אֶת־
אֲבוֹתֵינוּ לִגְדוּלָּתָם כֵּן יַדְרִיךְ אוֹתָנוּ וְאֶת־בָּנֵינוּ בַּיָּמִים
שֶׁיָּבוֹאוּ: לְפָנָיו בִּלְבַד אָנוּ כּוֹרְעִים אַךְ עוֹמְדִים זְקוּפִים
בִּפְנֵי־רֵעֵינוּ: עֲבוֹדָתוֹ הִיא חֵרוּתֵנוּ הַנּוֹתֶנֶת לָנוּ לְשָׁרֵת אֶת־
כָּל־בְּנֵי־אָדָם: צִדְקָתוֹ מְאַחֶדֶת אֶת־בֵּית־יִשְׂרָאֵל הַמְּפֻזָּר
בְּכָל־אַרְצוֹת־הַתֵּבֵל· הִיא מְדַבֶּרֶת אֵלֵינוּ בְּכָל־לָשׁוֹן
וּבְכָל־מָקוֹם· וְיוֹצֶרֶת אוֹתָנוּ כְּלִי־שְׁלוֹמוֹ: לֹא־יָנוּם וְלֹא
יִישָׁן שׁוֹמֵר יִשְׂרָאֵל: עוֹשֶׂה שָׁלוֹם בִּמְרוֹמָיו הוּא יַעֲשֶׂה שָׁלוֹם
עָלֵינוּ וְדֶרֶךְ־יִשְׂרָאֵל עַמּוֹ עַל־כָּל־בָּאֵי־עוֹלָם · אָמֵן:

VI

SABBATH MORNING SERVICE

Say this to the family of Jacob! Declare it to the children of Israel!

If you now obey My voice and keep My covenant, you of all nations shall be My very own though all the earth is Mine. You shall be My kingdom of priests, and My holy nation.

Exodus 19: 3, 5–6

DIRECTING THE HEART TO GOD
How good are your tents, O Jacob, and your homes, O Israel.

Through the greatness of Your love I enter Your house. In awe I worship before the ark of Your holiness.

Lord, as I loved the courts of Your temple, and the place where Your glory dwelt, so I still worship and bend low, humble before the Lord my maker.

As for me, let my prayer come before You at the proper time.

Answer me God, in the greatness of Your love, for Your deliverance is sure.

THE FAMILY OF ISRAEL
We are one small part of the family of Israel; together with all other holy communities we turn to God in whom we trust. He is the righteousness our prophets proclaimed and the wisdom our rabbis sought. He is the truth and glory of our history, our strength in all the changes of the world. He led our fathers to greatness. May He guide us and our children in the days that lie ahead. We bow to Him alone, and stand upright before our fellow men. By serving Him we are free to serve all mankind. His righteousness unites the family of Israel scattered throughout the world. It speaks to us in every tongue, in every place, to make us the instruments of His peace. The guardian of Israel never slumbers and never sleeps. He makes peace and harmony in the highest, may He bring this peace upon us, and through His people Israel to all mankind. Amen.

קכו שִׁיר הַמַּעֲלוֹת

בְּשׁוּב יְהֹוָה אֶת־שִׁיבַת צִיּוֹן הָיִינוּ כְּחֹלְמִים׃

אָז יִמָּלֵא שְׂחוֹק פִּינוּ וּלְשׁוֹנֵנוּ רִנָּה

אָז יֹאמְרוּ בַגּוֹיִם הִגְדִּיל יְהֹוָה לַעֲשׂוֹת עִם־אֵלֶּה׃

הִגְדִּיל יְהֹוָה לַעֲשׂוֹת עִמָּנוּ הָיִינוּ שְׂמֵחִים׃

שׁוּבָה יְהֹוָה אֶת־שְׁבִיתֵנוּ כַּאֲפִיקִים בַּנֶּגֶב׃

הַזֹּרְעִים בְּדִמְעָה בְּרִנָּה יִקְצֹרוּ׃

הָלוֹךְ יֵלֵךְ וּבָכֹה נֹשֵׂא מֶשֶׁךְ־הַזָּרַע

בֹּא־יָבֹא בְרִנָּה נֹשֵׂא אֲלֻמֹּתָיו׃

רִבּוֹן הָעוֹלָמִים וַאֲדֹנֵי הָאֲדֹנִים ׃ לֹא עַל־צִדְקֹתֵינוּ אֲנַחְנוּ מַפִּילִים תַּחֲנוּנֵינוּ לְפָנֶיךָ ׃ כִּי עַל־רַחֲמֶיךָ הָרַבִּים ׃ אֲדֹנָי שְׁמָעָה ׃ אֲדֹנָי סְלָחָה ׃ אֲדֹנָי הַקְשִׁיבָה וַעֲשֵׂה ׃ מָה־אָנוּ ׃ מֶה־חַיֵּינוּ ׃ מֶה־חַסְדֵּנוּ ׃ מַה־צִּדְקוֹתֵינוּ ׃ מַה־יְשׁוּעָתֵנוּ ׃ מַה־כֹּחֵנוּ ׃ מַה־גְּבוּרָתֵנוּ ׃ מַה־נֹּאמַר לְפָנֶיךָ יְיָ אֱלֹהֵינוּ וֵאלֹהֵי אֲבוֹתֵינוּ ׃ הֲלֹא הַגִּבּוֹרִים כְּאַיִן לְפָנֶיךָ ׃ וְאַנְשֵׁי הַשֵּׁם כְּלֹא הָיוּ ׃ וַחֲכָמִים כִּבְלִי מַדָּע ׃ וּנְבוֹנִים כִּבְלִי הַשְׂכֵּל ׃ כִּי רֹב מַעֲשֵׂינוּ תֹהוּ ׃ וִימֵי חַיֵּינוּ הֶבֶל לְפָנֶיךָ ׃ וּמוֹתַר הָאָדָם מִן הַבְּהֵמָה אָיִן ׃ כִּי הַכֹּל הָבֶל לְבַד הַנְּשָׁמָה הַטְּהוֹרָה ׃ שֶׁהִיא עֲתִידָה לִתֵּן דִּין וְחֶשְׁבּוֹן לִפְנֵי כִסֵּא כְבוֹדֶךָ ׃

אֲבָל אֲנַחְנוּ עַמְּךָ בְּנֵי בְרִיתֶךָ ׃ בְּנֵי אַבְרָהָם אֹהַבְךָ ׃ זֶרַע יִצְחָק ׃ עֲדַת יַעֲקֹב ׃ אַשְׁרֵינוּ מַה־טּוֹב חֶלְקֵנוּ וּמַה־נָּעִים גּוֹרָלֵנוּ וּמַה־יָּפָה יְרֻשָּׁתֵנוּ ׃

Psalm 126

A Pilgrim Song.

SONGS OF
PRAISE

When the Lord brought back the captives to Zion
  we felt as if in a dream.
Then our mouths were filled with laughter,
  and our tongues with song.

Even among the nations they said:
  'What great things the Lord has done for them!'
Indeed the Lord has done great things with us!
  How we rejoiced!

Lord, bring back those who cannot return,
  like streams in a dry land;
that those who sow in tears
  may reap in joy.

Though a man goes out weeping
  carrying seed to sow;
he shall come back singing
  carrying his sheaves.

Alternative Songs of Praise, pages 571–609.

THE
WEAKNESS
OF MAN

Master of existence, and Lord of lords, we do not rely on our own good deeds but on Your great mercy as we lay our needs before You. Lord, hear! Lord, pardon! Lord, listen and act! What are we? What is our life? What is our love? What is our justice? What is our success? What is our endurance? What is our power? Lord our God, and God of our fathers, what can we say before You, for in Your presence are not the powerful as nothing, the famous as if they had never existed, the learned as if without knowledge, and the intelligent as if without insight. To You most of our actions are pointless and our daily life is shallow. Even the superiority of man over the beasts is nothing. For everything is trivial except the pure soul which must one day give its account and reckoning before the judgment seat of Your glory.

THE CHOICE
OF ISRAEL

Yet we are Your people, the children of Your covenant, the children of Abraham, whom You loved, the descendants of Isaac, and the congregation of Jacob. We are happy! How good is our portion, how fine our destiny and how beautiful our heritage!

יְיָ מֶלֶךְ · יְיָ מָלָךְ · יְיָ יִמְלֹךְ לְעוֹלָם וָעֶד :

וְהָיָה יְיָ לְמֶלֶךְ עַל־כָּל־הָאָרֶץ · בַּיּוֹם הַהוּא יִהְיֶה יְיָ
אֶחָד וּשְׁמוֹ אֶחָד : הוֹשִׁיעֵנוּ יְיָ אֱלֹהֵינוּ · לְהוֹדוֹת לְשֵׁם קָדְשֶׁךָ
לְהִשְׁתַּבֵּחַ בִּתְהִלָּתֶךָ : בָּרוּךְ יְהוָה אֱלֹהֵי יִשְׂרָאֵל מִן־הָעוֹלָם
וְעַד הָעוֹלָם · וְאָמַר כָּל־הָעָם אָמֵן · הַלְלוּיָהּ : כֹּל הַנְּשָׁמָה
תְּהַלֵּל יָהּ · הַלְלוּיָהּ :

I

You are the Lord of creation and the guardian of Israel. Your truth has been our strength and Your righteousness our purpose in every generation.

We are Your people and You are our God.

> When is God exalted in heaven? When His people are one band on earth.
>
> *Leviticus Rabbah*

We are Your children and You are our father.

> When you act like children of God, then you deserve to be called His children.
>
> *Kiddushin*

We are Your servants and You are our master.

> To serve Him is perfect freedom, and to worship Him the soul's purest happiness.
>
> *Union Prayer Book*

We are Your community and You are our portion.

> When we are at one with the community our prayer becomes unselfish.
>
> *Moses Chasid*

We are Your inheritance and You are our destiny.

> Moses commanded us Torah, the heritage of the community of Jacob.
>
> *Deuteronomy 33: 4*

We are Your flock and You are our shepherd.

> He who scattered Israel will gather him, and guard him as a shepherd guards his flock.
>
> *Jeremiah 31: 10*

THE POWER
OF GOD

The Lord does rule, the Lord has ruled, the Lord shall rule forever and ever.

The Lord shall be as a king over the whole earth. On that day the Lord shall be One, and known as One.

Save us, Lord our God, to proclaim Your holy name and be honoured in praising You.

Blessed is the Lord God of Israel from everlasting to everlasting. Let all the people say: Amen! Praise the Lord!

May all who live praise the Lord. Hallelujah!

II

You are the Lord of creation and the guardian of Israel. Your truth has been our strength and Your righteousness our purpose in every generation.

We are Your vineyard and You are our keeper.

> As the vine will receive no graft from another tree, so the community of Israel accepts no master but God.
>
> *Zohar*

We are Your work and You are our creator.

> Everyone who acts in justice and truth is a partner with God in the work of creation.
>
> *Mechilta*

We are Your beloved and You are our friend.

> I have loved you with an everlasting love, and so I stretch My faithful care upon you.
>
> *Jeremiah 31: 3*

We are Your very own and You are our nearest.

> The Lord has declared you today to be His own people, as He promised you, to keep all His commands.
>
> *Deuteronomy 26: 18*

We are Your people and You are our king.

> Accept the yoke of the kingdom of heaven, and practise love and kindness to one another.
>
> *Sifre*

We are Your acknowledged people and You are our acknowledged God.

> It is our duty to praise the Lord of all, to recognise the greatness of the creator of first things.
>
> *Aleynu Prayer*

וַיְבָרֶךְ שְׁלֹמֹה אֵת כָּל־קְהַל יִשְׂרָאֵל קוֹל גָּדוֹל לֵאמֹר:
בָּרוּךְ יְהוָה אֲשֶׁר נָתַן מְנוּחָה לְעַמּוֹ יִשְׂרָאֵל כְּכֹל אֲשֶׁר דִּבֵּר
לֹא־נָפַל דָּבָר אֶחָד מִכֹּל דְּבָרוֹ הַטּוֹב אֲשֶׁר דִּבֶּר בְּיַד מֹשֶׁה
עַבְדּוֹ: יְהִי יְהוָה אֱלֹהֵינוּ עִמָּנוּ כַּאֲשֶׁר הָיָה עִם־אֲבֹתֵינוּ אַל־
יַעַזְבֵנוּ וְאַל־יִטְּשֵׁנוּ: לְהַטּוֹת לְבָבֵנוּ אֵלָיו לָלֶכֶת בְּכָל־
דְּרָכָיו וְלִשְׁמֹר מִצְוֹתָיו וְחֻקָּיו וּמִשְׁפָּטָיו אֲשֶׁר צִוָּה אֶת־
אֲבֹתֵינוּ: וְיִהְיוּ דְבָרַי אֵלֶּה אֲשֶׁר הִתְחַנַּנְתִּי לִפְנֵי יְהוָה קְרֹבִים
אֶל־יְהוָה אֱלֹהֵינוּ יוֹמָם וָלָיְלָה לַעֲשׂוֹת מִשְׁפַּט עַבְדּוֹ וּמִשְׁפַּט
עַמּוֹ יִשְׂרָאֵל דְּבַר־יוֹם בְּיוֹמוֹ: לְמַעַן דַּעַת כָּל־עַמֵּי הָאָרֶץ
כִּי יְהוָה הוּא הָאֱלֹהִים אֵין עוֹד: וְהָיָה לְבַבְכֶם שָׁלֵם עִם
יְהוָה אֱלֹהֵינוּ לָלֶכֶת בְּחֻקָּיו וְלִשְׁמֹר מִצְוֹתָיו כַּיּוֹם הַזֶּה:

בָּרוּךְ יְהוָה לְעוֹלָם · אָמֵן וְאָמֵן:
בָּרוּךְ יְהוָה אֱלֹהִים אֱלֹהֵי יִשְׂרָאֵל · עֹשֵׂה נִפְלָאוֹת לְבַדּוֹ:
וּבָרוּךְ שֵׁם כְּבוֹדוֹ לְעוֹלָם · וְיִמָּלֵא כְבוֹדוֹ אֶת־כָּל־הָאָרֶץ ·
אָמֵן וְאָמֵן:

בָּרוּךְ אַתָּה יְיָ אֱלֹהֵינוּ מֶלֶךְ הָעוֹלָם · אֲשֶׁר קִדְּשָׁנוּ
בְּמִצְוֹתָיו וְצִוָּנוּ לַעֲסוֹק בְּדִבְרֵי תוֹרָה:

Let us think of our past, of our common heritage as children of
Israel. A strange folk have we been all these years, a riddle and
bewilderment to men. Through centuries without number we have
wandered about on earth, fleeing from eternal Egypt through a shore-
less Red Sea. We have seen far-flung empires crack and crumble, and
mighty peoples dwindle to nothing. Armies beyond counting have
marched by us in pomp and glory. They marched by us in pride,
with kings and priests, with tyrants and princes. Yet of them all no
sign is left, for they fell and died by the roadside. But we the Jews
still march on. Obstinately we fight off time and man, contending at
each step with a thousand foes, yet ever marching on.

And Solomon blessed the whole community of Israel in a loud voice, and said: 'Blessed is the Lord who has given rest to His people Israel as He promised. Not one of the promises of God, that He made through Moses His servant, has failed. May the Lord our God be with us as He was with our fathers. May He never leave us nor cast us off. May He turn our hearts towards Him so that we walk in all His ways, and keep His commands, laws and judgments that He gave to our fathers. May the words of this prayer be with the Lord our God day and night, so that He may do justice for His servant and for His people Israel as each day requires. So may all the peoples of the earth know that the Lord is God, no other exists. Be whole-hearted with the Lord our God, following His laws and keeping His commands as at this day.'

1 Kings 8: 55–61

Blessed be the Lord forever. Amen and amen.

Blessed be the Lord God, the God of Israel, who alone works wonders.

Blessed be His glorious name forever. All the earth is full of His glory. Amen and amen.

THE DUTY TO STUDY   Blessed are You, Lord our God, king of the universe, who makes us holy through doing His commands, and who commands us to devote ourselves to the study of His teaching.

One of the following passages or one selected from the Anthology, pages 401–409.

I am a Jew because, born of Israel and having lost her, I have felt her live again in me, more living than myself.

I am a Jew because, born of Israel and having regained her, I wish her to live after me, more living than in myself.

I am a Jew because the faith of Israel demands of me no abdication of the mind.

I am a Jew because the faith of Israel requires of me all the devotion of my heart.

I am a Jew because in every place where suffering weeps, the Jew weeps.

May there be sense in our persistence and reason in our tenacity.
May our constancy as Jews not be thought an end in itself, but solely
a way and a means. May we live our lives as Jews only to keep alive
our heritage, to keep ablaze the fires our prophets lit. May we, like
our fathers, still stand out against the multitude, protesting with
all our might against its follies and its fears. May we still be a light
to those who stumble in darkness.

And in that hope let us repeat the cry our people uttered when
a thousand idols were still worshipped by man: 'Hear O Israel, the
Lord is our God, the Lord is One.'

Adapted from the Service of the Newark Free Synagogue 1924

יִשְׁתַּבַּח שִׁמְךָ לָעַד מַלְכֵּנוּ · הָאֵל הַמֶּלֶךְ הַגָּדוֹל וְהַקָּדוֹשׁ ·
בַּשָּׁמַיִם וּבָאָרֶץ · כִּי לְךָ נָאֶה יְיָ אֱלֹהֵינוּ וֵאלֹהֵי
אֲבוֹתֵינוּ לְעוֹלָם וָעֶד שִׁיר וּשְׁבָחָה · קְדֻשָּׁה וּמַלְכוּת · בְּרָכוֹת
וְהוֹדָאוֹת לְשִׁמְךָ הַגָּדוֹל וְהַקָּדוֹשׁ · וּמֵעוֹלָם וְעַד־עוֹלָם אַתָּה
אֵל : בָּרוּךְ אַתָּה יְיָ · בּוֹרֵא כָּל־הַנְּשָׁמוֹת · רִבּוֹן כָּל־
הַמַּעֲשִׂים · מֶלֶךְ חֵי הָעוֹלָמִים :

The half Kaddish on page 168 may be included here.

בָּרְכוּ אֶת־יְיָ הַמְבֹרָךְ :

בָּרוּךְ יְיָ הַמְבֹרָךְ לְעוֹלָם וָעֶד :

בָּרוּךְ אַתָּה יְיָ אֱלֹהֵינוּ מֶלֶךְ הָעוֹלָם · יוֹצֵר אוֹר וּבוֹרֵא
חֹשֶׁךְ · עֹשֶׂה שָׁלוֹם וּבוֹרֵא אֶת־הַכֹּל : הַכֹּל יוֹדוּךְ · וְהַכֹּל
יְשַׁבְּחוּךְ · וְהַכֹּל יֹאמְרוּ אֵין קָדוֹשׁ כַּיְיָ : הַמֵּאִיר לָעוֹלָם
כֻּלּוֹ וּלְיוֹשְׁבָיו וּבְטוּבוֹ מְחַדֵּשׁ בְּכָל־יוֹם תָּמִיד מַעֲשֵׂה
בְרֵאשִׁית : מָה רַבּוּ מַעֲשֶׂיךָ יְיָ · כֻּלָּם בְּחָכְמָה עָשִׂיתָ · מָלְאָה
הָאָרֶץ קִנְיָנֶךָ : הַמֶּלֶךְ הַמְרוֹמָם לְבַדּוֹ מֵאָז · הַמְשֻׁבָּח
וְהַמְפֹאָר וְהַמִּתְנַשֵּׂא מִימוֹת עוֹלָם : אֱלֹהֵי עוֹלָם · בְּרַחֲמֶיךָ
הָרַבִּים רַחֵם עָלֵינוּ · אֲדוֹן עֻזֵּנוּ · צוּר מִשְׂגַּבֵּנוּ · מָגֵן יִשְׁעֵנוּ ·
מִשְׂגָּב בַּעֲדֵנוּ : בָּרוּךְ אַתָּה יְיָ · יוֹצֵר הַמְּאוֹרוֹת :

I am a Jew because at every time when despair cries out, the Jew hopes.

I am a Jew because the word of Israel is the oldest and the newest.

I am a Jew because the promise of Israel is the universal promise.

I am a Jew because, for Israel, the world is not yet completed; men are completing it.

I am a Jew because above all the nations and Israel, Israel places man and his unity.

I am a Jew because above man, image of the divine Unity, Israel places the divine Unity and its divinity.

Edmond Fleg

THE DUTY OF PRAISE   Praised be Your name forever, for You are the God who is the great and holy king in heaven and on earth. Therefore, Lord our God, and God of our fathers, song and praise, holiness and majesty, blessing and gratitude belong to Your great and holy name forever and ever. From age to age You are God. Blessed are You Lord, creator of every living being, master of all deeds, the king, the life of all existence.

The half Kaddish on page 168 may be included here.

THE CALL TO COM- MUNITY PRAYER   Bless the Lord whom we are called to bless.

Blessed be the Lord whom we are called to bless forever and ever.

THE CREATOR OF THE UNIVERSE   Blessed are You, Lord our God, king of the universe, who forms light yet creates darkness, who makes peace yet creates all. All things proclaim You, all things honour You, and all say: 'None is holy like the Lord.' He gives light to all the world and those who live in it. In His goodness He renews the work of the creation day by day. Lord, how great are Your works; You made them all in wisdom; the earth is full of Your creatures. You are the only king exalted from the beginning of time, who has been worshipped, praised and glorified since days of old.

Everlasting God, in Your great mercy have mercy upon us; Lord of our strength, rock of our protection, shield of our safety, our true protector. Blessed are You Lord, who creates the lights of the universe.

אַהֲבָה רַבָּה אֲהַבְתָּנוּ יְיָ אֱלֹהֵינוּ. חֶמְלָה גְדוֹלָה וִיתֵרָה
חָמַלְתָּ עָלֵינוּ. אָבִינוּ מַלְכֵּנוּ. בַּעֲבוּר שִׁמְךָ הַגָּדוֹל וּבַעֲבוּר
אֲבוֹתֵינוּ שֶׁבָּטְחוּ בְךָ. וַתְּלַמְּדֵם חֻקֵּי חַיִּים לַעֲשׂוֹת רְצוֹנְךָ
בְּלֵבָב שָׁלֵם. כֵּן תְּחָנֵּנוּ: הָאֵר עֵינֵינוּ בְּתוֹרָתֶךָ. וְדַבֵּק לִבֵּנוּ
בְּמִצְוֹתֶיךָ. וְיַחֵד לְבָבֵנוּ לְאַהֲבָה וּלְיִרְאָה אֶת־שְׁמֶךָ. לְמַעַן
לֹא נֵבוֹשׁ וְלֹא נִכָּלֵם כִּי אֵל פּוֹעֵל יְשׁוּעוֹת אָתָּה. וּבָנוּ בָחַרְתָּ
מִכָּל־עַם וְלָשׁוֹן. וְקֵרַבְתָּנוּ מַלְכֵּנוּ לְשִׁמְךָ הַגָּדוֹל בְּאַהֲבָה.
לְהוֹדוֹת לְךָ וּלְיַחֶדְךָ וּלְאַהֲבָה אֶת־שְׁמֶךָ: בָּרוּךְ אַתָּה יְיָ.
הַבּוֹחֵר בְּעַמּוֹ יִשְׂרָאֵל בְּאַהֲבָה:

שְׁמַ**ע** יִשְׂרָאֵל. יְהֹוָה אֱלֹהֵינוּ יְהֹוָה אֶחָ**ד**:

בָּרוּךְ שֵׁם כְּבוֹד מַלְכוּתוֹ לְעוֹלָם וָעֶד:

וְאָהַבְתָּ אֵת יְהֹוָה אֱלֹהֶיךָ. בְּכָל־לְבָבְךָ וּבְכָל־נַפְשְׁךָ
וּבְכָל־מְאֹדֶךָ: וְהָיוּ הַדְּבָרִים הָאֵלֶּה אֲשֶׁר אָנֹכִי מְצַוְּךָ הַיּוֹם
עַל־לְבָבֶךָ: וְשִׁנַּנְתָּם לְבָנֶיךָ וְדִבַּרְתָּ בָּם. בְּשִׁבְתְּךָ בְּבֵיתֶךָ
וּבְלֶכְתְּךָ בַדֶּרֶךְ וּבְשָׁכְבְּךָ וּבְקוּמֶךָ: וּקְשַׁרְתָּם לְאוֹת עַל־
יָדֶךָ. וְהָיוּ לְטֹטָפֹת בֵּין עֵינֶיךָ: וּכְתַבְתָּם עַל־מְזֻזוֹת בֵּיתֶךָ
וּבִשְׁעָרֶיךָ:

וְעַתָּה שְׁמַע יַעֲקֹב עַבְדִּי וְיִשְׂרָאֵל בָּחַרְתִּי בוֹ:

כֹּה־אָמַר יְהֹוָה עֹשֶׂךָ וְיֹצֶרְךָ מִבֶּטֶן יַעְזְרֶךָ

אַל־תִּירָא עַבְדִּי יַעֲקֹב וִישֻׁרוּן בָּחַרְתִּי בוֹ:

כִּי אֶצָּק־מַיִם עַל־צָמֵא וְנֹזְלִים עַל־יַבָּשָׁה

אֶצֹּק רוּחִי עַל־זַרְעֶךָ וּבִרְכָתִי עַל־צֶאֱצָאֶיךָ:

HIS LOVE
FOR ISRAEL   With deep love You have loved us, and with great and overflowing tenderness You have taken pity on us. Our father, our king, show us compassion because of Your own greatness, and because of our fathers who trusted in You, for You taught them rules to live by, to do Your will with their whole heart. Let our eyes see the light of Your teaching and our hearts embrace Your commands. Give us integrity to love You and fear You. So shall we never lose our self-respect, nor be put to shame, for You are the power which works to save us. You chose us from all peoples and tongues, and in love drew us near to Your own greatness—to honour You, to declare Your unity, and to love You. Blessed are You Lord, who chooses His people Israel in love.

THE GOD
OF ISRAEL   Hear O Israel, the Lord is our God, the Lord is One.

Blessed is His name, whose glorious kingdom is forever and ever.

Love the Lord your God with all your heart, and all your soul, and all your might. These words that I command you today shall be upon your heart. Repeat them to your children, and talk about them when you sit in your home, and when you walk in the street; when you lie down, and when you rise up. Hold fast to them as a sign upon your hand, and let them be as reminders before your eyes. Write them on the doorposts of your home and at your gates.

Deuteronomy 6: 4–9

During the silence the second and third paragraphs of the Shema (pages 60–62) may be read, or the following:

Now listen Jacob My servant,
and Israel whom I have chosen!
Thus says the Lord who made you,
who formed you from the womb, who helps you.
Do not be afraid, Jacob My servant,
Yeshurun whom I have chosen.
For I will pour out water on the thirsty soil,
and streams on the dry ground.
I will pour out My spirit on your descendants,
and My blessing on your offspring.

וְצָמְחוּ בְּבֵין חָצִיר כַּעֲרָבִים עַל־יִבְלֵי־מָיִם:

זֶה יֹאמַר לַיהֹוָה אָנִי וְזֶה יִקְרָא בְשֵׁם־יַעֲקֹב

וְזֶה יִכְתֹּב יָדוֹ לַיהֹוָה וּבְשֵׁם יִשְׂרָאֵל יְכַנֶּה:

כֹּה־אָמַר יְהֹוָה מֶלֶךְ־יִשְׂרָאֵל וְגֹאֲלוֹ יְהֹוָה צְבָאוֹת

אֲנִי רִאשׁוֹן וַאֲנִי אַחֲרוֹן וּמִבַּלְעָדַי אֵין אֱלֹהִים:

כִּי עַם קָדוֹשׁ אַתָּה לַיהֹוָה אֱלֹהֶיךָ בְּךָ בָּחַר יְהֹוָה אֱלֹהֶיךָ לִהְיוֹת לוֹ לְעַם סְגֻלָּה מִכֹּל הָעַמִּים אֲשֶׁר עַל־פְּנֵי הָאֲדָמָה: לֹא מֵרֻבְּכֶם מִכָּל־הָעַמִּים חָשַׁק יְהֹוָה בָּכֶם וַיִּבְחַר בָּכֶם כִּי־אַתֶּם הַמְעַט מִכָּל־הָעַמִּים: כִּי מֵאַהֲבַת יְהֹוָה אֶתְכֶם וּמִשָּׁמְרוֹ אֶת־הַשְּׁבֻעָה אֲשֶׁר נִשְׁבַּע לַאֲבֹתֵיכֶם הוֹצִיא יְהֹוָה אֶתְכֶם בְּיָד חֲזָקָה וַיִּפְדְּךָ מִבֵּית עֲבָדִים מִיַּד פַּרְעֹה מֶלֶךְ־מִצְרָיִם: וְהָיָה עֵקֶב תִּשְׁמְעוּן אֶת הַמִּשְׁפָּטִים הָאֵלֶּה וּשְׁמַרְתֶּם וַעֲשִׂיתֶם אֹתָם וְשָׁמַר יְהֹוָה אֱלֹהֶיךָ לְךָ אֶת־הַבְּרִית וְאֶת־הַחֶסֶד אֲשֶׁר נִשְׁבַּע לַאֲבֹתֶיךָ:

Berdychev

They shall spring up among the grass
like willows by running streams.
One man will say: 'I belong to the Lord',
another will call himself by Jacob's name.
With his hand another will write: 'Belonging to the Lord',
and be known by the name of Israel.
Thus says the Lord, Israel's king and redeemer,
the Lord of all creation:
'I am the first and I am the last
and besides Me there is no God.'

Isaiah 44: 1–6

For you are a people holy to the Lord your God. It is you that the Lord your God has chosen to be His very own people out of all the peoples on the face of the earth. The Lord did not love you and choose you because you outnumbered other peoples, for you were the least of all peoples. It was for love alone and to keep the promise which He swore to your fathers that the Lord brought you out with His mighty hand and rescued you from the camp of slavery, from the power of Pharaoh, king of Egypt. Listen to these judgments, be true to them and do them, and then the Lord your God will be true to the covenant and faithful love which He promised your fathers.

Deuteronomy 7: 6–8, 12

After the silence the service continues on the following page.

Nuremberg

אֱמֶת וְיַצִּיב וְנָכוֹן וְקַיָּם וּמְקֻבָּל וְטוֹב הַדָּבָר הַזֶּה עָלֵינוּ לְעוֹלָם וָעֶד: אֱמֶת אֱלֹהֵי עוֹלָם מַלְכֵּנוּ· צוּר יַעֲקֹב מָגֵן יִשְׁעֵנוּ· לְדוֹר וָדוֹר הוּא קַיָּם· וּמַלְכוּתוֹ וֶאֱמוּנָתוֹ לָעַד קַיָּמֶת: אֱמֶת שָׁאַתָּה הוּא יְיָ אֱלֹהֵינוּ וֵאלֹהֵי אֲבוֹתֵינוּ· פּוֹדֵנוּ וּמַצִּילֵנוּ· מֵעוֹלָם הוּא שְׁמֶךָ· אֵין אֱלֹהִים זוּלָתֶךָ:

עֶזְרַת אֲבוֹתֵינוּ אַתָּה הוּא מֵעוֹלָם· מָגֵן וּמוֹשִׁיעַ לָהֶם וְלִבְנֵיהֶם אַחֲרֵיהֶם בְּכָל־דּוֹר וָדוֹר: אַשְׁרֵי אִישׁ שֶׁיִּשְׁמַע לְמִצְוֹתֶיךָ· וְתוֹרָתְךָ וּדְבָרְךָ יָשִׂים עַל־לִבּוֹ: אֱמֶת אַתָּה הוּא רִאשׁוֹן· וְאַתָּה הוּא אַחֲרוֹן· וּמִבַּלְעָדֶיךָ אֵין לָנוּ מֶלֶךְ גּוֹאֵל וּמוֹשִׁיעַ:

צוּר יִשְׂרָאֵל· קוּמָה בְּעֶזְרַת יִשְׂרָאֵל· וּגְאַל כִּנְאֻמֶךָ יְהוּדָה וְיִשְׂרָאֵל· גֹּאֲלֵנוּ יְיָ צְבָאוֹת שְׁמוֹ קְדוֹשׁ יִשְׂרָאֵל· בָּרוּךְ אַתָּה יְיָ· גָּאַל יִשְׂרָאֵל:

אֲדֹנָי שְׂפָתַי תִּפְתָּח· וּפִי יַגִּיד תְּהִלָּתֶךָ:

בָּרוּךְ אַתָּה יְיָ אֱלֹהֵינוּ וֵאלֹהֵי אֲבוֹתֵינוּ· אֱלֹהֵי אַבְרָהָם· אֱלֹהֵי יִצְחָק· וֵאלֹהֵי יַעֲקֹב· הָאֵל הַגָּדוֹל הַגִּבּוֹר וְהַנּוֹרָא· אֵל עֶלְיוֹן· גּוֹמֵל חֲסָדִים טוֹבִים קוֹנֵה הַכֹּל וְזוֹכֵר חַסְדֵי אָבוֹת וּמֵבִיא גוֹאֵל לִבְנֵי בְנֵיהֶם לְמַעַן שְׁמוֹ בְּאַהֲבָה: מֶלֶךְ עוֹזֵר וּמוֹשִׁיעַ וּמָגֵן· בָּרוּךְ אַתָּה יְיָ· מָגֵן אַבְרָהָם:

אַתָּה גִּבּוֹר לְעוֹלָם יְיָ· מְחַיֶּה מֵתִים אַתָּה רַב לְהוֹשִׁיעַ· מְכַלְכֵּל חַיִּים בְּחֶסֶד· מְחַיֶּה מֵתִים בְּרַחֲמִים רַבִּים· סוֹמֵךְ נוֹפְלִים· וְרוֹפֵא חוֹלִים· וּמַתִּיר אֲסוּרִים· וּמְקַיֵּם אֱמוּנָתוֹ לִישֵׁנֵי עָפָר· מִי כָמוֹךָ בַּעַל גְּבוּרוֹת וּמִי דוֹמֶה לָּךְ· מֶלֶךְ מֵמִית וּמְחַיֶּה· וּמַצְמִיחַ יְשׁוּעָה: וְנֶאֱמָן אַתָּה לְהַחֲיוֹת מֵתִים· בָּרוּךְ אַתָּה יְיָ· מְחַיֵּה הַמֵּתִים:

After the silence continue here.

TRUTH AND RE-DEMPTION Your word is true forever. It is certain for us, it is firm, accepted and good. It is true that the everlasting God is our king; the strength of Jacob, the defender of our safety. He endures from generation to generation, and His rule and His faithfulness stand firm forever. It is true that You are the Lord our God, and God of our fathers, who rescues and delivers us. So were You ever known. There is no God besides You.

It is You who always helped our fathers. In every generation You were the shield and saviour for them and their children after them. Happy indeed is the man who hears Your commands, and sets Your teaching and Your word upon his heart. It is true that You are the first, and that You are the last, and besides You we have no king who rescues and saves us.

Rock of Israel, rise up to the aid of Your people Israel. He rescues us, the Lord of all creation, the holiness of Israel. Blessed are You Lord, who rescues Israel.

THE AMIDAH Lord, open my lips and my mouth shall declare Your praise.

GOD OF HISTORY Blessed are You, Lord our God, and God of our fathers, God of Abraham, God of Isaac, and God of Jacob, the great, the mighty, and the awesome God, God beyond, generous in love and kindness, and possessing all. He remembers the good deeds of our fathers, and therefore in love brings rescue to the generations, for such is His being. The king who helps and saves and shields. Blessed are You Lord, the shield of Abraham.

GOD OF MIGHT You, O Lord, are the endless power that renews life beyond death; You are the greatness that saves. You care for the living with love. You renew life beyond death with unending mercy. You support the falling, and heal the sick. You free prisoners, and keep faith with those who sleep in the dust. Who can perform such mighty deeds, and who can compare with You, a king who brings death and life, and renews salvation. You are faithful to renew life beyond death. Blessed are You Lord, who renews life beyond death.

נַעֲרִיצְךָ וְנַקְדִּישְׁךָ כְּשֵׁם שֶׁמַּקְדִּישִׁים
אוֹתוֹ בִּשְׁמֵי מָרוֹם כַּכָּתוּב עַל יַד
נְבִיאֶךָ· וְקָרָא זֶה אֶל זֶה וְאָמַר·

קָדוֹשׁ קָדוֹשׁ קָדוֹשׁ יְיָ
צְבָאוֹת· מְלֹא כָל־הָאָרֶץ
כְּבוֹדוֹ:

כְּבוֹדוֹ מָלֵא עוֹלָם מְשָׁרְתָיו שׁוֹאֲלִים
זֶה לָזֶה אַיֵּה מְקוֹם כְּבוֹדוֹ· לְעֻמָּתָם
בָּרוּךְ יֹאמֵרוּ·

וְאַתָּה קָדוֹשׁ· יוֹשֵׁב תְּהִלּוֹת יִשְׂרָאֵל·

קָדוֹשׁ קָדוֹשׁ קָדוֹשׁ יְיָ
צְבָאוֹת· מְלֹא כָל־הָאָרֶץ
כְּבוֹדוֹ:

בָּרוּךְ כְּבוֹד יְהֹוָה מִמְּקוֹמוֹ·

יִמְלֹךְ יְהֹוָה לְעוֹלָם· אֱלֹהַיִךְ
צִיּוֹן לְדֹר וָדֹר הַלְלוּיָהּ:

בָּרוּךְ אַתָּה יְיָ· הָאֵל הַקָּדוֹשׁ:

בָּרוּךְ כְּבוֹד יְיָ מִמְּקוֹמוֹ:

מִמְּקוֹמוֹ הוּא יִפֶן בְּרַחֲמִים וְיָחֹן עַם הַמְיַחֲדִים שְׁמוֹ עֶרֶב וָבֹקֶר בְּכָל־
יוֹם תָּמִיד פַּעֲמַיִם בְּאַהֲבָה שְׁמַע אוֹמְרִים·

שְׁמַע יִשְׂרָאֵל יְיָ אֱלֹהֵינוּ יְיָ אֶחָד:

אֶחָד הוּא אֱלֹהֵינוּ הוּא אָבִינוּ הוּא מַלְכֵּנוּ הוּא מוֹשִׁיעֵנוּ· וְהוּא יַשְׁמִיעֵנוּ
בְּרַחֲמָיו שֵׁנִית לְעֵינֵי כָּל־חַי לִהְיוֹת לָכֶם לֵאלֹהִים:

אֲנִי יְיָ אֱלֹהֵיכֶם:

וּבְדִבְרֵי קָדְשְׁךָ כָּתוּב לֵאמֹר·

יִמְלֹךְ יְיָ לְעוֹלָם אֱלֹהַיִךְ צִיּוֹן לְדֹר וָדֹר· הַלְלוּיָהּ:

לְדוֹר וָדוֹר נַגִּיד גָּדְלֶךָ· וּלְנֵצַח נְצָחִים קְדֻשָּׁתְךָ נַקְדִּישׁ· וְשִׁבְחֲךָ אֱלֹהֵינוּ
מִפִּינוּ לֹא יָמוּשׁ לְעוֹלָם וָעֶד· כִּי אֵל מֶלֶךְ גָּדוֹל וְקָדוֹשׁ אָתָּה· בָּרוּךְ
אַתָּה יְיָ· הָאֵל הַקָּדוֹשׁ:

וְשָׁמְרוּ בְנֵי־יִשְׂרָאֵל אֶת־הַשַּׁבָּת לַעֲשׂוֹת אֶת־הַשַּׁבָּת לְדֹרֹתָם
בְּרִית עוֹלָם· בֵּינִי וּבֵין בְּנֵי יִשְׂרָאֵל אוֹת הִוא לְעֹלָם·
כִּי־שֵׁשֶׁת יָמִים עָשָׂה יְהֹוָה אֶת־הַשָּׁמַיִם וְאֶת־הָאָרֶץ· וּבַיּוֹם
הַשְּׁבִיעִי שָׁבַת וַיִּנָּפַשׁ:

We worship and sanctify You as they sanctify You in the highest heavens. As it is written by the hand of Your prophet: And they called to each other and said: Holy, holy, holy is the Lord of all creation, the whole earth is full of His glory. His glory fills the universe. Those who serve Him ask each other, 'Where is the place of His glory?' They cry in answer, 'Blessed!'

Blessed is His glory revealed in every place.

From His place may He turn in mercy, and be gracious to the people who in love declare His unity twice each day, evening and morning, with the words of the *Shema*.

You are holy, dwelling in the prayers of Israel.

Holy, holy, holy is the Lord of all creation, the whole earth is full of His glory.

Blessed is His glory revealed in every place.

The Lord shall rule forever! Zion, He is your God for all generations! Praise the Lord!

Blessed are You Lord, the holy God.

———

Hear O Israel, the Lord is our God, the Lord is One.

Our God is One. He is our father, He is our king, He is our deliverer, and in His mercy He will again announce to us in the presence of all living His promise to be your God.

I am the Lord your God!

And in Your holy writing it is said:

The Lord shall rule forever! Zion, He is your God for all generations! Praise the Lord!

We declare Your greatness to all generations, and to all eternity we proclaim Your holiness. Your praise shall never depart from our mouth, for You are God, the great and holy king. Blessed are You Lord, the holy God.

The children of Israel shall keep the Sabbath, observing the Sabbath as a timeless covenant for all generations. It is a sign between Me and the children of Israel forever. For in six days the Lord made heaven and earth and on the seventh day He ceased from work and was at rest.

Exodus 31: 16–17

אֱלֹהֵינוּ וֵאלֹהֵי אֲבוֹתֵינוּ · רְצֵה־נָא בִמְנוּחָתֵנוּ · קַדְּשֵׁנוּ בְּמִצְוֹתֶיךָ · שִׂים חֶלְקֵנוּ בְּתוֹרָתֶךָ · שַׂבְּעֵנוּ מִטּוּבֶךָ · שַׂמַּח נַפְשֵׁנוּ בִּישׁוּעָתֶךָ · וְטַהֵר לִבֵּנוּ לְעָבְדְּךָ בֶּאֱמֶת · וְהַנְחִילֵנוּ יְיָ אֱלֹהֵינוּ בְּאַהֲבָה וּבְרָצוֹן שַׁבַּת קָדְשֶׁךָ · וְיָנוּחוּ בָהּ כָּל־יִשְׂרָאֵל מְקַדְּשֵׁי שְׁמֶךָ : בָּרוּךְ אַתָּה יְיָ · מְקַדֵּשׁ הַשַּׁבָּת :

רְצֵה יְיָ אֱלֹהֵינוּ בְּעַמְּךָ יִשְׂרָאֵל · וְלִתְפִלָּתָם שְׁעֵה · וּבְרַחֲמֶיךָ הָרַבִּים תַּחְפֹּץ בָּנוּ וְתַשְׁרֶה שְׁכִינָתְךָ עַל צִיּוֹן · וְתֶחֱזֶינָה עֵינֵינוּ בְּשׁוּבְךָ לְצִיּוֹן בְּרַחֲמִים · בָּרוּךְ אַתָּה יְיָ · הַמַּחֲזִיר שְׁכִינָתוֹ לְצִיּוֹן :

מוֹדִים אֲנַחְנוּ לָךְ שֶׁאַתָּה הוּא יְיָ אֱלֹהֵינוּ וֵאלֹהֵי אֲבוֹתֵינוּ לְעוֹלָם וָעֶד · צוּרֵנוּ צוּר חַיֵּינוּ וּמָגֵן יִשְׁעֵנוּ אַתָּה הוּא לְדוֹר וָדוֹר : נוֹדֶה לְּךָ וּנְסַפֵּר תְּהִלָּתֶךָ עַל חַיֵּינוּ הַמְּסוּרִים בְּיָדֶךָ · וְעַל נִשְׁמוֹתֵינוּ הַפְּקוּדוֹת לָךְ · וְעַל נִסֶּיךָ שֶׁבְּכָל־יוֹם עִמָּנוּ · וְעַל נִפְלְאוֹתֶיךָ וְטוֹבוֹתֶיךָ שֶׁבְּכָל־עֵת עֶרֶב וָבֹקֶר וְצָהֳרָיִם : הַטּוֹב כִּי לֹא כָלוּ רַחֲמֶיךָ · הַמְרַחֵם כִּי לֹא תַמּוּ חֲסָדֶיךָ · כִּי מֵעוֹלָם קִוִּינוּ לָךְ :

וְעַל כֻּלָּם יִתְבָּרַךְ וְיִתְרוֹמַם וְיִתְנַשֵּׂא תָּמִיד שִׁמְךָ מַלְכֵּנוּ לְעוֹלָם וָעֶד : וְכָל־הַחַיִּים יוֹדוּךָ סֶּלָה · וִיהַלְלוּ וִיבָרְכוּ אֶת־שִׁמְךָ הַגָּדוֹל בֶּאֱמֶת · הָאֵל יְשׁוּעָתֵנוּ וְעֶזְרָתֵנוּ סֶלָה : בָּרוּךְ אַתָּה יְיָ · הַטּוֹב שִׁמְךָ וּלְךָ נָאֶה לְהוֹדוֹת :

שִׂים שָׁלוֹם טוֹבָה וּבְרָכָה חַיִּים חֵן וָחֶסֶד צְדָקָה וְרַחֲמִים עָלֵינוּ · וּבָרְכֵנוּ אָבִינוּ כֻּלָּנוּ יַחַד בְּאוֹר פָּנֶיךָ · כִּי בְאוֹר פָּנֶיךָ נָתַתָּ לָּנוּ יְיָ אֱלֹהֵינוּ תּוֹרָה וְחַיִּים · אַהֲבָה וָחֶסֶד · צְדָקָה וְרַחֲמִים · בְּרָכָה וְשָׁלוֹם · וְטוֹב בְּעֵינֶיךָ לְבָרֵךְ אֶת־עַמְּךָ יִשְׂרָאֵל בְּרָב־עֹז וּבְשָׁלוֹם : בָּרוּךְ אַתָּה יְיָ · הַמְבָרֵךְ אֶת־עַמּוֹ יִשְׂרָאֵל בַּשָּׁלוֹם :

Our God and God of our fathers, may our rest be pleasing to You. Make us holy by doing Your commands and let us share in the work of Your Torah. Make us content with Your goodness and let our souls know the joy of Your salvation. Purify our hearts to serve You in truth. In Your love and goodwill let us inherit Your holy Sabbath and may all Israel who seek holiness find in it their rest. Blessed are You Lord, who makes the Sabbath holy.

THANKS-GIVING AND PEACE Lord our God, be pleased with Your people Israel and listen to their prayers. In Your great mercy delight in us so that Your presence may rest upon Zion. Our eyes look forward to Your return to Zion in mercy! Blessed are You Lord, who restores His presence to Zion.

We declare with gratitude that You are our God and the God of our fathers forever. You are our rock, the rock of our life and the shield that saves us. In every generation we thank You and recount Your praise for our lives held in Your hand, for our souls that are in Your care, and for the signs of Your presence that are with us every day. At every moment, at evening, morning and noon, we experience Your wonders and Your goodness. You are goodness itself, for Your mercy has no end. You are mercy itself, for Your love has no limit. Forever have we put our hope in You.

And for all these things may Your name, our king, be blessed, exalted and honoured forever and ever. May every living being thank You; may they praise and bless Your great name in truth for You are the God who saves and helps us. Blessed are You Lord, known as goodness, whom it is right to praise.

Grant us peace, goodness and blessing; life, grace and kindness; justice and mercy. Our father, bless us all together with the light of Your presence, for in the light of Your presence You give us, Lord our God, law and life, love and kindness, justice and mercy, blessing and peace. And in Your eyes it is good to bless Your people Israel with great strength and peace. Blessed are You Lord, who blesses His people Israel with peace.

אֱלֹהַי נְצוֹר לְשׁוֹנִי מֵרָע · וּשְׂפָתוֹתַי מִדַּבֵּר מִרְמָה · וְלִמְקַלְלַי נַפְשִׁי תִדּוֹם · וְנַפְשִׁי כֶּעָפָר לַכֹּל תִּהְיֶה: פְּתַח לִבִּי בְּתוֹרָתֶךָ · וְאַחֲרֵי מִצְוֹתֶיךָ תִּרְדּוֹף נַפְשִׁי · וְכָל־הַקָּמִים עָלַי לְרָעָה מְהֵרָה הָפֵר עֲצָתָם וְקַלְקֵל מַחְשְׁבוֹתָם: יִהְיוּ לְרָצוֹן אִמְרֵי־פִי · וְהֶגְיוֹן לִבִּי לְפָנֶיךָ · יְהֹוָה צוּרִי וְגֹאֲלִי:

עֹשֶׂה שָׁלוֹם בִּמְרוֹמָיו · הוּא יַעֲשֶׂה שָׁלוֹם עָלֵינוּ וְעַל־כָּל־יִשְׂרָאֵל · וְאִמְרוּ אָמֵן:

אֵין כָּמוֹךָ בָאֱלֹהִים אֲדֹנָי וְאֵין כְּמַעֲשֶׂיךָ: מַלְכוּתְךָ מַלְכוּת כָּל־עֹלָמִים וּמֶמְשַׁלְתְּךָ בְּכָל־דּוֹר וָדֹר: יְיָ מֶלֶךְ יְיָ מָלָךְ יְיָ יִמְלֹךְ לְעֹלָם וָעֶד: יְיָ עֹז לְעַמּוֹ יִתֵּן יְיָ יְבָרֵךְ אֶת־עַמּוֹ בַשָּׁלוֹם:

אַב הָרַחֲמִים הֵיטִיבָה בִרְצוֹנְךָ אֶת־צִיּוֹן · כִּי־בְךָ לְבַד בָּטָחְנוּ · מֶלֶךְ אֵל רָם וְנִשָּׂא אֲדוֹן עוֹלָמִים:

I

וַיְדַבֵּר אֱלֹהִים אֵת כָּל־הַדְּבָרִים הָאֵלֶּה לֵאמֹר:

א   אָנֹכִי יְהֹוָה אֱלֹהֶיךָ אֲשֶׁר הוֹצֵאתִיךָ מֵאֶרֶץ מִצְרַיִם מִבֵּית עֲבָדִים:

ב   לֹא־יִהְיֶה לְךָ אֱלֹהִים אֲחֵרִים עַל־פָּנָי: לֹא־תַעֲשֶׂה לְךָ פֶסֶל וְכָל־תְּמוּנָה אֲשֶׁר בַּשָּׁמַיִם מִמַּעַל וַאֲשֶׁר בָּאָרֶץ מִתָּחַת וַאֲשֶׁר בַּמַּיִם מִתַּחַת לָאָרֶץ: לֹא־תִשְׁתַּחֲוֶה לָהֶם וְלֹא תָעָבְדֵם כִּי אָנֹכִי יְהֹוָה אֱלֹהֶיךָ אֵל קַנָּא פֹּקֵד עֲוֹן אָבֹת עַל־בָּנִים עַל־שִׁלֵּשִׁים וְעַל־רִבֵּעִים לְשֹׂנְאָי: וְעֹשֶׂה חֶסֶד לַאֲלָפִים לְאֹהֲבַי וּלְשֹׁמְרֵי מִצְוֹתָי:

ג   לֹא תִשָּׂא אֶת־שֵׁם־יְהֹוָה אֱלֹהֶיךָ לַשָּׁוְא כִּי לֹא יְנַקֶּה יְהֹוָה אֵת אֲשֶׁר־יִשָּׂא אֶת־שְׁמוֹ לַשָּׁוְא:

MEDI-
TATION

My God, keep my tongue from causing harm and my lips from telling lies. Let me be silent if people curse me, my soul still humble and at peace with all. Open my heart to Your teaching, and give me the will to practise it. May the plans and schemes of those who seek my harm come to nothing. May the words of my mouth and the meditation of my heart be acceptable to You, O Lord, my rock and my redeemer.

May He who makes peace in the highest bring this peace upon us and upon all Israel. Amen.

ORDER OF THE READING OF THE TORAH

Lord, there is no God like You, no deeds like Yours! Your kingdom is an everlasting kingdom. Your authority is for every generation! The Lord has ruled, the Lord does rule, the Lord shall rule forever and ever. The Lord will give strength to His people, the Lord will bless His people with peace.

Father of mercies, may it please You to be good to Zion, for we trust in You alone, king and God, supreme and sublime, Lord everlasting.

One of the following passages appropriate to the service.

I

THE TEN
COMMAND-
MENTS

Then God spoke all these words:

1. I am the Lord your God who brought you out of the land of Egypt, out of the camp of slavery.

2. You shall have no other gods but Me. You shall not make yourself an idol in the likeness of anything which is in the sky above or on the earth below, or in the deeps under the earth. You shall not worship them nor serve them, for I the Lord your God am a demanding God, burdening the children down to the third and fourth generations with their fathers' guilt, if they hate Me, but showing kindness to thousands of generations if they should love Me, and keep My commands.

3. You shall not use the name of the Lord your God falsely, for the Lord will not excuse anyone who uses His name falsely.

ד זָכוֹר אֶת־יוֹם הַשַּׁבָּת לְקַדְּשׁוֹ : שֵׁשֶׁת יָמִים תַּעֲבֹד
וְעָשִׂיתָ כָּל־מְלַאכְתֶּךָ : וְיוֹם הַשְּׁבִיעִי שַׁבָּת לַיהוָה אֱלֹהֶיךָ
לֹא־תַעֲשֶׂה כָל־מְלָאכָה אַתָּה וּבִנְךָ וּבִתֶּךָ עַבְדְּךָ וַאֲמָתְךָ
וּבְהֶמְתֶּךָ וְגֵרְךָ אֲשֶׁר בִּשְׁעָרֶיךָ : כִּי שֵׁשֶׁת־יָמִים עָשָׂה יְהוָה
אֶת־הַשָּׁמַיִם וְאֶת־הָאָרֶץ אֶת־הַיָּם וְאֶת־כָּל־אֲשֶׁר־בָּם וַיָּנַח
בַּיּוֹם הַשְּׁבִיעִי · עַל־כֵּן בֵּרַךְ יְהוָה אֶת־יוֹם הַשַּׁבָּת וַיְקַדְּשֵׁהוּ :

ה כַּבֵּד אֶת־אָבִיךָ וְאֶת־אִמֶּךָ לְמַעַן יַאֲרִכוּן יָמֶיךָ עַל
הָאֲדָמָה אֲשֶׁר־יְהוָה אֱלֹהֶיךָ נֹתֵן לָךְ :

ו לֹא תִּרְצָח :

ז לֹא תִּנְאָף :

ח לֹא תִּגְנֹב :

ט לֹא־תַעֲנֶה בְרֵעֲךָ עֵד שָׁקֶר :

י לֹא תַחְמֹד בֵּית רֵעֶךָ לֹא תַחְמֹד · אֵשֶׁת רֵעֶךָ וְעַבְדּוֹ
וַאֲמָתוֹ וְשׁוֹרוֹ וַחֲמֹרוֹ וְכֹל אֲשֶׁר לְרֵעֶךָ :

II

כִּי הַמִּצְוָה הַזֹּאת אֲשֶׁר אָנֹכִי מְצַוְּךָ הַיּוֹם לֹא־נִפְלֵאת
הִוא מִמְּךָ וְלֹא־רְחֹקָה הִוא : לֹא בַשָּׁמַיִם הִוא לֵאמֹר מִי
יַעֲלֶה־לָּנוּ הַשָּׁמַיְמָה וְיִקָּחֶהָ לָּנוּ וְיַשְׁמִעֵנוּ אֹתָהּ וְנַעֲשֶׂנָּה :
וְלֹא־מֵעֵבֶר לַיָּם הִוא לֵאמֹר מִי יַעֲבָר־לָנוּ אֶל־עֵבֶר הַיָּם
וְיִקָּחֶהָ לָּנוּ וְיַשְׁמִעֵנוּ אֹתָהּ וְנַעֲשֶׂנָּה : כִּי־קָרוֹב אֵלֶיךָ הַדָּבָר
מְאֹד בְּפִיךָ וּבִלְבָבְךָ לַעֲשֹׂתוֹ : רְאֵה נָתַתִּי לְפָנֶיךָ הַיּוֹם
אֶת־הַחַיִּים וְאֶת־הַטּוֹב וְאֶת־הַמָּוֶת וְאֶת־הָרָע : הַעִדֹתִי בָכֶם
הַיּוֹם אֶת־הַשָּׁמַיִם וְאֶת־הָאָרֶץ הַחַיִּים וְהַמָּוֶת נָתַתִּי לְפָנֶיךָ
הַבְּרָכָה וְהַקְּלָלָה וּבָחַרְתָּ בַּחַיִּים לְמַעַן תִּחְיֶה אַתָּה וְזַרְעֶךָ :
לְאַהֲבָה אֶת־יְהוָה אֱלֹהֶיךָ לִשְׁמֹעַ בְּקֹלוֹ וּלְדָבְקָה־בוֹ כִּי
הוּא חַיֶּיךָ וְאֹרֶךְ יָמֶיךָ :

4. Remember the Sabbath day and keep it holy. You have six days to labour and do all your work, but the seventh shall be a Sabbath for the Lord your God. That day you shall do no work, neither you, nor your son, nor your daughter, nor your servant, man or woman, nor your cattle, nor the stranger who lives in your home. For in six days the Lord made heaven and earth, the seas and all that is in them, and He rested on the seventh day. Therefore, He blessed the Sabbath day and made it holy.

5. Respect your father and your mother so that the days of your life be fulfilled on the land which the Lord your God gives you.

6. You shall not murder.

7. You shall not commit adultery.

8. You shall not steal.

9. You shall not give false evidence against your neighbour.

10. You shall not covet your neighbour's house, you shall not covet your neighbour's wife, nor his servant, man or woman, nor his ox, nor his ass, nor anything that is your neighbour's.

The service continues at the foot of page 154.   *Exodus 20: 1–14*

II

LIFE AND DEATH   This commandment which I place upon you today is not too wonderful for you nor too remote. It is not in heaven that you need to say: 'Who will go up to heaven for us to fetch it, and tell it to us so that we may hear it and do it'. It is not beyond the sea so that you need to say: 'Who will cross the sea for us to fetch it, and tell it to us so that we may hear it and keep it'. It is something very near to you, it is in your mouth and in your heart to do it. See, today I offer you life and good, and death and evil. On this day I call heaven and earth as witness against you that I have set before you life and death, blessing and curse. Choose life!—then you and your descendants will live. Love the Lord your God, obey His voice, and hold fast to Him, for He is your life and the measure of your days.

The service continues at the foot of page 154.   *From Deuteronomy 30*

III

וְהָיָה בְּאַחֲרִית הַיָּמִים יִהְיֶה הַר בֵּית־יְהֹוָה נָכוֹן בְּרֹאשׁ
הֶהָרִים וְנִשָּׂא הוּא מִגְּבָעוֹת
וְנָהֲרוּ עָלָיו עַמִּים: וְהָלְכוּ גּוֹיִם רַבִּים וְאָמְרוּ
לְכוּ וְנַעֲלֶה אֶל־הַר־יְהֹוָה וְאֶל־בֵּית אֱלֹהֵי יַעֲקֹב
וְיוֹרֵנוּ מִדְּרָכָיו וְנֵלְכָה בְּאֹרְחֹתָיו
כִּי מִצִּיּוֹן תֵּצֵא תוֹרָה וּדְבַר יְהֹוָה מִירוּשָׁלָיִם:
וְשָׁפַט בֵּין עַמִּים רַבִּים וְהוֹכִיחַ לְגוֹיִם עֲצֻמִים עַד־רָחוֹק
וְכִתְּתוּ חַרְבֹתֵיהֶם לְאִתִּים וַחֲנִיתֹתֵיהֶם לְמַזְמֵרוֹת
לֹא־יִשְׂאוּ גּוֹי אֶל־גּוֹי חֶרֶב וְלֹא־יִלְמְדוּן עוֹד מִלְחָמָה:
וְיָשְׁבוּ אִישׁ תַּחַת גַּפְנוֹ וְתַחַת תְּאֵנָתוֹ וְאֵין מַחֲרִיד
כִּי־פִי יְהֹוָה צְבָאוֹת דִּבֵּר:

IV

כֹּה־אָמַר הָאֵל יְהֹוָה
בּוֹרֵא הַשָּׁמַיִם וְנוֹטֵיהֶם רֹקַע הָאָרֶץ וְצֶאֱצָאֶיהָ
נֹתֵן נְשָׁמָה לָעָם עָלֶיהָ וְרוּחַ לַהֹלְכִים בָּהּ:
אֲנִי יְהֹוָה קְרָאתִיךָ בְצֶדֶק וְאַחְזֵק בְּיָדֶךָ וְאֶצָּרְךָ
וְאֶתֶּנְךָ לִבְרִית עָם לְאוֹר גּוֹיִם:
לִפְקֹחַ עֵינַיִם עִוְרוֹת לְהוֹצִיא מִמַּסְגֵּר אַסִּיר
מִבֵּית כֶּלֶא יֹשְׁבֵי חֹשֶׁךְ:
אַתֶּם עֵדַי נְאֻם־יְהֹוָה וְעַבְדִּי אֲשֶׁר בָּחָרְתִּי
לְמַעַן תֵּדְעוּ וְתַאֲמִינוּ לִי וְתָבִינוּ כִּי־אֲנִי הוּא
לְפָנַי לֹא־נוֹצַר אֵל וְאַחֲרַי לֹא יִהְיֶה:

III

THE
FUTURE

In the last days
the mountain of the Lord's house shall be set firm
on the top of the mountains,
and raised up above the hills.
All nations shall flow towards it
and many peoples shall go there, saying:
'Come, let us go up to the mountain of the Lord,
to the house of the God of Jacob,
so that He may teach us about His ways
and we may walk in His paths,
for Torah shall come out of Zion,
and the word of the Lord from Jerusalem.'
Then He shall judge between many nations
and decide for great powers.
Then they shall hammer their swords into ploughshares
and their spears into pruning-hooks.
Nation shall not lift up sword against nation,
never again shall they train for war.
But each man shall sit under his vine and under his fig-tree
and no one shall terrorise him.
For the mouth of the Lord of creation has spoken.

The service continues at the foot of page 154.

Micah 4: 1–4

IV

THE
JUST
SOCIETY

Thus speaks God, the Lord,
He who created the skies and stretched them out,
who shaped the earth and all that grows on it,
who gives breath to its people
and life to those who walk upon it:
I, the Lord, have called you for righteousness,
I have taken you by the hand and have formed you;
I have appointed you as covenant of the people
and light of the nations,
to open eyes that are blind,
to bring captives out of prison,
and those who live in darkness from the dungeon.
You are My witnesses, says the Lord,
My servant whom I have chosen,
that men may know and believe Me,
and understand that I am He.
No God was formed before Me,
nor ever shall be after Me.

The service continues at the foot of page 154.

From Isaiah 42 and 43

V

וּשְׁמַרְתֶּם אֶת־דִּבְרֵי הַבְּרִית הַזֹּאת וַעֲשִׂיתֶם אֹתָם לְמַעַן
תַּשְׂכִּילוּ אֵת כָּל־אֲשֶׁר תַּעֲשׂוּן: אַתֶּם נִצָּבִים הַיּוֹם כֻּלְּכֶם
לִפְנֵי יְהֹוָה אֱלֹהֵיכֶם רָאשֵׁיכֶם שִׁבְטֵיכֶם זִקְנֵיכֶם וְשֹׁטְרֵיכֶם
כֹּל אִישׁ יִשְׂרָאֵל: טַפְּכֶם נְשֵׁיכֶם וְגֵרְךָ אֲשֶׁר בְּקֶרֶב מַחֲנֶיךָ
מֵחֹטֵב עֵצֶיךָ עַד שֹׁאֵב מֵימֶיךָ: לְעָבְרְךָ בִּבְרִית יְהֹוָה
אֱלֹהֶיךָ וּבְאָלָתוֹ אֲשֶׁר יְהֹוָה אֱלֹהֶיךָ כֹּרֵת עִמְּךָ הַיּוֹם: לְמַעַן
הָקִים־אֹתְךָ הַיּוֹם לוֹ לְעָם וְהוּא יִהְיֶה־לְּךָ לֵאלֹהִים כַּאֲשֶׁר
דִּבֶּר־לָךְ וְכַאֲשֶׁר נִשְׁבַּע לַאֲבֹתֶיךָ לְאַבְרָהָם לְיִצְחָק וּלְיַעֲקֹב:
וְלֹא אִתְּכֶם לְבַדְּכֶם אָנֹכִי כֹּרֵת אֶת־הַבְּרִית הַזֹּאת וְאֶת־
הָאָלָה הַזֹּאת: כִּי אֶת־אֲשֶׁר יֶשְׁנוֹ פֹּה עִמָּנוּ עֹמֵד הַיּוֹם לִפְנֵי
יְהֹוָה אֱלֹהֵינוּ וְאֵת אֲשֶׁר אֵינֶנּוּ פֹּה עִמָּנוּ הַיּוֹם:

VI

שִׁמְעוּ אֵלַי רֹדְפֵי צֶדֶק מְבַקְשֵׁי יְהֹוָה
הַבִּיטוּ אֶל־צוּר חֻצַּבְתֶּם וְאֶל־מַקֶּבֶת בּוֹר נֻקַּרְתֶּם:
הַבִּיטוּ אֶל־אַבְרָהָם אֲבִיכֶם וְאֶל־שָׂרָה תְּחוֹלֶלְכֶם
כִּי־אֶחָד קְרָאתִיו וַאֲבָרְכֵהוּ וְאַרְבֵּהוּ:
כִּי־נִחַם יְהֹוָה צִיּוֹן נִחַם כָּל־חָרְבֹתֶיהָ
וַיָּשֶׂם מִדְבָּרָהּ כְּעֵדֶן וְעַרְבָתָהּ כְּגַן־יְהֹוָה
שָׂשׂוֹן וְשִׂמְחָה יִמָּצֵא בָהּ תּוֹדָה וְקוֹל זִמְרָה:
הַקְשִׁיבוּ אֵלַי עַמִּי וּלְאוּמִּי אֵלַי הַאֲזִינוּ
כִּי תוֹרָה מֵאִתִּי תֵצֵא וּמִשְׁפָּטִי לְאוֹר עַמִּים אַרְגִּיעַ:

וַיְהִי בִּנְסֹעַ הָאָרֹן· וַיֹּאמֶר מֹשֶׁה
קוּמָה יְיָ· וְיָפֻצוּ אֹיְבֶיךָ· וְיָנֻסוּ
מְשַׂנְאֶיךָ מִפָּנֶיךָ: כִּי מִצִּיּוֹן תֵּצֵא
תוֹרָה· וּדְבַר־יְיָ מִירוּשָׁלָיִם:

כִּי מִצִּיּוֹן תֵּצֵא תוֹרָה וּדְבַר־יְיָ
מִירוּשָׁלָיִם:

V

THE COM-
MUNITY

Keep the words of this covenant and observe them so that you may succeed in all that you do. All of you stand here today in the presence of the Lord your God, your leaders, your tribes, your elders and your officers, every man of Israel; your children, your wives, and the stranger who is in your camp, from those who chop wood to those who draw water. You are about to enter into the covenant of the Lord your God, and into His oath which the Lord your God makes with you today. By this He makes a people of you and He will be your God, as He promised you and as He swore to your fathers, to Abraham, Isaac and Jacob. It is not with you alone that I make this covenant and this oath, not only with those who stand here with us today before the Lord our God, but also with those who are not here with us today.

The service continues at the foot of the page.   *Deuteronomy 29: 8–14*

VI

THE FAMILY
OF ISRAEL

Listen to Me, you who pursue righteousness,
who seek the Lord.
Look to the rock from which you were hewn,
and the quarry from which you were cut.
Look to Abraham your father,
and to Sarah who gave you birth.
For when he was one alone I called him,
and I blessed him and increased him.
For the Lord has comforted Zion,
comforted all her waste places;
He makes her desert like Eden
and her dry land like the garden of the Lord.
Joy and gladness shall be found in her,
thanksgiving and the voice of song.
Attend to Me, My people,
and listen to Me, My nation;
for Torah comes from Me,
and My justice shall soon be the light of the peoples.
Isaiah 51: 1–4

For Torah shall come out of Zion and the word of the Lord from Jerusalem.

Whenever the ark moved forward then Moses said: 'Rise up, Lord, and let Your enemies be scattered, let those who hate You flee before You.' For Torah shall come out of Zion and the word of the Lord from Jerusalem.

בָּרוּךְ שֶׁנָּתַן תּוֹרָה לְעַמּוֹ יִשְׂרָאֵל בִּקְדֻשָּׁתוֹ:

שְׁמַע יִשְׂרָאֵל יְהוָֹה אֱלֹהֵינוּ יְהוָֹה אֶחָד:

אֶחָד אֱלֹהֵינוּ גָּדוֹל אֲדוֹנֵינוּ קָדוֹשׁ וְנוֹרָא שְׁמוֹ:

גַּדְּלוּ לַיהוָֹה אִתִּי וּנְרוֹמְמָה שְׁמוֹ יַחְדָּו:

לְךָ יְהוָֹה הַגְּדֻלָּה וְהַגְּבוּרָה וְהַתִּפְאֶרֶת וְהַנֵּצַח וְהַהוֹד כִּי־כֹל בַּשָּׁמַיִם וּבָאָרֶץ לְךָ יְהוָֹה הַמַּמְלָכָה וְהַמִּתְנַשֵּׂא לְכֹל לְרֹאשׁ: רוֹמְמוּ יְהוָֹה אֱלֹהֵינוּ · וְהִשְׁתַּחֲווּ לַהֲדֹם רַגְלָיו · קָדוֹשׁ הוּא: רוֹמְמוּ יְהוָֹה אֱלֹהֵינוּ · וְהִשְׁתַּחֲווּ לְהַר קָדְשׁוֹ · כִּי קָדוֹשׁ יְהוָֹה אֱלֹהֵינוּ:

אֵין קָדוֹשׁ כַּיהוָֹה כִּי־אֵין בִּלְתֶּךָ · וְאֵין צוּר כֵּאלֹהֵינוּ: כִּי מִי אֱלוֹהַּ מִבַּלְעֲדֵי יְהוָֹה · וּמִי צוּר זוּלָתִי אֱלֹהֵינוּ: תּוֹרָה צִוָּה־לָנוּ מֹשֶׁה · מוֹרָשָׁה קְהִלַּת יַעֲקֹב: עֵץ־חַיִּים הִיא לַמַּחֲזִיקִים בָּהּ · וְתֹמְכֶיהָ מְאֻשָּׁר: דְּרָכֶיהָ דַרְכֵי־נֹעַם · וְכָל־נְתִיבוֹתֶיהָ שָׁלוֹם: שָׁלוֹם רָב לְאֹהֲבֵי תוֹרָתֶךָ · וְאֵין־לָמוֹ מִכְשׁוֹל: יְהוָֹה עֹז לְעַמּוֹ יִתֵּן · יְהוָֹה יְבָרֵךְ אֶת־עַמּוֹ בַשָּׁלוֹם: כִּי שֵׁם יְהוָֹה אֶקְרָא · הָבוּ גֹדֶל לֵאלֹהֵינוּ: הַכֹּל תְּנוּ עֹז לֵאלֹהִים · וּתְנוּ כָבוֹד לַתּוֹרָה:

וְזֹאת הַתּוֹרָה אֲשֶׁר־שָׂם מֹשֶׁה · לִפְנֵי בְּנֵי יִשְׂרָאֵל: תּוֹרָה צִוָּה־לָנוּ מֹשֶׁה · מוֹרָשָׁה קְהִלַּת יַעֲקֹב: הָאֵל תָּמִים דַּרְכּוֹ · אִמְרַת יְהוָֹה צְרוּפָה · מָגֵן הוּא לְכֹל הַחוֹסִים בּוֹ:

Before reading the Torah

בָּרְכוּ אֶת־יְיָ הַמְבֹרָךְ:

בָּרוּךְ יְיָ הַמְבֹרָךְ לְעוֹלָם וָעֶד:

בָּרוּךְ אַתָּה יְיָ אֱלֹהֵינוּ מֶלֶךְ הָעוֹלָם · אֲשֶׁר בָּחַר־בָּנוּ מִכָּל־הָעַמִּים · וְנָתַן־לָנוּ אֶת־תּוֹרָתוֹ · בָּרוּךְ אַתָּה יְיָ · נוֹתֵן הַתּוֹרָה:

Blessed is He who in His holiness gave Torah to His people Israel.

Hear O Israel, the Lord is our God, the Lord is One.

Our God is One. Our Lord is great; holy and awesome is His name.

Declare the greatness of the Lord with me, and let us exalt His name together.

Lord, Yours is the greatness, the power, the beauty, the victory and the splendour, for everything in heaven and earth is Yours. Lord, Yours is the kingdom, and You are supreme over all. Exalt the Lord our God, and bow down before His footstool—holy is He. Exalt the Lord our God and bow down before the mountain of His holiness— for holy is the Lord our God.

There is none holy like the Lord, for nothing, Lord, is like You and there is no strength like our God. For who is God besides the Lord, and what is strength except our God! Moses commanded us Torah, the heritage of the community of Jacob. It is a tree of life to all who grasp it and those who hold fast to it are happy. Its ways are ways of pleasantness and all its paths are peace. There is great peace for those who love Your Torah, and for them there is no stumbling. The Lord will give strength to His people, the Lord will bless His people with peace. So I call out the name of the Lord:— Declare the greatness of our God! Let everything declare His strength and the glory of His Torah.

This is the Torah that Moses set before the children of Israel. Moses commanded us the Torah, the heritage of the community of Jacob. The way of God is perfect, and the word of the Lord is proved. He is a shield for all who trust in Him.

Before reading the Torah
Bless the Lord whom we are called to bless.

Blessed be the Lord whom we are called to bless forever and ever.

Blessed are You, Lord our God, king of the universe, who chose us from all peoples to give us His teaching. Blessed are You Lord, who gives us the Torah.

After reading the Torah

בָּרוּךְ אַתָּה יְיָ אֱלֹהֵינוּ מֶלֶךְ הָעוֹלָם · אֲשֶׁר נָתַן־לָנוּ
תּוֹרַת אֱמֶת · וְחַיֵּי עוֹלָם נָטַע בְּתוֹכֵנוּ · בָּרוּךְ אַתָּה יְיָ · נוֹתֵן
הַתּוֹרָה:

Before reading the Haftarah

בָּרוּךְ אַתָּה יְיָ אֱלֹהֵינוּ מֶלֶךְ הָעוֹלָם · אֲשֶׁר בָּחַר בִּנְבִיאִים
טוֹבִים וְרָצָה בְדִבְרֵיהֶם הַנֶּאֱמָרִים בֶּאֱמֶת: בָּרוּךְ אַתָּה יְיָ ·
הַבּוֹחֵר בַּתּוֹרָה וּבְמֹשֶׁה עַבְדּוֹ וּבְיִשְׂרָאֵל עַמּוֹ וּבִנְבִיאֵי
הָאֱמֶת וָצֶדֶק:

After reading the Haftarah

עַל־הַתּוֹרָה וְעַל־הָעֲבוֹדָה וְעַל־הַנְּבִיאִים וְעַל־יוֹם הַשַּׁבָּת
הַזֶּה שֶׁנָּתַתָּ־לָּנוּ יְיָ אֱלֹהֵינוּ לִקְדֻשָּׁה וְלִמְנוּחָה לְכָבוֹד
וּלְתִפְאָרֶת · עַל־הַכֹּל יְיָ אֱלֹהֵינוּ אֲנַחְנוּ מוֹדִים לָךְ וּמְבָרְכִים
אוֹתָךְ · יִתְבָּרַךְ שִׁמְךָ בְּפִי כָּל־חַי תָּמִיד לְעוֹלָם וָעֶד ·
בָּרוּךְ אַתָּה יְיָ · מְקַדֵּשׁ הַשַּׁבָּת:

אֱלֹהֵינוּ שֶׁמַּלְכוּתוֹ מַלְכוּת כָּל־עוֹלָמִים יְבָרֵךְ

Our Sovereign Lady, Queen Elizabeth,
and all the Royal Family, her advisers and her counsellors.

יִתֵּן לָנוּ כֹּחַ לְמַלֵּא חוֹבָתֵנוּ בְּאַהֲבָה · כָּךְ שֶׁצֶּדֶק וּנְדִיבוּת
יִשְׂרְרוּ בְּאַרְצֵנוּ · יְהִי שָׁלוֹם בִּלְבָבֵנוּ · אַנְשֵׁי־קְהִלּוֹת־
הַמַּלְכוּת יִתְוַדְּעוּ בְּהַכָּרָה הֲדָדִית · יִהְיוּ מְאֻחָדִים בְּאַהֲבַת־
הַטּוֹב וּמֵאֲלִימוּת וָרִיב יִרְחָקוּ · עִם כָּל־אֻמּוֹת־הָעוֹלָם
יַחְדָּיו נִשְׂאַף לְשַׁלְוָה וְלִצְדָקָה · וּבְשָׁלוֹם נִחְיֶה אָנוּ וּבָנֵינוּ ·
אָז תִּזְכֶּה מַלְכוּתֵנוּ לְכָבוֹד אֲמִיתִי וְלִגְדֻלָּה לִקְרַאת
הַגְּאֻלָּה וְלַהֲקָמַת־מַלְכוּת־הַשָּׁמַיִם עַל־הָאָרֶץ · אָמֵן:

After reading the Torah

Blessed are You, Lord our God, king of the universe, who gave us the teaching of truth and planted eternal life within us. Blessed are You Lord, who gives us the Torah.

Before reading the Haftarah

Blessed are You, Lord our God, king of the universe, who chose good prophets and was pleased by their words for they were spoken in truth. Blessed are You Lord, who chooses the Torah, Moses His servant, Israel His people and the true and righteous prophets.

After reading the Haftarah

For the Torah, for the service, for the prophets and for this Sabbath day which You gave us, Lord our God, for holiness and rest, for glory and beauty—for all these, Lord our God, we thank and bless You. May Your name be blessed by the mouth of all living forever and ever. Blessed are You Lord, who makes the Sabbath holy.

THE PRAYERS OF THE COMMUNITY

May He whose kingdom is an everlasting kingdom bless

Our Sovereign Lady, Queen Elizabeth,

and all the Royal Family, her advisers and her counsellors.

May He give His wisdom to the government of this country, to all who lead it and to all who have responsibility for its safety and its welfare. May He give us all the strength to do our duty, and the love to do it well, so that justice and kindness may dwell in our land. May His peace be in our hearts, so that every community of our nation may meet in understanding and respect, united by love of goodness, and keeping far from violence and strife. Together may we work for peace and justice among all nations, and may we and our children live in peace. So may this kingdom find its honour and greatness in the work of redemption, and the building of God's kingdom here on earth. May this be His will. Amen.

אֱלֹהֵינוּ וֵאלֹהֵי אֲבוֹתֵינוּ שְׁלַח־נָא בִּרְכָתְךָ עַל־מְדִינַת־
יִשְׂרָאֵל וְעַל־כָּל־יוֹשְׁבֶיהָ. שְׁלַח־נָא אוֹרְךָ וַאֲמִתְּךָ
לְמַנְהִיגֵי־הָעָם וְהַדְרִיכֵם בְּחָכְמָה וּבִתְבוּנָה כְּדֵי שֶׁיִּשְׂרוֹר
שָׁלוֹם בִּגְבוּלוֹתֶיהָ וְשַׁלְוָה בְּבָתֵּיהָ. רוּחַ־אַחֲוָה וַהֲבָנָה הָדָדִית
תְּרַפֵּא כָּל־פֶּצַע וְחַבּוּרָה. תִּקְוַת־עַמָּה וַעֲבוֹדַת־בָּנֶיהָ
תַּגְשֶׁמְנָה אֶת־חֲזוֹן־הַנְּבִיאִים: כִּי מִצִּיּוֹן תֵּצֵא תוֹרָה וּדְבַר־
יְהוָה מִירוּשָׁלָיִם. אָמֵן:

אַב הָרַחֲמִים חֲמָל־נָא וְחוּס־נָא עַל אָבוֹת וּבָנִים
הָאֲבֵלִים בְּקִרְבֵּנוּ: נַחֵם אוֹתָם בְּחַסְדְּךָ הַגָּדוֹל חַזְּקָם בְּתִקְוַת
אַלְמָוֶת לַחֲזוֹת בְּנֹעַם בְּרִכּוֹתֶיךָ בְּחַיֵּי־הַנֶּצַח: יְקַבְּלוּ
בְּהַכְנָעָה אֶת־מוּסָרְךָ וְיַעֲשׂוּ רְצוֹנְךָ כִרְצוֹנָם. אָמֵן:

אֵל מֶלֶךְ נֶאֱמָן הָרוֹפֵא לִשְׁבוּרֵי לֵב וּמְחַבֵּשׁ לְעַצְּבוֹתָם
שְׁלַח רְפוּאָה שְׁלֵמָה לְחוֹלֵי עַמֶּךְ: יֵדְעוּ כֻלָּם כִּי זִכְרוֹנָם
לְפָנֶיךָ תָּמִיד וְאַתָּה הוּא מָגֵן וּמוֹשִׁיעַ לְכֹל הַחוֹסִים בָּךְ. אָמֵן:

מִי שֶׁבֵּרַךְ אֲבוֹתֵינוּ אַבְרָהָם יִצְחָק וְיַעֲקֹב הוּא יְבָרֵךְ
אֶת־כָּל־הַקָּהָל הַקָּדוֹשׁ הַזֶּה עִם כָּל־קְהִלּוֹת הַקֹּדֶשׁ. הֵם
וּנְשֵׁיהֶם וּבְנֵיהֶם וּבְנוֹתֵיהֶם וְכָל אֲשֶׁר לָהֶם. וּמִי שֶׁמְּיַחֲדִים
בָּתֵּי כְנֵסִיּוֹת לִתְפִלָּה. וּמִי שֶׁבָּאִים בְּתוֹכָם לְהִתְפַּלֵּל. וּמִי
שֶׁנּוֹתְנִים נֵר לַמָּאוֹר וְיַיִן לְקִדּוּשׁ וּלְהַבְדָּלָה וּפַת לָאוֹרְחִים
וּצְדָקָה לָעֲנִיִּים. וְכָל־מִי שֶׁעוֹסְקִים בְּצָרְכֵי צִבּוּר בֶּאֱמוּנָה.
מֶלֶךְ עוֹלָמִים יְבָרֵךְ אֶתְכֶם וִיזַכֶּה אֶתְכֶם. וְיִשְׁמַע קוֹל
תְּפִלּוֹתֵיכֶם. וְיִפְדֶּה וְיַצִּיל אֶתְכֶם מִכָּל־צָרָה וְצוּקָה. וְחֶסֶד
יְיָ יְהִי בְּסַעֲדְכֶם וְיָגֵן בַּעַדְכֶם. וְיִפְרוֹשׂ סֻכַּת שְׁלוֹמוֹ עֲלֵיכֶם
וְיִטַּע בֵּינֵיכֶם אַהֲבָה וְאַחֲוָה. שָׁלוֹם וְרֵעוּת לְעוֹלָם:
יְיָ אֱלֹהֵי אֲבוֹתֵיכֶם יֹסֵף עֲלֵיכֶם כָּכֶם אֶלֶף פְּעָמִים וִיבָרֵךְ
אֶתְכֶם כַּאֲשֶׁר דִּבֶּר־לָכֶם. וְכֵן יְהִי רָצוֹן. וְנֹאמַר אָמֵן:

Our God and God of our fathers, we ask Your blessing upon the State of Israel and all who dwell in it. Send Your light and Your truth to the leaders of the people, and guide them with wisdom and understanding, so that peace may reign on its borders and tranquillity in its homes. May the spirit of friendship and understanding remove all fears and heal all wounds. There, may mercy and truth come together for the good of all mankind, so that Your promise is fulfilled: 'for Torah shall come out of Zion and the word of the Lord from Jerusalem.' Amen.

Father of mercies, whose all-embracing love is our refuge and our hope, support with tenderness the sorrowing hearts among us. Comfort them with the knowledge that they will be united with those who are dear to them in eternal blessedness. Give them faith and courage and acceptance of Your chastening hand. Amen.

God, may it please You to send healing to those who are in pain or in anxiety. Be their refuge through their time of trial. Make them secure in the knowledge that they will never be forgotten by You, for You are the shield of all who trust in You. Amen.

PRAYER FOR THE CON-GREGATION May He who blessed our fathers, Abraham, Isaac and Jacob, bless this holy community with all other holy communities; them, their families and all they have. May He bless those who come together to maintain synagogues for prayer, and those who come to pray in them; those who light the Sabbath candles, and those who make Kiddush and Havdalah. May He bless those who share their food with strangers, give charity to the poor, and devote themselves to the needs of society in a true spirit.

May the everlasting king bless you and consider you worthy; may He listen to your prayers, and free and release you from all trouble and anxiety. May the kindness of the Lord support you and protect you. May He spread over you the covering of His peace and plant among you enduring love and brotherhood, peace and friendship.

May the Lord God of your fathers increase you and bless you as He has promised. May this be His will. Amen.

יְהִי רָצוֹן מִלְּפָנֶיךָ יְיָ אֱלֹהֵינוּ וֵאלֹהֵי אֲבוֹתֵינוּ שֶׁתְּחַדֵּשׁ
עָלֵינוּ אֶת־הַחֹדֶשׁ הַזֶּה לְטוֹבָה וְלִבְרָכָה · וְתִתֶּן־לָנוּ חַיִּים
אֲרֻכִים חַיִּים שֶׁל־שָׁלוֹם חַיִּים שֶׁל־טוֹבָה חַיִּים שֶׁל־
בְּרָכָה חַיִּים שֶׁיֵּשׁ בָּהֶם יִרְאַת שָׁמַיִם וְיִרְאַת חֵטְא חַיִּים
שֶׁאֵין בָּהֶם בּוּשָׁה וּכְלִמָּה · חַיִּים שֶׁל אַהֲבַת תּוֹרָה
חַיִּים שֶׁיִּמָּלְאוּ מִשְׁאֲלוֹת לִבֵּנוּ לְטוֹבָה · אָמֵן :

רֹאשׁ חֹדֶשׁ   יִהְיֶה בְּיוֹם

הַבָּא עָלֵינוּ וְעַל כָּל־יִשְׂרָאֵל לְטוֹבָה :
יְחַדְּשֵׁהוּ הַקָּדוֹשׁ בָּרוּךְ הוּא עָלֵינוּ וְעַל כָּל־עַמּוֹ
בֵּית יִשְׂרָאֵל לְחַיִּים וּלְשָׁלוֹם · לְשָׂשׂוֹן וּלְשִׂמְחָה · לִישׁוּעָה
וּלְנֶחָמָה · וְנֹאמַר אָמֵן :

יְהַלְלוּ אֶת־שֵׁם יְהוָה כִּי־נִשְׂגָּב שְׁמוֹ לְבַדּוֹ ·
     הוֹדוֹ עַל־אֶרֶץ וְשָׁמָיִם : וַיָּרֶם קֶרֶן לְעַמּוֹ תְּהִלָּה
לְכָל־חֲסִידָיו לִבְנֵי יִשְׂרָאֵל עַם־קְרֹבוֹ · הַלְלוּיָהּ :

כד

לְדָוִד מִזְמוֹר

לַיהוָה הָאָרֶץ וּמְלוֹאָהּ תֵּבֵל וְיֹשְׁבֵי בָהּ :

כִּי־הוּא עַל־יַמִּים יְסָדָהּ וְעַל־נְהָרוֹת יְכוֹנְנֶהָ :

מִי־יַעֲלֶה בְהַר־יְהוָה וּמִי־יָקוּם בִּמְקוֹם קָדְשׁוֹ :

נְקִי כַפַּיִם וּבַר־לֵבָב אֲשֶׁר לֹא־נָשָׂא לַשָּׁוְא נַפְשׁוֹ וְלֹא נִשְׁבַּע
לְמִרְמָה :

יִשָּׂא בְרָכָה מֵאֵת יְהוָה וּצְדָקָה מֵאֱלֹהֵי יִשְׁעוֹ :

זֶה דּוֹר דֹּרְשָׁיו מְבַקְשֵׁי פָנֶיךָ יַעֲקֹב סֶלָה :

On the Sabbath preceding the New Moon, the following is said:

Lord our God, and God of our fathers, may it be Your will that the new moon come to us for goodness and blessing. May the new month bring us a life of fulfilment and peace, a life of goodness and blessing; a life filled with awe of God and fear of sin; a life without self-reproach and shame; a life marked by love of Your teaching; when the desires of our hearts may be fulfilled for good. Amen.

The new moon of .... will be on ....

May it come to us and to all Israel for good.

May the Holy One, blessed be He, bring us and all His people, the family of Israel, a new month of life and peace, of happiness and joy, of achievement and consolation. Amen.

RETURN OF THE SCROLL — Praise the name of the Lord, for His name alone is supreme. His majesty is beyond heaven and earth. He has restored the honour of His people, the praise of those who love Him—the children of Israel, a people so close to Him. Praise the Lord!

Psalm 24

David's psalm.

The earth and its fullness belong to the Lord,
   the world and those who dwell in it,
for it is He who set it on the seas
   and made it firm upon the depths.

Who may ascend the mountain of the Lord
   and who may stand in the place of His holiness?
He whose hands are clean,
   whose heart is pure,
who has not given up his soul to worthless things
   nor committed himself to deception.

He shall earn a blessing from the Lord
   and be justified by God who saves him.
This is a generation that searches for Him,
   those who seek Your presence are the family of Jacob.

שְׂאוּ שְׁעָרִים רָאשֵׁיכֶם וְהִנָּשְׂאוּ פִּתְחֵי עוֹלָם וְיָבוֹא מֶלֶךְ הַכָּבוֹד :

מִי זֶה מֶלֶךְ הַכָּבוֹד יְהֹוָה עִזּוּז וְגִבּוֹר יְהֹוָה גִּבּוֹר מִלְחָמָה :

שְׂאוּ שְׁעָרִים רָאשֵׁיכֶם וּשְׂאוּ פִּתְחֵי עוֹלָם וְיָבֹא מֶלֶךְ הַכָּבוֹד :

מִי הוּא זֶה מֶלֶךְ הַכָּבוֹד יְהֹוָה צְבָאוֹת הוּא מֶלֶךְ הַכָּבוֹד סֶלָה :

כט

מִזְמוֹר לְדָוִד

הָבוּ לַיהֹוָה בְּנֵי אֵלִים הָבוּ לַיהֹוָה כָּבוֹד וָעֹז :

הָבוּ לַיהֹוָה כְּבוֹד שְׁמוֹ הִשְׁתַּחֲווּ לַיהֹוָה בְּהַדְרַת־קֹדֶשׁ :

קוֹל יְהֹוָה עַל־הַמָּיִם אֵל־הַכָּבוֹד הִרְעִים יְהֹוָה עַל־מַיִם רַבִּים :

קוֹל־יְהֹוָה בַּכֹּחַ קוֹל יְהֹוָה בֶּהָדָר :

קוֹל יְהֹוָה שֹׁבֵר אֲרָזִים וַיְשַׁבֵּר יְהֹוָה אֶת־אַרְזֵי הַלְּבָנוֹן :

וַיַּרְקִידֵם כְּמוֹ־עֵגֶל לְבָנוֹן וְשִׂרְיוֹן כְּמוֹ בֶן־רְאֵמִים :

קוֹל־יְהֹוָה חֹצֵב לַהֲבוֹת אֵשׁ :

קוֹל יְהֹוָה יָחִיל מִדְבָּר יָחִיל יְהֹוָה מִדְבַּר קָדֵשׁ :

קוֹל יְהֹוָה יְחוֹלֵל אַיָּלוֹת וַיֶּחֱשֹׂף יְעָרוֹת וּבְהֵיכָלוֹ כֻּלּוֹ אֹמֵר כָּבוֹד :

יְהֹוָה לַמַּבּוּל יָשָׁב וַיֵּשֶׁב יְהֹוָה מֶלֶךְ לְעוֹלָם :

יְהֹוָה עֹז לְעַמּוֹ יִתֵּן יְהֹוָה יְבָרֵךְ אֶת־עַמּוֹ בַשָּׁלוֹם :

Gates, lift up your heads!
  Be raised, you everlasting doors!
  Let the king of glory enter!
'Who is this king of glory?'
    The Lord, strong and mighty,
    the Lord, mighty in battle!

Gates, lift up your heads!
  Rise up you everlasting doors!
  Let the king of glory enter!
'Who is He, this king of glory?'
    The Lord of all creation,
    He is the king of glory!

Psalm 29

A Psalm of David.

Praise the Lord, you children of God!
  Praise the Lord, for His glory and strength!
Praise the Lord, honouring His name!
  Worship the Lord in the beauty of holiness!

The voice of the Lord echoes over the waters,
  the God of glory thunders,
    the Lord is echoing over the mighty waters.
The voice of the Lord in power,
  the voice of the Lord in majesty!

The voice of the Lord breaks cedars;
  the Lord has shattered the cedars of Lebanon.
They begin to leap about,
  Lebanon like a calf and Sirion like a young ox.

The voice of the Lord splits the lightning shafts,
  the voice of the Lord whirls the desert sand,
    the voice of the Lord whirls the desert of Kadesh.

The voice of the Lord makes the wild deer calve,
  it strips the forest bare—
    while in the temple all cry 'Glory!'

The Lord sat enthroned at the flood;
  the Lord is enthroned, king forever.
The Lord will give strength to His people,
  the Lord will bless His people with peace.

שָׁכֵן יְהֹוָה בְּתוֹךְ עַמֶּךָ
וְתָנוּחַ רוּחֲךָ בְּבֵית תְּפִלָּתֶךָ
כִּי כָל־פֶּה וְכָל־לָשׁוֹן יִתְּנוּ
הוֹד וְהָדָר לְמַלְכוּתֶךָ : כִּי
לֶקַח טוֹב נָתַתִּי לָכֶם תּוֹרָתִי
אַל־תַּעֲזֹבוּ :
הֲשִׁיבֵנוּ יְהֹוָה אֵלֶיךָ וְנָשׁוּבָה
חַדֵּשׁ יָמֵינוּ כְּקֶדֶם :

וּבְנֻחֹה יֹאמַר : שׁוּבָה יְיָ רִבְבוֹת אַלְפֵי
יִשְׂרָאֵל : קוּמָה יְיָ לִמְנוּחָתֶךָ אַתָּה וַאֲרוֹן
עֻזֶּךָ : כֹּהֲנֶיךָ יִלְבְּשׁוּ־צֶדֶק וַחֲסִידֶיךָ יְרַנֵּנוּ :
בַּעֲבוּר דָּוִד עַבְדֶּךָ אַל־תָּשֵׁב פְּנֵי מְשִׁיחֶךָ :
כִּי לֶקַח טוֹב נָתַתִּי לָכֶם תּוֹרָתִי אַל־תַּעֲזֹבוּ :
עֵץ חַיִּים הִיא לַמַּחֲזִיקִים בָּהּ וְתֹמְכֶיהָ
מְאֻשָּׁר : דְּרָכֶיהָ דַרְכֵי־נֹעַם וְכָל־נְתִיבוֹתֶיהָ
שָׁלוֹם :
הֲשִׁיבֵנוּ יְהֹוָה אֵלֶיךָ וְנָשׁוּבָה חַדֵּשׁ יָמֵינוּ
כְּקֶדֶם :

אֵין כֵּאלֹהֵינוּ · אֵין כַּאדוֹנֵינוּ · אֵין כְּמַלְכֵּנוּ · אֵין
כְּמוֹשִׁיעֵנוּ :

מִי כֵאלֹהֵינוּ · מִי כַאדוֹנֵינוּ · מִי כְמַלְכֵּנוּ · מִי כְמוֹשִׁיעֵנוּ :

נוֹדֶה לֵאלֹהֵינוּ · נוֹדֶה לַאדוֹנֵינוּ · נוֹדֶה לְמַלְכֵּנוּ · נוֹדֶה
לְמוֹשִׁיעֵנוּ :

בָּרוּךְ אֱלֹהֵינוּ · בָּרוּךְ אֲדוֹנֵינוּ · בָּרוּךְ מַלְכֵּנוּ · בָּרוּךְ
מוֹשִׁיעֵנוּ :

אַתָּה הוּא אֱלֹהֵינוּ · אַתָּה הוּא אֲדוֹנֵינוּ · אַתָּה הוּא מַלְכֵּנוּ ·
אַתָּה הוּא מוֹשִׁיעֵנוּ :

עָלֵינוּ לְשַׁבֵּחַ לַאֲדוֹן הַכֹּל לָתֵת גְּדֻלָּה לְיוֹצֵר בְּרֵאשִׁית ·
אֲשֶׁר בָּחַר־בָּנוּ מִכָּל־הָעַמִּים · וְנָתַן־לָנוּ אֶת־
תּוֹרָתוֹ · וַאֲנַחְנוּ כֹּרְעִים וּמִשְׁתַּחֲוִים וּמוֹדִים לִפְנֵי מֶלֶךְ מַלְכֵי
הַמְּלָכִים הַקָּדוֹשׁ בָּרוּךְ הוּא · שֶׁהוּא נוֹטֶה שָׁמַיִם וְיוֹסֵד אָרֶץ ·
וּמוֹשַׁב יְקָרוֹ בַּשָּׁמַיִם מִמַּעַל וּשְׁכִינַת עֻזּוֹ בְּגָבְהֵי מְרוֹמִים :
הוּא אֱלֹהֵינוּ · אֵין עוֹד · אֱמֶת מַלְכֵּנוּ · אֶפֶס זוּלָתוֹ · כַּכָּתוּב
בְּתוֹרָתוֹ · וְיָדַעְתָּ הַיּוֹם וַהֲשֵׁבֹתָ אֶל־לְבָבֶךָ כִּי יְיָ הוּא
הָאֱלֹהִים בַּשָּׁמַיִם מִמַּעַל וְעַל־הָאָרֶץ מִתַּחַת אֵין עוֹד :

THE RETURN OF ISRAEL Lord, be present among Your people, and may Your spirit rest in Your house of prayer. For every voice and every tongue will speak of the glory and majesty of Your kingdom. 'For I have given you good instruction, do not forsake My teaching.'

Turn us back to You, Lord, and we shall return; renew our lives as of old.

And when the ark rested Moses used to say: 'Lord, return to the countless thousands of Israel.' Rise up, Lord, to Your place of rest, You and the ark of Your strength! Your priests will be clothed in righteousness and those who love You will shout for joy. For the sake of Your servant David, do not turn away the face of Your anointed. 'For I have given you good instruction, do not forsake My teaching.' It is a tree of life to all who grasp it and those who hold fast to it are happy. Its ways are ways of pleasantness and all its paths are peace.

Turn us back to You, Lord, and we shall return; renew our lives as of old.

There is none like our God; there is none like our Lord; there is none like our king; there is none like our saviour.

Who is like our God; who is like our Lord; who is like our king; who is like our saviour?

We give thanks to our God; we give thanks to our Lord; we give thanks to our king; we give thanks to our saviour.

Blessed is our God; blessed is our Lord; blessed is our king; blessed is our saviour.

You are our God; You are our Lord; You are our king; You are our saviour.

BUILDING THE KINGDOM OF GOD: THE DUTY OF ISRAEL It is our duty to praise the Lord of all, to recognise the greatness of the creator of first things, who has chosen us from all peoples by giving us His Torah. Therefore we bend low and submit, and give thanks before the King above the kings of kings, the Holy One, blessed be He. He extends the limits of space and makes the world firm. His glory extends through the universe beyond, and the presence of His strength into farthest space. He is our God; no other exists. Our king is truth; the rest is nothing. It is written in His Torah: 'Realise this today and take it to heart—it is the Lord who is God in the heavens above and on the earth beneath; no other exists.'

עַל־כֵּן נְקַוֶּה לְּךָ יְיָ אֱלֹהֵינוּ לִרְאוֹת מְהֵרָה בְּתִפְאֶרֶת
עֻזֶּךָ · לְהַעֲבִיר גִּלּוּלִים מִן הָאָרֶץ וְהָאֱלִילִים כָּרוֹת יִכָּרֵתוּן ·
לְתַקֵּן עוֹלָם בְּמַלְכוּת שַׁדַּי · וְכָל־בְּנֵי בָשָׂר יִקְרְאוּ בִשְׁמֶךָ ·
לְהַפְנוֹת אֵלֶיךָ כָּל־רִשְׁעֵי אָרֶץ: יַכִּירוּ וְיֵדְעוּ כָּל־יוֹשְׁבֵי
תֵבֵל כִּי לְךָ תִּכְרַע כָּל־בֶּרֶךְ תִּשָּׁבַע כָּל־לָשׁוֹן: לְפָנֶיךָ יְיָ
אֱלֹהֵינוּ יִכְרְעוּ וְיִפֹּלוּ · וְלִכְבוֹד שִׁמְךָ יְקָר יִתֵּנוּ · וִיקַבְּלוּ
כֻלָּם אֶת־עֹל מַלְכוּתֶךָ · וְתִמְלֹךְ עֲלֵיהֶם מְהֵרָה לְעוֹלָם
וָעֶד · כִּי הַמַּלְכוּת שֶׁלְּךָ הִיא וּלְעוֹלְמֵי עַד תִּמְלֹךְ בְּכָבוֹד
כַּכָּתוּב בְּתוֹרָתֶךָ · יְהֹוָה יִמְלֹךְ לְעוֹלָם וָעֶד: וְנֶאֱמַר · וְהָיָה
יְהֹוָה לְמֶלֶךְ עַל־כָּל־הָאָרֶץ בַּיּוֹם הַהוּא יִהְיֶה יְהֹוָה אֶחָד
וּשְׁמוֹ אֶחָד :

יִתְגַּדַּל וְיִתְקַדַּשׁ שְׁמֵהּ רַבָּא בְּעָלְמָא דִּי־בְרָא כִרְעוּתֵהּ ·
וְיַמְלִיךְ מַלְכוּתֵהּ בְּחַיֵּיכוֹן וּבְיוֹמֵיכוֹן וּבְחַיֵּי
דִי־כָל־בֵּית יִשְׂרָאֵל בַּעֲגָלָא וּבִזְמַן קָרִיב · וְאִמְרוּ אָמֵן :
יְהֵא שְׁמֵהּ רַבָּא מְבָרַךְ לְעָלַם וּלְעָלְמֵי עָלְמַיָּא ·
יִתְבָּרַךְ וְיִשְׁתַּבַּח וְיִתְפָּאַר וְיִתְרוֹמַם וְיִתְנַשֵּׂא וְיִתְהַדָּר
וְיִתְעַלֶּה וְיִתְהַלָּל שְׁמֵהּ דִּי־קֻדְשָׁא · בְּרִיךְ הוּא · לְעֵלָּא מִן־
כָּל־בִּרְכָתָא וְשִׁירָתָא תֻּשְׁבְּחָתָא וְנֶחֱמָתָא דִּי־אֲמִירָן בְּעָלְמָא ·
וְאִמְרוּ אָמֵן :
יְהֵא שְׁלָמָא רַבָּא מִן־שְׁמַיָּא וְחַיִּים עָלֵינוּ וְעַל־כָּל־
יִשְׂרָאֵל · וְאִמְרוּ אָמֵן :
עֹשֶׂה שָׁלוֹם בִּמְרוֹמָיו הוּא יַעֲשֶׂה שָׁלוֹם עָלֵינוּ וְעַל־כָּל־
יִשְׂרָאֵל · וְאִמְרוּ אָמֵן :

THE HOPE FOR MANKIND Therefore, Lord our God, we put our hope in You. Soon let us witness the glory of Your power; when the worship of material things shall pass away from the earth, and prejudice and superstition shall at last be cut off; when the world will be set right by the rule of God, and all mankind shall speak out in Your name, and all the wicked of the earth shall turn to You. Then all who inhabit this world shall meet in understanding, and shall know that to You alone each one shall submit, and pledge himself in every tongue. In Your presence, Lord our God, they shall bow down and be humble, honouring the glory of Your being. All shall accept the duty of building Your kingdom, so that Your reign of goodness shall come soon and last forever. For Yours alone is the true kingdom, and only the glory of Your rule endures forever. So it is written in Your Torah:

'The Lord shall rule forever and ever.'

So it is prophesied:

'The Lord shall be as a king over all the earth.

On that day the Lord shall be One, and known as One.'

Let us magnify and let us sanctify the great name of God in the world which He created according to His will. May His kingdom come in your lifetime, and in your days, and in the lifetime of the family of Israel—quickly and speedily may it come. Amen.

May the greatness of His being be blessed from eternity to eternity.

Let us bless and let us extol, let us tell aloud and let us raise aloft, let us set on high and let us honour, let us exalt and let us praise the Holy One—blessed be He!—though He is far beyond any blessing or song, any honour or any consolation that can be spoken of in this world. Amen.

May great peace from heaven and the gift of life be granted to us and to all the family of Israel. Amen.

May He who makes peace in the highest bring this peace upon us and upon all Israel. Amen.

אֲדוֹן עוֹלָם אֲשֶׁר מָלַךְ   בְּטֶרֶם כָּל־יְצִיר נִבְרָא:

לְעֵת נַעֲשָׂה בְחֶפְצוֹ כֹּל ·   אֲזַי מֶלֶךְ שְׁמוֹ נִקְרָא:

וְאַחֲרֵי כִּכְלוֹת הַכֹּל ·   לְבַדּוֹ יִמְלוֹךְ נוֹרָא:

וְהוּא הָיָה · וְהוּא הֹוֶה ·   וְהוּא יִהְיֶה בְּתִפְאָרָה:

וְהוּא אֶחָד וְאֵין שֵׁנִי   לְהַמְשִׁילוֹ לְהַחְבִּירָה:

בְּלִי רֵאשִׁית בְּלִי תַכְלִית ·   וְלוֹ הָעֹז וְהַמִּשְׂרָה:

וְהוּא אֵלִי וְחַי גּוֹאֲלִי ·   וְצוּר חֶבְלִי בְּיוֹם צָרָה:

וְהוּא נִסִּי וּמָנוּסִי ·   מְנָת כּוֹסִי בְּיוֹם אֶקְרָא:

בְּיָדוֹ אַפְקִיד רוּחִי ·   בְּעֵת אִישַׁן וְאָעִירָה:

וְעִם רוּחִי גְוִיָּתִי ·   אֲדֹנָי לִי וְלֹא אִירָא:

יְבָרֶכְךָ יְהוָֹה וְיִשְׁמְרֶךָ :
יָאֵר יְהוָֹה פָּנָיו אֵלֶיךָ וִיחֻנֶּךָ :
יִשָּׂא יְהוָֹה פָּנָיו אֵלֶיךָ וְיָשֵׂם לְךָ שָׁלוֹם:

Eternal Lord who ruled alone
before creation of all forms,
when all was made at His desire
then as the king was He revealed.

And after everything shall end
alone, in wonder, will He reign,
as once He was, so is He now,
the glory that will never change.

He is the One, no other is
to be compared, to stand beside,
neither before, nor following,
His is the strength and His the might.

This is my God, my life He saves,
the rock I grasp in deep despair,
the flag I wave, the place I hide,
He shares my cup the day I call.

Within His hand I lay my soul
both when I sleep and when I wake,
and with my soul my body too,
my Lord is close I shall not fear.

May the Lord bless you and keep you.

May the face of the Lord enlighten you and be gracious to you.

May the Lord turn His face towards you and give you peace.

תפלת מנחה לשבת

אַשְׁרֵי יוֹשְׁבֵי בֵיתֶךָ עוֹד יְהַלְלוּךָ סֶּלָה:

אַשְׁרֵי הָעָם שֶׁכָּכָה לּוֹ אַשְׁרֵי הָעָם שֶׁיֲיָ אֱלֹהָיו:

וּבָא לְצִיּוֹן גּוֹאֵל וּלְשָׁבֵי פֶשַׁע בְּיַעֲקֹב נְאֻם יְהֹוָה: וַאֲנִי זֹאת בְּרִיתִי אוֹתָם אָמַר יְהֹוָה רוּחִי אֲשֶׁר עָלֶיךָ וּדְבָרַי אֲשֶׁר־שַׂמְתִּי בְּפִיךָ לֹא־יָמוּשׁוּ מִפִּיךָ וּמִפִּי זַרְעֲךָ וּמִפִּי זֶרַע זַרְעֲךָ:

בָּרוּךְ אֱלֹהֵינוּ שֶׁבְּרָאָנוּ לִכְבוֹדוֹ וְהִבְדִּילָנוּ מִן־הַתּוֹעִים: הוּא יִפְתַּח לִבֵּנוּ בְּתוֹרָתוֹ וְיָשֵׂם בְּלִבֵּנוּ אַהֲבָתוֹ וְיִרְאָתוֹ לְמַעַן לֹא נִיגַע לָרִיק וְלֹא נֵלֵד לַבֶּהָלָה: יְהִי רָצוֹן מִלְּפָנֶיךָ יְיָ אֱלֹהֵינוּ וֵאלֹהֵי אֲבוֹתֵינוּ · שֶׁנִּשְׁמוֹר חֻקֶּיךָ בָּעוֹלָם הַזֶּה · וְנִזְכֶּה וְנִחְיֶה וְנִרְאֶה וְנִירַשׁ טוֹבָה וּבְרָכָה לִשְׁנֵי יְמוֹת הַמָּשִׁיחַ וּלְחַיֵּי הָעוֹלָם הַבָּא: וְיִבְטְחוּ בְךָ יוֹדְעֵי שְׁמֶךָ כִּי לֹא־עָזַבְתָּ דֹרְשֶׁיךָ יְיָ: יְיָ חָפֵץ לְמַעַן צִדְקוֹ יַגְדִּיל תּוֹרָה וְיַאְדִּיר:

וַאֲנִי תְפִלָּתִי־לְךָ יְהֹוָה עֵת רָצוֹן

אֱלֹהִים בְּרָב־חַסְדֶּךָ עֲנֵנִי בֶּאֱמֶת יִשְׁעֶךָ:

SABBATH AFTERNOON SERVICE

REJOICING IN GOD

Happy are those who live in Your house
and can always praise You.
Happy the people of whom this is true!
Happy the people whose God is the Lord!

A redeemer shall come to Zion and to those in Jacob who turn from wrong, says the Lord. As for Me, this is My covenant which I make with them, says the Lord. My spirit which is upon you and My words which I have put in your mouth will never leave your mouth, nor the mouth of your children nor the mouth of your children's children.

Isaiah 59: 20–21

TRUSTING IN GOD

Blessed is our God who created us for His glory, and who parts us from those who go astray. May He open our hearts to His teaching and set the love and fear of Him within them, so that we do not wear ourselves away for nothing only to produce confusion. Lord our God and God of our fathers, help us to keep to Your commands in this world, so that we earn the right to life, and inherit the goodness and blessing of the messianic days and the life of the world to come.

'And those who truly know You put their trust in You, for You never abandon those who seek You.'

'For the sake of His righteousness the Lord delighted in making His Torah great and splendid.'

As for me, let my prayer come before You at the proper time.
Answer me God, in the greatness of Your love, for Your deliverance is sure.

אֲדֹנָי שְׂפָתַי תִּפְתָּח ׃ וּפִי יַגִּיד תְּהִלָּתֶךָ ׃

בָּרוּךְ אַתָּה יְיָ אֱלֹהֵינוּ וֵאלֹהֵי אֲבוֹתֵינוּ ׃ אֱלֹהֵי אַבְרָהָם ׃ אֱלֹהֵי יִצְחָק ׃ וֵאלֹהֵי יַעֲקֹב ׃ הָאֵל הַגָּדוֹל הַגִּבּוֹר וְהַנּוֹרָא ׃ אֵל עֶלְיוֹן ׃ גּוֹמֵל חֲסָדִים טוֹבִים קוֹנֵה הַכֹּל וְזוֹכֵר חַסְדֵי אָבוֹת וּמֵבִיא גוֹאֵל לִבְנֵי בְנֵיהֶם לְמַעַן שְׁמוֹ בְּאַהֲבָה ׃ מֶלֶךְ עוֹזֵר וּמוֹשִׁיעַ וּמָגֵן ׃ בָּרוּךְ אַתָּה יְיָ ׃ מָגֵן אַבְרָהָם ׃

אַתָּה גִּבּוֹר לְעוֹלָם יְיָ ׃ מְחַיֵּה מֵתִים אַתָּה רַב לְהוֹשִׁיעַ ׃ מְכַלְכֵּל חַיִּים בְּחֶסֶד ׃ מְחַיֵּה מֵתִים בְּרַחֲמִים רַבִּים ׃ סוֹמֵךְ נוֹפְלִים ׃ וְרוֹפֵא חוֹלִים ׃ וּמַתִּיר אֲסוּרִים ׃ וּמְקַיֵּם אֱמוּנָתוֹ לִישֵׁנֵי עָפָר ׃ מִי כָמוֹךָ בַּעַל גְּבוּרוֹת וּמִי דוֹמֶה לָּךְ ׃ מֶלֶךְ מֵמִית וּמְחַיֶּה ׃ וּמַצְמִיחַ יְשׁוּעָה ׃ וְנֶאֱמָן אַתָּה לְהַחֲיוֹת מֵתִים ׃ בָּרוּךְ אַתָּה יְיָ ׃ מְחַיֵּה הַמֵּתִים ׃

נְקַדֵּשׁ אֶת־שִׁמְךָ בָּעוֹלָם כְּשֵׁם שֶׁמַּקְדִּישִׁים אוֹתוֹ בִּשְׁמֵי מָרוֹם כַּכָּתוּב עַל יַד נְבִיאֶךָ ׃ וְקָרָא זֶה אֶל זֶה וְאָמַר ׃

קָדוֹשׁ קָדוֹשׁ קָדוֹשׁ יְיָ צְבָאוֹת ׃ מְלֹא כָל־הָאָרֶץ כְּבוֹדוֹ ׃

לְעֻמָּתָם בָּרוּךְ יֹאמֵרוּ ׃

בָּרוּךְ כְּבוֹד יְיָ מִמְּקוֹמוֹ ׃

וּבְדִבְרֵי קָדְשְׁךָ כָּתוּב לֵאמֹר ׃

יִמְלֹךְ יְיָ לְעוֹלָם אֱלֹהַיִךְ צִיּוֹן לְדֹר וָדֹר ׃ הַלְלוּיָהּ ׃

לְדוֹר וָדוֹר נַגִּיד גָּדְלֶךָ ׃ וּלְנֵצַח נְצָחִים קְדֻשָּׁתְךָ נַקְדִּישׁ ׃ וְשִׁבְחֲךָ אֱלֹהֵינוּ מִפִּינוּ לֹא יָמוּשׁ לְעוֹלָם וָעֶד ׃ כִּי אֵל מֶלֶךְ גָּדוֹל וְקָדוֹשׁ אָתָּה ׃ בָּרוּךְ אַתָּה יְיָ ׃ הָאֵל הַקָּדוֹשׁ ׃

THE
AMIDAH   Lord, open my lips and my mouth shall declare Your praise.

GOD OF
HISTORY   Blessed are You, Lord our God, and God of our fathers, God of Abraham, God of Isaac, and God of Jacob, the great, the mighty, and the awesome God, God beyond, generous in love and kindness, and possessing all. He remembers the good deeds of our fathers, and therefore in love brings rescue to the generations, for such is His being. The king who helps and saves and shields. Blessed are You Lord, the shield of Abraham.

GOD OF
MIGHT   You, O Lord, are the endless power that renews life beyond death; You are the greatness that saves. You care for the living with love. You renew life beyond death with unending mercy. You support the falling, and heal the sick. You free prisoners, and keep faith with those who sleep in the dust. Who can perform such mighty deeds, and who can compare with You, a king who brings death and life, and renews salvation. You are faithful to renew life beyond death. Blessed are You Lord, who renews life beyond death.

GOD OF
HOLINESS   We sanctify Your name in the world as they sanctify it in the highest heavens; as it is written by the hand of Your prophet: And they called to each other and said:

Holy, holy, holy is the Lord of all creation, the whole earth is full of His glory.

They cry in answer, 'Blessed!'

Blessed is His glory revealed in every place.

And in Your holy writing it is said:

The Lord shall rule forever! Zion, He is your God for all generations! Praise the Lord!

We declare Your greatness to all generations, and to all eternity we proclaim Your holiness. Your praise shall never depart from our mouth, for You are God, the great and holy king.

Blessed are You Lord, the holy God.

אַתָּה אֶחָד וְשִׁמְךָ אֶחָד · וּמִי כְּעַמְּךָ יִשְׂרָאֵל גּוֹי אֶחָד בָּאָרֶץ · תִּפְאֶרֶת גְּדֻלָּה · וַעֲטֶרֶת יְשׁוּעָה · יוֹם מְנוּחָה וּקְדֻשָּׁה לְעַמְּךָ נָתָתָּ · אַבְרָהָם יָגֵל · יִצְחָק יְרַנֵּן · יַעֲקֹב וּבָנָיו יָנוּחוּ בוֹ · מְנוּחַת אַהֲבָה וּנְדָבָה · מְנוּחַת אֱמֶת וֶאֱמוּנָה · מְנוּחַת שָׁלוֹם וְשַׁלְוָה וְהַשְׁקֵט וָבֶטַח · מְנוּחָה שְׁלֵמָה שָׁאַתָּה רוֹצֶה בָּהּ · יַכִּירוּ בָנֶיךָ וְיֵדְעוּ כִּי מֵאִתְּךָ הִיא מְנוּחָתָם וְעַל מְנוּחָתָם יַקְדִּישׁוּ אֶת־שְׁמֶךָ:

אֱלֹהֵינוּ וֵאלֹהֵי אֲבוֹתֵינוּ · רְצֵה־נָא בִמְנוּחָתֵנוּ · קַדְּשֵׁנוּ בְּמִצְוֹתֶיךָ · שִׂים חֶלְקֵנוּ בְּתוֹרָתֶךָ · שַׂבְּעֵנוּ מִטּוּבֶךָ · שַׂמַּח נַפְשֵׁנוּ בִּישׁוּעָתֶךָ · וְטַהֵר לִבֵּנוּ לְעָבְדְּךָ בֶּאֱמֶת · וְהַנְחִילֵנוּ יְיָ אֱלֹהֵינוּ בְּאַהֲבָה וּבְרָצוֹן שַׁבַּת קָדְשֶׁךָ · וְיָנוּחוּ בָהּ כָּל־ יִשְׂרָאֵל מְקַדְּשֵׁי שְׁמֶךָ: בָּרוּךְ אַתָּה יְיָ · מְקַדֵּשׁ הַשַּׁבָּת:

רְצֵה יְיָ אֱלֹהֵינוּ בְּעַמְּךָ יִשְׂרָאֵל · וְלִתְפִלָּתָם שְׁעֵה · וּבְרַחֲמֶיךָ הָרַבִּים תַּחְפֹּץ בָּנוּ וְתַשְׁרֶה שְׁכִינָתְךָ עַל צִיּוֹן · וְתֶחֱזֶינָה עֵינֵינוּ בְּשׁוּבְךָ לְצִיּוֹן בְּרַחֲמִים · בָּרוּךְ אַתָּה יְיָ · הַמַּחֲזִיר שְׁכִינָתוֹ לְצִיּוֹן:

מוֹדִים אֲנַחְנוּ לָךְ שָׁאַתָּה הוּא יְיָ אֱלֹהֵינוּ וֵאלֹהֵי אֲבוֹתֵינוּ לְעוֹלָם וָעֶד · צוּרֵנוּ צוּר חַיֵּינוּ וּמָגֵן יִשְׁעֵנוּ אַתָּה הוּא לְדוֹר וָדוֹר: נוֹדֶה לְּךָ וּנְסַפֵּר תְּהִלָּתֶךָ עַל חַיֵּינוּ הַמְּסוּרִים בְּיָדֶךָ · וְעַל נִשְׁמוֹתֵינוּ הַפְּקוּדוֹת לָךְ · וְעַל נִסֶּיךָ שֶׁבְּכָל־יוֹם עִמָּנוּ · וְעַל נִפְלְאוֹתֶיךָ וְטוֹבוֹתֶיךָ שֶׁבְּכָל־עֵת עֶרֶב וָבֹקֶר וְצָהֳרָיִם: הַטּוֹב כִּי לֹא כָלוּ רַחֲמֶיךָ · הַמְרַחֵם כִּי לֹא תַמּוּ חֲסָדֶיךָ · כִּי מֵעוֹלָם קִוִּינוּ לָךְ:

You are One and Your name is One, and who is like Your people Israel, a nation unique on the earth. A splendid greatness, a crown of salvation is the day of rest and holiness You gave to Your people. Abraham was glad, Isaac rejoiced, Jacob and his sons rested on it. Rest given freely in love, true and faithful rest, peaceful, tranquil rest, quiet and secure—the perfect rest that You desire. May Your children realise and know that their rest comes from You, and through their rest they make Your name holy.

Our God and God of our fathers, may our rest be pleasing to You. Make us holy by doing Your commands and let us share in the work of Your Torah. Make us content with Your goodness and let our souls know the joy of Your salvation. Purify our hearts to serve You in truth. In Your love and goodwill let us inherit Your holy Sabbath and may all Israel who seek holiness find in it their rest. Blessed are You Lord, who makes the Sabbath holy.

THANKS-GIVING AND PEACE Lord our God, be pleased with Your people Israel and listen to their prayers. In Your great mercy delight in us so that Your presence may rest upon Zion. Our eyes look forward to Your return to Zion in mercy! Blessed are You Lord, who restores His presence to Zion.

We declare with gratitude that You are our God and the God of our fathers forever. You are our rock, the rock of our life and the shield that saves us. In every generation we thank You and recount Your praise for our lives held in Your hand, for our souls that are in Your care, and for the signs of Your presence that are with us every day. At every moment, at evening, morning and noon, we experience Your wonders and Your goodness. You are goodness itself, for Your mercy has no end. You are mercy itself, for Your love has no limit. Forever have we put our hope in You.

וְעַל כֻּלָּם יִתְבָּרַךְ וְיִתְרוֹמַם וְיִתְנַשֵּׂא תָּמִיד שִׁמְךָ מַלְכֵּנוּ
לְעוֹלָם וָעֶד: וְכָל־הַחַיִּים יוֹדוּךָ סֶּלָה· וִיהַלְלוּ וִיבָרְכוּ
אֶת־שִׁמְךָ הַגָּדוֹל בֶּאֱמֶת· הָאֵל יְשׁוּעָתֵנוּ וְעֶזְרָתֵנוּ סֶלָה:
בָּרוּךְ אַתָּה יְיָ· הַטּוֹב שִׁמְךָ וּלְךָ נָאֶה לְהוֹדוֹת:

שָׁלוֹם רָב עַל יִשְׂרָאֵל עַמְּךָ תָּשִׂים לְעוֹלָם· כִּי אַתָּה הוּא
מֶלֶךְ אָדוֹן לְכָל־הַשָּׁלוֹם· וְטוֹב בְּעֵינֶיךָ לְבָרֵךְ אֶת־עַמְּךָ
יִשְׂרָאֵל בְּכָל־עֵת וּבְכָל־שָׁעָה בִּשְׁלוֹמֶךָ: בָּרוּךְ אַתָּה יְיָ·
הַמְבָרֵךְ אֶת־עַמּוֹ יִשְׂרָאֵל בַּשָּׁלוֹם:

אֱלֹהַי נְצוֹר לְשׁוֹנִי מֵרָע· וּשְׂפָתוֹתַי מִדַּבֵּר מִרְמָה·
וְלִמְקַלְלַי נַפְשִׁי תִדּוֹם· וְנַפְשִׁי כֶּעָפָר לַכֹּל תִּהְיֶה: פְּתַח
לִבִּי בְּתוֹרָתֶךָ· וְאַחֲרֵי מִצְוֹתֶיךָ תִּרְדּוֹף נַפְשִׁי· וְכָל־הַקָּמִים
עָלַי לְרָעָה מְהֵרָה הָפֵר עֲצָתָם וְקַלְקֵל מַחְשְׁבוֹתָם: יִהְיוּ
לְרָצוֹן אִמְרֵי־פִי· וְהֶגְיוֹן לִבִּי לְפָנֶיךָ· יְהֹוָה צוּרִי וְגֹאֲלִי:
עֹשֶׂה שָׁלוֹם בִּמְרוֹמָיו הוּא יַעֲשֶׂה שָׁלוֹם עָלֵינוּ וְעַל
כָּל־יִשְׂרָאֵל· וְאִמְרוּ אָמֵן:

עָלֵינוּ לְשַׁבֵּחַ לַאֲדוֹן הַכֹּל לָתֵת גְּדֻלָּה לְיוֹצֵר בְּרֵאשִׁית·
אֲשֶׁר בָּחַר־בָּנוּ מִכָּל־הָעַמִּים· וְנָתַן־לָנוּ אֶת־
תּוֹרָתוֹ· וַאֲנַחְנוּ כּוֹרְעִים וּמִשְׁתַּחֲוִים וּמוֹדִים לִפְנֵי מֶלֶךְ מַלְכֵי
הַמְּלָכִים הַקָּדוֹשׁ בָּרוּךְ הוּא· שֶׁהוּא נוֹטֶה שָׁמַיִם וְיוֹסֵד
אָרֶץ· וּמוֹשַׁב יְקָרוֹ בַּשָּׁמַיִם מִמַּעַל וּשְׁכִינַת עֻזּוֹ בְּגָבְהֵי
מְרוֹמִים: הוּא אֱלֹהֵינוּ· אֵין עוֹד· אֱמֶת מַלְכֵּנוּ· אֶפֶס
זוּלָתוֹ· כַּכָּתוּב בְּתוֹרָתוֹ· וְיָדַעְתָּ הַיּוֹם וַהֲשֵׁבֹתָ אֶל־לְבָבֶךָ
כִּי יְיָ הוּא הָאֱלֹהִים בַּשָּׁמַיִם מִמַּעַל וְעַל־הָאָרֶץ מִתָּחַת
אֵין עוֹד:

And for all these things may Your name, our king, be blessed, exalted and honoured forever and ever. May every living being thank You; may they praise and bless Your great name in truth for You are the God who saves and helps us. Blessed are You Lord, known as goodness, whom it is right to praise.

Set true peace upon Your people Israel forever. For You are the king, the Lord of all peace, and in Your eyes it is good to bless Your people Israel at every time and in every hour with Your peace. Blessed are You Lord, who blesses His people Israel with peace.

MEDI-TATION My God, keep my tongue from causing harm and my lips from telling lies. Let me be silent if people curse me, my soul still humble and at peace with all. Open my heart to Your teaching, and give me the will to practise it. May the plans and schemes of those who seek my harm come to nothing. May the words of my mouth and the meditation of my heart be acceptable to You, O Lord, my rock and my redeemer.

May He who makes peace in the highest bring this peace upon us and upon all Israel. Amen.

BUILDING THE KINGDOM OF GOD: THE DUTY OF ISRAEL It is our duty to praise the Lord of all, to recognise the greatness of the creator of first things, who has chosen us from all peoples by giving us His Torah. Therefore we bend low and submit, and give thanks before the King above the kings of kings, the Holy One, blessed be He. He extends the limits of space and makes the world firm. His glory extends through the universe beyond, and the presence of His strength into farthest space. He is our God; no other exists. Our king is truth; the rest is nothing. It is written in His Torah: 'Realise this today and take it to heart—it is the Lord who is God in the heavens above and on the earth beneath; no other exists.'

עַל־כֵּן נְקַוֶּה לְךָ יְיָ אֱלֹהֵינוּ לִרְאוֹת מְהֵרָה בְּתִפְאֶרֶת עֻזֶּךָ · לְהַעֲבִיר גִּלּוּלִים מִן הָאָרֶץ וְהָאֱלִילִים כָּרוֹת יִכָּרֵתוּן · לְתַקֵּן עוֹלָם בְּמַלְכוּת שַׁדַּי וְכָל־בְּנֵי בָשָׂר יִקְרְאוּ בִשְׁמֶךָ · לְהַפְנוֹת אֵלֶיךָ כָּל־רִשְׁעֵי אָרֶץ : יַכִּירוּ וְיֵדְעוּ כָּל־יוֹשְׁבֵי תֵבֵל כִּי לְךָ תִּכְרַע כָּל־בֶּרֶךְ תִּשָּׁבַע כָּל־לָשׁוֹן : לְפָנֶיךָ יְיָ אֱלֹהֵינוּ יִכְרְעוּ וְיִפֹּלוּ · וְלִכְבוֹד שִׁמְךָ יְקָר יִתֵּנוּ · וִיקַבְּלוּ כֻלָּם אֶת־עֹל מַלְכוּתֶךָ · וְתִמְלוֹךְ עֲלֵיהֶם מְהֵרָה לְעוֹלָם וָעֶד · כִּי הַמַּלְכוּת שֶׁלְּךָ הִיא וּלְעוֹלְמֵי עַד תִּמְלוֹךְ בְּכָבוֹד · כַּכָּתוּב בְּתוֹרָתֶךָ · יְהֹוָה יִמְלֹךְ לְעוֹלָם וָעֶד : וְנֶאֱמַר · וְהָיָה יְהֹוָה לְמֶלֶךְ עַל־כָּל־הָאָרֶץ בַּיּוֹם הַהוּא יִהְיֶה יְהֹוָה אֶחָד וּשְׁמוֹ אֶחָד :

יִתְגַּדַּל וְיִתְקַדַּשׁ שְׁמֵהּ רַבָּא בְּעָלְמָא דִי־בְרָא כִרְעוּתֵהּ · וְיַמְלִיךְ מַלְכוּתֵהּ בְּחַיֵּיכוֹן וּבְיוֹמֵיכוֹן וּבְחַיֵּי דִי־כָל־בֵּית יִשְׂרָאֵל בַּעֲגָלָא וּבִזְמַן קָרִיב · וְאִמְרוּ אָמֵן :
יְהֵא שְׁמֵהּ רַבָּא מְבָרַךְ לְעָלַם וּלְעָלְמֵי עָלְמַיָּא ·
יִתְבָּרַךְ וְיִשְׁתַּבַּח וְיִתְפָּאַר וְיִתְרוֹמַם וְיִתְנַשֵּׂא וְיִתְהַדָּר וְיִתְעַלֶּה וְיִתְהַלָּל שְׁמֵהּ דִּי־קֻדְשָׁא · בְּרִיךְ הוּא · לְעֵלָּא מִן־כָּל־בִּרְכָתָא וְשִׁירָתָא תֻּשְׁבְּחָתָא וְנֶחֱמָתָא דִּי־אֲמִירָן בְּעָלְמָא · וְאִמְרוּ אָמֵן :
יְהֵא שְׁלָמָא רַבָּא מִן־שְׁמַיָּא וְחַיִּים עָלֵינוּ וְעַל־כָּל־יִשְׂרָאֵל · וְאִמְרוּ אָמֵן :
עֹשֶׂה שָׁלוֹם בִּמְרוֹמָיו הוּא יַעֲשֶׂה שָׁלוֹם עָלֵינוּ וְעַל־כָּל־יִשְׂרָאֵל · וְאִמְרוּ אָמֵן :

THE HOPE   Therefore, Lord our God, we put our hope in You. Soon let us
FOR   witness the glory of Your power; when the worship of material
MANKIND   things shall pass away from the earth, and prejudice and superstition shall at last be cut off; when the world will be set right by the
rule of God, and all mankind shall speak out in Your name, and all
the wicked of the earth shall turn to You. Then all who inhabit this
world shall meet in understanding, and shall know that to You alone
each one shall submit, and pledge himself in every tongue. In Your
presence, Lord our God, they shall bow down and be humble,
honouring the glory of Your being. All shall accept the duty of
building Your kingdom, so that Your reign of goodness shall come
soon and last forever. For Yours alone is the true kingdom, and only
the glory of Your rule endures forever. So it is written in Your Torah:

'The Lord shall rule forever and ever.'

So it is prophesied:

'The Lord shall be as a king over all the earth. On that day the
Lord shall be One, and known as One.'

Let us magnify and let us sanctify the great name of God in the
world which He created according to His will. May His kingdom
come in your lifetime, and in your days, and in the lifetime of the
family of Israel—quickly and speedily may it come. Amen.

May the greatness of His being be blessed from eternity to
eternity.

Let us bless and let us extol, let us tell aloud and let us raise aloft,
let us set on high and let us honour, let us exalt and let us praise the
Holy One—blessed be He!—though He is far beyond any blessing
or song, any honour or any consolation that can be spoken of in this
world. Amen.

May great peace from heaven and the gift of life be granted to us
and to all the family of Israel. Amen.

May He who makes peace in the highest bring this peace upon us
and upon all Israel. Amen.

A chapter from the Sayings of the Fathers is read here.

פרקי אבות

כָּל־יִשְׂרָאֵל יֵשׁ לָהֶם חֵלֶק לָעוֹלָם הַבָּא · שֶׁנֶּאֱמַר וְעַמֵּךְ
כֻּלָּם צַדִּיקִים לְעוֹלָם יִירְשׁוּ אָרֶץ · נֵצֶר מַטָּעַי מַעֲשֵׂי יָדַי
לְהִתְפָּאֵר :

פרק ראשון

א מֹשֶׁה קִבֵּל תּוֹרָה מִסִּינַי · וּמְסָרָהּ לִיהוֹשֻׁעַ וִיהוֹשֻׁעַ לִזְקֵנִים
וּזְקֵנִים לִנְבִיאִים וּנְבִיאִים מְסָרוּהָ לְאַנְשֵׁי כְנֶסֶת הַגְּדוֹלָה ·
הֵם אָמְרוּ שְׁלֹשָׁה דְבָרִים · הֱווּ מְתוּנִים בַּדִּין וְהַעֲמִידוּ
תַלְמִידִים הַרְבֵּה וַעֲשׂוּ סְיָג לַתּוֹרָה :

ב שִׁמְעוֹן הַצַּדִּיק הָיָה מִשְּׁיָרֵי כְנֶסֶת הַגְּדוֹלָה · הוּא הָיָה
אוֹמֵר · עַל־שְׁלֹשָׁה דְבָרִים הָעוֹלָם עוֹמֵד · עַל הַתּוֹרָה וְעַל
הָעֲבוֹדָה וְעַל גְּמִילוּת חֲסָדִים :

ג אַנְטִיגְנוֹס אִישׁ סוֹכוֹ קִבֵּל מִשִּׁמְעוֹן הַצַּדִּיק · הוּא הָיָה
אוֹמֵר · אַל־תִּהְיוּ כַּעֲבָדִים הַמְשַׁמְּשִׁים אֶת־הָרַב עַל־מְנָת
לְקַבֵּל פְּרָס · אֶלָּא הֱווּ כַּעֲבָדִים הַמְשַׁמְּשִׁים אֶת־הָרַב שֶׁלֹּא
עַל־מְנָת לְקַבֵּל פְּרָס · וִיהִי מוֹרָא שָׁמַיִם עֲלֵיכֶם :

ד יוֹסֵי בֶּן־יוֹעֶזֶר אִישׁ צְרֵדָה וְיוֹסֵי בֶּן־יוֹחָנָן אִישׁ יְרוּשָׁלַיִם
קִבְּלוּ מֵהֶם · יוֹסֵי בֶּן־יוֹעֶזֶר אִישׁ צְרֵדָה אוֹמֵר · יְהִי בֵיתְךָ
בֵית וַעַד לַחֲכָמִים וֶהֱוֵה מִתְאַבֵּק בַּעֲפַר רַגְלֵיהֶם וֶהֱוֵה
שׁוֹתֶה בַצָּמָא אֶת־דִּבְרֵיהֶם :

ה יוֹסֵי בֶּן־יוֹחָנָן אִישׁ יְרוּשָׁלַיִם אוֹמֵר · יְהִי בֵיתְךָ פָּתוּחַ
לָרְוָחָה וְיִהְיוּ עֲנִיִּים בְּנֵי בֵיתֶךָ :

FROM THE
SAYINGS OF THE FATHERS

All Israel has a share in the world to come, as it is said in the Prophets (*Isaiah 60: 21*): 'And your people shall all be righteous. They shall inherit the earth forever, the branch I planted, the work of My hands to bring Me glory.'

From Chapter 1

1. Moses received Torah on Sinai, and handed it on to Joshua, and Joshua to the elders, and the elders to the prophets, and the prophets handed it on to the men of the Great Assembly. They said three things, Be patient and careful in judgment, raise up many disciples, and make a fence to protect the Torah.

2. Simon the Just was one of the last survivors of the Great Assembly. He used to say, Civilisation is based on three things— on Torah, on service and on loving deeds.

3. Antigonos of Socho received tradition from Simon the Just. He used to say, Do not be like servants who serve their master in order to get a reward. Instead be like servants who serve their master with no thought of reward, and let the awe of heaven be upon you.

4. Yose ben Yoezer of Tseredah and Yose ben Yochanan of Jerusalem received tradition from those who came before. The former says, Let your house be a meeting-place for the wise, sit in the dust at their feet, and drink in their words thirstily.

5. The latter says, Let your house be open wide and the poor be members of your household.

ו יְהוֹשֻׁעַ בֶּן־פְּרַחְיָה וְנִתַּי הָאַרְבֵּלִי קִבְּלוּ מֵהֶם · יְהוֹשֻׁעַ בֶּן־
פְּרַחְיָה אוֹמֵר · עֲשֵׂה לְךָ רַב וּקְנֵה לְךָ חָבֵר וֶהֱוֵה דָן אֶת־
כָּל־הָאָדָם לְכַף זְכוּת:

ז נִתַּי הָאַרְבֵּלִי אוֹמֵר · הַרְחֵק מִשָּׁכֵן רָע וְאַל־תִּתְחַבֵּר לְרָשָׁע
וְאַל־תִּתְיָאֵשׁ מִן־הַפֻּרְעָנוּת:

ח יְהוּדָה בֶּן־טַבַּי וְשִׁמְעוֹן בֶּן־שָׁטַח קִבְּלוּ מֵהֶם · יְהוּדָה
בֶּן־טַבַּי אוֹמֵר · אַל־תַּעַשׂ עַצְמְךָ כְּעוֹרְכֵי הַדַּיָּנִים · וּכְשֶׁיִּהְיוּ
בַּעֲלֵי הַדִּין עוֹמְדִים לְפָנֶיךָ יִהְיוּ בְעֵינֶיךָ כִּרְשָׁעִים ·
וּכְשֶׁנִּפְטָרִים מִלְּפָנֶיךָ יִהְיוּ בְעֵינֶיךָ כְּזַכָּאִים כְּשֶׁקִּבְּלוּ עֲלֵיהֶם
אֶת־הַדִּין:

ט שִׁמְעוֹן בֶּן־שָׁטַח אוֹמֵר · הֱוֵה מַרְבֶּה לַחֲקוֹר אֶת־הָעֵדִים ·
וֶהֱוֵה זָהִיר בִּדְבָרֶיךָ שֶׁמָּא מִתּוֹכָם יִלְמְדוּ לְשַׁקֵּר:

י שְׁמַעְיָה וְאַבְטַלְיוֹן קִבְּלוּ מֵהֶם · שְׁמַעְיָה אוֹמֵר · אֱהַב אֶת־
הַמְּלָאכָה וּשְׂנָא אֶת־הָרַבָּנוּת וְאַל־תִּתְוַדַּע לָרָשׁוּת:

יא אַבְטַלְיוֹן אוֹמֵר · חֲכָמִים הִזָּהֲרוּ בְּדִבְרֵיכֶם · שֶׁמָּא יָשֻׁתּוּ
הַתַּלְמִידִים הַבָּאִים אַחֲרֵיכֶם וְיָמוּתוּ וְנִמְצָא שֵׁם שָׁמַיִם
מִתְחַלֵּל:

יב הִלֵּל וְשַׁמַּי קִבְּלוּ מֵהֶם · הִלֵּל אוֹמֵר · הֱוֵה מִתַּלְמִידָיו
שֶׁל־אַהֲרֹן · אוֹהֵב שָׁלוֹם וְרוֹדֵף שָׁלוֹם אוֹהֵב אֶת־הַבְּרִיּוֹת
וּמְקָרְבָן לַתּוֹרָה:

יג הוּא הָיָה אוֹמֵר · נְגִיד שְׁמָא אֲבַד שְׁמֵהּ · וּדְלָא מוֹסִיף יָסֵף
וּדְלָא יַלִּיף קְטָלָא חַיָּב · וּדְאִשְׁתַּמַּשׁ בְּתָגָא חֲלָף:

יד הוּא הָיָה אוֹמֵר · אִם אֵין אֲנִי לִי מִי לִי · וּכְשֶׁאֲנִי לְעַצְמִי
מָה אֲנִי · וְאִם לֹא עַכְשָׁו אֵימָתָי:

6. Joshua ben Perachyah and Nittai the Arbelite received tradition from those who came before. The former says, Find yourself a teacher, get yourself a friend, and put the best construction on every man's conduct.

7. The latter says, Keep away from a bad neighbour, do not associate with the wicked, and do not shrug off the thought of retribution.

8. Judah ben Tabbai and Simon ben Shetach received tradition from those who came before. The former says, Do not be like those who influence the judges in their favour. When the parties to a dispute are standing before you, consider them both equally guilty, but as soon as they have accepted the verdict consider them both equally innocent.

9. The latter says, Examine the witnesses thoroughly, and be careful what you say, for from your words they can learn to lie.

10. Shemayah and Avtalyon received tradition from those who came before. The former says, Love work, hate domination and do not get too familiar with a corrupt power.

11. The latter says, Wise men, watch your words! For your pupils may drink them up and die, and the name of heaven be despised.

12. Hillel and Shammai received tradition from those who came before. Hillel says, Be a disciple of Aaron, loving peace and pursuing peace, loving His creatures and drawing them close to the Torah.

13. He used to say, A name made great is a name destroyed. Whoever does not increase his knowledge decreases it; whoever does not learn destroys his life. Whoever uses the crown of religion for his own worldly advantage must perish.

14. He used to say, If I am not for myself, who is for me? But if I am only for myself, what am I? And if not now, when?

טו שַׁמַּאי אוֹמֵר· עֲשֵׂה תוֹרָתְךָ קֶבַע· אֱמוֹר מְעַט וַעֲשֵׂה הַרְבֵּה· וֶהֱוֵי מְקַבֵּל אֶת־כָּל־הָאָדָם בְּסֵבֶר פָּנִים יָפוֹת:

טז רַבָּן גַּמְלִיאֵל אוֹמֵר· עֲשֵׂה לְךָ רַב וְהִסְתַּלֵּק מִן הַסָּפֵק וְאַל־תַּרְבֶּה לְעַשֵּׂר אֻמָּדוֹת:

יז שִׁמְעוֹן בְּנוֹ אוֹמֵר· כָּל־יָמַי גָּדַלְתִּי בֵּין הַחֲכָמִים וְלֹא מָצָאתִי לַגּוּף טוֹב מִשְּׁתִיקָה· וְלֹא הַמִּדְרָשׁ עִקָּר אֶלָּא הַמַּעֲשֶׂה· וְכָל־הַמַּרְבֶּה דְבָרִים מֵבִיא חֵטְא:

יח רַבָּן שִׁמְעוֹן בֶּן־גַּמְלִיאֵל אוֹמֵר· עַל־שְׁלֹשָׁה דְבָרִים הָעוֹלָם קַיָּם· עַל־הָאֱמֶת וְעַל־הַדִּין וְעַל־הַשָּׁלוֹם:

פרק שני

א רַבִּי אוֹמֵר· אֵיזוֹ הִיא דֶרֶךְ יְשָׁרָה שֶׁיָּבוֹר לוֹ הָאָדָם· כָּל־שֶׁהִיא תִפְאֶרֶת לְעֹשֶׂהָ וְתִפְאֶרֶת לוֹ מִן הָאָדָם· וֶהֱוֵי זָהִיר בְּמִצְוָה קַלָּה כְּבַחֲמוּרָה שֶׁאֵין אַתָּה יוֹדֵעַ מַתַּן שְׂכָרָן שֶׁל־מִצְוֹת· וֶהֱוֵי מְחַשֵּׁב הֶפְסֵד מִצְוָה כְּנֶגֶד שְׂכָרָהּ וּשְׂכַר עֲבֵרָה כְּנֶגֶד הֶפְסֵדָהּ: הִסְתַּכֵּל בִּשְׁלֹשָׁה דְבָרִים וְאֵין אַתָּה בָא לִידֵי עֲבֵרָה· דַּע מַה־לְּמַעְלָה מִמְּךָ עַיִן רוֹאָה וְאֹזֶן שׁוֹמַעַת וְכָל־מַעֲשֶׂיךָ בַּסֵּפֶר נִכְתָּבִים:

ב רַבָּן גַּמְלִיאֵל בְּנוֹ שֶׁל־רַבִּי יְהוּדָה הַנָּשִׂיא אוֹמֵר· יָפֶה תַלְמוּד תּוֹרָה עִם דֶּרֶךְ אֶרֶץ שֶׁיְּגִיעַת שְׁנֵיהֶם מַשְׁכַּחַת עָוֹן· וְכָל־תּוֹרָה שֶׁאֵין עִמָּהּ מְלָאכָה סוֹפָהּ בְּטֵלָה וְגוֹרֶרֶת עָוֹן· וְכָל־הָעוֹסְקִים עִם־הַצִּבּוּר יִהְיוּ עוֹסְקִים עִמָּהֶם לְשֵׁם שָׁמַיִם שֶׁזְּכוּת אֲבוֹתָם מְסַיַּעְתָּם וְצִדְקָתָם עוֹמֶדֶת לָעַד· וְאַתֶּם מַעֲלֶה אֲנִי עֲלֵיכֶם שָׂכָר הַרְבֵּה כְּאִלּוּ עֲשִׂיתֶם:

15. Shammai says, Make Torah study a fixed habit. Say little and do much, and welcome everyone cheerfully.

16. Rabban Gamliel used to say, Find yourself a teacher and get rid of doubt, and do not get used to guessing your taxes.

17. Simon his son says, All my life I grew up among the wise and have found nothing better for anyone than silence. The main thing is not theory but practice, and one who talks too much causes sin.

18. Rabban Simon ben Gamliel says, Civilisation is preserved by three things: by truth, by justice and by peace.

From Chapter 2

1. Rabbi says, What is the upright course a man should choose? That which brings honour to the one who does it, and for which he is honoured by his fellow-men. Be just as careful with a light commandment as with a weighty one, for you do not know the reward given for each commandment. Reckon the loss incurred by fulfilling a commandment against the reward for it; and the profit gained by transgressing against the loss it entails. Consider three things and you will not come into the power of sin. Know what is above you—an eye that sees, an ear that hears, and that all your deeds are written in a book.

2. Rabban Gamliel, the son of Rabbi Judah the Prince, says, It is an excellent thing to combine the study of Torah with a trade or profession, for the labour necessary for both together puts sin out of mind. Study of Torah, however, which is not combined with work, ends in futility and becomes the cause of sin. Let all who work for the congregation do it for the sake of heaven. Then the merit of their fathers will come to their aid and their righteousness will last forever. (And God will say,) 'And as for you, I credit you with a great reward, as though you had done it all yourselves.'

ג הֱווּ זְהִירִים בִּרְשׁוּת שֶׁאֵין מְקָרְבִים לוֹ לְאָדָם אֶלָּא לְצֹרֶךְ עַצְמָם · נִרְאִים כְּאוֹהֲבִים בִּשְׁעַת הֲנָאָתָם וְאֵין עוֹמְדִים לוֹ לְאָדָם בִּשְׁעַת דָּחֳקוֹ:

ד הוּא הָיָה אוֹמֵר · עֲשֵׂה רְצוֹנוֹ כִרְצוֹנֶךָ כְּדֵי שֶׁיַּעֲשֶׂה רְצוֹנְךָ כִּרְצוֹנוֹ · בַּטֵּל רְצוֹנְךָ מִפְּנֵי רְצוֹנוֹ כְּדֵי שֶׁיְּבַטֵּל רְצוֹן אֲחֵרִים מִפְּנֵי רְצוֹנֶךָ:

ה הִלֵּל אוֹמֵר · אַל־תִּפְרֹשׁ מִן־הַצִּבּוּר · וְאַל־תַּאֲמֵן בְּעַצְמְךָ עַד יוֹם מוֹתְךָ · וְאַל־תָּדִין אֶת־חֲבֵרְךָ עַד שֶׁתַּגִּיעַ לִמְקוֹמוֹ · וְאַל־תֹּאמַר דָּבָר שֶׁאִי אֶפְשָׁר לִשְׁמוֹעַ שֶׁסּוֹפוֹ לְהִשָּׁמֵעַ · וְאַל־תֹּאמַר לִכְשֶׁאֶפָּנֶה אֶשְׁנֶה שֶׁמָּא לֹא תִפָּנֶה:

ו הוּא הָיָה אוֹמֵר · אֵין בּוֹר יְרֵא חֵטְא וְלֹא עַם הָאָרֶץ חָסִיד וְלֹא הַבַּיְשָׁן לָמֵד וְלֹא הַקַּפְּדָן מְלַמֵּד · וְלֹא כָל־הַמַּרְבֶּה בִסְחוֹרָה מַחְכִּים · וּבַמָּקוֹם שֶׁאֵין אֲנָשִׁים הִשְׁתַּדֵּל לִהְיוֹת אִישׁ:

ז אַף הוּא רָאָה גֻּלְגֹּלֶת אַחַת שֶׁצָּפָה עַל־פְּנֵי הַמָּיִם · אָמַר לָהּ · עַל דְּאַטֵּפְתְּ אַטְפוּךְ וְסוֹף מְטַיְּפַיִךְ יְטוּפוּן:

ט רַבָּן יוֹחָנָן בֶּן־זַכַּי קִבֵּל מֵהִלֵּל וּמִשַּׁמַּי · הוּא הָיָה אוֹמֵר · אִם לָמַדְתָּ תּוֹרָה הַרְבֵּה אַל־תַּחֲזֵק טוֹבָה לְעַצְמְךָ כִּי לְכָךְ נוֹצָרְתָּ:

יג אָמַר לָהֶם · צְאוּ וּרְאוּ אֵיזוֹ הִיא דֶרֶךְ טוֹבָה שֶׁיִּדְבַּק בָּהּ הָאָדָם · רַבִּי אֱלִיעֶזֶר אוֹמֵר עַיִן טוֹבָה · רַבִּי יְהוֹשֻׁעַ אוֹמֵר חָבֵר טוֹב · רַבִּי יוֹסֵי אוֹמֵר שָׁכֵן טוֹב · רַבִּי שִׁמְעוֹן אוֹמֵר הָרוֹאֶה אֶת־הַנּוֹלָד · רַבִּי אֶלְעָזָר אוֹמֵר לֵב טוֹב: אָמַר לָהֶם · רוֹאֶה אֲנִי אֶת־דִּבְרֵי אֶלְעָזָר בֶּן־עֲרָךְ מִדִּבְרֵיכֶם שֶׁבִּכְלַל דְּבָרָיו דִּבְרֵיכֶם:

3. Be careful of those in power! For they draw no man near them except in their own interest. They seem like friends when it is to their own advantage, but they do not stand by a man in his hour of need.

4. He used to say, Do His will as if it were your will, so that He may do your will as if it were His will. Destroy your will for the sake of His will, so that He may destroy the will of others for the sake of your will.

5. Hillel says, Do not separate yourself from the community. Do not trust in yourself until the day of your death. Do not judge your fellow-man until you have been in his position. Do not say anything which cannot be understood at once in the hope that it will be understood in the end. And do not say 'When I have leisure I will study', perhaps you will never have leisure.

6. He used to say, A crude man cannot fear sin, an ignorant man cannot be pious, nor can a timid man learn, nor a short-tempered man teach. A man who is too pre-occupied with business cannot grow wise. Where there are no men, try to be a man!

7. Also, when he saw a skull floating on the surface of the water, he said, Because you drowned others, they drowned you, and in the end those who drowned you shall themselves be drowned.

9. Rabban Yochanan ben Zakkai received tradition from Hillel and Shammai. He used to say, If you have learnt much Torah, do not congratulate yourself, for that is why you were created.

13. He said to his disciples, Go out and see the right course a man should adopt. Rabbi Eliezer says, A kindly eye. Rabbi Joshua says, A good companion. Rabbi Yose says, A good neighbour. Rabbi Simon says, One who foresees the consequences. Rabbi Elazar says, A good heart. He said to them, I agree with the words of Elazar ben Arach, for his words include yours.

יד אָמַר לָהֶם · צְאוּ וּרְאוּ אֵיזוֹ הִיא דֶרֶךְ רָעָה שֶׁיִתְרַחֵק
מִמֶּנָּה הָאָדָם · רַבִּי אֱלִיעֶזֶר אוֹמֵר עַיִן רָעָה · רַבִּי יְהוֹשֻׁעַ
אוֹמֵר חָבֵר רָע · רַבִּי יוֹסֵי אוֹמֵר שָׁכֵן רָע · רַבִּי שִׁמְעוֹן
אוֹמֵר הַלֹּוֶה וְאֵינוֹ מְשַׁלֵּם · אֶחָד הַלֹּוֶה מִן־הָאָדָם כְּלֹוֶה
מִן־הַמָּקוֹם · רַבִּי אֶלְעָזָר אוֹמֵר לֵב רָע: אָמַר לָהֶם רוֹאֶה
אֲנִי אֶת־דִּבְרֵי אֶלְעָזָר בֶּן־עֲרָךְ מִדִּבְרֵיכֶם שֶׁבִּכְלַל דְּבָרָיו
דִּבְרֵיכֶם :

טו הֵם אָמְרוּ שְׁלֹשָׁה דְבָרִים · רַבִּי אֱלִיעֶזֶר אוֹמֵר · יְהִי כְבוֹד
חֲבֵרְךָ חָבִיב עָלֶיךָ כְּשֶׁלָּךְ · וְאַל־תְּהִי נוֹחַ לִכְעוֹס · וְשׁוּב יוֹם
אֶחָד לִפְנֵי מִיתָתְךָ · וֶהֱוֵה מִתְחַמֵּם כְּנֶגֶד אוּרָם שֶׁל־חֲכָמִים
וֶהֱוֵה זָהִיר בְּגַחַלְתָּם שֶׁלֹּא תִכָּוֶה · שֶׁנְּשִׁיכָתָם נְשִׁיכַת שׁוּעָל
וַעֲקִיצָתָם עֲקִיצַת עַקְרָב וּלְחִישָׁתָם לְחִישַׁת שָׂרָף וְכָל־
דִּבְרֵיהֶם כְּגַחֲלֵי אֵשׁ :

טז רַבִּי יְהוֹשֻׁעַ אוֹמֵר · עַיִן הָרָע וְיֵצֶר הָרָע וְשִׂנְאַת הַבְּרִיּוֹת
מוֹצִיאִים אֶת־הָאָדָם מִן־הָעוֹלָם :

יז רַבִּי יוֹסֵי אוֹמֵר · יְהִי מָמוֹן חֲבֵרְךָ חָבִיב עָלֶיךָ כְּשֶׁלָּךְ
וְהַתְקֵן עַצְמְךָ לִלְמוֹד תּוֹרָה שֶׁאֵינָה יְרֻשָּׁה־לָךְ · וְכָל־מַעֲשֶׂיךָ
יִהְיוּ לְשֵׁם שָׁמָיִם :

יח רַבִּי שִׁמְעוֹן אוֹמֵר · הֱוֵה זָהִיר בִּקְרִיאַת שְׁמַע וּבִתְפִלָּה
וּכְשֶׁאַתָּה מִתְפַּלֵּל אַל־תַּעַשׂ תְּפִלָּתְךָ קֶבַע אֶלָּא רַחֲמִים
וְתַחֲנוּנִים לִפְנֵי הַמָּקוֹם · שֶׁנֶּאֱמַר כִּי־חַנּוּן וְרַחוּם הוּא אֶרֶךְ
אַפַּיִם וְרַב־חֶסֶד וְנִחָם עַל־הָרָעָה · וְאַל־תְּהִי רָשָׁע בִּפְנֵי
עַצְמֶךָ :

יט רַבִּי אֶלְעָזָר אוֹמֵר · הֱוֵה שָׁקוּד לִלְמוֹד תּוֹרָה וְדַע מַה־
שֶׁתָּשִׁיב לְאֶפִּיקוּרוֹס וְדַע לִפְנֵי מִי אַתָּה עָמֵל וּמִי הוּא בַּעַל
מְלַאכְתְּךָ שֶׁיְּשַׁלֶּם־לָךְ שְׂכַר פְּעֻלָּתֶךָ :

14. He said to them, Go out and see the wrong course, one that a man should avoid. Rabbi Eliezer says, A grudging eye. Rabbi Joshua says, A bad companion. Rabbi Yose says, A bad neighbour. Rabbi Simon says, A borrower who does not pay back. It is the same whether he borrows from man or whether he borrows from God who is present everywhere. Rabbi Elazar says, A mean heart. He said to them, I agree with the words of Elazar ben Arach, for his words include yours.

15. Each of them said three things. Rabbi Eliezer says, Let the honour of your fellow-man be as dear to you as your own. Do not be quick to anger. Repent even one day before your death. Warm yourself at the fire of the wise, but beware of their glowing coals lest you be scorched. For their bite is the bite of a fox, and their sting the sting of a scorpion, and their hiss the hiss of a serpent, for all their words are like coals of fire.

16. Rabbi Joshua says, A grudging eye, the impulse to evil, and hatred of mankind drive a man out of the world.

17. Rabbi Yose says, Let the property of your fellow-man be as dear to you as your own. Train yourself to study Torah, for it is not yours by inheritance. And let all your actions be for the sake of heaven.

18. Rabbi Simon says, Take care when you say the *Shema* and the *Amidah*. When you pray do not make your prayer a fixed formal thing, but an appeal for mercy, a supplication before God. As it is said (*Joel 2: 13*): 'For He is gracious and merciful, long-suffering and full of love and ready to relent from threatened evil.' And do not consider yourself completely wicked.

19. Rabbi Elazar says, Be diligent in the study of Torah and know how to answer an unbeliever. Also realise in whose presence you toil, and who is the Employer who will give you the wages for your work.

כ רַבִּי טַרְפוֹן אוֹמֵר · הַיּוֹם קָצֵר וְהַמְּלָאכָה מְרֻבָּה וְהַפּוֹעֲלִים עֲצֵלִים וְהַשָּׂכָר הַרְבֵּה וּבַעַל הַבַּיִת דּוֹחֵק:

כא הוּא הָיָה אוֹמֵר · לֹא עָלֶיךָ הַמְּלָאכָה לִגְמוֹר וְלֹא אַתָּה בֶן־חוֹרִין לְהִבָּטֵל מִמֶּנָּה · אִם לָמַדְתָּ תוֹרָה הַרְבֵּה נוֹתְנִים לְךָ שָׂכָר הַרְבֵּה וְנֶאֱמָן הוּא בַּעַל מְלַאכְתְּךָ שֶׁיְּשַׁלֶּם־לְךָ שְׂכַר פְּעֻלָּתֶךָ · וְדַע שֶׁמַּתַּן שְׂכָרָם שֶׁל־צַדִּיקִים לֶעָתִיד לָבוֹא:

פרק שלישי

א עֲקַבְיָא בֶּן־מַהֲלַלְאֵל אוֹמֵר · הִסְתַּכֵּל בִּשְׁלֹשָׁה דְבָרִים וְאֵין אַתָּה בָא לִידֵי עֲבֵרָה · דַּע מֵאַיִן בָּאתָ וּלְאָן אַתָּה הוֹלֵךְ וְלִפְנֵי מִי אַתָּה עָתִיד לִתֵּן דִּין וְחֶשְׁבּוֹן:

ב רַבִּי חֲנִינָא סְגַן הַכֹּהֲנִים אוֹמֵר · הֱוֵה מִתְפַּלֵּל בִּשְׁלוֹמָהּ שֶׁל־מַלְכוּת שֶׁאַלְמָלֵא מוֹרָאָהּ אִישׁ אֶת־רֵעֵהוּ חַיִּים בְּלָעוֹ:

ג רַבִּי חֲנַנְיָא בֶּן־תְּרַדְיוֹן אוֹמֵר · שְׁנַיִם שֶׁיּוֹשְׁבִים וְיֵשׁ בֵּינֵיהֶם דִּבְרֵי תוֹרָה שְׁכִינָה שְׁרוּיָה בֵינֵיהֶם:

ו רַבִּי נְחוּנְיָא בֶּן־הַקָּנָה אוֹמֵר · כָּל־הַמְקַבֵּל עָלָיו עֹל תּוֹרָה מַעֲבִירִים מִמֶּנּוּ עֹל מַלְכוּת וְעֹל דֶּרֶךְ אֶרֶץ · וְכָל־הַפּוֹרֵק מִמֶּנּוּ עֹל תּוֹרָה נוֹתְנִים עָלָיו עֹל מַלְכוּת וְעֹל דֶּרֶךְ אֶרֶץ:

ז רַבִּי חֲלַפְתָּא בֶּן־דּוֹסָא אִישׁ כְּפַר חֲנַנְיָא אוֹמֵר · עֲשָׂרָה שֶׁיּוֹשְׁבִים וְעוֹסְקִים בַּתּוֹרָה שְׁכִינָה שְׁרוּיָה בֵינֵיהֶם · שֶׁנֶּאֱמַר אֱלֹהִים נִצָּב בַּעֲדַת־אֵל · וּמִנַּיִן אֲפִילוּ אֶחָד שֶׁנֶּאֱמַר בְּכָל־ הַמָּקוֹם אֲשֶׁר אַזְכִּיר אֶת־שְׁמִי אָבֹא אֵלֶיךָ וּבֵרַכְתִּיךָ:

ח רַבִּי אֶלְעָזָר אִישׁ בַּרְתּוֹתָא אוֹמֵר · תֶּן־לוֹ מִשֶּׁלּוֹ שֶׁאַתָּה וְשֶׁלְּךָ שֶׁלּוֹ · וְכֵן בְּדָוִד הוּא אוֹמֵר כִּי־מִמְּךָ הַכֹּל וּמִיָּדְךָ נָתַנּוּ לָךְ:

20. Rabbi Tarfon says, The day is short, and the work is great, and the labourers are sluggish, and the wages are high, and the Master of the house is insistent.

21. He used to say, It is not your duty to finish the work but you are not free to neglect it. If you learn much Torah, you will be given much reward, and faithful is your Employer to pay you the reward of your labour. But know that the reward of the righteous is in the time to come.

From Chapter 3

1. Akavya ben Mahalalel says, Keep three things in sight and you will not fall into the power of sin. Know where you come from, and where you go to, and before whom you are destined to give an account and reckoning.

2. Rabbi Chanina, the deputy High Priest says, Pray for the welfare of the government, because but for the fear it inspires men would swallow each other up alive.

3. Rabbi Chananya ben Teradion says, When two people sit together, and words of Torah pass between them, the presence of God rests between them also.

6. Rabbi Nechunya ben Hakanah says, He who takes upon himself the yoke of Torah will find relief from the yoke of politics and worldly affairs. But whoever gets rid of the yoke of Torah will find the yoke of politics and worldly affairs weighing more heavily on him.

7. Rabbi Chalafta ben Dosa, of the village of Chananya, says, When ten people sit studying Torah, God's presence dwells among them, as it is said (*Psalm 82: 1*): 'God stands in the congregation of the godly.' How do we know that this even applies to one person only? Because it is said (*Exodus 20: 21*): 'In every place where I cause My name to be remembered, I will come to you and bless you.'

8. Rabbi Elazar of Bertota says, Give Him what is His, for what you are and what you have are His. Therefore in the case of David it is said (*1 Chronicles 29: 14*): 'For everything comes from You, and we have only given You what comes from Your hand.'

ט רַבִּי יַעֲקֹב אוֹמֵר · הַמְהַלֵּךְ בַּדֶּרֶךְ וְשׁוֹנֶה וּמַפְסִיק מִמִּשְׁנָתוֹ וְאוֹמֵר מַה־נָּאֶה אִילָן זֶה מַה־נָּאֶה נִיר זֶה מַעֲלֶה עָלָיו הַכָּתוּב כְּאִלּוּ מִתְחַיֵּב בְּנַפְשׁוֹ :

יא רַבִּי חֲנִינָא בֶּן־דּוֹסָא אוֹמֵר · כֹּל שֶׁיִּרְאַת חֶטְאוֹ קוֹדֶמֶת לְחָכְמָתוֹ חָכְמָתוֹ מִתְקַיֶּמֶת · וְכֹל שֶׁחָכְמָתוֹ קוֹדֶמֶת לְיִרְאַת חֶטְאוֹ אֵין חָכְמָתוֹ מִתְקַיֶּמֶת :

יב הוּא הָיָה אוֹמֵר · כֹּל שֶׁמַּעֲשָׂיו מְרֻבִּים מֵחָכְמָתוֹ חָכְמָתוֹ מִתְקַיֶּמֶת וְכֹל שֶׁחָכְמָתוֹ מְרֻבָּה מִמַּעֲשָׂיו אֵין חָכְמָתוֹ מִתְקַיֶּמֶת :

יג הוּא הָיָה אוֹמֵר · כֹּל שֶׁרוּחַ הַבְּרִיּוֹת נוֹחָה הֵימֶנּוּ רוּחַ הַמָּקוֹם נוֹחָה הֵימֶנּוּ · וְכֹל שֶׁאֵין רוּחַ הַבְּרִיּוֹת נוֹחָה הֵימֶנּוּ אֵין רוּחַ הַמָּקוֹם נוֹחָה הֵימֶנּוּ :

יד רַבִּי דּוֹסָא בֶּן־הָרְכִּינַס אוֹמֵר · שֵׁנָה שֶׁל־שַׁחֲרִית וְיַיִן שֶׁל־צָהֳרַיִם וְשִׂיחַת הַיְלָדִים וִישִׁיבַת בָּתֵּי כְנֵסִיּוֹת שֶׁל־עַמֵּי הָאָרֶץ מוֹצִיאִים אֶת־הָאָדָם מִן־הָעוֹלָם :

טז רַבִּי יִשְׁמָעֵאל אוֹמֵר · הֱוֵה קַל לְרֹאשׁ וְנוֹחַ לְתִשְׁחֹרֶת וֶהֱוֵה מְקַבֵּל אֶת־כָּל־הָאָדָם בְּשִׂמְחָה :

יז רַבִּי עֲקִיבָא אוֹמֵר · שְׂחוֹק וְקַלּוּת רֹאשׁ מַרְגִּילִים אֶת־הָאָדָם לְעֶרְוָה : מָסֹרֶת סְיָג לַתּוֹרָה · מַעְשְׂרוֹת סְיָג לָעֹשֶׁר · נְדָרִים סְיָג לַפְּרִישׁוּת · סְיָג לַחָכְמָה שְׁתִיקָה :

יח הוּא הָיָה אוֹמֵר · חָבִיב אָדָם שֶׁנִּבְרָא בְּצֶלֶם חִבָּה יְתֵרָה נוֹדַעַת לוֹ שֶׁנִּבְרָא בְּצֶלֶם אֱלֹהִים :

יט הַכֹּל צָפוּי וְהָרְשׁוּת נְתוּנָה וּבְטוֹב הָעוֹלָם נָדוֹן וְהַכֹּל לְפִי רֹב הַמַּעֲשֶׂה :

9. Rabbi Jacob says, If someone is studying as he walks along the road and interrupts his study and exclaims: 'How lovely is that tree! How lovely is this field!' Scripture considers that he had harmed his own soul.

11. Rabbi Chanina ben Dosa says, Everyone whose fear of sin comes before his wisdom, his wisdom will endure. And everyone whose wisdom comes before his fear of sin, his wisdom will not endure.

12. He used to say, Everyone whose deeds exceed his wisdom, his wisdom will endure. And everyone whose wisdom exceeds his deeds, his wisdom will not endure.

13. He used to say, Everyone who delights his fellow-creatures, God delights in him. And everyone who gives no delight to his fellow-creatures, God does not delight in him.

14. Rabbi Dosa ben Horkinas says, Sleeping late, mid-day drinking, childish chatter and attending meetings of ignorant people drive a man out of the world.

16. Rabbi Ishmael says, Be respectful to your senior, and be patient with your junior, and welcome everyone cheerfully.

17. Rabbi Akiba says, Joking and frivolity lead a man to immorality. Tradition is a safeguard around the Torah; giving regularly to charity is a safeguard to wealth; vows are a safeguard for self-restraint; a safeguard for wisdom is silence.

18. He used to say, Beloved is man for he was created in the image of God. Yet with even greater love it was revealed to him that he was so created in the image of God.

19. Everything is foreseen, yet free choice is granted. The world is judged with mercy, yet everything is according to the amount of work.

כ הוּא הָיָה אוֹמֵר ‧ הַכֹּל נָתוּן בָּעֵרָבוֹן וּמְצוּדָה פְרוּסָה עַל־כָּל־הַחַיִּים ‧ הֶחָנוּת פְּתוּחָה וְהַחֶנְוָנִי מַקִּיף וְהַפִּנְקָס פָּתוּחַ וְהַיָּד כּוֹתֶבֶת וְכָל־הָרוֹצֶה לִלְוֹות יָבֹא וְיִלְוֶה ‧ וְהַגַּבָּאִים מַחֲזִירִים תָּדִיר בְּכָל־יוֹם וְנִפְרָעִים מִן־הָאָדָם מִדַּעְתּוֹ וְשֶׁלֹּא מִדַּעְתּוֹ וְיֵשׁ לָהֶם עַל מַה שֶׁיִּסְמְכוּ וְהַדִּין דִּין אֱמֶת ‧ וְהַכֹּל מְתֻקָּן לִסְעוּדָה:

כא רַבִּי אֶלְעָזָר בֶּן־עֲזַרְיָה אוֹמֵר ‧ אִם אֵין תּוֹרָה אֵין דֶּרֶךְ אֶרֶץ ‧ אִם אֵין דֶּרֶךְ אֶרֶץ אֵין תּוֹרָה ‧ אִם אֵין חָכְמָה אֵין יִרְאָה ‧ אִם אֵין יִרְאָה אֵין חָכְמָה ‧ אִם אֵין דַּעַת אֵין בִּינָה ‧ אִם אֵין בִּינָה אֵין דַּעַת ‧ אִם אֵין קֶמַח אֵין תּוֹרָה ‧ אִם אֵין תּוֹרָה אֵין קֶמַח:

כב הוּא הָיָה אוֹמֵר ‧ כֹּל שֶׁחָכְמָתוֹ מְרֻבָּה מִמַּעֲשָׂיו לְמָה הוּא דוֹמֶה ‧ לְאִילָן שֶׁעֲנָפָיו מְרֻבִּים וְשָׁרָשָׁיו מוּעָטִים וְהָרוּחַ בָּאָה וְעוֹקַרְתּוֹ וְהוֹפַכְתּוֹ עַל פָּנָיו ‧ אֲבָל כֹּל שֶׁמַּעֲשָׂיו מְרֻבִּים מֵחָכְמָתוֹ לְמָה הוּא דוֹמֶה ‧ לְאִילָן שֶׁעֲנָפָיו מוּעָטִים וְשָׁרָשָׁיו מְרֻבִּים שֶׁאֲפִילוּ כָּל־הָרוּחוֹת שֶׁבָּעוֹלָם בָּאוֹת וְנוֹשְׁבוֹת בּוֹ אֵין מְזִיזִים אוֹתוֹ מִמְּקוֹמוֹ:

פרק רביעי

א בֶּן־זוֹמָא אוֹמֵר ‧ אֵיזֶהוּ חָכָם ‧ הַלּוֹמֵד מִכָּל־אָדָם ‧ אֵיזֶהוּ גִבּוֹר ‧ הַכּוֹבֵשׁ אֶת־יִצְרוֹ ‧ אֵיזֶהוּ עָשִׁיר ‧ הַשָּׂמֵחַ בְּחֶלְקוֹ ‧ אֵיזֶהוּ מְכֻבָּד ‧ הַמְכַבֵּד אֶת־הַבְּרִיּוֹת:

ב בֶּן־עַזַּי אוֹמֵר ‧ הֱוֵה רָץ לְמִצְוָה קַלָּה וּבוֹרֵחַ מִן־הָעֲבֵרָה ‧ שֶׁמִּצְוָה גוֹרֶרֶת מִצְוָה וַעֲבֵרָה גוֹרֶרֶת עֲבֵרָה שֶׁשְּׂכַר מִצְוָה מִצְוָה וּשְׂכַר עֲבֵרָה עֲבֵרָה:

ג אַל־תְּהִי בָז לְכָל־אָדָם וְאַל־תְּהִי מַפְלִיג לְכָל־דָּבָר שֶׁאֵין לְךָ אָדָם שֶׁאֵין לוֹ שָׁעָה וְאֵין לְךָ דָבָר שֶׁאֵין לוֹ מָקוֹם:

20. He used to say, Everything is given on pledge, and a net is spread for all living. The shop is open, and the shopkeeper gives credit, and the account is open and the hand writes, and whoever wishes to borrow may come and borrow. But the collectors go round every day, and exact payment from man with his consent or without it, and their claims are justified, and the judgment is a judgment of truth. Yet everything is prepared for the feast!

21. Rabbi Elazar ben Azaryah says, Where there is no Torah there are no manners; where there are no manners there is no Torah.
   Without wisdom there is no fear of God; without the fear of God there is no wisdom.
   Without insight there is no knowledge; without knowledge there is no insight.
   Without food there is no Torah; without Torah there is no food.

22. He used to say, A man whose wisdom exceeds his deeds is like a tree whose branches are many, but whose roots are few. Then the wind comes and uproots it and turns it over. But the man whose deeds exceed his wisdom is like a tree whose branches are few, but whose roots are many, so that even if all the winds in the world come and blow upon it, it cannot be moved from its place.

From Chapter 4

1. Ben Zoma says, Who is wise? He who learns from every man. Who is mighty? He who controls his passions. Who is rich? He who is happy with what he has. Who is honourable? He who honours mankind.

2. Ben Azzai says, Run to do even a small *mitzvah*, but run away from doing wrong. One good deed leads to another, and one sin leads to another. Virtue is its own reward, and the wages of sin are sin.

3. Hold no man insignificant and nothing improbable, for there is no man that has not his hour and no thing that has not its place.

ד רַבִּי לְוִיטַס אִישׁ יַבְנֶה אוֹמֵר · מְאֹד מְאֹד הֱוֵה שְׁפַל רוּחַ שֶׁתִּקְוַת אֱנוֹשׁ רִמָּה :

ו רַבִּי יִשְׁמָעֵאל אוֹמֵר · הַלּוֹמֵד עַל־מְנָת לְלַמֵּד מַסְפִּיקִים בְּיָדוֹ לִלְמוֹד וּלְלַמֵּד · וְהַלּוֹמֵד עַל־מְנָת לַעֲשׂוֹת מַסְפִּיקִים בְּיָדוֹ לִלְמוֹד וּלְלַמֵּד לִשְׁמוֹר וְלַעֲשׂוֹת :

ז רַבִּי צָדוֹק אוֹמֵר · אַל־תַּעֲשֵׂהָ עֲטָרָה לְהִתְגַּדֶּל־בָּהּ וְלֹא קַרְדּוּם לַחְפָּר־בָּהּ · וְכַךְ הָיָה הִלֵּל אוֹמֵר · וּדְאִשְׁתַּמַּשׁ בְּתָגָא חֲלָף · הָא לָמַדְתָּ כָּל־הַנֶּהֱנֶה מִדִּבְרֵי תוֹרָה נוֹטֵל חַיָּיו מִן־הָעֹלָם :

י רַבִּי יִשְׁמָעֵאל בֶּן־רַבִּי יוֹסֵי הָיָה אוֹמֵר · אַל־תְּהִי דָן יְחִידִי שֶׁאֵין דָּן יְחִידִי אֶלָּא אֶחָד · וְאַל־תֹּאמַר קַבְּלוּ דַעְתִּי שֶׁהֵן רַשָּׁאִים וְלֹא אָתָּה :

יב רַבִּי מֵאִיר אוֹמֵר · הֱוֵה מְמַעֵט בְּעֵסֶק וַעֲסֹק בַּתּוֹרָה וֶהֱוֵה שְׁפַל־רוּחַ בִּפְנֵי כָל־אָדָם · וְאִם־בָּטַלְתָּ מִן הַתּוֹרָה יֶשׁ־לְךָ בְּטֵלִים הַרְבֵּה כְּנֶגְדֶּךָ · וְאִם־עָמַלְתָּ בַתּוֹרָה יֶשׁ־לוֹ שָׂכָר הַרְבֵּה לִתֶּן־לָךְ :

יג רַבִּי אֱלִיעֶזֶר בֶּן יַעֲקֹב אוֹמֵר · הָעוֹשֶׂה מִצְוָה אַחַת קוֹנֶה לוֹ פְּרַקְלִיט אֶחָד · וְהָעוֹבֵר עֲבֵרָה אַחַת קוֹנֶה לוֹ קַטֵּגוֹר אֶחָד · תְּשׁוּבָה וּמַעֲשִׂים טוֹבִים כִּתְרִיס בִּפְנֵי הַפֻּרְעָנוּת :

יד רַבִּי יוֹחָנָן הַסַּנְדְּלָר אוֹמֵר · כָּל־כְּנֵסִיָּה שֶׁהִיא לְשֵׁם שָׁמַיִם סוֹפָהּ לְהִתְקַיֵּם · וְשֶׁאֵינָהּ לְשֵׁם שָׁמַיִם אֵין סוֹפָהּ לְהִתְקַיֵּם :

טו רַבִּי אֶלְעָזָר בֶּן־שַׁמּוּעַ אוֹמֵר · יְהִי כְבוֹד תַּלְמִידְךָ חָבִיב עָלֶיךָ כְּשֶׁלָּךְ וּכְבוֹד חֲבֵרְךָ כְּמוֹרָא רַבָּךְ וּמוֹרָא רַבָּךְ כְּמוֹרָא שָׁמַיִם :

טז רַבִּי יְהוּדָה אוֹמֵר · הֱוֵה זָהִיר בְּתַלְמוּד שֶׁשִּׁגְגַת תַּלְמוּד עוֹלָה זָדוֹן :

4. Rabbi Levitas of Yavneh says, Be very humble, for the hope of mortal man is the worm.

6. Rabbi Ishmael says, He who learns in order to teach will be given the opportunity to learn and to teach. But he who learns in order to practise will be given the opportunity both to learn and teach, and to observe and practise.

7. Rabbi Zadok says, Do not use the Torah as a crown for your own importance, or a spade to dig with. Hillel also used to say, He who puts the crown to his own use shall perish. Here you learn that he who makes a profit from the words of Torah helps to destroy himself.

10. Rabbi Ishmael ben Rabbi Yose used to say, Do not judge alone, for no-one judges alone except One. And do not say 'You must accept my view!'—the choice belongs to your colleagues and you have no right to compel them.

12. Rabbi Meir says, Decrease your concern for business affairs, concern yourself rather with religious affairs, and be humble before all men. If you neglect Torah, you will find many reasons for doing so, but if you labour in it, He has a great reward to give you.

13. Rabbi Eliezer ben Jacob says, He who does one *mitzvah* acquires a counsel for the defence, and he who commits one sin acquires a counsel for the prosecution. Repentance and good deeds serve as a shield against retribution.

14. Rabbi Yochanan the sandal-maker says, Every meeting which is for the sake of heaven will endure, and every meeting which is not for the sake of heaven will not endure.

15. Rabbi Elazar ben Shammua says, Let your pupil's honour be as dear to you as your own; and your colleague's honour be as your respect for your teacher; and your teacher's respect as the awe of heaven.

16. Rabbi Judah says, Take care when you study, for an error in teaching can do as much harm as a deliberate sin.

יז רַבִּי שִׁמְעוֹן אוֹמֵר · שְׁלֹשָׁה כְתָרִים הֵם · כֶּתֶר תּוֹרָה וְכֶתֶר כְּהֻנָּה וְכֶתֶר מַלְכוּת · וְכֶתֶר שֵׁם טוֹב עוֹלֶה עַל גַּבֵּיהֶם :

יח רַבִּי נְהוֹרַי אוֹמֵר · הֱוֵה גוֹלֶה לִמְקוֹם תּוֹרָה וְאַל־תֹּאמַר שֶׁהִיא תָבוֹא אַחֲרֶיךָ · שֶׁחֲבֵרֶיךָ יְקַיְּמוּהָ בְיָדֶיךָ · וְאֶל־בִּינָתְךָ אַל־תִּשָּׁעֵן :

יט רַבִּי יַנַּי אוֹמֵר · אֵין בְּיָדֵינוּ לֹא מִשַּׁלְוַת הָרְשָׁעִים וְאַף לֹא מִיִּסּוּרֵי הַצַּדִּיקִים :

כ רַבִּי מַתִּתְיָא בֶּן־חָרָשׁ אוֹמֵר · הֱוֵה מַקְדִּים בִּשְׁלוֹם כָּל־אָדָם וֶהֱוֵה זָנָב לָאֲרָיוֹת וְאַל־תְּהִי רֹאשׁ לַשּׁוּעָלִים :

כא רַבִּי יַעֲקֹב אוֹמֵר · הָעוֹלָם הַזֶּה דּוֹמֶה לִפְרוֹזְדוֹר בִּפְנֵי הָעוֹלָם הַבָּא · הַתְקֵן עַצְמְךָ בַּפְּרוֹזְדוֹר כְּדֵי שֶׁתִּכָּנֵס לַטְּרַקְלִין :

כב הוּא הָיָה אוֹמֵר · יָפָה שָׁעָה אַחַת בִּתְשׁוּבָה וּמַעֲשִׂים טוֹבִים בָּעוֹלָם הַזֶּה מִכָּל־חַיֵּי הָעוֹלָם הַבָּא · וְיָפָה שָׁעָה אַחַת שֶׁל־קֹרַת רוּחַ בָּעוֹלָם הַבָּא מִכָּל־חַיֵּי הָעוֹלָם הַזֶּה :

כג רַבִּי שִׁמְעוֹן בֶּן־אֶלְעָזָר אוֹמֵר · אַל־תְּרַצֶּה אֶת־חֲבֵרְךָ בִּשְׁעַת כַּעֲסוֹ וְאַל־תְּנַחֲמֵהוּ בְּשָׁעָה שֶׁמֵּתוֹ מֻטָּל לְפָנָיו וְאַל־תִּשְׁאַל לוֹ בִּשְׁעַת נִדְרוֹ וְאַל־תִּשְׁתַּדֵּל לִרְאוֹתוֹ בִּשְׁעַת קַלְקָלָתוֹ :

כד שְׁמוּאֵל הַקָּטָן אוֹמֵר · בִּנְפֹל אוֹיִבְךָ אַל־תִּשְׂמָח וּבִכָּשְׁלוֹ אַל־יָגֵל לִבֶּךָ · פֶּן־יִרְאֶה יְיָ וְרַע בְּעֵינָיו וְהֵשִׁיב מֵעָלָיו אַפּוֹ :

כה אֱלִישָׁע בֶּן־אֲבוּיָה אוֹמֵר · הַלּוֹמֵד יֶלֶד לְמָה הוּא דּוֹמֶה · לִדְיוֹ כְּתוּבָה עַל־נְיָר חָדָשׁ · וְהַלּוֹמֵד זָקֵן לְמָה הוּא דּוֹמֶה · לִדְיוֹ כְּתוּבָה עַל־נְיָר מָחוּק :

17. Rabbi Simon says, There are three crowns: the crown of Torah, the crown of priesthood, and the crown of royalty. But the crown of a good reputation excels them all.

18. Rabbi Nehorai says, Search for a place of Torah and do not say it will search for you. For there you will find companions to help you grasp it, and you will not have to rely on your own understanding alone.

19. Rabbi Yannai says, Neither the prosperity of the wicked nor even the suffering of the righteous are in our hands.

20. Rabbi Mattitya ben Cheresh says, Be first to greet every man. Be a tail to lions rather than a head to jackals.

21. Rabbi Jacob says, The world is like a corridor to the world to come. Prepare yourself in the corridor so that you may enter the inner chamber.

22. He used to say, One hour of repentance and good deeds in this world is better than all the life of the world to come; and one hour of calmness of spirit in the world to come is better than all the life of this world.

23. Rabbi Simon ben Elazar says, Do not try to calm your fellow-man when he is angry; do not console him when his dead lie before him; do not cross-question him when he makes a vow; and do not try to see him at the time of his disgrace.

24. Samuel the younger says, 'Do not rejoice when your enemy falls and do not let your heart be glad when he stumbles' (*Proverbs 24: 17*). 'For the Lord sees it and thinks it wicked and turns His anger from him' (*Proverbs 24: 18*).

25. Elisha ben Abuyah says, If someone learns as a child—what does he resemble? He resembles ink written on clean paper. If someone learns as an old man—what does he resemble? He resembles ink written on worn-out paper.

כו רַבִּי יוֹסֵי בַּר יְהוּדָה אִישׁ כְּפַר הַבַּבְלִי אוֹמֵר · הַלּוֹמֵד מִן־הַקְּטַנִּים לְמָה הוּא דוֹמֶה · לְאוֹכֵל עֲנָבִים קֵהוֹת וְשׁוֹתֶה יַיִן מִגִּתּוֹ · וְהַלּוֹמֵד מִן־הַזְּקֵנִים לְמָה הוּא דוֹמֶה · לְאוֹכֵל עֲנָבִים בְּשׁוּלוֹת וְשׁוֹתֶה יַיִן יָשָׁן :

כז רַבִּי מֵאִיר אוֹמֵר · אַל־תִּסְתַּכֵּל בְּקַנְקַן אֶלָּא בְּמַה שֶּׁיֶּשׁ־בּוֹ · יֵשׁ קַנְקַן חָדָשׁ מָלֵא יָשָׁן וְיָשָׁן שֶׁאֲפִילוּ חָדָשׁ אֵין בּוֹ :

כח רַבִּי אֶלְעָזָר הַקַּפָּר אוֹמֵר · הַקִּנְאָה וְהַתַּאֲוָה וְהַכָּבוֹד מוֹצִיאִים אֶת־הָאָדָם מִן הָעוֹלָם :

כט הוּא הָיָה אוֹמֵר · הַיְּלוֹדִים לָמוּת וְהַמֵּתִים לִחְיוֹת וְהַחַיִּים לָדוֹן לֵידַע וּלְהוֹדִיעַ וּלְהִוָּדַע שֶׁהוּא אֵל הוּא הַיּוֹצֵר הוּא הַבּוֹרֵא הוּא הַמֵּבִין הוּא הַדַּיָּן הוּא הָעֵד הוּא בַּעַל דִּין הוּא עָתִיד לָדוֹן בָּרוּךְ הוּא שֶׁאֵין לְפָנָיו לֹא עַוְלָה וְלֹא שִׁכְחָה וְלֹא מַשּׂוֹא פָנִים וְלֹא מִקַּח שֹׁחַד שֶׁהַכֹּל שֶׁלּוֹ · וְדַע שֶׁהַכֹּל לְפִי הַחֶשְׁבּוֹן · וְאַל־יַבְטִיחֲךָ יִצְרְךָ שֶׁהַשְּׁאוֹל בֵּית מָנוֹס לָךְ · שֶׁעַל כָּרְחֲךָ אַתָּה נוֹלָד וְעַל כָּרְחֲךָ אַתָּה חַי וְעַל כָּרְחֲךָ אַתָּה מֵת וְעַל כָּרְחֲךָ אַתָּה עָתִיד לִתֵּן דִּין וְחֶשְׁבּוֹן לִפְנֵי מֶלֶךְ מַלְכֵי הַמְּלָכִים הַקָּדוֹשׁ בָּרוּךְ הוּא :

פרק חמישי

י שִׁבְעָה דְבָרִים בְּגֹלֶם וְשִׁבְעָה בְּחָכָם · חָכָם אֵינוֹ מְדַבֵּר לִפְנֵי מִי שֶׁגָּדוֹל מִמֶּנּוּ בְּחָכְמָה · וְאֵינוֹ נִכְנָס לְתוֹךְ דִּבְרֵי חֲבֵרוֹ · וְאֵינוֹ נִבְהָל לְהָשִׁיב · שׁוֹאֵל כָּעִנְיָן וּמֵשִׁיב כַּהֲלָכָה · וְאוֹמֵר עַל־רִאשׁוֹן רִאשׁוֹן וְעַל־אַחֲרוֹן אַחֲרוֹן · וְעַל מַה־שֶּׁלֹּא שָׁמַע אוֹמֵר לֹא שָׁמָעְתִּי · וּמוֹדֶה עַל־הָאֱמֶת · וְחִלּוּפֵיהֶם בְּגֹלֶם :

26. Rabbi Yose bar Judah of K'far ha-Bavli says, If someone learns from the young, whom does he resemble? He resembles a person who eats unripe grapes, and drinks wine straight from the vat. If someone learns from the old, whom does he resemble? He resembles a person who eats ripe grapes and drinks mature wine.

27. Rabbi Meir says, Do not look at the bottle but at what it contains. You can find new bottles filled with old wine, and old ones in which there is not even new wine.

28. Rabbi Elazar Hakappar says, Envy, desire and ambition drive a man out of the world.

29. He used to say, Those who are born will die; those who are dead will live again; and those who live again will be judged, to know, to make known and to realise that He is God, He is the maker, He is the creator, He is the discerner, He is the judge, He is the witness, He is the plaintiff; and He will summon to judgment. Blessed be He, in whose presence there is no fault and no forgetfulness, who shows no favour and takes no bribe, for everything is His. Know that everything is according to the reckoning. Do not deceive yourself that the grave will be an excuse for you, for without your consent you were born, and without your consent you live, and without your consent you die, and without your consent you will have to give an account and a reckoning before the King above the kings of kings, the Holy One, blessed be He.

From Chapter 5

10. There are seven characteristics of an uncultured man, and seven of a wise man. A wise man does not speak before someone greater than himself in wisdom.

   He does not cut into his fellow's speech.
   He does not rush to reply.
   He asks what is relevant and answers to the point.
   He speaks about first things first, and about last things last.
   As to what he has not heard he says 'I did not hear it.'
   He acknowledges the truth.
The reverse of all these applies to the uncultured man.

יג אַרְבַּע מִדּוֹת בָּאָדָם · הָאוֹמֵר שֶׁלִּי שֶׁלִּי וְשֶׁלְּךָ שֶׁלָּךְ זוֹ מִדָּה בֵּינוֹנִית וְיֵשׁ אוֹמְרִים זוֹ מִדַּת סְדוֹם · שֶׁלִּי שֶׁלְּךָ וְשֶׁלְּךָ שֶׁלִּי עַם הָאָרֶץ · שֶׁלִּי שֶׁלְּךָ וְשֶׁלְּךָ שֶׁלָּךְ חָסִיד · שֶׁלְּךָ שֶׁלִּי וְשֶׁלִּי שֶׁלִּי רָשָׁע :

יד אַרְבַּע מִדּוֹת בַּדֵּעוֹת · נוֹחַ לִכְעוֹס וְנוֹחַ לִרְצוֹת יָצָא הֶפְסֵדוֹ בִּשְׂכָרוֹ · קָשֶׁה לִכְעוֹס וְקָשֶׁה לִרְצוֹת יָצָא שְׂכָרוֹ בְּהֶפְסֵדוֹ · קָשֶׁה לִכְעוֹס וְנוֹחַ לִרְצוֹת חָסִיד · נוֹחַ לִכְעוֹס וְקָשֶׁה לִרְצוֹת רָשָׁע :

טו אַרְבַּע מִדּוֹת בְּנוֹתְנֵי צְדָקָה · הָרוֹצֶה שֶׁיִּתֵּן וְלֹא יִתְּנוּ אֲחֵרִים עֵינוֹ רָעָה בְּשֶׁל־אֲחֵרִים · יִתְּנוּ אֲחֵרִים וְהוּא לֹא יִתֵּן עֵינוֹ רָעָה בְּשֶׁלּוֹ · יִתֵּן וְיִתְּנוּ אֲחֵרִים חָסִיד · לֹא יִתֵּן וְלֹא יִתְּנוּ אֲחֵרִים רָשָׁע :

יט כָּל־אַהֲבָה שֶׁהִיא־תְלוּיָה בְדָבָר בָּטֵל דָּבָר בְּטֵלָה אַהֲבָה · וְשֶׁאֵינָה תְלוּיָה בְדָבָר אֵינָהּ בְּטֵלָה לְעוֹלָם · אֵיזוֹ הִיא אַהֲבָה שֶׁהִיא־תְלוּיָה בְדָבָר זוֹ אַהֲבַת אַמְנוֹן וְתָמָר · וְשֶׁאֵינָהּ תְּלוּיָה בְדָבָר זוֹ אַהֲבַת דָּוִד וִיהוֹנָתָן :

כ כָּל־מַחֲלֹקֶת שֶׁהִיא לְשֵׁם שָׁמַיִם סוֹפָהּ לְהִתְקַיֵּם וְשֶׁאֵינָהּ לְשֵׁם שָׁמַיִם אֵין סוֹפָהּ לְהִתְקַיֵּם · אֵיזוֹ הִיא מַחֲלֹקֶת שֶׁהִיא לְשֵׁם שָׁמַיִם זוֹ מַחֲלֹקֶת הִלֵּל וְשַׁמַּאי · וְשֶׁאֵינָהּ לְשֵׁם שָׁמַיִם זוֹ מַחֲלֹקֶת קֹרַח וְכָל־עֲדָתוֹ :

13. There are four types of man: One who says, What is mine is mine, and what is yours is yours—this is the average type. (Some say this is the selfishness of Sodom.)

One who says, What is mine is yours, and what is yours is mine—he is an ignoramus.

One who says, What is mine is yours, and what is yours is yours—he is a *chasid*.

One who says, What is yours is mine, and what is mine is mine—he is wicked.

14. There are four kinds of temperament: Easily angered, and easily pacified—his gain is cancelled by his loss.

Difficult to anger, and difficult to pacify—his loss is cancelled by his gain.

Difficult to anger, and easy to pacify—he is a *chasid*.

Easy to anger, and difficult to pacify—he is wicked.

16. There are four types of people who give to charity—One who wishes to give, but that others should not give—his eye begrudges what belongs to others.

One who wishes others to give, but that he himself should not give—his eye begrudges what belongs to him.

One who wishes to give, and others to give as well—he is a *chasid*.

One who does not wish to give, nor others to give—he is wicked.

19. If love depends on some selfish cause when the cause disappears love disappears; but if love does not depend on a selfish cause it will never disappear. What love depended on a selfish cause? Amnon's love for Tamar (*2 Samuel 13*). What love did not depend on a selfish cause? David's love for Jonathan (*1 Samuel 18*).

20. Every controversy which is for the sake of heaven will in the end lead to a lasting result. But one which is not for the sake of heaven will not in the end lead to a lasting result. What was a dispute for the sake of heaven? The dispute of Hillel and Shammai! And one which was not for the sake of heaven? The dispute of Korach and all his company (*Numbers 16*)!

כא כָּל־הַמְזַכֶּה אֶת־הָרַבִּים אֵין חֵטְא בָּא עַל־יָדוֹ וְכָל־
הַמַּחֲטִיא אֶת־הָרַבִּים אֵין־מַסְפִּיקִים בְּיָדוֹ לַעֲשׂוֹת תְּשׁוּבָה ·
מֹשֶׁה זָכָה וְזִכָּה אֶת־הָרַבִּים זְכוּת הָרַבִּים תָּלוּי בּוֹ · יָרְבְעָם
חָטָא וְהֶחֱטִיא אֶת־הָרַבִּים חֵטְא הָרַבִּים תָּלוּי בּוֹ :

כג יְהוּדָה בֶּן־תֵּימָא אוֹמֵר · הֱוֵה עַז כַּנָּמֵר וְקַל כַּנֶּשֶׁר רָץ
כַּצְּבִי וְגִבּוֹר כָּאֲרִי לַעֲשׂוֹת רְצוֹן אָבִיךְ שֶׁבַּשָּׁמָיִם :

כה בֶּן־בַּג בַּג אוֹמֵר · הֲפָךְ־בַּהּ וַהֲפָךְ־בַּהּ דְּכֹלָּא בַהּ וּבַהּ
תֶּחֱזֵי וְסִיב וּבְלֵה בַהּ וּמִנַּהּ לָא תָזוּעַ שֶׁאֵין לְךָ מִדָּה טוֹבָה
הֵימֶנָּה :

כו בֶּן־הֵא הֵא אוֹמֵר · לְפֻם צַעֲרָא אַגְרָא :

פרק ששי

שָׁנוּ חֲכָמִים בִּלְשׁוֹן הַמִּשְׁנָה בָּרוּךְ שֶׁבָּחַר בָּהֶם וּבְמִשְׁנָתָם :

א רַבִּי מֵאִיר אוֹמֵר · כָּל־הָעוֹסֵק בַּתּוֹרָה לִשְׁמָהּ זוֹכֶה
לִדְבָרִים הַרְבֵּה וְלֹא עוֹד אֶלָּא שֶׁכָּל־הָעוֹלָם כֻּלּוֹ כְּדַי
הוּא לוֹ · נִקְרָא רֵעַ אָהוּב אוֹהֵב אֶת־הַמָּקוֹם אוֹהֵב אֶת־
הַבְּרִיּוֹת · מְשַׂמֵּחַ אֶת־הַמָּקוֹם מְשַׂמֵּחַ אֶת־הַבְּרִיּוֹת וּמַלְבַּשְׁתּוֹ
עֲנָוָה וְיִרְאָה וּמַכְשַׁרְתּוֹ לִהְיוֹת צַדִּיק חָסִיד יָשָׁר וְנֶאֱמָן
וּמְרַחַקְתּוֹ מִן־הַחֵטְא וּמְקָרַבְתּוֹ לִידֵי זְכוּת וְנֶהֱנִין מִמֶּנּוּ
עֵצָה וְתוּשִׁיָּה בִּינָה וּגְבוּרָה · וְנוֹתֶנֶת לוֹ מַלְכוּת וּמֶמְשָׁלָה
וּמְגַלִּים לוֹ רָזֵי תוֹרָה וְנַעֲשֶׂה כְּמַעְיָן שֶׁאֵינוֹ פוֹסֵק וּכְנָהָר
הַמִּתְגַּבֵּר וְהוֹלֵךְ וֶהֱוֵה צָנוּעַ וְאֶרֶךְ רוּחַ וּמוֹחֵל עַל־עֶלְבּוֹנוֹ
וּמְגַדַּלְתּוֹ וּמְרוֹמַמְתּוֹ עַל כָּל־הַמַּעֲשִׂים :

ב רַבִּי יְהוֹשֻׁעַ בֶּן־לֵוִי אוֹמֵר · וְהַלֻּחֹת מַעֲשֵׂה אֱלֹהִים הֵמָּה
וְהַמִּכְתָּב מִכְתַּב אֱלֹהִים הוּא חָרוּת עַל־הַלֻּחֹת · אַל־תִּקְרָא
חָרוּת אֶלָּא חֵרוּת שֶׁאֵין לְךָ בֶּן־חוֹרִין אֶלָּא מִי שֶׁעוֹסֵק
בְּתַלְמוּד תּוֹרָה :

21. When a man leads many to goodness no sin shall come through him. When a man leads many to sin he will not even have the means to repent. Moses was worthy and made many worthy, therefore the worth of many is linked to him. Jeroboam sinned and made many sin, and therefore the sin of many is linked to him.

23. Judah ben Tema says, Be strong as a leopard, light as an eagle, swift as a gazelle and strong as a lion to do the will of your father who is in heaven.

25. Ben Bag Bag says, Turn the Torah this way and turn it that way, for everything is in it. Look into it, grow old and grey over it, and do not turn away from it for you have nothing better than this.

26. Ben Hey Hey says, According to the labour is the reward.

From Chapter 6

The wise taught the following in the style of the Mishnah—blessed be He who chose them and their Mishnah.

1. Rabbi Meir says, He who labours in the Torah for its own sake merits many things. And not only that, the whole world is in his debt. He is called friend, beloved, one who loves God, one who loves mankind, one who gives joy to God and man. The Torah clothes him in humility and awe of God and fits him to be just, saintly, upright and faithful. It keeps him far from sin and draws him to virtue, and people benefit from his advice and knowledge, his understanding and strength. It gives him a royal dignity and power. The secrets of the Torah are revealed to him, and he becomes like an ever-growing stream, a river that does not cease. He becomes modest, longsuffering and forgiving. It gives him greatness and lifts him above all things.

2. Rabbi Joshua ben Levi said, 'And the tables of the Law were the work of God and the writing was the writing of God engraved on the tables' (*Exodus 32: 16*). Do not read '*charut*'—engraved, but '*cherut*'—freedom; for no man is free unless he labours in Torah.

ג הַלּוֹמֵד מֵחֲבֵרוֹ פֶּרֶק אֶחָד אוֹ הֲלָכָה אַחַת אוֹ דִּבּוּר אֶחָד אוֹ אֲפִילוּ אוֹת אַחַת צָרִיךְ לִנְהָג בּוֹ כָּבוֹד:

ד כַּךְ הִיא דַרְכָּהּ שֶׁל־תּוֹרָה · פַּת בְּמֶלַח תֹּאכֵל וּמַיִם בִּמְשׂוּרָה תִּשְׁתֶּה וְעַל הָאָרֶץ תִּישָׁן וְחַיֵּי צַעַר תִּחְיֶה וּבַתּוֹרָה אַתָּה עָמֵל · אִם־אַתָּה עָשֶׂה כֵן אַשְׁרֶיךָ בָּעוֹלָם הַזֶּה וְטוֹב לְךָ לָעוֹלָם הַבָּא:

ה אַל־תְּבַקֵּשׁ גְּדֻלָּה לְעַצְמֶךָ וְאַל־תַּחְמֹד כָּבוֹד · יוֹתֵר מִלִּמּוּדְךָ עֲשֵׂה · וְאַל־תִּתְאַוֶּה לְשֻׁלְחָנָם שֶׁל־מְלָכִים · שֶׁשֻּׁלְחָנְךָ גָּדוֹל מִשֻּׁלְחָנָם וְכִתְרְךָ גָּדוֹל מִכִּתְרָם · וְנֶאֱמָן הוּא בַּעַל מְלַאכְתְּךָ שֶׁיְּשַׁלֶּם לְךָ שְׂכַר פְּעֻלָּתֶךָ:

ט אָמַר רַבִּי יוֹסֵי בֶּן־קִסְמָא · פַּעַם אַחַת הָיִיתִי מְהַלֵּךְ בַּדֶּרֶךְ וּפָגַע בִּי אָדָם אֶחָד וְנָתַן־לִי שָׁלוֹם · אָמַר לִי · רַבִּי מֵאֵיזֶה מָקוֹם אָתָּה · אָמַרְתִּי לוֹ · מֵעִיר גְּדוֹלָה שֶׁל־חֲכָמִים וְשֶׁל־סוֹפְרִים אָנִי · אָמַר לִי · רַבִּי רְצוֹנְךָ שֶׁתָּדוּר עִמָּנוּ בִּמְקוֹמֵנוּ וַאֲנִי אֶתֵּן לְךָ אֶלֶף אֲלָפִים דִּינְרֵי זָהָב וַאֲבָנִים טוֹבוֹת וּמַרְגָּלִיּוֹת · אָמַרְתִּי לוֹ · אִם אַתָּה נוֹתֵן לִי כָּל־כֶּסֶף וְזָהָב וַאֲבָנִים טוֹבוֹת וּמַרְגָּלִיּוֹת שֶׁבָּעוֹלָם אֵינִי דָר אֶלָּא בִּמְקוֹם תּוֹרָה · שֶׁבִּשְׁעַת פְּטִירָתוֹ שֶׁל־אָדָם אֵין מְלַוִּים לוֹ לְאָדָם לֹא כֶסֶף וְלֹא זָהָב וְלֹא אֲבָנִים טוֹבוֹת וּמַרְגָּלִיּוֹת אֶלָּא תּוֹרָה וּמַעֲשִׂים טוֹבִים בִּלְבָד · שֶׁנֶּאֱמַר · בְּהִתְהַלֶּכְךָ תַּנְחֶה אֹתָךְ בְּשָׁכְבְּךָ תִּשְׁמֹר עָלֶיךָ וַהֲקִיצוֹתָ הִיא תְשִׂיחֶךָ · בְּהִתְהַלֶּכְךָ תַּנְחֶה אֹתָךְ בָּעוֹלָם הַזֶּה בְּשָׁכְבְּךָ תִּשְׁמוֹר עָלֶיךָ בַּקֶּבֶר וַהֲקִיצוֹתָ הִיא תְשִׂיחֶךָ לָעוֹלָם הַבָּא:

3. If a man learns from his fellow a single chapter, a single rule, a single expression, or even a single letter, he should treat him with honour.

4. This is the way of the Torah! A piece of bread with salt you will eat, a ration of water you will drink, upon the ground you will lie, a life of hardship you will lead, and you will labour in the Torah. If you do this, 'happy shall you be'—in this world. 'And it shall be well with you'—in the world to come.

5. Seek no greatness for yourself, no honours, and let your deeds be greater than your learning. Do not long for the table of kings, for your table is greater than theirs, and your crown is greater than theirs. Faithful is your Employer to pay you the reward of your labour.

9. Rabbi Yose ben Kisma said, Once I was walking along the road and a man came up to me and greeted me. He said to me, 'Rabbi, where are you from?' I told him, 'I come from a great city of wise men and teachers.' He said to me, 'Rabbi, if you would care to settle among us in our place, I would give you thousands of gold dinars, and precious stones and pearls.' I told him, 'If you give me all the silver and gold and precious stones and pearls in the world, I would still only settle in a place of Torah. When a man dies neither silver nor gold nor precious stones nor pearls accompany him, only Torah and good deeds. For it is said (*Proverbs 6: 22*): "When you walk it shall lead you; when you lie down it shall watch over you; and when you awake it shall speak with you." "When you walk it shall lead you"—in this world. "When you lie down it shall watch over you"—in the grave. "When you awake it shall speak with you"—in the world to come.'

יא כֹּל מַה־שֶּׁבָּרָא הַקָּדוֹשׁ בָּרוּךְ הוּא בְּעוֹלָמוֹ לֹא בְרָאוֹ
אֶלָּא לִכְבוֹדוֹ · שֶׁנֶּאֱמַר כֹּל הַנִּקְרָא בִשְׁמִי וְלִכְבוֹדִי בְּרָאתִיו
יְצַרְתִּיו אַף עֲשִׂיתִיו · וְאוֹמֵר · יְיָ יִמְלֹךְ לְעֹלָם וָעֶד :

רַבִּי חֲנַנְיָא בֶּן־עֲקַשְׁיָא אוֹמֵר · רָצָה הַקָּדוֹשׁ בָּרוּךְ הוּא
לְזַכּוֹת אֶת־יִשְׂרָאֵל לְפִיכָךְ הִרְבָּה לָהֶם תּוֹרָה וּמִצְווֹת ·
שֶׁנֶּאֱמַר · יְיָ חָפֵץ לְמַעַן צִדְקוֹ יַגְדִּיל תּוֹרָה וְיַאְדִּיר :

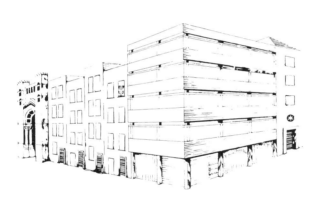

Leo Baeck College, London

11. Everything that the Holy One, blessed be He, created in this world, He created for His glory alone, as it is said (*Isaiah 43: 7*): 'Everything that is called by My name, I created for My glory, it is I who formed it, I made it.' And it says (*Exodus 15: 18*): 'The Lord shall rule forever and ever.'

Rabbi Chananya ben Akashya says, It pleased the Holy One, blessed be He, to make Israel worthy. Because of this He gave them much Torah and many commandments, as it is said (*Isaiah 42: 21*): 'It pleased the Lord because of His righteousness to make the Torah great and glorious.'

DAILY MORNING SERVICE

בָּרְכִי נַפְשִׁי אֶת־יְהֹוָה יְהֹוָה אֱלֹהַי גָּדַלְתָּ מְּאֹד הוֹד וְהָדָר לָבָשְׁתָּ ׃ עֹטֶה־אוֹר כַּשַּׂלְמָה נוֹטֶה שָׁמַיִם כַּיְרִיעָה ׃

הִנְנִי מִתְעַטֵּף בְּטַלִּית שֶׁל־צִיצִת כְּדֵי לְקַיֵּם מִצְוַת בּוֹרְאִי ׃ כַּכָּתוּב בַּתּוֹרָה ׃ וְעָשׂוּ לָהֶם צִיצִת עַל־כַּנְפֵי בִגְדֵיהֶם לְדֹרֹתָם ׃ וּכְשֵׁם שֶׁאֲנִי מִתְכַּסֶּה בְּטַלִּית בָּעוֹלָם הַזֶּה כֵּן תִּזְכֶּה נִשְׁמָתִי לְהִתְלַבֵּשׁ בְּטַלִּית נָאָה לָעוֹלָם הַבָּא בְּגַן עֵדֶן ׃ אָמֵן ׃

בָּרוּךְ אַתָּה יְיָ אֱלֹהֵינוּ מֶלֶךְ הָעוֹלָם ׃ אֲשֶׁר קִדְּשָׁנוּ בְּמִצְוֹתָיו וְצִוָּנוּ לְהִתְעַטֵּף בַּצִּיצִת ׃

הִנְנִי מְכַוֵּן בְּהַנָּחַת תְּפִלִּין לְקַיֵּם מִצְוַת בּוֹרְאִי שֶׁצִּוָּנוּ לְהָנִיחַ תְּפִלִּין ׃ כַּכָּתוּב בַּתּוֹרָה ׃ וּקְשַׁרְתָּם לְאוֹת עַל־יָדֶךָ וְהָיוּ לְטֹטָפֹת בֵּין עֵינֶיךָ ׃ וְהֵם אַרְבַּע פָּרָשׁוֹת אֵלּוּ ׃ שְׁמַע ׃ וְהָיָה אִם־שָׁמֹעַ ׃ קַדֶּשׁ ׃ וְהָיָה כִּי יְבִאֲךָ ׃ שֶׁיֵּשׁ בָּהֶם יִחוּדוֹ וְאַחְדוּתוֹ יִתְבָּרַךְ שְׁמוֹ ׃ וְשֶׁנִּזְכֹּר נִסִּים וְנִפְלָאוֹת שֶׁעָשָׂה עִמָּנוּ בְּהוֹצִיאוֹ אוֹתָנוּ מִמִּצְרָיִם ׃ וַאֲשֶׁר לוֹ הַכֹּחַ וְהַמֶּמְשָׁלָה בָּעֶלְיוֹנִים וּבַתַּחְתּוֹנִים לַעֲשׂוֹת בָּהֶם כִּרְצוֹנוֹ ׃ וְצִוָּנוּ לְהָנִיחַ עַל־הַיָּד לְזִכְרוֹן זְרוֹעַ הַנְּטוּיָה ׃ וְשֶׁהִיא נֶגֶד הַלֵּב לְשַׁעְבֵּד בָּזֶה תַּאֲוַת וּמַחְשְׁבוֹת לִבֵּנוּ לַעֲבֹדָתוֹ יִתְבָּרַךְ שְׁמוֹ ׃ וְעַל־הָרֹאשׁ נֶגֶד הַמֹּחַ שֶׁהַנְּשָׁמָה שֶׁבְּמוֹחִי עִם־חוּשַׁי וְכֹחוֹתַי כֻּלָּם יִהְיוּ מְשֻׁעְבָּדִים לַעֲבֹדָתוֹ יִתְבָּרַךְ שְׁמוֹ ׃ וּמִשֶּׁפַע מִצְוַת תְּפִלִּין יִתְמַשֵּׁךְ עָלַי לִהְיוֹת לִי חַיִּים אֲרֻכִים וְשֶׁפַע קֹדֶשׁ וּמַחֲשָׁבוֹת קְדוֹשׁוֹת בְּלִי הַרְהוֹר חֵטְא וְעָוֹן כְּלָל ׃ וְשֶׁלֹּא יְפַתֵּנוּ וְלֹא יִתְגָּרֶה בָּנוּ יֵצֶר הָרָע וַיַנִּיחֵנוּ לַעֲבֹד אֶת־יְיָ כַּאֲשֶׁר עִם־לְבָבֵנוּ ׃ אָמֵן ׃

DAILY MORNING SERVICE

When Tallit and Tefillin are worn, the following are said:
Meditation before putting on the Tallit

Bless the Lord, my soul! Lord my God, how great You are, clothed in majesty and glory, wrapped in light like a robe. You spread out the heavens like a tent. (*Psalm 104: 1–2.*)

I prepare to wrap myself in this *Tallit* to fulfil the command of my creator. As it is written in the Torah: 'Each generation shall put a tassel on the corners of their clothes.' And just as I cover myself with a robe in this world, so may my soul deserve to be robed in a beautiful robe in the world to come, as in Eden. Amen.

On putting on the Tallit

Blessed are You, Lord our God, king of the universe, who makes us holy through doing His commands and commands us to wrap ourselves in the *Tallit*.

Meditation before putting on the Tefillin

I now prepare myself to lay *Tefillin* to fulfil the command of my creator who commanded us to lay *Tefillin*, as it is written in the Torah: 'Hold fast to them as a sign upon your hand and let them be as reminders before your eyes.' And in them are these four sections of the Torah: 'Hear O Israel . . .' (*Deuteronomy 6: 4–9*); 'This will happen . . .' (*Deuteronomy 11: 13–21*); 'Sanctify . . .' (*Exodus 13: 1–10*); 'And when the Lord shall bring you . . .' (*Exodus 13: 11–16*). They state His uniqueness and His unity, may His name be blessed. They also record the signs and the wonders that He did for us when He brought us out from Egypt—He, whose power and authority extend over the highest and the lowest, to deal with them according to His plan. He commanded us to lay *Tefillin* on the hand as a reminder of His 'outstretched arm', and opposite the heart to show in this way that the longings and desires of our heart should be controlled for His service, may His name be blessed. And on the head over the brain, showing that the mind that is in my brain, with all my senses and faculties, should be committed to His service, may His name be blessed. By keeping the commandment of *Tefillin* may fulfilment in my life increase, together with holiness and holy thought, undisturbed by sin and wrong. Do not let the desire for evil deceive us nor provoke us. Let us be led to serve the Lord as it is in our hearts to do. Amen.

בָּרוּךְ אַתָּה יְיָ אֱלֹהֵינוּ מֶלֶךְ הָעוֹלָם · אֲשֶׁר קִדְּשָׁנוּ
בְּמִצְוֹתָיו וְצִוָּנוּ לְהָנִיחַ תְּפִלִּין:

בָּרוּךְ אַתָּה יְיָ אֱלֹהֵינוּ מֶלֶךְ הָעוֹלָם · אֲשֶׁר קִדְּשָׁנוּ
בְּמִצְוֹתָיו וְצִוָּנוּ עַל־מִצְוַת תְּפִלִּין:
בָּרוּךְ שֵׁם כְּבוֹד מַלְכוּתוֹ לְעוֹלָם וָעֶד:

וְאֵרַשְׂתִּיךְ לִי לְעוֹלָם ·
וְאֵרַשְׂתִּיךְ לִי בְּצֶדֶק וּבְמִשְׁפָּט וּבְחֶסֶד וּבְרַחֲמִים ·
וְאֵרַשְׂתִּיךְ לִי בֶּאֱמוּנָה וְיָדַעַתְּ אֶת־יְיָ:

_____

אֱלֹהַי · נְשָׁמָה שֶׁנָּתַתָּ־בִּי טְהוֹרָה · אַתָּה בְרָאתָהּ · אַתָּה
יְצַרְתָּהּ · אַתָּה נְפַחְתָּהּ בִּי · וְאַתָּה מְשַׁמְּרָהּ בְּקִרְבִּי · וְאַתָּה
עָתִיד לִטְּלָהּ מִמֶּנִּי לְחַיֵּי עוֹלָם: כָּל־זְמַן שֶׁהַנְּשָׁמָה בְקִרְבִּי
מוֹדֶה אֲנִי לְפָנֶיךָ יְיָ אֱלֹהַי וֵאלֹהֵי אֲבוֹתַי · שֶׁאַתָּה הוּא רִבּוֹן
כָּל־הַמַּעֲשִׂים · מוֹשֵׁל בְּכָל־הַבְּרִיּוֹת · אֲדוֹן כָּל־הַנְּשָׁמוֹת:
בָּרוּךְ אַתָּה יְיָ · הַמַּחֲזִיר נְשָׁמוֹת לִפְגָרִים מֵתִים:

בָּרוּךְ אַתָּה יְיָ אֱלֹהֵינוּ מֶלֶךְ הָעוֹלָם · מַתִּיר אֲסוּרִים:
בָּרוּךְ אַתָּה יְיָ אֱלֹהֵינוּ מֶלֶךְ הָעוֹלָם · זוֹקֵף כְּפוּפִים:
בָּרוּךְ אַתָּה יְיָ אֱלֹהֵינוּ מֶלֶךְ הָעוֹלָם · שֶׁעָשָׂה־לִי כָּל־
צָרְכִּי:
בָּרוּךְ אַתָּה יְיָ אֱלֹהֵינוּ מֶלֶךְ הָעוֹלָם · אֲשֶׁר הֵכִין מִצְעֲדֵי־
גָבֶר:
בָּרוּךְ אַתָּה יְיָ אֱלֹהֵינוּ מֶלֶךְ הָעוֹלָם · עוֹטֵר יִשְׂרָאֵל
בְּתִפְאָרָה:

On putting the Tefillin on the arm

Blessed are You, Lord our God, king of the universe, who makes us holy through doing His commands and commands us to lay *Tefillin.*

On putting the Tefillin on the head

Blessed are You, Lord our God, king of the universe, who makes us holy through doing His commands and commands us concerning the commandment of *Tefillin.*

Blessed is His name, whose glorious kingdom is forever and ever.

As the strap is wound three times round the middle finger

I betroth you to Me forever.
I betroth you to Me with integrity and justice,
    with tenderness and love.
I betroth you to Me with faithfulness
    and you will know the Lord.

Hosea 2: 21–22

The Yigdal *(page* 44*) or* Adon Olam *(page* 170*) is sung here.*

THE GOODNESS OF MAN My God, the soul You have given me is pure, for You created it, You formed it and You made it live within me. You watch over it within me, but one day You will take it from me to everlasting life. My God and God of my fathers, as long as the soul is within me, I will declare that You are the master of all deeds, the ruler of all creatures and the Lord of every soul. Blessed are You Lord, who brings the dead into everlasting life.

Blessed are You, Lord our God, king of the universe, who frees those who are bound.

Blessed are You, Lord our God, king of the universe, who lifts up those bent low.

Blessed are You, Lord our God, king of the universe, who provides for my every need.

Blessed are You, Lord our God, king of the universe, who strengthens the steps of man.

Blessed are You, Lord our God, king of the universe, who crowns Israel with glory.

בָּרוּךְ אַתָּה יְיָ אֱלֹהֵינוּ מֶלֶךְ הָעוֹלָם · הַנּוֹתֵן לַיָּעֵף כֹּחַ:

בָּרוּךְ אַתָּה יְיָ אֱלֹהֵינוּ מֶלֶךְ הָעוֹלָם · הַמַּעֲבִיר שֵׁנָה מֵעֵינַי וּתְנוּמָה מֵעַפְעַפָּי:

לְעוֹלָם יְהֵא אָדָם יְרֵא שָׁמַיִם בַּסֵּתֶר כְּבַגָּלוּי · וּמוֹדֶה עַל־הָאֱמֶת וְדוֹבֵר אֱמֶת בִּלְבָבוֹ:

יְהִי רָצוֹן מִלְּפָנֶיךָ יְיָ אֱלֹהֵינוּ וֵאלֹהֵי אֲבוֹתֵינוּ · שֶׁתַּרְגִּילֵנוּ בְּתוֹרָתֶךָ וְדַבְּקֵנוּ בְּמִצְוֹתֶיךָ · וְאַל תְּבִיאֵנוּ לֹא לִידֵי חֵטְא וְלֹא לִידֵי עֲבֵרָה וְלֹא לִידֵי נִסָּיוֹן וְלֹא לִידֵי בִזָּיוֹן · וְאַל תַּשְׁלֶט־בָּנוּ יֵצֶר הָרָע · וְהַרְחִיקֵנוּ מֵאָדָם רַע וּמֵחָבֵר רַע · וְדַבְּקֵנוּ בְּיֵצֶר הַטּוֹב וּבְמַעֲשִׂים טוֹבִים · וְכֹף אֶת־יִצְרֵנוּ לְהִשְׁתַּעְבֶּד־לָךְ · וּתְנֵנוּ הַיּוֹם וּבְכָל־יוֹם לְחֵן וּלְחֶסֶד וּלְרַחֲמִים בְּעֵינֶיךָ וּבְעֵינֵי כָל־רוֹאֵינוּ · וְתִגְמְלֵנוּ חֲסָדִים טוֹבִים: בָּרוּךְ אַתָּה יְיָ · גּוֹמֵל חֲסָדִים טוֹבִים לְעַמּוֹ יִשְׂרָאֵל:

רִבּוֹן הָעוֹלָמִים וַאֲדֹנֵי הָאֲדֹנִים · לֹא עַל־צִדְקוֹתֵינוּ אֲנַחְנוּ מַפִּילִים תַּחֲנוּנֵינוּ לְפָנֶיךָ · כִּי עַל־רַחֲמֶיךָ הָרַבִּים: אֲדֹנָי שְׁמָעָה · אֲדֹנָי סְלָחָה · אֲדֹנָי הַקְשִׁיבָה וַעֲשֵׂה · מָה־אָנוּ · מֶה־חַיֵּינוּ · מֶה־חַסְדֵּנוּ · מַה־צִּדְקוֹתֵינוּ · מַה־יְּשׁוּעָתֵנוּ · מַה־כֹּחֵנוּ · מַה־גְּבוּרָתֵנוּ · מַה־נֹּאמַר לְפָנֶיךָ יְיָ אֱלֹהֵינוּ וֵאלֹהֵי אֲבוֹתֵינוּ · הֲלֹא הַגִּבּוֹרִים כְּאַיִן לְפָנֶיךָ · וְאַנְשֵׁי הַשֵּׁם כְּלֹא הָיוּ · וַחֲכָמִים כִּבְלִי מַדָּע · וּנְבוֹנִים כִּבְלִי הַשְׂכֵּל · כִּי רֹב מַעֲשֵׂינוּ תֹּהוּ · וִימֵי חַיֵּינוּ הֶבֶל לְפָנֶיךָ · וּמוֹתַר הָאָדָם מִן הַבְּהֵמָה אָיִן · כִּי הַכֹּל הָבֶל לְבַד הַנְּשָׁמָה הַטְּהוֹרָה · שֶׁהִיא עֲתִידָה לִתֵּן דִּין וְחֶשְׁבּוֹן לִפְנֵי כִסֵּא כְבוֹדֶךָ:

בָּרוּךְ אַתָּה יְיָ אֱלֹהֵינוּ מֶלֶךְ הָעוֹלָם· אֲשֶׁר קִדְּשָׁנוּ בְּמִצְוֹתָיו וְצִוָּנוּ לַעֲסוֹק בְּדִבְרֵי תוֹרָה:

Blessed are You, Lord our God, king of the universe, who gives strength to the weary.

Blessed are You, Lord our God, king of the universe, who takes away sleep from my eyes and slumber from my eyelids.

Man should always be in awe of heaven in private as well as in public. He should tell the truth and speak it in his heart.

Lord our God and God of our fathers, help us to live according to Your teaching and to hold fast to Your commands. Let us not come into the power of sin or wrong-doing, temptation or disgrace. Let no evil within us control us, and keep us far from bad people and bad company. Help us hold fast to the good within us and to good deeds, and bend our will and our desires to serve You. Give us today, and every day, grace, kindness and mercy in Your sight and in the sight of all who regard us, and grant us Your love and kindness. Blessed are You Lord, who grants love and kindness to His people Israel.

THE WEAKNESS OF MAN Master of existence, and Lord of lords, we do not rely on our own good deeds but on Your great mercy as we lay our needs before You. Lord, hear! Lord, pardon! Lord, listen and act! What are we? What is our life? What is our love? What is our justice? What is our success? What is our endurance? What is our power? Lord our God, and God of our fathers, what can we say before You, for in Your presence are not the powerful as nothing, the famous as if they had never existed, the learned as if without knowledge, and the intelligent as if without insight. To You most of our actions are pointless and our daily life is shallow. Even the superiority of man over the beasts is nothing. For everything is trivial except the pure soul which must one day give its account and reckoning before the judgment seat of Your glory.

THE DUTY TO STUDY Blessed are You, Lord our God, king of the universe, who makes us holy through doing His commands, and who commands us to devote ourselves to the study of His teaching.

One of the passages selected from the Anthology, pages 352–409 may be read here.

וַיְבָרֶךְ דָּוִיד אֶת־יְהֹוָה לְעֵינֵי כָּל־הַקָּהָל · וַיֹּאמֶר דָּוִיד ·

בָּרוּךְ אַתָּה יְהֹוָה אֱלֹהֵי יִשְׂרָאֵל אָבִינוּ מֵעוֹלָם וְעַד־עוֹלָם :

לְךָ יְהֹוָה הַגְּדֻלָּה וְהַגְּבוּרָה וְהַתִּפְאֶרֶת וְהַנֵּצַח וְהַהוֹד · כִּי־

כֹל בַּשָּׁמַיִם וּבָאָרֶץ לְךָ יְהֹוָה הַמַּמְלָכָה וְהַמִּתְנַשֵּׂא לְכֹל

לְרֹאשׁ : וְהָעשֶׁר וְהַכָּבוֹד מִלְּפָנֶיךָ · וְאַתָּה מוֹשֵׁל בַּכֹּל ·

וּבְיָדְךָ כֹּחַ וּגְבוּרָה · וּבְיָדְךָ לְגַדֵּל וּלְחַזֵּק לַכֹּל : וְעַתָּה

אֱלֹהֵינוּ מוֹדִים אֲנַחְנוּ לָךְ · וּמְהַלְלִים לְשֵׁם תִּפְאַרְתֶּךָ :

וִיבָרְכוּ שֵׁם כְּבֹדֶךָ · וּמְרוֹמַם עַל־כָּל־בְּרָכָה וּתְהִלָּה :

אַתָּה־הוּא יְהֹוָה לְבַדֶּךָ · אַתָּה עָשִׂיתָ אֶת־הַשָּׁמַיִם שְׁמֵי

הַשָּׁמַיִם וְכָל־צְבָאָם · הָאָרֶץ וְכָל־אֲשֶׁר עָלֶיהָ · הַיַּמִּים

וְכָל־אֲשֶׁר בָּהֶם · וְאַתָּה מְחַיֶּה אֶת־כֻּלָּם · וּצְבָא הַשָּׁמַיִם

לְךָ מִשְׁתַּחֲוִים :

יְיָ מֶלֶךְ · יְיָ מָלָךְ · יְיָ יִמְלֹךְ לְעוֹלָם וָעֶד :

וְהָיָה יְיָ לְמֶלֶךְ עַל־כָּל־הָאָרֶץ · בַּיּוֹם הַהוּא יִהְיֶה יְיָ

אֶחָד וּשְׁמוֹ אֶחָד : הוֹשִׁיעֵנוּ יְיָ אֱלֹהֵינוּ · לְהוֹדוֹת לְשֵׁם קָדְשֶׁךָ

לְהִשְׁתַּבֵּחַ בִּתְהִלָּתֶךָ : בָּרוּךְ יְהֹוָה אֱלֹהֵי יִשְׂרָאֵל מִן־הָעוֹלָם

וְעַד הָעוֹלָם · וְאָמַר כָּל־הָעָם אָמֵן · הַלְלוּיָהּ : כֹּל הַנְּשָׁמָה

תְּהַלֵּל יָהּ · הַלְלוּיָהּ :

יִשְׁתַּבַּח שִׁמְךָ לָעַד מַלְכֵּנוּ · הָאֵל הַמֶּלֶךְ הַגָּדוֹל

וְהַקָּדוֹשׁ בַּשָּׁמַיִם וּבָאָרֶץ · כִּי לְךָ נָאֶה יְיָ

אֱלֹהֵינוּ וֵאלֹהֵי אֲבוֹתֵינוּ לְעוֹלָם וָעֶד שִׁיר וּשְׁבָחָה · קְדֻשָּׁה

וּמַלְכוּת · בְּרָכוֹת וְהוֹדָאוֹת לְשִׁמְךָ הַגָּדוֹל וְהַקָּדוֹשׁ · וּמֵעוֹלָם

וְעַד־עוֹלָם אַתָּה אֵל : בָּרוּךְ אַתָּה יְיָ · בּוֹרֵא כָּל־הַנְּשָׁמוֹת ·

רִבּוֹן כָּל־הַמַּעֲשִׂים · מֶלֶךְ חַי הָעוֹלָמִים :

The half Kaddish on page 168 may be included here.

בָּרְכוּ אֶת־יְיָ הַמְבֹרָךְ :

בָּרוּךְ יְיָ הַמְבֹרָךְ לְעוֹלָם וָעֶד :

Then David blessed the Lord in the sight of all the congregation, and David said: 'Blessed are You Lord, the God of our father Israel from everlasting to everlasting. Yours is the greatness, the power, the splendour, the glory and the majesty, for everything in heaven and earth is Yours. Yours is the kingdom and You are exalted supreme over all. Wealth and honour come from You, for You rule over all. In Your hand are strength and might. It is in Your power to give greatness and strength to all. And now, our God, we give You thanks and praise Your glorious name.' (*I Chronicles 29: 10–13.*) May the people bless Your glorious name, though it is beyond all blessing and praise. You are the Lord alone; You made the sky, the reaches of space and its countless lights, the earth and everything on it, the seas and everything in them; You give life to them all, and the universe worships You. (*Nehemiah 9: 5–6.*)

THE POWER OF GOD   The Lord does rule, the Lord has ruled, the Lord shall rule forever and ever.

The Lord shall be as a king over the whole earth. On that day the Lord shall be One, and known as One.

Save us, Lord our God, to proclaim Your holy name and be honoured in praising You.

Blessed is the Lord God of Israel from everlasting to everlasting. Let all the people say: Amen! Praise the Lord!

May all who live praise the Lord. Hallelujah!

A selected psalm is included here.

THE DUTY OF PRAISE   Praised be Your name forever, for You are the God who is the great and holy king in heaven and on earth. Therefore, Lord our God, and God of our fathers, song and praise, holiness and majesty, blessing and gratitude belong to Your great and holy name forever and ever. From age to age You are God. Blessed are You Lord, creator of every living being, master of all deeds, the king, the life of all existence.

The half Kaddish on page 168 may be included here.

THE CALL TO COM- MUNITY PRAYER   Bless the Lord whom we are called to bless.

Blessed be the Lord whom we are called to bless forever and ever.

בָּרוּךְ אַתָּה יְיָ אֱלֹהֵינוּ מֶלֶךְ הָעוֹלָם · יוֹצֵר אוֹר וּבוֹרֵא חֹשֶׁךְ · עֹשֶׂה שָׁלוֹם וּבוֹרֵא אֶת־הַכֹּל: הַכֹּל יוֹדוּךָ · וְהַכֹּל יְשַׁבְּחוּךָ · וְהַכֹּל יֹאמְרוּ אֵין קָדוֹשׁ כַּיְיָ: הַמֵּאִיר לָעוֹלָם כֻּלּוֹ וּלְיוֹשְׁבָיו וּבְטוּבוֹ מְחַדֵּשׁ בְּכָל־יוֹם תָּמִיד מַעֲשֵׂה בְרֵאשִׁית: מָה רַבּוּ מַעֲשֶׂיךָ יְיָ · כֻּלָּם בְּחָכְמָה עָשִׂיתָ · מָלְאָה הָאָרֶץ קִנְיָנֶךָ: הַמֶּלֶךְ הַמְרוֹמָם לְבַדּוֹ מֵאָז · הַמְשֻׁבָּח וְהַמְפֹאָר וְהַמִּתְנַשֵּׂא מִימוֹת עוֹלָם: אֱלֹהֵי עוֹלָם · בְּרַחֲמֶיךָ הָרַבִּים רַחֵם עָלֵינוּ · אֲדוֹן עֻזֵּנוּ · צוּר מִשְׂגַּבֵּנוּ · מָגֵן יִשְׁעֵנוּ · מִשְׂגָּב בַּעֲדֵנוּ: בָּרוּךְ אַתָּה יְיָ · יוֹצֵר הַמְּאוֹרוֹת:

אַהֲבָה רַבָּה אֲהַבְתָּנוּ יְיָ אֱלֹהֵינוּ · חֶמְלָה גְדוֹלָה וִיתֵרָה חָמַלְתָּ עָלֵינוּ: אָבִינוּ מַלְכֵּנוּ · בַּעֲבוּר שִׁמְךָ הַגָּדוֹל וּבַעֲבוּר אֲבוֹתֵינוּ שֶׁבָּטְחוּ בָךְ · וַתְּלַמְּדֵם חֻקֵּי חַיִּים לַעֲשׂוֹת רְצוֹנְךָ בְּלֵבָב שָׁלֵם · כֵּן תְּחָנֵּנוּ: הָאֵר עֵינֵינוּ בְּתוֹרָתֶךָ · וְדַבֵּק לִבֵּנוּ בְּמִצְוֹתֶיךָ · וְיַחֵד לְבָבֵנוּ לְאַהֲבָה וּלְיִרְאָה אֶת־שְׁמֶךָ · לְמַעַן לֹא נֵבוֹשׁ וְלֹא נִכָּלֵם כִּי אֵל פּוֹעֵל יְשׁוּעוֹת אָתָּה · וּבָנוּ בָחַרְתָּ מִכָּל־עַם וְלָשׁוֹן · וְקֵרַבְתָּנוּ מַלְכֵּנוּ לְשִׁמְךָ הַגָּדוֹל בְּאַהֲבָה · לְהוֹדוֹת לְךָ וּלְיַחֶדְךָ וּלְאַהֲבָה אֶת־שְׁמֶךָ: בָּרוּךְ אַתָּה יְיָ · הַבּוֹחֵר בְּעַמּוֹ יִשְׂרָאֵל בְּאַהֲבָה:

שְׁמַ**ע** יִשְׂרָאֵל · יְהֹוָה אֱלֹהֵינוּ יְהֹוָה אֶחָ**ד**:

בָּרוּךְ שֵׁם כְּבוֹד מַלְכוּתוֹ לְעוֹלָם וָעֶד:

וְאָהַבְתָּ אֵת יְהֹוָה אֱלֹהֶיךָ · בְּכָל־לְבָבְךָ וּבְכָל־נַפְשְׁךָ וּבְכָל־מְאֹדֶךָ: וְהָיוּ הַדְּבָרִים הָאֵלֶּה אֲשֶׁר אָנֹכִי מְצַוְּךָ הַיּוֹם עַל־לְבָבֶךָ: וְשִׁנַּנְתָּם לְבָנֶיךָ וְדִבַּרְתָּ בָּם · בְּשִׁבְתְּךָ בְּבֵיתֶךָ וּבְלֶכְתְּךָ בַדֶּרֶךְ וּבְשָׁכְבְּךָ וּבְקוּמֶךָ: וּקְשַׁרְתָּם לְאוֹת עַל־יָדֶךָ · וְהָיוּ לְטֹטָפֹת בֵּין עֵינֶיךָ: וּכְתַבְתָּם עַל־מְזֻזוֹת בֵּיתֶךָ וּבִשְׁעָרֶיךָ:

THE CREATOR OF THE UNIVERSE

Blessed are You, Lord our God, king of the universe, who forms light yet creates darkness, who makes peace yet creates all. All things proclaim You, all things honour You, and all say: 'None is holy like the Lord.' He gives light to all the world and those who live in it. In His goodness He renews the work of the creation day by day. Lord, how great are Your works; You made them all in wisdom; the earth is full of Your creatures. You are the only king exalted from the beginning of time, who has been worshipped, praised and glorified since days of old.

Everlasting God, in Your great mercy have mercy upon us; Lord of our strength, rock of our protection, shield of our safety, our true protector. Blessed are You Lord, who creates the lights of the universe.

HIS LOVE FOR ISRAEL

With deep love You have loved us, and with great and overflowing tenderness You have taken pity on us. Our father, our king, show us compassion because of Your own greatness, and because of our fathers who trusted in You, for You taught them rules to live by, to do Your will with their whole heart. Let our eyes see the light of Your teaching and our hearts embrace Your commands. Give us integrity to love You and fear You. So shall we never lose our self-respect, nor be put to shame, for You are the power which works to save us. You chose us from all peoples and tongues, and in love drew us near to Your own greatness—to honour You, to declare Your unity, and to love You. Blessed are You Lord, who chooses His people Israel in love.

THE GOD OF ISRAEL

Hear O Israel, the Lord is our God, the Lord is One.

Blessed is His name, whose glorious kingdom is forever and ever.

Love the Lord your God with all your heart, and all your soul, and all your might. These words that I command you today shall be upon your heart. Repeat them to your children, and talk about them when you sit in your home, and when you walk in the street; when you lie down, and when you rise up. Hold fast to them as a sign upon your hand, and let them be as reminders before your eyes. Write them on the doorposts of your home and at your gates.

Deuteronomy 6: 4–9

וְהָיָה אִם־שָׁמֹעַ תִּשְׁמְעוּ אֶל־מִצְוֹתַי אֲשֶׁר אָנֹכִי מְצַוֶּה
אֶתְכֶם הַיּוֹם · לְאַהֲבָה אֶת־יְהֹוָה אֱלֹהֵיכֶם וּלְעָבְדוֹ בְּכָל־
לְבַבְכֶם וּבְכָל־נַפְשְׁכֶם : וְנָתַתִּי מְטַר־אַרְצְכֶם בְּעִתּוֹ יוֹרֶה
וּמַלְקוֹשׁ · וְאָסַפְתָּ דְגָנֶךָ וְתִירשְׁךָ וְיִצְהָרֶךָ : וְנָתַתִּי עֵשֶׂב בְּשָׂדְךָ
לִבְהֶמְתֶּךָ · וְאָכַלְתָּ וְשָׂבָעְתָּ : הִשָּׁמְרוּ לָכֶם פֶּן־יִפְתֶּה
לְבַבְכֶם · וְסַרְתֶּם וַעֲבַדְתֶּם אֱלֹהִים אֲחֵרִים וְהִשְׁתַּחֲוִיתֶם
לָהֶם : וְחָרָה אַף־יְהֹוָה בָּכֶם וְעָצַר אֶת־הַשָּׁמַיִם וְלֹא־יִהְיֶה
מָטָר וְהָאֲדָמָה לֹא תִתֵּן אֶת־יְבוּלָהּ · וַאֲבַדְתֶּם מְהֵרָה מֵעַל
הָאָרֶץ הַטֹּבָה אֲשֶׁר יְהֹוָה נֹתֵן לָכֶם : וְשַׂמְתֶּם אֶת־דְּבָרַי
אֵלֶּה עַל־לְבַבְכֶם וְעַל־נַפְשְׁכֶם · וּקְשַׁרְתֶּם אֹתָם לְאוֹת
עַל־יֶדְכֶם וְהָיוּ לְטוֹטָפֹת בֵּין עֵינֵיכֶם : וְלִמַּדְתֶּם אֹתָם אֶת־
בְּנֵיכֶם לְדַבֵּר בָּם · בְּשִׁבְתְּךָ בְּבֵיתֶךָ וּבְלֶכְתְּךָ בַדֶּרֶךְ
וּבְשָׁכְבְּךָ וּבְקוּמֶךָ : וּכְתַבְתָּם עַל־מְזוּזוֹת בֵּיתֶךָ וּבִשְׁעָרֶיךָ :
לְמַעַן יִרְבּוּ יְמֵיכֶם וִימֵי בְנֵיכֶם עַל הָאֲדָמָה אֲשֶׁר נִשְׁבַּע
יְהֹוָה לַאֲבֹתֵיכֶם לָתֵת לָהֶם · כִּימֵי הַשָּׁמַיִם עַל־הָאָרֶץ :

וַיֹּאמֶר יְהֹוָה אֶל־מֹשֶׁה לֵּאמֹר : דַּבֵּר אֶל־בְּנֵי יִשְׂרָאֵל
וְאָמַרְתָּ אֲלֵהֶם וְעָשׂוּ לָהֶם צִיצִת עַל־כַּנְפֵי בִגְדֵיהֶם
לְדֹרֹתָם · וְנָתְנוּ עַל־צִיצִת הַכָּנָף פְּתִיל תְּכֵלֶת : וְהָיָה לָכֶם
לְצִיצִת וּרְאִיתֶם אֹתוֹ וּזְכַרְתֶּם אֶת־כָּל־מִצְוֹת יְהֹוָה וַעֲשִׂיתֶם
אֹתָם · וְלֹא־תָתוּרוּ אַחֲרֵי לְבַבְכֶם וְאַחֲרֵי עֵינֵיכֶם אֲשֶׁר־
אַתֶּם זֹנִים אַחֲרֵיהֶם : לְמַעַן תִּזְכְּרוּ וַעֲשִׂיתֶם אֶת־כָּל־
מִצְוֹתָי · וִהְיִיתֶם קְדֹשִׁים לֵאלֹהֵיכֶם : אֲנִי יְהֹוָה אֱלֹהֵיכֶם
אֲשֶׁר הוֹצֵאתִי אֶתְכֶם מֵאֶרֶץ מִצְרַיִם לִהְיוֹת לָכֶם לֵאלֹהִים ·
אֲנִי יְהֹוָה אֱלֹהֵיכֶם:

This will happen if you listen carefully to My commands which I give you today, to love the Lord your God and to serve Him with all your heart and all your soul. I shall then give your land rain at the right time, the autumn rain and the spring rain, so that you can harvest your corn, your wine and your oil. I shall also give grass in your fields to your cattle, and you will eat and be full. Take care that your heart is not deceived into straying, obeying other gods and worshipping them. The anger of God will then blaze out against you. He will shut up the sky. There will be no rain. The land will not produce, and you will quickly be destroyed from the good land which the Lord gives you. So put these words of Mine in your heart and in your soul, and hold fast to them as a sign upon your hand and as reminders before your eyes. Repeat them to your children, and talk about them when you sit in your home, and when you walk in the street, when you lie down and when you rise up. Write them on the doorposts of your home and at your gates. Then you and your children may live long on the good land that God promised to give your fathers as long as there is a sky over the earth.

Deuteronomy 11: 13–21

The Lord said to Moses: 'Speak to the children of Israel and tell them that each generation shall put tassels on the corner of their clothes, and put a blue thread on the corner tassel. Then when this tassel catches your eye, you will remember all the Lord's commands and do them. Then you will no longer wander after the desires of your heart and your eyes which led you to lust. Then you will remember all My commands and do them and you will be set apart for your God. I am the Lord your God, who brought you out of the land of Egypt, to be your own God. I, the Lord, am your God.'

Numbers 15: 37–41

אֱמֶת וְיַצִּיב וְנָכוֹן וְקַיָּם וּמְקֻבָּל וְטוֹב הַדָּבָר הַזֶּה עָלֵינוּ
לְעוֹלָם וָעֶד: אֱמֶת אֱלֹהֵי עוֹלָם מַלְכֵּנוּ · צוּר
יַעֲקֹב מָגֵן יִשְׁעֵנוּ · לְדוֹר וָדוֹר הוּא קַיָּם · וּמַלְכוּתוֹ וֶאֱמוּנָתוֹ
לָעַד קַיֶּמֶת: אֱמֶת שָׁאַתָּה הוּא יְיָ אֱלֹהֵינוּ וֵאלֹהֵי אֲבוֹתֵינוּ ·
פּוֹדֵנוּ וּמַצִּילֵנוּ · מֵעוֹלָם הוּא שְׁמֶךָ · אֵין אֱלֹהִים זוּלָתֶךָ:
עֶזְרַת אֲבוֹתֵינוּ אַתָּה הוּא מֵעוֹלָם · מָגֵן וּמוֹשִׁיעַ לָהֶם
וְלִבְנֵיהֶם אַחֲרֵיהֶם בְּכָל־דּוֹר וָדוֹר: אַשְׁרֵי אִישׁ שֶׁיִּשְׁמַע
לְמִצְוֹתֶיךָ · וְתוֹרָתְךָ וּדְבָרְךָ יָשִׂים עַל־לִבּוֹ: אֱמֶת אַתָּה
הוּא רִאשׁוֹן · וְאַתָּה הוּא אַחֲרוֹן · וּמִבַּלְעָדֶיךָ אֵין לָנוּ מֶלֶךְ
גּוֹאֵל וּמוֹשִׁיעַ:

צוּר יִשְׂרָאֵל · קוּמָה בְּעֶזְרַת יִשְׂרָאֵל · גְּאָלֵנוּ יְיָ צְבָאוֹת
שְׁמוֹ קְדוֹשׁ יִשְׂרָאֵל · בָּרוּךְ אַתָּה יְיָ · גָּאַל יִשְׂרָאֵל:

Wilkowiszki, Russia

TRUTH
AND RE-
DEMPTION
     Your word is true forever. It is certain for us, it is firm, accepted and good. It is true that the everlasting God is our king; the strength of Jacob, the defender of our safety. He endures from generation to generation, and His rule and His faithfulness stand firm forever. It is true that You are the Lord our God, and God of our fathers, who rescues and delivers us. So were You ever known. There is no God besides You.

It is You who always helped our fathers. In every generation You were the shield and saviour for them and their children after them. Happy indeed is the man who hears Your commands, and sets Your teaching and Your word upon his heart. It is true that You are the first, and that You are the last, and besides You we have no king who rescues and saves us.

Rock of Israel, rise up to the aid of Your people Israel. He rescues us, the Lord of all creation, the holiness of Israel. Blessed are You Lord, who rescues Israel.

The service continues with the Amidah, page 232. (On the Days of Repentance, page 240.)

Zolkiew, Galicia

DAILY AFTERNOON AND EVENING
SERVICES

וְהוּא רַחוּם יְכַפֵּר עָוֹן וְלֹא
יַשְׁחִית וְהִרְבָּה לְהָשִׁיב אַפּוֹ
וְלֹא יָעִיר כָּל־חֲמָתוֹ:

אַשְׁרֵי יוֹשְׁבֵי בֵיתֶךָ עוֹד
יְהַלְלוּךָ סֶּלָה:
אַשְׁרֵי הָעָם שֶׁכָּכָה לּוֹ אַשְׁרֵי
הָעָם שֶׁיְיָ אֱלֹהָיו:

בָּרְכוּ אֶת־יְיָ הַמְבֹרָךְ:

בָּרוּךְ יְיָ הַמְבֹרָךְ לְעוֹלָם וָעֶד:

בָּרוּךְ אַתָּה יְיָ אֱלֹהֵינוּ מֶלֶךְ הָעוֹלָם · אֲשֶׁר בִּדְבָרוֹ מַעֲרִיב
עֲרָבִים · בְּחָכְמָה פּוֹתֵחַ שְׁעָרִים · וּבִתְבוּנָה מְשַׁנֶּה עִתִּים ·
וּמַחֲלִיף אֶת־הַזְּמַנִּים · וּמְסַדֵּר אֶת־הַכּוֹכָבִים בְּמִשְׁמְרוֹתֵיהֶם
בָּרָקִיעַ כִּרְצוֹנוֹ: בּוֹרֵא יוֹם וָלַיְלָה · גּוֹלֵל אוֹר מִפְּנֵי חֹשֶׁךְ
וְחֹשֶׁךְ מִפְּנֵי אוֹר: הַמַּעֲבִיר יוֹם וּמֵבִיא לָיְלָה · וּמַבְדִּיל בֵּין
יוֹם וּבֵין לָיְלָה · יְיָ צְבָאוֹת שְׁמוֹ: בָּרוּךְ אַתָּה יְיָ · הַמַּעֲרִיב
עֲרָבִים:

אַהֲבַת עוֹלָם בֵּית יִשְׂרָאֵל עַמְּךָ אָהַבְתָּ · תּוֹרָה וּמִצְוֹת
חֻקִּים וּמִשְׁפָּטִים אוֹתָנוּ לִמַּדְתָּ: עַל־כֵּן יְיָ אֱלֹהֵינוּ · בְּשָׁכְבֵנוּ
וּבְקוּמֵנוּ נָשִׂיחַ בְּחֻקֶּיךָ · וְנִשְׂמַח וְנַעֲלֹז בְּדִבְרֵי תוֹרָתֶךָ
וּמִצְוֹתֶיךָ וְחֻקּוֹתֶיךָ לְעוֹלָם וָעֶד: כִּי הֵם חַיֵּינוּ וְאֹרֶךְ יָמֵינוּ ·
וּבָהֶם נֶהְגֶּה יוֹמָם וָלָיְלָה · וְאַהֲבָתְךָ אַל־תָּסִיר מִמֶּנּוּ
לְעוֹלָמִים: בָּרוּךְ אַתָּה יְיָ · אוֹהֵב אֶת־עַמּוֹ יִשְׂרָאֵל:

DAILY AFTERNOON AND EVENING SERVICES

Evening

Psalm 134 (page 550) or another suitable psalm may be read.

Because He is merciful He forgives sin and does not destroy. Many times He turns aside His rage and does not rouse His anger.

The evening service continues here.

Afternoon

Happy are those who live in
　Your house,
　and can always praise You.
Happy the people of whom this
　is true!
　Happy the people whose God
　is the Lord!

Psalm 145 (page 556) or another suitable psalm may be read.
The service continues with the Amidah, page 232. (On the Days of Repentance, page 240.)

THE CALL TO COMMUNITY PRAYER

Bless the Lord whom we are called to bless.

Blessed be the Lord whom we are called to bless forever and ever.

THE CREATOR OF THE UNIVERSE

Blessed are You, Lord our God, king of the universe. By His word He brings on the evening twilight; in wisdom He opens the gates of dawn, and with foresight makes times pass and seasons change. He sets the stars in their courses in the sky according to His plan. He creates day and night, turning light into darkness and darkness into light. He makes the day fade away and brings on the night, and separates day and night, for He is the Lord of the hosts of heaven. Blessed are You Lord, who brings on the evening twilight.

HIS LOVE FOR ISRAEL

With everlasting love have You loved Your people the family of Israel. Teaching and practice, duty and justice—these You have taught us. Therefore, Lord our God, we think upon all this before we sleep and when we wake, and rejoice and delight in Your teaching and its practice forever and ever, for they are our life and the measure of our days. We keep them in mind both day and night. Never take Your love away from us. Blessed are You Lord, who loves His people Israel.

שְׁמַ**ע** יִשְׂרָאֵל · יְהֹוָה אֱלֹהֵינוּ יְהֹוָה אֶחָ**ד** :

בָּרוּךְ שֵׁם כְּבוֹד מַלְכוּתוֹ לְעוֹלָם וָעֶד :

וְאָהַבְתָּ אֵת יְהֹוָה אֱלֹהֶיךָ · בְּכָל־לְבָבְךָ וּבְכָל־נַפְשְׁךָ
וּבְכָל־מְאֹדֶךָ : וְהָיוּ הַדְּבָרִים הָאֵלֶּה אֲשֶׁר אָנֹכִי מְצַוְּךָ הַיּוֹם
עַל־לְבָבֶךָ : וְשִׁנַּנְתָּם לְבָנֶיךָ וְדִבַּרְתָּ בָּם · בְּשִׁבְתְּךָ בְּבֵיתֶךָ
וּבְלֶכְתְּךָ בַדֶּרֶךְ וּבְשָׁכְבְּךָ וּבְקוּמֶךָ : וּקְשַׁרְתָּם לְאוֹת עַל־
יָדֶךָ · וְהָיוּ לְטֹטָפֹת בֵּין עֵינֶיךָ : וּכְתַבְתָּם עַל־מְזֻזוֹת בֵּיתֶךָ
וּבִשְׁעָרֶיךָ :

אֱמֶת וֶאֱמוּנָ**ה** כָּל־זֹאת וְקַיָּם עָלֵינוּ כִּי הוּא יְיָ
אֱלֹהֵינוּ וְאֵין זוּלָתוֹ וַאֲנַחְנוּ יִשְׂרָאֵל
עַמּוֹ · הָעֹשֶׂה גְדֹלוֹת עַד־אֵין חֵקֶר וְנִפְלָאוֹת עַד־אֵין
מִסְפָּר · וְרָאוּ בָנָיו גְּבוּרָתוֹ שִׁבְּחוּ וְהוֹדוּ לִשְׁמוֹ וּמַלְכוּתוֹ
בְּרָצוֹן קִבְּלוּ עֲלֵיהֶם · מֹשֶׁה וּבְנֵי יִשְׂרָאֵל לְךָ עָנוּ שִׁירָה
בְּשִׂמְחָה רַבָּה · וְאָמְרוּ כֻלָּם ·
מִי־כָמֹכָה בָּאֵלִם יְהֹוָה מִי כָּמֹכָה נֶאְדָּר בַּקֹּדֶשׁ נוֹרָא
תְהִלֹּת עֹשֵׂה פֶלֶא :
מַלְכוּתְךָ יְיָ אֱלֹהֵינוּ רָאוּ בָנֶיךָ עַל הַיָּם · יַחַד כֻּלָּם הוֹדוּ
וְהִמְלִיכוּ וְאָמְרוּ · יְהֹוָה יִמְלֹךְ לְעֹלָם וָעֶד :
וְנֶאֱמַר כִּי־פָדָה יְיָ אֶת־יַעֲקֹב וּגְאָלוֹ מִיַּד חָזָק מִמֶּנּוּ ·
בָּרוּךְ אַתָּה יְיָ · גָּאַל יִשְׂרָאֵל :

הַשְׁכִּיבֵנוּ אָבִינוּ לְשָׁלוֹם וְהַעֲמִידֵנוּ מַלְכֵּנוּ לְחַיִּים ·
וּפְרוֹשׂ עָלֵינוּ סֻכַּת שְׁלוֹמֶךָ וְתַקְּנֵנוּ בְּעֵצָה טוֹבָה מִלְּפָנֶיךָ
וְהוֹשִׁיעֵנוּ לְמַעַן שְׁמֶךָ · וְהָגֵן בַּעֲדֵנוּ וְהָסֵר מֵעָלֵינוּ אוֹיֵב
דֶּבֶר וְחֶרֶב וְרָעָב וְיָגוֹן · וּבְצֵל כְּנָפֶיךָ תַּסְתִּירֵנוּ כִּי אֵל

THE GOD OF ISRAEL

Hear O Israel, the Lord is our God, the Lord is One.

Blessed is His name, whose glorious kingdom is forever and ever.

Love the Lord your God with all your heart, and all your soul, and all your might. These words that I command you today shall be upon your heart. Repeat them to your children, and talk about them when you sit in your home, and when you walk in the street; when you lie down, and when you rise up. Hold fast to them as a sign upon your hand, and let them be as reminders before your eyes. Write them on the doorposts of your home and at your gates.

Deuteronomy 6: 4–9

The second and third paragraphs of the Shema are on page 222.

OUR REDEEMER

All this is true and firmly held by us, that He is the Lord our God, for no other exists, and that we are Israel, His people. He performs great deeds beyond research, too wonderful to tell. His children saw His power, praised and thanked His name, and willingly accepted His rule over them. With great joy Moses and the children of Israel answered You in song, all of them saying:
'Who is like You, Lord, among the gods men worship!
Who is like You, majestic in holiness,
awesome in praise, working wonders!'
Lord our God, Your children saw Your rule over the Red Sea. All of them as one honoured You as king, saying:
'The Lord shall rule forever and ever!'
And it is prophesied:
'For the Lord has set Jacob free and rescued him from a hand stronger than his own.'
Blessed are You Lord, who rescues Israel.

HIS GIFT PEACE, JOY AND REST

Cause us, our father, to lie down in peace, and rise again to enjoy life. Spread over us the covering of Your peace, guide us with Your good counsel and save us for the sake of Your name. Be a shield about us, turning away every enemy, disease, violence, hunger and sorrow.

שׁוֹמְרֵנוּ וּמַצִּילֵנוּ אָתָּה כִּי אֵל מֶלֶךְ חַנּוּן וְרַחוּם אָתָּה · וּשְׁמוֹר
צֵאתֵנוּ וּבוֹאֵנוּ לְחַיִּים וּלְשָׁלוֹם מֵעַתָּה וְעַד עוֹלָם : בָּרוּךְ
אַתָּה יְיָ · שׁוֹמֵר עַמּוֹ יִשְׂרָאֵל לָעַד :

בָּרוּךְ יְיָ בַּיּוֹם · בָּרוּךְ יְיָ בַּלָּיְלָה · בָּרוּךְ יְיָ בְּשָׁכְבֵּנוּ ·
בָּרוּךְ יְיָ בְּקוּמֵנוּ : כִּי בְיָדְךָ נַפְשׁוֹת הַחַיִּים וְהַמֵּתִים : אֲשֶׁר
בְּיָדוֹ נֶפֶשׁ כָּל־חָי וְרוּחַ כָּל־בְּשַׂר־אִישׁ : בְּיָדְךָ אַפְקִיד
רוּחִי פָּדִיתָה אוֹתִי יְיָ אֵל אֱמֶת : אֱלֹהֵינוּ שֶׁבַּשָּׁמַיִם יַחֵד
שִׁמְךָ וְקַיֵּם מַלְכוּתְךָ תָּמִיד וּמְלוֹךְ עָלֵינוּ לְעוֹלָם וָעֶד :

The half Kaddish on page 168 may be included here.

The service continues on the following page. (On the Days of Repentance, page 240.)

Pesaro

Shelter us in the shadow of Your wings, for You are a God who guards and protects us, a ruler of mercy and compassion. Guard us when we go out and when we come in, to enjoy life and peace both now and forever. Blessed are You Lord, who guards His people Israel forever.

Blessed be the Lord by day. Blessed be the Lord by night. Blessed be the Lord when we lie down. Blessed be the Lord when we rise up. For in Your hand are the souls of the living and the dead. 'In His hand is the soul of every creature and the soul of human flesh.' 'Within His hand I lay my soul, You have redeemed me, Lord God of truth.' Our God who is in heaven, reveal Your unity, establish Your kingdom for all time and rule over us forever and ever.

The half Kaddish on page 168 may be included here.

The service continues on the following page. (On the Days of Repentance, page 240.)

Toledo

DAILY AMIDAH

אֲדֹנָי שְׂפָתַי תִּפְתָּח · וּפִי יַגִּיד תְּהִלָּתֶךָ :

בָּרוּךְ אַתָּה יְיָ אֱלֹהֵינוּ וֵאלֹהֵי אֲבוֹתֵינוּ · אֱלֹהֵי אַבְרָהָם ·
אֱלֹהֵי יִצְחָק · וֵאלֹהֵי יַעֲקֹב · הָאֵל הַגָּדוֹל הַגִּבּוֹר
וְהַנּוֹרָא · אֵל עֶלְיוֹן · גּוֹמֵל חֲסָדִים טוֹבִים קוֹנֵה הַכֹּל וְזוֹכֵר
חַסְדֵי אָבוֹת וּמֵבִיא גוֹאֵל לִבְנֵי בְנֵיהֶם לְמַעַן שְׁמוֹ בְּאַהֲבָה :
מֶלֶךְ עוֹזֵר וּמוֹשִׁיעַ וּמָגֵן · בָּרוּךְ אַתָּה יְיָ · מָגֵן אַבְרָהָם :

אַתָּה גִּבּוֹר לְעוֹלָם יְיָ · מְחַיֵּה מֵתִים אַתָּה רַב לְהוֹשִׁיעַ ·
מְכַלְכֵּל חַיִּים בְּחֶסֶד · מְחַיֵּה מֵתִים בְּרַחֲמִים
רַבִּים · סוֹמֵךְ נוֹפְלִים · וְרוֹפֵא חוֹלִים · וּמַתִּיר אֲסוּרִים ·
וּמְקַיֵּם אֱמוּנָתוֹ לִישֵׁנֵי עָפָר : מִי כָמוֹךָ בַּעַל גְּבוּרוֹת וּמִי
דוֹמֶה לָּךְ · מֶלֶךְ מֵמִית וּמְחַיֶּה · וּמַצְמִיחַ יְשׁוּעָה : וְנֶאֱמָן אַתָּה
לְהַחֲיוֹת מֵתִים · בָּרוּךְ אַתָּה יְיָ · מְחַיֵּה הַמֵּתִים :

Evening	*Morning and afternoon*
נְקַדֵּשׁ אֶת־שִׁמְךָ בָּעוֹלָם	אַתָּה קָדוֹשׁ וְשִׁמְךָ קָדוֹשׁ
כְּשֵׁם שֶׁמַּקְדִּישִׁים אוֹתוֹ בִּשְׁמֵי	וּקְדוֹשִׁים בְּכָל־יוֹם יְהַלְלוּךָ
מָרוֹם כַּכָּתוּב עַל יַד נְבִיאֶךָ ·	סֶלָה · בָּרוּךְ אַתָּה יְיָ · הָאֵל
וְקָרָא זֶה אֶל זֶה וְאָמַר ·	הַקָּדוֹשׁ :

קָדוֹשׁ קָדוֹשׁ קָדוֹשׁ יְיָ צְבָאוֹת · מְלֹא כָל־הָאָרֶץ
כְּבוֹדוֹ :

לְעֻמָּתָם בָּרוּךְ יֹאמֵרוּ ·

בָּרוּךְ כְּבוֹד יְיָ מִמְּקוֹמוֹ :

וּבְדִבְרֵי קָדְשְׁךָ כָּתוּב לֵאמֹר ·

יִמְלֹךְ יְיָ לְעוֹלָם אֱלֹהַיִךְ צִיּוֹן לְדֹר וָדֹר · הַלְלוּיָהּ :

DAILY AMIDAH

Lord, open my lips and my mouth shall declare Your praise.

GOD OF HISTORY Blessed are You, Lord our God, and God of our fathers, God of Abraham, God of Isaac, and God of Jacob, the great, the mighty, and the awesome God, God beyond, generous in love and kindness, and possessing all. He remembers the good deeds of our fathers, and therefore in love brings rescue to the generations, for such is His being. The king who helps and saves and shields. Blessed are You Lord, the shield of Abraham.

GOD OF MIGHT You, O Lord, are the endless power that renews life beyond death; You are the greatness that saves. You care for the living with love. You renew life beyond death with unending mercy. You support the falling, and heal the sick. You free prisoners, and keep faith with those who sleep in the dust. Who can perform such mighty deeds, and who can compare with You, a king who brings death and life, and renews salvation. You are faithful to renew life beyond death. Blessed are You Lord, who renews life beyond death.

GOD OF HOLINESS

Morning and afternoon

We sanctify Your name in the world as they sanctify it in the highest heavens. As it is written by the hand of Your prophet: And they called to each other and said:

Evening

You are holy and Your name is holy, and those who seek holiness praise You day by day.

Blessed are You Lord, the holy God.

_____

Holy, holy, holy is the Lord of all creation, the whole earth is full of His glory.

They cry in answer, 'Blessed!'

Blessed is His glory revealed in every place.

And in Your holy writing it is said:

The Lord shall rule forever! Zion, He is your God for all generations! Praise the Lord!

לְדוֹר וָדוֹר נַגִּיד גָּדְלֶךָ · וּלְנֵצַח נְצָחִים קְדֻשָּׁתְךָ נַקְדִּישׁ · וְשִׁבְחֲךָ אֱלֹהֵינוּ מִפִּינוּ לֹא יָמוּשׁ לְעוֹלָם וָעֶד · כִּי אֵל מֶלֶךְ גָּדוֹל וְקָדוֹשׁ אָתָּה · בָּרוּךְ אַתָּה יְיָ · הָאֵל הַקָּדוֹשׁ:

אַתָּה חוֹנֵן לְאָדָם דַּעַת · וּמְלַמֵּד לֶאֱנוֹשׁ בִּינָה · חָנֵּנוּ מֵאִתְּךָ דֵּעָה וּבִינָה וְהַשְׂכֵּל · בָּרוּךְ אַתָּה יְיָ · חוֹנֵן הַדָּעַת:

הֲשִׁיבֵנוּ אָבִינוּ לְתוֹרָתֶךָ · וְקָרְבֵנוּ מַלְכֵּנוּ לַעֲבוֹדָתֶךָ · וְהַחֲזִירֵנוּ בִּתְשׁוּבָה שְׁלֵמָה לְפָנֶיךָ · בָּרוּךְ אַתָּה יְיָ · הָרוֹצֶה בִּתְשׁוּבָה:

סְלַח־לָנוּ אָבִינוּ כִּי חָטָאנוּ · מְחַל־לָנוּ מַלְכֵּנוּ כִּי פָשָׁעְנוּ · כִּי אֵל טוֹב וְסַלָּח אָתָּה · בָּרוּךְ אַתָּה יְיָ · חַנּוּן הַמַּרְבֶּה לִסְלוֹחַ:

רְאֵה בְעָנְיֵנוּ וְרִיבָה רִיבֵנוּ · וּגְאָלֵנוּ מְהֵרָה לְמַעַן שְׁמֶךָ · כִּי גּוֹאֵל חָזָק אָתָּה · בָּרוּךְ אַתָּה יְיָ · גּוֹאֵל יִשְׂרָאֵל:

רְפָאֵנוּ יְיָ וְנֵרָפֵא · הוֹשִׁיעֵנוּ וְנִוָּשֵׁעָה · כִּי תְהִלָּתֵנוּ אָתָּה · וְהַעֲלֵה אֲרֻכָה וּמַרְפֵּא לְכָל־תַּחֲלוּאֵינוּ וּלְכָל־מַכְאוֹבֵינוּ וּלְכָל־מַכּוֹתֵינוּ · כִּי אֵל רוֹפֵא רַחֲמָן וְנֶאֱמָן אָתָּה · בָּרוּךְ אַתָּה יְיָ · רוֹפֵא הַחוֹלִים:

בָּרֵךְ עָלֵינוּ יְיָ אֱלֹהֵינוּ אֶת־הַשָּׁנָה הַזֹּאת וְאֶת־כָּל־מִינֵי תְבוּאָתָהּ לְטוֹבָה · וְתֵן בְּרָכָה עַל פְּנֵי הָאֲדָמָה · וְשַׂבְּעֵנוּ מִטּוּבֶךָ · וּבָרֵךְ שְׁנוֹתֵינוּ כַּשָּׁנִים הַטּוֹבוֹת · בָּרוּךְ אַתָּה יְיָ · מְבָרֵךְ הַשָּׁנִים:

תְּקַע בְּשׁוֹפָר גָּדוֹל לְחֵרוּתֵנוּ · וְתִשָּׂא מְהֵרָה פְּדוּת בְּעָרֵי־אַרְצֵנוּ כִּי אֵל פּוֹדֶה וְגוֹאֵל אָתָּה · בָּרוּךְ אַתָּה יְיָ · הַפּוֹדֶה עַמּוֹ יִשְׂרָאֵל בְּרַחֲמִים:

הָשֵׁב מִשְׁפַּט־צִדְקָתֶךָ בָּעוֹלָם וְהָסֵר מִמֶּנּוּ יָגוֹן וַאֲנָחָה · וּמְלוֹךְ עָלֵינוּ אַתָּה יְיָ לְבַדְּךָ בְּחֶסֶד וּבְרַחֲמִים · וְצַדְּקֵנוּ בַּמִּשְׁפָּט · בָּרוּךְ אַתָּה יְיָ · מֶלֶךְ אוֹהֵב צְדָקָה וּמִשְׁפָּט:

We declare Your greatness to all generations, and to all eternity we proclaim Your holiness. Your praise shall never depart from our mouth, for You are God, the great and holy king. Blessed are You Lord, the holy God.

You favour mankind with knowledge, and teach mortals understanding. Favour us with the knowledge, understanding and discernment that come from You. Blessed are You Lord, who favours us with knowledge.

Turn us back to Your teaching, our father, and draw us near to Your service, our king. Bring us back in perfect repentance to Your presence. Blessed are You Lord, who desires repentance.

Forgive us, our father, for we have sinned; pardon us, our king, for we have disobeyed; for You are a God who is good and forgiving. Blessed are You Lord, who is generous to forgive.

Look upon our affliction and defend our cause, and rescue us quickly for the sake of Your name. For You are a mighty redeemer. Blessed are You Lord, the redeemer of Israel.

Heal us, Lord, and we shall be healed; save us, and we shall be saved; for it is You we praise. Send relief and healing for all our diseases, our sufferings and our wounds; for You are a merciful and faithful healer. Blessed are You Lord, who heals the sick.

Bless this year, O Lord our God, and may all that it brings be good for us; send Your blessings over the face of the earth, satisfy us with Your goodness, and make our years good years. Blessed are You Lord, who blesses the years.

Sound the great horn for our freedom, and speedily may the voice of liberty be heard in the cities of our lands, for You are a God who redeems and rescues. Blessed are You Lord, who redeems His people Israel in mercy.

Restore Your judgment of righteousness in the world. Turn away from us sorrow and pain, rule over us with love and mercy, and judge us with righteousness. Blessed are You Lord, the king who loves righteousness and truth.

וְלַמַּלְשִׁינוּת אַל תְּהִי תִקְוָה וְכָל־הָרִשְׁעָה כְּרֶגַע תֹּאבֵד. כִּי אַתָּה יוֹדֵעַ אֶת־עֲצַת־אָדָם. בָּרוּךְ אַתָּה יְיָ. הַמַּעֲבִיר רִשְׁעָה מִן־הָאָרֶץ:

עַל־הַצַּדִּיקִים וְעַל־הַחֲסִידִים וְעַל־הַתְּמִימִים וְעַל גֵּרֵי הַצֶּדֶק וְעָלֵינוּ יֶהֱמוּ רַחֲמֶיךָ יְיָ אֱלֹהֵינוּ. וְתֵן שָׂכָר טוֹב לְכָל הַבּוֹטְחִים בְּשִׁמְךָ בֶּאֱמֶת. בָּרוּךְ אַתָּה יְיָ. מִשְׁעָן וּמִבְטָח לַצַּדִּיקִים:

וְלִירוּשָׁלַיִם עִירְךָ בְּרַחֲמִים תָּשׁוּב. וְתִשְׁכּוֹן בְּתוֹכָהּ וּבְנֵה אוֹתָהּ בְּקָרוֹב בְּיָמֵינוּ בִּנְיַן עוֹלָם. וְכִסֵּא דָוִד מְהֵרָה לְתוֹכָהּ תָּכִין. בָּרוּךְ אַתָּה יְיָ. בּוֹנֵה יְרוּשָׁלָיִם:

אֶת־צֶמַח דָּוִד עַבְדְּךָ מְהֵרָה תַצְמִיחַ. וְקַרְנוֹ תָּרוּם בִּישׁוּעָתֶךָ. כִּי לִישׁוּעָתְךָ קִוִּינוּ כָּל־הַיּוֹם. בָּרוּךְ אַתָּה יְיָ. מַצְמִיחַ קֶרֶן יְשׁוּעָה:

שְׁמַע קוֹלֵנוּ יְיָ אֱלֹהֵינוּ אָב הָרַחֲמָן. חוּס וְרַחֵם עָלֵינוּ. וְקַבֵּל בְּרַחֲמִים וּבְרָצוֹן אֶת־תְּפִלָּתֵנוּ. כִּי אֵל שׁוֹמֵעַ תְּפִלּוֹת וְתַחֲנוּנִים אָתָּה. וּמִלְּפָנֶיךָ מַלְכֵּנוּ רֵיקָם אַל־תְּשִׁיבֵנוּ. כִּי אַתָּה שׁוֹמֵעַ תְּפִלַּת כָּל־פֶּה. בָּרוּךְ אַתָּה יְיָ. שׁוֹמֵעַ תְּפִלָּה:

רְצֵה יְיָ אֱלֹהֵינוּ בְּעַמְּךָ יִשְׂרָאֵל. וְלִתְפִלָּתָם שְׁעֵה. וּבְרַחֲמֶיךָ הָרַבִּים תַּחְפֹּץ בָּנוּ וְתִשְׁרֶה שְׁכִינָתְךָ עַל צִיּוֹן. וְתֶחֱזֶינָה עֵינֵינוּ בְּשׁוּבְךָ לְצִיּוֹן בְּרַחֲמִים. בָּרוּךְ אַתָּה יְיָ. הַמַּחֲזִיר שְׁכִינָתוֹ לְצִיּוֹן:

מוֹדִים אֲנַחְנוּ לָךְ שָׁאַתָּה הוּא יְיָ אֱלֹהֵינוּ וֵאלֹהֵי אֲבוֹתֵינוּ לְעוֹלָם וָעֶד. צוּרֵנוּ צוּר חַיֵּינוּ וּמָגֵן יִשְׁעֵנוּ אַתָּה הוּא לְדוֹר וָדוֹר: נוֹדֶה לְךָ וּנְסַפֵּר תְּהִלָּתֶךָ עַל חַיֵּינוּ הַמְּסוּרִים בְּיָדֶךָ. וְעַל נִשְׁמוֹתֵינוּ הַפְּקוּדוֹת לָךְ. וְעַל נִסֶּיךָ שֶׁבְּכָל־יוֹם עִמָּנוּ. וְעַל נִפְלְאוֹתֶיךָ וְטוֹבוֹתֶיךָ שֶׁבְּכָל־עֵת עֶרֶב וָבֹקֶר וְצָהֳרָיִם: הַטּוֹב כִּי לֹא כָלוּ רַחֲמֶיךָ. הַמְרַחֵם כִּי לֹא תַמּוּ חֲסָדֶיךָ. כִּי מֵעוֹלָם קִוִּינוּ לָךְ:

And may there be no hope for slander, and may all evil come to nothing, for You know the motives of man. Blessed are You Lord, who makes evil pass away from the earth.

To the righteous, the pious, and the honest, to those who join us in righteousness, and us ourselves, be merciful Lord our God. Grant a good reward to all who sincerely trust in You. Blessed are You Lord, the support and safety of the righteous.

Turn in mercy to Jerusalem and may Your presence dwell within it. Rebuild the city of righteousness soon in our days, and may it be a centre of prayer for all people. Blessed are You Lord, who builds Jerusalem.

Fulfil in our time the words of Your servant David, so that men are again ruled in justice and in the fear of God. Let light dawn in the world in our days, for we wait and work for Your salvation. Blessed are You Lord, who makes the power of salvation flourish.

Hear our voice, Lord our God, father of mercy. Spare us and have pity on us, and receive our prayer with love and favour. For You are a God who listens to our prayers and needs. Our king, do not turn us away empty from Your presence, for You hear the prayers of all lips. Blessed are You Lord, who listens to prayers.

On the Days of Repentance continue on page 244.

THANKS-
GIVING
AND PEACE

Lord our God, be pleased with Your people Israel and listen to their prayers. In Your great mercy delight in us so that Your presence may rest upon Zion. Our eyes look forward to Your return to Zion in mercy! Blessed are You Lord, who restores His presence to Zion.

We declare with gratitude that You are our God and the God of our fathers forever. You are our rock, the rock of our life and the shield that saves us. In every generation we thank You and recount Your praise for our lives held in Your hand, for our souls that are in Your care, and for the signs of Your presence that are with us every day. At every moment, at evening, morning and noon, we experience Your wonders and Your goodness. You are goodness itself, for Your mercy has no end. You are mercy itself, for Your love has no limit. Forever have we put our hope in You.

וְעַל כֻּלָּם יִתְבָּרַךְ וְיִתְרוֹמֵם וְיִתְנַשֵּׂא תָּמִיד שִׁמְךָ מַלְכֵּנוּ
לְעוֹלָם וָעֶד: וְכָל־הַחַיִּים יוֹדוּךָ סֶּלָה ׃ וִיהַלְלוּ וִיבָרְכוּ
אֶת־שִׁמְךָ הַגָּדוֹל בֶּאֱמֶת ׃ הָאֵל יְשׁוּעָתֵנוּ וְעֶזְרָתֵנוּ סֶלָה:
בָּרוּךְ אַתָּה יְיָ ׃ הַטּוֹב שִׁמְךָ וּלְךָ נָאֶה לְהוֹדוֹת:

<table>
<tr><td>For an afternoon or evening service</td><td>For a morning service</td></tr>
</table>

שָׁלוֹם רָב עַל
יִשְׂרָאֵל עַמְּךָ תָּשִׂים
לְעוֹלָם ׃ כִּי אַתָּה הוּא
מֶלֶךְ אָדוֹן לְכָל־
הַשָּׁלוֹם ׃ וְטוֹב בְּעֵינֶיךָ
לְבָרֵךְ אֶת־עַמְּךָ
יִשְׂרָאֵל בְּכָל־עֵת
וּבְכָל־שָׁעָה בִּשְׁלוֹמֶךָ:
בָּרוּךְ אַתָּה יְיָ ׃
הַמְבָרֵךְ אֶת־עַמּוֹ
יִשְׂרָאֵל בַּשָּׁלוֹם:

שִׂים שָׁלוֹם טוֹבָה וּבְרָכָה חַיִּים חֵן
וָחֶסֶד צְדָקָה וְרַחֲמִים עָלֵינוּ ׃ וּבָרְכֵנוּ
אָבִינוּ כֻּלָּנוּ יַחַד בְּאוֹר פָּנֶיךָ ׃ כִּי
בְאוֹר פָּנֶיךָ נָתַתָּ לָנוּ יְיָ אֱלֹהֵינוּ תּוֹרָה
וְחַיִּים ׃ אַהֲבָה וָחֶסֶד ׃ צְדָקָה וְרַחֲמִים ׃
בְּרָכָה וְשָׁלוֹם ׃ וְטוֹב בְּעֵינֶיךָ לְבָרֵךְ
אֶת־עַמְּךָ יִשְׂרָאֵל בְּרֹב־עֹז וּבְשָׁלוֹם:
בָּרוּךְ אַתָּה יְיָ ׃ הַמְבָרֵךְ אֶת־עַמּוֹ
יִשְׂרָאֵל בַּשָּׁלוֹם:

אֱלֹהַי נְצוֹר לְשׁוֹנִי מֵרָע ׃ וּשְׂפָתוֹתַי מִדַּבֵּר מִרְמָה ׃
וְלִמְקַלְלַי נַפְשִׁי תִדּוֹם ׃ וְנַפְשִׁי כֶּעָפָר לַכֹּל תִּהְיֶה: פְּתַח
לִבִּי בְּתוֹרָתֶךָ ׃ וְאַחֲרֵי מִצְוֹתֶיךָ תִּרְדּוֹף נַפְשִׁי ׃ וְכָל־הַקָּמִים
עָלַי לְרָעָה מְהֵרָה הָפֵר עֲצָתָם וְקַלְקֵל מַחְשְׁבוֹתָם: יִהְיוּ
לְרָצוֹן אִמְרֵי־פִי ׃ וְהֶגְיוֹן לִבִּי לְפָנֶיךָ ׃ יְהֹוָה צוּרִי וְגֹאֲלִי:

עֹשֶׂה שָׁלוֹם בִּמְרוֹמָיו ׃ הוּא יַעֲשֶׂה שָׁלוֹם עָלֵינוּ וְעַל כָּל־
יִשְׂרָאֵל ׃ וְאִמְרוּ אָמֵן:

And for all these things may Your name, our king, be blessed, exalted and honoured forever and ever. May every living being thank You; may they praise and bless Your great name in truth for You are the God who saves and helps us. Blessed are You Lord, known as goodness, whom it is right to praise.

For a morning service

Grant us peace, goodness and blessing; life, grace and kindness; justice and mercy. Our father, bless us all together with the light of Your presence, for in the light of Your presence You give us, Lord our God, law and life, love and kindness, justice and mercy, blessing and peace. And in Your eyes it is good to bless Your people Israel with great strength and peace. Blessed are You Lord, who blesses His people Israel with peace.

For an afternoon or evening service

Set true peace upon Your people Israel forever. For You are the king, the Lord of all peace, and in Your eyes it is good to bless Your people Israel at every time and in every hour with Your peace. Blessed are You Lord, who blesses His people Israel with peace.

MEDI-TATION   My God, keep my tongue from causing harm and my lips from telling lies. Let me be silent if people curse me, my soul still humble and at peace with all. Open my heart to Your teaching, and give me the will to practise it. May the plans and schemes of those who seek my harm come to nothing. May the words of my mouth and the meditation of my heart be acceptable to You, O Lord, my rock and my redeemer.

May He who makes peace in the highest bring this peace upon us and upon all Israel. Amen.

Aleynu, Kaddish and Hymns on page 166.

AMIDAH FOR SPECIAL SERVICES

אֲדֹנָי שְׂפָתַי תִּפְתָּח. וּפִי יַגִּיד תְּהִלָּתֶךָ:

בָּרוּךְ אַתָּה יְיָ אֱלֹהֵינוּ וֵאלֹהֵי אֲבוֹתֵינוּ · אֱלֹהֵי אַבְרָהָם ·
אֱלֹהֵי יִצְחָק. וֵאלֹהֵי יַעֲקֹב · הָאֵל הַגָּדוֹל הַגִּבּוֹר
וְהַנּוֹרָא · אֵל עֶלְיוֹן · גּוֹמֵל חֲסָדִים טוֹבִים קוֹנֵה הַכֹּל
וְזוֹכֵר חַסְדֵי אָבוֹת וּמֵבִיא גוֹאֵל לִבְנֵי בְנֵיהֶם לְמַעַן שְׁמוֹ
בְּאַהֲבָה :

(זָכְרֵנוּ לַחַיִּים מֶלֶךְ חָפֵץ בַּחַיִּים · וְכָתְבֵנוּ בְּסֵפֶר הַחַיִּים ·
לְמַעַנְךָ אֱלֹהִים חַיִּים:)

מֶלֶךְ עוֹזֵר וּמוֹשִׁיעַ וּמָגֵן · בָּרוּךְ אַתָּה יְיָ · מָגֵן אַבְרָהָם :

אַתָּה גִּבּוֹר לְעוֹלָם יְיָ · מְחַיֵּה מֵתִים אַתָּה רַב לְהוֹשִׁיעַ ·
מְכַלְכֵּל חַיִּים בְּחֶסֶד · מְחַיֵּה מֵתִים בְּרַחֲמִים רַבִּים ·
סוֹמֵךְ נוֹפְלִים · וְרוֹפֵא חוֹלִים · וּמַתִּיר אֲסוּרִים · וּמְקַיֵּם אֱמוּנָתוֹ
לִישֵׁנֵי עָפָר : מִי כָמוֹךָ בַּעַל גְּבוּרוֹת וּמִי דּוֹמֶה לָּךְ · מֶלֶךְ
מֵמִית וּמְחַיֶּה · וּמַצְמִיחַ יְשׁוּעָה :

(מִי כָמוֹךָ אַב הָרַחֲמִים זוֹכֵר יְצוּרָיו לַחַיִּים בְּרַחֲמִים:)

וְנֶאֱמָן אַתָּה לְהַחֲיוֹת מֵתִים · בָּרוּךְ אַתָּה יְיָ · מְחַיֵּה
הַמֵּתִים :

AMIDAH FOR SPECIAL SERVICES

Lord, open my lips and my mouth shall declare Your praise.

GOD OF HISTORY   Blessed are You, Lord our God, and God of our fathers, God of Abraham, God of Isaac, and God of Jacob, the great, the mighty, and the awesome God, God beyond, generous in love and kindness, and possessing all. He remembers the good deeds of our fathers, and therefore in love brings rescue to the generations, for such is His being. (*On the Days of Repentance*: King who delights in life, recall us to life and record us in the Book of Life for Your own sake, God of Life!) The king who helps and saves and shields. Blessed are You Lord, the shield of Abraham.

GOD OF MIGHT   You, O Lord, are the endless power that renews life beyond death; You are the greatness that saves. You care for the living with love. You renew life beyond death with unending mercy. You support the falling, and heal the sick. You free prisoners, and keep faith with those who sleep in the dust. Who can perform such mighty deeds, and who can compare with You, a king who brings death and life, and renews salvation. (*On the Days of Repentance*: Who is like You, father of mercies, recalling His creatures to life in mercy.) You are faithful to renew life beyond death. Blessed are You Lord, who renews life beyond death.

נְקַדֵּשׁ אֶת־שִׁמְךָ בָּעוֹלָם
כְּשֵׁם שֶׁמַּקְדִּישִׁים אוֹתוֹ בִּשְׁמֵי
מָרוֹם כַּכָּתוּב עַל יַד נְבִיאֶךָ.
וְקָרָא זֶה אֶל זֶה וְאָמָר.

קָדוֹשׁ קָדוֹשׁ קָדוֹשׁ
יְיָ צְבָאוֹת. מְלֹא כָל־
הָאָרֶץ כְּבוֹדוֹ:

לְעֻמָּתָם בָּרוּךְ יֹאמֵרוּ.

בָּרוּךְ כְּבוֹד יְיָ
מִמְּקוֹמוֹ:

וּבְדִבְרֵי קָדְשְׁךָ כָּתוּב לֵאמֹר.

יִמְלֹךְ יְיָ לְעוֹלָם
אֱלֹהַיִךְ צִיּוֹן לְדֹר וָדֹר.
הַלְלוּיָהּ:

לְדוֹר וָדוֹר נַגִּיד גָּדְלֶךָ.
וּלְנֵצַח נְצָחִים קְדֻשָּׁתְךָ נַקְדִּישׁ.
וְשִׁבְחֲךָ אֱלֹהֵינוּ מִפִּינוּ לֹא
יָמוּשׁ לְעוֹלָם וָעֶד. כִּי אֵל
מֶלֶךְ גָּדוֹל וְקָדוֹשׁ אָתָּה.
בָּרוּךְ אַתָּה יְיָ. הָאֵל
הַקָּדוֹשׁ: (הַמֶּלֶךְ הַקָּדוֹשׁ:)

אַתָּה קָדוֹשׁ וְשִׁמְךָ קָדוֹשׁ
וּקְדוֹשִׁים בְּכָל־יוֹם יְהַלְלוּךָ
סֶּלָה. בָּרוּךְ אַתָּה יְיָ. הָאֵל
הַקָּדוֹשׁ: (הַמֶּלֶךְ הַקָּדוֹשׁ:)

נַעֲרִיצְךָ וְנַקְדִּישְׁךָ כְּשֵׁם שֶׁמַּקְדִּישִׁים
אוֹתוֹ בִּשְׁמֵי מָרוֹם כַּכָּתוּב עַל יַד נְבִיאֶךָ.
וְקָרָא זֶה אֶל זֶה וְאָמָר.

קָדוֹשׁ קָדוֹשׁ קָדוֹשׁ יְיָ צְבָאוֹת
מְלֹא כָל־הָאָרֶץ כְּבוֹדוֹ:

כְּבוֹדוֹ מָלֵא עוֹלָם מְשָׁרְתָיו שׁוֹאֲלִים זֶה
לָזֶה אַיֵּה מְקוֹם כְּבוֹדוֹ. לְעֻמָּתָם בָּרוּךְ
יֹאמֵרוּ.

בָּרוּךְ כְּבוֹד יְיָ מִמְּקוֹמוֹ:

מִמְּקוֹמוֹ הוּא יִפֶן בְּרַחֲמִים וְיָחֹן עַם
הַמְיַחֲדִים שְׁמוֹ עֶרֶב וָבֹקֶר בְּכָל־יוֹם תָּמִיד
פַּעֲמַיִם בְּאַהֲבָה שְׁמַע אוֹמְרִים.

שְׁמַע יִשְׂרָאֵל יְיָ אֱלֹהֵינוּ יְיָ
אֶחָד:

אֶחָד הוּא אֱלֹהֵינוּ הוּא אָבִינוּ הוּא
מַלְכֵּנוּ הוּא מוֹשִׁיעֵנוּ. וְהוּא יַשְׁמִיעֵנוּ
בְּרַחֲמָיו שֵׁנִית לְעֵינֵי כָּל־חַי לִהְיוֹת לָכֶם
לֵאלֹהִים:

אֲנִי יְיָ אֱלֹהֵיכֶם:

וּבְדִבְרֵי קָדְשְׁךָ כָּתוּב לֵאמֹר.

יִמְלֹךְ יְיָ לְעוֹלָם אֱלֹהַיִךְ צִיּוֹן
לְדֹר וָדֹר. הַלְלוּיָהּ:

לְדוֹר וָדוֹר נַגִּיד גָּדְלֶךָ. וּלְנֵצַח נְצָחִים
קְדֻשָּׁתְךָ נַקְדִּישׁ. וְשִׁבְחֲךָ אֱלֹהֵינוּ מִפִּינוּ
לֹא יָמוּשׁ לְעוֹלָם וָעֶד. כִּי אֵל מֶלֶךְ גָּדוֹל
וְקָדוֹשׁ אָתָּה. בָּרוּךְ אַתָּה יְיָ. הָאֵל הַקָּדוֹשׁ:
(הַמֶּלֶךְ הַקָּדוֹשׁ:)

GOD OF HOLINESS

Sabbath afternoon, daily morning and afternoon

We sanctify Your name in the world as they sanctify it in the highest heavens. As it is written according to the vision of Your prophet: And they called to each other and said:

Holy, holy, holy is the Lord of all creation, the whole earth is full of His glory.

They cry in answer, 'Blessed!'

Blessed is His glory revealed in every place.

And in Your holy writing it is said:

The Lord shall rule forever! Zion, He is your God for all generations! Praise the Lord!

We declare Your greatness to all generations, and to all eternity we proclaim Your holiness. Your praise shall never depart from our mouth, for You are God, the great and holy king. Blessed are You Lord, the holy God. (*On the Days of Repentance*: the holy king.)

Sabbath and daily eve

You are holy and Your name is holy, and those who seek holiness praise You day by day.

Blessed are You Lord, the holy God. (*On the Days of Repentance*: the holy king.)

Sabbath morning

We worship and sanctify You as they sanctify You in the highest heavens. As it is written by the hand of Your prophet: And they called to each other and said:

Holy, holy, holy is the Lord of all creation, the whole earth is full of His glory.

His glory fills the universe. Those who serve Him ask each other, 'Where is the place of His glory?' They cry in answer, 'Blessed!'

Blessed is His glory revealed in every place.

From His place may He turn in mercy, and be gracious to the people who in love declare His unity twice each day, evening and morning, with the words of the *Shema*.

Hear O Israel, the Lord is our God, the Lord is One.

Our God is One. He is our father, He is our king, He is our deliverer, and in His mercy He will again announce to us in the presence of all living His promise to be your God.

I am the Lord your God!

And in Your holy writing it is said:

The Lord shall rule forever! Zion, He is your God for all generations! Praise the Lord!

We declare Your greatness to all generations, and to all eternity we proclaim Your holiness. Your praise shall never depart from our mouth, for You are God, the great and holy king. Blessed are You Lord, the holy God. (*On the Days of Repentance*: the holy king.)

On weekdays continue on page 234.

On Sabbath continue on the following page.

וַיְכֻלּוּ הַשָּׁמַיִם וְהָאָרֶץ וְכָל־צְבָאָם: וַיְכַל אֱלֹהִים בַּיּוֹם הַשְּׁבִיעִי מְלַאכְתּוֹ אֲשֶׁר עָשָׂה · וַיִּשְׁבֹּת בַּיּוֹם הַשְּׁבִיעִי מִכָּל־מְלַאכְתּוֹ אֲשֶׁר עָשָׂה: וַיְבָרֶךְ אֱלֹהִים אֶת־יוֹם הַשְּׁבִיעִי וַיְקַדֵּשׁ אֹתוֹ · כִּי בוֹ שָׁבַת מִכָּל־מְלַאכְתּוֹ אֲשֶׁר בָּרָא אֱלֹהִים לַעֲשׂוֹת:

וְשָׁמְרוּ בְנֵי־יִשְׂרָאֵל אֶת־הַשַּׁבָּת לַעֲשׂוֹת אֶת־הַשַּׁבָּת לְדֹרֹתָם בְּרִית עוֹלָם: בֵּינִי וּבֵין בְּנֵי יִשְׂרָאֵל אוֹת הִוא לְעֹלָם כִּי־שֵׁשֶׁת יָמִים עָשָׂה יְהוָֹה אֶת־הַשָּׁמַיִם וְאֶת־הָאָרֶץ וּבַיּוֹם הַשְּׁבִיעִי שָׁבַת וַיִּנָּפַשׁ:

אַתָּה אֶחָד וְשִׁמְךָ אֶחָד · וּמִי כְּעַמְּךָ יִשְׂרָאֵל גּוֹי אֶחָד בָּאָרֶץ: תִּפְאֶרֶת גְּדֻלָּה · וַעֲטֶרֶת יְשׁוּעָה · יוֹם מְנוּחָה וּקְדֻשָּׁה לְעַמְּךָ נָתָתָּ: אַבְרָהָם יָגֵל · יִצְחָק יְרַנֵּן · יַעֲקֹב וּבָנָיו יָנוּחוּ בוֹ: מְנוּחַת אַהֲבָה וּנְדָבָה · מְנוּחַת אֱמֶת וֶאֱמוּנָה · מְנוּחַת שָׁלוֹם וְשַׁלְוָה וְהַשְׁקֵט וָבֶטַח · מְנוּחָה שְׁלֵמָה שָׁאַתָּה רוֹצֶה בָּהּ · יַכִּירוּ בָנֶיךָ וְיֵדְעוּ כִּי מֵאִתְּךָ הִיא מְנוּחָתָם וְעַל מְנוּחָתָם יַקְדִּישׁוּ אֶת־שְׁמֶךָ:

אֱלֹהֵינוּ וֵאלֹהֵי אֲבוֹתֵינוּ · רְצֵה־נָא בִמְנוּחָתֵנוּ · קַדְּשֵׁנוּ בְּמִצְוֹתֶיךָ · שִׂים חֶלְקֵנוּ בְּתוֹרָתֶךָ · שַׂבְּעֵנוּ מִטּוּבֶךָ · שַׂמַּח נַפְשֵׁנוּ בִּישׁוּעָתֶךָ · וְטַהֵר לִבֵּנוּ לְעָבְדְּךָ בֶּאֱמֶת · וְהַנְחִילֵנוּ יְיָ אֱלֹהֵינוּ בְּאַהֲבָה וּבְרָצוֹן שַׁבַּת קָדְשֶׁךָ · וְיָנוּחוּ בָהּ כָּל־יִשְׂרָאֵל מְקַדְּשֵׁי שְׁמֶךָ: בָּרוּךְ אַתָּה יְיָ · מְקַדֵּשׁ הַשַּׁבָּת:

רְצֵה יְיָ אֱלֹהֵינוּ בְּעַמְּךָ יִשְׂרָאֵל · וְלִתְפִלָּתָם שְׁעֵה · וּבְרַחֲמֶיךָ הָרַבִּים תַּחְפֹּץ בָּנוּ וְתַשְׁרֶה שְׁכִינָתְךָ עַל צִיּוֹן ·

The following paragraph is said on Sabbath eve

THE
HOLINESS
OF THE
SABBATH
Heaven and earth were finished and all their host. On the seventh day God finished the work that He had done, and He ceased on the seventh day from all the work that He had done. God blessed the seventh day, and made it holy, because on it God ceased from all the work of creation that He had done.

Genesis 2: 1–3

The following paragraph is said on Sabbath morning

The children of Israel shall keep the Sabbath, observing the Sabbath as a timeless covenant for all generations. It is a sign between Me and the children of Israel forever. For in six days the Lord made heaven and earth and on the seventh day He ceased from work and was at rest.

Exodus 31: 16–17

The following paragraph is said on Sabbath afternoon

You are One and Your name is One, and who is like Your people Israel, a nation unique on the earth. A splendid greatness, a crown of salvation is the day of rest and holiness You gave to Your people. Abraham was glad, Isaac rejoiced, Jacob and his sons rested on it. Rest given freely in love, true and faithful rest, peaceful, tranquil rest, quiet and secure—the perfect rest that You desire. May Your children realise and know that their rest comes from You, and through their rest they make Your name holy.

Sabbath services continue here

Our God and God of our fathers, may our rest be pleasing to You. Make us holy by doing Your commands and let us share in the work of Your Torah. Make us content with Your goodness and let our souls know the joy of Your salvation. Purify our hearts to serve You in truth. In Your love and goodwill let us inherit Your holy Sabbath and may all Israel who seek holiness find in it their rest. Blessed are You Lord, who makes the Sabbath holy.

Daily services continue here

THANKS-
GIVING
AND PEACE
Lord our God, be pleased with Your people Israel and listen to their prayers. In Your great mercy delight in us so that Your presence may rest upon Zion.

אֱלֹהֵינוּ וֵאלֹהֵי אֲבוֹתֵינוּ יַעֲלֶה וְיָבֹא וְיַגִּיעַ וְיֵרָאֶה· זִכְרוֹנֵנוּ
וּפִקְדוֹנֵנוּ· וְזִכְרוֹן אֲבוֹתֵינוּ· וְזִכְרוֹן מָשִׁיחַ בֶּן־דָּוִד עַבְדֶּךָ·
וְזִכְרוֹן יְרוּשָׁלַיִם עִיר קָדְשֶׁךָ· וְזִכְרוֹן כָּל־עַמְּךָ בֵּית
יִשְׂרָאֵל לְפָנֶיךָ· לִפְלֵיטָה וּלְטוֹבָה· לְחֵן וּלְחֶסֶד·
וּלְרַחֲמִים· בְּיוֹם

בראש החדש: רֹאשׁ הַחֹדֶשׁ הַזֶּה·

בפסח: חַג הַמַּצּוֹת הַזֶּה·

בסכות: חַג הַסֻּכּוֹת הַזֶּה·

זָכְרֵנוּ יְיָ אֱלֹהֵינוּ בּוֹ לְטוֹבָה·   אָמֵן:

וּפָקְדֵנוּ בוֹ לִבְרָכָה·   אָמֵן:

וְהוֹשִׁיעֵנוּ בוֹ לְחַיִּים טוֹבִים: אָמֵן:

וּבִדְבַר יְשׁוּעָה וְרַחֲמִים חוּס וְחָנֵּנוּ· כִּי אֵלֶיךָ עֵינֵינוּ· כִּי
אֵל מֶלֶךְ חַנּוּן וְרַחוּם אָתָּה:

וְתֶחֱזֶינָה עֵינֵינוּ בְּשׁוּבְךָ לְצִיּוֹן בְּרַחֲמִים· בָּרוּךְ אַתָּה יְיָ·
הַמַּחֲזִיר שְׁכִינָתוֹ לְצִיּוֹן:

מוֹדִים אֲנַחְנוּ לָךְ שָׁאַתָּה הוּא יְיָ אֱלֹהֵינוּ וֵאלֹהֵי אֲבוֹתֵינוּ
לְעוֹלָם וָעֶד· צוּרֵנוּ צוּר חַיֵּינוּ וּמָגֵן יִשְׁעֵנוּ אַתָּה הוּא לְדוֹר
וָדוֹר: נוֹדֶה לְךָ וּנְסַפֵּר תְּהִלָּתֶךָ עַל חַיֵּינוּ הַמְּסוּרִים
בְּיָדֶךָ· וְעַל נִשְׁמוֹתֵינוּ הַפְּקוּדוֹת לָךְ· וְעַל נִסֶּיךָ שֶׁבְּכָל־יוֹם
עִמָּנוּ· וְעַל נִפְלְאוֹתֶיךָ וְטוֹבוֹתֶיךָ שֶׁבְּכָל־עֵת עֶרֶב וָבֹקֶר
וְצָהֳרָיִם: הַטּוֹב כִּי לֹא כָלוּ רַחֲמֶיךָ· הַמְּרַחֵם כִּי לֹא תַמּוּ
חֲסָדֶיךָ· כִּי מֵעוֹלָם קִוִּינוּ לָךְ:

וְעַל כֻּלָּם יִתְבָּרַךְ וְיִתְרוֹמֵם וְיִתְנַשֵּׂא תָּמִיד שִׁמְךָ מַלְכֵּנוּ
לְעוֹלָם וָעֶד: (וּכְתֹב לְחַיִּים טוֹבִים כָּל־בְּנֵי בְרִיתֶךָ:)
וְכָל־הַחַיִּים יוֹדוּךָ סֶּלָה· וִיהַלְלוּ וִיבָרְכוּ אֶת־שִׁמְךָ הַגָּדוֹל
בֶּאֱמֶת· הָאֵל יְשׁוּעָתֵנוּ וְעֶזְרָתֵנוּ סֶלָה: בָּרוּךְ אַתָּה יְיָ· הַטּוֹב
שִׁמְךָ וּלְךָ נָאֶה לְהוֹדוֹת:

On the new moon and middle days of festivals add here:

Our God and God of our fathers, may Your regard and concern for us and our fathers, for the time of our redemption, for Jerusalem the city of Your holiness, and for all Your people the family of Israel, be close to You and be pleasing to You. Favour us all with freedom and goodness, with grace, love and mercy, on this day of

(On the New Moon)	the New Moon.
(On Pesach)	the Feast of Unleavened Bread.
(On Succot)	the Feast of *Succot*.

Lord our God, remember us for our good,	(Amen)
bring us Your blessing,	(Amen)
and save us for a good life.	(Amen)

Spare us and be kind to us according to Your promise of deliverance and mercy. Our eyes are turned towards You, for You are a king of mercy and compassion.

Our eyes look forward to Your return to Zion in mercy! Blessed are You Lord, who restores His presence to Zion.

We declare with gratitude that You are our God and the God of our fathers forever. You are our rock, the rock of our life and the shield that saves us. In every generation we thank You and recount Your praise for our lives held in Your hand, for our souls that are in Your care, and for the signs of Your presence that are with us every day. At every moment, at evening, morning and noon, we experience Your wonders and Your goodness. You are goodness itself, for Your mercy has no end. You are mercy itself, for Your love has no limit. Forever have we put our hope in You.

(On Chanukah add the prayer on page 267)
(On Purim add the prayer on page 264)

And for all these things may Your name, our king, be blessed exalted and honoured forever and ever. (*On the Days of Repentance*: Record all the children of Your covenant for a good life.) May every living being thank You; may they praise and bless Your great name in truth for You are the God who saves and helps us. Blessed are You Lord, known as goodness, whom it is right to praise.

For an afternoon or evening service

For a morning service

שִׂים שָׁלוֹם טוֹבָה וּבְרָכָה חַיִּים חֵן
וָחֶסֶד צְדָקָה וְרַחֲמִים עָלֵינוּ. וּבָרְכֵנוּ
אָבִינוּ כֻּלָּנוּ יַחַד בְּאוֹר פָּנֶיךָ. כִּי
בְאוֹר פָּנֶיךָ נָתַתָּ לָנוּ יְיָ אֱלֹהֵינוּ תּוֹרָה
וְחַיִּים. אַהֲבָה וָחֶסֶד. צְדָקָה וְרַחֲמִים.
בְּרָכָה וְשָׁלוֹם. וְטוֹב בְּעֵינֶיךָ לְבָרֵךְ
אֶת־עַמְּךָ יִשְׂרָאֵל בְּרָב־עֹז וּבְשָׁלוֹם:

שָׁלוֹם רָב עַל
יִשְׂרָאֵל עַמְּךָ תָּשִׂים
לְעוֹלָם. כִּי אַתָּה הוּא
מֶלֶךְ אָדוֹן לְכָל־
הַשָּׁלוֹם. וְטוֹב בְּעֵינֶיךָ
לְבָרֵךְ אֶת־עַמְּךָ
יִשְׂרָאֵל בְּכָל־עֵת
וּבְכָל־שָׁעָה בִּשְׁלוֹמֶךָ:

(בְּסֵפֶר חַיִּים נִזָּכֵר וְנִכָּתֵב לְפָנֶיךָ אֲנַחְנוּ וְכָל־עַמְּךָ בֵּית
יִשְׂרָאֵל לְחַיִּים טוֹבִים וּלְשָׁלוֹם:)
בָּרוּךְ אַתָּה יְיָ. הַמְבָרֵךְ אֶת־עַמּוֹ יִשְׂרָאֵל בַּשָּׁלוֹם:

אֱלֹהַי נְצוֹר לְשׁוֹנִי מֵרָע. וּשְׂפָתוֹתַי מִדַּבֵּר מִרְמָה.
וְלִמְקַלְלַי נַפְשִׁי תִדּוֹם. וְנַפְשִׁי כֶּעָפָר לַכֹּל תִּהְיֶה: פְּתַח
לִבִּי בְּתוֹרָתֶךָ. וְאַחֲרֵי מִצְוֹתֶיךָ תִּרְדּוֹף נַפְשִׁי. וְכָל־הַקָּמִים
עָלַי לְרָעָה מְהֵרָה הָפֵר עֲצָתָם וְקַלְקֵל מַחְשְׁבוֹתָם: יִהְיוּ
לְרָצוֹן אִמְרֵי־פִי. וְהֶגְיוֹן לִבִּי לְפָנֶיךָ. יְהֹוָה צוּרִי וְגֹאֲלִי:

עֹשֶׂה שָׁלוֹם בִּמְרוֹמָיו. הוּא יַעֲשֶׂה שָׁלוֹם עָלֵינוּ וְעַל
כָּל־יִשְׂרָאֵל. וְאִמְרוּ אָמֵן:

For a morning service

Grant us peace, goodness and blessing; life, grace and kindness; justice and mercy. Our father, bless us all together with the light of Your presence, for in the light of Your presence You give us, Lord our God, law and life, love and kindness, justice and mercy, blessing and peace. And in Your eyes it is good to bless Your people Israel with great strength and peace.

For an afternoon or evening service

Set true peace upon Your people Israel forever. For You are the king, the Lord of all peace, and in Your eyes it is good to bless Your people Israel at every time and in every hour with Your peace.

(*On the Days of Repentance*: In Your presence may we and all Your people, the family of Israel, be remembered and recorded in the Book of Life for a good life and for peace.) Blessed are You Lord, who blesses His people Israel with peace.

MEDI-TATION My God, keep my tongue from causing harm and my lips from telling lies. Let me be silent if people curse me, my soul still humble and at peace with all. Open my heart to Your teaching, and give me the will to practise it. May the plans and schemes of those who seek my harm come to nothing. May the words of my mouth and the meditation of my heart be acceptable to You, O Lord, my rock and my redeemer.

May He who makes peace in the highest bring this peace upon us and upon all Israel. Amen.

On new moon and festivals the service continues with the Hallel on page 528.
On other sabbaths the service continues on pages 40 (*evening*), 148 (*morning*) or 178 (*afternoon*).
On other days the service continues on page 166.

PRAYERS FOR THE DAYS OF REPENTANCE

Introductory prayer

The old year has died, and the new year has scarcely begun. In this pause before the account is made of the past, and my life is judged for what it is, I ask for honesty, vision and courage. Honesty to see myself as I am, vision to see myself as I should be, and the courage to change and realise myself.

Many obstacles block my return: my lack of trust, my anxieties and fears, and old habits of selfishness and greed. They separate me from You. They divide me from my true nature, and deny me the contentment and the peace You offer.

Your hand is open to every living being. At the smallest sign You come to meet us for You are generous to forgive. On this day of repentance and return, stretch out Your hand to me, so that I may grasp it, and lead me along the paths of love and duty into the harmony and peace which You have prepared for me.

הֲשִׁיבֵנוּ יְהֹוָה אֵלֶיךָ וְנָשׁוּבָה חַדֵּשׁ יָמֵינוּ כְּקֶדֶם:

'Turn us back to You, Lord, and we shall return; renew our lives as of old.'

Evening service

מַה־נֹּאמַר לְפָנֶיךָ יוֹשֵׁב מָרוֹם · וּמַה־נְּסַפֵּר לְפָנֶיךָ שׁוֹכֵן שְׁחָקִים · הֲלֹא הַנִּסְתָּרוֹת וְהַנִּגְלוֹת אַתָּה יוֹדֵעַ: אַתָּה יוֹדֵעַ רָזֵי עוֹלָם · וְתַעֲלֻמוֹת סִתְרֵי כָל־חָי · אַתָּה חוֹפֵשׂ כָּל־חַדְרֵי בָטֶן · רוֹאֶה כְלָיוֹת וָלֵב: אֵין דָּבָר נֶעְלָם מִמֶּךָ · וְאֵין נִסְתָּר מִנֶּגֶד עֵינֶיךָ:

יְהִי רָצוֹן מִלְּפָנֶיךָ יְיָ אֱלֹהֵינוּ וֵאלֹהֵי אֲבוֹתֵינוּ שֶׁתְּרַחֵם
עָלֵינוּ · וְתִמְחֹל לָנוּ אֶת־כָּל־חַטֹּאתֵינוּ · וּתְכַפֶּר־לָנוּ אֶת־
כָּל־עֲוֹנוֹתֵינוּ · וְתִמְחֹל וְתִסְלַח לְכָל־פְּשָׁעֵינוּ · וְסָלַחְתָּ לַעֲוֹנֵנוּ
וּלְחַטָּאתֵנוּ וּנְחַלְתָּנוּ : סְלַח לָנוּ אָבִינוּ כִּי חָטָאנוּ · מְחַל לָנוּ
מַלְכֵּנוּ כִּי פָשָׁעְנוּ : כִּי־אַתָּה אֲדֹנָי טוֹב וְסַלָּח · וְרַב־חֶסֶד
לְכָל־קֹרְאֶיךָ : לְמַעַן־שִׁמְךָ יְהוָה · וְסָלַחְתָּ לַעֲוֹנֵנוּ כִּי רַב־
הוּא · לְמַעַן שִׁמְךָ יְהוָה תְּחַיֵּינוּ · בְּצִדְקָתְךָ תּוֹצִיא מִצָּרָה
נַפְשֵׁנוּ : יְהוָה צְבָאוֹת עִמָּנוּ · מִשְׂגָּב לָנוּ אֱלֹהֵי יַעֲקֹב : יְהוָה
צְבָאוֹת · אַשְׁרֵי אָדָם בֹּטֵחַ בָּךְ :

What shall we say in Your presence, You who dwell on high?
What shall we declare to You, who are in heaven beyond? For You
know things secret as well as revealed. You know the mysteries of
the universe and the unconscious thoughts of everyone alive. You
search the innermost parts, You watch our motives and our passions.
Nothing is concealed from You. Nothing is hidden from Your gaze.

Lord our God, and God of our fathers, have mercy on us. Pardon
our sins, forgive our wrongdoing and pardon and set aside our
misdeeds. Forgive our sin and our wrongdoing, and accept us as
Your heritage. Forgive us, our father, for we have sinned. Blot out,
our king, the wrong that we have done, for You, O Lord, are good
and forgiving, and full of love to all who call upon You. For Your
own sake, O Lord, forgive our failure for it is great. For Your own
sake, give us life. In Your righteousness bring our souls out of trouble.
The Lord of all creation is with us, the God of Jacob is our refuge.
Lord of creation, happy is the man who trusts in You.

נִפְלָאִים מַעֲשֶׂיךָ וְנַפְשִׁי יֹדַעַת מְאֹד ·

מִי יְמַלֵּל גְּבוּרוֹתֶיךָ · מִי יְחַוֶּה גְדֻלּוֹתֶיךָ ·

מִי יַזְכִּיר תְּהִלּוֹתֶיךָ · מִי יְסַפֵּר צִדְקוֹתֶיךָ ·

מִי יַכִּיר אוֹתוֹתֶיךָ · מִי יֵדַע פְּלִיאוֹתֶיךָ ·

מִי יַבִּיעַ נוֹרְאוֹתֶיךָ · מִי יֵדַע הֲלִיכוֹתֶיךָ :

יָּךְ מִי יַחְקוֹר תַּעֲלֻמוֹתֶיךָ · יְּךָ מִי יַעֲמִיק לְמַחְשְׁבוֹתֶיךָ :

מִי יַעֲשֶׂה כְמַעֲשֶׂיךָ · מִי יִגְמוֹל עַל טוֹבוֹתֶיךָ :

אֱלֹהַי בֹּשְׁתִּי וְנִכְלַמְתִּי · לַעֲמוֹד לְפָנֶיךָ לְדַעְתִּי ·

כִּי כְפִי עָצְמַת גְּדֻלָּתְךָ כֵּן תַּכְלִית דַּלּוּתִי וְשִׁפְלוּתִי ·

וּכְפִי שְׁלֵימוּתְךָ כֵּן חֶסְרוֹנִי :

כִּי אַתָּה אֶחָד · וְאַתָּה חַי · וְאַתָּה גִבּוֹר · וְאַתָּה קַיָּם ·

וְאַתָּה גָדוֹל · וְאַתָּה חָכָם · וְאַתָּה אֱלוֹהַּ :

וַאֲנִי גוּשׁ וְרִמָּה · עָפָר מִן הָאֲדָמָה ·

כְּלִי מָלֵא כְלִמָּה · צֵל עוֹבֵר · רוּחַ הוֹלֵךְ וְלֹא יָשׁוּב :

מָה־אֲנִי מֶה־חַיָּי וּמַה־גְּבוּרָתִי · וּמַה־צִּדְקָתִי :

אֱלֹהַי יָדַעְתִּי כִּי עֲוֹנוֹתַי עָצְמוּ מִסַּפֵּר ·

וְאַשְׁמוֹתַי עָצְמוּ מִלִּזְכּוֹר ·

אַךְ אֶזְכּוֹר מֵהֶם כְּטִפָּה מִן הַיָּם · וְאֶתְוַדֶּה בָהֶם ·

אוּלַי אַשְׁבִּיחַ שְׁאוֹן גַּלֵּיהֶם וְדָכְיָם ·

וְאַתָּה תִּשְׁמַע הַשָּׁמַיִם וְסָלָחְתָּ :

חָטָאתִי וּפָשַׁעְתִּי · וְיָשָׁר הֶעֱוֵיתִי · וְלֹא־שָׁוָה לִי :

Morning service

Your works are wonderful—I know it so well.

Who can speak about Your might, who can tell Your greatness?

Who can record Your glory, who can recount Your righteousness?

Who can perceive Your signs, who can know Your marvels?

Who can comprehend their awe and wonder? Who can know Your ways?

Lord, who can investigate Your secrets? Who could penetrate Your thoughts?

Whose works can equal Yours? Who can repay You for Your goodness?

My God, I am ashamed and confused as I stand in Your presence, for I know that compared to Your greatness, I am so frail and weak and compared to Your perfection, I am so lacking.

For You are One, and You are true life, and You are mighty, and You remain firm, and You are great, and You are wise, and You are God.

And I am just a lump of earth, and a worm; dust from the ground, a cup full of shame, a fleeting shadow, a breeze that goes and does not return.

What am I? What is my life? How strong am I? How righteous am I?

God, I know that the wrongs I have done are too many to be told, and my faults too many to recall.

Nevertheless, I shall recall some of them and confess, though they are like a drop from the ocean.

Perhaps I can calm their uproar and tumult, like the waves and breakers of the sea,
and You will listen and forgive.

I have sinned and I have done wrong. I damaged what was right, and it did not help me.

סַרְתִּי מִמִּצְוֹתֶיךָ וּמִמִּשְׁפָּטֶיךָ הַטּוֹבִים ·

וְאַתָּה צַדִּיק עַל כָּל־הַבָּא עָלָי ·

כִּי אֱמֶת עָשִׂיתָ וַאֲנִי הִרְשָׁעְתִּי :

יְהִי רָצוֹן מִלְפָנֶיךָ יְיָ אֱלֹהַי לָכֹף אֶת־יִצְרִי ·

וְהַסְתֵּר פָּנֶיךָ מֵחַטָּאַי וּמֵאַשְׁמָי · אַל תַּעֲלֵנִי בַּחֲצִי יָמָי :

אָנָּא הָאֱלֹהִים · בְּמִדַּת רַחֲמֶיךָ שְׁפְטֵנִי ·

אַל־בְּאַפְּךָ פֶּן תַּמְעִיטֵנִי ·

וְשׁוּב אֵלַי בְּרַחֲמִים · וַהֲשִׁיבֵנִי בִתְשׁוּבָה שְׁלֵמָה לְפָנֶיךָ ·

וֶהֱיֵה עִם פִּי וְהִגְיוֹנִי · וּשְׁמוֹר דְּרָכַי מֵחֲטוֹא בִלְשׁוֹנִי ·

וְזָכְרֵנִי לְחֶסֶד וּלְרַחֲמִים לַנְחֵנִי בְּמַעְגְּלֵי צֶדֶק לְמַעַן שְׁמְךָ הַגָּדוֹל :

וּלְךָ יְיָ חֶסֶד עַל כָּל־הַטּוֹבָה אֲשֶׁר גְּמַלְתָּנִי ·

וַאֲשֶׁר עַד־יוֹם מוֹתִי תִּגְמְלֵנִי ·

וּבְיִרְאָתְךָ הַטְּהוֹרָה תְּחַזְּקֵנִי ·

וְעַל כָּל־זֶה אֲנִי חַיָּב לְהוֹדוֹת וּלְיַחֵד אֶת־שִׁמְךָ הַגָּדוֹל ·

כִּי אֵין כָּמוֹךָ בָאֱלֹהִים אֲדֹנָי וְאֵין כְּמַעֲשֶׂיךָ :

Dresden

I turned away from Your commands and decisions which were good, but You were just in everything that happened to me because You did rightly, and I acted wickedly.

May it be Your will, Lord my God, to crush my evil impulse.

Cover Your face so that You do not see my sins and my faults! Do not take me away in the prime of life.

Lord, I beg You, judge me with mercy and not in anger, lest You annihilate me.

Turn to me in mercy, and bring me back to You in complete repentance, and be with my speech, and with my thoughts, and keep me from sinning with my tongue.

Think of me with love and mercy, and lead me in good ways because of Your greatness.

I love You, Lord, for all the goodness which You granted me, and which You will grant me until my dying day.

Strengthen me in the pure love and awe I feel for You.

For all this, I am in duty bound to thank You, and declare the unity of Your great name.

For, Lord, there is no God like You, and no deeds like Yours.

Ibn Gabirol from 'The Crown of Glory'

Warsaw

IN MEMORY

אלה אזכרה

Who knows, it might even be our religion
from which the world and all peoples
learn good, and for that reason and that
reason only do we have to suffer now.
Anne Frank

MEMORIAL SERVICE FOR THE SIX MILLION

PRAYER

We remember our six million dead, who died when madness ruled the world and evil dwelt on earth. We remember those we knew, and those whose very name is lost.

We mourn for all that died with them; their goodness and their wisdom, which could have saved the world and healed so many wounds. We mourn for the genius and the wit that died, the learning and the laughter that were lost. The world has become a poorer place and our hearts become cold as we think of the splendour that might have been.

We stand in gratitude for their example of decency and goodness. They are like candles which shine out from the darkness of those years, and in their light we know what goodness is—and evil.

We salute those men and women who were not Jews, who had the courage to stand outside the mob and suffer with us. They, too, are Your witnesses, a source of hope when we despair.

Because of our people's suffering, may such times never come again, and may their sacrifice not be in vain. In our daily fight against cruelty and prejudice, against tyranny and persecution, their memory gives us strength and leads us on.

In silence we remember those who sanctified His name on earth.

PASSAGES FOR STUDY

With the full weight of the authority granted to me as your Rabbi, I command you to leave me here. You must flee and save yourselves! Take heed of your bodies and your souls. Do not place your lives in danger unnecessarily because of the lightning bolt that strikes from without, but do not think for one fleeting instant that you must

sacrifice your lives for inner spiritual matters. I beseech and adjure you to remember always those of our people who fell at the hands of the murderers. It is not for man to judge which one of them shall be a saint and which not. Everyone slaughtered by the wicked ones is to be judged a saint. My dear students, always remember the Nehardea of Lithuania, the Yeshiva of Slabodka. And when the world returns again to stability and quiet, never become weary of teaching the glories, the wisdom, the Torah and the *Musar* of Lithuania, the beautiful and ethical life which Jews lived here. Do not become embittered by wailing and tears. Speak of these matters with calmness and serenity, as did our holy Sages in the Midrash, '*Lamentations Rabbati*'. And do as our holy Sages have done—pour forth your words and cast them into letters. This will be the greatest retribution which you can wreak upon these wicked ones. Despite the raging wrath of our foes the holy souls of your brothers and sisters will then remain alive. These evil ones schemed to blot out their names from the face of the earth; but a man cannot destroy letters. For words have wings; they mount up to the heavenly heights and they endure for eternity.

Rabbi Nachum Yanchiker—the last Musar talk delivered in the Slabodka Musar–Yeshiva, Kovno, moments before the German invasion.

We have been pointedly reminded that we are in hiding, that we are Jews in chains, chained to one spot, without any rights, but with a thousand duties. We Jews mustn't show our feelings, must be brave and strong, must accept all inconveniences and not grumble, must do what is within our power and trust in God. Sometime this terrible war will be over. Surely the time will come when we are people again, and not just Jews.

Who has inflicted this upon us? Who has made us Jews different from all other people? Who has allowed us to suffer so terribly up till now? It is God that has made us as we are, but it will be God, too, who will raise us up again. If we bear all this suffering and if there are still Jews left when it is over, then Jews, instead of being doomed, will be held up as an example. Who knows, it might even be our religion from which the world and all peoples learn good, and for that reason and that reason only do we have to suffer now.

Let us remain aware of our task and not grumble, a solution will come, God has never deserted our people. Right through the ages there have been Jews, through all the ages they have had to suffer, but it has made them strong too; the weak fall, but the strong will remain and never go under!

If God lets me live, I shall attain more than my mother ever has done, I shall not remain insignificant, I shall work in the world and for mankind!

And now I know that first and foremost I shall require courage and cheerfulness!

Anne Frank

MEMORIAL PRAYER

אֵל מָלֵא רַחֲמִים שׁוֹכֵן בַּמְּרוֹמִים · הַמְצֵא מְנוּחָה נְכוֹנָה
תַּחַת כַּנְפֵי הַשְּׁכִינָה בְּמַעֲלוֹת קְדוֹשִׁים וּטְהוֹרִים · כְּזוֹהַר
הָרָקִיעַ מַזְהִירִים · לְנִשְׁמוֹת שִׁשָּׁה מִלְיוֹן אַחֵינוּ וְאַחְיוֹתֵינוּ
שֶׁמֵּתוּ עַל־קִדּוּשׁ הַשֵּׁם · יָנוּחוּ בַּשַּׁלְוָה וּבַשָּׁלוֹם שֶׁלֹּא יָדְעוּ
בְחַיֵּיהֶם · בְּעַל הָרַחֲמִים הַסְתִּירֵם בְּסֵתֶר כְּנָפֶיךָ לְעוֹלָמִים ·
וּצְרוֹר בִּצְרוֹר הַחַיִּים אֶת־נִשְׁמָתָם · יְיָ הוּא נַחֲלָתָם וְיָנוּחוּ
בְשָׁלוֹם עַל מִשְׁכָּבָם · וְנֹאמַר אָמֵן :

God full of compassion whose presence is over us, may the souls of our six million dead who have gone to their everlasting home with the holy and pure on high who shine as the lights of heaven, find the safety and rest denied them on earth beneath the shelter of Your presence. Master of mercy, cover them in the shelter of Your wings forever, and bind their souls into the gathering of life. It is the Lord who is their heritage. May they be at peace in their place of rest. Amen.

ISRAEL INDEPENDENCE DAY

PRAYER

אֱלֹהֵינוּ וֵאלֹהֵי־אֲבוֹתֵינוּ בְּיָדְךָ גּוֹרַל־עַמֵּנוּ וַעֲתִיד־כָּל־
אוּמָה וְלָשׁוֹן: אַתָּה הוּא הַמְפַזְּרֵנוּ בְּאַרְצוֹת־תֵּבֵל וְאַתָּה
הוּא הַמְקַבְּצֵנוּ: אַתָּה מַנְחֵינוּ מֵעַבְדוּת לְחֵרוּת· מִצָּרָה
לְשִׂמְחָה· וְאָנוּ עֵדֶיךָ נָאִיר אוֹרְךָ בֵּין־הָעַמִּים: חַזְּקֵנוּ־נָא
לַעֲשׂוֹת רְצוֹנֶךָ:

כַּאֲבוֹתֵינוּ לְפָנֵינוּ לְצִיּוֹן בְּאַהֲבָה נִפְנֶה: זִכְרוֹנוֹתֶיהָ
מְקָרְבִים אוֹתָנוּ זֶה לָזֶה· חֶזְיוֹנָה מְקָרֵב אוֹתָנוּ אֵלֶיךָ: זַכֵּנוּ
לִרְאוֹת בְּבִנְיַן־יְרוּשָׁלַיִם בְּיָמֵינוּ: יִהְיוּ־נָא חָזְקָה בְּמִשְׁפָּט
הַגֻּנָּתָהּ בְּצִדְקָה וּשְׂכָרָהּ שָׁלוֹם:

לְשִׁמְךָ נִתֵּן כָּבוֹד עַל־הַנִּפְלָאוֹת שֶׁרָאוּ עֵינֵינוּ כִּי תִקְוָה
קָמָה מְשׁוֹאָה· מַעְיָנוֹת בְּתוֹךְ בִּקְעוֹת־צִיָּה נִפְתְּחוּ וַעֲרָבָה
תִּפְרַח כַּחֲבַצָּלֶת:

מִבַּעַד לְצָרוֹת־זְמַנֵּנוּ שָׁמַעְנוּ דִּבְרֵי־נְבִיאֶיךָ וְרָאִינוּ קִיּוּם־
דְּבָרֶךָ: שׁוּב פְּדִיתָנוּ אֲדוֹן־הָאֱמֶת: חַזְּקֵנוּ וְאַמְּצֵנוּ לְכַלּוֹת
מְלַאכְתֶּךָ וְלִפְתֹּחַ שַׁעֲרֵי־פְדוּת לְיִשְׂרָאֵל וְלָעַמִּים· אָמֵן:

Our God and God of our fathers, in Your hand is the destiny of
our people and the fate of all nations. You scatter us through the world
and it is You who gather us in. You lead us through slavery and from
pain to freedom and joy, to be Your light and witness among the
nations. Give us strength to do Your will!

We turn to Zion in love, like our fathers before us. Its memories
draw us nearer to each other, its vision draws us nearer to You.
Give us honour to rebuild Jerusalem in our time. Let justice be its
strength and righteousness its defence, and may its reward be peace.

We praise You for the wonders our eyes have seen: the hope that was born out of suffering, the springs that came to the dry sad valley, the rose that blossomed in the desert.

In the troubles of our time we have heard the message of Your prophets and seen the fulfilment of Your word. Again You have redeemed us, Lord of truth. Give us courage to complete Your work, and bring redemption to mankind. Amen.

PASSAGES FOR STUDY

I belong to a group of people who from the time Britain conquered Palestine have not ceased to strive for the concluding of a genuine peace between Jew and Arab.

By a genuine peace we inferred and still infer that both peoples together should develop the land without the one imposing its will on the other. In view of the international usages of our generation, this appeared to us to be very difficult but not impossible. We were and still are well aware that in this unusual—yes, unprecedented case, it is a question of seeking new ways of understanding and cordial agreement between the nations. Here again we stood and still stand under the sway of a commandment.

We considered it a fundamental point that in this case two vital claims are opposed to each other, two claims of a different nature and a different origin which cannot objectively be pitted against one another and between which no objective decision can be made as to which is just, which unjust. We considered and still consider it our duty to understand and to honour the claim which is opposed to ours and to endeavour to reconcile both claims. We could not and cannot renounce the Jewish claim; something even higher than the life of our people is bound up with this land, namely its work, its divine mission. But we have been and still are convinced that it must be possible to find some compromise between this claim and the other; for we love this land and we believe in its future; since such love and such faith are surely present on the other side as well, a union in the common service of the land must be within the range of possibility. Where there is faith and love, a solution may be found even to what appears to be a tragic opposition.

... It seems to me that God does not give any one portion of the earth away, so that the owner may say as God says in the Bible: 'For all the earth is Mine' (*Exodus 19: 5*). The conquered land is, in my opinion, only lent even to the conqueror who has settled on it—and God waits to see what he will make of it.

Martin Buber

Accordingly we, the members of the National Council, representing the Jewish people in the Land of Israel and the Zionist Movement, have assembled on the day of the termination of the British Mandate for Palestine, and, by virtue of our natural and historic right and of the resolution of the United Nations, do hereby proclaim the establishment of a Jewish State in the Land of Israel—the State of Israel.

The State of Israel will be open to Jewish immigration and the ingathering of exiles. It will devote itself to developing the land for the good of all its inhabitants. It will rest upon foundations of liberty, justice and peace as envisioned by the prophets of Israel. It will maintain complete equality of social and political rights for all its citizens, without distinction of creed, race or sex. It will guarantee freedom of religion and conscience, of language, education and culture. It will safeguard the Holy Places of all religions. It will be loyal to the principles of the United Nations Charter.

Even amidst the violent attacks launched against us for months past, we call upon the sons of the Arab people dwelling in Israel to keep the peace and to play their part in building the State on the basis of full and equal citizenship and due representation in all its institutions, provisional and permanent.

We extend the hand of peace and good-neighbourliness to all the states around us and to their peoples, and we call upon them to co-operate in mutual helpfulness with the independent Jewish nation in its land. The State of Israel is prepared to make its contribution in a concerted effort for the advancement of the entire Middle East.

We call upon the Jewish people throughout the Diaspora to join forces with us in immigration and construction, and to be at our right hand in the great endeavour to fulfil the age-old longing for the redemption of Israel.

With trust in Almighty God, we set our hands in witness to this Proclamation, at this session of the Provisional Council of State, on the soil of the homeland, in the city of Tel Aviv, this Sabbath Eve, the fifth of Iyar, 5708, the 14th of May 1948.

From the Declaration of Independence

קכב

שִׁיר הַמַּעֲלוֹת לְדָוִד

שָׂמַחְתִּי בְּאֹמְרִים לִי בֵּית יְהֹוָה נֵלֵךְ :
עֹמְדוֹת הָיוּ רַגְלֵינוּ בִּשְׁעָרַיִךְ יְרוּשָׁלָיִם :
יְרוּשָׁלַיִם הַבְּנוּיָה כְּעִיר שֶׁחֻבְּרָה־לָּהּ יַחְדָּו :
שֶׁשָּׁם עָלוּ שְׁבָטִים שִׁבְטֵי־יָהּ
עֵדוּת לְיִשְׂרָאֵל לְהֹדוֹת לְשֵׁם יְהֹוָה :
כִּי שָׁמָּה יָשְׁבוּ כִסְאוֹת לְמִשְׁפָּט כִּסְאוֹת לְבֵית דָּוִד :
שַׁאֲלוּ שְׁלוֹם יְרוּשָׁלָיִם יִשְׁלָיוּ אֹהֲבָיִךְ :
יְהִי־שָׁלוֹם בְּחֵילֵךְ שַׁלְוָה בְּאַרְמְנוֹתָיִךְ :
לְמַעַן אַחַי וְרֵעָי אֲדַבְּרָה־נָּא שָׁלוֹם בָּךְ :
לְמַעַן בֵּית־יְהֹוָה אֱלֹהֵינוּ אֲבַקְשָׁה טוֹב לָךְ :

Psalm 122

A pilgrim Song. David's.

I rejoiced when they said to me:
'Let us go to the house of the Lord!'
And now our feet are standing
inside your gates, O Jerusalem!

Jerusalem rebuilt! As a city
where all are united together.
Here the tribes came up,
the tribes of the Lord

—for it is the mark of Israel
  to thank the name of the Lord.
There were the seats of justice,
  the thrones of the house of David.

Pray for the peace of Jerusalem,
  may those who love you prosper.
Peace be within your walls,
  tranquillity inside your homes.

For the sake of my brothers and friends
  I call out, 'Peace be with you!'
For the sake of the house of the Lord our God,
  I will seek your good.

MEMORIAL PRAYER

אֵל מָלֵא רַחֲמִים שׁוֹכֵן בַּמְּרוֹמִים · הַמְצֵא מְנוּחָה נְכוֹנָה
תַּחַת כַּנְפֵי הַשְּׁכִינָה בְּמַעֲלוֹת קְדוֹשִׁים וּטְהוֹרִים · כְּזוֹהַר
הָרָקִיעַ מַזְהִירִים · לְנִשְׁמוֹת אֵלֶּה שֶׁהִקְרִיבוּ אֶת־חַיֵּיהֶם עַל
הֲקָמַת־הַמְּדִינָה וּבְעֵת צָרָה נָטְעוּ תִקְוָה חֲדָשָׁה בְּלֵב עַמְּךָ
יִשְׂרָאֵל · בַּעַל הָרַחֲמִים הַסְתִּירֵם בְּסֵתֶר כְּנָפֶיךָ לְעוֹלָמִים ·
וּצְרוֹר בִּצְרוֹר הַחַיִּים אֶת־נִשְׁמָתָם · יְיָ הוּא נַחֲלָתָם וְיָנוּחוּ
בְשָׁלוֹם עַל מִשְׁכָּבָם · וְנֹאמַר אָמֵן:

God full of compassion whose presence is over us, may the souls
of those who gave their lives to rebuild the land, and in times of
disaster gave new hope to Your people Israel, find safety and rest
with the holy and pure on high who shine as the lights of heaven,
beneath the shelter of Your presence. Master of mercy, cover
them in the shelter of Your wings forever, and bind their souls into
the gathering of life. It is the Lord who is their heritage. May they
be at peace in their place of rest. Amen.

PURIM

PURIM PRAYER

עַל הַנִּסִּים · וְעַל הַגְּבוּרוֹת · וְעַל הַתְּשׁוּעוֹת · וְעַל
הַנִּפְלָאוֹת וְעַל הַנֶּחָמוֹת שֶׁעָשִׂיתָ לַאֲבוֹתֵינוּ בַּיָּמִים הָהֵם
וּבַזְּמַן הַזֶּה: בִּימֵי מָרְדְּכַי וְאֶסְתֵּר בְּשׁוּשַׁן הַבִּירָה · כְּשֶׁעָמַד
עֲלֵיהֶם הָמָן הָרָשָׁע בִּקֵּשׁ לְהַשְׁמִיד לַהֲרוֹג וּלְאַבֵּד אֶת־כָּל־
הַיְּהוּדִים · מִנַּעַר וְעַד־זָקֵן טַף וְנָשִׁים בְּיוֹם אֶחָד · בִּשְׁלשָׁה
עָשָׂר לְחֹדֶשׁ שְׁנֵים־עָשָׂר הוּא חֹדֶשׁ אֲדָר · וּשְׁלָלָם לָבוֹז:
וְאַתָּה בְּרַחֲמֶיךָ הָרַבִּים הֵפַרְתָּ אֶת־עֲצָתוֹ · וְקִלְקַלְתָּ אֶת־
מַחֲשַׁבְתּוֹ · וַהֲשֵׁבוֹתָ לּוֹ גְּמוּלוֹ בְּרֹאשׁוֹ: וְעָשִׂיתָ עִמָּהֶם נֵס
וָפֶלֶא · וְנוֹדֶה לְשִׁמְךָ הַגָּדוֹל:

We thank You for the wonders, for the heroic acts, for the victories,
for the marvellous and consoling deeds which You performed for
our fathers, in those days at this season. In the days of Mordechai and
Esther, in Shushan the capital, when the wicked Haman rose up
against them, he sought to destroy, kill and exterminate all the Jews,
both young and old, little children and women, on one day, and
plunder their possessions. (That is on the 13th day of the twelfth
month, which is the month of Adar.) Then You, in Your great mercy,
upset his plan and overthrew his design, and made his acts recoil
upon his own head. And You performed a wonder and a marvel for
them, therefore we thank Your great name.

Before reading the Scroll of Esther.

בָּרוּךְ אַתָּה יְיָ אֱלֹהֵינוּ מֶלֶךְ הָעוֹלָם · אֲשֶׁר קִדְּשָׁנוּ
בְּמִצְוֹתָיו וְצִוָּנוּ עַל מִקְרָא מְגִלָּה:
בָּרוּךְ אַתָּה יְיָ אֱלֹהֵינוּ מֶלֶךְ הָעוֹלָם · שֶׁעָשָׂה נִסִּים
לַאֲבוֹתֵינוּ בַּיָּמִים הָהֵם וּבַזְּמַן הַזֶּה:
בָּרוּךְ אַתָּה יְיָ אֱלֹהֵינוּ מֶלֶךְ הָעוֹלָם · שֶׁהֶחֱיָנוּ וְקִיְּמָנוּ
וְהִגִּיעָנוּ לַזְּמַן הַזֶּה:

Blessed are You, Lord our God, king of the universe, who makes us holy through doing His commands, and commands us to read the Scroll of Esther.

Blessed are You, Lord our God, king of the universe, who did wonders for our fathers in those days at this season.

Blessed are You, Lord our God, king of the universe, who has kept us alive and supported us and brought us to this season.

After reading the Scroll of Esther

בָּרוּךְ אַתָּה יְיָ אֱלֹהֵינוּ מֶלֶךְ הָעוֹלָם · הָרָב אֶת־רִיבֵנוּ וְהַדָּן אֶת־דִּינֵנוּ · תְּשׁוּעָתֵנוּ הָיִיתָ לָנֶצַח וְתִקְוָתֵנוּ בְּכָל־דּוֹר וָדוֹר · לֹא־יֵבְוֹשׁוּ וְלֹא־יִכָּלְמוּ לָנֶצַח כָּל־הַחוֹסִים בָּךְ · בָּרוּךְ אַתָּה יְיָ · הָאֵל הַמּוֹשִׁיעַ:

Blessed are You, Lord our God, king of the universe, who heard our plea and judged our cause. You are the one who has always saved us, our hope in every generation. May those who trust in You never be ashamed nor humiliated. Blessed are You Lord, the God who saves us.

PURIM SONG

שׁוֹשַׁנַּת יַעֲקֹב צָהֲלָה וְשָׂמֵחָה בִּרְאוֹתָם יַחַד תְּכֵלֶת מָרְדְּכָי: תְּשׁוּעָתָם הָיִיתָ לָנֶצַח וְתִקְוָתָם בְּכָל־דּוֹר וָדוֹר: לְהוֹדִיעַ שֶׁכָּל־קוֹיֶךָ לֹא יֵבְשׁוּ וְלֹא יִכָּלְמוּ לָנֶצַח כָּל־הַחוֹסִים בָּךְ:

The Jews of Shushan, the flower of Jacob, were joyful and glad when all of them saw Mordechai clothed in the royal purple. You have always been the one who saved them, and their hope in every generation, to make known that all who hope in You shall never be ashamed, nor shall any be humiliated who put their trust in You.

Other Purim songs, page 592.

CHANUKAH

Before lighting the Chanukiah

בָּרוּךְ אַתָּה יְיָ אֱלֹהֵינוּ מֶלֶךְ הָעוֹלָם · אֲשֶׁר קִדְּשָׁנוּ
בְּמִצְוֹתָיו וְצִוָּנוּ לְהַדְלִיק נֵר שֶׁל חֲנֻכָּה:

בָּרוּךְ אַתָּה יְיָ אֱלֹהֵינוּ מֶלֶךְ הָעוֹלָם · שֶׁעָשָׂה נִסִּים
לַאֲבוֹתֵינוּ בַּיָּמִים הָהֵם וּבַזְּמַן הַזֶּה:

Blessed are You, Lord our God, king of the universe, who makes
us holy through doing His commands, and commands us to kindle
the lights of Chanukah.

Blessed are You, Lord our God, king of the universe, who did
wonders for our fathers in those days at this season.

On the first night add

בָּרוּךְ אַתָּה יְיָ אֱלֹהֵינוּ מֶלֶךְ הָעוֹלָם · שֶׁהֶחֱיָנוּ וְקִיְּמָנוּ
וְהִגִּיעָנוּ לַזְּמַן הַזֶּה:

Blessed are You, Lord our God, king of the universe, who has
kept us alive and supported us and brought us to this season.

After lighting the Chanukiah

הַנֵּרוֹת הַלָּלוּ אָנוּ מַדְלִיקִים עַל הַנִּסִּים וְעַל הַגְּבוּרוֹת
וְעַל הַתְּשׁוּעוֹת וְעַל הַנִּפְלָאוֹת וְעַל הַנֶּחָמוֹת · שֶׁעָשִׂיתָ
לַאֲבוֹתֵינוּ בַּיָּמִים הָהֵם וּבַזְּמַן הַזֶּה עַל יְדֵי כֹּהֲנֶיךָ הַקְּדוֹשִׁים ·
וְכָל־שְׁמֹנַת יְמֵי הֲנֻכָּה הַנֵּרוֹת הַלָּלוּ קֹדֶשׁ וְאֵין לָנוּ רְשׁוּת
לְהִשְׁתַּמֵּשׁ בָּהֶם אֶלָּא לִרְאוֹתָם בִּלְבַד · כְּדֵי לְהוֹדוֹת לְשִׁמְךָ
עַל־נִסֶּיךָ וְעַל־יְשׁוּעָתֶךָ וְעַל־נִפְלְאוֹתֶיךָ:

We kindle these lights to commemorate the wonders, the heroic acts, the victories and the marvellous and consoling deeds which You performed for our fathers through Your holy priests in those days at this season. During all the eight days of Chanukah these lights are holy and we are not permitted to make use of them, but only to see them in order to thank Your name for the wonders, the victories and the marvellous deeds.

CHANUKAH PRAYER

עַל הַנִּסִּים · וְעַל הַגְּבוּרוֹת · וְעַל הַתְּשׁוּעוֹת · וְעַל הַנִּפְלָאוֹת
שֶׁעָשִׂיתָ לַאֲבוֹתֵינוּ בַּיָּמִים הָהֵם וּבַזְּמַן הַזֶּה: בִּימֵי מַתִּתְיָהוּ
בֶּן־יוֹחָנָן הַכֹּהֵן הַחַשְׁמוֹנַאי וּבָנָיו · כְּשֶׁעָמְדָה מַלְכוּת אַנְטִיוֹכוֹס
עַל עַמְּךָ יִשְׂרָאֵל לְהַשְׁכִּיחָם תּוֹרָתֶךָ: וְאַתָּה בְּרַחֲמֶיךָ
הָרַבִּים עָמַדְתָּ לָהֶם בְּעֵת צָרָתָם · רַבְתָּ אֶת־רִיבָם · דַּנְתָּ
אֶת־דִּינָם · מָסַרְתָּ גִבּוֹרִים בְּיַד חַלָּשִׁים · וְרַבִּים בְּיַד מְעַטִּים ·
וּלְךָ עָשִׂיתָ שֵׁם גָּדוֹל וְקָדוֹשׁ בְּעוֹלָמֶךָ · וּלְעַמְּךָ יִשְׂרָאֵל
עָשִׂיתָ תְּשׁוּעָה גְדוֹלָה כְּהַיּוֹם הַזֶּה: וְאַחֲרֵי־כֵן בָּאוּ בָנֶיךָ
לִדְבִיר בֵּיתֶךָ · וּפִנּוּ אֶת־הֵיכָלֶךָ · וְהִדְלִיקוּ נֵרוֹת בְּחַצְרוֹת
קָדְשֶׁךָ · וְקָבְעוּ שְׁמוֹנַת יְמֵי חֲנֻכָּה לְהוֹדוֹת וּלְהַלֵּל לְשִׁמְךָ
הַגָּדוֹל:

We thank You for the wonders, the heroic acts, the victories and the marvellous and consoling deeds You performed for our fathers, in those days at this season. In the days of Mattathias, the Hasmonean, the son of Yochanan the priest, and his sons, when the kingdom of Antiochus rose up against Your people Israel to make them forget Your teaching, then You in Your great mercy stood up for them in their hour of need. You heard their plea. You judged their cause. You delivered the strong into the hands of the weak, and the many into the hands of the few. You made Your name great and holy in Your world, and gave a great victory to Your people Israel as at this day. Afterwards Your children entered the inner sanctuary of Your house, they cleared the Temple, and lit the lamps in Your holy courts. Then they appointed eight days of dedication to thank and honour Your great name.

CHANUKAH HYMN—MAOZ TZUR

מָעוֹז צוּר יְשׁוּעָתִי · לְךָ נָאֶה לְשַׁבֵּחַ · תִּכּוֹן בֵּית
תְּפִלָּתִי · וְשָׁם תּוֹדָה נְזַבֵּחַ · לְעֵת תָּכִין
מַטְבֵּחַ מִצָּר הַמְנַבֵּחַ · אָז אֶגְמוֹר · בְּשִׁיר מִזְמוֹר · חֲנֻכַּת
הַמִּזְבֵּחַ :

רָעוֹת שָׂבְעָה נַפְשִׁי · בְּיָגוֹן כֹּחִי כָלָה · חַיַּי מֵרְרוּ בְקֹשִׁי ·
בְּשִׁעְבּוּד מַלְכוּת עֶגְלָה · וּבְיָדוֹ הַגְּדוֹלָה · הוֹצִיא אֶת־
הַסְּגֻלָּה · חֵיל פַּרְעֹה · וְכָל־זַרְעוֹ · יָרְדוּ כְּאֶבֶן מְצוּלָה :

דְּבִיר קָדְשׁוֹ הֱבִיאַנִי · וְגַם שָׁם לֹא שָׁקַטְתִּי · וּבָא נוֹגֵשׂ
וְהִגְלַנִי · כִּי זָרִים עָבַדְתִּי · וְיֵין רַעַל מָסַכְתִּי · כִּמְעַט
שֶׁעָבַרְתִּי · קֵץ בָּבֶל · זְרֻבָּבֶל · לְקֵץ שִׁבְעִים נוֹשַׁעְתִּי :

יְוָנִים נִקְבְּצוּ עָלַי · אֲזַי בִּימֵי חַשְׁמַנִּים · וּפָרְצוּ חוֹמוֹת
מִגְדָּלַי · וְטִמְּאוּ כָּל־הַשְּׁמָנִים · וּמִנּוֹתַר קַנְקַנִּים · נַעֲשָׂה נֵס
לַשּׁוֹשַׁנִּים · בְּנֵי בִינָה · יְמֵי שְׁמוֹנָה · קָבְעוּ שִׁיר וּרְנָנִים :

Fortress, rock who sets me free,
how fine it is to sing Your praise.
When my house of prayer shall be,
our offerings of thanks we'll raise.
The time You end all slaughter,
enemies shall falter.
I'll complete
a song to greet
and dedicate the altar.

How my soul was filled with strife,
sorrow robbed my strength from me.
Bitter hardship ruled my life,
bound by Egypt's slavery.
God let His mighty hand show,
to help His chosen people go.
Pharaoh's power,
his finest flower,
sank into the depths below.

Brought to God's own holy place
even there no peace I found.
Sent to exile in disgrace,
to other gods I still felt bound.
I drank the wine of madness,
seventy years of sadness.
Babylon fell;
Zerubavel
brought salvation's gladness.

When the Greeks were gathered round
in the Maccabean days,
broke my towers to the ground,
spoilt the oil used for Your praise.
Your sign then guided our fate,
one day's oil lasted for eight.
Our wise men
established then
this festival we celebrate.

Other Chanukah Songs, pages 590–592.

A PRAYER FOR CHANUKAH

O Lord, creator and ruler of all things, by Your command light
springs out of darkness, and order out of chaos. In Your wisdom,
You granted us the power to struggle against falsehood and oppression, and through this struggle to gain liberty and truth.

You appointed Israel a champion of justice, and the guardian of
Your teaching. Today we remember, in joy and gratitude, the courage
of the Maccabees and their victory against tyranny. Your servants
rescued Your house from destruction, and Your Torah from shame.
They rededicated the Temple in Jerusalem and heralded for all men
the ultimate triumph of their trust in You. With reverence we recall
their loyalty and thank You for the wonders that You did for us
through them. May their example and their sacrifice never fail us in
the time to come.

As the lights of Chanukah shed their radiance in our homes, may
they kindle in us the flame of faithfulness. May they help us to
struggle more bravely for justice and for truth, and guide us towards
You, the light everlasting. Amen.

BLESSINGS FOR VARIOUS OCCASIONS

Washing the hands before a meal

בָּרוּךְ אַתָּה יְיָ אֱלֹהֵינוּ מֶלֶךְ הָעוֹלָם · אֲשֶׁר קִדְּשָׁנוּ בְּמִצְוֹתָיו וְצִוָּנוּ עַל נְטִילַת יָדָיִם:

For wine

בָּרוּךְ אַתָּה יְיָ אֱלֹהֵינוּ מֶלֶךְ הָעוֹלָם · בּוֹרֵא פְּרִי הַגָּפֶן:

For bread

בָּרוּךְ אַתָּה יְיָ אֱלֹהֵינוּ מֶלֶךְ הָעוֹלָם · הַמּוֹצִיא לֶחֶם מִן הָאָרֶץ:

For cake and pastry

בָּרוּךְ אַתָּה יְיָ אֱלֹהֵינוּ מֶלֶךְ הָעוֹלָם · בּוֹרֵא מִינֵי מְזוֹנוֹת:

For fruits which grow on trees

בָּרוּךְ אַתָּה יְיָ אֱלֹהֵינוּ מֶלֶךְ הָעוֹלָם · בּוֹרֵא פְּרִי הָעֵץ:

For vegetables

בָּרוּךְ אַתָּה יְיָ אֱלֹהֵינוּ מֶלֶךְ הָעוֹלָם · בּוֹרֵא פְּרִי הָאֲדָמָה:

For all other food

בָּרוּךְ אַתָּה יְיָ אֱלֹהֵינוּ מֶלֶךְ הָעוֹלָם · שֶׁהַכֹּל נִהְיֶה בִּדְבָרוֹ:

After eating any food except bread

בָּרוּךְ אַתָּה יְיָ אֱלֹהֵינוּ מֶלֶךְ הָעוֹלָם · בּוֹרֵא נְפָשׁוֹת רַבּוֹת וְחֶסְרוֹנָן · עַל כָּל־מַה־שֶּׁבָּרֵאתָ לְהַחֲיוֹת בָּהֶם נֶפֶשׁ כָּל־חָי · בָּרוּךְ חֵי הָעוֹלָמִים:

On smelling flowers

בָּרוּךְ אַתָּה יְיָ אֱלֹהֵינוּ מֶלֶךְ הָעוֹלָם · בּוֹרֵא עִשְׂבוֹר בְּשָׂמִים:

BLESSINGS FOR VARIOUS OCCASIONS

BLESSINGS CONCERNING FOOD

Washing the hands before a meal

Blessed are You, Lord our God, king of the universe, who makes us holy through doing His commands, and commands us concerning washing the hands.

For wine

Blessed are You, Lord our God, king of the universe, who creates the fruit of the vine.

For bread

Blessed are You, Lord our God, king of the universe, who brings forth food out of the earth.

For cake and pastry

Blessed are You, Lord our God, king of the universe, who creates different kinds of food.

For fruits which grow on trees

Blessed are You, Lord our God, king of the universe, who creates the fruit of the tree.

For vegetables

Blessed are You, Lord our God, king of the universe, who creates the fruit of the earth.

For all other food

Blessed are You, Lord our God, king of the universe, by whose word all things exist.

After eating any food except bread

Blessed are You, Lord our God, king of the universe, who creates many living things and their needs, with all that You created to keep each one of them alive. Blessed are You, the life of all existence.

BLESSINGS CONCERNING NATURE

On smelling flowers

Blessed are You, Lord our God, king of the universe, who creates fragrant plants.

On smelling spices

בָּרוּךְ אַתָּה יְיָ אֱלֹהֵינוּ מֶלֶךְ הָעוֹלָם · בּוֹרֵא מִינֵי בְשָׂמִים:

On smelling perfumes

בָּרוּךְ אַתָּה יְיָ אֱלֹהֵינוּ מֶלֶךְ הָעוֹלָם · בּוֹרֵא שֶׁמֶן עָרֵב:

On seeing the wonders of nature

בָּרוּךְ אַתָּה יְיָ אֱלֹהֵינוּ מֶלֶךְ הָעוֹלָם · עֹשֶׂה מַעֲשֵׂה בְרֵאשִׁית:

For thunder

בָּרוּךְ אַתָּה יְיָ אֱלֹהֵינוּ מֶלֶךְ הָעוֹלָם · שֶׁכֹּחוֹ וּגְבוּרָתוֹ מָלֵא עוֹלָם:

On seeing a rainbow

בָּרוּךְ אַתָּה יְיָ אֱלֹהֵינוּ מֶלֶךְ הָעוֹלָם · זוֹכֵר הַבְּרִית וְנֶאֱמָן בִּבְרִיתוֹ וְקַיָּם בְּמַאֲמָרוֹ:

On seeing the sea

בָּרוּךְ אַתָּה יְיָ אֱלֹהֵינוּ מֶלֶךְ הָעוֹלָם · שֶׁעָשָׂה אֶת־הַיָּם הַגָּדוֹל:

On seeing the beauties of nature

בָּרוּךְ אַתָּה יְיָ אֱלֹהֵינוּ מֶלֶךְ הָעוֹלָם · שֶׁכָּכָה לוֹ בְּעוֹלָמוֹ:

On seeing trees in blossom for the first time in the year

בָּרוּךְ אַתָּה יְיָ אֱלֹהֵינוּ מֶלֶךְ הָעוֹלָם · שֶׁלֹּא חִסַּר בְּעוֹלָמוֹ דָּבָר · וּבָרָא בוֹ בְּרִיּוֹת טוֹבוֹת וְאִילָנוֹת טוֹבִים לְהַנּוֹת בָּהֶם בְּנֵי אָדָם:

On seeing people of unusual appearance

בָּרוּךְ אַתָּה יְיָ אֱלֹהֵינוּ מֶלֶךְ הָעוֹלָם · מְשַׁנֶּה הַבְּרִיּוֹת:

On seeing kings and rulers

בָּרוּךְ אַתָּה יְיָ אֱלֹהֵינוּ מֶלֶךְ הָעוֹלָם · שֶׁנָּתַן מִכְּבוֹדוֹ לְבָשָׂר וָדָם:

On seeing people with religious knowledge and wisdom

בָּרוּךְ אַתָּה יְיָ אֱלֹהֵינוּ מֶלֶךְ הָעוֹלָם · שֶׁחָלַק מֵחָכְמָתוֹ לִירֵאָיו:

On smelling spices

Blessed are You, Lord our God, king of the universe, who creates different kinds of spices.

On smelling perfumes

Blessed are You, Lord our God, king of the universe, who creates sweet smelling oil.

On seeing the wonders of nature

Blessed are You, Lord our God, king of the universe, who performs the work of creation.

For thunder

Blessed are You, Lord our God, king of the universe, whose strength and power fill the world.

On seeing a rainbow

Blessed are You, Lord our God, king of the universe, who remembers His covenant and is faithful to it, and keeps His promise.

On seeing the sea

Blessed are You, Lord our God, king of the universe, who made the great sea.

On seeing the beauties of nature

Blessed are You, Lord our God, king of the universe, who has such as these in His world.

On seeing trees in blossom for the first time in the year

Blessed are You, Lord our God, king of the universe, who has not made His world lack for anything, and has created in it fine creatures and trees to give pleasure to mankind.

BLESSINGS CONCERNING PEOPLE

On seeing people of unusual appearance

Blessed are You, Lord our God, king of the universe, who varies the forms of creation.

On seeing kings and rulers

Blessed are You, Lord our God, king of the universe, who has given of His glory to flesh and blood.

On seeing people with religious knowledge and wisdom

Blessed are You, Lord our God, king of the universe, who has given a share of His wisdom to those in awe of Him.

On seeing people with great secular learning

בָּרוּךְ אַתָּה יְיָ אֱלֹהֵינוּ מֶלֶךְ הָעוֹלָם · שֶׁנָּתַן מֵחָכְמָתוֹ לְבָשָׂר וָדָם:

On fixing a mezuzah

בָּרוּךְ אַתָּה יְיָ אֱלֹהֵינוּ מֶלֶךְ הָעוֹלָם · אֲשֶׁר קִדְּשָׁנוּ בְּמִצְוֹתָיו וְצִוָּנוּ לִקְבּוֹעַ מְזוּזָה:

On tasting new fruits, on moving into a new home and on using new clothes

בָּרוּךְ אַתָּה יְיָ אֱלֹהֵינוּ מֶלֶךְ הָעוֹלָם · שֶׁהֶחֱיָנוּ וְקִיְּמָנוּ וְהִגִּיעָנוּ לַזְּמַן הַזֶּה:

On hearing bad news

בָּרוּךְ אַתָּה יְיָ אֱלֹהֵינוּ מֶלֶךְ הָעוֹלָם · דַּיַּן הָאֱמֶת:

On hearing news which is good for you and for others

בָּרוּךְ אַתָּה יְיָ אֱלֹהֵינוּ מֶלֶךְ הָעוֹלָם · הַטּוֹב וְהַמֵּטִיב:

On seeing one who has recovered from serious illness

בְּרִיךְ רַחֲמָנָא מַלְכָּא דְעָלְמָא דִי יַהֲבָךְ לָן וְלָא יַהֲבָךְ לְעַפְרָא:

On seeing synagogues which remain after a destruction

בָּרוּךְ אַתָּה יְיָ אֱלֹהֵינוּ מֶלֶךְ הָעוֹלָם· מַצִּיב גְּבוּל אַלְמָנָה:

On seeing a place where a wonderful thing happened to you

בָּרוּךְ אַתָּה יְיָ אֱלֹהֵינוּ מֶלֶךְ הָעוֹלָם· שֶׁעָשָׂה לִי נֵס בַּמָּקוֹם הַזֶּה:

On seeing people with great secular learning

Blessed are You, Lord our God, king of the universe, who has given of His wisdom to flesh and blood.

BLESSINGS CONCERNING EVENTS

On fixing a mezuzah

Blessed are You, Lord our God, king of the universe, who makes us holy through doing His commands, and commands us to fix the *mezuzah*.

On tasting new fruits, on moving into a new home and on using new clothes

Blessed are You, Lord our God, king of the universe, who has kept us alive and supported us and brought us to this season.

On hearing bad news

Blessed are You, Lord our God, king of the universe, the true judge.

On hearing news which is good for you and for others

Blessed are You, Lord our God, king of the universe, who is good and does good.

On seeing one who has recovered from serious illness

Blessed is the All-merciful, king of the universe, who has restored you to us and not to the dust.

On seeing synagogues which remain after a destruction

Blessed are You, Lord our God, king of the universe, who '(destroys the possessions of the proud and) preserves the portion of the defenceless.'

On seeing a place where a wonderful thing happened to you

Blessed are You, Lord our God, king of the universe, who performed a wonderful thing for me at this place.

MY FAMILY

אלה תולדות

Give these, companions in love, great happiness, the happiness of Your creatures in Eden long ago. Blessed are You Lord, who rejoices the bridegroom and the bride.

Marriage Service

MARRIAGE SERVICE

פד

לַמְנַצֵּחַ עַל־הַגִּתִּית לִבְנֵי־קֹרַח מִזְמוֹר:

מַה־יְּדִידוֹת מִשְׁכְּנוֹתֶיךָ יְהֹוָה צְבָאוֹת:
נִכְסְפָה וְגַם־כָּלְתָה נַפְשִׁי לְחַצְרוֹת יְהֹוָה
לִבִּי וּבְשָׂרִי יְרַנְּנוּ אֶל אֵל־חָי:

גַּם־צִפּוֹר מָצְאָה בַיִת וּדְרוֹר קֵן לָהּ אֲשֶׁר־שָׁתָה אֶפְרֹחֶיהָ
אֶת־מִזְבְּחוֹתֶיךָ יְהֹוָה צְבָאוֹת מַלְכִּי וֵאלֹהָי:

אַשְׁרֵי יוֹשְׁבֵי בֵיתֶךָ עוֹד יְהַלְלוּךָ סֶּלָה:
אַשְׁרֵי אָדָם עוֹז־לוֹ בָךְ מְסִלּוֹת בִּלְבָבָם:
עֹבְרֵי בְּעֵמֶק הַבָּכָא מַעְיָן יְשִׁיתוּהוּ גַּם־בְּרָכוֹת יַעְטֶה מוֹרֶה:
יֵלְכוּ מֵחַיִל אֶל־חָיִל יֵרָאֶה אֶל־אֱלֹהִים בְּצִיּוֹן:

MARRIAGE SERVICE

Psalm 84

For the choirmaster. Upon the Gittit. For the sons of Korach. A psalm.

How lovely where Your presence dwells
    Lord of all creation.
My soul is longing, pining
    for the courts of the Lord.
My heart and my flesh sing out
    to the living God.

Even a sparrow finds a home
    and a swallow her own nest
    in which to lay her young—
    such are Your altars, Lord of all creation,
    my ruler and my God.

Happy are those who live in Your house
    and can always praise You.
Happy the pilgrim inspired by You,
    they journey to You in their heart.
They pass through the dry sad valley
    and make it seem a place of springs,
    as if the early rain covered it with blessings.
They go from strength to strength
    to appear before God in Zion.

יְהֹוָה אֱלֹהִים צְבָאוֹת שִׁמְעָה תְפִלָּתִי

הַאֲזִינָה אֱלֹהֵי יַעֲקֹב סֶלָה:

מָגִנֵּנוּ רְאֵה אֱלֹהִים וְהַבֵּט פְּנֵי מְשִׁיחֶךָ:

כִּי טוֹב־יוֹם בַּחֲצֵרֶיךָ מֵאָלֶף

בָּחַרְתִּי הִסְתּוֹפֵף בְּבֵית אֱלֹהַי מִדּוּר בְּאָהֳלֵי־רֶשַׁע:

כִּי שֶׁמֶשׁ וּמָגֵן יְהֹוָה אֱלֹהִים חֵן וְכָבוֹד יִתֵּן יְהֹוָה

לֹא יִמְנַע־טוֹב לַהֹלְכִים בְּתָמִים:

יְהֹוָה צְבָאוֹת אַשְׁרֵי אָדָם בֹּטֵחַ בָּךְ:

ק

מִזְמוֹר לְתוֹדָה

הָרִיעוּ לַיהֹוָה כָּל־הָאָרֶץ:

עִבְדוּ אֶת־יְהֹוָה בְּשִׂמְחָה בֹּאוּ לְפָנָיו בִּרְנָנָה:

דְּעוּ כִּי־יְהֹוָה הוּא אֱלֹהִים הוּא עָשָׂנוּ וְלוֹ אֲנַחְנוּ
עַמּוֹ וְצֹאן מַרְעִיתוֹ:

בֹּאוּ שְׁעָרָיו בְּתוֹדָה חֲצֵרֹתָיו בִּתְהִלָּה הוֹדוּ־לוֹ בָּרְכוּ שְׁמוֹ:

כִּי־טוֹב יְהֹוָה לְעוֹלָם חַסְדּוֹ וְעַד־דֹּר וָדֹר אֱמוּנָתוֹ:

Lord, God of all creation, hear my prayer,
　　listen, God of Jacob!
God, our shield, look
　　and watch over Your anointed!
For one day in Your courts is better
　　than a thousand elsewhere.
I would rather stand at the doorway
　　of the house of my God
　　than live at ease in the tents of the wicked.

For the Lord God is a sun and a shield,
　　the Lord gives favour and glory.
He will not withhold goodness
　　from those who walk in integrity.

Lord of all creation,
　　happy the man who trusts in You!

Psalm 100

A psalm of thanksgiving.

Shout to the Lord all the earth,
　　serve the Lord with joy,
　　come before Him with singing.

Know that the Lord is God.
　　It is He who made us and we are His,
　　His own people and the flock of His pasture.

Come into His gates with thanks,
　　into His courts with praise,
　　thank Him, bless His name.

For the Lord is good,
　　His love is everlasting
　　and His faithfulness for all generations.

בָּרוּךְ הַבָּא בְּשֵׁם יְהֹוָה ·　　בֵּרַכְנוּכֶם מִבֵּית יְהֹוָה:

Blessed are those who come in the name of the Lord! We bless you from the house of the Lord.

מִי אַדִּיר עַל הַכֹּל · מִי בָּרוּךְ עַל הַכֹּל · מִי גָּדוֹל
עַל הַכֹּל · הוּא יְבָרֵךְ הֶחָתָן וְהַכַּלָּה:

May He who is supreme above all, who is blessed above all, who is great above all—may He bless the bridegroom and the bride.

One of the following prayers:

Lord, at the quietness of this time, and in the holiness of this place, give Your blessing to Your children. You have given them youth with its hopes and love with its dreams. May these come true through their faith in each other and their trust in You. Let them be devoted to each other, and as the years go by, teach them how great is the joy that comes from sharing, and how deep the love that grows with giving. May Your presence dwell among them in the warmth of their love, in the kindness of their home, and in their charity for others.

Lord, who taught men and women to help and serve each other in marriage, and lead each other into happiness, bless this covenant of affection, these promises of truth. Protect and care for the bridegroom and bride as they go through life together. May they be loving companions, secure in their devotion which deepens with the passing years. In their respect and honour for each other may they find their peace, and in their affection and tenderness their happiness. May Your presence be in their home and in their hearts.

Lord our God, we stand before Your holiness, and in quietness thank You for bringing us to this time. May Your love protect .... and .... who ask You to bless them. They ask Your blessing not for themselves alone but for each other, and for their life together, for in Your blessing is loyalty and devotion, love and trust. Be with them Lord, so that they may know true happiness and bring joy to all who love them. Let them honour You, and so bring honour to themselves. Blessed are You, who teaches mankind the way to happiness.

MARRIAGE   2.

בָּרוּךְ אַתָּה יְיָ אֱלֹהֵינוּ מֶלֶךְ הָעוֹלָם · בּוֹרֵא פְּרִי הַגָּפֶן:

Blessed are You, Lord our God, king of the universe, who creates the fruit of the vine.

בָּרוּךְ אַתָּה יְיָ אֱלֹהֵינוּ מֶלֶךְ הָעוֹלָם · אֲשֶׁר קִדְּשָׁנוּ בְּמִצְוֹתָיו וּמְקַדֵּשׁ עַמּוֹ יִשְׂרָאֵל עַל יְדֵי חֻפָּה וְקִדּוּשִׁין:

Blessed are You, Lord our God, king of the universe, who makes us holy through doing His commands, and who makes His people Israel holy by the ceremony of the *chuppah* and the sanctity of marriage.

Do you .... enter into this holy covenant of affection and truth to take .... to be your wife in the sight of God and man?

And do you faithfully promise to be a true and devoted husband to her?

Do you .... enter into this holy covenant of affection and truth to take .... to be your husband in the sight of God and man?

And do you faithfully promise to be a true and devoted wife to him?

הֲרֵי אַתְּ מְקֻדֶּשֶׁת לִי בְּטַבַּעַת זוֹ כְּדַת מֹשֶׁה וְיִשְׂרָאֵל:

By this ring you are married to me in holiness according to the law of Moses and Israel.

הֲרֵי אַתָּה מְקֻדָּשׁ לִי כְּדַת מֹשֶׁה וְיִשְׂרָאֵל:

And you are married to me in holiness according to the law of Moses and Israel.

בָּרוּךְ אַתָּה יְיָ אֱלֹהֵינוּ מֶלֶךְ הָעוֹלָם · בּוֹרֵא פְּרִי הַגָּפֶן :

בָּרוּךְ אַתָּה יְיָ אֱלֹהֵינוּ מֶלֶךְ הָעוֹלָם · שֶׁהַכֹּל בָּרָא
לִכְבוֹדוֹ :

בָּרוּךְ אַתָּה יְיָ אֱלֹהֵינוּ מֶלֶךְ הָעוֹלָם · יוֹצֵר הָאָדָם :

בָּרוּךְ אַתָּה יְיָ אֱלֹהֵינוּ מֶלֶךְ הָעוֹלָם · אֲשֶׁר יָצַר אֶת־
הָאָדָם בְּצַלְמוֹ · בְּצֶלֶם דְּמוּת תַּבְנִיתוֹ · וְהִתְקִין לוֹ מִמֶּנּוּ
בִּנְיַן עֲדֵי עַד · בָּרוּךְ אַתָּה יְיָ · יוֹצֵר הָאָדָם :

שׂוֹשׂ תָּשִׂישׂ וְתָגֵל הָעֲקָרָה · בְּקִבּוּץ בָּנֶיהָ לְתוֹכָהּ בְּשִׂמְחָה ·
בָּרוּךְ אַתָּה יְיָ · מְשַׂמֵּחַ צִיּוֹן בְּבָנֶיהָ :

שַׂמֵּחַ תְּשַׂמַּח רֵעִים הָאֲהוּבִים · כְּשַׂמֵּחֲךָ יְצִירְךָ בְּגַן עֵדֶן
מִקֶּדֶם · יִזְכּוּ בָנֶיךָ הָאֵלֶּה לִבְנוֹת בֵּית בְּיִשְׂרָאֵל לִכְבוֹד שְׁמֶךָ ·
בָּרוּךְ אַתָּה יְיָ · מְשַׂמֵּחַ חָתָן וְכַלָּה :

בָּרוּךְ אַתָּה יְיָ אֱלֹהֵינוּ מֶלֶךְ הָעוֹלָם · אֲשֶׁר בָּרָא שָׂשׂוֹן
וְשִׂמְחָה חָתָן וְכַלָּה · אַהֲבָה וְאַחֲוָה וְשָׁלוֹם וְרֵעוּת · מְהֵרָה יְיָ
אֱלֹהֵינוּ יִשָּׁמַע בְּעָרֵי יְהוּדָה וּבְחוּצוֹת יְרוּשָׁלַיִם קוֹל שָׂשׂוֹן
וְקוֹל שִׂמְחָה · קוֹל חָתָן וְקוֹל כַּלָּה · בָּרוּךְ אַתָּה יְיָ · מְשַׂמֵּחַ
חָתָן עִם הַכַּלָּה :

קנ

הַלְלוּ־יָהּ

הַלְלוּ־אֵל בְּקָדְשׁוֹ ·   הַלְלוּהוּ בִּרְקִיעַ עֻזּוֹ :

הַלְלוּהוּ בִגְבוּרֹתָיו ·   הַלְלוּהוּ כְּרֹב גֻּדְלוֹ :

הַלְלוּהוּ בְּתֵקַע שׁוֹפָר ·   הַלְלוּהוּ בְּנֵבֶל וְכִנּוֹר :

הַלְלוּהוּ בְּתֹף וּמָחוֹל ·   הַלְלוּהוּ בְּמִנִּים וְעֻגָב :

הַלְלוּהוּ בְּצִלְצְלֵי־שָׁמַע ·   הַלְלוּהוּ בְּצִלְצְלֵי תְרוּעָה :

כֹּל הַנְּשָׁמָה תְּהַלֵּל יָהּ   הַלְלוּ־יָהּ :

Blessed are You, Lord our God, king of the universe, who creates the fruit of the vine.

Blessed are You, Lord our God, king of the universe, who created everything for His glory.

Blessed are You, Lord our God, king of the universe, who forms mankind.

Blessed are You, Lord our God, king of the universe, who formed mankind in His own image, to be like Him, to imitate Him and to resemble Him, and prepared from mankind and for mankind a constant sharing and renewal. Blessed are You Lord, who forms mankind.

Let Zion, deprived of her young, rise up again and cry out for joy as her children are gathered around her in happiness. Blessed are You Lord, who gives joy to Zion through her children.

Give these, companions in love, great happiness, the happiness of Your creatures in Eden long ago. May Your children be worthy to create a Jewish home, that honours You and honours them. Blessed are You Lord, who rejoices the bridegroom and the bride.

Blessed are You, Lord our God, king of the universe, who created joy and happiness, bridegroom and bride, love and companionship, peace and friendship. Soon, O Lord our God, may the sound of happiness and rejoicing be heard in the towns of Judah and in the streets of Jerusalem, the voice of the bridegroom and the voice of the bride. Blessed are You Lord, who causes the bridegroom to rejoice with the bride.

Psalm 150

Praise the Lord!

Praise God in His holy place.
  Praise Him in His mighty heavens.
Praise Him for His powerful deeds.
  Praise Him for His surpassing greatness.

Praise Him with the *shofar* blast.
  Praise Him with the lyre and harp.
Praise Him with drums and dancing.
  Praise Him with the lute and pipe.

Praise Him with the clash of cymbals.
  Praise Him with the clanging cymbals.
Let everything that has breath
  praise the Lord.

Praise the Lord!

THANKSGIVING SERVICE FOR PARENTS
(NAMING OF A CHILD)

To be recited by the father

אָהַבְתִּי כִּי־יִשְׁמַע יְהוָה אֶת־קוֹלִי תַּחֲנוּנָי:

כִּי־הִטָּה אָזְנוֹ לִי וּבְיָמַי אֶקְרָא:

חַנּוּן יְהוָה וְצַדִּיק וֵאלֹהֵינוּ מְרַחֵם:

שׁוּבִי נַפְשִׁי לִמְנוּחָיְכִי כִּי־יְהוָה גָּמַל עָלָיְכִי:

מָה־אָשִׁיב לַיהוָה כָּל־תַּגְמוּלוֹהִי עָלָי:

נְדָרַי לַיהוָה אֲשַׁלֵּם נֶגְדָה־נָּא לְכָל־עַמּוֹ:

לְךָ־אֶזְבַּח זֶבַח תּוֹדָה וּבְשֵׁם יְהוָה אֶקְרָא:

הַלְלוּ־יָהּ:

I love the Lord for He hears
my voice, my pleading.
Because He turned His ear to me
throughout my days I will call Him.
Merciful is the Lord and just,
and our God has compassion.
Return, my soul, to your rest,
for the Lord has been generous to you.
What can I return to the Lord
for all His generosity to me?
I will fulfil my promises to the Lord
in the presence of all His people.
To You I offer the offering of gratitude
and call in the name of the Lord.
Praise the Lord!

From Psalm 116

The Mother's Prayer

Father of all mankind, and source of all life, through Your great love I enter Your house to thank You and to bless Your name. You have given me the joy of creation, which supported me in my weakness, and comforted me in my anxiety. Your mercy has restored me. I thank You for my life and for the life of my child, for You renew the wonder of creation.

The Mother's Prayer
(For an Adopted Child)

Father of all mankind, and source of all life, through Your great love I enter Your house to thank You and to bless Your name. I give You thanks for You have found me worthy. I turn to You in awe because You have put Your trust in me. I bless You for the love which binds me to my child; and for the wonder of creation which You have renewed within my heart.

The mother continues here

For a boy

As he grows in body and in mind, may the law of truth be found on his lips and the love of justice in his heart. May he be a blessing to those around him and bring honour to Israel in the sight of all mankind.

Lord, be with me and my husband; may our love for our child draw us even more closely together in helpfulness and in trust.

Teach us to carry on through our child the heritage of Israel, so that its tradition of wisdom and holiness may never cease.

Now in love we comfort him; may he comfort us in future years. Amen.

For a girl

As she grows in body and in mind, may the law of truth be found on her lips and the love of justice in her heart. May she be a blessing to those around her and bring honour to Israel in the sight of all mankind.

Lord, be with me and my husband; may our love for our child draw us even more closely together in helpfulness and in trust.

Teach us to carry on through our child the heritage of Israel, so that its tradition of wisdom and holiness may never cease.

Now in love we comfort her; may she comfort us in future years. Amen.

Prayer by the Rabbi

Father of love, accept the thanksgiving of this mother in Israel. May her spirit lifted to You now in humble gratitude be ever directed to You for help and strength. Bless her and her husband with wisdom to guide their child according to Your will, giving examples in their lives of Your care and understanding. May the light of love fill their home, and Your blessing be upon them and all who are dear to them. Amen.

For a boy

מִי שֶׁבֵּרַךְ אֲבוֹתֵינוּ אַבְרָהָם
יִצְחָק וְיַעֲקֹב הוּא יְבָרֵךְ אֶת־
הַיֶּלֶד הַזֶּה וְיִקָּרֵא שְׁמוֹ
בְּיִשְׂרָאֵל ...... וְיִתֶּן לוֹ
אֱלֹהִים חַיִּים אֲרֻכִּים וְחִלּוּץ־
עֲצָמוֹת· יִשְׂמְחוּ בוֹ אָבִיו וְאִמּוֹ·
וִיהִי בְּרָכָה לְכָל־מַכָּרָיו
וְכָבוֹד לְיִשְׂרָאֵל וּלְשֵׁם־
קָדְשֶׁךָ· אָמֵן:

May He who blessed our ancestors Abraham, Isaac and Jacob, bless this child, who shall be known in Israel as ....

God, grant him life and health of body and mind, and make him a constant joy to his parents, a blessing to all who know him, an honour to Israel and to Your holy name. Amen.

For a girl

מִי שֶׁבֵּרַךְ אִמּוֹתֵינוּ שָׂרָה
רִבְקָה רָחֵל וְלֵאָה הוּא יְבָרֵךְ
אֶת־הַיַּלְדָּה הַזֹּאת וְיִקָּרֵא
שְׁמָהּ בְּיִשְׂרָאֵל ...... וְיִתֶּן לָהּ
אֱלֹהִים חַיִּים אֲרֻכִּים וְחִלּוּץ־
עֲצָמוֹת· יִשְׂמְחוּ בָהּ אָבִיהָ
וְאִמָּהּ· וּתְהִי בְּרָכָה לְכָל־
מַכָּרֶיהָ וְכָבוֹד לְיִשְׂרָאֵל
וּלְשֵׁם־קָדְשֶׁךָ· אָמֵן:

May He who blessed our ancestors Sarah, Rebecca, Rachel and Leah, bless this child, who shall be known in Israel as ....

God, grant her life and health of body and mind, and make her a constant joy to her parents, a blessing to all who know her, an honour to Israel and to Your holy name. Amen.

BLESSING

SERVICE UPON ADMISSION TO THE JEWISH FAITH

Psalm 15 (page 422) and Psalm 121 (page 540)

To be recited by the convert

My God, the father of all mankind, accept the offering of my heart at this solemn time. I have chosen to enter the family of Israel. I stand in Your presence as a member of Your people and ask for Your blessing. Help me to follow the teachings of Judaism, to live a Jewish life and to be part of Israel's destiny. Give me the strength and courage to share its dangers and difficulties as well as its responsibilities and opportunities. I thank You for this moment and all the future offers me. Be the light which guides me through my life. May my words and actions earn Your blessing; may they bring honour to Israel; may they make Your name holy in the world.

Hear O Israel, the Lord is our God, the Lord is One.

שְׁמַע יִשְׂרָאֵל · יְהֹוָה אֱלֹהֵינוּ יְהֹוָה אֶחָד׃

Love the Lord your God with all your heart, and all your soul, and all your might.

וְאָהַבְתָּ אֵת יְהֹוָה אֱלֹהֶיךָ · בְּכָל־לְבָבְךָ וּבְכָל־נַפְשְׁךָ וּבְכָל־מְאֹדֶךָ׃

Prayer by the Rabbi

For a man

Almighty God, we welcome into our community our brother

. . . .

whose name shall be called in Israel. . . . .
Care for him and hear his prayer for he has been called to serve

For a woman

Almighty God, we welcome into our community our sister

. . . .

whose name shall be called in Israel. . . . .
Care for her and hear her prayer for she has been called to serve

For a man, continued

You. May Your image in him be a light for him and for us. May his love for You and Your teaching grow stronger as the years increase. May he be a loyal member of the community of Israel, gaining respect for it in the eyes of the world, and so helping mankind to righteousness and truth.

He has declared his belief in You, the one and only God, who has formed the souls of all mankind and in whose love they are equal. He has declared his belief in You, who judges mankind by their righteousness alone, and whom all may approach through prayer and integrity. On Your love and mercy he relies.

Keep this knowledge alive within him. May his devotion to Judaism and his love for the family of Israel grow from strength to strength. In sorrow may this be his comfort; in weakness may this be his strength; in all the changes and chances of life may it bring him joy. Filled with awe and trust, he has come to live under the shelter of Your wings. God of Israel, be his refuge and his shield for evermore. Amen.

For a woman, continued

You. May Your image in her be a light for her and for us. May her love for You and Your teaching grow stronger as the years increase. May she be a loyal member of the community of Israel, gaining respect for it in the eyes of the world, and so helping mankind to righteousness and truth.

She has declared her belief in You, the one and only God, who has formed the souls of all mankind and in whose love they are equal. She has declared her belief in You, who judges mankind by their righteousness alone, and whom all may approach through prayer and integrity. On Your love and mercy she relies.

Keep this knowledge alive within her. May her devotion to Judaism and her love for the family of Israel grow from strength to strength. In sorrow may this be her comfort; in weakness may this be her strength; in all the changes and chances of life may it bring her joy. Filled with awe and trust, she has come to live under the shelter of Your wings. God of Israel, be her refuge and her shield for evermore. Amen.

THE TEN COMMANDMENTS

(According to Deuteronomy 5: 6–18)

א· אָנֹכִי יְיָ אֱלֹהֶיךָ אֲשֶׁר הוֹצֵאתִיךָ מֵאֶרֶץ מִצְרַיִם מִבֵּית
עֲבָדִים:

ב· לֹא יִהְיֶה־לְךָ אֱלֹהִים אֲחֵרִים עַל־פָּנָי: לֹא־תַעֲשֶׂה
לְךָ פֶסֶל כָּל־תְּמוּנָה אֲשֶׁר בַּשָּׁמַיִם מִמַּעַל וַאֲשֶׁר בָּאָרֶץ
מִתָּחַת וַאֲשֶׁר בַּמַּיִם מִתַּחַת לָאָרֶץ: לֹא־תִשְׁתַּחֲוֶה לָהֶם
וְלֹא תָעָבְדֵם כִּי אָנֹכִי יְיָ אֱלֹהֶיךָ אֵל קַנָּא פֹּקֵד עֲוֹן אָבוֹת
עַל־בָּנִים וְעַל־שִׁלֵּשִׁים וְעַל־רִבֵּעִים לְשֹׂנְאָי: וְעֹשֶׂה חֶסֶד
לַאֲלָפִים לְאֹהֲבַי וּלְשֹׁמְרֵי מִצְוֹתָי:

ג· לֹא תִשָּׂא אֶת־שֵׁם־יְיָ־אֱלֹהֶיךָ לַשָּׁוְא כִּי לֹא יְנַקֶּה
יְיָ אֵת אֲשֶׁר־יִשָּׂא אֶת־שְׁמוֹ לַשָּׁוְא:

ד· שָׁמוֹר אֶת־יוֹם הַשַּׁבָּת לְקַדְּשׁוֹ כַּאֲשֶׁר צִוְּךָ יְיָ אֱלֹהֶיךָ:
שֵׁשֶׁת יָמִים תַּעֲבֹד וְעָשִׂיתָ כָּל־מְלַאכְתֶּךָ: וְיוֹם הַשְּׁבִיעִי שַׁבָּת
לַיְיָ אֱלֹהֶיךָ · לֹא תַעֲשֶׂה כָל־מְלָאכָה אַתָּה וּבִנְךָ וּבִתֶּךָ
וְעַבְדְּךָ וַאֲמָתֶךָ וְשׁוֹרְךָ וַחֲמֹרְךָ וְכָל־בְּהֶמְתֶּךָ וְגֵרְךָ אֲשֶׁר
בִּשְׁעָרֶיךָ לְמַעַן יָנוּחַ עַבְדְּךָ וַאֲמָתְךָ כָּמוֹךָ: וְזָכַרְתָּ כִּי־עֶבֶד
הָיִיתָ בְּאֶרֶץ מִצְרַיִם וַיֹּצִאֲךָ יְיָ אֱלֹהֶיךָ מִשָּׁם בְּיָד חֲזָקָה
וּבִזְרֹעַ נְטוּיָה עַל־כֵּן צִוְּךָ יְיָ אֱלֹהֶיךָ לַעֲשׂוֹת אֶת־יוֹם הַשַּׁבָּת:

ה· כַּבֵּד אֶת־אָבִיךָ וְאֶת־אִמֶּךָ כַּאֲשֶׁר צִוְּךָ יְיָ אֱלֹהֶיךָ
לְמַעַן יַאֲרִיכֻן יָמֶיךָ וּלְמַעַן יִיטַב לָךְ עַל הָאֲדָמָה אֲשֶׁר־יְיָ
אֱלֹהֶיךָ נֹתֵן לָךְ:

ו· לֹא תִּרְצָח:

ז· וְלֹא תִּנְאָף:

ח· וְלֹא תִּגְנֹב:

ט· וְלֹא־תַעֲנֶה בְרֵעֲךָ עֵד שָׁוְא:

י· וְלֹא תַחְמֹד אֵשֶׁת רֵעֶךָ וְלֹא תִתְאַוֶּה בֵּית רֵעֶךָ שָׂדֵהוּ
וְעַבְדּוֹ וַאֲמָתוֹ שׁוֹרוֹ וַחֲמֹרוֹ וְכֹל אֲשֶׁר לְרֵעֶךָ:

1. I am the Lord your God who brought you out of the land of Egypt, out of the camp of slavery.

2. You shall have no other gods but Me. You shall not make yourself an idol in the likeness of anything which is in the sky above or on the earth below or in the deeps under the earth. You shall not worship them nor serve them, for I the Lord your God am a demanding God, burdening the children down to the third and fourth generations with their fathers' guilt if they hate Me, but showing kindness to thousands of generations if they should love Me, and keep My commands.

3. You shall not use the name of the Lord your God falsely, for the Lord will not excuse anyone who uses His name falsely.

4. Observe the Sabbath day and keep it holy as the Lord your God commanded you. You have six days to labour and do all your work, but the seventh shall be a Sabbath for the Lord your God. That day you shall do no work, neither you, nor your son, nor your daughter, nor your servant, man or woman, nor your ox nor your ass, nor any of your animals, nor the stranger who lives in your home; so that those who serve you, men and women, shall rest like you. Remember you served as slaves in the land of Egypt and from there the Lord your God brought you out with a mighty hand and an outstretched arm. Therefore the Lord your God commanded you to keep the Sabbath day.

5. Respect your father and your mother as the Lord your God has commanded you, so that the days of your life be fulfilled and it be well with you on the land which the Lord your God gives you.

6. You shall not murder.

7. You shall not commit adultery.

8. You shall not steal.

9. You shall not give false evidence against your neighbour.

10. You shall not covet your neighbour's wife. You shall not long for your neighbour's house, his land, his servant, man or woman, his ox, his ass or anything that is your neighbour's.

PRAYER OF BARMITZVAH

In the presence of my teachers, the leaders and the members of this holy congregation, I now prepare to take upon myself the duties which are binding on all the family of Israel. I ask their help in the years that lie ahead to strengthen my loyalty and devotion so that I may grow in charity and good deeds. I think also of those who have gone before me, who through all the troubles of the world preserved this heritage of holiness and goodness, so that I should enter into it now.

May I be a true Barmitzvah, a son of the commandment, taking my place in the community of Israel, accepting its responsibilities, rejoicing in its blessing. May I be a witness to the living God and His goodness, and the tradition that lives within me.

I remember all those who have helped me reach this time. I give thanks for the love and care of my family, the patience and instruction of my teachers, and the support and companionship of my friends.

In the Torah I have read the word of God. With Your help may I go on to fulfil it in my life. Amen.

PRAYER OF BATMITZVAH

In the presence of my teachers, the leaders and the members of this holy congregation, I now prepare to take upon myself the duties which are binding on all the family of Israel. I ask their help in the years that lie ahead to strengthen my loyalty and devotion so that I may grow in charity and good deeds. I think also of those who have gone before me, who through all the troubles of the world preserved this heritage of holiness and goodness, so that I should enter into it now.

May I be a true Batmitzvah, a daughter of the commandment, taking my place in the community of Israel, accepting its responsibilities, rejoicing in its blessing. May I be a witness to the living God and His goodness, and the tradition that lives within me.

I remember all those who have helped me reach this time. I give thanks for the love and care of my family, the patience and instruction of my teachers, and the support and companionship of my friends.

In the Torah I have read the word of God. With Your help may I go on to fulfil it in my life. Amen.

PRAYER FOR A JOURNEY

May God who called our father Abraham to journey into the unknown, and guarded him, and blessed him, may He protect me too and bless my journey. May His confidence support me as I set out, may His spirit be with me on the way, and may He lead me back to my home in peace. Those I love, I commend to His care. He is with them, I shall not fear. As for myself, may His presence be my companion, so that blessing comes to me, and to everyone I meet.

Blessed are You Lord, whose presence journeys with His people.

PRAYER FOR AN ANNIVERSARY

Lord, who makes times pass and seasons change, You appointed for our people festivals of gladness and seasons of joy, for our remembrance is always before You. On this day I come before You with my private memories, and thank You for my own experience, and for companionship and love. Whatever the future brings may this day always renew my spirit, giving me happiness on my journey through life. My heart is grateful for the kindness You have shown me. Bless me also in the years that lie ahead.

PRAYER DURING SICKNESS

In my sickness Lord, I turn to You, for I am Your creation. Your strength and courage are in my spirit, and Your powers of healing are within my body. May it be Your will to restore me to health.

In my illness I have learnt what is great and what is small. I know how dependent I am upon You. My own pain and anxiety have been my teachers. May I never forget this precious knowledge when I am well again.

Comfort me, Lord, and shelter me in Your love. Heal me and I shall be healed, save me and I shall be saved.

Blessed are You Lord, the faithful and merciful healer.

בָּרוּךְ אַתָּה יְיָ · רוֹפֵא חוֹלִים:

PRAYER ON BEHALF OF THE SICK

For a man

Lord, I pray for . . . . who is sick and in pain. May it be Your will to renew his strength and bring him back to health. Renew his spirit also and free him from anxiety for You watch over his body and his soul.

Though I cannot share his pain, help me to bring him good cheer and comfort. Give us the joy of helping each other through all the fortunes of life.

For a woman

Lord, I pray for . . . . who is sick and in pain. May it be Your will to renew her strength and bring her back to health. Renew her spirit also and free her from anxiety for You watch over her body and her soul.

Though I cannot share her pain, help me to bring her good cheer and comfort. Give us the joy of helping each other through all the fortunes of life.

Blessed are You Lord, the faithful and merciful healer.

בָּרוּךְ אַתָּה יְיָ · רוֹפֵא חוֹלִים:

PRAYER BEFORE AN OPERATION

Before my operation I turn to You, because You are always beside me.

You created the healing powers of my body and the strength and courage of my spirit. They are Your gifts to carry me from fear to confidence.

Yours are the wonder of science and the marvel of creation. I thank You for the wisdom of my doctors, the skill of my surgeon's hands and the devotion of my nurses. They are Your helpers in the work of healing. They comfort me.

Lord, I am Your child whom You created. Lead me gently into sleep and waken me to health. In Your love I trust.

PRAYER DURING DANGEROUS ILLNESS

As a child turns to his father, I turn to You, my God who created me. You are the master of my life and death, may it be Your will to heal me and keep me in life. But if it is time for me to go forward, through death to life everlasting, give me courage and trust to ease my journey.

Forgive my sins, and my soul will be pure as it returns to You. Protect those I love whom I leave behind, for their lives are in Your care. Through Your mercy we shall come together in the gathering of life. In Your hand I lay my soul, when I sleep and when I wake, and with my soul my body too. You are with me, I shall not fear.

יְיָ מֶלֶךְ · יְיָ מָלָךְ · יְיָ יִמְלֹךְ לְעוֹלָם וָעֶד :

The Lord does rule, the Lord has ruled, the Lord shall rule forever and ever.

בָּרוּךְ שֵׁם כְּבוֹד מַלְכוּתוֹ לְעוֹלָם וָעֶד :

Blessed is His name, whose glorious kingdom is forever and ever.

יְיָ הוּא הָאֱלֹהִים :

The Lord, He is God.

שְׁמַע יִשְׂרָאֵל · יְהֹוָה אֱלֹהֵינוּ יְהֹוָה אֶחָד :

Hear O Israel, the Lord is our God, the Lord is One.

PRAYER ON BEHALF OF THE DANGEROUSLY ILL

For a man

I pray to You for my beloved .... who approaches the frontiers of this life. You are the master over life and death and his fate is in Your hands. Heal his body and restore him to me, if this is Your will. If it is not, be with him where I cannot follow, and give him courage to conquer pain, and hope to overcome fear. Lead him forwards in peace from this world into the life that has no end, supported by his own good deeds, and accompanied by my love. Help me too, and teach me that though we may part now, we shall come together once again in the gathering of life. His soul is in Your hand, and with his soul, his body too. You are with him, I shall not fear.

For a woman

I pray to You for my beloved .... who approaches the frontiers of this life. You are the master over life and death and her fate is in Your hands. Heal her body and restore her to me, if this is Your will. If it is not, be with her where I cannot follow, and give her courage to conquer pain, and hope to overcome fear. Lead her forwards in peace from this world into the life that has no end, supported by her own good deeds, and accompanied by my love. Help me too, and teach me that though we may part now, we shall come together once again in the gathering of life. Her soul is in Your hand, and with her soul, her body too. You are with her, I shall not fear.

THANKSGIVING FOR RECOVERY AND AFTER DANGER (GOMEL)

I thank You, Lord my God and God of my fathers, God of the spirits of all flesh. You were with me in the time of my affliction, and You helped me. In a time of trouble You showed me the path of life and the fullness of joy. You showed me the sweetness which is at Your right hand forever.

בָּרוּךְ אַתָּה יְיָ אֱלֹהֵינוּ מֶלֶךְ הָעוֹלָם · הַגּוֹמֵל לְחַיָּבִים
טוֹבוֹת · שֶׁגְּמָלַנִי כָּל־טוֹב:

Blessed are You, Lord our God, king of the universe, who shows favour to the undeserving, even to me.

Response:

מִי שֶׁגְּמָלְךָ כָּל־טוֹב הוּא יִגְמָלְךָ כָּל־טוֹב:

May He who has shown favour to you, continue to favour you with all that is good.

PRAYER FOR COMMITTEE MEETINGS

Let us come together in God's name and prepare ourselves to do His will. May His presence dwell among us, drawing us to serve Him and His creatures with justice and with love. Let us listen to each other with respect, and treat each other with wisdom and generosity, so that we witness to the master whom we serve, and justify His choice of us. May none of our controversies rise up like those of Korach, from ambition and self-seeking. Let them only be for the sake of heaven, like those of Hillel and Shammai. May our eyes be open to see His greatness in the smallest things we do.

Through our faithfulness may the cause of goodness prosper in the world.

May the favour of the Lord our God be upon us, to support us in the work we do.

וִיהִי נֹעַם אֲדֹנָי אֱלֹהֵינוּ
עָלֵינוּ וּמַעֲשֵׂה יָדֵינוּ כּוֹנְנָה
עָלֵינוּ:

Response:

May He support the work we do.

וּמַעֲשֵׂה יָדֵינוּ כּוֹנְנֵהוּ:

PRAYER FOR INTERFAITH MEETINGS

Lord of all creation, we stand in awe before You, impelled by visions of the harmony of man. We are children of many traditions—inheritors of shared wisdom and tragic misunderstandings, of proud hopes and humble successes. Now it is time for us to meet—in memory and truth, in courage and trust, in love and promise.

In that which we share, let us see the common prayer of humanity; in that in which we differ, let us wonder at the freedom of man; in our unity and our differences, let us know the uniqueness that is God.

May our courage match our convictions, and our integrity match our hope.

May our faith in You bring us closer to each other.

May our meeting with past and present bring blessing for the future. Amen.

PRAYER FOR INTERNATIONAL UNDERSTANDING

Lord of peace, be with those who guide the destinies of the world so that an end may come to boasting and vainglory, and the reign of arrogance dwindle in our time. Give them the courage to speak the truth and the humility to listen. Help us all to put the good of our fellowmen above our own ambitions, and the truth which does not profit us above the lie which does. So may we stand upright, freed from the burden of fear and the weight of suspicion, learning to trust each other.

Help each one of us to bring his own offering of understanding, and his own sacrifice for peace, so that we are at peace with ourselves and live in peace with those around us. Then in tranquillity may we all go forward to build Your kingdom in the world until the earth shall be filled with Your knowledge as the waters cover the sea. Amen.

PRAYER IN THE HOME BEFORE A FUNERAL

For a man

Merciful Father, be with us as we gather in this house, the home of our dear one who has gone forward to life everlasting. We remember all his goodness. May his memory be a blessing.

Help us to remember that the soul does not die, and our dear one has gone to that eternal home which You prepared for us when our work on earth is done, and our time here has ended. Open the gates of mercy for him. May he enter into everlasting peace. In Your light we see beyond the frontiers of death to the life that has no end.

For a woman

Merciful Father, be with us as we gather in this house, the home of our dear one who has gone forward to life everlasting. We remember all her goodness. May her memory be a blessing.

Help us to remember that the soul does not die, and our dear one has gone to that eternal home which You prepared for us when our work on earth is done, and our time here has ended. Open the gates of mercy for her. May she enter into everlasting peace. In Your light we see beyond the frontiers of death to the life that has no end.

This house was built by human hands, but we shall come together in a home where we shall never part, surrounded by Your presence. Amen.

Psalm 23 (page 430).

MEMORIAL SERVICE

The souls of the righteous are in the hands of God, and no harm shall touch them. In the eyes of the ignorant they appeared to die, and their going seemed to be their hurt. But they are at peace, and their hope is full of immortality. Their chastening was slight compared to the great good they shall receive. God has put them to the test and proved them worthy to be with Him.

Wisdom of Solomon 3: 1–5

Psalm 23 (page 430) and Psalm 103 (page 512).

Lord God, source of all being and fountain of life, what can we say to You, for You see and know all things. In Your wisdom You formed the universe and in Your love You provide for all Your creatures. What can we do, but acknowledge Your power, accept Your gifts with gratitude, and according to Your will, give You back Your own.

Lord God, may the light of Your presence shine on us as we gather here, our hearts bowed down by the loss of . . . . whom You have gathered to Yourself. Accept in Your great mercy the earthly life which has now ended and shelter with Your tender care this soul that is so precious to our hearts.

For a man

We thank You for all that was gentle and noble in his life. Through his name inspire us with strength and light. Help us to use our grief itself for acts of service and of love.

Everlasting God, help us to realise more and more that time and space are not the measure of all things. Though our eyes do not see, teach us to understand that the soul of our dear one is not cut off. Love does not die, and truth is stronger than the grave. Just as our affection and the memory of the good he did unite us with him at this time, so may our trust in You lift us to the vision of the life that knows no death.

For a woman

We thank You for all that was gentle and noble in her life. Through her name inspire us with strength and light. Help us to use our grief itself for acts of service and of love.

Everlasting God, help us to realise more and more that time and space are not the measure of all things. Though our eyes do not see, teach us to understand that the soul of our dear one is not cut off. Love does not die, and truth is stronger than the grave. Just as our affection and the memory of the good she did unite us with her at this time, so may our trust in You lift us to the vision of the life that knows no death.

God of our strength, in our weakness help us; in our sorrow comfort us; in our confusion guide us. Without You our lives are nothing; with You there is fullness of life for evermore.

May the words of my mouth and the meditation of my heart be acceptable to You, O Lord, my rock and my redeemer.

אֵל מָלֵא רַחֲמִים

שׁוֹכֵן בַּמְּרוֹמִים· הַמְצֵא מְנוּחָה
נְכוֹנָה תַּחַת כַּנְפֵי הַשְּׁכִינָה·
בְּמַעֲלוֹת קְדוֹשִׁים וּטְהוֹרִים·
כְּזֹהַר הָרָקִיעַ מַזְהִירִים אֶת־
נִשְׁמַת · · · · · · · · שֶׁהָלַךְ
לְעוֹלָמוֹ · אָנָּא בַּעַל הָרַחֲמִים
הַסְתִּירֵהוּ בְּסֵתֶר כְּנָפֶיךָ
לְעוֹלָמִים · וּצְרוֹר בִּצְרוֹר
הַחַיִּים אֶת־נִשְׁמָתוֹ · יְיָ הוּא
נַחֲלָתוֹ וְיָנוּחַ בְּשָׁלוֹם עַל
מִשְׁכָּבוֹ וְנֹאמַר אָמֵן:

God full of compassion whose
presence is over us, grant perfect
rest beneath the shelter of Your
presence with the holy and pure
on high who shine as the lights of
heaven, to..................
who has gone to his everlasting
home. Master of mercy, cover
him in the shelter of Your wings
forever, and bind his soul into
the gathering of life. It is the
Lord who is his heritage. May he
be at peace in his place of rest.
Amen.

אֵל מָלֵא רַחֲמִים

שׁוֹכֵן בַּמְּרוֹמִים· הַמְצֵא מְנוּחָה
נְכוֹנָה תַּחַת כַּנְפֵי הַשְּׁכִינָה·
בְּמַעֲלוֹת קְדוֹשִׁים וּטְהוֹרִים·
כְּזֹהַר הָרָקִיעַ מַזְהִירִים אֶת־
נִשְׁמַת · · · · · · · · שֶׁהָלְכָה
לְעוֹלָמָהּ · אָנָּא בַּעַל הָרַחֲמִים
הַסְתִּירֶהָ בְּסֵתֶר כְּנָפֶיךָ
לְעוֹלָמִים · וּצְרוֹר בִּצְרוֹר
הַחַיִּים אֶת־נִשְׁמָתָהּ · יְיָ הוּא
נַחֲלָתָהּ וְתָנוּחַ בְּשָׁלוֹם עַל
מִשְׁכָּבָהּ וְנֹאמַר אָמֵן:

God full of compassion whose
presence is over us, grant perfect
rest beneath the shelter of Your
presence with the holy and pure
on high who shine as the lights of
heaven, to...................
who has gone to her everlasting
home. Master of mercy, cover
her in the shelter of Your wings
forever, and bind her soul into
the gathering of life. It is the
Lord who is her heritage. May
she be at peace in her place of
rest. Amen.

יִתְגַּדַּל וְיִתְקַדַּשׁ שְׁמֵהּ רַבָּא בְּעָלְמָא דִי־בְרָא כִרְעוּתֵהּ·
וְיַמְלִיךְ מַלְכוּתֵהּ בְּחַיֵּיכוֹן וּבְיוֹמֵיכוֹן וּבְחַיֵּי
דִי־כָל־בֵּית יִשְׂרָאֵל בַּעֲגָלָא וּבִזְמַן קָרִיב · וְאִמְרוּ אָמֵן:
יְהֵא שְׁמֵהּ רַבָּא מְבָרַךְ לְעָלַם וּלְעָלְמֵי עָלְמַיָּא·

יִתְבָּרַךְ וְיִשְׁתַּבַּח וְיִתְפָּאַר וְיִתְרוֹמַם וְיִתְנַשֵּׂא וְיִתְהַדָּר
וְיִתְעַלֶּה וְיִתְהַלָּל שְׁמֵהּ דִּי־קֻדְשָׁא · בְּרִיךְ הוּא · לְעֵלָּא
מִן־כָּל־בִּרְכָתָא וְשִׁירָתָא תֻּשְׁבְּחָתָא וְנֶחֱמָתָא דִּי־אֲמִירָן
בְּעָלְמָא · וְאִמְרוּ אָמֵן :
יְהֵא שְׁלָמָא רַבָּא מִן־שְׁמַיָּא וְחַיִּים עָלֵינוּ וְעַל־כָּל־
יִשְׂרָאֵל · וְאִמְרוּ אָמֵן :
עֹשֶׂה שָׁלוֹם בִּמְרוֹמָיו הוּא יַעֲשֶׂה שָׁלוֹם עָלֵינוּ וְעַל־כָּל־
יִשְׂרָאֵל · וְאִמְרוּ אָמֵן :

Let us magnify and let us sanctify the great name of God in the world which He created according to His will. May His kingdom come in your lifetime, and in your days, and in the lifetime of the family of Israel—quickly and speedily may it come. Amen.

May the greatness of His being be blessed from eternity to eternity.

Let us bless and let us extol, let us tell aloud and let us raise aloft, let us set on high and let us honour, let us exalt and let us praise the Holy One—blessed be He!—though He is far beyond any blessing or song, any honour or any consolation that can be spoken of in this world. Amen.

May great peace from heaven and the gift of life be granted to us and to all the family of Israel. Amen.

May He who makes peace in the highest bring this peace upon us and upon all Israel. Amen.

Adon Olam, page 170.

PRAYER FOR THE YAHRZEIT

(*Anniversary of a death*)

For a woman

Today I remember with love .... who has gone to everlasting life, and I honour her memory. As this light burns pure and clear, so may the thought of her goodness shine in my heart and strengthen me, Lord, to do Your will. Amen.

On lighting the Yahrzeit candle say:

זֵכֶר צַדִּיק לִבְרָכָה:

'The memory of the righteous is as a blessing.'

אֵל מָלֵא רַחֲמִים שׁוֹכֵן בַּמְּרוֹמִים · הַמְצֵא
מְנוּחָה נְכוֹנָה תַּחַת כַּנְפֵי
הַשְּׁכִינָה · בְּמַעֲלוֹת קְדוֹשִׁים וּטְהוֹרִים · כְּזוֹהַר הָרָקִיעַ
מַזְהִירִים · אֶת־נִשְׁמַת . . . . . שֶׁהָלְכָה לְעוֹלָמָהּ · אָנָּא בַּעַל
הָרַחֲמִים הַסְתִּירֶהָ בְּסֵתֶר כְּנָפֶיךָ לְעוֹלָמִים · וּצְרוֹר בִּצְרוֹר
הַחַיִּים אֶת־נִשְׁמָתָהּ · יְיָ הוּא נַחֲלָתָהּ וְתָנוּחַ בְּשָׁלוֹם עַל
מִשְׁכָּבָהּ וְנֹאמַר אָמֵן:

God full of compassion whose presence is over us, grant perfect rest beneath the shelter of Your presence with the holy and pure on high who shine as the lights of heaven, to . . . . who has gone to her everlasting home. Master of mercy, cover her in the shelter of Your wings forever, and bind her soul into the gathering of life. It is the Lord who is her heritage. May she be at peace in her place of rest. Amen.

For a man

Today I remember with love . . . . who has gone to everlasting life, and I honour his memory. As this light burns pure and clear, so may the thought of his goodness shine in my heart and strengthen me, Lord, to do Your will. Amen.

On lighting the Yahrzeit candle say:

זֵכֶר צַדִּיק לִבְרָכָה:

'The memory of the righteous is as a blessing.'

אֵל מָלֵא רַחֲמִים שׁוֹכֵן בַּמְּרוֹמִים · הַמְצֵא
מְנוּחָה נְכוֹנָה תַּחַת כַּנְפֵי
הַשְּׁכִינָה · בְּמַעֲלוֹת קְדוֹשִׁים וּטְהוֹרִים · כְּזוֹהַר הָרָקִיעַ

מַזְהִירִים · אֶת־נִשְׁמַת . . . . . שֶׁהָלַךְ לְעוֹלָמוֹ · אָנָּא בַּעַל
הָרַחֲמִים הַסְתִּירֵהוּ בְּסֵתֶר כְּנָפֶיךָ לְעוֹלָמִים · וּצְרוֹר בִּצְרוֹר
הַחַיִּים אֶת־נִשְׁמָתוֹ · יְיָ הוּא נַחֲלָתוֹ וְיָנְוּחַ בְּשָׁלוֹם עַל
מִשְׁכָּבוֹ וְנֹאמַר אָמֵן:

God full of compassion whose presence is over us, grant perfect
rest beneath the shelter of Your presence with the holy and pure on
high who shine as the lights of heaven, to . . . . who
has gone to his everlasting home. Master of mercy, cover him in the
shelter of Your wings forever, and bind his soul into the gathering of
life. It is the Lord who is his heritage. May he be at peace in his place
of rest. Amen.

Trani, Italy

KADDISH D'RABANAN

יִתְגַּדַּל וְיִתְקַדַּשׁ שְׁמֵהּ רַבָּא בְּעָלְמָא דִּי־בְרָא כִרְעוּתֵהּ ׃
וְיַמְלִיךְ מַלְכוּתֵהּ בְּחַיֵּיכוֹן וּבְיוֹמֵיכוֹן וּבְחַיֵּי דִּי־כָל־בֵּית
יִשְׂרָאֵל בַּעֲגָלָא וּבִזְמַן קָרִיב ׃ וְאִמְרוּ אָמֵן ׃

יְהֵא שְׁמֵהּ רַבָּא מְבָרַךְ לְעָלַם וּלְעָלְמֵי עָלְמַיָּא ׃

יִתְבָּרַךְ וְיִשְׁתַּבַּח וְיִתְפָּאַר וְיִתְרוֹמַם וְיִתְנַשֵּׂא וְיִתְהַדַּר וְיִתְעַלֶּה
וְיִתְהַלָּל שְׁמֵהּ דִּי־קֻדְשָׁא ׃ בְּרִיךְ הוּא ׃ לְעֵלָּא מִן־כָּל־
בִּרְכָתָא וְשִׁירָתָא תֻּשְׁבְּחָתָא וְנֶחֱמָתָא דִּי־אֲמִירָן בְּעָלְמָא ׃
וְאִמְרוּ אָמֵן ׃

עַל יִשְׂרָאֵל וְעַל רַבָּנָן וְעַל תַּלְמִידֵיהוֹן וְעַל כָּל־תַּלְמִידֵי
תַלְמִידֵיהוֹן וְעַל כָּל־מָן דִּי עָסְקִין בְּאוֹרַיְתָא דִּי בְּאַתְרָא
הָדֵן וְדִי בְכָל־אֲתַר וַאֲתַר יְהֵא לְהוֹן וּלְכוֹן שְׁלָמָא רַבָּא
חִנָּא וְחִסְדָּא וְרַחֲמִין וְחַיִּין אֲרִיכִין וּמְזוֹנָא רְוִיחָא וּפָרְקָנָא
מִן־קֳדָם אֲבוּהוֹן דִּי בִשְׁמַיָּא ׃ וְאִמְרוּ אָמֵן ׃

יְהִי שֵׁם יְיָ מְבֹרָךְ מֵעַתָּה וְעַד עוֹלָם ׃

יְהֵא שְׁלָמָא רַבָּא מִן־שְׁמַיָּא וְחַיִּים טוֹבִים עָלֵינוּ וְעַל־כָּל־
יִשְׂרָאֵל ׃ וְאִמְרוּ אָמֵן ׃

עֶזְרִי מֵעִם יְיָ עֹשֵׂה שָׁמַיִם וָאָרֶץ ׃

עֹשֶׂה שָׁלוֹם בִּמְרוֹמָיו הוּא בְּרַחֲמָיו יַעֲשֶׂה שָׁלוֹם עָלֵינוּ
וְעַל־כָּל־יִשְׂרָאֵל ׃ וְאִמְרוּ אָמֵן ׃

KADDISH D'RABANAN

Let us magnify and let us sanctify the great name of God in the world which He created according to His will. May His kingdom come in your lifetime, and in your days, and in the lifetime of the family of Israel—quickly and speedily may it come. Amen.

May the greatness of His being be blessed from eternity to eternity.

Let us bless and let us extol, let us tell aloud and let us raise aloft, let us set on high and let us honour, let us exalt and let us praise the Holy One—blessed be He!—though He is far beyond any blessing or song, any honour or any consolation that can be spoken of in this world. Amen.

For Israel and for the Rabbis, for their pupils, and the pupils of their pupils, who devote themselves to the study of Torah, in this place and every other place; let there be for them and for you great peace and favour, love and mercy, a life of fulfilment and of plenty, and redemption from their father who is in heaven. Amen.

May the name of the Lord be blessed from now and forever.

May great peace from heaven and the gift of good life be granted to us and to all the family of Israel. Amen.

My help is from the Lord alone, maker of heaven and earth.

May He who makes peace in the highest, in His mercy bring this peace upon us and upon all Israel. Amen.

HEBREW KADDISH

יִתְגַּדַּל וְיִתְקַדַּשׁ שְׁמוֹ הַגָּדוֹל · בָּעוֹלָם אֲשֶׁר בָּרָא כִרְצוֹנוֹ ·
וְיַמְלִיךְ מַלְכוּתוֹ · וְיַצְמִיחַ יְשׁוּעָתוֹ · בְּחַיֵּיכֶם וּבִימֵיכֶם וּבְחַיֵּי
כָל־בֵּית יִשְׂרָאֵל בִּמְהֵרָה וּבִזְמַן קָרוֹב · וְאִמְרוּ אָמֵן :

יְהִי שְׁמוֹ הַגָּדוֹל מְבֹרָךְ לְעוֹלָם וּלְעוֹלְמֵי עוֹלָמִים :

יִתְבָּרַךְ וְיִשְׁתַּבַּח וְיִתְפָּאַר וְיִתְרוֹמַם וְיִתְנַשֵּׂא וְיִתְהַדָּר וְיִתְעַלֶּה
וְיִתְהַלָּל שֵׁם הַקָּדוֹשׁ בָּרוּךְ הוּא · עַל כָּל־בִּרְכוֹת שִׁירוֹת
וְתִשְׁבָּחוֹת הַנֶּאֱמָרוֹת בָּעוֹלָם · וְאִמְרוּ אָמֵן :

יְהִי שָׁלוֹם רַב מִן הַשָּׁמַיִם · חַיִּים וְשָׂבָע וִישׁוּעָה וְנֶחָמָה
וּרְפוּאָה וּגְאֻלָּה וּסְלִיחָה וְכַפָּרָה וְרֶוַח וְהַצָּלָה לָנוּ וּלְכָל־
יִשְׂרָאֵל · וְאִמְרוּ אָמֵן :

עֹשֶׂה שָׁלוֹם בִּמְרוֹמָיו · הוּא יַעֲשֶׂה שָׁלוֹם עָלֵינוּ וְעַל כָּל־
יִשְׂרָאֵל · וְאִמְרוּ אָמֵן :

Mannheim New Synagogue

HEBREW KADDISH

Let us magnify and let us sanctify the great name of God in the world which He created according to His will. May His kingdom come, and His salvation flourish in your lifetime, and in your days, and in the lifetime of the family of Israel—quickly and speedily may they come. Amen.

May the greatness of His being be blessed from eternity to eternity.

Let us bless and let us extol, let us tell aloud and let us raise aloft, let us set on high and let us honour, let us exalt and let us praise the Holy One—blessed be He!—though He is far beyond all blessings, songs and honours that can be spoken of in this world. Amen.

May great peace from heaven, life and fulfilment, salvation and consolation, healing and redemption, forgiveness and atonement, relief and deliverance be granted to us and to all the family of Israel. Amen.

May He who makes peace in the highest bring this peace upon us and upon all Israel. Amen.

Hamburg Temple

Your home should be a place of quietness and happiness, where no harsh word is ever heard, but love, friendship, modesty, and a spirit of gentleness and reverence rules all the time.

Judah ben Abraham Shemariah

SERVICE AT DEDICATION OF A HOME

אִם־יְהֹוָה לֹא־יִבְנֶה בַיִת　שָׁוְא עָמְלוּ בוֹנָיו בּוֹ:

'Unless the Lord builds the house,
its builders toil in vain.'

Psalm 127: 1

We fix the *mezuzah* to the doorpost of this home to fulfil the command of our creator and to remind ourselves and all who enter that we should love Him with all our heart and all our soul and all our might.

We ask His blessing on this home and all who live in it. May its doors be open to those in need and its rooms be filled with kindness. May love dwell within its walls, and joy shine from its windows. May His peace protect it and His presence never leave it.

שְׁמַע יִשְׂרָאֵל · יְהֹוָה אֱלֹהֵינוּ יְהֹוָה אֶחָד:

בָּרוּךְ שֵׁם כְּבוֹד מַלְכוּתוֹ לְעוֹלָם וָעֶד:

וְאָהַבְתָּ אֵת יְהֹוָה אֱלֹהֶיךָ · בְּכָל־לְבָבְךָ וּבְכָל־נַפְשְׁךָ וּבְכָל־מְאֹדֶךָ: וְהָיוּ הַדְּבָרִים הָאֵלֶּה אֲשֶׁר אָנֹכִי מְצַוְּךָ הַיּוֹם עַל־לְבָבֶךָ: וְשִׁנַּנְתָּם לְבָנֶיךָ וְדִבַּרְתָּ בָּם · בְּשִׁבְתְּךָ בְּבֵיתֶךָ וּבְלֶכְתְּךָ בַדֶּרֶךְ וּבְשָׁכְבְּךָ וּבְקוּמֶךָ: וּקְשַׁרְתָּם לְאוֹת עַל־יָדֶךָ · וְהָיוּ לְטֹטָפֹת בֵּין עֵינֶיךָ: וּכְתַבְתָּם עַל־מְזֻזוֹת בֵּיתֶךָ וּבִשְׁעָרֶיךָ:

Hear O Israel, the Lord is our God, the Lord is One.

Blessed is His name, whose glorious kingdom is forever and ever.

Love the Lord your God with all your heart, and all your soul, and all your might. These words that I command you today shall be upon your heart. Repeat them to your children, and talk about them when you sit in your home, and when you walk in the street; when you lie down, and when you rise up. Hold fast to them as a sign upon your hand, and let them be as reminders before your eyes. Write them on the doorposts of your home and at your gates.

Deuteronomy 6: 4–9

בָּרוּךְ אַתָּה יְיָ אֱלֹהֵינוּ מֶלֶךְ הָעוֹלָם · אֲשֶׁר קִדְּשָׁנוּ בְּמִצְוֹתָיו וְצִוָּנוּ לִקְבּוֹעַ מְזוּזָה:

Blessed are You, Lord our God, king of the universe, who makes us holy through doing His commands, and commands us to fix the *mezuzah*.

בָּרוּךְ אַתָּה יְיָ אֱלֹהֵינוּ מֶלֶךְ הָעוֹלָם · שֶׁהֶחֱיָנוּ וְקִיְּמָנוּ וְהִגִּיעָנוּ לַזְּמַן הַזֶּה:

Blessed are You, Lord our God, king of the universe, who has kept us alive and supported us and brought us to this season.

SERVICE AT CIRCUMCISION

בָּרוּךְ הַבָּא בְּשֵׁם יְהוָֹה: בְּרוּכִים אַתֶּם לַיהוָֹה עֹשֵׂה שָׁמַיִם וָאָרֶץ:

The father says:

הִנְנִי מוּכָן לְקַיֵּם מִצְוַת עֲשֵׂה שֶׁצִּוָּנוּ הַבּוֹרֵא יִתְבָּרַךְ לָמוּל אֶת־בְּנִי · כַּכָּתוּב בַּתּוֹרָה · וַיֹּאמֶר אֱלֹהִים אֶל־אַבְרָהָם וְאַתָּה אֶת־בְּרִיתִי תִשְׁמֹר אַתָּה וְזַרְעֲךָ אַחֲרֶיךָ לְדֹרֹתָם: זֹאת בְּרִיתִי אֲשֶׁר תִּשְׁמְרוּ בֵּינִי וּבֵינֵיכֶם וּבֵין זַרְעֲךָ אַחֲרֶיךָ הִמּוֹל לָכֶם כָּל־זָכָר:

וְנֶאֱמָר · וּמָל יְהוָֹה אֱלֹהֶיךָ אֶת־לְבָבְךָ וְאֶת־לְבַב זַרְעֶךָ לְאַהֲבָה אֶת־יְהוָֹה אֱלֹהֶיךָ בְּכָל־לְבָבְךָ וּבְכָל־נַפְשְׁךָ לְמַעַן חַיֶּיךָ:

The Mohel says:

זֶה הַכִּסֵּא שֶׁל אֵלִיָּהוּ זָכוּר לַטּוֹב:

בָּרוּךְ אַתָּה יְיָ אֱלֹהֵינוּ מֶלֶךְ הָעוֹלָם · אֲשֶׁר קִדְּשָׁנוּ בְּמִצְוֹתָיו וְצִוָּנוּ עַל הַמִּילָה:

The father says:

בָּרוּךְ אַתָּה יְיָ אֱלֹהֵינוּ מֶלֶךְ הָעוֹלָם · אֲשֶׁר קִדְּשָׁנוּ בְּמִצְוֹתָיו וְצִוָּנוּ לְהַכְנִיסוֹ בִּבְרִיתוֹ שֶׁל אַבְרָהָם אָבִינוּ:

בָּרוּךְ אַתָּה יְיָ אֱלֹהֵינוּ מֶלֶךְ הָעוֹלָם · שֶׁהֶחֱיָנוּ וְקִיְּמָנוּ וְהִגִּיעָנוּ לַזְּמַן הַזֶּה:

All present reply:

כְּשֵׁם שֶׁנִּכְנַס לַבְּרִית כֵּן יִכָּנֵס לַתּוֹרָה וּלְחֻפָּה וּלְמַעֲשִׂים טוֹבִים:

SERVICE AT CIRCUMCISION

Blessed be he who comes in the name of the Lord. You are blessed by the Lord, maker of heaven and earth.

The father says:

I am ready to fulfil the commandment to circumcise my son, as the creator, blessed be He, has commanded us. For it is written in the Torah: 'And God said to Abraham, You shall keep My covenant, you and your children after you throughout their generations. This is My covenant which you shall keep, between Me and you and your children after you; every male among you shall be circumcised.'

Genesis 17: 9–10

And it is also written in the Torah: 'And the Lord your God will circumcise your heart, and the heart of your children, to love the Lord your God, with all your heart and with all your soul, that you may live.'

Deuteronomy 30: 6

The Mohel says:

This is the chair of Elijah. May he be remembered for good.

Blessed are You, Lord our God, king of the universe, who makes us holy through doing His commands, and commands us concerning circumcision.

The father says:

Blessed are You, Lord our God, king of the universe, who makes us holy through doing His commands, and commands us to bring our sons into the covenant of our father, Abraham.

Blessed are You, Lord our God, king of the universe, who has kept us alive and supported us and brought us to this season.

All present reply:

Just as he has entered into the covenant, so may he also enter into the blessings of Torah, of marriage and of good deeds.

The Mohel or Rabbi says:

בָּרוּךְ אַתָּה יְיָ אֱלֹהֵינוּ מֶלֶךְ הָעוֹלָם · בּוֹרֵא פְּרִי הַגָּפֶן:

אֱלֹהֵינוּ וֵאלֹהֵי אֲבוֹתֵינוּ · קַיֵּם אֶת־הַיֶּלֶד הַזֶּה וְיִקָּרֵא שְׁמוֹ
בְּיִשְׂרָאֵל . . . . . יִשְׂמְחוּ בוֹ אָבִיו וְאִמּוֹ וִילַמְּדוּהוּ בְּאַהֲבָה
וּבְחָכְמָה אֶת־פֵּשֶׁר־הַבְּרִית הַזֹּאת אֲשֶׁר נִכְנַס בָּהּ הַיּוֹם ·
לְמַעַן יִרְדֹּף צֶדֶק וֶאֱמֶת וְיֵלֶךְ בְּדַרְכֵי־שָׁלוֹם · יִגְדַּל הַיֶּלֶד
הַזֶּה לְהָבִיא בְרָכָה עַל־מִשְׁפַּחְתּוֹ וְעַל־בֵּית־יִשְׂרָאֵל וְעַל־
כָּל־מִשְׁפְּחוֹת־הָאֲדָמָה · כְּשֵׁם שֶׁנִּכְנַס לַבְּרִית כֵּן יִכָּנֵס
לַתּוֹרָה וּלְחֻפָּה וּלְמַעֲשִׂים טוֹבִים:

SABBATH EVE HOME SERVICE

הִנְנִי מוּכָן וּמְזֻמָּן לְכַבֵּד אֶת־הַשַּׁבָּת בְּנֶאֱמָנוּת אֵלֶיךָ
וְאֶל־הַדּוֹרוֹת שֶׁקְּדָמוּ לִי · הִנְנִי מַשְׁלִיךְ מִלִּבִּי כָּל־שִׂנְאָה
וְכָל־מְרִירוּת שֶׁנִּשְׁתַּיְּרוּ מֵהַשָּׁבוּעַ שֶׁעָבַר לְמַעַן תִּהְיֶה רוּחִי
שְׁלֵוָה וְאֶקְרָא בְשִׁמְךָ בֶּאֱמֶת: לְאוֹר־נֵרוֹת־הַשַּׁבָּת רוֹאָה אֲנִי
אֶת־הַמְסוּבִּים בְּבֵיתִי כְּצַוֹּךְ אוֹתִי לִרְאוֹתָם · וּמוֹדָה אֲנִי
לְפָנֶיךָ עַל־מִשְׁפָּחָה וִידִידוּת · עַל־נֶאֱמָנוּת וְאַהֲבָה · בְּקַדְּשִׁי
עַל־הַיַּיִן אַבִּיעַ לַשָּׁלוֹם הַשּׁוֹפֵעַ מִקְּדָשָׁהּ וְלַשִּׂמְחָה הַנּוֹבַעַת
מִנִּדְבַת־הַלֵּב · בְּאָכְלִי אֶת־פִּתִּי אַכִּיר בְּחוֹבָתִי לַאֲחֵרִים
וַאֲצַפֶּה לְיוֹם שֶׁכֻּלּוֹ שַׁבָּת וְשִׂמְחָה וְשָׁלוֹם לַכֹּל:

After lighting the candles

בָּרוּךְ אַתָּה יְיָ אֱלֹהֵינוּ מֶלֶךְ הָעוֹלָם · אֲשֶׁר קִדְּשָׁנוּ
בְּמִצְוֺתָיו וְצִוָּנוּ לְהַדְלִיק נֵר שֶׁל שַׁבָּת:

The Mohel or Rabbi says:

Blessed are You, Lord our God, king of the universe, who creates the fruit of the vine.

Our God and God of our fathers, support this child, and may his name be called in Israel . . . . May his father and mother rejoice in him. With love and wisdom may they teach him the meaning of the covenant which he has entered today, so that he may practise righteousness, seeking truth and walking in the ways of peace. May this young child grow into manhood as a blessing to his family, the family of Israel and the family of mankind. Just as he has entered into the covenant, so may he also enter into the blessings of Torah, of marriage and of good deeds.

SABBATH EVE HOME SERVICE

Meditation

Lord, I prepare to honour the Sabbath, keeping faith with You and the generations that have gone before. I cast away any hatred or bitterness that lingers from the week that is past, so that my spirit may be at rest, and I can truly speak Your name. I see those about me in the light of the Sabbath candles as You want me to see them, and thank You for family and friendship, loyalty and love. I make *kiddush*, and receive the gift of happiness, the peace that comes from holiness, the joy that comes from giving. As I eat the bread, I remember all I owe to others, and look forward to that great Sabbath when all shall find their joy and peace.

After lighting the candles

Blessed are You, Lord our God, king of the universe, who makes us holy through doing His commands, and commands us to light the Sabbath candles.

אֵל שַׁדַּי אוֹר־הָעוֹלָם · בָּרְכֵנוּ בִּבְרָכָה שְׁלֵמָה מִלְפָנֶיךָ :
רְצֵה־נָא בָנוּ וְהָאֵר אֶת־עֵינֵינוּ בְּאוֹרֶךָ וּבַאֲמִתֶּךָ כְּמוֹ
שֶׁהִדְלַקְנוּ לְפָנֶיךָ אֶת־נֵרוֹת הַשַּׁבָּת · וְהַשְׁכֵּן בִּנְאוֹתֵינוּ רוּחַ
אֱמוּנִים וְאַהֲבָה : הַדְרִיכֵנוּ בְּאוֹר פָּנֶיךָ וּבְאוֹרֶךָ נִרְאֶה
אוֹר : שְׁלַח־נָא אֶת־בִּרְכָתְךָ לְכָל־בֵּית בְּיִשְׂרָאֵל וּבָעוֹלָם
כֻּלּוֹ וְתֵן שָׁלוֹם וְשִׂמְחַת עוֹלָם עַל רֹאשָׁם · אָמֵן :

Blessing the children

For Boys

For Girls

יְשִׂמְךָ אֱלֹהִים כְּאֶפְרַיִם
וְכִמְנַשֶּׁה :

יְשִׂמֵךְ אֱלֹהִים כְּשָׂרָה רִבְקָה
רָחֵל וְלֵאָה :

יְבָרֶכְךָ יְהֹוָה וְיִשְׁמְרֶךָ ·
יָאֵר יְהֹוָה פָּנָיו אֵלֶיךָ וִיחֻנֶּךָּ ·
יִשָּׂא יְהֹוָה פָּנָיו אֵלֶיךָ וְיָשֵׂם לְךָ שָׁלוֹם :

שָׁלוֹם עֲלֵיכֶם מַלְאֲכֵי הַשָּׁרֵת מַלְאֲכֵי עֶלְיוֹן מֶלֶךְ
מַלְכֵי הַמְּלָכִים הַקָּדוֹשׁ בָּרוּךְ הוּא :

בּוֹאֲכֶם לְשָׁלוֹם מַלְאֲכֵי הַשָּׁלוֹם מַלְאֲכֵי עֶלְיוֹן מֶלֶךְ מַלְכֵי
הַמְּלָכִים הַקָּדוֹשׁ בָּרוּךְ הוּא :

בָּרְכוּנִי לְשָׁלוֹם מַלְאֲכֵי הַשָּׁלוֹם מַלְאֲכֵי עֶלְיוֹן מֶלֶךְ מַלְכֵי
הַמְּלָכִים הַקָּדוֹשׁ בָּרוּךְ הוּא :

צֵאתְכֶם לְשָׁלוֹם מַלְאֲכֵי הַשָּׁלוֹם מַלְאֲכֵי עֶלְיוֹן מֶלֶךְ
מַלְכֵי הַמְּלָכִים הַקָּדוֹשׁ בָּרוּךְ הוּא :

God of might, light of the world, bless us with a perfect blessing in Your presence. Enlighten our eyes with Your light and Your truth, just as we light the Sabbath candles before You, and so make a spirit of trust and love dwell in our homes. Guide us with the light of Your presence, for in Your light we see light. Send Your blessing to every home of Israel and to the whole world, and set peace and eternal blessing upon them. Amen.

Blessing the children

For Boys

May God make you like Ephraim and Manasseh.

For Girls

May God make you like Sarah, Rebecca, Rachel and Leah.

May the Lord bless you and keep you.
May the face of the Lord enlighten you and be gracious to you.
May the Lord turn His face towards you and give you peace.

Peace and welcome to you, servants of the Lord, messengers of the Most High, of the King above the kings of kings, the Holy One, blessed be He.

Enter in peace, you servants of peace, messengers of the Most High, of the King above the kings of kings, the Holy One, blessed be He.

Bless me with peace, you servants of peace, messengers of the Most High, of the King above the kings of kings, the Holy One, blessed be He.

Go forth in peace, you servants of peace, messengers of the Most High, of the King above the kings of kings, the Holy One, blessed be He.

אֵשֶׁת־חַיִל מִי יִמְצָא וְרָחֹק מִפְּנִינִים מִכְרָהּ:

בָּטַח בָּהּ לֵב בַּעְלָהּ וְשָׁלָל לֹא יֶחְסָר:

גְּמָלַתְהוּ טוֹב וְלֹא־רָע כֹּל יְמֵי חַיֶּיהָ:

כַּפָּהּ פָּרְשָׂה לֶעָנִי וְיָדֶיהָ שִׁלְּחָה לָאֶבְיוֹן:

עֹז־וְהָדָר לְבוּשָׁהּ וַתִּשְׂחַק לְיוֹם אַחֲרוֹן:

פִּיהָ פָּתְחָה בְחָכְמָה וְתוֹרַת־חֶסֶד עַל־לְשׁוֹנָהּ:

צוֹפִיָּה הֲלִיכוֹת בֵּיתָהּ וְלֶחֶם עַצְלוּת לֹא תֹאכֵל:

קָמוּ בָנֶיהָ וַיְאַשְּׁרוּהָ בַּעְלָהּ וַיְהַלְלָהּ:

רַבּוֹת בָּנוֹת עָשׂוּ חָיִל וְאַתְּ עָלִית עַל־כֻּלָּנָה:

שֶׁקֶר הַחֵן וְהֶבֶל הַיֹּפִי אִשָּׁה יִרְאַת־יְהֹוָה הִיא תִתְהַלָּל:

תְּנוּ־לָהּ מִפְּרִי יָדֶיהָ וִיהַלְלוּהָ בַשְּׁעָרִים מַעֲשֶׂיהָ:

KIDDUSH

וַיְכֻלּוּ הַשָּׁמַיִם וְהָאָרֶץ וְכָל־צְבָאָם: וַיְכַל אֱלֹהִים בַּיּוֹם הַשְּׁבִיעִי מְלַאכְתּוֹ אֲשֶׁר עָשָׂה · וַיִּשְׁבֹּת בַּיּוֹם הַשְּׁבִיעִי מִכָּל־מְלַאכְתּוֹ אֲשֶׁר עָשָׂה: וַיְבָרֶךְ אֱלֹהִים אֶת־יוֹם הַשְּׁבִיעִי וַיְקַדֵּשׁ אֹתוֹ · כִּי בוֹ שָׁבַת מִכָּל־מְלַאכְתּוֹ אֲשֶׁר בָּרָא אֱלֹהִים לַעֲשׂוֹת:

Eshet Chayil

A woman of worth, who can find her,
   for she is more precious than rubies.
Her husband trusts her in his heart
   and has no loss by it.
Every day of her life
   she does him good, not harm.
Her hand is held out open to the poor,
   reaching out to those in need.
She is clothed in strength and dignity,
   serene before the time to come.
When she speaks, it is with wisdom
   and on her tongue is the guidance of love.
She looks after her home with care,
   and does not idle away her time.
Her children stand up and honour her,
   and her husband sings her praises.
'Many a woman has done splendid deeds,
   but you surpass them all.'
Charm deceives and beauty fades,
   so praise the woman who honours God.
Give her honour for the work of her hands,
   and her own good deeds will praise her in public.

From Proverbs 31

KIDDUSH

THE
HOLINESS
OF THE
SABBATH
   Heaven and earth were finished and all their host. On the seventh day God finished the work that He had done, and He ceased on the seventh day from all the work that He had done. God blessed the seventh day, and made it holy, because on it God ceased from all the work of creation that He had done.

Genesis 2: 1–3

Blessing for wine

בָּרוּךְ אַתָּה יְיָ אֱלֹהֵינוּ מֶלֶךְ הָעוֹלָם · בּוֹרֵא פְּרִי הַגָּפֶן:

Blessing for the day

בָּרוּךְ אַתָּה יְיָ אֱלֹהֵינוּ מֶלֶךְ הָעוֹלָם · אֲשֶׁר קִדְּשָׁנוּ
בְּמִצְוֹתָיו · וְרָצָה בָנוּ · וְשַׁבַּת קָדְשׁוֹ בְּאַהֲבָה וּבְרָצוֹן
הִנְחִילָנוּ · זִכָּרוֹן לְמַעֲשֵׂה בְרֵאשִׁית · כִּי הוּא יוֹם תְּחִלָּה
לְמִקְרָאֵי קֹדֶשׁ · זֵכֶר לִיצִיאַת מִצְרָיִם: כִּי־בָנוּ בָחַרְתָּ
וְאוֹתָנוּ קִדַּשְׁתָּ מִכָּל־הָעַמִּים · וְשַׁבַּת קָדְשְׁךָ בְּאַהֲבָה וּבְרָצוֹן
הִנְחַלְתָּנוּ: בָּרוּךְ אַתָּה יְיָ · מְקַדֵּשׁ הַשַּׁבָּת:

Blessing for bread

בָּרוּךְ אַתָּה יְיָ אֱלֹהֵינוּ מֶלֶךְ הָעוֹלָם · הַמּוֹצִיא לֶחֶם מִן
הָאָרֶץ:

Fürth

Blessing for wine

Blessed are You, Lord our God, king of the universe, who creates the fruit of the vine.

Blessing for the day

Blessed are You, Lord our God, king of the universe, who makes us holy through doing His commands, and delights in us. Willingly and with love He gives us His holy Sabbath to inherit, for it recalls the act of creation. This is the first day of holy gatherings, a reminder of the exodus from Egypt. Because You chose us to be holy among all peoples, willingly and with love You gave us Your holy Sabbath to inherit. Blessed are You Lord, who makes the Sabbath holy.

Blessing for bread

Blessed are You, Lord our God, king of the universe, who brings forth food out of the earth.

Songs to be sung round the Sabbath table can be found on pages 572–578.

Berlin

KIDDUSH FOR SABBATH MORNING

וְשָׁמְרוּ בְנֵי־יִשְׂרָאֵל אֶת־הַשַּׁבָּת לַעֲשׂוֹת אֶת־הַשַּׁבָּת
לְדֹרֹתָם בְּרִית עוֹלָם: בֵּינִי וּבֵין בְּנֵי יִשְׂרָאֵל
אוֹת הִוא לְעֹלָם כִּי־שֵׁשֶׁת יָמִים עָשָׂה יְהוָֹה אֶת־הַשָּׁמַיִם
וְאֶת־הָאָרֶץ וּבַיּוֹם הַשְּׁבִיעִי שָׁבַת וַיִּנָּפַשׁ:

זָכוֹר אֶת־יוֹם הַשַּׁבָּת לְקַדְּשׁוֹ: שֵׁשֶׁת יָמִים תַּעֲבֹד וְעָשִׂיתָ
כָל־מְלַאכְתֶּךָ: וְיוֹם הַשְּׁבִיעִי שַׁבָּת לַיהוָֹה אֱלֹהֶיךָ לֹא־
תַעֲשֶׂה כָל־מְלָאכָה אַתָּה וּבִנְךָ וּבִתֶּךָ עַבְדְּךָ וַאֲמָתְךָ
וּבְהֶמְתֶּךָ וְגֵרְךָ אֲשֶׁר בִּשְׁעָרֶיךָ: כִּי שֵׁשֶׁת־יָמִים עָשָׂה יְהוָֹה
אֶת־הַשָּׁמַיִם וְאֶת־הָאָרֶץ אֶת־הַיָּם וְאֶת־כָּל־אֲשֶׁר־בָּם וַיָּנַח
בַּיּוֹם הַשְּׁבִיעִי · עַל־כֵּן בֵּרַךְ יְהוָֹה אֶת־יוֹם הַשַּׁבָּת
וַיְקַדְּשֵׁהוּ:

Blessing for wine

בָּרוּךְ אַתָּה יְיָ אֱלֹהֵינוּ מֶלֶךְ הָעוֹלָם · בּוֹרֵא פְּרִי הַגָּפֶן:

Blessing for bread

בָּרוּךְ אַתָּה יְיָ אֱלֹהֵינוּ מֶלֶךְ הָעוֹלָם · הַמּוֹצִיא לֶחֶם מִן
הָאָרֶץ:

KIDDUSH FOR SABBATH MORNING

The children of Israel shall keep the Sabbath, observing the Sabbath as a timeless covenant for all generations. It is a sign between Me and the children of Israel forever. For in six days the Lord made heaven and earth and on the seventh day He ceased from work and was at rest.

Exodus 31: 16–17

Remember the Sabbath day and keep it holy. You have six days to labour and do all your work, but the seventh shall be a Sabbath for the Lord your God. That day you shall do no work, neither you, nor your son, nor your daughter, nor your servant, man or woman, nor your cattle, nor the stranger who lives in your home. For in six days the Lord made heaven and earth, the seas and all that is in them, and He rested on the seventh day. Therefore, He blessed the Sabbath day and made it holy.

Exodus 20: 8–11

Blessing for wine

Blessed are You, Lord our God, king of the universe, who creates the fruit of the vine.

Blessing for bread

Blessed are You, Lord our God, king of the universe, who brings forth food out of the earth.

CLOSE OF SABBATH

וִיהִי נֹעַם אֲדֹנָי אֱלֹהֵינוּ עָלֵינוּ וּמַעֲשֵׂה יָדֵינוּ כּוֹנְנָה עָלֵינוּ
וּמַעֲשֵׂה יָדֵינוּ כּוֹנְנֵהוּ׃

צא

יֹשֵׁב בְּסֵתֶר עֶלְיוֹן בְּצֵל שַׁדַּי יִתְלוֹנָן׃

אֹמַר לַיהוָה מַחְסִי וּמְצוּדָתִי אֱלֹהַי אֶבְטַח־בּוֹ׃

כִּי הוּא יַצִּילְךָ מִפַּח יָקוּשׁ מִדֶּבֶר הַוּוֹת׃

בְּאֶבְרָתוֹ יָסֶךְ לָךְ וְתַחַת־כְּנָפָיו תֶּחְסֶה צִנָּה וְסֹחֵרָה אֲמִתּוֹ׃

לֹא־תִירָא מִפַּחַד לָיְלָה מֵחֵץ יָעוּף יוֹמָם׃

מִדֶּבֶר בָּאֹפֶל יַהֲלֹךְ מִקֶּטֶב יָשׁוּד צָהֳרָיִם׃

יִפֹּל מִצִּדְּךָ אֶלֶף וּרְבָבָה מִימִינֶךָ אֵלֶיךָ לֹא יִגָּשׁ׃

רַק בְּעֵינֶיךָ תַבִּיט וְשִׁלֻּמַת רְשָׁעִים תִּרְאֶה׃

כִּי־אַתָּה יְהוָה מַחְסִי עֶלְיוֹן שַׂמְתָּ מְעוֹנֶךָ׃

לֹא־תְאֻנֶּה אֵלֶיךָ רָעָה וְנֶגַע לֹא־יִקְרַב בְּאָהֳלֶךָ׃

כִּי מַלְאָכָיו יְצַוֶּה־לָּךְ לִשְׁמָרְךָ בְּכָל־דְּרָכֶיךָ׃

עַל־כַּפַּיִם יִשָּׂאוּנְךָ פֶּן־תִּגֹּף בָּאֶבֶן רַגְלֶךָ׃

עַל־שַׁחַל וָפֶתֶן תִּדְרֹךְ תִּרְמֹס כְּפִיר וְתַנִּין׃

כִּי בִי חָשַׁק וַאֲפַלְּטֵהוּ אֲשַׂגְּבֵהוּ כִּי־יָדַע שְׁמִי׃

יִקְרָאֵנִי וְאֶעֱנֵהוּ עִמּוֹ־אָנֹכִי בְצָרָה אֲחַלְּצֵהוּ וַאֲכַבְּדֵהוּ׃

אֹרֶךְ יָמִים אַשְׂבִּיעֵהוּ וְאַרְאֵהוּ בִּישׁוּעָתִי׃

CLOSE OF SABBATH

May the favour of the Lord our God be upon us to support us in the work we do, and support the work we do.

Psalm 90: 17

Psalm 91

He who dwells in the mystery of the Most High
 rests in the shadow of the Almighty.
Therefore I say that the Lord is my shelter,
 my fortress, my God in whom I trust!
For He rescues you from the hunter's trap,
 from a death that is final destruction.
He covers you with His strength,
 you find shelter beneath His wings.
His truth surrounds and shields you.

Do not fear the terror of the night,
 nor the sharp blows that fly by day,
the disease that walks in darkness,
 the sickness that destroys at noon.

Though a thousand fall at your side,
 ten thousand at your right hand,
 no harm can come to you.
Just look with your eyes
 and see the results of wickedness.

Because you say: 'The Lord is my refuge',
 and make the Most High your dwelling,
no evil shall come upon you,
 no blow shall come near your house.

For He commands His messengers to watch over you,
 to keep you in all your ways.
They bear you in their hands
 lest your feet stumble on a stone.
Through terror and venom you will find your way,
 you will crush down new fears and evil.

'When a man has clung to Me in love, I set him free,
 I protect him for he knows My being.
When he calls Me I answer him.
 I will be with him in trouble.
 I will rescue him and bring him honour.
I give him the span of his life,
 then I show him My salvation.'

בָּרוּךְ אַתָּה בָּעִיר וּבָרוּךְ אַתָּה בַּשָּׂדֶה:

בָּרוּךְ אַתָּה בְּבֹאֶךָ וּבָרוּךְ אַתָּה בְּצֵאתֶךָ:

יִשְׂרָאֵל נוֹשַׁע בַּיָי תְּשׁוּעַת עוֹלָמִים ·

לֹא־תֵבשׁוּ וְלֹא־תִכָּלְמוּ עַד־עוֹלְמֵי עַד:

כִּי־בְשִׂמְחָה תֵצֵאוּ וּבְשָׁלוֹם תּוּבָלוּן:

שָׁלוֹם שָׁלוֹם לָרָחוֹק וְלַקָּרוֹב אָמַר יְיָ:

יְיָ עֹז לְעַמּוֹ יִתֵּן יְיָ יְבָרֵךְ אֶת־עַמּוֹ בַשָּׁלוֹם:

קכח

שִׁיר הַמַּעֲלוֹת ·

אַשְׁרֵי כָּל־יְרֵא יְהֹוָה הַהֹלֵךְ בִּדְרָכָיו:

יְגִיעַ כַּפֶּיךָ כִּי תֹאכֵל אַשְׁרֶיךָ וְטוֹב לָךְ:

אֶשְׁתְּךָ כְּגֶפֶן פֹּרִיָּה בְּיַרְכְּתֵי בֵיתֶךָ ·

בָּנֶיךָ כִּשְׁתִלֵי זֵיתִים סָבִיב לְשֻׁלְחָנֶךָ:

הִנֵּה כִי־כֵן יְבֹרַךְ גָּבֶר יְרֵא יְהֹוָה:

יְבָרֶכְךָ יְהֹוָה מִצִּיּוֹן וּרְאֵה בְּטוּב יְרוּשָׁלָיִם
כֹּל יְמֵי חַיֶּיךָ:

וּרְאֵה־בָנִים לְבָנֶיךָ · שָׁלוֹם עַל־יִשְׂרָאֵל:

Blessed shall you be in the city,
　　and blessed shall you be in the field.
Blessed shall you be when you come in,
　　and blessed shall you be when you go out.
Israel is saved by the Lord
　　with an everlasting salvation;
　　　you shall not be disgraced nor ashamed forever and ever.
You shall go out with joy
　　and be guided in peace.
Peace, peace to him that is far,
　　and to him that is near,
　　　says the Lord.
The Lord will give strength to His people,
　　the Lord will bless His people with peace.

Psalm 128

A pilgrim song.

Happy is everyone who fears the Lord,
　　who walks in His ways.
When you eat the work of your hands,
　　happy shall you be and it shall go well with you:
your wife, like a fruitful vine,
　　in the heart of your house;
your children, like shoots of the olive tree,
　　around your table.
Surely this is how a man is blessed
　　who fears the Lord!
The Lord bless you from Zion!
May you see the good of Jerusalem
　　all the days of your life,
　　　and see your children's children!
Peace upon Israel!

Passages concerning peace, hope and consolation can be read here.

HAVDALAH SERVICE

הִנֵּה אֵל יְשׁוּעָתִי אֶבְטַח וְלֹא אֶפְחָד · כִּי עָזִּי וְזִמְרָת יָהּ יְיָ
וַיְהִי־לִי לִישׁוּעָה: וּשְׁאַבְתֶּם מַיִם בְּשָׂשׂוֹן מִמַּעַיְנֵי הַיְשׁוּעָה:
לַיְיָ הַיְשׁוּעָה עַל־עַמְּךָ בִרְכָתֶךָ סֶּלָה: יְיָ צְבָאוֹת עִמָּנוּ
מִשְׂגָּב־לָנוּ אֱלֹהֵי יַעֲקֹב סֶלָה: לַיְּהוּדִים הָיְתָה אוֹרָה
וְשִׂמְחָה וְשָׂשׂוֹן וִיקָר · כֵּן תִּהְיֶה לָּנוּ: כּוֹס־יְשׁוּעוֹת אֶשָּׂא
וּבְשֵׁם יְיָ אֶקְרָא:

Raising the cup of wine

בָּרוּךְ אַתָּה יְיָ אֱלֹהֵינוּ מֶלֶךְ הָעוֹלָם · בּוֹרֵא פְּרִי הַגָּפֶן:

Taking the spice box

בָּרוּךְ אַתָּה יְיָ אֱלֹהֵינוּ מֶלֶךְ הָעוֹלָם · בּוֹרֵא מִינֵי בְשָׂמִים:

Spreading the hands towards the light

בָּרוּךְ אַתָּה יְיָ אֱלֹהֵינוּ מֶלֶךְ הָעוֹלָם · בּוֹרֵא מְאוֹרֵי הָאֵשׁ:

בָּרוּךְ אַתָּה יְיָ אֱלֹהֵינוּ מֶלֶךְ הָעוֹלָם · הַמַּבְדִּיל בֵּין קֹדֶשׁ
לְחוֹל וּבֵין אוֹר לְחֹשֶׁךְ וּבֵין יִשְׂרָאֵל לָעַמִּים · וּבֵין יוֹם
הַשְּׁבִיעִי לְשֵׁשֶׁת יְמֵי הַמַּעֲשֶׂה · בָּרוּךְ אַתָּה יְיָ · הַמַּבְדִּיל
בֵּין קֹדֶשׁ לְחוֹל:

SONGS AT THE CLOSE OF SABBATH

הַמַּבְדִּיל בֵּין קֹדֶשׁ לְחוֹל · חַטֹּאתֵינוּ יִמְחֹל ·
זַרְעֵנוּ יַרְבֶּה כַחוֹל · וְכַכּוֹכָבִים בַּלָּיְלָה:

יוֹם פָּנָה כְּצֵל תֹּמֶר · אֶקְרָא לָאֵל עָלַי גֹּמֵר ·
אָמַר שׁוֹמֵר · אָתָא בֹקֶר וְגַם־לָיְלָה:

HAVDALAH SERVICE

See how God is my salvation! I trust and shall not fear, for God the Lord is my strength and song, and He has become my salvation! And you shall draw water with joy from the wells of salvation. Deliverance comes from the Lord; Your blessing on Your people! The Lord of all creation is with us, the God of Jacob is our refuge. The Jews had light and joy, gladness and honour—so may it be with us! I lift the cup of salvation and call in the name of the Lord.

Raising the cup of wine

Blessed are You, Lord our God, king of the universe, who creates the fruit of the vine.

Taking the spice box

Blessed are You, Lord our God, king of the universe, who creates different kinds of spices.

Spreading the hands towards the light

Blessed are You, Lord our God, king of the universe, who creates the lights of the fire.

Blessed are You, Lord our God, king of the universe, who distinguishes between holy and profane, between light and darkness, between Israel and the nations, between the seventh day and the six working days. Blessed are You Lord, who distinguishes between holy and profane.

SONGS AT THE CLOSE OF SABBATH

1

Hamavdil

May He who divides holy from profane
pardon our sins,
and increase our offspring as the sand
and as the stars at night.

As day turns, like the palm-tree's shade,
I call on God to complete for me
that day of which the watchman says:
'Morning will come, though it still be night!'

הֶעָתֵר נוֹרָא וְאָיוֹם · אֲשַׁוֵּעַ תְּנָה פִדְיוֹם · בְּנֶשֶׁף בְּעֶרֶב יוֹם · בְּאִישׁוֹן לָיְלָה:

נַחְנוּ בְיָדְךָ כַּחֹמֶר · סְלַח נָא עַל קַל וָחֹמֶר · יוֹם לְיוֹם יַבִּיעַ אֹמֶר · וְלַיְלָה לְלָיְלָה:

הַמַּבְדִּיל בֵּין קֹדֶשׁ לְחוֹל · חַטֹּאתֵינוּ יִמְחֹל · זַרְעֵנוּ יַרְבֶּה כַחוֹל · וְכַכּוֹכָבִים בַּלָּיְלָה:

אֵלִיָּהוּ הַנָּבִיא.

אֵלִיָּהוּ הַתִּשְׁבִּי ·
אֵלִיָּהוּ הַגִּלְעָדִי ·
בִּמְהֵרָה יָבֹא אֵלֵינוּ
עִם מָשִׁיחַ בֶּן־דָּוִד:

שָׁבְוּעַ טוֹב:

Be moved, awesome and wondrous God!
I cry to You to grant redemption,
at sunset, the evening of the day,
in the darkness of the night.

We are like clay in Your hands;
forgive our sins, light and grave,
as day pours out Your word to day,
and night to night.

May He who divides holy from profane
pardon our sins,
and increase our offspring as the sand
and as the stars at night.

2

Elijah the Prophet

Elijah the prophet,
Elijah the Tishbite,
Elijah the man of Gilead
—may he come to us soon,
with the Messiah, son of David.

3

A happy week.

BLESSINGS BEFORE MEALS

בָּרוּךְ אַתָּה יְיָ אֱלֹהֵינוּ מֶלֶךְ הָעוֹלָם · אֲשֶׁר קִדְּשָׁנוּ
בְּמִצְוֹתָיו וְצִוָּנוּ עַל נְטִילַת יָדָיִם:

בָּרוּךְ אַתָּה יְיָ אֱלֹהֵינוּ מֶלֶךְ הָעוֹלָם · הַמּוֹצִיא לֶחֶם מִן
הָאָרֶץ:

THANKSGIVING AFTER MEALS

קכו

שִׁיר הַמַּעֲלוֹת.

בְּשׁוּב יְהוָֹה אֶת־שִׁיבַת צִיּוֹן הָיִינוּ כְּחֹלְמִים:
אָז יִמָּלֵא שְׂחוֹק פִּינוּ וּלְשׁוֹנֵנוּ רִנָּה

אָז יֹאמְרוּ בַגּוֹיִם הִגְדִּיל יְהוָֹה לַעֲשׂוֹת עִם־אֵלֶּה:
הִגְדִּיל יְהוָֹה לַעֲשׂוֹת עִמָּנוּ הָיִינוּ שְׂמֵחִים:

שׁוּבָה יְהוָֹה אֶת־שְׁבִיתֵנוּ כַּאֲפִיקִים בַּנֶּגֶב:
הַזֹּרְעִים בְּדִמְעָה בְּרִנָּה יִקְצֹרוּ:

הָלוֹךְ יֵלֵךְ וּבָכֹה נֹשֵׂא מֶשֶׁךְ־הַזָּרַע
בֹּא־יָבֹא בְרִנָּה נֹשֵׂא אֲלֻמֹּתָיו:

BLESSINGS BEFORE MEALS

Washing the hands

Blessed are You, Lord our God, king of the universe, who makes us holy through doing His commands, and commands us concerning washing the hands.

Over bread

Blessed are You, Lord our God, king of the universe, who brings forth food out of the earth.

THANKSGIVING AFTER MEALS

On Sabbaths and joyful days Psalm 126 is sung.

Psalm 126
A pilgrim song.

When the Lord brought back the captives to Zion
    we felt as if in a dream.
Then our mouths were filled with laughter,
    and our tongues with song.

Even among the nations they said:
    'What great things the Lord has done for them!'
Indeed the Lord has done great things with us!
    How we rejoiced!

Lord, bring back those who cannot return,
    like streams in a dry land;
that those who sow in tears
    may reap in joy.

Though a man goes out weeping
    carrying seed to sow;
he shall come back singing
    carrying his sheaves.

רַבּוֹתַי נְבָרֵךְ :

יְהִי שֵׁם יְיָ מְבֹרָךְ מֵעַתָּה וְעַד עוֹלָם :

בִּרְשׁוּת רַבּוֹתַי נְבָרֵךְ (אֱלֹהֵינוּ) שֶׁאָכַלְנוּ מִשֶּׁלּוֹ :

בָּרוּךְ (אֱלֹהֵינוּ) שֶׁאָכַלְנוּ מִשֶּׁלּוֹ וּבְטוּבוֹ חָיִינוּ :

בָּרוּךְ הוּא וּבָרוּךְ שְׁמוֹ :

בָּרוּךְ אַתָּה יְיָ אֱלֹהֵינוּ מֶלֶךְ הָעוֹלָם · הַזָּן אֶת־הָעוֹלָם כֻּלּוֹ · בְּטוּבוֹ בְּחֵן בְּחֶסֶד וּבְרַחֲמִים · הוּא נוֹתֵן לֶחֶם לְכָל־בָּשָׂר · כִּי לְעוֹלָם חַסְדּוֹ : וּבְטוּבוֹ הַגָּדוֹל תָּמִיד לֹא־חָסַר לָנוּ וְאַל יֶחְסַר־לָנוּ מָזוֹן לְעוֹלָם וָעֶד בַּעֲבוּר שְׁמוֹ הַגָּדוֹל · כִּי הוּא זָן וּמְפַרְנֵס לַכֹּל וּמֵטִיב לַכֹּל וּמֵכִין מָזוֹן לְכָל־בְּרִיּוֹתָיו אֲשֶׁר בָּרָא · בָּרוּךְ אַתָּה יְיָ · הַזָּן אֶת־ הַכֹּל :

נוֹדֶה לְךָ יְיָ אֱלֹהֵינוּ עַל שֶׁהִנְחַלְתָּ לַאֲבוֹתֵינוּ אֶרֶץ חֶמְדָּה טוֹבָה וּרְחָבָה · בְּרִית וְתוֹרָה · וְלֶחֶם לִשְׂוֹבַע · כַּכָּתוּב · וְאָכַלְתָּ וְשָׂבָעְתָּ וּבֵרַכְתָּ אֶת־יְיָ אֱלֹהֶיךָ עַל־הָאָרֶץ הַטֹּבָה אֲשֶׁר נָתַן־לָךְ · בָּרוּךְ אַתָּה יְיָ · עַל־ הָאָרֶץ וְעַל־הַמָּזוֹן :

רַחֵם יְיָ אֱלֹהֵינוּ עַל־יִשְׂרָאֵל עַמֶּךָ · וְעַל יְרוּשָׁלַיִם עִירֶךָ · וְעַל צִיּוֹן מִשְׁכַּן כְּבוֹדֶךָ · אֱלֹהֵינוּ אָבִינוּ · רְעֵנוּ זוּנֵנוּ פַּרְנְסֵנוּ וְכַלְכְּלֵנוּ וְהַרְוִיחֵנוּ · וְהַרְוַח־לָנוּ יְיָ אֱלֹהֵינוּ מְהֵרָה מִכָּל־צָרוֹתֵינוּ : וְנָא אַל־תַּצְרִיכֵנוּ יְיָ אֱלֹהֵינוּ לֹא לִידֵי מַתְּנַת בָּשָׂר וָדָם וְלֹא לִידֵי הַלְוָאָתָם · כִּי אִם לְיָדְךָ הַמְּלֵאָה הַפְּתוּחָה הַקְּדוֹשָׁה וְהָרְחָבָה · שֶׁלֹּא נֵבוֹשׁ וְלֹא נִכָּלֵם לְעוֹלָם וָעֶד :

Ladies and gentlemen, let us say grace.

All reply

Blessed be the name of the Lord from now and forever.

With your permission, let us bless our God whose food we have eaten.

All reply

Blessed be the Lord our God whose food we have eaten, and through whose goodness we live.

Blessed be He, and blessed be His name.

Blessed are You, Lord our God, king of the universe, who feeds the whole world through His goodness, with grace, kindness and mercy. He gives food to all flesh, for His love is forever. Through His great goodness food has never failed us, and may it never fail us because of His greatness; for He feeds and provides for all and does good to all, and prepares food for all His creatures that He has created. Blessed are You Lord, who gives food to all.

We thank You, Lord our God, for giving our ancestors the heritage of a desirable, good and ample land, covenant and Torah, and food to satisfy, as it is written in the Torah: 'And you shall eat and be satisfied and bless the Lord your God for the good land which He gave you.' Blessed are You Lord, for the land and for the food.

Lord our God, be merciful to Israel Your people, to Jerusalem Your city, and to Zion where Your glory appeared. Our God, our father, be our shepherd and feed us, provide for us, sustain us and support us, and relieve us speedily from all our troubles. Let us never be in need of the charity of our fellowmen nor their loans, but dependent on Your hand alone which is full, open, holy and ample, so shall we never lose our self-respect nor be put to shame.

On Sabbath add

רְצֵה וְהַחֲלִיצֵנוּ יְיָ אֱלֹהֵינוּ בְּמִצְוֹתֶיךָ וּבְמִצְוַת יוֹם
הַשְּׁבִיעִי הַשַּׁבָּת הַגָּדוֹל וְהַקָּדוֹשׁ הַזֶּה · כִּי יוֹם זֶה גָּדוֹל
וְקָדוֹשׁ הוּא לְפָנֶיךָ לִשְׁבָּת־בּוֹ וְלָנֽוּחַ בּוֹ בְּאַהֲבָה
כְּמִצְוַת רְצוֹנֶךָ · בִּרְצוֹנְךָ הָנִיחַ לָנוּ יְיָ אֱלֹהֵינוּ שֶׁלֹּא
תְהִי צָרָה וְיָגוֹן וַאֲנָחָה בְּיוֹם מְנוּחָתֵנוּ · וְהַרְאֵנוּ יְיָ
אֱלֹהֵינוּ בְּנֶחָמַת צִיּוֹן עִירֶךָ · וּבְבִנְיַן יְרוּשָׁלַיִם עִיר
קָדְשֶׁךָ · כִּי אַתָּה הוּא בַּעַל הַיְשׁוּעוֹת וּבַעַל הַנֶּחָמוֹת :

On New Moon and festivals add יַעֲלֶה *page 246.*
On Chanukah add "... עַל הַנִּסִּים" *page 267.*
On Purim add "... עַל הַנִּסִּים" *page 264.*

וּבְנֵה יְרוּשָׁלַיִם עִיר הַקֹּדֶשׁ בִּמְהֵרָה בְיָמֵינוּ ·
בָּרוּךְ אַתָּה יְיָ · בּוֹנֶה בְרַחֲמָיו
יְרוּשָׁלָיִם · אָמֵן :

בָּרוּךְ אַתָּה יְיָ אֱלֹהֵינוּ מֶֽלֶךְ הָעוֹלָם · הָאֵל אָבִֽינוּ מַלְכֵּֽנוּ ·
אַדִּירֵֽנוּ בּוֹרְאֵֽנוּ גֹּאֲלֵֽנוּ יוֹצְרֵֽנוּ קְדוֹשֵֽׁנוּ קְדוֹשׁ יַעֲקֹב · רוֹעֵֽנוּ
רוֹעֵה יִשְׂרָאֵל · הַמֶּֽלֶךְ הַטּוֹב וְהַמֵּטִיב לַכֹּל · שֶׁבְּכָל־יוֹם
וָיוֹם הוּא הֵטִיב הוּא מֵטִיב הוּא יֵיטִיב לָֽנוּ : הוּא גְמָלָֽנוּ הוּא
גוֹמְלֵֽנוּ הוּא יִגְמְלֵֽנוּ לָעַד · לְחֵן לְחֶֽסֶד וּלְרַחֲמִים וּלְרֶֽוַח ·
הַצָּלָה וְהַצְלָחָה בְּרָכָה וִישׁוּעָה · נֶחָמָה פַּרְנָסָה וְכַלְכָּלָה ·
וְרַחֲמִים וְחַיִּים וְשָׁלוֹם וְכָל־טוֹב · וּמִכָּל־טוּב אַל־יְחַסְּרֵֽנוּ :

הָרַחֲמָן · הוּא יִמְלוֹךְ עָלֵֽינוּ לְעוֹלָם וָעֶד :
הָרַחֲמָן · הוּא יִתְבָּרַךְ בַּשָּׁמַֽיִם וּבָאָֽרֶץ :
הָרַחֲמָן · הוּא יִשְׁתַּבַּח לְדוֹר דּוֹרִים · וְיִתְפָּאַר בָּֽנוּ לָנֵֽצַח
נְצָחִים · וְיִתְהַדַּר בָּֽנוּ לָעַד וּלְעוֹלְמֵי עוֹלָמִים :
הָרַחֲמָן · הוּא יְפַרְנְסֵֽנוּ בְּכָבוֹד :

הָרַחֲמָן · הוּא יִשְׁבּוֹר עֻלֵּֽנוּ מֵעַל צַוָּארֵֽנוּ · וְהוּא יוֹלִיכֵֽנוּ קוֹמְמִיּוּת
לְאַרְצֵֽנוּ :

הָרַחֲמָן · הוּא יִשְׁלַח בְּרָכָה מְרֻבָּה בַּבַּֽיִת הַזֶּה · וְעַל
שֻׁלְחָן זֶה שֶׁאָכַֽלְנוּ עָלָיו :

On Sabbath add

Lord our God, strengthen us by Your commandments and by the commandment of the seventh day, this great and holy Sabbath; for You this day is a great and holy one to cease from work and be at rest according to Your will in love. Give us rest so that there shall be no trouble, grief or crying on our day of rest; and show us the consolation of Zion, Your city, and the building of Jerusalem, city of Your holiness, for You are the source of salvation and consolation.

On New Moon and festivals add "Our God..." page 247.
On Chanukah add "We thank you..." page 267.
On Purim add "We thank you..." page 264.

And build Jerusalem, city of holiness, soon in our days. Blessed are You Lord, who builds Jerusalem in His compassion. Amen.

Blessed are You, Lord our God, king of the universe; the God who is our father, our king, our source of power, our creator, our redeemer, our maker, our Holy One, the Holy One of Jacob; our shepherd, the shepherd of Israel, the good king who does good to all. Every day He has done good, does good and will do good for us. Generously He has provided for us, He does provide for us and always will provide for us grace, kindness, mercy and relief, deliverance and prosperity, blessing and salvation, consolation, provision and support, mercy, life, peace and all good. Let us never be in want of any goodness.

The All-merciful, may He rule over us forever and ever.

The All-merciful, may He be blessed in heaven and on earth.

The All-merciful, may He be praised through all generations, glorified among us for eternity, and honoured among us forever.

The All-merciful, may He give us an honourable livelihood.

The All-merciful, may He break off the yoke from our neck, and lead us with uprightness to our land.

The All-merciful, may He send a plentiful blessing on this house, and on this table at which we have eaten.

הָרַחֲמָן · הוּא יִשְׁלַח לָנוּ אֶת־אֵלִיָּה הַנָּבִיא זָכוּר לַטּוֹב ·
וִיבַשֶּׂר־לָנוּ בְּשׂוֹרוֹת טוֹבוֹת יְשׁוּעוֹת וְנֶחָמוֹת :

הָרַחֲמָן · הוּא יְבָרֵךְ אֶת־כָּל־הַמְסֻבִּין כָּאן (אֶת־בַּעַל
הַבַּיִת הַזֶּה אוֹתוֹ וְאֶת־אִשְׁתּוֹ וְאֶת־כָּל־אֲשֶׁר לָהֶם) · אוֹתָנוּ
וְאֶת־כָּל־אֲשֶׁר לָנוּ · כְּמוֹ שֶׁנִּתְבָּרְכוּ אֲבוֹתֵינוּ אַבְרָהָם יִצְחָק
וְיַעֲקֹב בַּכֹּל מִכֹּל כֹּל · כֵּן יְבָרֵךְ אוֹתָנוּ כֻּלָּנוּ יַחַד בִּבְרָכָה
שְׁלֵמָה · וְנֹאמַר אָמֵן :

בַּמָּרוֹם יְלַמְּדוּ עֲלֵיהֶם וְעָלֵינוּ זְכוּת שֶׁתְּהִי לְמִשְׁמֶרֶת
שָׁלוֹם · וְנִשָּׂא בְרָכָה מֵאֵת יְיָ וּצְדָקָה מֵאֱלֹהֵי יִשְׁעֵנוּ ·
וְנִמְצָא־חֵן וְשֵׂכֶל טוֹב בְּעֵינֵי אֱלֹהִים וְאָדָם :

שבת : הָרַחֲמָן . הוּא יַנְחִילֵנוּ יוֹם שֶׁכֻּלּוֹ שַׁבָּת וּמְנוּחָה לְחַיֵּי הָעוֹלָמִים :

ראש חדש : הָרַחֲמָן . הוּא יְחַדֵּשׁ עָלֵינוּ אֶת־הַחֹדֶשׁ הַזֶּה לְטוֹבָה
וְלִבְרָכָה :

יום טוב : הָרַחֲמָן . הוּא יַנְחִילֵנוּ יוֹם שֶׁכֻּלּוֹ טוֹב :

הָרַחֲמָן · הוּא יְזַכֵּנוּ לִימוֹת הַמָּשִׁיחַ וּלְחַיֵּי הָעוֹלָם הַבָּא :

מַגְדִּיל (מִגְדּוֹל) יְשׁוּעוֹת מַלְכּוֹ וְעֹשֶׂה חֶסֶד לִמְשִׁיחוֹ לְדָוִד
וּלְזַרְעוֹ עַד־עוֹלָם : עֹשֶׂה שָׁלוֹם בִּמְרוֹמָיו הוּא יַעֲשֶׂה
שָׁלוֹם עָלֵינוּ וְעַל כָּל־יִשְׂרָאֵל וְאִמְרוּ אָמֵן :

אָכַלְנוּ וְשָׂבָעְנוּ · אַל־נָא נִתְעַלֵּם מִצָּרְכֵי־רֵעֵינוּ וְאַל־
תֵּאָטַמְנָה אָזְנֵינוּ מִצַּעֲקָתָם לְמָזוֹן · פְּקַח עֵינֵינוּ וּפְתַח לִבֵּנוּ
וְנִתְחַלְּקָה בְּמַתְּנוֹתֶיךָ לְמַעַן חֲסוֹל־הָרָעָב וְהַמַּחְסוֹר מֵעוֹלָמֵנוּ :

יְיָ עֹז לְעַמּוֹ יִתֵּן יְיָ יְבָרֵךְ אֶת־עַמּוֹ בַשָּׁלוֹם :

The All-merciful, may He send us Elijah the prophet—may he be remembered for good!—who will bring us good news of salvation and comfort.

The All-merciful, may He bless all who are seated here (the master of this house, the mistress of this house, and all that is theirs), us and all that is ours, as our fathers Abraham, Isaac and Jacob were each of them blessed with 'everything'. So may He bless all of us together with a perfect blessing. Amen.

On high may they plead for them and for us, so that we merit a lasting peace, and may gain a blessing from the Lord and justice from the God of our salvation. May we find grace and understanding in the sight of God and man.

On Sabbath add

> The All-merciful, may He let us inherit a day that shall be wholly a Sabbath and rest in life everlasting.

On New Moon add

> The All-merciful, may He renew to us this month for goodness and blessing.

On festivals add

> The All-merciful, may He let us inherit a day that shall be wholly good.

The All-merciful, may He make us worthy of the messianic days and the life of the world to come.

He gives great salvation to His king (*On Sabbath and festivals*: He is a tower of strength to His king), and shows love and kindness to His anointed, to David and his seed forever. May He who makes peace in the highest bring this peace upon us and upon all Israel. Amen.

We have eaten and been satisfied. May we not be blind to the needs of others, nor deaf to their cry for food. Open our eyes and our hearts so that we may share Your gifts, and help to remove hunger and want from our world.

The Lord gives strength to His people, the Lord blesses His people with peace.

A SHORTER FORM OF THANKSGIVING AFTER MEALS

מַה שֶּׁאָכַלְנוּ יִהְיֶה לְשָׂבְעָה · וּמַה שֶּׁשָּׁתִינוּ יִהְיֶה לִרְוָיָה ·
וּמַה שֶּׁהוֹתַרְנוּ יִהְיֶה לִבְרָכָה · כְּדִכְתִיב · וַיִּתֵּן לִפְנֵיהֶם ·
וַיֹּאכְלוּ וַיּוֹתִירוּ כִּדְבַר יְיָ:

בְּרוּכִים אַתֶּם לַיְיָ · עֹשֵׂה שָׁמַיִם וָאָרֶץ:

בָּרוּךְ הַגֶּבֶר אֲשֶׁר יִבְטַח בַּיְיָ · וְהָיָה יְיָ מִבְטַחוֹ:

יְיָ עֹז לְעַמּוֹ יִתֵּן · יְיָ יְבָרֵךְ אֶת־עַמּוֹ בַשָּׁלוֹם:

THANKSGIVING AFTER MEALS AS A SONG

צוּר מִשֶּׁלּוֹ אָכַלְנוּ · בָּרְכוּ אֱמוּנַי · שָׂבַעְנוּ וְהוֹתַרְנוּ ·
כִּדְבַר יְיָ:

הַזָּן אֶת־עוֹלָמוֹ · רוֹעֵנוּ אָבִינוּ · אָכַלְנוּ אֶת־לַחְמוֹ · וְיֵינוֹ
שָׁתִינוּ · עַל־כֵּן נוֹדֶה לִשְׁמוֹ · וּנְהַלְלוֹ בְּפִינוּ · אָמַרְנוּ וְעָנִינוּ
אֵין־קָדוֹשׁ כַּיְיָ:

צוּר מִשֶּׁלּוֹ אָכַלְנוּ · בָּרְכוּ אֱמוּנַי · שָׂבַעְנוּ וְהוֹתַרְנוּ ·
כִּדְבַר יְיָ:

בְּשִׁיר וְקוֹל תּוֹדָה · נְבָרֵךְ אֱלֹהֵינוּ · עַל אֶרֶץ חֶמְדָּה ·
שֶׁהִנְחִיל לַאֲבוֹתֵינוּ · מָזוֹן וְצֵידָה · הִשְׂבִּיעַ לְנַפְשֵׁנוּ · חַסְדּוֹ
גָּבַר עָלֵינוּ · וֶאֱמֶת יְיָ:

צוּר מִשֶּׁלּוֹ אָכַלְנוּ · בָּרְכוּ אֱמוּנַי · שָׂבַעְנוּ וְהוֹתַרְנוּ ·
כִּדְבַר יְיָ:

A SHORTER FORM OF THANKSGIVING AFTER MEALS

May what we have eaten satisfy us, what we have drunk refresh us, and what we have left be for a blessing. For it is written: 'So he set it before them, and they ate and some was left over, as the Lord had said.' (*II Kings 4: 44*)

You are blessed by the Lord, maker of heaven and earth.

Blessed is the man who trusts in the Lord and puts his confidence in Him.

The Lord gives strength to His people. The Lord blesses His people with peace.

THANKSGIVING AFTER MEALS AS A SONG

Rock by whose gift we eat,
bless Him, my faithful ones,
for we have been satisfied
and food is left over,
   as was the word of the Lord.

He feeds all His world,
our shepherd, our father.
We have eaten His bread,
we have drunk of His wine,
now therefore we thank Him
and praise with our mouths;
we say and we sing
   none is holy as the Lord.

Rock by whose gift we eat,
bless Him, my faithful ones,
for we have been satisfied
and food is left over,
   as was the word of the Lord.

With song and thanksgiving
let us now bless our God
for the plentiful land
which our fathers received.
He has given us food
for our bodies and souls.
His mercy protects us,
   ever true is the Lord.

Rock by whose gift we eat,
bless Him, my faithful ones,
for we have been satisfied
and food is left over,
   as was the word of the Lord.

כִּי אֶשְׁמְרָה שַׁבָּת אֵל יִשְׁמְרֵנִי

הַשְׁכִּיבֵנִי יְהֹוָה לְשָׁלוֹם · וְהַעֲמִידֵנִי לְחַיִּים טוֹבִים · וּפְרוֹשׂ
עָלַי סֻכַּת שְׁלוֹמֶךָ · וְשׁוֹמְרֵנִי לְמַעַן שְׁמֶךָ:

הִנֵּה לֹא יָנוּם וְלֹא יִישָׁן שׁוֹמֵר יִשְׂרָאֵל:

יְהֹוָה יִשְׁמָר־צֵאתְךָ וּבוֹאֶךָ מֵעַתָּה וְעַד־עוֹלָם:

שְׁמַע יִשְׂרָאֵל יְיָ אֱלֹהֵינוּ יְיָ אֶחָד:
וְאָהַבְתָּ אֵת יְיָ אֱלֹהֶיךָ בְּכָל־לְבָבְךָ וּבְכָל־נַפְשְׁךָ
וּבְכָל־מְאֹדֶךָ:

בְּיָדוֹ אַפְקִיד רוּחִי ·   בְּעֵת אִישָׁן וְאָעִירָה:
וְעִם רוּחִי גְוִיָּתִי ·   אֲדֹנָי לִי וְלֹא אִירָא:

בָּרוּךְ יְיָ בַּיּוֹם · בָּרוּךְ יְיָ בַּלָּיְלָה · בָּרוּךְ יְיָ בְּשָׁכְבֵנוּ ·
בָּרוּךְ יְיָ בְּקוּמֵנוּ:

בְּשֵׁם יְיָ אֱלֹהֵי יִשְׂרָאֵל מִימִינִי מִיכָאֵל · וּמִשְּׂמֹאלִי גַּבְרִיאֵל ·
וּמִלְּפָנַי אוּרִיאֵל · וּמֵאֲחוֹרַי רְפָאֵל · וְעַל רֹאשִׁי שְׁכִינַת אֵל:

EVENING PRAYERS
FOR CHILDREN

Any of these passages can be used together with the first lines of the Shema and with any prayers of the child.

Lord, may I sleep in peace and wake up to a good life. Cover me with the shelter of Your peace and protect me because You are good.

Know that the guardian of Israel never slumbers and never sleeps.

The Lord will guard your going out and your coming in, now and for evermore.

HEAR O ISRAEL, THE LORD IS OUR GOD, THE LORD IS ONE. LOVE THE LORD YOUR GOD WITH ALL YOUR HEART, AND ALL YOUR SOUL, AND ALL YOUR MIGHT.

> Within His hand I lay my soul
> both when I sleep and when I wake,
> an 1 with my soul my body too,
> my Lord is close, I shall not fear.

Blessed be the Lord by day; blessed be the Lord by night. Blessed be the Lord when we lie down; blessed be the Lord when we rise up.

In the name of the Lord God of Israel, may Michael, the protection of God, be at my right hand; and Gabriel, the power of God, at my left; before me Uriel, the light of God; behind me Raphael, the healing of God; and above my head Shechinat El, the presence of God.

מְנוּחָה וְשִׂמְחָה

בָּרוּךְ אַתָּה יְיָ אֱלֹהֵינוּ מֶלֶךְ הָעוֹלָם · הַמַּעֲבִיר שֵׁנָה מֵעֵינַי וּתְנוּמָה מֵעַפְעַפָּי:

יְהֹוָה רֹעִי · לֹא אֶחְסָר:
בִּנְאוֹת דֶּשֶׁא יַרְבִּיצֵנִי · עַל־מֵי מְנֻחוֹת יְנַהֲלֵנִי:
אַךְ טוֹב וָחֶסֶד יִרְדְּפוּנִי כָּל־יְמֵי חַיָּי ·
וְשַׁבְתִּי בְּבֵית־יְהֹוָה לְאֹרֶךְ יָמִים:

לְעוֹלָם יְהֵא אָדָם יְרֵא שָׁמַיִם בַּסֵּתֶר כְּבַגָּלוּי · וּמוֹדֶה עַל־הָאֱמֶת וְדוֹבֵר אֱמֶת בִּלְבָבוֹ:

שְׁמַע יִשְׂרָאֵל יְיָ אֱלֹהֵינוּ יְיָ אֶחָד:
וְאָהַבְתָּ אֵת יְיָ אֱלֹהֶיךָ בְּכָל־לְבָבְךָ וּבְכָל־נַפְשְׁךָ וּבְכָל־מְאֹדֶךָ:

אֱלֹהַי נְצוֹר לְשׁוֹנִי מֵרָע · וּשְׂפָתוֹתַי מִדַּבֵּר מִרְמָה · פְּתַח לִבִּי בְּתוֹרָתֶךָ · וְאַחֲרֵי מִצְוֹתֶיךָ תִּרְדּוֹף נַפְשִׁי:
יִהְיוּ לְרָצוֹן אִמְרֵי פִי וְהֶגְיוֹן לִבִּי לְפָנֶיךָ · יְיָ צוּרִי וְגוֹאֲלִי:

וְגָר זְאֵב עִם־כֶּבֶשׂ · וְנָמֵר עִם־גְּדִי יִרְבָּץ ·
וְעֵגֶל וּכְפִיר וּמְרִיא יַחְדָּו · וְנַעַר קָטֹן נֹהֵג בָּם:
לֹא־יָרֵעוּ וְלֹא־יַשְׁחִיתוּ בְּכָל־הַר קָדְשִׁי:

MORNING PRAYERS
FOR CHILDREN

Any of these passages can be used together with the first lines of the Shema and with any prayers of the child.

Blessed are You, Lord our God, king of the universe, who takes away sleep from my eyes and slumber from my eyelids.

> The Lord is my shepherd
> I shall not want.
> In green fields He lets me lie
> by quiet streams He leads me.
> Surely goodness and mercy will be with me
> all the days of my life,
> and I shall live in the house of the Lord forever.

May I always remember God when I am alone and when I am with others; speak the truth and keep the truth in my heart.

HEAR O ISRAEL, THE LORD IS OUR GOD, THE LORD IS ONE. LOVE THE LORD YOUR GOD WITH ALL YOUR HEART, AND ALL YOUR SOUL, AND ALL YOUR MIGHT.

My God, keep my tongue from causing harm and my lips from telling lies. Open my heart to Your teachings and help me to do them.

May the words I speak aloud and the thoughts that lie within my heart always please You, Lord, who gives me strength and saves me.

> The wolf shall live with the lamb,
> the leopard lie down with the kid,
> the calf and the young lion shall feed together,
> and a little child shall lead them.
> They shall not hurt nor destroy
> in all My holy mountain.

PASSAGES FOR SILENT DEVOTION AND FOR PERIODS OF SILENCE IN SERVICES

CONCERNING MEDITATION

Every man should devote much time to meditation between his Creator and himself. He should judge himself and determine whether his actions are correct, and whether they are appropriate before the Lord who has granted him life, and who is gracious to him every moment. If he finds that he has acted properly, he should fear no one—no officials, no robbers, no beasts—and nothing in the universe except the Lord. When he learns this, he will have attained, first: perfection in the study of the Torah and in meekness; and second: perfect worship wherein all material considerations are forgotten, worship which asks for no personal benefits, and which prompts one to forget his very existence.

Meditation before God brings forth the holy spark that is found in every Jew; for it lights up his heart, and thereby deprives him of all desire for evil.

In meditation a man may discuss his tribulations with God: he may excuse himself for his misdeeds and implore the Lord to grant him his desire to approach nearer to God. A man's offences separate him from his Maker.

It is impossible to be a good Jew without devoting each day a portion of the time to commune with the Lord in solitude, and to have a conversation from the heart with Him.

Even though a man may feel he cannot concentrate adequately upon the theme of his meditation, he should nevertheless continue to express his thoughts in words. Words are like water which falls continually upon a rock until it breaks it through. In similar fashion they will break through a man's flinty heart.

In true meditation a man cries to the Lord like a child to his father who is about to go on a journey. There is no sadness in this weeping—only longing and yearning.

Nachman of Bratzlav

Words are the shell, meditation the kernel. Words are the body of the prayer, and meditation its spirit.

Bachya

We do not even know how we are supposed to pray. All we do is call for help because of the need of the moment. But what the soul intends is spiritual need, only we are not able to express what the soul means. That is why we do not merely ask God to hear our call for help, but also beg Him who knows what is hidden, to hear the silent cry of the soul.

Martin Buber

The following prayers are based on those in the sixth edition of Forms of Prayer

I

God, I thank You for this time of prayer, when I become conscious of Your presence, and lay before You my desires, my hopes and my gratitude. This consciousness, this inner certainty of Your presence is my greatest blessing. My life would be empty if I did not have it, if I lost You in the maze of the world, and if I did not return to You from time to time, to be at one with You, certain of Your existence and Your love. It is good that You are with me in all my difficulties and troubles, and that I have in You a friend whose help is sure and whose love never changes.

I thank You for the prayers I share with others, which bind me to them. May my prayers be warmer because of their devotion, and together may we be joined to the whole family of Israel. The splendour of our tradition lives again in me, with its tragic memories and its call to holiness and service.

I thank You also for the light and truth which shine out from Your word; for the holy words written down by those whose souls were touched by Your spirit; for the teaching and the call which reach me from Your messengers, which come from their very lips. Help me to transform my thanks into service. Let my mind and my soul add to the holiness of life. May all that I have learnt in my worship here stay with me and keep me in goodness, so that my actions may be pure and my soul be at peace in the dust and heat of the world. Amen.

II

Almighty God, I praise You, and bless You for the week that has passed, for Your protection and Your mercy which have brought me safely through its difficulties and dangers. I thank You for the joys which have lightened it, for the strength which has upheld me in the worldly fight, and for the joy and rapture of the struggle itself. If the swift passing of the days has dulled their true meaning, if I have failed to hear Your voice in the clamour of the world and recognise Your presence in its blinding glare, please forgive me. I will try to do better in the days to come. You are my father, and what can I do alone? What is my strength—without Your aid!

Help me then, I beg You. Strengthen and bless the goodness in me. Help me to see more clearly what is worthwhile, and to keep to it more faithfully. Help me to pursue the true ideals I know with more purpose and determination. Then when this holy day of rest comes round again, it may mark another step on my way through life, on my way to the perfect peace that dwells forever with You. Amen.

III

Father, I thank You for the precious gift of this Sabbath, and for the rest it brings to my body and spirit. I thank You for the opportunities it gives me to come closer to those I love and to those who worship with me. I thank You for this welcome break in the round of toil and worldly occupations, for this chance of reading my own heart, of estimating more accurately how I stand towards You, and towards my own soul. On this day of calm and holiness I see my life more clearly and in its true perspective. My judgment of it comes nearer to Yours. The things I thought were big now seem pitifully small; and what I thought was worthless or unimportant now seems filled with significance and meaning. I compare my pleasures and possessions to the knowledge of Your truth and goodness and they fade into nothingness. Bless this clearer insight, this truer judgment. Give me the strength and integrity to go forward in joy, with this light which illuminates my being, into the coming week. Amen.

IV

I turn towards You, and pray for those I love, who are dearer to me than life. Protect them as a father, and keep them from harm, in

body, mind and spirit. Deepen their desire to know Your will, and strengthen them to do it. Help them in their struggle with the world, with selfishness, with laziness, and with forgetfulness of their own souls. Lord, help me as well, so that my own life does not contradict the life I desire for them. Let it serve them as an example, and help them in their struggle for goodness.

I thank You for those who are dear to me, for the privilege of guiding their steps towards You, for the love which binds our hearts together, for its joy, for its solace, and for the strength it gives me in trouble and temptation. Help me to keep that love strong. May no selfishness or misunderstanding weaken it. May it bless me to the end! Amen.

V

Even on this day of rest, I think of the working days which lie ahead, and ask for Your blessing on them. You are with me in the peace and holiness of the Sabbath, be with me even more in the stress and strain of the world. Therefore I ask You above all to bless my daily work. Let me do it for its own sake, and not for my own advantage; and let it show my service, not my selfishness. In this way I shall be at peace with my soul, and closer in sympathy and friendship to my fellow men. Keep me from laziness, and help me to perfect myself, so that the world in which I live comes nearer to its perfection. Help me to measure all things by the standard of goodness and not by the standard of worldly success. Let humble work be honourable for me. Let me prefer it to works whose fruits are vanity and strife. Help me to realise that there is a goal beyond my livelihood, and that there is a purpose on earth greater than comfort. Let this knowledge save me from undue sadness and despair when I have my share of failure. I cast on You my burden of anxiety and fear, for You know what is best for me. In riches and poverty, success and failure, You are with me, and in them all I learn to see Your face. Amen.

VI

Lord, I have not always been true to You in my thoughts. I have doubted Your goodness, Your justice and Your very existence. The pressures of life were too strong, its bitterness more than I could bear. Everything went wrong with my hopes and my plans, and there

seemed no way out, no way to turn. I said, 'There is no justice in this life of ours!' Sometimes my own suffering, but still more the suffering of others, strengthened my doubts. 'Why,' I asked, 'does God make His own children suffer? Where is His love? Where is His power?' At this point, You almost ceased to exist for me. Your hand would have held me, guided me, comforted me, but I lost touch with You. I should have looked for You more steadily, searched for You more diligently.

Out of my limited experience and my small knowledge, I judged the source of justice, and set my cleverness higher than the ultimate wisdom. I saw only one side of truth—the darkness, not the light. I forgot the smiling face of life and its beauty. I also forgot that the pain of life itself can lead to deeper compassion, and is a teacher of great wisdom. Because I was proud, and claimed to understand what was beyond me, I did not see that human goodness is a token of its creator's goodness.

Pardon my conceit and my blindness. Help me to greater detachment so that I may see with greater steadiness and calm. Help me to find order in the apparent chaos of human life, and love even in its defeats and trials. Your mercy is always there; You know and feel our pain. Amen.

———————

Master of all the worlds, fountainhead of all happiness . . .
Help me to immerse my meditations and all the impulses of my heart
   and the depths of my thought in the mysteries of joy . . .
And grant, O my Creator,
That I believe with complete faith that all fires of suffering
And all the nine measures of destitution and illness and pain, and the
   heaps of trouble in this world, and punishment in the next world,
   and
All the deaths—
That they are as nothing:
As absolutely nothing
As absolutely nothing
Against the wondrous joy of clinging to Your godliness,
And the sweetness of the Torah . . .
Therefore does my prayer stretch itself before You,

My Father in heaven,

Save me and help me from this moment to be alone in the fields
every night . . .

To cry out to You from the depths of my heart . . .

To set forth all the burdens and negations that remove me from You,
Light of Life,

And give strength to strengthen myself in spite of everything—

To strengthen myself with great happiness,

With happiness that has no end,

Until my heart lifts up my hands to clap, to clap, to clap, and my legs
to dance until the soul swoons, swoons.

And help me ever to make a new beginning and to be a flowering well
of Torah and prayer,

To work always with quickened spirit,

And to stand with powerful strength against the scoffers and mockers,

Who go about in our days—days of double darkness . . .

But oh, against all the trouble and burdens,

Your joys and Your delights are strong and powerful . . .

Oh our great Father, home of delights and wellspring of joy.

Nachman of Bratzlav

Worms, The Old Synagogue

Do not say 'When I have leisure I will study'; perhaps you will never have leisure.

Sayings of the Fathers

STUDY ANTHOLOGY

CONTENTS

THE SABBATH

Our Father, Source of all blessings, be with us on this Sabbath
eve. Thou hast ordained for us times and seasons, so that every day
brings its opportunities, and each Sabbath its beneficent power.
Even as joy succeeds to sorrow, so does the Sabbath peace follow
the turmoil of our work-a-day lives. With gratitude and with hope we
lift up our hearts to thee, and ask thee to sanctify this day of rest.
Bless our toil in the days just gone: for that wherein we have failed,
do thou forgive us; and that which we have achieved do thou make
pure. Purge away our vain self-seeking, and renew in us our strivings
after truth. Send the light of joy and peace into our homes on this
Sabbath day, so that its holiness may illumine the coming week.
Unite us with our dear ones in thine all-hallowing love. So may we
keep faith with thine ancient covenant, and find acceptance in thy
sight. Amen.

LISTENING

Six days he has worked and attended to all his affairs; now, on the
seventh, he rests. Six days he has uttered the many useful and useless
things the workday demanded of him, but on the seventh he obeys
the command of the prophet; he lets his tongue rest from the talk of
every day, and learns to be silent, to *listen*. And this sanctifying of
the day of rest by listening to God's voice in silence must be shared
by all members of his house. It must not be fretted by the voice of

command. The man-servant and the maid-servant must also rest; and it is even said that just for the sake of their rest the day of rest was instituted, for when rest has penetrated to them, then all the house is, indeed, freed from the noise and chatter of the weekday, and redeemed to rest.

Franz Rosenzweig

BUSINESS PERMITTED ON THE SABBATH

Rabbi Chisda and Rabbi Hamnuna said that it is permissible to make plans for good deeds on the Sabbath; and Rabbi Elazar said that one may arrange about alms to the poor on Sabbath. Rabbi Yochanan said: One may transact business which has to do with the saving of life or with public health on Sabbath, and one may go to synagogue to discuss public affairs on Sabbath. Rabbi Jonathan said: One may even go to theatres and circuses on Sabbath for such a purpose. And in the school of Manasseh it was said that one may talk about the future marriage of one's children on Sabbath, or about the children's education, or about teaching them a handicraft, for the Scripture forbids 'your business', but *God's* business is permitted.

Shabbat

PEACE AND HARMONY

The goal of man is to live again in peace and harmony with his fellow men, with animals, with the soil. But this new harmony is different from that in paradise. It can now be obtained only if man develops fully in order to become truly human, by knowing the truth and doing justly, by developing his power of reason to a point which frees him from the bondage of man and of irrational passions. . . . On the Sabbath, in the state of rest, man anticipates the state of human freedom that will be fulfilled eventually, when the Messiah will come. The relationship of man and nature and of man and man is one of harmony, peace and non-interference. Where work is a symbol of conflict and disharmony, rest is an expression of dignity, peace and freedom. . . . That is why the Sabbath commandment is at one time motivated by God's rest and at the other by the liberation from Egypt. Both mean the same and interpret each other: rest is freedom.

Erich Fromm

SOME SABBATH LAWS

It is written: 'Remember the Sabbath day to keep it holy', which means to remember daily the Sabbath day to keep it holy; thus on coming across a delicious food of a rare kind, and which is not liable to be spoilt through keeping it, it should be purchased in honour of the Sabbath. . . .

It is mandatory upon all, even upon one having numerous domestics, to do something in honour of the Sabbath, thereby doing homage to it. . . .

A man who eats ordinary bread on week-days, must surely take care to eat on the holy Sabbath *challah*. . . .

One should prepare choice meat, fish, dessert and good wines, in accordance with his means. . . .

All deeds should be reviewed on the day preceding the Sabbath and repentance aroused, resolving to amend all misdeeds committed during the six days. . . .

It is mandatory to honour the Sabbath by the lighting of many candles—no less than two. . . . The candles should be big so that they should burn at least till after the meal, and one should take care to buy nice candles.

It is well that women should give some charity before lighting the candles.

Kitzur Shulchan Aruch

HIGHER THAN SUCCESS

There are objects in life higher than success. The Sabbath, with its exhortation to the worship of God and the doing of kindly deeds, reminds us week by week of these higher objects. It prevents us reducing our life to the level of a machine. The gathered experience of mankind, that the break in the routine of work one day in seven will heighten the value of the very work itself, is not lightly to be put aside. The Sabbath is one of the glories of our humanity. For if to labour is noble, of our own free will to pause in that labour which may lead to success, to money, or to fame, may be nobler still. To dedicate one day a week to rest and to God, this is the prerogative and privilege of man alone. It is an ordinance which we may rightly call Divine.

C. G. Montefiore

A SIMPLE MEAL

A simple vegetable meal on the Sabbath in a home where there is love between husband, wife and children is better than a fatted ox in a home where there is hatred. A man should not plan to honour the Sabbath with delicacies while he knows that he will quarrel with his wife, or father, or mother. Whether it be Sabbath or festival—'Better a dry morsel and quietness therewith, than a house full of feasting with strife' (*Proverbs 17 : 1*). One should honour the Sabbath by having no strife thereon.

Judah HeChasid

SOME SAYINGS OF THE RABBIS

The Sabbath was made for man, not man for the Sabbath.

Mechilta

On Sabbath a man should always walk with an easy and leisured gait; but to do a good act, interposed Rabbi Joshua ben Levi, a man should always run, even on Sabbath.

Tanchuma

Rabbi Jose ben Judah said: The angels of the service accompany a man on Friday evening from the Synagogue to his house, one good and one bad angel; and if, when he comes to his house, the lamp is lit, and the table spread, and the couch arranged, the good angel says: 'May it be God's will that the next Sabbath may be as this one', to which the bad angel, even against his will, says: 'Amen'. But if it is not so, then the bad angel says: 'May it be God's will that thus it may be on the next Sabbath also', and the good angel, against his will, says: 'Amen'.

Shabbat

The Sassover Rabbi narrated the following parable: 'A man invited an important personage for a Sabbath meal, and prepared a sumptuous meal for him. Later, however, he changed his mind, and did not call for his guest.'

In similar fashion, many persons make elaborate preparations to welcome the Sabbath, but the atmosphere at their table is the same as on a week-day, and no Sabbath hymns are chanted.

Chasidic

GOD'S PROPERTY

The Sabbath is a proclamation and acknowledgement of our task as man and Jews.

It is a 'covenant', the basis of every relationship between God and the Jew. For if we consider the world and ourselves as God's property, and regard our power over the earth as lent to us by God for the fulfilment of our task in life, then will our life be lived in accordance with the Torah. But if we regard the world as our own and ourselves as its master, then the contract is torn up.

Finally it is a 'Blessing'; if we renew our covenant with God every Sabbath, and dedicate ourself as God's servant then, on every Sabbath, God will give us renewed enlightenment of the spirit. Our Teachers describe this higher state of the soul by saying that the Sabbath provides us with an 'extra soul'.

Samson Raphael Hirsch

THE CREATION OF PEACE

The Bible tells us that on the seventh day God *finished* His work. Our Teachers concluded from this that there was an act of creation on the seventh day.

What was created on the seventh day? Tranquillity, serenity, peace and repose.

Rest (*M'nucha*) is the same as happiness and stillness, as peace and harmony. . . . It is the state in which there is no strife and no fighting, no fear and no distrust. The essence of good life is *m'nucha*. . . .

Six evenings a week we pray: 'Guard our going out and our coming in'; on the Sabbath eve, however, we pray: 'Spread over us the shelter of Your peace.'

Abraham Joshua Heschel

TRADITION

Sovereign of the universe, thou hast sustained us day by day during the week that is past, and hast brought us to this holy Sabbath with all its precious opportunities. Help us to be worthy of these thy mercies. Thou hast lent us this day; help us to give it back to thee by devoting it to thy service. O God, when our worship is ended, let its benign influence remain with us to sanctify the whole of this coming week, ennobling our most familiar tasks, hallowing our worldly work

with sincerity and rectitude, putting to shame every base longing. May our pleasures leave behind them no regret, no self-reproach. Amen.

PRAYER

The one who prays, knows, with the knowledge of experience, that beyond the visible dimensions of this world there is a hidden dimension of our existence in which something of the significance of a man's being is revealed to him, revealed to a greater or lesser degree, in keeping with the strength of the communion. It is a matter of experience, and experience, as is well known, is not debatable.

S. H. Bergman

The Baal Shem said: Imagine a man whose business hounds him through many streets and across the market-place the livelong day. He almost forgets that there is a Maker of the World. Only when the time for the Afternoon Prayer comes, does he remember: 'I must pray.' And then, from the bottom of his heart, he heaves a sigh of regret that he has spent his day on vain and idle matters, and he runs into a side-street and stands there and prays: God holds him dear, very dear, and his prayer pierces the firmament.

TRADITION

Why do we say: 'Our God and the God of our fathers'? There are two sorts of persons who believe in God. The one believes because his faith has been handed down to him by his fathers; and his faith is strong. The other has arrived at faith by dint of searching thought. And this is the difference between the two; the first has the advantage that his faith cannot be shaken, no matter how many objections are raised to it, for his faith is firm because he has taken it over from his fathers. But there is a flaw in it: it is a commandment given by man, and it has been learned without thought or reasoning. The advantage of the second man is that he has reached faith through his own power, through much searching and thinking. But his faith too has a flaw; it is easy to shake it by offering contrary evidence. But he who combines both kinds of faith is invulnerable. That is why we say: 'Our God', because of our searching, and 'the God of our fathers', because of our tradition.

Baal Shem Tov

A man must not depend on the work of his ancestors. If a man does not do good in this world, he cannot fall back on the merit of his fathers. No man will eat in the Time-To-Come of his father's works, but only of his own.

Midrash Tehillim

Said the 'Yud': 'We find that a father strives to help his son to become a learned man and pious Jew. When the son grows up, he in turn endeavours to make his own son become a good Jew. But will the time ever come when the father himself will strive to be a good Jew, instead of leaving the task to his son?'

Do not consider a thing as proof because you find it written in books: for just as a liar will deceive with his tongue, he will not be deterred from doing the same thing with his pen. They are utter fools who accept a thing as convincing proof simply because it is in writing.

Maimonides

A truth, once established by proof, neither gains force by the consent of all scholars, nor loses certainty because of the general dissent.

Maimonides

One fate *all* the Judaisms of the past shared in common. All of them began as rebellions, as great reformations, but after receiving widespread acceptance, developed vested 'priestly' interests, failed their people, and were forced to retreat before the onslaught of new rebellions, new philosophies, new challenges. . . .

Is there, then, nothing but change? Is change the end of all our history and all our striving? No, there is something else, the desire to be free. If the Jew has survived from Bible days to our own time, it is because at crucial moments he has refused to let others think and decide for him; he has in the end always chosen to be free, and never, never will he allow any one religion of Judaism eternal domination over him. In the end, he has always understood that changelessness is spiritual death. The Jew who would *live* must never completely surrender himself to one truth, but constantly, desperately, and—if need be—with anguish, must reach out for the farther and faint horizons of an ever Greater God and a more sublime faith.

Jacob Rader Marcus

When the great Rabbi Israel Baal Shem Tov saw misfortune threatening the Jews it was his custom to go into a certain part of the forest to meditate. There he would light a fire, say a special prayer, and the miracle would be accomplished and the misfortune averted.

Later, when his disciple, the celebrated Magid of Mezritch, had occasion, for the same reason, to intercede with heaven, he would go to the same place in the forest and say: 'Master of the Universe, listen! I do not know how to light the fire, but I am still able to say the prayer', and again the miracle would be accomplished.

Still later, Rabbi Moshe-Leib of Sasov, in order to save his people once more, would go into the forest and say: 'I do not know how to light the fire, I do not know the prayer, but I know the place and this must be sufficient.' It was sufficient and the miracle was accomplished.

Then it fell to Rabbi Israel of Rizhyn to overcome misfortune. Sitting in his armchair, his head in his hands, he spoke to God: 'I am unable to light the fire and I do not know the prayer, I cannot even find the place in the forest. All I can do is to tell the story, and this must be sufficient.' And it was sufficient.

Elie Wiesel

Many people prowl round Mount Sinai. Their speech is blurred, either they are garrulous or they shout or they are taciturn. But none of them comes straight down a broad, newly made, smooth road that does its own part in making one's strides long and swifter.

Franz Kafka

TORAH AND INTERPRETATION

The Law of Moses does not include philosophical theories, or logical investigations, or proofs involving high inquiries. For man's success is above Reason and beyond Nature.

Abravanel

The Torah does not oblige us to believe absurdities.

Joseph Albo

Those who learn for the sake of learning find the Torah sweet; those who learn for ulterior purposes find it bitter.

Zohar

He who feels, after many trials, that the soul within him can find repose only when it is occupied with the mysteries of the Torah, should know that for this has he been destined.

May no obstacle in the world, fleshly or even spiritual, confuse or turn him from the pursuit of the fountain of his life, his true fulfilment.

And it is well for him to know that not only his own self-fulfilment and salvation wait upon the satisfaction of this tendency within him. . . . . The saving of society and the perfecting of the world also depend upon it. For a soul fulfilled helps to fulfil the world. True thoughts, when they flow without hindrance into any one of the corners of life, bless all of life.

But should he abandon his search, and wander about seeking water from wells which are not really his, then, though he draw water as much as the ocean, and take from streams in every part of the earth, yet will he not find peace. For like a bird who has wandered from his nest, so is the man who wanders from his place.

Rav Kook

Rabbi Simlai taught: Six hundred and thirteen commandments were given to Moses. Then David reduced them to eleven in Psalm 15, beginning: 'He who follows integrity, who does what is right and speaks the truth in his heart'.

Micah reduced them to three (*Micah 6 : 8*):
'Act justly, love mercy and walk humbly with your God.'
Then came Isaiah and reduced them to two (*Isaiah 56 : 1*):
'Keep justice and act with integrity.'
Amos reduced them to one (*Amos 5 : 4*):
'Seek Me and live.'
Habakuk also contained them in one (*Habakuk 2 : 4*):
'But the righteous shall live by his faith.'
Akiba taught: 'The great principle of the Torah is expressed in the commandment: "Love your neighbour as you love yourself; I am the Lord".' (*Leviticus 19 : 18*).
But Ben Azai taught a greater principle (*Genesis 5 : 1*):
'This is the book of the generations of man. When God created man, He made him in the likeness of God.'

Makkot

Make not the fence higher than the law itself.

Chiyya Rabbah

The Torah was not given to angels.

Berachot

The Torah is eternal, but its explanation is to be made by the spiritual leaders of Judaism . . . in accordance with the age.

Baal Shem Tov

A man should always study the Torah even if his motives are not worthy, for by studying out of unworthy motives he will come to study out of worthy ones.

Shulchan Aruch

HALACHAH AND AGGADAH

Halachah represents the strength to shape one's life according to a fixed pattern; it is a form-giving force. *Aggadah* is the expression of man's ceaseless striving, which often defies all limitations. *Halachah* is the rationalisation and schematisation of living; it defines, specifies, sets measure and limit, placing life into an exact system. *Aggadah* deals with man's ineffable relations to God, to other men, and to the world. *Halachah* deals with details, with each commandment separately; *aggadah* with the whole of life, with the totality of religious life. *Halachah* deals with the law, *aggadah* with the meaning of the law. *Halachah* deals with subjects that can be expressed literally; *aggadah* introduces us to a realm which lies beyond the range of expression. *Halachah* teaches us how to perform common acts; *aggadah* tells us how to participate in the eternal drama. *Halachah* gives us knowledge; *aggadah* exaltation. *Halachah* prescribes, *aggadah* suggests; *halachah* decrees, *aggadah* inspires; *halachah* is definite, *aggadah* is allusive.

To maintain that the essence of Judaism consists exclusively of *halachah* is as erroneous as to maintain that the essence of Judaism consists exclusively of *aggadah*.

The interrelationship of *halachah* and *aggadah* is the very heart of Judaism. *Halachah* without *aggadah* is dead, *aggadah* without *halachah* is wild.

Abraham Joshua Heschel

AVODAH—SERVICE

If you weary in the service of God, it means you are carrying other burdens, not that of the yoke of heaven.

Dubner Maggid

This is the service man must perform all of his days: to shape matter into form, to refine the flesh, and to let the light penetrate the

darkness, until the darkness itself shines and there is no longer any division between the two. As it is written: 'And there was evening and there was morning, one day.'

One should not make a great to-do about serving God. Does the hand boast when it carries out what the heart wills?

Chasidic

Faith, love and sorrow are three elements that mysteriously blend in human experience, each having its own tale to tell of the relation which we bear to the Supreme Being.

O. J. Simon

Our religion has three elements: fear, love and joy, by each of which one can draw near to God.

Judah Halevi

Worship inspired by fear is worship, but it does not rise to the highest part of the supernal sphere. That is reserved for worship inspired by love.

Zohar

GEMILUT CHASADIM—LOVING DEEDS

Simon the Just said: 'Civilization is based on three things—on Torah, on service and on loving deeds.' As regards the third, it is said (*Hosea 6: 6*): 'I desired love, and not sacrifice.' The world at the beginning was created only by love, as it is said (*Psalm 89: 3*): 'The world is built by love.' It happened that Rabbi Yochanan ben Zakkai went out from Jerusalem, and Rabbi Joshua followed him, and he saw the burnt ruins of the Temple, and he said: 'Woe is it that the place where the sins of Israel find atonement is laid waste.' Then said Rabbi Yochanan: 'Grieve not, we have an atonement equal to the Temple, the doing of loving deeds', as it is said: 'I desire love, and not sacrifice'.

Avot d'Rabbi Natan

In the future world man will be asked: 'What was your occupation?' If he replies: 'I fed the hungry', then they reply: 'This is the gate of the Lord; he who feeds the hungry, let him enter' (*Psalm 118: 20*). So with giving drink to the thirsty, clothing the naked, with those who look after orphans, and with those, generally, who do deeds of loving kindness. All these are gates of the Lord, and those who do such deeds shall enter within them.

Midrash Tehillim

DERECH ERETZ—CONDUCT AND RESPECT

If you have a guest, never speak to him about learned matters unless you know he is able to take part in the conversation.

Judah HeChasid

In the academy, follow wisdom; at a banquet, age.

Ammi ben Nathan

How foolish are those who rise before a scroll and not before a great man!

Raba

Respect an old man who has lost his learning through no fault of his own. The fragments of the Tablets broken by Moses were kept in the Ark of the Covenant alongside the new ones.

Judah bar Ilai

The best security for old age: respect your children.

Sholem Asch

God spoke to Moses respectfully, not like a tyrant.

Eleazar ben Arak

BIKKUR CHOLIM—VISITING THE SICK

One should not neglect to invoke Divine compassion on every sick person he visits. If one spent time with the sick but forgot to pray for Divine compassion, he has not fulfilled the *mitzvah* completely . . . . One may pray for the sick in any language he wishes since he is addressing his words directly to the *Shechinah* (the presence of God) which is at the side of the patient . . . . He should say: 'May the All-present have mercy upon you among the sick ones of Israel.' For Sabbath the formula is: 'It is Sabbath, to cry out is forbidden. But the cure will come speedily, and His mercies are many. Have a peaceful Sabbath.'

Chafetz Chaim

THE WILL OF GOD

Said Rabbi Bunam: 'Two merchants go to the Leipzig Fair. One goes by a direct route, another by an indirect, but both reach the same destination. Likewise, the aim of service to God is to attain holiness, and to arrive at the point where we make God's will our own. Hence, as long as we reach this point, it makes no difference how long we have served the Lord. One may die young or in the prime of life and

become just as holy as one who has died in old age. We are taught by
the Talmud: "It is the same whether one does much or little, so long
as he has aimed to do God's will."'

BLESSING

The Rabbis asked: What is meant by the phrase: 'May the Lord
bless you and keep you'? One Rabbi explained it: 'God will bless you
with wealth and He will watch over you, that with that wealth you
shall perform *mitzvot*, good and beautiful deeds that shall resound
to the glory of our God, to the honour and blessedness of our people!'

Numbers Rabbah

First become a blessing to yourself that you may be a blessing to
others.

Samson Raphael Hirsch

TESHUVAH—REPENTANCE

What is the punishment of a sinner?

Wisdom Literature answered: 'Evil pursues sinners!' (*Proverbs
13: 21*)

Prophetical Literature answered: 'The soul that sins, it shall die!'
(*Ezekiel 18: 4*)

The Torah answered: 'Let him bring a trespass-offering and he
will be forgiven.' (*Based on Leviticus 1: 4*)

When the question was asked of the Holy One, blessed be He, He
replied: 'Let him repent and he will be forgiven, as it is said: "Good
and upright is the Lord, therefore He shows the way to sinners."'
(*Psalm 25: 8*)

Yerushalmi

A king had a son who had gone astray from his father a journey of
a hundred days. His friends said to him: 'Return to your father.'
He said: 'I cannot; it is too far.' Then his father sent to say: 'Return
as far as you can, and I will come to you the rest of the way.' So God
says to man: 'Return to Me, and I will return to you.'

Pesikta Rabbati

The first step towards repentance, which is the most essential and
at the same time the most difficult, is confession, or rather 'the
admission to oneself' that one has sinned. It is not God who needs an
avowal or confession from us, for He knows us through and through;

in fact, much better than we know ourselves. But we ourselves stand very much in need of honest and unreserved confession; it is to our own selves that we must admit that we have done wrong.

Samson Raphael Hirsch

A *chasid* complained to Rabbi Zev Wolf of Zbarazh that certain persons were turning night into day, playing cards. 'That is good,' said the Zaddik. 'Like all people, they want to serve God and don't know how. But now they are learning to stay awake and persist in doing something. When they have become perfect in this, all they need do is turn to God—and what excellent servants they will make for Him then!'

SHEMA

Whom does one address when one says: 'Hear O Israel'?

Each person addresses his neighbour, to encourage him in his affirmation of his faith.

Each person is both Jacob, the trickster, and Israel, the patriarch. In the Shema he speaks to Israel, to encourage the higher self within him.

A man must recite a blessing for evil, just as he recites a blessing for good. For it is said:

'Love the Lord your God with all your heart, and all your soul, and all your might.'

'With all your heart'—with your two wills, with your good will and your will towards evil.

'And all your soul'—even if He takes your soul from you.

'And all your strength'—for every measure that He measures out to you, thank Him with all your might.

Mishnah

'Love the Lord your God with all your heart, and all your soul . . .'

Rabbi Akiba says 'all your soul'—even if He takes away your soul from you. . . .

When Rabbi Akiba was taken out to be killed by the Romans, it was the time for the reading of the Shema, and they kept flaying his flesh with iron combs, yet he accepted upon himself the yoke of the kingdom of heaven (by reciting the Shema). His disciples said to him: 'Still constant, master?' He said to them: 'All my days I was troubled

by this explanation: "with all your soul"—even if He takes your soul from you. I said: "O that it were in my power to fulfil this!" And now that it is in my power, shall I not fulfil it?' He kept prolonging the 'One', until his spirit left him at 'One'. A voice issued from heaven and said: 'Happy are you, Rabbi Akiba, that your spirit has left you at "One".'

Berachot

'With all your heart . . . soul . . . strength.' Rabbi Eliezer said: 'After we are told to love God with our whole life, why are we then told to love Him with all our strength i.e. our wealth? There are persons to whom life is more precious than wealth. They are admonished to love Him with all their life. But there are others whose actions show that wealth is dearer to them than life. Such people are asked to love God with all their wealth.'

Berachot

Said the Koretzer: 'We recite in the Shema: "These things . . . shall be upon your heart. Repeat them to your children. . . ." When these words go forth from your heart, they will truly influence your children for good.'

'This will happen if you listen carefully to My commands which I give you today, to love the Lord your God . . .' (Second paragraph of Shema).

Beware lest you be tempted to think: 'I shall study in order to acquire wealth, or to have the honour of being addressed as Rabbi, or that I may earn a reward in the world to come.' The Torah says: 'to love'. All that you do must have the pure aim of expressing your love for God.

Sifre

LIFE AND DEATH

We come to thee, O God, for thy gracious help. Give us strength to bear our load of care; give us clearness of vision so that we may see the wisdom and the love which have laid it upon us. Help us to be true to our better selves, to discern our real work in life, and to do it with all our might. Be by our side when we are struggling with our own hearts, when we seek to rise above our failings and weaknesses. Help us to realise life's meaning, to understand its solemnity, so that each day we live may be yet another step leading us nearer to thee. Amen.

BIRTH

Rabbi Chanina bar Pappa expounded: The name of the angel appointed over conception is *Laylah* (Night). He takes the seed and lays it before the Holy One, blessed be He, and says to Him: 'Master of the universe, what is this seed to be—mighty or weak, wise or foolish, rich or poor?' But he does not say 'wicked or righteous'— for all is in the hands of heaven, except the fear of heaven.

Niddah

Before a child is born, a light is held behind its head with which it can see from one end of the world to the other, and they teach it the whole of the Torah. But at the moment of birth an angel touches it on the lips, and it forgets all. So all of life is spent remembering what we once knew.

Based on Niddah

Unless we believe that God renews the work of creation every day, our prayers and doing of the commandments grow old and accustomed and tedious. As it is written in the psalm (*Psalm 71: 9*): 'Cast me not off in the time of old age'—that is to say, do not let my world grow old.

Chasidic

YOUTH AND MANHOOD

In Genesis we read of Abraham and Isaac on their way to an altar. We can read this chapter and discover something which refers to every man throughout the ages. It tells of a change which takes place when a youngster leaves adolescence and enters mature manhood. Noble youth is full of the desire to sacrifice itself. There is a cause. How else can youth serve the good cause than through readiness for sacrifice? Youth has no experience and no skill to serve mankind. But it has its life. To give their lives so that others may benefit is the desire of noble hearts. But there comes a moment which brings the understanding that the good cause can be served by hard work into which goes much sacrifice. But this sacrifice is without self-immolation. It is a sacrifice in which life is not sacrificed but is rendered in obedience to demands as they appear in the course of life itself. When the understanding of this sacrifice arrives in the heart of a youth, he leaves adolescence behind and enters manhood. He ceases to be a 'son' and can become what a father is: a man obedient to the duties which have to be performed in life. Isaac's sacrifice is no longer what the noble heart demands. Isaac can leave the place

where life is sacrificed. Isaac can grow up, marry and become what Abraham is: a *Baal Habayit*, the priestly father of a home. This is the story which happens eternally when history does not consume, as it so often does, the hecatombs of sacrifices and lets the young grow old.

Ignaz Maybaum

LIFE'S JOURNEY

O my soul, prepare provision in abundance, prepare not little, while you are yet alive, and while your hand has yet strength, because the journey is too great for you. And say not: 'I shall prepare provision tomorrow'; for the day has declined, and you do not know what the next day may bring. Know likewise that yesterday shall never come back, and that whatever you have done therein is weighed, numbered and counted. Nor should you say: 'I shall do it tomorrow'; for the day of death is hidden from all the living. Hasten to your task every day.

Bachya

As the hand held before the eye hides the tallest mountain, so this small earthly life hides from our gaze the vast radiance and secrets of which the world is full, and whoever can take life from before his eyes, as one takes away one's hand, will see the great radiance within the world.

Chasidic

PURPOSE

Rabbi Zusya of Hanipol said: In the coming world they will not ask me 'Why were you not Moses?' but 'Why were you not Zusya?'

The Bratslaver said: Declare at all times: 'The world was created for my sake.' Do not declare: 'Of what concern is this to me?' But do your share to add some improvement, to supply something that is missing, and to leave the world a little better for your sojourn in it.

On the dark path on which a man is to walk here on earth just as much light is provided as he wants in order to make the next step. More would only dazzle, and every side-light bewilder him.

Moses Mendelssohn

Scholars passed by a dead dog. The disciples said: 'How awful its smell!' Their master said: 'How white its teeth!'

Bachya

LOVE

To serve God out of love is to fulfil the Torah . . . . But this is a high level of piety, and not every sage attains it.

Maimonides

To love God truly, one must first love man. And if anyone tells you that he loves God and does not love his fellow-man, you will know that he is lying.

Chasidic

EARNING LOVE

What you must do is love your neighbour as yourself. There is no one who knows your many faults better than you! But you love yourself notwithstanding. And so you must love your neighbour, no matter how many faults you see in him.

Chasidic

When love was strong, we could have made our bed on a sword's blade; now, when it has become weak, a bed of sixty cubits is not large enough for us.

Sanhedrin

There is none more lonely than the man who loves only himself.

Abraham Ibn Ezra

Everyone has in his life a beautiful day when, like the first human beings in Eden, he finds love without care and trouble. But when this day is past, you earn love, as you earn bread, by the sweat of the brow.

Ludwig Boerne

LEARNING FROM LIFE

There was that law of life, so cruel and so just, which demanded that one must grow or else pay more for remaining the same.

Norman Mailer

He who does not increase his knowledge, decreases it.

Sayings of the Fathers

What is it that troubles you? Death?—Who lives forever?
Or because your foot has stumbled on the earth? There is no man who has never stumbled.

Shmuel HaNagid

Sadness is the worst quality in a man. It is the attribute of an incurable egotist. He is always thinking: 'Something should rightfully come to me; something is wrongfully lacking to me.' Whether in relation to substance or spirit, it is always 'I'.

The Alexanderer Rabbi

He who in his life has never made a fool of himself has also never been wise.

Heinrich Heine

THE PATH OF LIFE

The world is like a fair: People gather for a while, then part; some profit and rejoice, others lose and grieve.

Bachya

Days are scrolls: write on them what you want to be remembered.

Bachya

One thing acquired through pain is better for man than one hundred things easily acquired.

Midrash

A man cannot say to the Angel of Death: 'I wish to arrange my affairs before I die.'

Midrash

What should a man do that he may live? Destroy his self.

Tamid

There is no room for God in a man who is full of himself.

Chasidic

Every day man is sold, and every day redeemed.
Every day man's spirit is taken from him and . . . returned to him in the morning.
Every day miracles are worked for him as for those who went out of Egypt.
Every day redemption is worked for him as for those who went out of Egypt.
Every day he is fed on the breasts of his mother.
Every day he is chastised for his deeds, like a child by his teacher.

Seder Eliyahu Rabbah

LIVELIHOOD

They tell a story of the Dubner Maggid, the famous preacher of the east European ghettos. Once he was asked by the mighty scholar

called the Vilna Gaon to tell him his faults. The Maggid at first declined. When the Gaon pressed him, he at last spoke somewhat like this: 'Very well. You are the most pious man of our age. You study night and day, retired from the world, surrounded by the rows of your books, the Holy Ark, the faces of devout scholars. You have reached high holiness. How have you achieved it? Go down in the market place, Gaon, with the rest of the Jews. Endure their work, their strains, their distractions. Mingle in the world, hear the scepticism and irreligion they hear, take the blows they take. Submit to the ordinary trials of the ordinary Jew. Let us see then if you will remain the Vilna Gaon!' They say the Gaon broke down and wept.

Herman Wouk

Some people think of business when they are at the Synagogue. Is it too much to ask them to think of God when they are at business?

Nachman of Kosov

OLD AGE

A Rabbi was once passing through a field where he saw a very old man planting an oak-tree. 'Why are you planting that tree?' said he. 'You surely do not expect to live long enough to see the acorn growing up into an oak-tree?'

'Ah,' replied the old man, 'my ancestors planted trees not for themselves, but for us, in order that we might enjoy their shade and fruit. I am doing likewise for those who will come after me.'

Ta'anit

Grant me clearness of vision to see life as a whole from youth to age and to be comforted in the faith that the best is yet to be. In moments of doubt and despondency when, like the patriarch Jacob, I count my days as few and evil and when the waning of my bodily powers makes me declare with the sage, I have no pleasure in them, then sustain me with a realization of those blessings which the maturity of age alone can bring and the ripeness of experience alone can yield. Give me the sweetness of that joy which is reserved for those who serve others through the counsel and guidance learned in the school of life's experience. . . .

Enable me to hold fast, however old I may grow, to the spirit of youth. Suffer me not to lose that sense of wonder which stirs within me in the presence of Your creation. Renew me from day to day with that power of communion with You which restores my soul.

I crave the power to see ever more clearly that other half of life's plan, which youth cannot discern. Sustain me with the faith that wrong, cruelty, and injustice cannot prevail, but that the right, the pure and true shall endure. And may the imperishable worth of life uphold me in the deathless hope of the hereafter.

Let me not be afraid! As one by one my bodily powers weaken, may my soul enter into greater freedom and be purified and atoned in Your sight. Let me die the death of the righteous and let my end be like his. Amen.

Union Prayer Book

HUMILITY

Do not resemble a big door which lets in the wind; or a small door which makes the worthy bend down; but resemble the threshold on which all may tread, or a low peg on which all can hang their things.

Derech Eretz Zuta

Everyone must have two pockets, so that he can reach into the one or the other, according to his needs. In his right pocket are to be the words: 'For my sake was the world created', and in his left: 'I am dust and ashes.'

Rabbi Bunam of Pzhysha

A man of piety complained to the Besht, saying, 'I have laboured hard and long in the service of the Lord, and yet I have received no improvement. I am still an ordinary and ignorant person.'

The Besht answered: 'You have gained the realization that you are ordinary and ignorant, and this in itself is a worthy accomplishment.'

Chasidic

The difficulty is, of course, that too many people, when they evaluate the events of their lives, seem to take it for granted that the universe was created especially for them. Such a self-centered theory holds a great appeal for the egotist but, judging from the monotonous regularity with which nature makes and destroys every kind of living organism, it is rationally unsound. Much more realistic and much more sensible is the Jewish point of view that one must attempt to accommodate himself to the world as he finds it, rather than expect the world to accommodate itself fully to his human wishes and his human dreams.

David Max Eichhorn

REALITY

Man is afraid of things that cannot harm him, and he knows it. And he longs for things that cannot help him, and he knows it. But actually it is something within man that he is afraid of, and it is something within man that he longs for.

Chasidic

In a dream we live seventy years and discover, on awakening, that it was a quarter of an hour. In our life which passes as a dream, we live seventy years, and then we waken to a greater understanding which shows us that it was a quarter of an hour.

Chasidic

JOY

Rav said: A man will have to give account in the judgment day of every good thing which he might have enjoyed and did not.

Yerushalmi

One should not stand up to say the Tefillah (the Amidah) while immersed in sorrow, or idleness, or laughter, or frivolity, or chatter, or idle talk, but only while rejoicing in the performance of a religious act.

Berachot

SHARING JOY

Rabbi Baruka of Huza frequented the market of Lapet. One day Elijah appeared to him there, and Rabbi Baruka asked him: 'Is there among the people of this market anyone that is destined to share in the world to come?' Elijah replied, 'There is none' . . . . Then two men appeared on the scene and Elijah said, 'These two will share in the world to come.' Rabbi Baruka asked them, 'What is your occupation?' They said, 'We are merry-makers; when we see a man who is downcast, we cheer him up; also when we see two people quarrelling with one another, we try to make peace between them.'

Ta'anit

Show business has been good to me all these years, and the biggest bonus has really been the pleasure of making people laugh and helping them to forget their troubles for a few hours.

Bud Flanagan

There are men who suffer terrible distress and are unable to tell what they feel in their hearts, and they go their way and suffer and

suffer. But if they meet one with a laughing face, he can revive them with his joy. And to revive a man is no slight thing.

Nachman of Bratzlav

SUFFERING

Whenever one is confronted with an inescapable, unavoidable situation, whenever one has to face a fate which cannot be changed, e.g. an incurable disease, such as an incurable cancer; just then one is given a last chance to actualize the highest value, to fulfil the deepest meaning, the meaning of suffering. For what matters above all is the attitude we take towards suffering, the attitude in which we take our suffering upon ourselves.

Viktor Frankl

Do we not all make the experience that the most precious possessions we call our own must be gained and earned by fight and suffering and pain? We should not know how to estimate their true value, if they fell into our lap without endeavour. Health is appreciated as a possession only by him who has passed through illness, freedom only by him who has seen oppression, and we should not cling to life if there were no death. We just do not know whether what we call an evil fate will not later prove to be good fortune. When Mephisto calls himself 'Part of that force which ever wants the evil and ever forms the good,' he thereby expresses that owing to some higher wisdom the good, even through the evil, reaches its goal. It is this deep, religious thought with which Joseph consoles his brothers: 'You indeed thought to do evil unto me, but God has thought it for good.' Nahum of Gimzo is said to have received this name because he used to say about all that occurred to him: 'Gam zu le-tauvoh' this also is for the good. To be able to speak like that from the depths of one's heart, one must to be sure have unshakeable faith in God, who always means well with His creatures, and, even where He visits us, chastises us, 'as a father chastises his son.' (*Deuteronomy 8 : 5*). This is a faith which knows the 'secret things belong unto the Lord, our God' (*Deuteronomy 29: 28*), that there are not only riddles in the world—riddles may be solved after all—but also eternal secrets before which we can only bow in humility. It is a faith which confronted with the eternal problem of evil, utters the brave words 'and nevertheless' (*Leviticus 26: 44*). Even when death bereaves man of his dearest, the faithful devoutly prays: 'Yitgadal ve-yitkaddash sheme rabbo,'

'His great name be praised and sanctified in the world, which He has created according to His will.'

G. Salzberger

DEATH

When we are dead, and people weep for us and grieve, let it be because we touched their lives with beauty and simplicity. Let it not be said that life was good to us, but, rather, that we were good to life.

Jacob P. Rudin

When Adam saw for the first time the sun go down and an ever-deepening gloom enfold creation, his mind was filled with terror. God then took pity on him, and endowed him with the divine intuition to take two stones—the name of one was 'Darkness' and the name of the other 'Shadow of Death'—and rub them against each other, and so discover fire. Thereupon Adam exclaimed with grateful joy: 'Blessed be the creator of light!'

Talmud

If you would endure life, be prepared for death.

Sigmund Freud

Is there not a certain satisfaction in the fact that natural limits are set to the life of the individual, so that at the conclusion it may appear as a work of art?

Albert Einstein

One wears his mind out in study, and yet has more mind with which to study. One gives away his heart in love and yet has more heart to give away. One perishes out of pity for a suffering world, and is the stronger therefor. So, too, it is possible at one and the same time to hold on to life and let it go.

Milton Steinberg

LIFE BEYOND DEATH

As for myself, I am content with the conviction that God's eyes are forever upon me, that His providence and justice will follow me into the future life as it has protected me in this, and that my true happiness consists in the development of the powers of my soul. It is such felicity that awaits me in the life to come. More I do not desire to know.

Moses Mendelssohn

The day of death is when two worlds meet with a kiss: this world going out, the future world coming in.

Jose ben Abin

THE FUTURE

Almighty God, thou who hearest prayer, hearken unto us, we beseech thee, in this solemn hour. Bless our worship this day. May our prayers win for us thy mercy and thy love. May the gleams of thy light, the visions of thy truth, which come to bless us here, abide with us when we are mingling with the world, so that, whatever our trials, we may still hold fast to our faith in thee, and whatever our temptations, we may still feel the sanctifying influence of thy presence. Amen.

FAITH

There are two kinds of love: one man loves whatever his clever son does and says, and boasts about his doing clever things and speaking clever words; the other loves his son for himself, no matter what he may say or do.

It is the same with the love of God for man. When a tried and proven man keeps the commandments and does good works wisely and well, God loves what he does and is present in all that he does, and thus the outer being of the universe is bound to God. But when the tried and proven man clings to God with his own being, then God loves him even when he does not work wisely and well, but goes his way with a simple mind and clings to God. God loves him just for that reason. And so the inner being of the universe is lifted to God.

Chasidic

Faith is still the central word in our radical tradition . . . Neither land nor ancestors, power nor riches, codes nor scientific theories, institutions nor conventions, will of themselves avail. Only atonement, the return of the heart in humility to the throne of grace. This and this alone is the essential element in the Jewish tradition.

Harold F. Reinhart

Faith does not spring out of nothing. It comes with the discovery of the holy dimension of our existence . . . .

Faith does not detach man from thinking, it does not suspend reason. It is opposed not to knowledge but to indifferent aloofness to the essence of living.

Faith means to hold small things great, to take light matters seriously, to distinguish the common and the passing from the aspect of the lasting. . . .

Faith is a dynamic, personal act, flowing between the heart of man and the love of God. . . .

Faith is the insight that life is not a self-maintaining, private affair, not a chaos of whims and instincts, but an aspiration, a way, not a refuge.

Faith is real only when it is not one-sided but reciprocal. Man can rely on God, if God can rely on man.

Abraham J. Heschel

Man must beware of looking upon religion as an ideal to be *yearned* for, it should be an ideal to be applied.

S. Dubnow

Learn, with the whole of your ability to learn, all that you can of '*devekut*' (communion with God). Learn in the place where you are, within the circumstances, complexities, joys and sorrows in which you find yourself, learn *through* these involvements, to understand—with heart, not head—the meanings that emanate from them. No one can take this task from you. No one else can do this work for you. Faith speaks to you and me, and it relies on the experience of those greater than us. The world is not blind, is not meaningless. Redemption awaits us just behind the curtain. It is not given to an individual man to draw this curtain aside and bring about the redemption. But he isn't compelled to sit and wait, without doing anything. It is given to him to be a *partner* in the act of redemption. By a man's opening in himself the inner sources through which flows and rises the light of redemption for the individual, in keeping with his ability to receive it, the kingdom of heaven grows and increases in the world. And the active hope of many individuals will bring the total redemption nearer. That is the hope of Israel.

S. H. Bergman

CREATION

Our masters taught: For two and a half years the Schools of Shammai and Hillel have maintained a dispute; the former said: It would have been better if man had not been created; the School of Hillel said: It is better for man to have been created than not to have been created. They took a vote and came to this decision: It would have been better had man not been created; yet, since he has been created, let him pay close attention to his actions, those past and those before him.

Erubin

Rabbi Bunam said: The Lord created the world in a state of beginning. The universe is always in an uncompleted state, in the form of its beginning. It is not like a vessel at which the master works and he finishes it; it requires continuous labour and unceasing renewal by creative forces. Were there a second's pause by these forces, the universe would return to primaeval chaos.

God within Himself separates into the God who creates and the God who reveals, the God of omnipotent justice, and the God of love and mercy. Man within himself separates into the soul beloved by God and the lover who loves his neighbour.

Franz Rosenzweig

REVELATION

The Torah was given in public, for all to see, in the open. For if it had been given in the land of Israel, Israel would have said to the nations of the world: 'You have no share in it!' Therefore the Torah was given in the wilderness, in public, for all to see, in the open, and everyone who wishes to receive it, let him come and receive it.

Mechilta

The ideal of man is to be a revelation himself, clearly to recognize himself as a manifestation of God.

Baal Shem Tov

Revelation is the silent, imperceptible manifestation of God in history. It is the still, small voice: it is the inevitableness, the regularity of nature. Not the whirlwind or earthquake, but the orderly movements of the heavens, the successions of harvests. God reveals Himself by the fact that while man has freedom to choose evil, yet he has, in fact, chosen good, though he knew not that his choice was guided. Revelation, then, is the denial of chance.

Herbert Loewe

The God of Israel is not a nature God but one who proves Himself by His deeds. He is the God of the perpetual flow of creation and action; His name is interpreted as 'I Am Who I Shall Be'. He is the God of history. Each experience Israel undergoes is viewed as a continuation of previous events and a link to future ones. No other

people has felt so deeply the flow, the dynamics of what they experienced as a community; nor has any other people experienced as
intensively the ever-enduring, the permanence within this eternal
change. The waves roll on, the river remains the same.

Lion Feuchtwanger

Did God wait for Mount Sinai or, perhaps, Golgotha? No paths
that lead from Sinai and Golgotha are guaranteed to lead to Him, but
neither can He possibly have failed to come to one who sought Him
on the trails skirting Olympus. There is no temple built so close
to Him as to give man reassurance in its closeness, and none is so far
from Him as to make it too difficult for man's hand to reach. There
is no direction from which it would not be possible for Him to come,
and none from which He must come; no block of wood in which He
may not once take up His dwelling, and no psalm of David that will
always reach His ear.

Franz Rosenzweig

REDEMPTION

A man cannot find redemption until he sees the flaws in his soul,
and tries to efface them. Nor can a people be redeemed until it sees
the flaws in its soul and tries to efface them. But whether it be a man
or a people, whoever shuts out the realization of his flaws is shutting
out redemption. We can be redeemed only to the extent to which
we see ourselves.

Chasidic

Nor does salvation exactly depend on the number of the commandments man accomplishes. It is true that every law gives Israel
an opportunity of acquiring merit, and inheriting thereby the world
to come; for which reason the Holy One, blessed be He, multiplied
to them Torah and commandments. But this multiplication only
aims at an increase of opportunities enabling man to accomplish at
least *one* law in a perfect manner, which alone possesses the virtue
of saving.

Solomon Schechter

Redemption, like a livelihood, must be earned each day.

Genesis Rabbah

Rabbi Yochanan said: 'A man was walking on a road at night, and
his lantern went out. He lighted it, but it went out again. Finally he
said to himself: 'Why shall I bother with the lantern? I will sit down

at the roadside and when the sunlight arrives, I will continue my journey.'

By the same token, the Children of Israel were enslaved in Egypt, and Moses led them forth; they were enslaved in Babylon, and Zerubbabel led them forth; they were enslaved in Persia, and Mordecai led them forth; they were enslaved by Greece, and the Maccabees freed them. When they were once more enslaved by Rome, they said: 'O Lord, free us no longer through the intervention of a man; we are weary of the succession of enslavement, freedom and enslavement. Be our Redeemer, Lord, not a mortal man. Let not a man lighten us, but lighten us Yourself, as it is written: 'For with You is the fountain of life; in Your light, do we see light.' (*Psalm 36: 10*)

Midrash Tehillim

If salvation lay ready to hand and could be discovered without great labour, how could it come about that it should be neglected almost by all? . . . . But every excellent thing is as difficult as it is rare.

Spinoza

The world is a spinning die, and everything turns and changes: man is turned into angel, and angel into man, and the head into the foot, and the foot into the head. Thus all things turn and spin and change, this into that, and that into this, the topmost into the undermost, and the undermost into the topmost. For at the root all is one, and salvation inheres in the change and return of things.

Chasidic

THE MESSIAH

Rabbi Joshua came upon the prophet Elijah as he was standing at the entrance of Rabbi Simeon ben Yochai's cave.

He asked him: 'When is the Messiah coming?'

The other replied: 'Go and ask him yourself.'

'Where shall I find him?'

'Before the gates of Rome.'

'By what sign shall I know him?'

'He is sitting among poor people covered with wounds. The others unbind all their wounds at once, and then bind them up again. But he unbinds one wound at a time, and then binds it up again straightaway. He tells himself: "Perhaps I shall be needed (to appear as the Messiah)—and I must not take time and be late!" '

So he went and found him and said: 'Peace be with you, my master and teacher!'

He answered him: 'Peace be with you, son of Levi!'

Then he asked him: 'When are you coming, master?'

He answered him: 'Today!'

Thereupon he returned to Elijah and said to him: 'He has deceived me, he has indeed deceived me! He told me, "Today I am coming!" and he has not come.'

But the other said to him: 'This is what he told you, "Today—if you would only hear His voice". ' (*Psalm 95: 7*)

Sanhedrin

THE PROBLEM

Let me spell out this passional experience of contemporary man of faith.

He looks upon himself as a stranger in modern society which is technically minded, self-centered and self-loving, almost in a sickly narcissistic fashion, scoring honour upon honour, piling up victory upon victory, reaching for the distant galaxies, and seeing in the here-and-now sensible world the only manifestation of being. What can a man of faith like myself, living by a doctrine which has no technical potential, by a law which cannot be tested in the laboratory, steadfast in his loyalty to an eschatological vision whose fulfillment cannot be predicted with any degree of probability, let alone certainty, even by the most complex, advanced mathematical calculations— what can such a man say to a functional utilitarian society which is *saeculum*-orientated and whose practical reasons of the mind have long ago supplanted the sensitive reasons of the heart?

Joseph D. Soloveitchik

Those who do not walk in loneliness will be bewildered when the Messiah comes and they are called. But we will be as one who has been asleep and whose spirit is quiet and calm.

Chasidic

THE COMING

Israel required no Messiah in the generally accepted sense of the word because it itself suffered and agonized for its faith . . . died for its faith and was resurrected time and again.

Samuel Holdheim

Three pillars support the world: teaching, service, and good deeds, and, as the world approaches its end, the first two will shrink, and only good deeds will grow. And then what is written will become truth: 'Zion shall be redeemed with justice.'

Chasidic

Rabbi Bunam said: 'Before the Messiah will come, there will be Rabbis without Torah, Chasidim without Chasidism, rich men without riches, summers without heat, winters without cold, and grain stalks without grain.'

Chasidic

I believe with perfect faith in the coming of the Messiah; and, though he tarry, I will wait daily for his coming.

Maimonides

Rabbi Yochanan ben Zakkai used to say: If there be a plant in your hand when they say to you: 'Behold the Messiah!'—Go and plant the plant, and afterwards go out to greet him.

Avot d'Rabbi Natan

All the calculated ends have already passed, and it now depends entirely on repentance and good deeds.

Sanhedrin

In the days of the Messiah, the Holy One will execute the urge to evil. The righteous, to whom it will then seem as an enormous mountain, will weep and say: 'How did we conquer such a height?' The wicked, to whom it will look like a hair, will weep and say: 'Why did we not overcome it?'

Judah bar Ilai

In free space there is neither right nor left. In the same way, there is reward and punishment only in this, and not in the Messianic world.

Chasidic

Said the Stretiner: Each Jew has within himself an element of the Messiah which he is required to purify and mature. The Messiah will come when Israel has brought him to the perfection of growth and purity within themselves.

Chasidic

THE PERFECTION OF MAN

The Old Testament figures are themselves always on the verge of getting somewhere, and becoming themselves. They do not move

towards a fated end, but *with* God, arguing and creating as they go. They do not have to cheat time of their bit of eternity, but to fill it. So they continue to give meaning to their life and the life of those who come in touch with them, by their moving, searching, insisting, dreaming, by their appeal which death or fate cannot silence . . . I am attracted by the Jewish hero because in him I see that I am yet to become, that I am not to take too seriously what I am, for it is only the mud out of which I am yet to be made.

Werner and Lotte Pelz

THE PERFECTION OF THE WORLD

I make a sharp distinction between the present realities and the Messianic hope, . . . a hope which the nation cannot forget without ceasing to be a nation. A time will come when there shall be neither enemies nor frontiers, when war shall be no more, and men will be secure in the dignity of man.

Chaim Weizmann

The redemption toward which Jews have striven for thousands of years, is not identical with State, government, military power, war and diplomacy, but is as different from all this as day is from night.

Nathan Hofshi

Bar Kochba had many regiments of brave soldiers in whose valour he trusted. When he went forth to do battle he was accustomed to say: 'O Lord, help neither us nor our enemy!'

Yerushalmi

OUR MESSIANIC TASK

We should also pray for the wicked among the peoples of the world; we should love them too. As long as we do not pray in this way, as long as we do not love in this way, the Messiah will not come.

Chasidic

At the close of the seventy-second Psalm are the words: 'And let the whole earth be filled with His glory. Amen and Amen. The prayers of David, the son of Jesse, are ended.' All prayers and hymns are a plea for His glory to be revealed throughout the world. But if once the whole earth is indeed filled with it, there will be no further need to pray.

Chasidic

The Messiah will come only when he is no longer necessary; he will come only on the day after his arrival; he will come, not on the last day, but on the very last.

Franz Kafka

THE FUTURE

What crazy existence is this we've had
    that so undermined us?
We have kept pace with progress and rushed straight ahead
    and left ourselves behind us.

Karl Kraus

Nobody, nobody, can point you the way to India. Even then (in the time of Alexander) the gates of India were inaccessible, but the King's sword pointed the way. Today the gates have been conveyed elsewhere, to a more distant, a higher place, nobody points the way; many carry swords; but only to flourish them, and the gaze that would follow them is confused.

Franz Kafka

We know that Jews were prohibited from investigating the future. The Torah and the prayers instruct them in remembrance, however. This stripped the future of its magic, to which all those succumb who turn to the soothsayers for enlightenment. This does not imply, however, that for the Jews the future turned into homogeneous, empty time. For every second of time was the strait gate through which the Messiah might enter.

Walter Benjamin

PEACE

Rabbi Bunam taught: Our sages say: 'Seek peace in your own place.' You cannot find peace anywhere save in your own self. In the psalm we read: 'There is no peace in my bones because of my sin.' When a man has made peace within himself, he will be able to make peace in the whole world.

The Torah enjoins us not to run after a mitzvah, but to perform it only if it comes to us. With regard to peace, however, it enjoins us to pursue it.

Numbers Rabbah

God is peace, His name is peace, and all is bound together in peace.

Zohar

THE JUST SOCIETY

Be with us, O God, during the coming week. Teach us to do thy will, and make us brave in performing it. Help us to overcome our failings, our forgetfulness of thee, our indifference to the needs of others, our heedlessness of the claims of our souls. Help us in our daily work, so that in very truth we may live by it, making it the source of our ennoblement, the instrument of the higher life. Help us to be better Israelites, to realise the splendour of our religious heritage, and to fulfil more faithfully the high responsibilities it lays upon us. For so shall we work for thy greater glory and for the establishment of thy Kingdom on earth. Amen.

> May the will come from You
> to annul wars and the shedding of blood from the
>   universe,
> and to extend a peace, great and wondrous, in the
>   universe.
> Nor again shall one people raise the sword against
>   another
> and they shall learn war no more.
> But let all the residents of earth recognize and know
>   the innermost truth:
> that we are not come into this world for quarrel and
>   division,
> nor for hate and jealousy, contrariness and bloodshed;
> but we are come into this world
> You to recognize and know,
> may You be blessed forever.
>
> And let Your glory fill all our wits and minds,
>   knowledge and hearts;
> and may I be a chariot for the presence of Your
>   divinity.
> May I not again depart from holiness as much as
>   a hairsbreadth.
> May I not think one extraneous thought.
> But may I ever cling to You and to Your sacred Torah,
> until I be worthy to introduce others into the
>   knowledge of the truth of Your divinity.

To announce to the sons of men Your power,
and the honour of the glory of Your kingdom.

Nachman of Bratzlav

JUSTICE

One can always find warm hearts who in a glow of emotion would like to make the whole world happy but who have never attempted the sober experiment of bringing a real blessing to a single human being. It is easy to revel enthusiastically in one's love of man, but it is more difficult to do good to someone solely because he is a human being. When we are approached by a human being demanding his right, we cannot replace definite ethical action by mere vague goodwill.

Leo Baeck

The wife of Rabbi Wolf of Zbarazh accused her maidservant of having stolen a costly vessel. The girl denied the deed. The woman, being angry, prepared herself to go out and appeal to the rabbinical court. Rabbi Wolf, seeing her preparations, put on his Sabbath garment also. His wife said that it was not fitting for him to go, and that she knew well enough how to conduct herself in the court's presence.

'Truly,' replied the Zaddik, 'you do. But the poor orphan, your maid, as whose counsel I am going, does not. And who but I will see that justice is done her?'

RESPONSIBILITY

There are all sorts of flight from responsibility: there is flight into death, flight into sickness, and finally flight into folly. The last is the least dangerous and most convenient and, even to the wise, the way to it is usually not as far as they like to imagine.

Arthur Schnitzler

What makes God happy? To see a poor devil who finds a treasure and returns it.

Yiddish Proverb

One who transgresses cannot justify himself by the claim that he was sent by another. The law of Moses is directed to each and every person, and the individual as such is personally responsible for his deeds.

S. H. Bergman

TRUTH

I believe in God as the God of truth. Liberal Jews have subscribed consistently to the doctrine that we cannot serve God by juggling with truth, and the stronger the intellectual grasp of a man, the more likely he is to be a good servant. It matters infinitely what we think and believe, for thought and belief *do* affect conduct.

Lily H. Montagu

Reason is an inadequate tool for the comprehension of ultimate reality, but it is the only tool we have for distinguishing faith from credulity, true religion from superstition, enthusiasm from fanaticism.

Louis Jacobs

Religion offers answers without obliterating the questions. They become blunted and will not attack you with the same ferocity. But without them the answer would dry up and wither away. The question is a great religious act; it helps you live great religious truth.

Shmuel Sperber

CHARITY

There are eight degrees in the giving of charity, one higher than the other:

He who gives grudgingly, reluctantly, or with regret.

He who gives less than he should, but gives graciously.

He who gives what he should, but only after he is asked.

He who gives before he is asked.

He who gives without knowing to whom he gives, although the recipient knows the identity of the donor.

He who gives without making his identity known.

He who gives without knowing to whom he gives, and the recipient not knowing from whom he receives.

He who helps a fellowman to support himself by a gift, or a loan, or by finding employment for him, thus helping him to become self-supporting.

Maimonides

No man is ever impoverished through giving charity, nor is evil or harm ever caused by it; as it is written (*Isaiah 32 : 17*): 'And the work of righteousness shall be peace.'

Whosoever has compassion on the poor, the Holy One, blessed be He, has compassion on him.

(Note by Isserles: Let man realise that he himself is forever seeking sustenance at the hand of God, and just as God answers his prayer, so should he answer the prayer of the poor. Let him also realize that the world is a revolving sphere, and that eventually he or his son or his grandson may be reduced to poor circumstances.)

Shulchan Aruch

If a man sees that his income is meagre, let him practise charity.

Gittin

More than the householder does for the beggar, the beggar does for the householder.

Leviticus Rabbah

A man may give liberally, and yet because he gives unlovingly and wounds the heart of the poor, his gift is in vain, for it has lost the attribute of charity; a man may give little, but because his heart goes with it his deed and himself are blessed.

Baba Batra

It is the duty of the Zaddikim to aid the wicked; of the wise to aid the unwise; of the rich to aid the poor. Each man should aid his fellowman according to his talent.

Zohar

BUSINESS

Be honourable in your business dealings. Do not say that such and such a price has been offered you for your wares, when the thing is not true; and do not act as though you had a desire to sell what you possess, when there is in your mind no serious thought of doing so. Such things are unworthy of a Jew.

On the worldly possessions of those who oppress the workman or who buy stolen goods, rests no blessing.

Judah HeChasid

Above all, my children, be honest in money matters with Jews and non-Jews alike. If you have money or possessions belonging to other people, take better care of them than you would if they were your own. The first question that is put to a man on entering the next world is whether or not he was faithful in his business dealings.

Glueckel of Hameln

THE ETHICAL LIFE

Just as it is forbidden to wrong another in buying and selling, it is forbidden to wrong him with words.

What is meant by 'wronging with words'? A man should not ask his neighbour how much he wants for a certain object if he has no intention of buying it. If someone was looking round for corn to buy he should not tell him: 'Go to so-and-so' knowing full well that that person has no corn to sell. If, God forbid, his neighbour was suffering he should not say to him as Job's friends said to him 'Remember, I pray thee, who ever perished being innocent?' (*Job 4 : 7*) If someone asked him a question which involves learning he should not turn to an unlearned person to ask him what he thinks about it. There are other examples, all of which cause someone's heart to ache.

Kitzur Shulchan Aruch

It is forbidden for a man to accustom himself to use smooth and deceptive language. He should not say one thing when he means another, but his inner thoughts should be in accord with the impression he gives, and his mouth should utter that which he really thinks. Even one word of smooth talk or misrepresentation is forbidden, but a man should have true lips, a sincere spirit and a heart free of any trickery and deceit.

Maimonides

A man should not invite his neighbour to eat at his table if he knows quite well that the invitation will be refused. He should not pretend to give him a present knowing full well that he will not accept it. And the same applies to whenever he does similar things, saying one thing with his mouth and meaning something different in his heart, showing his neighbour that he intends to honour him but not really meaning it deep in his heart. A man's mouth and heart should be as one and he should train his lips to speak honestly, his spirit to be one of integrity and his heart pure.

Kitzur Shulchan Aruch

No crown carries such royalty with it as does humility; no monument gives such glory as an unsullied name; no worldly gain can equal that which comes from observing God's laws. The highest sacrifice is a broken and contrite heart; the highest wisdom is that which is found in the Torah; the noblest of all ornaments is modesty; and the most beautiful thing that man can do is to forgive a wrong.

Eleazar of Worms

The thread on which the different good qualities of human beings are strung as pearls, is the fear of God. When the fastenings of this fear are unloosed, the pearls roll in all directions, and are lost one by one.

Orchot Zaddikim

If the means of your support in life be measured out scantily to you, remember that you have to be thankful and grateful even for the mere privilege to breathe, and that you must look upon that suffering as a test of your piety and a preparation for better things. But if worldly wealth be lent to you, exalt not yourself above your brother; for both of you came naked into the world, and both of you will surely have to sleep at last together in the dust.

Eleazar of Worms

POWER OVER ONESELF

There are so-called leaders versed only in superficialities and outward values. They cannot lead even themselves, and evil impulse prompts them to lead others. They are not so much to be blamed as those who vote for them and support them. These adherents will be called upon eventually to give an accounting for their action.

Nachman of Bratzlav

Darkness is not the road to light, dictatorship and paternalism are not the paths to freedom and independence, terror is no express train to the golden age.

C. Greenberg

'A man should concern himself more that he not injure others than that he not be injured.' For when a man tries to keep a watch that his fist not injure others, by that very act he enthrones in the world the God of truth and righteousness and adds power to the kingdom of justice; and it is precisely this power which will defend him against injury by others. . . . When a man constantly portrays to himself scenes of terror, when he asserts that everyone wants to obliterate him and that he can rely only on the power of his own fist, by this he denies the kingdom of truth and justice and enthrones the power of the fist. And since the fist is by nature poor at making distinctions, in the end defence and attack become reversed: instead of defending himself by means of the fist, such a man becomes himself the assailant and destroyer of others. Hence, like begetting like, others

repay him in kind, and so the earth is filled with violence and oppression.

Aaron Samuel Tamaret

THE GOD OF JUSTICE

Thus says the Lord, Let not the wise man glory in his wisdom, neither let the mighty man glory in his might, let not the rich man glory in his riches, but let him that glories glory in this, that he understands and knows Me, that I am the Lord who acts with love, justice and righteousness in the earth, for in these things I delight, says the Lord.

Jeremiah 9 : 22–23

AWARENESS

One of the causes of Auschwitz was—technology. Our actions now have effects which are beyond our awareness. This conflict between man and his technology, the concept of alienation, has been assimilated into modern life. A new dimension is here, a growing darkness. In the last century, man suffered from a lack of knowledge; in our time, man suffers from too much knowledge, from intentionally produced false knowledge. And if our intellect is insufficient or misdirected, this also applies to our feelings. All of us know this. The death of an infant moves us; the death of six million people simply stuns our senses.

We are Eichmann's sons, removed from the consequences of our actions. The fine edge of our sensibilities has been worn away by the monstrosities of our age. The six o'clock news is the most brutal programme on television—and we do not even turn it off. Each day, murder and destruction flicker across the screen as part of our home life. Is it any wonder that we have learned to live comfortably with the knowledge of the death of the six million? We can keep a body count of our own, right in the privacy of our living-room.

Yet there are moments in every life when we break out of the structure, when we are no longer controlled but, suddenly, are in control. And then we can be human beings. We can be humane. We can reach out toward our fellowman. And our shared suffering and our shame can be a bridge and can cease to be a barrier. Auschwitz—remembered within the community of human fellowship —can then become a question addressed to God. Then. But not until then.

Albert H. Friedlander

THE COMMUNITY

Merciful Father, we thank thee for this Sabbath day. We thank thee for the opportunity of uttering our praise and our gratitude, our hopes and our desires. We thank thee for the joy of worshipping thee, for the privilege of drawing near to thy holy presence. O God, thy mercies are new every morning. Not a day passes without leaving with us some token of thy lovingkindness. Thou hast given us life with all its delights. Thou hast placed us in a wonderful and beautiful world. Thou hast given us the joys of the mind and the spirit. Thou hast given us dear ones whose love is our stay and our treasure. For these and all our blessings we praise thy holy name. Amen.

THE INDIVIDUAL

One who thinks he can live without others is mistaken. One who thinks others cannot live without him is more mistaken.

Chasidic

Question: Our sages say: 'And there is not a thing that has not its place.' And so man too has his place. Then why do people sometimes feel so crowded?

Answer: Because each wants to occupy the place of the other.

Chasidic

The Kariver said: 'Do not hate your erring brother on the ground that you have not erred like him. Had he possessed your nature, he might not have sinned, and had you possessed his nature, you might have been the sinner. A man's transgressions depend not entirely upon his free choice, but often upon many other circumstances.'

Everyone of Israel should know and consider the fact that he, in the particular way he is made, is unique in the world, and that no one like him has ever been. For if someone like him had already been, there would be no reason for him to be in this world. Actually, everyone is something new in this world, and here he must perfect his particular being, for because it is still imperfect the coming of the Messiah is delayed.

Chasidic

MAN AND WOMAN

When Adam awakened from the divine surgery and beheld the beautiful Eve at his side, he asked: 'What is going to be the plan of

our life together?' She replied: 'We shall have a common table, you will seek to provide it with bread, and I shall cover it with fresh flowers.'

W. H. Gold

When a soul is sent down from heaven, it is a combined male and female soul. The male part enters the male child and the female part enters the female. If they are worthy, God causes them to re-unite in marriage. This is true mating.

Zohar

To love somebody is not just a strong feeling—it is a decision, it is a judgment, it is a promise. If love were only a feeling, there would be no basis for the promise to love each other for ever. A feeling comes and it may go. How can I judge that it will stay for ever, when my act does not involve judgment and decision?

Erich Fromm

HUSBAND AND WIFE

If your wife is small, bend down to her and whisper in her ear.

Baba Metzia

Let a man eat and drink under his means, and clothe himself according to his means, and honour his wife and children beyond his means, because they depend on him, while he depends on Him who spoke and the world came into being.

Chullin

Be careful not to hurt your wife, because woman is prone to tears and sensitive to wrong. Be careful about the honour of your wife, for blessing enters the house only because of the wife.

Baba Metzia

Your wife has been given to you in order that you may realize with her life's great plan; she is not yours to vex or grieve. Vex her not, for God notes her tears.

Ketubot

He who wins a wise woman by his own worth, has won the chief victory in life.

Zohar

MOTHER

Jewish custom bids the Jewish mother, after her preparations for the Sabbath have been completed on Friday evening, kindle the

Sabbath lamp. That is symbolic of the Jewish woman's influence on her own home, and through it upon larger circles. She is the inspirer of a pure, chaste, family life whose hallowing influences are incalculable; she is the centre of all spiritual endeavours, the confidante and fosterer of every undertaking. To her the Talmudic sentence applies: 'It is a woman alone through whom God's blessings are vouchsafed to a house.'

Henrietta Szold

But the child must grow. It must emerge from mother's womb, from mother's breast; it must eventually become a completely separate human being. The very essence of motherly love is to care for the child's growth, and that means to want the child's separation from herself. Here lies the basic difference to erotic love. In erotic love, two people who were separate become one. In motherly love, two people who were one become separate. The mother must not only tolerate, she must wish and support the child's separation. It is only at this stage that motherly love becomes such a difficult task, that it requires unselfishness, the ability to give everything and to want nothing but the happiness of the loved one.

Erich Fromm

FATHER

And I say to myself: from this remote father right up to my own father, all these fathers have handed on to me a truth which flowed in their blood, which flows in mine; and shall I not hand it on, with my blood, to those of my blood?

Will you take it from me, my child? Will you hand it on? Perhaps you will wish to abandon it. If so, let it be for a greater truth, if there is one. I shall not blame you. It will be my fault; I shall have failed to hand it on as I received it.

But, whether you abandon it or whether you follow it, Israel will journey on to the end of days.

Edmond Fleg

When a father gives to his son, both laugh; when a son gives to his father, both cry.

One father supports ten children, but ten children do not support one father.

Yiddish Proverbs

CHILDREN

Do not threaten a child. Either punish or forgive him.

Semachot

Parents should never make a favourite of one child. For some ells of bright cloth the children of Israel were made slaves in Egypt.

Midrash

A person should never tell a child he will give him something and not keep his promise, because in this way he teaches the child to tell lies.

Sukkah

A father complained to the Besht that his son had forsaken God. 'What, Rabbi, shall I do?'

'Love him more than ever,' was the Besht's reply.

CHILDREN AND PRAYER

It must be the task of all religious education once again to teach the child to pray. It is of course obvious that this must be undertaken primarily in the parental home. Mothers who are concerned that their children should have a religious education, must pray with their children daily, whether in Hebrew or in their native tongue. But there is one essential element in this: the inner approach to prayer and the personal relationship. The familiar approach to God must already be expressed in prayer at a very early age. . . . There is one thing in prayer that we all need so greatly and which children can already learn: a few minutes each day of peace and quiet with oneself, at least a minute fragment of the day to listen within oneself, attending to the voice of God.

Ellen Littmann

HOME

Never enter your house with abrupt and startling step, and do not behave so that those who live under your roof dread your presence.

Eliezer ben Isaac

He who maintains peace at home helps to maintain it in Israel.

Simeon ben Gamliel

Build your home in such a way that a stranger may feel happy in your midst.

Theodor Herzl

Make not heavy the burden of a non-Jewish person who works for you; oppress him not; give him all you eat and drink; offend him not with words.

Shulchan Aruch

Behave to those who work for you as you desire God to behave to you.

Philo

OUR NEIGHBOUR

Said the 'Yud': 'Accustom yourself to generosity by degrees. At first refuse not a request for a pinch of snuff, for the light of a match, or for other small gifts. Such petty kindnesses will broaden your heart so that you can acquire the habit of helping your fellow-man in greater ways.'

Chasidic

Judaism teaches the unity of mankind. We all have one Father, one God has created us all.

Judaism demands that we respect the life, the health, the strength and the possessions of our neighbour. It therefore forbids to damage our fellow men through violence or cunning, or in any other illegal fashion, to rob him of his possessions or to leave him helpless against illegal attack.

Judaism demands that we consider the honour of our neighbour as sacred as our own. It therefore prohibits the derogation of our neighbour through evil gossip or hurting him through mockery and shame.

Judaism demands that we respect the religious convictions of others. It therefore prohibits any derogation or disrespect of religious customs and symbols of people of other faiths.

Judaism demands that we exercise loving-kindness towards everyone. . . . It therefore prohibits to limit our concern only to ourselves and our relatives and to remain unmoved by the suffering of strangers.

Judaism demands 'Love your neighbour as yourself' and declares this command of love which encompasses all humanity to be a fundamental principle of Judaism.

Prayerbook of Berlin Liberal Synagogue

There is no quality and there is no power in man that was created to no purpose. And even base and corrupt qualities can be uplifted to

serve God. When, for example, self-assurance is uplifted, it changes into proud assurance of the ways of God. But to what end can the denial of God have been created? It, too, can be uplifted through deeds of charity. For if someone comes to you and asks your help, you shall not turn him off with pious words, saying: 'Have faith, and take your troubles to God!' You shall act as though there were no God, as though there were only one person in all the world who could help this man—only yourself.

Chasidic

COMMUNITY

The Rabbis teach: When Israel is in trouble, and one among them separates himself, the two angels of the service who accompany a man lay their hands on his head, and say: 'This man who has separated himself from the community, shall not see its consolation.' And it is taught: If the community is in trouble, a man must not say: 'I will go to my house, and eat and drink and peace shall be with you, my soul.' But a man must share in the trouble of the community, even as Moses did. He who shares in its troubles is worthy to see its consolation.

Ta'anit

Judaism did not turn heavenward and create in heaven an eternal habitation of souls. It found 'eternal life' on earth, by strengthening the social feeling in the individual by making him regard himself not as an isolated being with an existence bounded by birth and death, but as part of a larger whole, as a limb of the social body .... I live for the sake of the member. I die to make room for new individuals, who will mould the community afresh and not allow it to stagnate and remain forever in one position. When the individual thus values the community as his own life, and strives after its happiness as though it were his individual wellbeing, he finds satisfaction, and no longer feels so keenly the bitterness of his individual existence, because he sees the end for which he lives and suffers.

Achad Ha-am

THE COMMUNITY AT PRAYER

Because I have seen reflected in your eyes the rising flame of the two Sabbath candles, your attention stretched out towards the movements of the young girl who lit them, as if you wished to help her and take part in her prayer;

Because, some moments after you began the call to the 'Sabbath Bride', you rose with a single move, bowed with fervour while the *Chazan* sang: 'Come my bride, come my bride . . .';

Because as one you acknowledged the sweetness of the psalm, praising the Eternal and accepting His special day;

Because you questioned yourself when saying 'Hear, O Israel . . .' whether you had really united your voices in the proclamation of the divine unity;

Because you communed during the silence of the Eighteen Benedictions, and at the end called with fervour for an era of peace for Israel and all the world;

Because you listened with closest attention to the words I spoke to you at the end of your week of labour;

Because you called within you the words of the blessing of God which I transmitted;

Because you began the *Kiddush* so strongly that our friends of the choir became unnecessary, and the *Chazan* yielded his place, smiling;

Because you saluted with joy the angels of Sabbath;

Because some very old faithfuls were a little bit out musically, following their own interior rhythm, rather than that of the others;

Because a baby cried, but you smiled, accepting his cry as a prayer;

Because someone among you remained standing while the others sat down, yet you accepted and understood;

Because families united together in the same row two or three generations of Jews at prayer;

Because at the moment of shaking hands I know what there is within you of joys, of problems, of dramas, sometimes also of hopes;

Because you delayed leaving this synagogue, and formed groups in the exitway;

Because there shines out from the whole of you sympathy, kindness, tolerance, the desire to understand and to act; because I love you deeply.

You have really prayed, O my community.

Daniel Farhi

LEADERSHIP

And they spoke to him (King Rehoboam) saying: If you will be a servant to this people this day. (*1 Kings 12: 7*) This teaches that

he who is appointed leader over the community becomes the servant of the community.

Midrash

While Moses was feeding the sheep of his father-in-law in the wilderness, a young kid ran away. Moses followed it until it reached a ravine, where it found a well to drink from. When Moses reached it, he said, 'I did not know that you ran away because you were thirsty. Now you must be weary.' He carried the kid back. Then God said: 'Because you have shown pity in leading back one of a flock belonging to a man, you shall lead My flock, Israel.'

Exodus Rabbah

If God has granted you the privilege of being a leader in Israel, do not rebuke your people with an angry heart, but with a soft tongue. For Israel is a holy congregation, blessed of the Lord. Let every man be important in your eyes, and not inconsequential. For you cannot know who is worthy and who is unworthy. Man often looks upon a fellowman as despicable and worthless, but God looks into the very ·heart.

Chasidic

PROBLEMS OF LEADERSHIP

A Zaddik was asked: 'Why is it that the pious man seems less eager to persuade others to become virtuous than the impious man to gain companions in wickedness?'

He replied: 'The man of piety walks in light and is not afraid to walk alone, whereas the man of impiety walks in darkness and is anxious for company.'

Chasidic

A man complained to Rabbi Bunam: 'The Talmud (*Erubin 13a*) tells us that when a man runs away from honours, honours run after him. Now I have run away from honours, but no honours pursue me.'

'The reason,' explained the Rabbi, 'is that you keep looking backwards.'

Chasidic

SOCIETY

In the Talmud it says that the stork is called *chasidah* in Hebrew, i.e. the devout or the loving one, because he gives so much love to his mate and his young. Then why is he classed in the Scriptures among the unclean birds? Because he gives love only to his own.

Chasidic

Give me your tired, your poor,
Your huddled masses yearning to breathe free,
The wretched refuse of your teeming shore,
Send these, the homeless, tempest-tost, to me,
I lift my lamp beside the golden door.

Emma Lazarus

From each according to his abilities, to each according to his needs.

Karl Marx

THE CREATURES OF GOD

'The Lord is good to all; and His tender mercies are over all His works.' (*Psalm 145: 9*)

The Patriarch, Rabbi Judah I, suffered from toothache for many years. Why was he thus punished? Because he once saw a bound calf being taken to the slaughter. The calf bleated and appealed for his aid, but the Rabbi said: 'Go, since it is for this that you have been created.'

And how was the Patriarch cured? He once saw a litter of mice being carried to the river to be drowned. He said: 'Let them go free, for it is written that "His mercies are over all His works".'

Yerushalmi

THE TREATMENT OF ANIMALS

Do not eat before you have fed your beast.

Rav

A good man does not sell his beast to a cruel person.

Sefer Chasidim

To relieve an animal of pain or danger is a biblical law, superseding any rabbinic law on Sabbath observance.

Shabbat

No man may buy a beast, an animal or a bird until he has provided food for it.

Yerushalmi

In the World-to-come God will punish riders who wound their horses with spurs.

Sefer Chasidim

When a Jew says he's going hunting to amuse himself, he lies.

Walter Rathenau

THE FAMILY OF ISRAEL

Our Father in heaven, help us, we beseech thee, to labour for the joy of others. Help us to spread happiness about us, to have a piteous heart for suffering, to be charitable in thought as well as in deed, to be just and patient and forgiving to all. God of our fathers, teach us to be worthy of the name of Israelite. May all that we do tend to its honour and to thy glory. Give us an understanding heart, so that we may feel how solemn is our responsibility as members of thy people, witnesses before men to thine everlasting truth. Amen.

THE BLESSING

Now the Lord said to Abram: 'Go out from your country, and from your family and your father's house, to the land that I will show you. And I will make a great nation of you, and I will bless you and make your name great; and be you a blessing . . . and all the families of the earth shall be blessed in you.'

Genesis 12: 1-3

Israel is likened to the dust and the sand. As nothing can grow without the dust of the soil, so the nations of the world cannot exist without Israel, through whom they receive their blessing.

As the myrtle is sweet to him who smells it, but bitter to him who bites it, so Israel brings prosperity to the nation which grants it kindness, and depression to the people which afflicts it with evil.

Esther Rabbah

Israel among the nations is like the heart amidst the organs of the body: it is the sickest and healthiest of them.

Judah Halevi

THE PURPOSE

A difficult task was assigned this people in its history. It is so easy to listen to the voices of idols, and it is so hard to receive the word of the One God into oneself. It is so easy to remain a slave, and it is so difficult to become a free man. But this people can only exist in the full seriousness of its task. It can only exist in this freedom which reaches beyond all other freedoms. Its history began when it heard the word, rising out of the mystery, and emerging into clarity: 'I am He-Who-Is your God, who brought you out of the land of Egypt, out of the house of bondage.'

Leo Baeck

To open eyes when others close them
to hear when others do not wish to listen
to look when others turn away
to seek to understand when others give up
to rouse oneself when others accept
to continue the struggle even when one is not the strongest
to cry out when others keep silent

to be a Jew
it is that
it is first of all that

and further
to live when others are dead
and to remember when others have forgotten.

Emmanuel Eydoux

To act out of love and to be willing to bear the suffering which the good and true man must inevitably bear in a world like ours, in a world which is only partly divine and which must be won for God through the efforts of man—that is the deepest utterance of the rabbis and the culminating idea of Jewish religiosity and of Jewish prayer.

Henry Slonimsky

IN OUR NOBILITY AND IN OUR SHABBINESS

The Jewish people, the separated people, therefore the holy people, is a God-made people. In our nobility and in our shabbiness, in our cultural refinement and in our vulgarity, in our endurance and in our weakness, in our glory and in the shame of our dehumanisation in Auschwitz—we are the people of God; a people not merely of believers in God—that we are too—but a people in whom everyone, Jew himself and gentile alike, meets his father in heaven who 'will swallow up death forever . . . and the shame of His people will He take away from off all the earth' (*Isaiah 25 : 8*). We did not choose to be Jews, God has chosen us.

Ignaz Maybaum

It is in no arrogant temper that we claim to be the chosen people. We thereby affirm, not that we are better than others, but that we ought to be better.

Morris Joseph

On the side of the road
there are leaves
so tired of being leaves
they have fallen.

On the side of the road
there are Jews
so tired of being Jews
they have fallen.

Sweep away the leaves.
Sweep away the Jews.

The same leaves, will they
grow again in spring?

Will there be a spring
for the downtrodden Jews?

Edmond Jabès

K'LAL YISRAEL—THE COMMUNITY OF ISRAEL

'And they shall stumble, one man with his brother' (*Leviticus 26 : 37*). This means that one man will stumble because of the sin of his brother. Hence learn that every Israelite is surety for every other.

Sifra

Said the Kozmirer: When all Jews cherish love for each other, they become together as one giant man and their arms together become one long arm. Then in truth it is possible for this mighty arm to reach into heaven itself and bring down to earth all gracious things.

As the ethrog has taste and fragrance, the palm taste but no fragrance, the myrtle fragrance but no taste, and the willow neither taste nor fragrance, so some Jews have learning and good deeds, some learning but no deeds, some deeds but no learning, and some neither learning nor deeds. Said the Holy One: let them all be tied together and they will atone one for the other.

Leviticus Rabbah

THE CHOOSING OF ISRAEL

The Jews regarded themselves as the chosen people not because of their racial qualities, but because of having been selected to be the servants of God to carry His moral law to the world. They looked

upon themselves as a covenantal people, a kingdom, not of supermen, but of priests. This covenant with God was an act of will on both sides, a matter not of the fatalism of blood but of choice. Admission into this covenant was open to all men of all races at all times, also as a matter of choice. The prophets of Israel constantly reminded the Jews of the non-racial character of their especial relationship to the Lord: 'Are you not as the children of the Ethiopians to Me, O children of Israel?' said the Lord. 'Have not I brought up Israel out of the land of Egypt, and the Philistines from Caphtor, and Aram from Kir?'

Abba Hillel Silver

The 'chosen people', but chosen for what? Not for pleasure, surely, not for power. No religion is an acceptance of the present condition or a warrant for terrestrial happiness. If happiness comes, it is incidental to the performance of function, or, in more solemn language, of mission; and the human situation, spiritual as well as material, is never so satisfactory that it should not, and cannot, be bettered. The 'choice' of a people means the acceptance by them of a specific vocation; and in this case the nature of the vocation is indicated clearly from the first: it is to practise and exemplify a new way of living.

Leon Roth

Given the freedom to choose I have decided to embrace Judaism. I have not done so out of loyalty to the Jewish people or the Jewish state. My choice was religious. I chose to believe in the God of Abraham, Isaac, and Jacob, to acknowledge the law of Moses as the Word of God; to accept the people of Israel as the holy instrument of divine fulfilment; to await the coming of the Messiah and the redemption of history.

Arthur A. Cohen

Every people is a question which God addresses to humanity; and every people, from its place, with its special talents and possibilities, must answer for its own sake and for the sake of humanity . . . This people Israel developed and grew in one millennium and formed the question that rests within it. It has kept arising ever again, through rebirths, in new epochs, for more than two millennia now. Through its prophets, its poets, its teachers, its righteous ones, Israel was able to learn how to listen to the question which God addressed to it. Its question proved, in Israel's experience, to be the deepest of all

questions which live within and from humanity. This people's hope is, therefore, the greatest of all hopes; it is the great expectation to which the way of all ways leads. The iniquity of this people is, therefore, deeper iniquity than any other. And offences against this people signify more than other offences. Both need 'God's reconciliation'. This people is 'a covenant for the nations', a law for the peoples.

Leo Baeck

THE SUFFERING OF ISRAEL

If there are ranks in suffering, Israel takes precedence of all the nations; if the duration of sorrows and the patience with which they are borne ennoble, the Jews can challenge the aristocracy of every land; if a literature is called rich in the possession of a few classic tragedies—what shall we say to a national tragedy lasting for fifteen hundred years, in which the poets and the actors were also the heroes?

Leopold Zunz

WITHOUT JEWS

Without Jews there will be no Jewish God.
If we should depart from the world in the end,
the light will go out in Your tattered tent.
Since Abraham has first discovered You,
You shone in the face of every Jew.
You radiated from Jewish eyes.
We formed Your image in that of our own.
Wherever we went, in each country and town,
our Jewish God went, too, a stranger like us.
Each fallen head of a Jewish dead
is a broken vessel empty of sound.
For we were the carriers of Your light,
the living sign of Your miraculous sight.
Our dead are counted in millions now.
The stars that surround You grow dim and low,
and with them recedes the memory of You.
Soon Your kingdom will vanish, too.
That which was planted and sown by Jews
lies burned on the ground.
On dead grass weeps the morning dew. . . .

Who will dream You up again?
Who will recall You?
Who will defy You?
Who long for You?
Who will, bridging his pain,
turn away from You, to return again?

Jacob Glatstein

EXILE

When exile will be comprehended and accepted as it should be, when in suffering, the service of God and His Torah will be understood as the only task of life, when even in misery God will be served, and external abundance esteemed only as a means of this service, then, perhaps, Israel will be ready for the greater temptations of prosperity and happiness in dispersion.

Samson Raphael Hirsch

Rabbi Chenoch of Alexander once said: The real exile of Israel in Egypt was that they learned to endure it.

Said the Belzer: There are three kinds of exile: exile among the nations; exile among Jews; and exile among one's own desires. . . . The worst exile is the exile from peace of mind. It is suffered by one who is overpowered by his evil desires at the same time that he is aware of their wickedness. The last-named needs redemption most urgently.

THE CONVERT OF RIGHTEOUSNESS

Maimonides' reply to a proselyte who asked if he could say the prayers which began: '*Our* God and God of *our* fathers . . .'

Pronounce all prayers as they are written and do not change anything. Your prayers and blessings should be the same as that of any other Israelite, regardless of whether you pray in private or conduct the service. The explanation is as follows: Abraham, our father, taught mankind the true belief and the unity of God, repudiating idolatry; through him many of his own household and also others were guided 'to keep the way of the Lord, to do righteousness and justice'. Thus he who becomes a proselyte and confesses the unity of God, as taught in the Torah, is a disciple of Abraham, our father. Such persons are of his household. . . .

You should therefore pray: 'Our God and God of our fathers', for Abraham is also *your* father. In no respect is there a difference between us and you.

Do not think little of your origin: we are descended from Abraham, Isaac and Jacob, but your descent is from the Creator, for in the words of Isaiah: 'One shall say: "I am the Lord's"; and another shall call himself by the name of Jacob.'

The Rabbis say: If anyone comes nowadays, and desires to become a proselyte, they say to him: 'Why do you want to become a proselyte? Do you not know that the Israelites are harried, hounded, persecuted and harassed, and that sufferings befall them?' If he says: 'I know it, and I am not worthy', they receive him without further argument.

Yebamot

Dearer to God is the proselyte who has come of his own accord than all the crowds of Israelites who stood around Mount Sinai. For had the Israelites not witnessed the thunder and lightning, the quaking mountain and sounding trumpets, they would not have accepted the Torah. But the proselyte, who saw none of these things, came and surrendered himself to the Holy One, blessed be He, and took the yoke of heaven upon himself. Can anyone be dearer to God than this man?

Tanchuma

ERETZ YISRAEL

The living Jewish people is primary. It is the living carrier and vessel of Judaism, the Jewish spirit. It has used even its Exile for spreading light and learning. Palestine can help this people to understand itself, to give an account of itself, to an intensification of its culture, a deepening of its philosophy, a renewal of its religion. Palestine can help this people perform its great ethical mission as a national-international entity. But this eternal and far-flung people does not need a Jewish state for the purpose of maintaining its very existence. The Jewish community throughout the world is a wondrous and paradoxical organism. It participates in the life of many nations, yet in spite of numberless predictions in the past and present, it is not absorbed by them. It is patriotic in every land, yet it is international, cosmopolitan. Palestine cannot solve the Jewish

problem. It is part of the Jewish destiny to face this problem and make it mean something of good for mankind.

Judah Leon Magnes

Ishmael, my brother,
How long shall we fight each other?

My brother from times bygone,
My brother—Hagar's son,
My brother, the wandering one.

One angel was sent to us both,
One angel watched over our growth—
There in the wilderness, death threatening through thirst,
I a sacrifice on the altar, Sarah's first.

Ishmael, my brother, hear my plea:
It was the angel who tied thee to me. . . .

Time is running out, put hatred to sleep.
Shoulder to shoulder, let's water our sheep.

Shin Shalom

For a Jew, the word nationalism should mean freedom. A Jew who today may declare: 'I am a nationalist', will not be saying in any special, precise, or clear-cut way: 'I am a man who seeks to rebuild a Jewish state in Palestine and who dreams of conquering Jerusalem.' He will be saying: 'I want to be a man fully free, I want to enjoy the sunshine, I want to escape the oppression, to escape the outrage, to escape the scorn with which men seek to overwhelm me.' At certain moments in history, nationalism is for human groups the manifestation of the spirit of freedom.

Bernard Lazare

The future is full of the gravest responsibilities. We are promised a place in the sun—not to ravage and dominate, but to serve our people, ourselves, the world. Standing in the sun we shall be seen clearly as never before. Our abilities will be on trial before a world full of nations, who will judge us in the light of a glorious past of ideal service to mankind. For Israel, election has never meant anything but obligation. Clearly, rehabilitating a nation is not a pastime. It is a task, a heavy task, a holy task.

Henrietta Szold

Our attitude to the country is complex, one of longing and attachment, starting with the dreams of our childhood and involving a deep desire to take root, a desire which is sometimes the expression

of fear of being torn away. This desire also embraces the people in the country, the people living here. Once Jewish sovereignty was gained, once it became clear that this was the home of the whole Jewish people, that it was their shelter, the home of their dreams, their creative spirit, then we were left with another great dream, one no less fantastic, perhaps, than the vision of the establishment of the State: that we should be able to take root not only on the mountains, in the soil, but also in the human scene—among the Arabs.

What we do is more important than what we dream, but there are dreams which cannot be forgotten. . . .

Muki Tzur

RETURN

No matter where I go, it is always to Israel.

Nachman of Bratzlav

The Land of Israel will be small . . . but the people of Israel will make it great . . . not in opulence but in eminence will their destiny be fulfilled, and the elixir of their pride will be distilled not out of dominion or far-flung borders, but out of the faithful and skilful building of the good society.

Abba Hillel Silver

The State of Israel will prove itself not by material wealth, not by military might or technical achievement, but by its moral character and human values.

David Ben Gurion

'Gather in the exiles' is the messianic prayer for integration of all nations into one mankind under the kingship of God. Men in fear of men, men lacking freedom are the exiles who turn to God with the prayer for the ingathering of the exiles. The exiles crave to return to God's peace, to *shalom*. The Jewish people with its messianic prayer for the redemption of the exiles is like the priest who prays for mankind. In the diaspora we are without the protection of the nation state, we are entirely thrown upon God. He is our shield, or we are lost. This is the prophetic situation of every Jew, be he a simple small shopkeeper or a luminary of science or art. The diaspora makes the Jew. This is how the election of God works.

Ignaz Maybaum

Said the Ropshitzer: By our service to God we build Jerusalem daily. One of us adds a row, another only a brick. When Jerusalem is completed, the Redemption will come.

Every single person, according to what he is, is able to find himself within the book of psalms, and earn repentance through reading the psalms.

Nachman of Bratzlav

אם אשכחך ירושלים
תשכח ימיני

PSALM ANTHOLOGY

DESCRIPTIONS OF PSALMS

1. The way of the righteous and the way of the wicked.
3. Confidence under persecution.
4. Confidence in God.
8. Man's place in creation.
11. Reliance on God's judgment in persecution.
12. Truth in a world of lies.
14. God looks down on corruption in the world.
15. Who may dwell with God.
16. Happiness and trust.
17. An upright man appeals to God.
19. The universe and Torah, witnesses to God.
20. A prayer before battle.
23. The Lord is my shepherd.
24. Greeting the universal king at the temple doors.
25. The prayer of the humble man. An alphabetic psalm.
27. Trust triumphs over fear.
29. God in the storm.
30. Thanksgiving after danger.
33. A national hymn of thanks.
34. A man praises God's justice. An alphabetic psalm.
36. The inner conflict between good and evil.
37. The problem of the prosperity of the wicked. An alphabetic psalm.
40. A prayer for God's help.
42/43. The lament of the exile.
46. God, the nation's fortress.
47. God, the ruler over the nations.
49. Death makes rich and poor alike.
50. God accuses His people of insincerity.
51. The repentant sinner.
57. God, the refuge in danger.
62. Safety is from God and not from man.
63. Longing for God in the wilderness.
67. A harvest hymn for all peoples.
71. A prayer in old age.
72. God's perfect ruler.
73. A man's faith is tested.
77. Hope in God after national disaster.
82. Against corrupt authority.
84. The pilgrim's song of joy.
85. Past captivity and future peace.

א

אַשְׁרֵי־הָאִישׁ אֲשֶׁר לֹא הָלַךְ בַּעֲצַת רְשָׁעִים

וּבְדֶרֶךְ חַטָּאִים לֹא עָמָד וּבְמוֹשַׁב לֵצִים לֹא יָשָׁב׃

כִּי אִם־בְּתוֹרַת יְהוָֹה חֶפְצוֹ וּבְתוֹרָתוֹ יֶהְגֶּה יוֹמָם וָלָיְלָה׃

וְהָיָה כְּעֵץ שָׁתוּל עַל־פַּלְגֵי מָיִם אֲשֶׁר פִּרְיוֹ יִתֵּן בְּעִתּוֹ

וְעָלֵהוּ לֹא־יִבּוֹל וְכֹל אֲשֶׁר־יַעֲשֶׂה יַצְלִיחַ׃

לֹא־כֵן הָרְשָׁעִים כִּי אִם־כַּמֹּץ אֲשֶׁר־תִּדְּפֶנּוּ רוּחַ׃

עַל־כֵּן לֹא־יָקֻמוּ רְשָׁעִים בַּמִּשְׁפָּט וְחַטָּאִים בַּעֲדַת צַדִּיקִים׃

כִּי־יוֹדֵעַ יְהוָֹה דֶּרֶךְ צַדִּיקִים וְדֶרֶךְ רְשָׁעִים תֹּאבֵד׃

ג

מִזְמוֹר לְדָוִד בְּבָרְחוֹ מִפְּנֵי אַבְשָׁלוֹם בְּנוֹ׃

יְהוָֹה מָה־רַבּוּ צָרָי רַבִּים קָמִים עָלָי׃

רַבִּים אֹמְרִים לְנַפְשִׁי אֵין יְשׁוּעָתָה לּוֹ בֵאלֹהִים סֶלָה׃

וְאַתָּה יְהוָֹה מָגֵן בַּעֲדִי כְּבוֹדִי וּמֵרִים רֹאשִׁי׃

קוֹלִי אֶל־יְהוָֹה אֶקְרָא וַיַּעֲנֵנִי מֵהַר קָדְשׁוֹ סֶלָה׃

אֲנִי שָׁכַבְתִּי וָאִישָׁנָה הֱקִיצוֹתִי כִּי יְהוָֹה יִסְמְכֵנִי׃

לֹא־אִירָא מֵרִבְבוֹת עָם אֲשֶׁר סָבִיב שָׁתוּ עָלָי׃

1

Happy is the man
who does not follow the advice of the wicked,
nor take his stand on the sinner's road,
nor sit at ease among the scornful.
But his delight is in the teaching of the Lord,
reflecting on His teaching day and night.

He is like a tree
planted by streams of water.
It gives its fruit in its season,
its leaf never fades.
Everything he does shall prosper.

It is not like this with the wicked,
for they are like chaff blown by the wind.
Therefore the wicked shall not withstand the judgment,
nor sinners stand in the company of the just.
For the Lord watches over the way of the just,
but the way of the wicked is doomed.

3

A psalm of David, when he fled from Absalom his son.

Lord, how many are closing in on me,
how many are rising against me,
how many are saying about my life:
'No help for him in God!'

But Lord, You are the shield about me,
You are my glory, You hold my head up high.
I cry aloud, I call to the Lord,
and He answers me from His holy mountain.

Now I can lie down and go to sleep,
and then awake, for the Lord upholds me.
I need not fear the thousands of people
surrounding me, ranged against me.

קוּמָה יְהוָה הוֹשִׁיעֵנִי אֱלֹהַי

כִּי־הִכִּיתָ אֶת־כָּל־אֹיְבַי לֶחִי שִׁנֵּי רְשָׁעִים שִׁבַּרְתָּ׃

לַיהוָה הַיְשׁוּעָה עַל־עַמְּךָ בִרְכָתֶךָ סֶּלָה׃

ד

לַמְנַצֵּחַ בִּנְגִינוֹת מִזְמוֹר לְדָוִד׃

בְּקָרְאִי עֲנֵנִי אֱלֹהֵי צִדְקִי בַּצָּר הִרְחַבְתָּ לִּי חָנֵּנִי וּשְׁמַע תְּפִלָּתִי׃

בְּנֵי אִישׁ עַד־מֶה כְבוֹדִי לִכְלִמָּה תֶּאֱהָבוּן רִיק תְּבַקְשׁוּ כָזָב סֶלָה׃

וּדְעוּ כִּי־הִפְלָה יְהוָה חָסִיד לוֹ יְהוָה יִשְׁמַע בְּקָרְאִי אֵלָיו׃

רִגְזוּ וְאַל־תֶּחֱטָאוּ אִמְרוּ בִלְבַבְכֶם עַל־מִשְׁכַּבְכֶם וְדֹמּוּ סֶלָה׃

זִבְחוּ זִבְחֵי־צֶדֶק וּבִטְחוּ אֶל־יְהוָה׃

רַבִּים אֹמְרִים מִי־יַרְאֵנוּ טוֹב נְסָה־עָלֵינוּ אוֹר פָּנֶיךָ יְהוָה׃

נָתַתָּה שִׂמְחָה בְלִבִּי מֵעֵת דְּגָנָם וְתִירוֹשָׁם רָבּוּ׃

בְּשָׁלוֹם יַחְדָּו אֶשְׁכְּבָה וְאִישָׁן כִּי־אַתָּה יְהוָה לְבָדָד לָבֶטַח תּוֹשִׁיבֵנִי׃

ח

לַמְנַצֵּחַ עַל־הַגִּתִּית מִזְמוֹר לְדָוִד׃

יְהוָה אֲדֹנֵינוּ מָה־אַדִּיר שִׁמְךָ בְּכָל־הָאָרֶץ אֲשֶׁר תְּנָה הוֹדְךָ עַל־הַשָּׁמָיִם׃

מִפִּי עוֹלְלִים וְיֹנְקִים יִסַּדְתָּ עֹז לְמַעַן צוֹרְרֶיךָ לְהַשְׁבִּית אוֹיֵב וּמִתְנַקֵּם׃

Lord, rise up!
 My God, save me!
For You struck all my enemies in the face,
 shattered the teeth of the wicked!

Deliverance comes from the Lord.
 Your blessing on Your people!

4

For the choirmaster.   With string music.   A psalm of David.

When I call, answer me, God of justice!
 You set me free when troubles close me in.
 Show me Your favour and hear my prayer!

Mortal men, how long will you put My glory to shame?
 What you love is illusion, what you seek is a lie.

But know this! The Lord has set apart those devoted to Him.
 The Lord hears whenever I call Him.

Tremble and do not sin! Search your heart as you lie in bed and
 be still.
 Let justice be your offering, and trust in the Lord.

'Who can bring us happiness?' many people say.
 Lord, show us the light of Your face!

You put in my heart a greater joy than theirs,
 for all the abundance of their corn and wine.

In peace I lie down and fall asleep,
 for, Lord, You alone let me live in safety.

8

For the choirmaster.   Upon the gittit.   A psalm of David.

Lord, our Lord, how glorious is Your name
 in all the earth!

Your majesty is proclaimed beyond the heavens.
 In the mouths of children and babes in arms
You placed strength to rebuke Your foes,
 silencing enmity and vengeance.

כִּי־אֶרְאֶה שָׁמֶיךָ מַעֲשֵׂה אֶצְבְּעֹתֶיךָ יָרֵחַ וְכוֹכָבִים אֲשֶׁר
כּוֹנָנְתָּה:

מָה־אֱנוֹשׁ כִּי־תִזְכְּרֶנּוּ וּבֶן־אָדָם כִּי תִפְקְדֶנּוּ:

וַתְּחַסְּרֵהוּ מְּעַט מֵאֱלֹהִים וְכָבוֹד וְהָדָר תְּעַטְּרֵהוּ:
תַּמְשִׁילֵהוּ בְּמַעֲשֵׂי יָדֶיךָ כֹּל שַׁתָּה תַחַת־רַגְלָיו:

צֹנֶה וַאֲלָפִים כֻּלָּם וְגַם בַּהֲמוֹת שָׂדָי:
צִפּוֹר שָׁמַיִם וּדְגֵי הַיָּם עֹבֵר אָרְחוֹת יַמִּים:

יְהוָה אֲדֹנֵינוּ מָה־אַדִּיר שִׁמְךָ בְּכָל־הָאָרֶץ:

יא

לַמְנַצֵּחַ לְדָוִד

בַּיהוָה חָסִיתִי אֵיךְ תֹּאמְרוּ לְנַפְשִׁי נוּדִי הַרְכֶם צִפּוֹר:

כִּי הִנֵּה הָרְשָׁעִים יִדְרְכוּן קֶשֶׁת כּוֹנְנוּ חִצָּם עַל־יֶתֶר
לִירוֹת בְּמוֹ־אֹפֶל לְיִשְׁרֵי־לֵב:

כִּי הַשָּׁתוֹת יֵהָרֵסוּן צַדִּיק מַה־פָּעָל:

יְהוָה בְּהֵיכַל קָדְשׁוֹ יְהוָה בַּשָּׁמַיִם כִּסְאוֹ עֵינָיו יֶחֱזוּ
עַפְעַפָּיו יִבְחֲנוּ בְּנֵי אָדָם:

יְהוָה צַדִּיק יִבְחָן וְרָשָׁע וְאֹהֵב חָמָס שָׂנְאָה נַפְשׁוֹ:

יַמְטֵר עַל־רְשָׁעִים פַּחִים אֵשׁ וְגָפְרִית
וְרוּחַ זִלְעָפוֹת מְנָת כּוֹסָם:

כִּי־צַדִּיק יְהוָה צְדָקוֹת אָהֵב יָשָׁר יֶחֱזוּ פָנֵימוֹ:

When I look up at Your heavens, the work of Your hands,
the moon and the stars You set in place,
what is man that You should remember him,
or the son of man that You should care for him.

You have made him little less than divine,
and crowned him with glory and splendour.
You gave him power over the works of Your hands,
You put all things beneath his feet.

Sheep and cattle, all of them,
also the beasts of the field,
the birds of the air, and the fish of the sea,
who make their way through the oceans.

Lord, our Lord, how glorious is Your name
in all the earth!

11

For the choirmaster.   David's.

In the Lord I have taken shelter!
How can you say to me,
'Fly back like a bird to its mountain!'

See how the wicked are bending the bow,
fitting their arrow to the string,
to shoot the honest man from the shadow.

When the foundations are undermined,
what can a righteous man do!

The Lord is in His holy temple,
the Lord whose throne is in heaven.
His eyes can see!
His gaze searches all mankind!

The Lord may test the just, but the wicked
and the lover of violence, His being hates.

He rains coals of fire and brimstone on the wicked;
from their cup they shall drink a burning wind.

The Lord is just and loves justice,
the upright shall see His face!

יב

לַמְנַצֵּחַ עַל־הַשְּׁמִינִית מִזְמוֹר לְדָוִד:

הוֹשִׁיעָה יְהוָה כִּי־גָמַר חָסִיד כִּי־פַסּוּ אֱמוּנִים מִבְּנֵי אָדָם:
שָׁוְא יְדַבְּרוּ אִישׁ אֶת־רֵעֵהוּ שְׂפַת חֲלָקוֹת בְּלֵב וָלֵב יְדַבֵּרוּ:

יַכְרֵת יְהוָה כָּל־שִׂפְתֵי חֲלָקוֹת לָשׁוֹן מְדַבֶּרֶת גְּדֹלוֹת:
אֲשֶׁר אָמְרוּ לִלְשֹׁנֵנוּ נַגְבִּיר שְׂפָתֵינוּ אִתָּנוּ מִי אָדוֹן לָנוּ:

מִשֹּׁד עֲנִיִּים מֵאֶנְקַת אֶבְיוֹנִים עַתָּה אָקוּם יֹאמַר יְהוָה
אָשִׁית בְּיֵשַׁע יָפִיחַ לוֹ:

אִמְרוֹת יְהוָה אֲמָרוֹת טְהֹרוֹת כֶּסֶף צָרוּף בַּעֲלִיל לָאָרֶץ
מְזֻקָּק שִׁבְעָתָיִם:

אַתָּה־יְהוָה תִּשְׁמְרֵם תִּצְּרֶנּוּ מִן־הַדּוֹר זוּ לְעוֹלָם:
סָבִיב רְשָׁעִים יִתְהַלָּכוּן כְּרֻם זֻלּוּת לִבְנֵי אָדָם:

יד

לַמְנַצֵּחַ לְדָוִד

אָמַר נָבָל בְּלִבּוֹ אֵין אֱלֹהִים הִשְׁחִיתוּ הִתְעִיבוּ עֲלִילָה אֵין
עֹשֵׂה־טוֹב:

יְהוָה מִשָּׁמַיִם הִשְׁקִיף עַל־בְּנֵי־אָדָם לִרְאוֹת הֲיֵשׁ מַשְׂכִּיל
דֹּרֵשׁ אֶת־אֱלֹהִים:

הַכֹּל סָר יַחְדָּו נֶאֱלָחוּ אֵין עֹשֵׂה־טוֹב אֵין גַּם־אֶחָד:

12

For the choirmaster.   On the sheminit.   A psalm of David.

Save us, Lord, for the pious are no more
    and the faithful have vanished from mankind.
People lie to one another,
    they speak with flattering lips and with false hearts.

May the Lord cut off all flattering lips
    and tongues that speak high-sounding words
saying, 'We shall strengthen our tongue,
    our lips are our own; who is Lord over us!'

'Because of the oppression of the poor,
    and the groaning of the needy,
    now I shall arise,' says the Lord,
    'and make them secure though they are despised.'

The words of the Lord are pure words,
    silver from the furnace, poured into a mould,
    seven times refined.

It is You, Lord, who will guard the oppressed,
    and ever protect us from this generation.
The wicked go about on every side,
    and the worthless are prized by mankind.

14

For the choirmaster.   David's.

The fool has said in his heart,
    'There is no God!'
People deal corruptly, they are depraved,
    none of them does good.

The Lord looks down from heaven
    on every man alive,
to see if there is anyone who understands,
    who searches for God.

All of them have fallen away,
    they have gone rotten together.
None of them does good,
    not even one.

הֲלֹא יָדְעוּ כָּל־פֹּעֲלֵי אָוֶן אֹכְלֵי עַמִּי אָכְלוּ לֶחֶם
יְהוָה לֹא קָרָאוּ׃

שָׁם פָּחֲדוּ פָחַד כִּי־אֱלֹהִים בְּדוֹר צַדִּיק׃

עֲצַת־עָנִי תָבִישׁוּ כִּי יְהוָה מַחְסֵהוּ׃

מִי־יִתֵּן מִצִּיּוֹן יְשׁוּעַת יִשְׂרָאֵל בְּשׁוּב יְהוָה שְׁבוּת עַמּוֹ
יָגֵל יַעֲקֹב יִשְׂמַח יִשְׂרָאֵל׃

טו

מִזְמוֹר לְדָוִד

יְהוָה מִי־יָגוּר בְּאָהֳלֶךָ מִי־יִשְׁכֹּן בְּהַר קָדְשֶׁךָ׃

הוֹלֵךְ תָּמִים וּפֹעֵל צֶדֶק וְדֹבֵר אֱמֶת בִּלְבָבוֹ׃

לֹא־רָגַל עַל־לְשֹׁנוֹ לֹא־עָשָׂה לְרֵעֵהוּ רָעָה
וְחֶרְפָּה לֹא־נָשָׂא עַל־קְרֹבוֹ׃

נִבְזֶה בְּעֵינָיו נִמְאָס וְאֶת־יִרְאֵי יְהוָה יְכַבֵּד
נִשְׁבַּע לְהָרַע וְלֹא יָמִר׃

כַּסְפּוֹ לֹא־נָתַן בְּנֶשֶׁךְ וְשֹׁחַד עַל־נָקִי לֹא לָקָח
עֹשֵׂה־אֵלֶּה לֹא יִמּוֹט לְעוֹלָם׃

טז

מִכְתָּם לְדָוִד

שָׁמְרֵנִי אֵל כִּי־חָסִיתִי בָךְ׃

אָמַרְתְּ לַיהוָה אֲדֹנָי אָתָּה טוֹבָתִי בַּל־עָלֶיךָ׃

Are they so ignorant,
    all of those who do evil,
devouring my people as they devour food,
    never mentioning the Lord?

But look how they tremble with fear,
    for God is on the side of the just.
You may mock the poor man's hope,
    but the Lord is his protection.

If only Israel's salvation would come from Zion,
    when the Lord brings His people home!
    What joy for Jacob! What happiness for Israel!

15

A psalm of David.

Lord, who may live in Your tent,
    who may dwell on the mountain of Your holiness?
He who follows integrity
    and does what is right
    and speaks the truth in his heart.
No malice is on his tongue,
    he never wrongs his fellowman,
    casts no discredit on his neighbour.
A worthless man is rejected in his eyes,
    but he honours those who fear the Lord.
He swears to his own hurt, but does not retract,
    he does not give his money expecting gain
    and takes no bribe against the innocent.
Such a man will never be shaken.

16

A michtam of David.

Keep me, God, for in You I found refuge.
I said to the Lord, 'You are my Lord,
    my happiness lies in You alone.'

לִקְדוֹשִׁים אֲשֶׁר־בָּאָרֶץ הֵמָּה וְאַדִּירֵי כָּל־חֶפְצִי־בָם :

יִרְבּוּ עַצְּבוֹתָם אַחֵר מָהָרוּ בַּל־אַסִּיךְ נִסְכֵּיהֶם מִדָּם
וּבַל־אֶשָּׂא אֶת־שְׁמוֹתָם עַל־שְׂפָתָי :

יְהוָה מְנָת חֶלְקִי וְכוֹסִי אַתָּה תּוֹמִיךְ גּוֹרָלִי :

חֲבָלִים נָפְלוּ־לִי בַּנְּעִימִים אַף־נַחֲלָת שָׁפְרָה עָלָי :

אֲבָרֵךְ אֶת־יְהוָה אֲשֶׁר יְעָצָנִי אַף־לֵילוֹת יִסְּרוּנִי כִלְיוֹתָי :

שִׁוִּיתִי יְהוָה לְנֶגְדִּי תָמִיד כִּי מִימִינִי בַּל־אֶמּוֹט :

לָכֵן שָׂמַח לִבִּי וַיָּגֶל כְּבוֹדִי אַף־בְּשָׂרִי יִשְׁכֹּן לָבֶטַח :

כִּי לֹא־תַעֲזֹב נַפְשִׁי לִשְׁאוֹל לֹא־תִתֵּן חֲסִידְךָ לִרְאוֹת שָׁחַת :

תּוֹדִיעֵנִי אֹרַח חַיִּים שֹׂבַע שְׂמָחוֹת אֶת־פָּנֶיךָ
נְעִמוֹת בִּימִינְךָ נֶצַח :

יז

תְּפִלָּה לְדָוִד

שִׁמְעָה יְהוָה צֶדֶק הַקְשִׁיבָה רִנָּתִי
הַאֲזִינָה תְפִלָּתִי בְּלֹא שִׂפְתֵי מִרְמָה :

מִלְּפָנֶיךָ מִשְׁפָּטִי יֵצֵא עֵינֶיךָ תֶּחֱזֶינָה מֵישָׁרִים :

בָּחַנְתָּ לִבִּי פָּקַדְתָּ לַּיְלָה
צְרַפְתַּנִי בַל־תִּמְצָא זַמֹּתִי בַּל־יַעֲבָר־פִּי :

לִפְעֻלּוֹת אָדָם בִּדְבַר שְׂפָתֶיךָ אֲנִי שָׁמַרְתִּי אָרְחוֹת פָּרִיץ :

All my desire is to be among
   the holy men of the land, them and the noble-hearted.
Sorrows increase for those who follow another god;
   never will I pour out their offerings of blood,
   never will I bring their names to my lips.

Lord, my share of the heritage, my cup,
   it is You who keep my fate secure.
The lines have fallen for me in pleasant places;
   a wonderful heritage is mine.

I will bless the Lord who gives me counsel,
   even at night my inner self instructs me.
I keep the Lord before me always;
   with Him at my right hand I cannot be shaken.

So my heart is glad, and my soul rejoices,
   even my body shall rest in safety,
for You will not abandon my soul in death,
   nor let Your faithful know corruption.

You will show me the path of life,
   the fullness of joy in Your presence,
   everlasting happiness at Your right hand.

17

A prayer of David.

Listen, Lord! Hear my call for justice!
   Listen to my plea.
Hear my prayer,
   for my lips do not deceive.
My judgment comes from You,
   for Your eyes see what is right.

You search my heart,
   and come to me at night.
You test me, but do not find
   a thought that should not pass my lips.
As for men's actions,
   I kept far from violent ways
   at the command of Your lips.

תָּמֹךְ אֲשֻׁרַי בְּמַעְגְּלוֹתֶיךָ בַּל־נָמוֹטוּ פְעָמָי :

אֲנִי־קְרָאתִיךָ כִי־תַעֲנֵנִי אֵל הַט־אָזְנְךָ לִי שְׁמַע אִמְרָתִי :

הַפְלֵה חֲסָדֶיךָ מוֹשִׁיעַ חוֹסִים מִמִּתְקוֹמְמִים בִּימִינֶךָ :

שָׁמְרֵנִי כְּאִישׁוֹן בַּת־עָיִן בְּצֵל כְּנָפֶיךָ תַּסְתִּירֵנִי :

מִפְּנֵי רְשָׁעִים זוּ שַׁדּוּנִי אֹיְבַי בְּנֶפֶשׁ יַקִּיפוּ עָלָי :

חֶלְבָּמוֹ סָגְרוּ פִּימוֹ דִּבְּרוּ בְגֵאוּת :

אַשֻּׁרֵנוּ עַתָּה סְבָבוּנוּ עֵינֵיהֶם יָשִׁיתוּ לִנְטוֹת בָּאָרֶץ :

דִּמְיֹנוֹ כְּאַרְיֵה יִכְסוֹף לִטְרוֹף וְכִכְפִיר יֹשֵׁב בְּמִסְתָּרִים :

קוּמָה יְהֹוָה קַדְּמָה פָנָיו הַכְרִיעֵהוּ פַּלְּטָה נַפְשִׁי מֵרָשָׁע חַרְבֶּךָ :

מִמְתִים יָדְךָ יְהֹוָה מִמְתִים מֵחֶלֶד חֶלְקָם בַּחַיִּים וּצְפוּנְךָ

תְּמַלֵּא בִטְנָם יִשְׂבְּעוּ בָנִים וְהִנִּיחוּ יִתְרָם לְעוֹלְלֵיהֶם :

אֲנִי בְּצֶדֶק אֶחֱזֶה פָנֶיךָ אֶשְׂבְּעָה בְהָקִיץ תְּמוּנָתֶךָ :

יט

לַמְנַצֵּחַ מִזְמוֹר לְדָוִד :

הַשָּׁמַיִם מְסַפְּרִים כְּבוֹד־אֵל וּמַעֲשֵׂה יָדָיו מַגִּיד הָרָקִיעַ :

יוֹם לְיוֹם יַבִּיעַ אֹמֶר וְלַיְלָה לְּלַיְלָה יְחַוֶּה־דָּעַת :

My steps kept firmly to Your paths,
   my feet never slipped.
It is I who call You, for You answer me, God;
   turn to me, listen to what I say!

Show the wonder of Your love!
   Your right hand saves those who trust in You
   from their attackers.
Keep me as the apple of Your eye,
   hide me in the shadow of Your wings
from the wicked who oppress me,
   from the enemies who besiege my soul.

They are buried in their fat,
   their mouths drip with pride.
At every step they surround us now
   looking for a chance to cast us to the ground.
They are like lions ready to claw,
   like a young lion crouched in ambush.

Rise up Lord! Confront them, bring them down!
   Rescue my soul from the wicked by Your sword.
Rescue me from such men by Your hand,
   from men whose real concern is worldly life.
You give them their fill of affluence
   they have children in plenty,
   yet to babies they shall leave their wealth.
Yet for me the reward of righteousness is to see Your face
   and be satisfied with Your likeness as I awake.

19

For the choirmaster.   A psalm of David.

Heaven declares the glory of God
   and the sky reveals the work of His hands.
Each day pours out speech to the other
   and night to night passes on the knowledge.

אֵין־אֹמֶר וְאֵין דְּבָרִים בְּלִי נִשְׁמָע קוֹלָם:

בְּכָל־הָאָרֶץ יָצָא קַוָּם וּבִקְצֵה תֵבֵל מִלֵּיהֶם

לַשֶּׁמֶשׁ שָׂם־אֹהֶל בָּהֶם:

וְהוּא כְּחָתָן יֹצֵא מֵחֻפָּתוֹ יָשִׂישׂ כְּגִבּוֹר לָרוּץ אֹרַח:

מִקְצֵה הַשָּׁמַיִם מוֹצָאוֹ וּתְקוּפָתוֹ עַל־קְצוֹתָם

וְאֵין נִסְתָּר מֵחַמָּתוֹ:

תּוֹרַת יְהֹוָה תְּמִימָה מְשִׁיבַת נָפֶשׁ

עֵדוּת יְהֹוָה נֶאֱמָנָה מַחְכִּימַת פֶּתִי:

פִּקּוּדֵי יְהֹוָה יְשָׁרִים מְשַׂמְּחֵי־לֵב

מִצְוַת יְהֹוָה בָּרָה מְאִירַת עֵינָיִם:

יִרְאַת יְהֹוָה טְהוֹרָה עוֹמֶדֶת לָעַד

מִשְׁפְּטֵי־יְהֹוָה אֱמֶת צָדְקוּ יַחְדָּו:

הַנֶּחֱמָדִים מִזָּהָב וּמִפַּז רָב וּמְתוּקִים מִדְּבַשׁ וְנֹפֶת צוּפִים:

גַּם־עַבְדְּךָ נִזְהָר בָּהֶם בְּשָׁמְרָם עֵקֶב רָב:

שְׁגִיאוֹת מִי־יָבִין מִנִּסְתָּרוֹת נַקֵּנִי:

גַּם מִזֵּדִים חֲשֹׁךְ עַבְדֶּךָ אַל־יִמְשְׁלוּ־בִי אָז אֵיתָם

וְנִקֵּיתִי מִפֶּשַׁע רָב:

יִהְיוּ לְרָצוֹן אִמְרֵי־פִי וְהֶגְיוֹן לִבִּי לְפָנֶיךָ יְהֹוָה צוּרִי וְגֹאֲלִי:

No speech at all! There are no words!
   Their sound cannot be heard!
And yet their scope extends through all the earth
   and their message to the end of the world.
In it He set a tent for the sun;
   it is like a bridegroom coming from his bridal chamber,
   like a champion who rejoices in running a race.
At one end of heaven is the rising of the sun
   and its course to the other end;
   nothing can escape from its heat.

The teaching of the Lord is perfect,
   restoring the soul.
The evidence of the Lord can be trusted,
   making wise the simple.
The duties of the Lord are right,
   rejoicing the heart.
The command of the Lord is clear,
   enlightening the eyes.
The fear of the Lord is pure,
   standing forever.
The judgments of the Lord are true,
   all of them just.

They are more to be desired than gold,
   even the finest gold.
They are even sweeter than the honey
   as it drips from the honeycomb.
Through them Your servant is warned,
   in keeping them much follows.
Who can detect his own failings,
   cleanse me from hidden faults.
Preserve Your servant from sins of pride,
   do not let them control me!
Then I shall be blameless,
   innocent of grave sin.
May the words of my mouth
   and the meditation of my heart
   be acceptable to You,
O Lord, my rock and my redeemer.

כ

לַמְנַצֵּחַ מִזְמוֹר לְדָוִד:

יַעַנְךָ יְהֹוָה בְּיוֹם צָרָה יְשַׂגֶּבְךָ שֵׁם אֱלֹהֵי יַעֲקֹב:

יִשְׁלַח־עֶזְרְךָ מִקֹּדֶשׁ וּמִצִּיּוֹן יִסְעָדֶךָּ:

יִזְכֹּר כָּל־מִנְחֹתֶיךָ וְעוֹלָתְךָ יְדַשְּׁנֶה סֶלָה:

יִתֶּן־לְךָ כִלְבָבֶךָ וְכָל־עֲצָתְךָ יְמַלֵּא:

נְרַנְּנָה בִּישׁוּעָתֶךָ וּבְשֵׁם־אֱלֹהֵינוּ נִדְגֹּל
יְמַלֵּא יְהֹוָה כָּל־מִשְׁאֲלוֹתֶיךָ:

עַתָּה יָדַעְתִּי כִּי הוֹשִׁיעַ יְהֹוָה מְשִׁיחוֹ יַעֲנֵהוּ מִשְּׁמֵי קָדְשׁוֹ
בִּגְבֻרוֹת יֵשַׁע יְמִינוֹ:

אֵלֶּה בָרֶכֶב וְאֵלֶּה בַסּוּסִים וַאֲנַחְנוּ בְּשֵׁם־יְהֹוָה אֱלֹהֵינוּ נַזְכִּיר:

הֵמָּה כָּרְעוּ וְנָפָלוּ וַאֲנַחְנוּ קַּמְנוּ וַנִּתְעוֹדָד:

יְהֹוָה הוֹשִׁיעָה הַמֶּלֶךְ יַעֲנֵנוּ בְיוֹם־קָרְאֵנוּ:

כג

מִזְמוֹר לְדָוִד

יְהֹוָה רֹעִי לֹא אֶחְסָר:

בִּנְאוֹת דֶּשֶׁא יַרְבִּיצֵנִי עַל־מֵי מְנֻחוֹת יְנַהֲלֵנִי:

נַפְשִׁי יְשׁוֹבֵב יַנְחֵנִי בְמַעְגְּלֵי־צֶדֶק לְמַעַן שְׁמוֹ:

20

For the choirmaster.   A psalm of David.

May the Lord answer you on the day of trouble,
    may the name of Jacob's God protect you.
May He send you help from the sanctuary,
    and give you support from Zion.

May He remember all you have sacrificed,
    and accept your offerings.
May He give you your heart's desire,
    and make all your plans succeed.

We shout for joy at your victory,
    and we in God's name plant our banners.
'May the Lord grant all you ask!'

Now I know that God
    saves His anointed.
He answers him from His holy heaven,
    with the mighty victories of His right hand.

Some trust in chariots, and some in horses,
    but we proclaim the name of the Lord our God.
They crumple and fall!
    But we rise up and stand firm.

Save us Lord! May the king answer us
    on the day we call!

23

A psalm of David.

The Lord is my shepherd
    I shall not want.

In green fields He lets me lie
    by quiet streams He leads me.
    He restores my soul.

He guides me in paths of truth
    for such is His name.

גַּם כִּי־אֵלֵךְ בְּגֵיא צַלְמָוֶת לֹא־אִירָא רָע כִּי־אַתָּה עִמָּדִי
שִׁבְטְךָ וּמִשְׁעַנְתֶּךָ הֵמָּה יְנַחֲמֻנִי:

תַּעֲרֹךְ לְפָנַי שֻׁלְחָן נֶגֶד צֹרְרָי דִּשַּׁנְתָּ בַשֶּׁמֶן רֹאשִׁי כּוֹסִי רְוָיָה:

אַךְ טוֹב וָחֶסֶד יִרְדְּפוּנִי כָּל־יְמֵי חַיָּי
וְשַׁבְתִּי בְּבֵית־יְהוָה לְאֹרֶךְ יָמִים:

כד

לְדָוִד מִזְמוֹר

לַיהוָה הָאָרֶץ וּמְלוֹאָהּ תֵּבֵל וְיֹשְׁבֵי בָהּ:
כִּי־הוּא עַל־יַמִּים יְסָדָהּ וְעַל־נְהָרוֹת יְכוֹנְנֶהָ:

מִי־יַעֲלֶה בְהַר־יְהוָה וּמִי־יָקוּם בִּמְקוֹם קָדְשׁוֹ:
נְקִי כַפַּיִם וּבַר־לֵבָב אֲשֶׁר לֹא־נָשָׂא לַשָּׁוְא נַפְשׁוֹ
וְלֹא נִשְׁבַּע לְמִרְמָה:

יִשָּׂא בְרָכָה מֵאֵת יְהוָה וּצְדָקָה מֵאֱלֹהֵי יִשְׁעוֹ:
זֶה דּוֹר דֹּרְשָׁיו מְבַקְשֵׁי פָנֶיךָ יַעֲקֹב סֶלָה:

שְׂאוּ שְׁעָרִים רָאשֵׁיכֶם וְהִנָּשְׂאוּ פִּתְחֵי עוֹלָם
וְיָבוֹא מֶלֶךְ הַכָּבוֹד:

מִי זֶה מֶלֶךְ הַכָּבוֹד יְהוָה עִזּוּז וְגִבּוֹר יְהוָה גִּבּוֹר מִלְחָמָה:

Though I walk through the valley of the shadow of death
    I fear no harm
    for You are beside me;
    Your rod and staff
    they comfort me.

You spread a table before me
    in front of my enemies.
    You soothe my head with oil;
    my cup runs over.

Surely goodness and mercy seek me
    all the days of my life
    and I shall dwell in the house of the Lord
    forever.

24

David's psalm.

The earth and its fullness belong to the Lord,
    the world and those who dwell in it,
for it is He who set it on the seas
    and made it firm upon the depths.

Who may ascend the mountain of the Lord
    and who may stand in the place of His holiness?
He whose hands are clean,
    whose heart is pure,
who has not given up his soul to worthless things
    nor committed himself to deception.

He shall earn a blessing from the Lord
    and be justified by God who saves him.
This is a generation that searches for Him,
    those who seek Your presence are the family of Jacob.

Gates, lift up your heads!
    Be raised, you everlasting doors!
    Let the king of glory enter!
'Who is this king of glory?'
    The Lord, strong and mighty,
    the Lord, mighty in battle!

שְׂאוּ שְׁעָרִים רָאשֵׁיכֶם וּשְׂאוּ פִּתְחֵי עוֹלָם וְיָבֹא מֶלֶךְ הַכָּבוֹד :

מִי הוּא זֶה מֶלֶךְ הַכָּבוֹד יְהֹוָה צְבָאוֹת הוּא מֶלֶךְ הַכָּבוֹד

סֶלָה :

כה

לְדָוִד

אֵלֶיךָ יְהֹוָה נַפְשִׁי אֶשָּׂא :

אֱלֹהַי בְּךָ בָטַחְתִּי אַל־אֵבוֹשָׁה אַל־יַעַלְצוּ אֹיְבַי לִי :

גַּם כָּל־קֹוֶיךָ לֹא יֵבֹשׁוּ יֵבֹשׁוּ הַבּוֹגְדִים רֵיקָם :

דְּרָכֶיךָ יְהֹוָה הוֹדִיעֵנִי אֹרְחוֹתֶיךָ לַמְּדֵנִי :

הַדְרִיכֵנִי בַאֲמִתֶּךָ וְלַמְּדֵנִי כִּי־אַתָּה אֱלֹהֵי יִשְׁעִי

אוֹתְךָ קִוִּיתִי כָּל־הַיּוֹם :

זְכֹר־רַחֲמֶיךָ יְהֹוָה וַחֲסָדֶיךָ כִּי מֵעוֹלָם הֵמָּה :

חַטֹּאות נְעוּרַי וּפְשָׁעַי אַל־תִּזְכֹּר כְּחַסְדְּךָ זְכָר־לִי־אַתָּה

לְמַעַן טוּבְךָ יְהֹוָה :

טוֹב־וְיָשָׁר יְהֹוָה עַל־כֵּן יוֹרֶה חַטָּאִים בַּדָּרֶךְ :

יַדְרֵךְ עֲנָוִים בַּמִּשְׁפָּט וִילַמֵּד עֲנָוִים דַּרְכּוֹ :

כָּל־אָרְחוֹת יְהֹוָה חֶסֶד וֶאֱמֶת לְנֹצְרֵי בְרִיתוֹ וְעֵדֹתָיו :

לְמַעַן־שִׁמְךָ יְהֹוָה וְסָלַחְתָּ לַעֲוֹנִי כִּי רַב־הוּא :

Gates, lift up your heads!
    Rise up you everlasting doors!
    Let the king of glory enter!
'Who is He, this king of glory?'
    The Lord of all creation,
    He is the king of glory!

25

David's.

Lord, I set my hope on You.
My God, I put my trust in You,
    let me not be put to shame,
    do not let my enemies triumph over me.
No, those who hope in You are never shamed;
    ashamed are traitors without a cause.

Lord, let me know Your ways,
    teach me Your paths.
Guide me in Your truth and teach me,
    for You are the God of my salvation
    for whom I wait all day long.
Remember Your compassion Lord, and Your mercies,
    for they have existed since ages past.
Do not remember the sins of my youth and my wrongdoing,
    but remember me in love,
    for the sake of Your righteousness, Lord.
Good and upright is the Lord,
    therefore He shows the way to sinners.
He guides the humble in justice,
    He teaches the humble His way.

All the Lord's paths are mercy and truth
    for those who keep His covenant and do His will.
Lord, for the sake of Your name, forgive my guilt
    pardon my iniquity for it is great.

מִי־זֶה הָאִישׁ יְרֵא יְהוָה יוֹרֶנּוּ בְּדֶרֶךְ יִבְחָר:

נַפְשׁוֹ בְּטוֹב תָּלִין וְזַרְעוֹ יִירַשׁ אָרֶץ:

סוֹד יְהוָה לִירֵאָיו וּבְרִיתוֹ לְהוֹדִיעָם:

עֵינַי תָּמִיד אֶל־יְהוָה כִּי הוּא־יוֹצִיא מֵרֶשֶׁת רַגְלָי:

פְּנֵה־אֵלַי וְחָנֵּנִי כִּי־יָחִיד וְעָנִי אָנִי:

צָרוֹת לְבָבִי הִרְחִיבוּ מִמְּצוּקוֹתַי הוֹצִיאֵנִי:

רְאֵה עָנְיִי וַעֲמָלִי וְשָׂא לְכָל־חַטֹּאותָי:

רְאֵה־אוֹיְבַי כִּי־רָבּוּ וְשִׂנְאַת חָמָס שְׂנֵאוּנִי:

שָׁמְרָה נַפְשִׁי וְהַצִּילֵנִי אַל־אֵבוֹשׁ כִּי־חָסִיתִי בָךְ:

תֹּם־וָיֹשֶׁר יִצְּרוּנִי כִּי קִוִּיתִיךָ:

פְּדֵה אֱלֹהִים אֶת־יִשְׂרָאֵל מִכֹּל צָרוֹתָיו:

כז

לְדָוִד

יְהוָה אוֹרִי וְיִשְׁעִי מִמִּי אִירָא יְהוָה מָעוֹז־חַיַּי מִמִּי אֶפְחָד:

בִּקְרֹב עָלַי מְרֵעִים לֶאֱכֹל אֶת־בְּשָׂרִי צָרַי וְאֹיְבַי לִי

הֵמָּה כָּשְׁלוּ וְנָפָלוּ:

Anyone who fears the Lord,
   the Lord will show him the way he should choose.
His soul shall live in goodness
   and his children inherit the land.
The hidden purpose of the Lord is kept for those who fear Him,
   His covenant also to give them knowledge.

My eyes are ever on the Lord,
   for it is He who releases my foot from the snare.
Turn to me and take pity on me
   for I am lonely and poor.
The sorrows of my heart have increased,
   release me from my distress.
See my misery and pain,
   and take away all my sins.

See my enemies, how many they are,
   and how violently they hate me.
Guard my soul and deliver me;
   I fear no shame for I shelter in You.
Innocence and integrity shall preserve me
   because I waited for You.

God, redeem Israel
   from all its troubles!

27

David's.

The Lord is my light and my safety
   whom shall I fear?
The Lord is the strength of my life
   of whom shall I be afraid?
When evil men advance to attack me
   to eat up my flesh,
it is my oppressors and enemies
   who stumble and fall.

אִם־תַּחֲנֶה עָלַי מַחֲנֶה לֹא־יִירָא לִבִּי
אִם־תָּקוּם עָלַי מִלְחָמָה בְּזֹאת אֲנִי בוֹטֵחַ:

אַחַת שָׁאַלְתִּי מֵאֵת־יְהֹוָה אוֹתָהּ אֲבַקֵּשׁ
שִׁבְתִּי בְּבֵית־יְהֹוָה כָּל־יְמֵי חַיַּי
לַחֲזוֹת בְּנֹעַם־יְהֹוָה וּלְבַקֵּר בְּהֵיכָלוֹ:

כִּי יִצְפְּנֵנִי בְּסֻכֹּה בְּיוֹם רָעָה יַסְתִּרֵנִי בְּסֵתֶר אָהֳלוֹ
בְּצוּר יְרוֹמְמֵנִי:

וְעַתָּה יָרוּם רֹאשִׁי עַל אֹיְבַי סְבִיבוֹתַי
וְאֶזְבְּחָה בְאָהֳלוֹ זִבְחֵי תְרוּעָה
אָשִׁירָה וַאֲזַמְּרָה לַיהֹוָה:

שְׁמַע־יְהֹוָה קוֹלִי אֶקְרָא וְחָנֵּנִי וַעֲנֵנִי:
לְךָ אָמַר לִבִּי בַּקְּשׁוּ פָנָי אֶת־פָּנֶיךָ יְהֹוָה אֲבַקֵּשׁ:

אַל־תַּסְתֵּר פָּנֶיךָ מִמֶּנִּי אַל־תַּט־בְּאַף עַבְדֶּךָ
עֶזְרָתִי הָיִיתָ אַל־תִּטְּשֵׁנִי וְאַל־תַּעַזְבֵנִי אֱלֹהֵי יִשְׁעִי:
כִּי־אָבִי וְאִמִּי עֲזָבוּנִי וַיהֹוָה יַאַסְפֵנִי:

הוֹרֵנִי יְהֹוָה דַּרְכֶּךָ וּנְחֵנִי בְּאֹרַח מִישׁוֹר לְמַעַן שׁוֹרְרָי:
אַל־תִּתְּנֵנִי בְּנֶפֶשׁ צָרָי כִּי קָמוּ־בִי עֵדֵי־שֶׁקֶר וִיפֵחַ חָמָס:

Even if an army camped against me
  my heart would not fear.
Even if war broke out against me,
  even then I would trust.

One thing I ask of the Lord,
  that only do I seek:
to live in the house of the Lord
  all the days of my life,
to look on the beauty of the Lord
  and pray each morning in His temple.

For He shelters me under His protection
  in times of trouble.
He hides me in the cover of His tent,
  lifting me to safety on a rock.

So my head is held up high
  above my enemies around me
and I offer inside His tent
  an offering of joy.
I shall sing my psalms of joy to the Lord.

Lord, hear my voice when I call!
  Take pity on me, and answer me!
Of You my heart has said,
  'Seek My face!'
Lord, it is Your face I seek,
  do not hide Your face from me.

Do not turn away Your servant in anger,
  You have been my help.
Never leave me, never desert me,
  God of my safety.
Even if my father and mother desert me,
  the Lord will care for me still.

Lord, direct me in Your way,
  lead me in the path of integrity,
  for people lie in wait for me.
Do not put me in the power of my foes;
  the false witnesses, who pant for violence,
  are rising up against me.

לוּלֵא הֶאֱמַנְתִּי לִרְאוֹת בְּטוּב־יְהוָה בְּאֶרֶץ חַיִּים:
קַוֵּה אֶל־יְהוָה חֲזַק וְיַאֲמֵץ לִבֶּךָ וְקַוֵּה אֶל־יְהוָה:

כט

מִזְמוֹר לְדָוִד

הָבוּ לַיהוָה בְּנֵי אֵלִים הָבוּ לַיהוָה כָּבוֹד וָעֹז:
הָבוּ לַיהוָה כְּבוֹד שְׁמוֹ הִשְׁתַּחֲווּ לַיהוָה בְּהַדְרַת־קֹדֶשׁ:

קוֹל יְהוָה עַל־הַמָּיִם אֵל־הַכָּבוֹד הִרְעִים
יְהוָה עַל־מַיִם רַבִּים:
קוֹל־יְהוָה בַּכֹּחַ קוֹל יְהוָה בֶּהָדָר:

קוֹל יְהוָה שֹׁבֵר אֲרָזִים וַיְשַׁבֵּר יְהוָה אֶת־אַרְזֵי הַלְּבָנוֹן:
וַיַּרְקִידֵם כְּמוֹ־עֵגֶל לְבָנוֹן וְשִׂרְיֹן כְּמוֹ בֶן־רְאֵמִים:

קוֹל־יְהוָה חֹצֵב לַהֲבוֹת אֵשׁ:
קוֹל יְהוָה יָחִיל מִדְבָּר יָחִיל יְהוָה מִדְבַּר קָדֵשׁ:

קוֹל יְהוָה יְחוֹלֵל אַיָּלוֹת וַיֶּחֱשֹׂף יְעָרוֹת
וּבְהֵיכָלוֹ כֻּלּוֹ אֹמֵר כָּבוֹד:

יְהוָה לַמַּבּוּל יָשָׁב וַיֵּשֶׁב יְהוָה מֶלֶךְ לְעוֹלָם:
יְהוָה עֹז לְעַמּוֹ יִתֵּן יְהוָה יְבָרֵךְ אֶת־עַמּוֹ בַשָּׁלוֹם:

So I trusted—to see the goodness of the Lord
  in the land of the living.
Wait for the Lord! Be strong and let your heart take courage!
  Wait for the Lord!

29

A psalm of David.

Praise the Lord, you children of God!
  Praise the Lord for His glory and strength!
Praise the Lord, honouring His name!
  Worship the Lord in the beauty of holiness!

The voice of the Lord echoes over the waters,
  the God of glory thunders,
  the Lord is echoing over the mighty waters.
The voice of the Lord in power,
  the voice of the Lord in majesty!

The voice of the Lord breaks cedars;
  the Lord has shattered the cedars of Lebanon.
They begin to leap about,
  Lebanon like a calf and Sirion like a young ox.

The voice of the Lord splits the lightning shafts,
  the voice of the Lord whirls the desert sand,
  the voice of the Lord whirls the desert of Kadesh.

The voice of the Lord makes the wild deer calve,
  it strips the forest bare—
  while in His temple all cry 'Glory!'

The Lord sat enthroned at the flood;
  the Lord is enthroned, king forever.
The Lord will give strength to His people,
  the Lord will bless His people with peace.

ל

מִזְמוֹר שִׁיר־חֲנֻכַּת הַבַּיִת לְדָוִד׃

אֲרוֹמִמְךָ יְהוָה כִּי דִלִּיתָנִי וְלֹא־שִׂמַּחְתָּ אֹיְבַי לִי׃

יְהוָה אֱלֹהָי שִׁוַּעְתִּי אֵלֶיךָ וַתִּרְפָּאֵנִי׃

יְהוָה הֶעֱלִיתָ מִן־שְׁאוֹל נַפְשִׁי חִיִּיתַנִי מִיָּרְדִי־בוֹר׃

זַמְּרוּ לַיהוָה חֲסִידָיו וְהוֹדוּ לְזֵכֶר קָדְשׁוֹ׃

כִּי רֶגַע בְּאַפּוֹ חַיִּים בִּרְצוֹנוֹ בָּעֶרֶב יָלִין בֶּכִי וְלַבֹּקֶר רִנָּה׃

וַאֲנִי אָמַרְתִּי בְשַׁלְוִי בַּל־אֶמּוֹט לְעוֹלָם׃

יְהוָה בִּרְצוֹנְךָ הֶעֱמַדְתָּה לְהַרְרִי עֹז הִסְתַּרְתָּ פָנֶיךָ הָיִיתִי נִבְהָל׃

אֵלֶיךָ יְהוָה אֶקְרָא וְאֶל־אֲדֹנָי אֶתְחַנָּן׃

מַה־בֶּצַע בְּדָמִי בְּרִדְתִּי אֶל־שָׁחַת הֲיוֹדְךָ עָפָר הֲיַגִּיד אֲמִתֶּךָ׃

שְׁמַע־יְהוָה וְחָנֵּנִי יְהוָה הֱיֵה־עֹזֵר לִי׃

הָפַכְתָּ מִסְפְּדִי לְמָחוֹל לִי פִּתַּחְתָּ שַׂקִּי וַתְּאַזְּרֵנִי שִׂמְחָה׃

לְמַעַן יְזַמֶּרְךָ כָבוֹד וְלֹא יִדֹּם יְהוָה אֱלֹהַי לְעוֹלָם אוֹדֶךָּ׃

לג

רַנְּנוּ צַדִּיקִים בַּיהוָה לַיְשָׁרִים נָאוָה תְהִלָּה׃

הוֹדוּ לַיהוָה בְּכִנּוֹר בְּנֵבֶל עָשׂוֹר זַמְּרוּ־לוֹ׃

שִׁירוּ־לוֹ שִׁיר חָדָשׁ הֵיטִיבוּ נַגֵּן בִּתְרוּעָה׃

30

A psalm.   A song for the dedication of the House.   David's.

I exalt You, Lord, for You raised me up,
  and did not let my enemies gloat over me.
Lord, my God, I cried out to You
  and You healed me.
Lord, You brought up my soul from below,
  You kept me alive, stopped me sinking into the grave.

Sing psalms to the Lord, you who love Him,
  and give thanks to His holy name!
His anger lasts only a moment, His favour for a lifetime.
  Tears may linger at evening, but in the morning comes joy.

I, too, once said in my success,
  'I shall never slip'.
Lord, Your favour set me on a mountain stronghold—
  but then You hid Your face, and I was in terror.

To You, O Lord, I call,
  from my Lord I ask pity.

'What profit is there in shedding my blood when I go down to the
    grave?
  Can the dust praise You? Can it proclaim Your truth?
Hear me, Lord, and take pity on me!
  Lord, be my helper!'

You turned my mourning into dancing;
  You stripped away my sackcloth, and wrapped me in joy.
So my soul sings Your psalms, silent no longer;
  Lord, my God, I praise You forever and ever.

33

Shout for joy to the Lord, men of justice,
  such praise is right for upright men.
Thank the Lord on the harp,
  play for Him on the ten-stringed lute.
Sing Him a song that is new,
  play it aloud with shouts of joy.

כִּי־יָשָׁר דְּבַר־יְהֹוָה וְכָל־מַעֲשֵׂהוּ בֶּאֱמוּנָה:

אֹהֵב צְדָקָה וּמִשְׁפָּט חֶסֶד יְהֹוָה מָלְאָה הָאָרֶץ:

בִּדְבַר יְהֹוָה שָׁמַיִם נַעֲשׂוּ וּבְרוּחַ פִּיו כָּל־צְבָאָם:

כֹּנֵס כַּנֵּד מֵי הַיָּם נֹתֵן בְּאוֹצָרוֹת תְּהוֹמוֹת:

יִירְאוּ מֵיְהֹוָה כָּל־הָאָרֶץ מִמֶּנּוּ יָגוּרוּ כָּל־יֹשְׁבֵי תֵבֵל:

כִּי הוּא אָמַר וַיֶּהִי הוּא־צִוָּה וַיַּעֲמֹד:

יְהֹוָה הֵפִיר עֲצַת־גּוֹיִם הֵנִיא מַחְשְׁבוֹת עַמִּים:

עֲצַת יְהֹוָה לְעוֹלָם תַּעֲמֹד מַחְשְׁבוֹת לִבּוֹ לְדֹר וָדֹר:

אַשְׁרֵי הַגּוֹי אֲשֶׁר־יְהֹוָה אֱלֹהָיו הָעָם בָּחַר לְנַחֲלָה לוֹ:

מִשָּׁמַיִם הִבִּיט יְהֹוָה רָאָה אֶת־כָּל־בְּנֵי הָאָדָם:

מִמְּכוֹן־שִׁבְתּוֹ הִשְׁגִּיחַ אֶל כָּל־יֹשְׁבֵי הָאָרֶץ:

הַיֹּצֵר יַחַד לִבָּם הַמֵּבִין אֶל־כָּל־מַעֲשֵׂיהֶם:

אֵין־הַמֶּלֶךְ נוֹשָׁע בְּרָב־חָיִל גִּבּוֹר לֹא־יִנָּצֵל בְּרָב־כֹּחַ:

שֶׁקֶר הַסּוּס לִתְשׁוּעָה וּבְרֹב חֵילוֹ לֹא יְמַלֵּט:

הִנֵּה עֵין יְהֹוָה אֶל־יְרֵאָיו לַמְיַחֲלִים לְחַסְדּוֹ:

לְהַצִּיל מִמָּוֶת נַפְשָׁם וּלְחַיּוֹתָם בָּרָעָב:

נַפְשֵׁנוּ חִכְּתָה לַיהֹוָה עֶזְרֵנוּ וּמָגִנֵּנוּ הוּא:

כִּי־בוֹ יִשְׂמַח לִבֵּנוּ כִּי בְשֵׁם קָדְשׁוֹ בָטָחְנוּ:

יְהִי־חַסְדְּךָ יְהֹוָה עָלֵינוּ כַּאֲשֶׁר יִחַלְנוּ לָךְ:

For the word of the Lord is honest
  and all His work can be trusted.
He loves what is right and just,
  the earth is full of His love.

By the word of the Lord the heavens were made,
  by the breath of His mouth their host of stars.
He heaps up the waves of the ocean,
  He stores up the depths of the sea.

Let all the earth fear the Lord,
  and all who inhabit the world revere Him.
For He spoke—and it was!
  He commanded—and there it stood!

The Lord upsets the plans of nations,
  He frustrates the peoples' intentions;
but the plans of the Lord stand firm forever,
  the intentions of His heart from age to age.

Happy the nation whose God is the Lord,
  the people He chose for His heritage.
The Lord looks down from heaven,
  He sees the whole human race.

From where He dwells, He watches
  all who live on earth.
He moulds the heart of them all,
  He considers all their deeds.

No king is saved by military might,
  no hero preserved by great strength.
It is delusion to rely on a horse for safety;
  despite its power, it cannot save.

See! The eye of the Lord is on those who fear Him,
  on those who rely on His love;
to rescue their souls from death
  and keep them alive in famine.

Our souls are waiting for the Lord,
  He is our help and shield.
In Him our hearts rejoice,
  because we trust His holy name.
Lord, may Your love rest upon us,
  as our hope has rested in You!

לד

לְדָוִד

בְּשַׁנּוֹתוֹ אֶת־טַעְמוֹ לִפְנֵי אֲבִימֶלֶךְ וַיְגָרֲשֵׁהוּ וַיֵּלַךְ׃

אֲבָרְכָה אֶת־יְהֹוָה בְּכָל־עֵת תָּמִיד תְּהִלָּתוֹ בְּפִי׃
בַּיהֹוָה תִּתְהַלֵּל נַפְשִׁי יִשְׁמְעוּ עֲנָוִים וְיִשְׂמָחוּ׃

גַּדְּלוּ לַיהֹוָה אִתִּי וּנְרוֹמְמָה שְׁמוֹ יַחְדָּו׃
דָּרַשְׁתִּי אֶת־יְהֹוָה וְעָנָנִי וּמִכָּל־מְגוּרוֹתַי הִצִּילָנִי׃

הִבִּיטוּ אֵלָיו וְנָהָרוּ וּפְנֵיהֶם אַל־יֶחְפָּרוּ׃
זֶה עָנִי קָרָא וַיהֹוָה שָׁמֵעַ וּמִכָּל־צָרוֹתָיו הוֹשִׁיעוֹ׃

חֹנֶה מַלְאַךְ־יְהֹוָה סָבִיב לִירֵאָיו וַיְחַלְּצֵם׃
טַעֲמוּ וּרְאוּ כִּי־טוֹב יְהֹוָה אַשְׁרֵי הַגֶּבֶר יֶחֱסֶה־בּוֹ׃

יְראוּ אֶת־יְהֹוָה קְדֹשָׁיו כִּי־אֵין מַחְסוֹר לִירֵאָיו׃
כְּפִירִים רָשׁוּ וְרָעֵבוּ וְדֹרְשֵׁי יְהֹוָה לֹא־יַחְסְרוּ כָל־טוֹב׃

לְכוּ־בָנִים שִׁמְעוּ־לִי יִרְאַת יְהֹוָה אֲלַמֶּדְכֶם׃
מִי־הָאִישׁ הֶחָפֵץ חַיִּים אֹהֵב יָמִים לִרְאוֹת טוֹב׃

נְצֹר לְשׁוֹנְךָ מֵרָע וּשְׂפָתֶיךָ מִדַּבֵּר מִרְמָה׃
סוּר מֵרָע וַעֲשֵׂה־טוֹב בַּקֵּשׁ שָׁלוֹם וְרָדְפֵהוּ׃

34

David's. When after feigning madness in the presence of Avimelech, he
was driven away and escaped.

I will bless the Lord at all times,
His praise shall always be in my mouth.
My soul shall glory in the Lord.
Let the humble hear, and be glad!

Declare the greatness of the Lord with me
and let us exalt His name together!
I sought the Lord and He answered me.
He released me from all my fears.

Those who gazed at Him were radiant,
they did not hang their heads in shame.
This poor man cried out—the Lord heard,
and saved him from all his troubles.

A messenger of the Lord is stationed
around those who fear Him, to deliver them.
Taste and see that the Lord is good!
Happy the man who shelters in Him.

Fear the Lord, His holy ones!
Those who fear Him lack nothing.
Strong lions suffer want and go hungry,
but those who seek the Lord lack nothing.

Come children, listen to me
and I will teach you respect for the Lord.
Who is the man who longs for life,
who desires many days to enjoy prosperity?

Keep your tongue from evil,
and your lips from telling lies.
Turn away from evil, and do good,
seek peace, and pursue it.

עֵינֵי יְהוָֹה אֶל־צַדִּיקִים וְאָזְנָיו אֶל־שַׁוְעָתָם:

פְּנֵי יְהוָֹה בְּעֹשֵׂי רָע לְהַכְרִית מֵאֶרֶץ זִכְרָם:

צָעֲקוּ וַיהוָֹה שָׁמֵעַ וּמִכָּל־צָרוֹתָם הִצִּילָם:

קָרוֹב יְהוָֹה לְנִשְׁבְּרֵי־לֵב וְאֶת־דַּכְּאֵי־רוּחַ יוֹשִׁיעַ:

רַבּוֹת רָעוֹת צַדִּיק וּמִכֻּלָּם יַצִּילֶנּוּ יְהוָֹה:

שֹׁמֵר כָּל־עַצְמוֹתָיו אַחַת מֵהֵנָּה לֹא נִשְׁבָּרָה:

תְּמוֹתֵת רָשָׁע רָעָה וְשֹׂנְאֵי צַדִּיק יֶאְשָׁמוּ:

פֹּדֶה יְהוָֹה נֶפֶשׁ עֲבָדָיו וְלֹא יֶאְשְׁמוּ כָּל־הַחֹסִים בּוֹ:

לו

לַמְנַצֵּחַ לְעֶבֶד־יְהוָֹה לְדָוִד:

נְאֻם־פֶּשַׁע לָרָשָׁע בְּקֶרֶב לִבִּי אֵין־פַּחַד אֱלֹהִים לְנֶגֶד עֵינָיו:

כִּי־הֶחֱלִיק אֵלָיו בְּעֵינָיו לִמְצֹא עֲוֹנוֹ לִשְׂנֹא:

דִּבְרֵי־פִיו אָוֶן וּמִרְמָה חָדַל לְהַשְׂכִּיל לְהֵיטִיב:

אָוֶן יַחְשֹׁב עַל־מִשְׁכָּבוֹ יִתְיַצֵּב עַל־דֶּרֶךְ לֹא־טוֹב רָע לֹא יִמְאָס:

יְהוָֹה בְּהַשָּׁמַיִם חַסְדֶּךָ אֱמוּנָתְךָ עַד־שְׁחָקִים:

צִדְקָתְךָ כְּהַרְרֵי־אֵל מִשְׁפָּטֶיךָ תְּהוֹם רַבָּה

The eyes of the Lord are upon the righteous,
  and His ears are open to their cries.
The face of the Lord is turned against those who do wrong,
  cutting off their memory from the earth.

When they cry out, the Lord hears,
  and delivers them from their troubles.
The Lord is near to the broken-hearted,
  and saves those whose spirit is crushed.

Many trials befall a righteous man,
  but the Lord rescues him from all of them.
He watches over all his bones—
  not one of them is broken.

Evil brings death to the wicked.
  Those who hate the righteous are doomed.
The Lord redeems the soul of His servants.
  Those who take refuge in Him shall never come to harm.

36

For the choirmaster.   The servant of the Lord's.   David's.

Sin speaks to the sinner,
  deep in the heart;
there is no dread of God
  before his eyes.

It flatters him too much in his own eyes
  to detect and hate his guilt.
The words of his mouth become mischief and deceit,
  the urge for wisdom and goodness has gone.

He thinks up mischief
  as he lies in bed.
He is set on a way that is not good.
  He does not reject evil.

Lord, Your love reaches to heaven,
  Your faithfulness up to the skies.
Your righteousness is like the mighty mountains,
  Your judgments like the great deep.

אָדָם וּבְהֵמָה תוֹשִׁיעַ יְהֹוָה:

מַה־יָּקָר חַסְדְּךָ אֱלֹהִים וּבְנֵי אָדָם בְּצֵל כְּנָפֶיךָ יֶחֱסָיוּן:

יִרְוְיֻן מִדֶּשֶׁן בֵּיתֶךָ וְנַחַל עֲדָנֶיךָ תַשְׁקֵם:

כִּי־עִמְּךָ מְקוֹר חַיִּים בְּאוֹרְךָ נִרְאֶה־אוֹר:

מְשֹׁךְ חַסְדְּךָ לְיֹדְעֶיךָ וְצִדְקָתְךָ לְיִשְׁרֵי־לֵב:

אַל־תְּבוֹאֵנִי רֶגֶל גַּאֲוָה וְיַד־רְשָׁעִים אַל־תְּנִדֵנִי:

שָׁם נָפְלוּ פֹּעֲלֵי אָוֶן דֹּחוּ וְלֹא־יָכְלוּ קוּם:

לז (א־יא)

לְדָוִד

אַל־תִּתְחַר בַּמְּרֵעִים אַל־תְּקַנֵּא בְּעֹשֵׂי עַוְלָה:

כִּי כֶחָצִיר מְהֵרָה יִמָּלוּ וּכְיֶרֶק דֶּשֶׁא יִבּוֹלוּן:

בְּטַח בַּיהוָה וַעֲשֵׂה־טוֹב שְׁכָן־אֶרֶץ וּרְעֵה אֱמוּנָה:

וְהִתְעַנַּג עַל־יְהֹוָה וְיִתֶּן־לְךָ מִשְׁאֲלֹת לִבֶּךָ:

גּוֹל עַל־יְהֹוָה דַּרְכֶּךָ וּבְטַח עָלָיו וְהוּא יַעֲשֶׂה:

וְהוֹצִיא כָאוֹר צִדְקֶךָ וּמִשְׁפָּטֶךָ כַּצָּהֳרָיִם:

דּוֹם לַיהוָה וְהִתְחוֹלֵל לוֹ אַל־תִּתְחַר בְּמַצְלִיחַ דַּרְכּוֹ בְּאִישׁ עֹשֶׂה מְזִמּוֹת:

הֶרֶף מֵאַף וַעֲזֹב חֵמָה אַל־תִּתְחַר אַךְ־לְהָרֵעַ:

כִּי־מְרֵעִים יִכָּרֵתוּן וְקֹוֵי יְהֹוָה הֵמָּה יִירְשׁוּ־אָרֶץ:

Lord, You save man and beast!
  God, how precious is Your love!
The sons of men take refuge
  in the shadow of Your wings.

They feast on the bounty of Your house,
  You let them drink from the stream of Your pleasures,
for with You is the fountain of life.
  In Your light, we see light.

Continue Your love to those who love You,
  and Your faithfulness to the upright in heart.
Do not let the foot of the proud crush me,
  nor the hand of the wicked drive me away.

The workers of iniquity have fallen, there they lie;
  flung down, they cannot rise again.

37: 1–11

David's.

Do not worry because of the wicked.
  Do not envy those who do wrong,
for like the grass they quickly wither,
  like the green of the field they fade away.

Trust in the Lord, and do good,
  live in the land, and keep faith.
Find your delight in the Lord,
  and He will give you your heart's desires.

Commit your way to the Lord,
  rely on Him, and He will act,
for He will bring your righteousness to light
  and your integrity into the light of noon.

Be still before the Lord, and wait patiently for Him,
  do not fret about those who push their way to success.
Cease from anger, leave your rage.
  Do not fret—it only leads to wrong.
For those who do wrong will be cut off,
  but those who wait for the Lord shall inherit the earth.

וְעוֹד מְעַט וְאֵין רָשָׁע וְהִתְבּוֹנַנְתָּ עַל־מְקוֹמוֹ וְאֵינֶנּוּ:

וַעֲנָוִים יִירְשׁוּ־אָרֶץ וְהִתְעַנְּגוּ עַל־רֹב שָׁלוֹם:

מ

לַמְנַצֵּחַ לְדָוִד מִזְמוֹר:

קַוֹּה קִוִּיתִי יְהוָה וַיֵּט אֵלַי וַיִּשְׁמַע שַׁוְעָתִי:

וַיַּעֲלֵנִי מִבּוֹר שָׁאוֹן מִטִּיט הַיָּוֵן וַיָּקֶם עַל־סֶלַע רַגְלַי כּוֹנֵן
אֲשֻׁרָי:

וַיִּתֵּן בְּפִי שִׁיר חָדָשׁ תְּהִלָּה לֵאלֹהֵינוּ יִרְאוּ רַבִּים וְיִירָאוּ
וְיִבְטְחוּ בַּיהוָה:

אַשְׁרֵי־הַגֶּבֶר אֲשֶׁר־שָׂם יְהוָה מִבְטַחוֹ וְלֹא־פָנָה אֶל־רְהָבִים
וְשָׂטֵי כָזָב:

רַבּוֹת עָשִׂיתָ אַתָּה יְהוָה אֱלֹהַי נִפְלְאֹתֶיךָ וּמַחְשְׁבֹתֶיךָ אֵלֵינוּ
אֵין עֲרֹךְ אֵלֶיךָ אַגִּידָה וַאֲדַבֵּרָה עָצְמוּ מִסַּפֵּר:

זֶבַח וּמִנְחָה לֹא־חָפַצְתָּ אָזְנַיִם כָּרִיתָ לִּי עוֹלָה וַחֲטָאָה לֹא
שָׁאָלְתָּ:

אָז אָמַרְתִּי הִנֵּה־בָאתִי בִּמְגִלַּת־סֵפֶר כָּתוּב עָלָי:

לַעֲשׂוֹת־רְצוֹנְךָ אֱלֹהַי חָפָצְתִּי וְתוֹרָתְךָ בְּתוֹךְ מֵעָי:

A little while longer—and the wicked is no more.
   Search for his place—nothing is there!
But the humble shall inherit the earth,
   delighting in abundant peace.

40

For the choirmaster.   David's psalm.

I waited and hoped for the Lord
   and He bent down to me
   and heard my cry for help.
He pulled me out of a quaking pit,
   out of clinging mud.
Then He set my foot upon a rock
   and steadied my steps.
He put a new song in my mouth,
   praising our God.
Many shall see and fear,
   and trust in the Lord.
Happy the man who has put
   his trust in the Lord,
who has not turned to the arrogant,
   to those who rely on a lie.

You have done so many things, Lord, my God,
   so many wonderful things—
   made so many plans for us—
   You have no equal!
   If I proclaim and speak of them
   they are more than can be told.
You did not want sacrifices and offerings—
   instead You opened my ears!
You asked for no burnt or sin offerings—
So therefore I said:
   'See! I have come
   with a scroll of a book written about myself.
   To do Your will, God, has been my desire,
   with Your teaching in the depths of my being.'

בִּשַּׂרְתִּי צֶדֶק בְּקָהָל רָב הִנֵּה שְׂפָתַי לֹא אֶכְלָא יְהֹוָה אַתָּה
יָדָעְתָּ:

צִדְקָתְךָ לֹא־כִסִּיתִי בְּתוֹךְ לִבִּי אֱמוּנָתְךָ וּתְשׁוּעָתְךָ אָמַרְתִּי
לֹא־כִחַדְתִּי חַסְדְּךָ וַאֲמִתְּךָ לְקָהָל רָב:

אַתָּה יְהֹוָה לֹא־תִכְלָא רַחֲמֶיךָ מִמֶּנִּי חַסְדְּךָ וַאֲמִתְּךָ תָּמִיד
יִצְּרוּנִי:

כִּי אָפְפוּ־עָלַי רָעוֹת עַד־אֵין מִסְפָּר הִשִּׂיגוּנִי עֲוֹנֹתַי וְלֹא־
יָכֹלְתִּי לִרְאוֹת עָצְמוּ מִשַּׂעֲרוֹת רֹאשִׁי וְלִבִּי עֲזָבָנִי:

רְצֵה יְהֹוָה לְהַצִּילֵנִי יְהֹוָה לְעֶזְרָתִי חוּשָׁה:

יֵבֹשׁוּ וְיַחְפְּרוּ יַחַד מְבַקְשֵׁי נַפְשִׁי לִסְפּוֹתָהּ יִסֹּגוּ אָחוֹר וְיִכָּלְמוּ
חֲפֵצֵי רָעָתִי:
יָשֹׁמּוּ עַל־עֵקֶב בָּשְׁתָּם הָאֹמְרִים לִי הֶאָח הֶאָח:

יָשִׂישׂוּ וְיִשְׂמְחוּ בְּךָ כָּל־מְבַקְשֶׁיךָ יֹאמְרוּ תָמִיד יִגְדַּל יְהֹוָה
אֹהֲבֵי תְּשׁוּעָתֶךָ:

וַאֲנִי עָנִי וְאֶבְיוֹן אֲדֹנָי יַחֲשָׁב־לִי עֶזְרָתִי וּמְפַלְטִי אַתָּה אֱלֹהַי
אַל־תְּאַחַר:

I have preached righteousness in the great congregation,
  I have not curbed my lips
  as You know, O Lord!
I did not hide Your righteousness in my heart
    but I declared Your faithfulness and Your salvation;
    I never concealed Your love and Your truth
    in the great congregation.

But You, Lord, will not withold Your mercy from me,
  Your love and Your truth will always preserve me.

More evils have gathered around me
  than I can count.
My sins have closed in on me
    so that I can hardly see—
    for they are more than the hairs of my head,
    my courage fails me.

Lord, may it be Your will to deliver me.
  Lord, come quickly to my aid!

Let them be ashamed and humbled together
  who seek my life to destroy it.
Sweep them away in confusion
  who delight in my harm!
Let them be appalled by their shame,
  for taunting me and jeering.

Let there be joy and gladness
  for all who seek You.
  Let those who love Your salvation
  always have cause to say, 'The Lord is great!'

As for me, poor and in need,
  may the Lord think of me.
  You are my help, my deliverer.
  My God, do not delay!

מב

לַמְנַצֵּחַ מַשְׂכִּיל לִבְנֵי־קֹרַח:

כְּאַיָּל תַּעֲרֹג עַל־אֲפִיקֵי־מָיִם כֵּן נַפְשִׁי תַעֲרֹג אֵלֶיךָ אֱלֹהִים:

צָמְאָה נַפְשִׁי לֵאלֹהִים לְאֵל חָי מָתַי אָבוֹא וְאֵרָאֶה פְּנֵי אֱלֹהִים:

הָיְתָה־לִּי דִמְעָתִי לֶחֶם יוֹמָם וָלָיְלָה בֶּאֱמֹר אֵלַי כָּל־הַיּוֹם
אַיֵּה אֱלֹהֶיךָ:

אֵלֶּה אֶזְכְּרָה וְאֶשְׁפְּכָה עָלַי נַפְשִׁי כִּי אֶעֱבֹר בַּסָּךְ אֶדַּדֵּם
עַד־בֵּית אֱלֹהִים בְּקוֹל־רִנָּה וְתוֹדָה הָמוֹן חוֹגֵג:

מַה־תִּשְׁתּוֹחֲחִי נַפְשִׁי וַתֶּהֱמִי עָלָי הוֹחִלִי לֵאלֹהִים כִּי־עוֹד
אוֹדֶנּוּ יְשׁוּעוֹת פָּנָיו:

אֱלֹהַי עָלַי נַפְשִׁי תִשְׁתּוֹחָח עַל־כֵּן אֶזְכָּרְךָ מֵאֶרֶץ יַרְדֵּן
וְחֶרְמוֹנִים מֵהַר מִצְעָר:

תְּהוֹם־אֶל־תְּהוֹם קוֹרֵא לְקוֹל צִנּוֹרֶיךָ כָּל־מִשְׁבָּרֶיךָ וְגַלֶּיךָ
עָלַי עָבָרוּ:

יוֹמָם יְצַוֶּה יְהֹוָה חַסְדּוֹ וּבַלַּיְלָה שִׁירֹה עִמִּי תְּפִלָּה לְאֵל חַיָּי:

אוֹמְרָה לְאֵל סַלְעִי לָמָה שְׁכַחְתָּנִי לָמָּה־קֹדֵר אֵלֵךְ בְּלַחַץ
אוֹיֵב:

בְּרֶצַח בְּעַצְמוֹתַי חֵרְפוּנִי צוֹרְרָי בְּאָמְרָם אֵלַי כָּל־הַיּוֹם אַיֵּה
אֱלֹהֶיךָ:

מַה־תִּשְׁתּוֹחֲחִי נַפְשִׁי וּמַה־תֶּהֱמִי עָלָי הוֹחִילִי לֵאלֹהִים
כִּי־עוֹד אוֹדֶנּוּ יְשׁוּעֹת פָּנַי וֵאלֹהָי:

42

For the choirmaster.   A poem of the sons of Korach.

As a deer longs for running streams,
  so my soul longs for You, my God.

My soul thirsts for God, the living God.
  'When shall I come and appear before God?'

My tears have been my food, by day and night,
  as all day long men say to me, 'Where is your God?'

These things I remember, as I pour out my soul—
  how I would pass by with the throng
  leading them to the house of God,
  with voices raised in joy and praise, the noise of celebration.

Why are you cast down my soul, and why do you moan within me?
  Hope in God! I praise Him still, for the salvation of His presence.

My God, when my soul is cast down within me, I think of You,
  from the land of Jordan, and the Hermons, from the hill of Mitzar.

Deep calls to deep in the roar of Your cataracts,
  all Your waves and breakers swept over me.

By day the Lord will send His lovingkindness,
  at night His song shall be with me, a prayer to the God of my life.

I will say to God, my rock, 'Why have You forgotten me?
  Why must I go about mournfully, oppressed by the enemy?'

My enemies taunt me, as if crushing my bones,
  as all day long they ask me, 'Where is your God?'

Why are you cast down my soul, and why do you moan within me?
  Hope in God! I praise Him still, my own salvation, and my God.

מג

שָׁפְטֵנִי אֱלֹהִים וְרִיבָה רִיבִי מִגּוֹי לֹא־חָסִיד מֵאִישׁ־מִרְמָה
וְעַוְלָה תְפַלְּטֵנִי:

כִּי־אַתָּה אֱלֹהֵי מָעוּזִּי לָמָה זְנַחְתָּנִי לָמָּה־קֹדֵר אֶתְהַלֵּךְ
בְּלַחַץ אוֹיֵב:

שְׁלַח־אוֹרְךָ וַאֲמִתְּךָ הֵמָּה יַנְחוּנִי יְבִיאוּנִי אֶל־הַר־קָדְשְׁךָ
וְאֶל־מִשְׁכְּנוֹתֶיךָ:

וְאָבוֹאָה אֶל־מִזְבַּח אֱלֹהִים אֶל־אֵל שִׂמְחַת גִּילִי וְאוֹדְךָ
בְכִנּוֹר אֱלֹהִים אֱלֹהָי:

מַה־תִּשְׁתּוֹחֲחִי נַפְשִׁי וּמַה־תֶּהֱמִי עָלָי הוֹחִילִי לֵאלֹהִים כִּי־
עוֹד אוֹדֶנּוּ יְשׁוּעֹת פָּנַי וֵאלֹהָי:

מו

לַמְנַצֵּחַ לִבְנֵי־קֹרַח עַל־עֲלָמוֹת שִׁיר:

אֱלֹהִים לָנוּ מַחֲסֶה וָעֹז עֶזְרָה בְצָרוֹת נִמְצָא מְאֹד:
עַל־כֵּן לֹא־נִירָא בְּהָמִיר אָרֶץ וּבְמוֹט הָרִים בְּלֵב יַמִּים:
יֶהֱמוּ יֶחְמְרוּ מֵימָיו יִרְעֲשׁוּ־הָרִים בְּגַאֲוָתוֹ סֶלָה:

נָהָר פְּלָגָיו יְשַׂמְּחוּ עִיר־אֱלֹהִים קְדֹשׁ מִשְׁכְּנֵי עֶלְיוֹן:
אֱלֹהִים בְּקִרְבָּהּ בַּל־תִּמּוֹט יַעְזְרֶהָ אֱלֹהִים לִפְנוֹת בֹּקֶר:
הָמוּ גוֹיִם מָטוּ מַמְלָכוֹת נָתַן בְּקוֹלוֹ תָּמוּג אָרֶץ:

יְהֹוָה צְבָאוֹת עִמָּנוּ מִשְׂגָּב־לָנוּ אֱלֹהֵי יַעֲקֹב סֶלָה:

43

God be my judge, and plead my cause against a nation with no mercy,
  from men of deceit and lies deliver me!

Since You are the God of my strength why have You rejected me?
  Why do I walk alone, mourning, oppressed by the enemy?

Send out Your light and Your truth—may they guide me!
  Let them bring me to Your holy mountain and to Your dwelling
    places.

And I shall come to the altar of God, the God of joy, my delight,
  and I shall praise You with the harp, O God, my God.

Why are you cast down my soul, and why do you moan within me?
  Hope in God! I praise Him still, my own salvation, and my God.

46

For the choirmaster.   Of the sons of Korach.   Upon Alamot.   A song.

God is our refuge and strength,
  an ever-present help in trouble.
Therefore we shall not fear though the earth is changed
  and the mountains fall into the depths of the sea;
even though its waters roar and foam
  though the mountains shake as they swell.

There is a river whose waters give joy to the city of God,
  the holy place of the presence of God.
God is within, it cannot be shaken.
  God will help it at the dawning of the day.
Nations are in tumult, kingdoms totter;
  He speaks out, the earth melts away.

The Lord of all creation is with us,
  the God of Jacob is our refuge.

לְכוּ־חֲזוּ מִפְעֲלוֹת יְהֹוָה אֲשֶׁר־שָׂם שַׁמּוֹת בָּאָרֶץ:

מַשְׁבִּית מִלְחָמוֹת עַד־קְצֵה הָאָרֶץ קֶשֶׁת יְשַׁבֵּר וְקִצֵּץ חֲנִית

עֲגָלוֹת יִשְׂרֹף בָּאֵשׁ:

הַרְפּוּ וּדְעוּ כִּי־אָנֹכִי אֱלֹהִים אָרוּם בַּגּוֹיִם אָרוּם בָּאָרֶץ:

יְהֹוָה צְבָאוֹת עִמָּנוּ מִשְׂגָּב־לָנוּ אֱלֹהֵי יַעֲקֹב סֶלָה:

מז

לַמְנַצֵּחַ לִבְנֵי־קֹרַח מִזְמוֹר:

כָּל־הָעַמִּים תִּקְעוּ־כָף הָרִיעוּ לֵאלֹהִים בְּקוֹל רִנָּה:

כִּי־יְהֹוָה עֶלְיוֹן נוֹרָא מֶלֶךְ גָּדוֹל עַל־כָּל־הָאָרֶץ:

יַדְבֵּר עַמִּים תַּחְתֵּינוּ וּלְאֻמִּים תַּחַת רַגְלֵינוּ:

יִבְחַר־לָנוּ אֶת־נַחֲלָתֵנוּ אֶת גְּאוֹן יַעֲקֹב אֲשֶׁר־אָהֵב סֶלָה:

עָלָה אֱלֹהִים בִּתְרוּעָה יְהֹוָה בְּקוֹל שׁוֹפָר:

זַמְּרוּ אֱלֹהִים זַמֵּרוּ זַמְּרוּ לְמַלְכֵּנוּ זַמֵּרוּ:

כִּי מֶלֶךְ כָּל־הָאָרֶץ אֱלֹהִים זַמְּרוּ מַשְׂכִּיל:

מָלַךְ אֱלֹהִים עַל־גּוֹיִם אֱלֹהִים יָשַׁב עַל־כִּסֵּא קָדְשׁוֹ:

נְדִיבֵי עַמִּים נֶאֱסָפוּ עַם אֱלֹהֵי אַבְרָהָם

כִּי לֵאלֹהִים מָגִנֵּי־אֶרֶץ מְאֹד נַעֲלָה:

Come and consider what the Lord has done,
   the astonishing things He has done on earth.
He makes wars end throughout the earth,
   He breaks the bow, He snaps the spear,
   He burns the chariots with fire.
'Be still and know that I am God,
   supreme among the nations, supreme on earth!'

The Lord of all creation is with us,
   the God of Jacob is our refuge.

47

For the choirmaster.   A psalm of the sons of Korach.

All peoples, clap your hands!
   Cry out to God with shouts of joy,
for the Lord is exalted and awesome,
   a great king over all the earth.

He subdues the peoples beneath us
   and nations under our foot.
He chose our destiny for us,
   the pride of Jacob whom He loved.

God is exalted with shouts of joy,
   the Lord with the sound of the *shofar*.
Sing praise to God, sing praise;
   sing praise to our king, sing praise.

For God is king of all the earth,
   sing praise with all your skill!
God reigns over all the nations,
   God sits on His holy throne.

The princes of the peoples are assembled,
   the people of the God of Abraham.
For those who govern the earth belong to God;
   He is supreme above them.

מט

לַמְנַצֵּחַ לִבְנֵי־קֹרַח מִזְמוֹר׃

שִׁמְעוּ־זֹאת כָּל־הָעַמִּים הַאֲזִינוּ כָּל־יֹשְׁבֵי חָלֶד׃

גַּם־בְּנֵי אָדָם גַּם־בְּנֵי־אִישׁ יַחַד עָשִׁיר וְאֶבְיוֹן׃

פִּי יְדַבֵּר חָכְמוֹת וְהָגוּת לִבִּי תְבוּנוֹת׃

אַטֶּה לְמָשָׁל אָזְנִי אֶפְתַּח בְּכִנּוֹר חִידָתִי׃

לָמָּה אִירָא בִּימֵי רָע עֲוֹן עֲקֵבַי יְסוּבֵּנִי׃

הַבֹּטְחִים עַל־חֵילָם וּבְרֹב עָשְׁרָם יִתְהַלָּלוּ׃

אָח לֹא־פָדֹה יִפְדֶּה אִישׁ לֹא־יִתֵּן לֵאלֹהִים כָּפְרוֹ׃

וְיֵקַר פִּדְיוֹן נַפְשָׁם וְחָדַל לְעוֹלָם׃

וִיחִי־עוֹד לָנֶצַח לֹא יִרְאֶה הַשָּׁחַת׃

כִּי יִרְאֶה חֲכָמִים יָמוּתוּ יַחַד כְּסִיל וָבַעַר יֹאבֵדוּ וְעָזְבוּ
לַאֲחֵרִים חֵילָם׃

קִרְבָּם בָּתֵּימוֹ לְעוֹלָם מִשְׁכְּנֹתָם לְדוֹר וָדֹר קָרְאוּ בִשְׁמוֹתָם
עֲלֵי אֲדָמוֹת׃

וְאָדָם בִּיקָר בַּל־יָלִין נִמְשַׁל כַּבְּהֵמוֹת נִדְמוּ׃

זֶה דַרְכָּם כֵּסֶל לָמוֹ וְאַחֲרֵיהֶם בְּפִיהֶם יִרְצוּ סֶלָה׃

כַּצֹּאן לִשְׁאוֹל שַׁתּוּ מָוֶת יִרְעֵם וַיִּרְדּוּ בָם יְשָׁרִים לַבֹּקֶר
וְצוּרָם לְבַלּוֹת שְׁאוֹל מִזְּבֻל לוֹ׃

אַךְ־אֱלֹהִים יִפְדֶּה־נַפְשִׁי מִיַּד־שְׁאוֹל כִּי יִקָּחֵנִי סֶלָה׃

49

For the choirmaster.　A psalm of the sons of Korach.

Hear this, all peoples,
　listen you worldly men.
Sons of the masses, sons of the masters,
　rich and poor alike!
My mouth shall speak wisdom
　and the meditations of my heart bring understanding.
I turn my ear to catch a parable,
　I give my interpretation on the harp.
Why should I fear in evil days,
　surrounded by the crookedness
　of those who want to steal my place;
men who trust in their wealth
　and glory in the greatness of their riches.
But no man can even redeem his brother
　or pay the price of his ransom to God.
The redemption of his soul is too dear,
　it is always beyond the power of payment.
He cannot buy life without end,
　or avoid the sight of the grave.
Let him see that wise men die,
　the fool and the brute perish alike,
　and they leave their wealth to others.
They think to themselves that their houses will last forever,
　and their homes for generations to come.
　They even name lands after themselves.
But man even in his splendour cannot remain,
　he is like the animals that pass away.
This is the way of the self-assured—more fool them!—
　and their successors who enjoy the same opinions:
like sheep herded to the world below,
　death shall shepherd them.
With dawn the upright shall have the better of them,
　their outward form will rot,
　the grave will be their home.
But God will redeem my soul from the power of the grave
　for He shall take me.

אַל־תִּירָא כִּי־יַעֲשִׁר אִישׁ כִּי־יִרְבֶּה כְּבוֹד בֵּיתוֹ׃

כִּי לֹא בְמוֹתוֹ יִקַּח הַכֹּל לֹא־יֵרֵד אַחֲרָיו כְּבוֹדוֹ׃

כִּי־נַפְשׁוֹ בְּחַיָּיו יְבָרֵךְ וְיוֹדֻךָ כִּי־תֵיטִיב לָךְ׃

תָּבוֹא עַד־דּוֹר אֲבוֹתָיו עַד־נֵצַח לֹא יִרְאוּ־אוֹר׃

אָדָם בִּיקָר וְלֹא יָבִין נִמְשַׁל כַּבְּהֵמוֹת נִדְמוּ׃

נ

מִזְמוֹר לְאָסָף

אֵל אֱלֹהִים יְהוָה דִּבֶּר וַיִּקְרָא־אָרֶץ מִמִּזְרַח־שֶׁמֶשׁ עַד־מְבֹאוֹ׃

מִצִּיּוֹן מִכְלַל־יֹפִי אֱלֹהִים הוֹפִיעַ׃

יָבֹא אֱלֹהֵינוּ וְאַל־יֶחֱרַשׁ אֵשׁ־לְפָנָיו תֹּאכֵל וּסְבִיבָיו נִשְׂעֲרָה מְאֹד׃

יִקְרָא אֶל־הַשָּׁמַיִם מֵעָל וְאֶל־הָאָרֶץ לָדִין עַמּוֹ׃

אִסְפוּ־לִי חֲסִידָי כֹּרְתֵי בְרִיתִי עֲלֵי־זָבַח׃

וַיַּגִּידוּ שָׁמַיִם צִדְקוֹ כִּי־אֱלֹהִים שֹׁפֵט הוּא סֶלָה׃

שִׁמְעָה עַמִּי וַאֲדַבֵּרָה יִשְׂרָאֵל וְאָעִידָה בָּךְ אֱלֹהִים אֱלֹהֶיךָ אָנֹכִי׃

לֹא עַל־זְבָחֶיךָ אוֹכִיחֶךָ וְעוֹלֹתֶיךָ לְנֶגְדִּי תָמִיד׃

לֹא־אֶקַּח מִבֵּיתְךָ פָר מִמִּכְלְאֹתֶיךָ עַתּוּדִים׃

Do not be afraid when a man gets rich
    and the glory of his house increases,
for when he dies, he takes nothing with him,
    his wealth will not follow him down.
Though he congratulated himself while he lived:
    'How men praise you because you have done so well by yourself!'
His soul will go to join the generation of his fathers
    who never see the light anymore.

Man even in his splendour does not understand.
    He is like the animals that pass away.

50

A psalm of Asaph.

God of Might, God of Justice, Lord of Mercy!
    He speaks and summons the earth
from the rising of the sun to its setting.
    From Zion, the perfection of beauty, God shines forth.

Our God is coming and will not be silent!
    A fire devours before Him
    and around Him a raging storm!
He summons the heavens above and the earth
    to the judgment of His people.

'Gather My faithful to Me,
    who made a covenant with Me by sacrifice!'
The heavens declare His righteousness,
    for God, He is judge.

'Listen My people, and I will speak;
    Israel, I will testify against you:
    God, your God, am I!

I do not complain of your sacrifices,
    your offerings are always before Me.
I need no young bull from your home,
    nor your goats from the pens.

כִּי־לִי כָל־חַיְתוֹ־יָעַר בְּהֵמוֹת בְּהַרְרֵי־אָלֶף :
יָדַעְתִּי כָּל־עוֹף הָרִים וְזִיז שָׂדַי עִמָּדִי :

אִם־אֶרְעַב לֹא־אֹמַר לָךְ כִּי־לִי תֵבֵל וּמְלֹאָהּ :
הַאוֹכַל בְּשַׂר אַבִּירִים וְדַם עַתּוּדִים אֶשְׁתֶּה :

זְבַח לֵאלֹהִים תּוֹדָה וְשַׁלֵּם לְעֶלְיוֹן נְדָרֶיךָ :
וּקְרָאֵנִי בְּיוֹם צָרָה אֲחַלֶּצְךָ וּתְכַבְּדֵנִי :

וְלָרָשָׁע אָמַר אֱלֹהִים מַה־לְּךָ לְסַפֵּר חֻקָּי וַתִּשָּׂא בְרִיתִי
עֲלֵי־פִיךָ :
וְאַתָּה שָׂנֵאתָ מוּסָר וַתַּשְׁלֵךְ דְּבָרַי אַחֲרֶיךָ :

אִם־רָאִיתָ גַנָּב וַתִּרֶץ עִמּוֹ וְעִם מְנָאֲפִים חֶלְקֶךָ :
פִּיךָ שָׁלַחְתָּ בְרָעָה וּלְשׁוֹנְךָ תַּצְמִיד מִרְמָה :

תֵּשֵׁב בְּאָחִיךָ תְדַבֵּר בְּבֶן־אִמְּךָ תִּתֶּן־דֹּפִי :
אֵלֶּה עָשִׂיתָ וְהֶחֱרַשְׁתִּי דִּמִּיתָ הֱיוֹת־אֶהְיֶה כָמוֹךָ אוֹכִיחֲךָ
וְאֶעֶרְכָה לְעֵינֶיךָ :

בִּינוּ־נָא זֹאת שֹׁכְחֵי אֱלוֹהַּ פֶּן־אֶטְרֹף וְאֵין מַצִּיל :
זֹבֵחַ תּוֹדָה יְכַבְּדָנְנִי וְשָׂם דֶּרֶךְ אַרְאֶנּוּ בְּיֵשַׁע אֱלֹהִים :

For every beast of the wood is Mine,
   the cattle on thousands of hills.
I know every bird on the hills,
   all that moves in the field is Mine.

If I were hungry, I should not tell you,
   for the world is Mine and all it holds.
Do I eat the flesh of bulls
   or drink the blood of goats?

Offer God your gratitude
   and fulfil your promises to the Most High;
then call upon Me on the day of trouble,
   I will rescue you, and you shall honour Me.'

But to the wicked God says:
   'How can you recite My laws
   and take My covenant on your lips,
for you hate My laws
   and thrust My words behind you.

You see a thief and want to be with him,
   you throw in your lot with adulterers.
With your mouth you stir up evil
   and weave deceit with your tongue.

You sit and speak against your brother
   and slander your own mother's son.
You do all this—can I be silent?
   Did you really think that I was like you?
   Point by point I will rebuke you before your eyes.

Consider this, you who forget God,
   lest I tear you in pieces
   and there is no escape:
He who shows Me gratitude
   gives Me honour,
and to the man who follows the right way
   I shall show the salvation of God.'

נא (א‎־יט)

לַמְנַצֵּחַ מִזְמוֹר לְדָוִד :

בְּבוֹא‎־אֵלָיו נָתָן הַנָּבִיא כַּאֲשֶׁר‎־בָּא אֶל‎־בַּת‎־שָׁבַע :

חָנֵּנִי אֱלֹהִים כְּחַסְדֶּךָ כְּרֹב רַחֲמֶיךָ מְחֵה פְשָׁעָי :

הֶרֶב כַּבְּסֵנִי מֵעֲוֹנִי וּמֵחַטָּאתִי טַהֲרֵנִי :

כִּי‎־פְשָׁעַי אֲנִי אֵדָע וְחַטָּאתִי נֶגְדִּי תָמִיד :

לְךָ לְבַדְּךָ חָטָאתִי וְהָרַע בְּעֵינֶיךָ עָשִׂיתִי לְמַעַן תִּצְדַּק

בְּדָבְרֶךָ תִּזְכֶּה בְשָׁפְטֶךָ :

הֵן‎־בְּעָווֹן חוֹלָלְתִּי וּבְחֵטְא יֶחֱמַתְנִי אִמִּי :

הֵן‎־אֱמֶת חָפַצְתָּ בַטֻּחוֹת וּבְסָתֻם חָכְמָה תוֹדִיעֵנִי :

תְּחַטְּאֵנִי בְאֵזוֹב וְאֶטְהָר תְּכַבְּסֵנִי וּמִשֶּׁלֶג אַלְבִּין :

תַּשְׁמִיעֵנִי שָׂשׂוֹן וְשִׂמְחָה תָּגֵלְנָה עֲצָמוֹת דִּכִּיתָ :

הַסְתֵּר פָּנֶיךָ מֵחֲטָאָי וְכָל‎־עֲוֹנֹתַי מְחֵה :

לֵב טָהוֹר בְּרָא‎־לִי אֱלֹהִים וְרוּחַ נָכוֹן חַדֵּשׁ בְּקִרְבִּי :

אַל‎־תַּשְׁלִיכֵנִי מִלְּפָנֶיךָ וְרוּחַ קָדְשְׁךָ אַל‎־תִּקַּח מִמֶּנִּי :

הָשִׁיבָה לִּי שְׂשׂוֹן יִשְׁעֶךָ וְרוּחַ נְדִיבָה תִסְמְכֵנִי :

אֲלַמְּדָה פֹשְׁעִים דְּרָכֶיךָ וְחַטָּאִים אֵלֶיךָ יָשׁוּבוּ :

הַצִּילֵנִי מִדָּמִים אֱלֹהִים אֱלֹהֵי תְּשׁוּעָתִי תְּרַנֵּן לְשׁוֹנִי צִדְקָתֶךָ :

אֲדֹנָי שְׂפָתַי תִּפְתָּח וּפִי יַגִּיד תְּהִלָּתֶךָ :

51: 1–19

For the choirmaster. A psalm of David when Nathan the prophet came
to him after he had been with Bath-sheba.

Be kind to me, God, in Your mercy,
in Your great compassion blot out my misdeeds.
Wash me free from my guilt
and cleanse me from my sin.

For my misdeeds I know too well
and my sin is always before me.
Against You, You only, have I sinned,
and done what is evil in Your sight.
Therefore, You are just in Your sentence,
and right in Your judgment.
But even though I was born to err,
and my mother conceived me in sin,
the truth is still what You desire within me
and in my inmost heart You show me wisdom.

Purify me with hyssop, and I shall be clean,
wash me, and I shall be whiter than snow.
Let me hear joy and gladness,
so that the bones You crushed dance again.
Turn Your gaze away from my sins
and blot out all my guilt.

Create a pure heart for me, God,
and put a firm and steadfast spirit in me.
Do not cast me away from Your presence,
nor take Your holy spirit from me.

Give me back the joy of Your salvation
and let a willing spirit uphold me.
Then I will teach transgressors the way
so that sinners may return to You.

Keep me from bloodshed, O God.
You are the God who saves me.
My tongue shall ring out Your justice.
Lord, open my lips
and my mouth shall declare Your praise.

כִּי לֹא־תַחְפֹּץ זֶבַח וְאֶתֵּנָה עוֹלָה לֹא תִרְצֶה:

זִבְחֵי אֱלֹהִים רוּחַ נִשְׁבָּרָה לֵב־נִשְׁבָּר וְנִדְכֶּה אֱלֹהִים לֹא תִבְזֶה:

נז

לַמְנַצֵּחַ אַל־תַּשְׁחֵת לְדָוִד מִכְתָּם בְּבָרְחוֹ מִפְּנֵי־שָׁאוּל בַּמְּעָרָה:

חָנֵּנִי אֱלֹהִים חָנֵּנִי כִּי בְךָ חָסָיָה נַפְשִׁי וּבְצֵל־כְּנָפֶיךָ אֶחְסֶה עַד יַעֲבֹר הַוּוֹת:

אֶקְרָא לֵאלֹהִים עֶלְיוֹן לָאֵל גֹּמֵר עָלָי:

יִשְׁלַח מִשָּׁמַיִם וְיוֹשִׁיעֵנִי חֵרֵף שֹׁאֲפִי סֶלָה יִשְׁלַח אֱלֹהִים חַסְדּוֹ וַאֲמִתּוֹ:

נַפְשִׁי בְּתוֹךְ לְבָאִם אֶשְׁכְּבָה לֹהֲטִים בְּנֵי־אָדָם שִׁנֵּיהֶם חֲנִית וְחִצִּים וּלְשׁוֹנָם חֶרֶב חַדָּה:

רוּמָה עַל־הַשָּׁמַיִם אֱלֹהִים עַל כָּל־הָאָרֶץ כְּבוֹדֶךָ:

רֶשֶׁת הֵכִינוּ לִפְעָמַי כָּפַף נַפְשִׁי כָּרוּ לְפָנַי שִׁיחָה נָפְלוּ בְתוֹכָהּ סֶלָה:

נָכוֹן לִבִּי אֱלֹהִים נָכוֹן לִבִּי אָשִׁירָה וַאֲזַמֵּרָה:

עוּרָה כְבוֹדִי עוּרָה הַנֵּבֶל וְכִנּוֹר אָעִירָה שָּׁחַר:

אוֹדְךָ בָעַמִּים אֲדֹנָי אֲזַמֶּרְךָ בַּלְאֻמִּים:

כִּי־גָדֹל עַד־שָׁמַיִם חַסְדֶּךָ וְעַד־שְׁחָקִים אֲמִתֶּךָ:

רוּמָה עַל־שָׁמַיִם אֱלֹהִים עַל כָּל־הָאָרֶץ כְּבוֹדֶךָ:

For You desire no sacrifice, or I would give it,
   burnt offerings You do not want.
God's sacrifices are a humbled spirit,
   a broken and a contrite heart You will not despise.

57

For the choirmaster.   To the tune 'Do not destroy'.   David's michtam
     when he fled from Saul, in the cave.

Take pity on me God, take pity,
   for in You my soul has taken refuge.
I take refuge in the shadow of Your wings
   until the storms are past.
I call to God, the highest,
   to God who has a purpose for me.
He will send from heaven and save me
   from the taunts of my persecutor.
   God will send His mercy and His truth.

My soul is in the midst of lions,
   I lie down among those ablaze with hatred,
   men whose teeth are spears and arrows,
   whose tongue is a sharp sword.

God, show Yourself exalted beyond the heavens,
   Your glory over all the earth.

They set a trap for my steps,
   my soul was bowed down.
They dug a pit before me,
   they fell into it themselves.

Firm is my heart, O God, firm is my heart.
   I shall sing and play music.
Awake my glory!
   Awake lyre and harp!
   I will awake the dawn.

I will thank You, Lord, among the peoples,
   and praise You among the nations.
For Your love is great, reaching up to heaven
   and Your truth up to the skies.

God, show Yourself exalted beyond the heavens,
   Your glory over all the earth.

סב

לַמְנַצֵּחַ עַל־יְדוּתוּן מִזְמוֹר לְדָוִד׃

אַךְ אֶל־אֱלֹהִים דּוּמִיָּה נַפְשִׁי מִמֶּנּוּ יְשׁוּעָתִי׃

אַךְ־הוּא צוּרִי וִישׁוּעָתִי מִשְׂגַּבִּי לֹא־אֶמּוֹט רַבָּה׃

עַד־אָנָה תְּהוֹתְתוּ עַל־אִישׁ תְּרָצְּחוּ כֻלְּכֶם כְּקִיר נָטוּי גָּדֵר
הַדְּחוּיָה׃

אַךְ מִשְּׂאֵתוֹ יָעֲצוּ לְהַדִּיחַ יִרְצוּ כָזָב
בְּפִיו יְבָרֵכוּ וּבְקִרְבָּם יְקַלְלוּ־סֶלָה׃

אַךְ לֵאלֹהִים דּוֹמִּי נַפְשִׁי כִּי־מִמֶּנּוּ תִּקְוָתִי׃

אַךְ־הוּא צוּרִי וִישׁוּעָתִי מִשְׂגַּבִּי לֹא אֶמּוֹט׃

עַל־אֱלֹהִים יִשְׁעִי וּכְבוֹדִי צוּר־עֻזִּי מַחְסִי בֵּאלֹהִים׃

בִּטְחוּ בוֹ בְכָל־עֵת עָם שִׁפְכוּ־לְפָנָיו לְבַבְכֶם אֱלֹהִים
מַחֲסֶה־לָּנוּ סֶלָה׃

אַךְ הֶבֶל בְּנֵי־אָדָם כָּזָב בְּנֵי אִישׁ בְּמֹאזְנַיִם לַעֲלוֹת הֵמָּה
מֵהֶבֶל יָחַד׃

אַל־תִּבְטְחוּ בְעֹשֶׁק וּבְגָזֵל אַל־תֶּהְבָּלוּ חַיִל כִּי־יָנוּב אַל־
תָּשִׁיתוּ לֵב׃

אַחַת דִּבֶּר אֱלֹהִים שְׁתַּיִם־זוּ שָׁמָעְתִּי כִּי עֹז לֵאלֹהִים׃

וּלְךָ־אֲדֹנָי חָסֶד כִּי־אַתָּה תְּשַׁלֵּם לְאִישׁ כְּמַעֲשֵׂהוּ׃

62

For the choirmaster.   Setting by Yedutun.   A psalm of David.

Only in God is there rest for my soul,
   from Him comes my safety.
Only He is my rock and my safety,
   my fortress so that I never fall.

How long will you threaten a man,
   all of you trying to destroy him,
like a wall already tottering,
   a toppling rampart!

They only scheme to throw him off his height,
   they delight in deceit;
they bless him with their mouth,
   but inwardly they curse him.

Only in God find your rest, my soul,
   for from Him comes my hope.
Only He is my rock and my safety,
   my fortress so that I never fall.

My safety, my honour, depend on God,
   the rock of my strength—my shelter is in God.
Rely on Him, people, at all times!
   Pour out your hearts before Him.
   God is a shelter for us!

The 'common man' is an empty wind,
   the 'superman' a tiny speck.
Put them in the scales together—they go up,
   lighter even than an empty wind.

Put no trust in extortion,
   no empty hopes in robbery.
Though wealth breeds wealth,
   keep your heart detached.

One thing God has said—
   twice I have learnt it—
that 'strength depends on God'
   and 'Lord, faithful love is Yours!'
For You repay a man
   according to what he does.

סג (א‑ט)

מִזְמוֹר לְדָוִד בִּהְיוֹתוֹ בְּמִדְבַּר יְהוּדָה:

אֱלֹהִים אֵלִי אַתָּה אֲשַׁחֲרֶךָּ צָמְאָה לְךָ נַפְשִׁי כָּמַהּ לְךָ בְשָׂרִי בְּאֶרֶץ‑צִיָּה וְעָיֵף בְּלִי‑מָיִם:

כֵּן בַּקֹּדֶשׁ חֲזִיתִךָ לִרְאוֹת עֻזְּךָ וּכְבוֹדֶךָ:
כִּי‑טוֹב חַסְדְּךָ מֵחַיִּים שְׂפָתַי יְשַׁבְּחוּנְךָ:
כֵּן אֲבָרֶכְךָ בְחַיָּי בְּשִׁמְךָ אֶשָּׂא כַפָּי:

כְּמוֹ חֵלֶב וָדֶשֶׁן תִּשְׂבַּע נַפְשִׁי וְשִׂפְתֵי רְנָנוֹת יְהַלֶּל‑פִּי:
אִם‑זְכַרְתִּיךָ עַל‑יְצוּעָי בְּאַשְׁמֻרוֹת אֶהְגֶּה‑בָּךְ:
כִּי‑הָיִיתָ עֶזְרָתָה לִּי וּבְצֵל כְּנָפֶיךָ אֲרַנֵּן:

דָּבְקָה נַפְשִׁי אַחֲרֶיךָ בִּי תָּמְכָה יְמִינֶךָ:

סז

לַמְנַצֵּחַ בִּנְגִינֹת מִזְמוֹר שִׁיר:

אֱלֹהִים יְחָנֵּנוּ וִיבָרְכֵנוּ יָאֵר פָּנָיו אִתָּנוּ סֶלָה:
לָדַעַת בָּאָרֶץ דַּרְכֶּךָ בְּכָל‑גּוֹיִם יְשׁוּעָתֶךָ:

יוֹדוּךָ עַמִּים אֱלֹהִים יוֹדוּךָ עַמִּים כֻּלָּם:
יִשְׂמְחוּ וִירַנְּנוּ לְאֻמִּים כִּי‑תִשְׁפֹּט עַמִּים מִישֹׁר וּלְאֻמִּים בָּאָרֶץ תַּנְחֵם סֶלָה:

63: 1–9

A psalm of David when he was in the desert of Judah.

God, You are my God,
   with longing do I seek You.
My soul is thirsty for You,
   my flesh is pining for You
in a dry and weary land
   where there is no water.

So I looked for You in the holy place,
   to see Your power and glory.
Because Your love is better than life,
   my lips shall praise You.
So I bless You as long as I live,
   in Your name I raise my hands in prayer.

My soul is satisfied as at a feast,
   my mouth and lips sing out Your praise.
I remember You on my bed,
   and think about You through the night,
for You have been my help,
   and in the shadow of Your wings I sing for joy.

My soul clings to You,
   Your right hand supports me.

67

For the choirmaster.   For strings.   A psalm.   A song.

May God be gracious to us and bless us
   and let His face shed its light among us.
Then Your way will be known on earth,
   Your saving power among all nations.

Let the peoples praise You, God,
   let all the peoples praise You!
Let the nations be glad and sing out for joy,
   for You will rule the peoples in fairness
   and guide the nations of the earth.

יוֹדוּךָ עַמִּים אֱלֹהִים יוֹדוּךָ עַמִּים כֻּלָּם:

אֶרֶץ נָתְנָה יְבוּלָהּ יְבָרְכֵנוּ אֱלֹהִים אֱלֹהֵינוּ:

יְבָרְכֵנוּ אֱלֹהִים וְיִירְאוּ אוֹתוֹ כָּל־אַפְסֵי־אָרֶץ:

עא

בְּךָ־יְהֹוָה חָסִיתִי אַל־אֵבוֹשָׁה לְעוֹלָם:

בְּצִדְקָתְךָ תַּצִּילֵנִי וּתְפַלְּטֵנִי הַטֵּה־אֵלַי אָזְנְךָ וְהוֹשִׁיעֵנִי:

הֱיֵה לִי לְצוּר מָעוֹן לָבוֹא תָּמִיד צִוִּיתָ לְהוֹשִׁיעֵנִי

כִּי־סַלְעִי וּמְצוּדָתִי אָתָּה:

אֱלֹהַי פַּלְּטֵנִי מִיַּד רָשָׁע מִכַּף מְעַוֵּל וְחוֹמֵץ:

כִּי־אַתָּה תִקְוָתִי אֲדֹנָי יֱהֹוִה מִבְטַחִי מִנְּעוּרָי:

עָלֶיךָ נִסְמַכְתִּי מִבֶּטֶן מִמְּעֵי אִמִּי אַתָּה גוֹזִי

בְּךָ תְהִלָּתִי תָמִיד:

כְּמוֹפֵת הָיִיתִי לְרַבִּים וְאַתָּה מַחֲסִי־עֹז:

יִמָּלֵא פִי תְּהִלָּתֶךָ כָּל־הַיּוֹם תִּפְאַרְתֶּךָ:

אַל־תַּשְׁלִיכֵנִי לְעֵת זִקְנָה כִּכְלוֹת כֹּחִי אַל־תַּעַזְבֵנִי:

כִּי־אָמְרוּ אוֹיְבַי לִי וְשֹׁמְרֵי נַפְשִׁי נוֹעֲצוּ יַחְדָּו:

לֵאמֹר אֱלֹהִים עֲזָבוֹ רִדְפוּ וְתִפְשׂוּהוּ כִּי־אֵין מַצִּיל:

Let the peoples praise You, God,
　let all the peoples praise You!
The earth has given her harvest,
　may God, our God, bless us.
May God bless us
　and let the ends of the earth revere Him.

71

Lord, in You I have taken refuge,
　let me never be ashamed.
In Your justice, rescue me and free me,
　listen to me and save me.
Be my sheltering rock,
　where I may always come,
which You prepared for my safety—
　You are my rock and my fortress!

My God, rescue me from the hand of the wicked,
　from the power of the unjust and the ruthless.
Lord, You are my hope,
　the Lord God I trusted since my childhood.
Since my birth I have relied upon You,
　for You delivered me from my mother's womb—
I praise You always.

My life has been a mystery to many
　but You are my strong refuge.
My mouth shall be filled with Your praise
　and Your glory all day long.
Do not reject me in old age;
　when my strength is feeble, do not abandon me.
My enemies are plotting against me,
　those who watch me take counsel together,
saying, 'God has forsaken him,
　let us follow him, and catch him,
　for no-one comes to his rescue'.

אֱלֹהִים אַל־תִּרְחַק מִמֶּנִּי אֱלֹהַי לְעֶזְרָתִי חוּשָׁה:

יֵבֹשׁוּ יִכְלוּ שֹׂטְנֵי נַפְשִׁי יַעֲטוּ חֶרְפָּה וּכְלִמָּה מְבַקְשֵׁי רָעָתִי:

וַאֲנִי תָּמִיד אֲיַחֵל וְהוֹסַפְתִּי עַל־כָּל־תְּהִלָּתֶךָ:

פִּי יְסַפֵּר צִדְקָתֶךָ כָּל־הַיּוֹם תְּשׁוּעָתֶךָ כִּי לֹא יָדַעְתִּי סְפֹרוֹת:

אָבוֹא בִּגְבֻרוֹת אֲדֹנָי יֱהוִֹה אַזְכִּיר צִדְקָתְךָ לְבַדֶּךָ:

אֱלֹהִים לִמַּדְתַּנִי מִנְּעוּרָי וְעַד־הֵנָּה אַגִּיד נִפְלְאוֹתֶיךָ:

וְגַם עַד־זִקְנָה וְשֵׂיבָה אֱלֹהִים אַל־תַּעַזְבֵנִי עַד־אַגִּיד זְרוֹעֲךָ

לְדוֹר לְכָל־יָבוֹא גְּבוּרָתֶךָ:

וְצִדְקָתְךָ אֱלֹהִים עַד־מָרוֹם אֲשֶׁר־עָשִׂיתָ גְדֹלוֹת

אֱלֹהִים מִי כָמוֹךָ:

אֲשֶׁר הִרְאִיתַנִי צָרוֹת רַבּוֹת וְרָעוֹת תָּשׁוּב תְּחַיֵּינִי

וּמִתְּהֹמוֹת הָאָרֶץ תָּשׁוּב תַּעֲלֵנִי:

תֶּרֶב גְּדֻלָּתִי וְתִסֹּב תְּנַחֲמֵנִי:

גַּם־אֲנִי אוֹדְךָ בִכְלִי־נֶבֶל אֲמִתְּךָ אֱלֹהַי אֲזַמְּרָה לְךָ בְכִנּוֹר

קְדוֹשׁ יִשְׂרָאֵל:

תְּרַנֵּנָּה שְׂפָתַי כִּי אֲזַמְּרָה־לָּךְ וְנַפְשִׁי אֲשֶׁר פָּדִיתָ:

God, do not stay so far from me,
   my God, hurry to help me.
Let those who seek my life
   be ashamed and destroyed.
Let those who try to harm me
   be covered with shame and confusion.
But I shall always hope
   and praise You more and more.
My lips will speak of Your righteousness
   and Your salvation all day long,
     though it is more than I can understand.

I shall declare Your mighty deeds, Lord God,
   declaring Your righteousness, Yours alone.
God, You have taught me since my youth,
   and even now I still proclaim Your wonders.
Now that I am old and grey,
   do not abandon me, God,
until I have told the next generation
   of Your outstretched arm,
     of Your might to all who come after.

Your righteousness, O God, extends to heaven.
   You have done great things,
     there is no-one like You, God.
You have shown me many bitter troubles,
   but You will revive me again
     and raise me up again from the depths of the earth.
You will make me greater than ever
   and comfort me again.

And I will praise You on the lyre
   for Your truth, my God.
On my harp I will play to You,
   Holy One of Israel.
When I sing for You
   my lips will rejoice.
So will my soul
   which You have redeemed.

גַּם־לְשׁוֹנִי כָּל־הַיּוֹם תֶּהְגֶּה צִדְקָתֶךָ כִּי־בֹשׁוּ
כִי־חָפְרוּ מְבַקְשֵׁי רָעָתִי:

עב

לִשְׁלֹמֹה

אֱלֹהִים מִשְׁפָּטֶיךָ לְמֶלֶךְ תֵּן וְצִדְקָתְךָ לְבֶן־מֶלֶךְ:
יָדִין עַמְּךָ בְצֶדֶק וַעֲנִיֶּיךָ בְמִשְׁפָּט:

יִשְׂאוּ הָרִים שָׁלוֹם לָעָם וּגְבָעוֹת בִּצְדָקָה:
יִשְׁפֹּט עֲנִיֵּי־עָם יוֹשִׁיעַ לִבְנֵי אֶבְיוֹן וִידַכֵּא עוֹשֵׁק:

יִירָאוּךָ עִם־שָׁמֶשׁ וְלִפְנֵי יָרֵחַ דּוֹר דּוֹרִים:
יֵרֵד כְּמָטָר עַל־גֵּז כִּרְבִיבִים זַרְזִיף אָרֶץ:

יִפְרַח־בְּיָמָיו צַדִּיק וְרֹב שָׁלוֹם עַד־בְּלִי יָרֵחַ:
וְיֵרְדְּ מִיָּם עַד־יָם וּמִנָּהָר עַד־אַפְסֵי־אָרֶץ:

לְפָנָיו יִכְרְעוּ צִיִּים וְאֹיְבָיו עָפָר יְלַחֵכוּ:
מַלְכֵי תַרְשִׁישׁ וְאִיִּים מִנְחָה יָשִׁיבוּ
מַלְכֵי שְׁבָא וּסְבָא אֶשְׁכָּר יַקְרִיבוּ:
וְיִשְׁתַּחֲווּ־לוֹ כָל־מְלָכִים כָּל־גּוֹיִם יַעַבְדוּהוּ:

כִּי־יַצִּיל אֶבְיוֹן מְשַׁוֵּעַ וְעָנִי וְאֵין־עֹזֵר לוֹ:
יָחֹס עַל־דַּל וְאֶבְיוֹן וְנַפְשׁוֹת אֶבְיוֹנִים יוֹשִׁיעַ:
מִתּוֹךְ וּמֵחָמָס יִגְאַל נַפְשָׁם וְיֵיקַר דָּמָם בְּעֵינָיו:

My tongue will speak of Your righteousness
all day long—
for shamed and disgraced
are those who try to hurt me.

72

Solomon's.

God, grant the king Your own judgment
and Your righteousness to a king's son,
that he may rule Your people rightly
and Your poor with justice.

May the mountains bring peace to the people
and the hills righteousness.
May he defend the poor of the people,
save the children of those in need,
and crush the oppressor.

They shall fear You while the sun endures,
and as long as the moon lasts throughout all generations.
He shall descend like rain upon the meadows,
like showers that water the earth.

In his days the righteous shall flourish,
and universal peace till the moon fails.
He shall rule from sea to sea,
from the Great River to the ends of the earth.

The bedouin shall submit to him,
and his enemies lick the dust.
The kings of Tarshish and the islands
shall pay him tribute.
The kings of Sheba and Seba
shall bring him gifts.
All kings shall pay him homage,
all nations shall serve him.

Because he rescues the needy when they cry,
the poor, and those who have no helper;
because he has pity on the weak and needy
and saves the lives of the poor;
because he rescues their lives from oppression and violence
and their blood is precious in his sight.

וִיחִי וְיִתֶּן־לוֹ מִזְּהַב שְׁבָא וְיִתְפַּלֵּל בַּעֲדוֹ תָמִיד
כָּל־הַיּוֹם יְבָרֲכֶנְהוּ:

יְהִי פִסַּת־בַּר בָּאָרֶץ בְּרֹאשׁ הָרִים יִרְעַשׁ כַּלְּבָנוֹן פִּרְיוֹ
וְיָצִיצוּ מֵעִיר כְּעֵשֶׂב הָאָרֶץ:

יְהִי שְׁמוֹ לְעוֹלָם לִפְנֵי־שֶׁמֶשׁ יִנּוֹן שְׁמוֹ וְיִתְבָּרֲכוּ בוֹ
כָּל־גּוֹיִם יְאַשְּׁרוּהוּ:

בָּרוּךְ יְהוָה אֱלֹהִים אֱלֹהֵי יִשְׂרָאֵל עֹשֵׂה נִפְלָאוֹת לְבַדּוֹ:
וּבָרוּךְ שֵׁם כְּבוֹדוֹ לְעוֹלָם וְיִמָּלֵא כְבוֹדוֹ אֶת־כָּל־הָאָרֶץ
אָמֵן וְאָמֵן:

כָּלּוּ תְפִלּוֹת דָּוִד בֶּן־יִשָׁי:

עג

מִזְמוֹר לְאָסָף
אַךְ טוֹב לְיִשְׂרָאֵל אֱלֹהִים לְבָרֵי לֵבָב:
וַאֲנִי כִּמְעַט נָטָיוּ רַגְלָי כְּאַיִן שֻׁפְּכוּ אֲשֻׁרָי:

כִּי־קִנֵּאתִי בַּהוֹלְלִים שְׁלוֹם רְשָׁעִים אֶרְאֶה:
כִּי אֵין חַרְצֻבּוֹת לְמוֹתָם וּבָרִיא אוּלָם:

בַּעֲמַל אֱנוֹשׁ אֵינֵמוֹ וְעִם־אָדָם לֹא יְנֻגָּעוּ:
לָכֵן עֲנָקַתְמוֹ גַאֲוָה יַעֲטָף־שִׁית חָמָס לָמוֹ:

May his name live forever,
   let them give him the gold of Sheba!
May they always pray for him,
   blessing him all the day.

May corn be abundant in the land,
   even on the peaks of the mountains.
May its fruit rustle like that of Lebanon,
   may men flourish in cities
   like grass on the earth!

May his name live forever,
   enduring as long as the sun!
Through him may all men find their blessing,
   and all nations their happiness.

Blessed be the Lord God, the God of Israel,
   who alone works wonders.
Blessed be His glorious name forever.
   All the earth is full of His glory.
Amen and amen!

   The prayers of David the son of Jesse are ended.

73

A psalm of Asaph.

How good is God to Israel!
   to those who are pure in heart!
Yet my foot came close to stumbling,
   my footsteps almost slipped.

For I was envious of the arrogant
   when I saw the ease of the wicked.
No anguished death for them,
   their bodies are perfectly sound.

They are not burdened like the rest of mankind,
   nor stricken like honest men.
Pride is their chain of honour,
   they clothe themselves in violence.

יָצָא מֵחֵלֶב עֵינֵמוֹ עָבְרוּ מַשְׂכִּיּוֹת לֵבָב׃

יָמִיקוּ וִידַבְּרוּ בְרָע עֹשֶׁק מִמָּרוֹם יְדַבֵּרוּ׃

שַׁתּוּ בַשָּׁמַיִם פִּיהֶם וּלְשׁוֹנָם תִּהֲלַךְ בָּאָרֶץ׃

לָכֵן יָשׁוּב עַמּוֹ הֲלֹם וּמֵי מָלֵא יִמָּצוּ לָמוֹ׃

וְאָמְרוּ אֵיכָה יָדַע־אֵל וְיֵשׁ דֵּעָה בְעֶלְיוֹן׃

הִנֵּה־אֵלֶּה רְשָׁעִים וְשַׁלְוֵי עוֹלָם הִשְׂגּוּ־חָיִל׃

אַךְ־רִיק זִכִּיתִי לְבָבִי וָאֶרְחַץ בְּנִקָּיוֹן כַּפָּי׃

וָאֱהִי נָגוּעַ כָּל־הַיּוֹם וְתוֹכַחְתִּי לַבְּקָרִים׃

אִם־אָמַרְתִּי אֲסַפְּרָה כְמוֹ הִנֵּה דוֹר בָּנֶיךָ בָגָדְתִּי׃

וָאֲחַשְּׁבָה לָדַעַת זֹאת עָמָל הוּא בְעֵינָי׃

עַד־אָבוֹא אֶל־מִקְדְּשֵׁי־אֵל אָבִינָה לְאַחֲרִיתָם׃

אַךְ בַּחֲלָקוֹת תָּשִׁית לָמוֹ הִפַּלְתָּם לְמַשּׁוּאוֹת׃

אֵיךְ הָיוּ לְשַׁמָּה כְרָגַע סָפוּ תַמּוּ מִן־בַּלָּהוֹת׃

כַּחֲלוֹם מֵהָקִיץ אֲדֹנָי בָּעִיר צַלְמָם תִּבְזֶה׃

כִּי יִתְחַמֵּץ לְבָבִי וְכִלְיוֹתַי אֶשְׁתּוֹנָן׃

וַאֲנִי־בַעַר וְלֹא אֵדַע בְּהֵמוֹת הָיִיתִי עִמָּךְ׃

וַאֲנִי תָמִיד עִמָּךְ אָחַזְתָּ בְּיַד־יְמִינִי׃

בַּעֲצָתְךָ תַנְחֵנִי וְאַחַר כָּבוֹד תִּקָּחֵנִי׃

Their eyes bulge out of fatness,
the insolence in their hearts overflows.
They scoff and talk of evil,
planning oppression from above.
They set their mouth against the very heavens
and their tongue struts through the earth.

So His people turn towards them
drinking in their words to the full.
And they say: 'How can God know?
Does the Most High take notice?
Look! Such are the wicked,
always at ease and growing in power!'

How useless it seemed to cleanse my heart
and wash my hands in innocence!
For I was stricken all the day long,
tormented morning after morning.

Yet if I had said: 'I will tell this aloud!'
I would have betrayed a generation of Your children
But the more I tried to understand it,
this burden was always before my eyes.

Then I came into God's holy place
and realised their final end.
You set them on a slippery path,
hurl them into utter ruin.

One moment and they will be a desolation,
completely engulfed in terrors.
Like a dream to one suddenly awake, O Lord,
You shake off these phantoms when You arise!

How bitter was my heart
and sharp the pain within me.
For I was stupid and did not understand,
behaving like an animal before You.

Yet I am always with You.
You have grasped me by the hand.
You will guide me with Your counsel
and afterwards receive me in glory.

מִי־לִי בַשָּׁמָיִם וְעִמְּךָ לֹא־חָפַצְתִּי בָאָרֶץ:

כָּלָה שְׁאֵרִי וּלְבָבִי צוּר־לְבָבִי וְחֶלְקִי אֱלֹהִים לְעוֹלָם:

כִּי־הִנֵּה רְחֵקֶיךָ יֹאבֵדוּ הִצְמַתָּה כָּל־זוֹנֶה מִמֶּךָּ:

וַאֲנִי קִרְבַת אֱלֹהִים לִי טוֹב שַׁתִּי בַּאדֹנָי יֱהוִֹה מַחְסִי

לְסַפֵּר כָּל־מַלְאֲכוֹתֶיךָ:

עז

לַמְנַצֵּחַ עַל־יְדוּתוּן לְאָסָף מִזְמוֹר:

קוֹלִי אֶל־אֱלֹהִים וְאֶצְעָקָה קוֹלִי אֶל־אֱלֹהִים וְהַאֲזִין אֵלָי:

בְּיוֹם צָרָתִי אֲדֹנָי דָּרָשְׁתִּי יָדִי לַיְלָה נִגְּרָה וְלֹא תָפוּג

מֵאֲנָה הִנָּחֵם נַפְשִׁי:

אֶזְכְּרָה אֱלֹהִים וְאֶהֱמָיָה אָשִׂיחָה וְתִתְעַטֵּף רוּחִי סֶלָה:

אָחַזְתָּ שְׁמֻרוֹת עֵינָי נִפְעַמְתִּי וְלֹא אֲדַבֵּר:

חִשַּׁבְתִּי יָמִים מִקֶּדֶם שְׁנוֹת עוֹלָמִים:

אֶזְכְּרָה נְגִינָתִי בַּלַּיְלָה עִם־לְבָבִי אָשִׂיחָה וַיְחַפֵּשׂ רוּחִי:

הַלְעוֹלָמִים יִזְנַח אֲדֹנָי וְלֹא־יֹסִיף לִרְצוֹת עוֹד:

הֶאָפֵס לָנֶצַח חַסְדּוֹ גָּמַר אֹמֶר לְדֹר וָדֹר:

הֲשָׁכַח חַנּוֹת אֵל אִם־קָפַץ בְּאַף רַחֲמָיו סֶלָה:

Whom have I in heaven but You?
    Beside You, I desire nothing on earth.
My flesh and heart may fail
    but God is the rock of my heart
    and my portion forever.

For those who go far from You perish,
    You destroy all who betray Your trust.
But for me, the nearness of God is my good.
    I have made the Lord God my refuge
    that I might tell of all Your works.

77

For the choirmaster.   Setting by Yedutun.   Asaph's psalm.

I cried aloud to God, I shouted out,
    I cried aloud to God, and He heard me.
In the day of my distress I searched for the Lord,
    my hand was stretched out all night long,
    my soul refused all comfort.
I moaned when I remembered God;
    as I lay thinking, my spirit sank.

You stopped me closing my eyes,
    so disturbed that I could not speak.
I thought over days long past,
    the years of former times.
I remembered my old song of happiness in the night.
    I prayed in my heart, and my spirit asked this question:

Will the Lord reject us forever
    and show His favour no more?
Has His love vanished to nothing,
    is the promise He made to all generations finished?
Has God forgotten His mercy
    and shut up His compassion in anger?

וָאֹמַר חַלּוֹתִי הִיא שְׁנוֹת יְמִין עֶלְיוֹן:

אֶזְכּוֹר מַעַלְלֵי־יָהּ כִּי־אֶזְכְּרָה מִקֶּדֶם פִּלְאֶךָ:

וְהָגִיתִי בְכָל־פָּעֳלֶךָ וּבַעֲלִילוֹתֶיךָ אָשִׂיחָה:

אֱלֹהִים בַּקֹּדֶשׁ דַּרְכֶּךָ מִי־אֵל גָּדוֹל כֵּאלֹהִים:

אַתָּה הָאֵל עֹשֵׂה פֶלֶא הוֹדַעְתָּ בָעַמִּים עֻזֶּךָ:

גָּאַלְתָּ בִּזְרוֹעַ עַמֶּךָ בְּנֵי־יַעֲקֹב וְיוֹסֵף סֶלָה:

רָאוּךָ מַּיִם אֱלֹהִים רָאוּךָ מַּיִם יָחִילוּ אַף יִרְגְּזוּ תְּהֹמוֹת:

זֹרְמוּ מַיִם עָבוֹת קוֹל נָתְנוּ שְׁחָקִים אַף־חֲצָצֶיךָ יִתְהַלָּכוּ:

קוֹל רַעַמְךָ בַּגַּלְגַּל הֵאִירוּ בְרָקִים תֵּבֵל רָגְזָה וַתִּרְעַשׁ הָאָרֶץ:

בַּיָּם דַּרְכֶּךָ וּשְׁבִילְךָ בְּמַיִם רַבִּים וְעִקְּבוֹתֶיךָ לֹא נֹדָעוּ:

נָחִיתָ כַצֹּאן עַמֶּךָ בְּיַד־מֹשֶׁה וְאַהֲרֹן:

פב

מִזְמוֹר לְאָסָף

אֱלֹהִים נִצָּב בַּעֲדַת־אֵל בְּקֶרֶב אֱלֹהִים יִשְׁפֹּט:

עַד־מָתַי תִּשְׁפְּטוּ־עָוֶל וּפְנֵי רְשָׁעִים תִּשְׂאוּ־סֶלָה:

שִׁפְטוּ־דַל וְיָתוֹם עָנִי וָרָשׁ הַצְדִּיקוּ:

פַּלְּטוּ־דַל וְאֶבְיוֹן מִיַּד רְשָׁעִים הַצִּילוּ:

But then I said, 'This is my weakness,
does the right hand of the Most High change?'
I remember the deeds of the Lord,
I remember Your wonders of old.
I think over all Your works
and ponder about all You have done.

God, Your way leads through holiness;
what power is great as God!
You are the God who does wonders,
You showed Your power among the peoples.
You redeemed, with arm outstretched,
the sons of Jacob and Joseph.

Then the waters saw You, O God,
the waters saw You and whirled about,
they trembled to their depths.
The clouds poured out rain,
the skies thundered,
Your shafts flashed down.

The roar of Your thunder rolled by,
Your lightning lit up the world,
the earth trembled and shook.
Your way was through the sea,
Your path through mighty waters
but Your steps could not be known.

You led Your people like a flock
by the hand of Moses and Aaron.

82

A psalm of Asaph.

God stands in the congregation of the godly,
in the midst of the mighty He judges.

'How long will you judge unjustly,
and show favour to the wicked?
Do justice for the weak and the orphan,
act rightly for the afflicted and the destitute!
Rescue the weak and the needy,
save them from the clutches of the wicked!'

לֹא יָדְעוּ וְלֹא יָבִינוּ בַּחֲשֵׁכָה יִתְהַלָּכוּ יִמּוֹטוּ כָּל־מוֹסְדֵי אָרֶץ:

אֲנִי־אָמַרְתִּי אֱלֹהִים אַתֶּם וּבְנֵי עֶלְיוֹן כֻּלְּכֶם:

אָכֵן כְּאָדָם תְּמוּתוּן וּכְאַחַד הַשָּׂרִים תִּפֹּלוּ:

קוּמָה אֱלֹהִים שָׁפְטָה הָאָרֶץ כִּי־אַתָּה תִנְחַל בְּכָל־הַגּוֹיִם:

פד

לַמְנַצֵּחַ עַל־הַגִּתִּית לִבְנֵי־קֹרַח מִזְמוֹר:

מַה־יְּדִידוֹת מִשְׁכְּנוֹתֶיךָ יְהוָה צְבָאוֹת:

נִכְסְפָה וְגַם־כָּלְתָה נַפְשִׁי לְחַצְרוֹת יְהוָה

לִבִּי וּבְשָׂרִי יְרַנְּנוּ אֶל אֵל־חָי:

גַּם־צִפּוֹר מָצְאָה בַיִת וּדְרוֹר קֵן לָהּ אֲשֶׁר־שָׁתָה אֶפְרֹחֶיהָ

אֶת־מִזְבְּחוֹתֶיךָ יְהוָה צְבָאוֹת מַלְכִּי וֵאלֹהָי:

אַשְׁרֵי יוֹשְׁבֵי בֵיתֶךָ עוֹד יְהַלְלוּךָ סֶּלָה:

אַשְׁרֵי אָדָם עוֹז־לוֹ בָךְ מְסִלּוֹת בִּלְבָבָם:

עֹבְרֵי בְּעֵמֶק הַבָּכָא מַעְיָן יְשִׁיתוּהוּ גַּם־בְּרָכוֹת יַעְטֶה מוֹרֶה:

יֵלְכוּ מֵחַיִל אֶל־חָיִל יֵרָאֶה אֶל־אֱלֹהִים בְּצִיּוֹן:

יְהוָה אֱלֹהִים צְבָאוֹת שִׁמְעָה תְפִלָּתִי

הַאֲזִינָה אֱלֹהֵי יַעֲקֹב סֶלָה:

מָגִנֵּנוּ רְאֵה אֱלֹהִים וְהַבֵּט פְּנֵי מְשִׁיחֶךָ:

They do not realise, they do not understand;
   they grope in the dark
   and the order of the world is shaken.
I said, 'You are godlike beings,
   sons of the Highest all of you.
Yet you shall die like men;
   princes fall, so shall you.'

God, arise, judge the earth!
   For You possess all the nations.

84

For the choirmaster.   Upon the Gittit.   For the sons of Korach.   A psalm.

How lovely where Your presence dwells
   Lord of all creation.
My soul is longing, pining
   for the courts of the Lord.
My heart and my flesh sing out
   to the living God.

Even a sparrow finds a home
   and a swallow her own nest
   in which to lay her young—
   such are Your altars, Lord of all creation,
   my ruler and my God.

Happy are those who live in Your house
   and can always praise You.
Happy the pilgrim inspired by You,
   they journey to You in their heart.
They pass through the dry sad valley
   and make it seem a place of springs,
   as if the early rain covered it with blessings.
They go from strength to strength
   to appear before God in Zion.

Lord, God of all creation, hear my prayer,
   listen, God of Jacob!
God, our shield, look
   and watch over Your anointed!

כִּי טוֹב־יוֹם בַּחֲצֵרֶיךָ מֵאָלֶף בָּחַרְתִּי הִסְתּוֹפֵף בְּבֵית אֱלֹהַי
מִדּוּר בְּאָהֳלֵי־רֶשַׁע:

כִּי שֶׁמֶשׁ וּמָגֵן יְהֹוָה אֱלֹהִים חֵן וְכָבוֹד יִתֵּן יְהֹוָה
לֹא יִמְנַע־טוֹב לַהֹלְכִים בְּתָמִים:

יְהֹוָה צְבָאוֹת אַשְׁרֵי אָדָם בֹּטֵחַ בָּךְ:

פה

לַמְנַצֵּחַ לִבְנֵי־קֹרַח מִזְמוֹר:

רָצִיתָ יְהֹוָה אַרְצֶךָ שַׁבְתָּ שְׁבִית יַעֲקֹב:

נָשָׂאתָ עֲוֹן עַמֶּךָ כִּסִּיתָ כָל־חַטָּאתָם סֶלָה:

אָסַפְתָּ כָל־עֶבְרָתֶךָ הֱשִׁיבוֹתָ מֵחֲרוֹן אַפֶּךָ:

שׁוּבֵנוּ אֱלֹהֵי יִשְׁעֵנוּ וְהָפֵר כַּעַסְךָ עִמָּנוּ:

הַלְעוֹלָם תֶּאֱנַף־בָּנוּ תִּמְשֹׁךְ אַפְּךָ לְדֹר וָדֹר:

הֲלֹא־אַתָּה תָּשׁוּב תְּחַיֵּינוּ וְעַמְּךָ יִשְׂמְחוּ־בָךְ:

הַרְאֵנוּ יְהֹוָה חַסְדֶּךָ וְיֶשְׁעֲךָ תִּתֶּן־לָנוּ:

אֶשְׁמְעָה מַה־יְדַבֵּר הָאֵל יְהֹוָה כִּי יְדַבֵּר שָׁלוֹם אֶל־עַמּוֹ
וְאֶל־חֲסִידָיו וְאַל־יָשׁוּבוּ לְכִסְלָה:

אַךְ קָרוֹב לִירֵאָיו יִשְׁעוֹ לִשְׁכֹּן כָּבוֹד בְּאַרְצֵנוּ:

חֶסֶד־וֶאֱמֶת נִפְגָּשׁוּ צֶדֶק וְשָׁלוֹם נָשָׁקוּ:

אֱמֶת מֵאֶרֶץ תִּצְמָח וְצֶדֶק מִשָּׁמַיִם נִשְׁקָף:

For one day in Your courts is better
than a thousand elsewhere.
I would rather stand at the doorway
of the house of my God
than live at ease in the tents of the wicked.

For the Lord God is a sun and a shield,
the Lord gives favour and glory.
He will not withhold goodness
from those who walk in integrity.

Lord of all creation,
happy the man who trusts in You!

85

For the choirmaster. For the sons of Korach. A psalm.

Lord, You have shown favour to Your land,
You reversed the captivity of Jacob.
You forgave the guilt of Your people,
You covered all their sins.
You retracted all Your anger,
You turned away from Your bitter rage.
Bring us back, O God, our saviour
and cancel Your indignation against us.
Will You be angry with us forever,
prolonging Your anger to all generations?
Will You not bring us back to life
so that Your people may rejoice in You!
Lord, show us Your mercy
and grant us Your salvation.

I will hear what God, the Lord, has to say
for He means peace for His people, all those who love Him,
if they renounce their folly.
Very close is His help to those who fear Him,
so that glory may dwell in our land.
Mercy and truth have met together,
righteousness and peace have kissed each other.
Truth springs up from the earth
and righteousness looks down from heaven.

גַּם־יְהוָה יִתֵּן הַטּוֹב וְאַרְצֵנוּ תִּתֵּן יְבוּלָהּ׃

צֶדֶק לְפָנָיו יְהַלֵּךְ וְיָשֵׂם לְדֶרֶךְ פְּעָמָיו׃

פו

תְּפִלָּה לְדָוִד

הַטֵּה־יְהוָה אָזְנְךָ עֲנֵנִי כִּי־עָנִי וְאֶבְיוֹן אָנִי׃

שָׁמְרָה נַפְשִׁי כִּי־חָסִיד אָנִי הוֹשַׁע עַבְדְּךָ אַתָּה אֱלֹהַי

הַבּוֹטֵחַ אֵלֶיךָ׃

חָנֵּנִי אֲדֹנָי כִּי־אֵלֶיךָ אֶקְרָא כָּל־הַיּוֹם׃

שַׂמֵּחַ נֶפֶשׁ עַבְדֶּךָ כִּי אֵלֶיךָ אֲדֹנָי נַפְשִׁי אֶשָּׂא׃

כִּי־אַתָּה אֲדֹנָי טוֹב וְסַלָּח וְרַב־חֶסֶד לְכָל־קֹרְאֶיךָ׃

הַאֲזִינָה יְהוָה תְּפִלָּתִי וְהַקְשִׁיבָה בְּקוֹל תַּחֲנוּנוֹתָי׃

בְּיוֹם צָרָתִי אֶקְרָאֶךָּ כִּי תַעֲנֵנִי׃

אֵין־כָּמוֹךָ בָאֱלֹהִים אֲדֹנָי וְאֵין כְּמַעֲשֶׂיךָ׃

כָּל־גּוֹיִם אֲשֶׁר עָשִׂיתָ יָבוֹאוּ וְיִשְׁתַּחֲווּ לְפָנֶיךָ אֲדֹנָי

וִיכַבְּדוּ לִשְׁמֶךָ׃

כִּי־גָדוֹל אַתָּה וְעֹשֵׂה נִפְלָאוֹת אַתָּה אֱלֹהִים לְבַדֶּךָ׃

הוֹרֵנִי יְהוָה דַּרְכֶּךָ אֲהַלֵּךְ בַּאֲמִתֶּךָ יַחֵד לְבָבִי לְיִרְאָה שְׁמֶךָ׃

אוֹדְךָ אֲדֹנָי אֱלֹהַי בְּכָל־לְבָבִי וַאֲכַבְּדָה שִׁמְךָ לְעוֹלָם׃

כִּי־חַסְדְּךָ גָּדוֹל עָלָי וְהִצַּלְתָּ נַפְשִׁי מִשְּׁאוֹל תַּחְתִּיָּה׃

Yes the Lord gives what is good
and our land shall give its harvest.
Righteousness shall go before Him
and make a way for His footsteps.

86

A prayer of David.

Turn Your ear to me, Lord! Answer me!
For I am poor and in need.
Guard my soul, for I am devoted to You.
You are my God, save Your servant who trusts in You.

Lord be gracious to me
for I cry to You all day long.
Rejoice the soul of Your servant,
for Lord, I put my hope in You.

Lord, You are good and forgiving,
full of mercy to all who call upon You.
Listen, Lord, to my prayer,
and hear my voice when I plead.

In my day of distress I call to You,
for You will answer me.
Lord, there is no god like You,
no deeds like Yours!

All the nations that You made
shall come and worship before You, O Lord,
and glorify Your name.
For You are great and do such wonders,
You, God, only You.

Show me, Lord, Your way
so that I may walk in Your truth.
Give my heart integrity
to revere Your name.
Then I will thank You, Lord my God, with all my heart
and glorify Your name forever.
Your love for me has been so great
that You rescued me from the lower world.

אֱלֹהִים זֵדִים קָמוּ עָלַי וַעֲדַת עָרִיצִים בִּקְשׁוּ נַפְשִׁי
וְלֹא שָׂמוּךָ לְנֶגְדָּם:

וְאַתָּה אֲדֹנָי אֵל־רַחוּם וְחַנּוּן אֶרֶךְ אַפַּיִם וְרַב־חֶסֶד וֶאֱמֶת:

פְּנֵה אֵלַי וְחָנֵּנִי תְּנָה־עֻזְּךָ לְעַבְדֶּךָ וְהוֹשִׁיעָה לְבֶן־אֲמָתֶךָ:

עֲשֵׂה־עִמִּי אוֹת לְטוֹבָה וְיִרְאוּ שֹׂנְאַי וְיֵבֹשׁוּ

כִּי־אַתָּה יְהוָֹה עֲזַרְתַּנִי וְנִחַמְתָּנִי:

צ

תְּפִלָּה לְמֹשֶׁה אִישׁ־הָאֱלֹהִים

אֲדֹנָי מָעוֹן אַתָּה הָיִיתָ לָּנוּ בְּדֹר וָדֹר:

בְּטֶרֶם הָרִים יֻלָּדוּ וַתְּחוֹלֵל אֶרֶץ וְתֵבֵל
וּמֵעוֹלָם עַד־עוֹלָם אַתָּה אֵל:

תָּשֵׁב אֱנוֹשׁ עַד־דַּכָּא וַתֹּאמֶר שׁוּבוּ בְנֵי־אָדָם:

כִּי אֶלֶף שָׁנִים בְּעֵינֶיךָ כְּיוֹם אֶתְמוֹל כִּי יַעֲבֹר
וְאַשְׁמוּרָה בַלָּיְלָה:

זְרַמְתָּם שֵׁנָה יִהְיוּ בַּבֹּקֶר כֶּחָצִיר יַחֲלֹף:

בַּבֹּקֶר יָצִיץ וְחָלָף לָעֶרֶב יְמוֹלֵל וְיָבֵשׁ:

כִּי־כָלִינוּ בְאַפֶּךָ וּבַחֲמָתְךָ נִבְהָלְנוּ:

שַׁתָּה עֲוֺנֹתֵינוּ לְנֶגְדֶּךָ עֲלֻמֵנוּ לִמְאוֹר פָּנֶיךָ:

כִּי כָל־יָמֵינוּ פָּנוּ בְעֶבְרָתֶךָ כִּלִּינוּ שָׁנֵינוּ כְמוֹ־הֶגֶה:

יְמֵי־שְׁנוֹתֵינוּ בָהֶם שִׁבְעִים שָׁנָה וְאִם בִּגְבוּרֹת שְׁמוֹנִים שָׁנָה
וְרָהְבָּם עָמָל וָאָוֶן כִּי־גָז חִישׁ וַנָּעֻפָה:

O God, proud men rise against me,
a violent mob, who seek my life,
people to whom You mean nothing.
But You are the Lord, the God of mercy and compassion,
slow to anger, ever loving and ever true.

Turn to me, God, and be gracious to me.
Give Your strength to Your servant.
Rescue the child of a woman who served You.
Show me a sign of Your goodness,
let my enemies see it and be ashamed.
Because You, Lord, have been my help and my comfort.

90

A prayer of Moses, the man of God.

Lord, You have been our home from age to age.
Before the mountains were born,
before You brought the earth and world to birth,
You were God from eternity, and will be forever.

You turn mankind back to dust
yet You say: 'Sons of man, turn back to Me!'
To You a thousand years
are like a yesterday gone by,
a passing hour in the night.
You sweep men away,
they are frail as sleep;
like grass that grows in the morning,
that grows so fresh in the morning,
and in the evening fades and dies.
We are burnt up by Your anger
and dismayed by Your wrath.
You lay bare our sins before You,
our secret sins in the light of Your presence.
Our days pass away in Your anger,
so we end our years like a sigh.

Our lives can reach seventy years,
eighty years with strength,
and they are troubled with grief and emptiness,
but this is soon over and then we move on.

מִי־יוֹדֵעַ עֹז אַפֶּךָ וּכְיִרְאָתְךָ עֶבְרָתֶךָ׃

לִמְנוֹת יָמֵינוּ כֵּן הוֹדַע וְנָבִא לְבַב חָכְמָה׃

שׁוּבָה יְהֹוָה עַד־מָתָי וְהִנָּחֵם עַל־עֲבָדֶיךָ׃

שַׂבְּעֵנוּ בַבֹּקֶר חַסְדֶּךָ וּנְרַנְּנָה וְנִשְׂמְחָה בְּכָל־יָמֵינוּ׃

שַׂמְּחֵנוּ כִּימוֹת עִנִּיתָנוּ שְׁנוֹת רָאִינוּ רָעָה׃

יֵרָאֶה אֶל־עֲבָדֶיךָ פָעֳלֶךָ וַהֲדָרְךָ עַל־בְּנֵיהֶם׃

וִיהִי נֹעַם אֲדֹנָי אֱלֹהֵינוּ עָלֵינוּ וּמַעֲשֵׂה יָדֵינוּ כּוֹנְנָה עָלֵינוּ

וּמַעֲשֵׂה יָדֵינוּ כּוֹנְנֵהוּ׃

צא

יֹשֵׁב בְּסֵתֶר עֶלְיוֹן בְּצֵל שַׁדַּי יִתְלוֹנָן׃

אֹמַר לַיהֹוָה מַחְסִי וּמְצוּדָתִי אֱלֹהַי אֶבְטַח־בּוֹ׃

כִּי הוּא יַצִּילְךָ מִפַּח יָקוּשׁ מִדֶּבֶר הַוּוֹת׃

בְּאֶבְרָתוֹ יָסֶךְ לָךְ וְתַחַת־כְּנָפָיו תֶּחְסֶה צִנָּה וְסֹחֵרָה אֲמִתּוֹ׃

לֹא־תִירָא מִפַּחַד לָיְלָה מֵחֵץ יָעוּף יוֹמָם׃

מִדֶּבֶר בָּאֹפֶל יַהֲלֹךְ מִקֶּטֶב יָשׁוּד צָהֳרָיִם׃

יִפֹּל מִצִּדְּךָ אֶלֶף וּרְבָבָה מִימִינֶךָ אֵלֶיךָ לֹא יִגָּשׁ׃

רַק בְּעֵינֶיךָ תַבִּיט וְשִׁלֻּמַת רְשָׁעִים תִּרְאֶה׃

Who knows the power of Your anger
   and fears the strength of Your wrath!
So show us how to spend our time
   and acquire a heart of wisdom.

Lord, turn back to us!
   How long till You take pity on Your servants?
Fill the morning of our life with Your love
   to be glad and sing all our days.
Give us happiness to match our sadness,
   for times when we knew misfortune.
Let the meaning of Your work be clear to Your servants
   and Your glory to their children.
May the favour of the Lord our God be upon us
   to support us in the work we do,
     and support the work we do.

91

He who dwells in the mystery of the Most High
   rests in the shadow of the Almighty.
Therefore I say that the Lord is my shelter,
   my fortress, my God in whom I trust!
For He rescues you from the hunter's trap,
   from a death that is final destruction.
He covers you with His strength,
   you find shelter beneath His wings.
   His truth surrounds and shields you.

Do not fear the terror of the night,
   nor the sharp blows that fly by day,
the disease that walks in darkness,
   the sickness that destroys at noon.

Though a thousand fall at your side,
   ten thousand at your right hand,
   no harm can come to you.
Just look with your eyes
   and see the results of wickedness.

כִּי־אַתָּה יְהוָֹה מַחְסִי עֶלְיוֹן שַׂמְתָּ מְעוֹנֶךָ：

לֹא־תְאֻנֶּה אֵלֶיךָ רָעָה וְנֶגַע לֹא־יִקְרַב בְּאָהֳלֶךָ：

כִּי מַלְאָכָיו יְצַוֶּה־לָּךְ לִשְׁמָרְךָ בְּכָל־דְּרָכֶיךָ：

עַל־כַּפַּיִם יִשָּׂאוּנְךָ פֶּן־תִּגֹּף בָּאֶבֶן רַגְלֶךָ：

עַל־שַׁחַל וָפֶתֶן תִּדְרֹךְ תִּרְמֹס כְּפִיר וְתַנִּין：

כִּי בִי חָשַׁק וַאֲפַלְּטֵהוּ אֲשַׂגְּבֵהוּ כִּי־יָדַע שְׁמִי：

יִקְרָאֵנִי וְאֶעֱנֵהוּ עִמּוֹ־אָנֹכִי בְצָרָה אֲחַלְּצֵהוּ וַאֲכַבְּדֵהוּ：

אֹרֶךְ יָמִים אַשְׂבִּיעֵהוּ וְאַרְאֵהוּ בִּישׁוּעָתִי：

צב

מִזְמוֹר שִׁיר לְיוֹם הַשַּׁבָּת：

טוֹב לְהֹדוֹת לַיהוָֹה וּלְזַמֵּר לְשִׁמְךָ עֶלְיוֹן：

לְהַגִּיד בַּבֹּקֶר חַסְדֶּךָ וֶאֱמוּנָתְךָ בַּלֵּילוֹת：

עֲלֵי־עָשׂוֹר וַעֲלֵי־נָבֶל עֲלֵי הִגָּיוֹן בְּכִנּוֹר：

כִּי שִׂמַּחְתַּנִי יְהוָֹה בְּפָעֳלֶךָ בְּמַעֲשֵׂי יָדֶיךָ אֲרַנֵּן：

מַה־גָּדְלוּ מַעֲשֶׂיךָ יְהוָֹה מְאֹד עָמְקוּ מַחְשְׁבֹתֶיךָ：

אִישׁ־בַּעַר לֹא יֵדָע וּכְסִיל לֹא־יָבִין אֶת־זֹאת：

בִּפְרֹחַ רְשָׁעִים כְּמוֹ עֵשֶׂב וַיָּצִיצוּ כָּל־פֹּעֲלֵי אָוֶן

לְהִשָּׁמְדָם עֲדֵי־עַד：

וְאַתָּה מָרוֹם לְעֹלָם יְהוָֹה：

Because you say: 'The Lord is my refuge',
   and make the Most High your dwelling,
no evil shall come upon you,
   no blow shall come near your house.

For He commands His messengers to watch over you,
   to keep you in all your ways.
They bear you in their hands
   lest your feet stumble on a stone.
Through terror and venom you will find your way,
   you will crush down new fears and evil.

   'When a man has clung to Me in love, I set him free,
      I protect him for he knows My being.
   When he calls Me I answer him.
      I will be with him in trouble.
      I will rescue him and bring him honour.
   I give him the span of his life,
      then I show him My salvation.'

92

A psalm to sing for the Sabbath day.

It is good to give thanks to the Lord
   to praise Your name, O God beyond all,
to tell of Your love in the morning
   and Your faithfulness every night.
With the ten-stringed lute, with the lyre
   with the gentle sound of the harp.
For You made me rejoice in Your deeds, O Lord,
   at the works of Your hand I sing out.
Lord, how great are Your works,
   Your thoughts are so very deep.
A stupid man does not know this
   nor can a foolish man understand
that when the wicked flourish
   they are only like grass
and when all who do evil spring up
   their end is always destruction,
      and only You, Lord, are exalted forever.

כִּי הִנֵּה אֹיְבֶיךָ יְהוָה כִּי־הִנֵּה אֹיְבֶיךָ יֹאבֵדוּ

יִתְפָּרְדוּ כָּל־פֹּעֲלֵי אָוֶן:

וַתָּרֶם כִּרְאֵים קַרְנִי בַּלֹּתִי בְּשֶׁמֶן רַעֲנָן:

וַתַּבֵּט עֵינִי בְּשׁוּרָי בַּקָּמִים עָלַי מְרֵעִים תִּשְׁמַעְנָה אָזְנָי:

צַדִּיק כַּתָּמָר יִפְרָח כְּאֶרֶז בַּלְּבָנוֹן יִשְׂגֶּה:

שְׁתוּלִים בְּבֵית יְהוָה בְּחַצְרוֹת אֱלֹהֵינוּ יַפְרִיחוּ:

עוֹד יְנוּבוּן בְּשֵׂיבָה דְּשֵׁנִים וְרַעֲנַנִּים יִהְיוּ:

לְהַגִּיד כִּי־יָשָׁר יְהוָה צוּרִי וְלֹא־עַוְלָתָה בּוֹ:

צג

יְהוָה מָלָךְ גֵּאוּת לָבֵשׁ לָבֵשׁ יְהוָה עֹז הִתְאַזָּר

אַף־תִּכּוֹן תֵּבֵל בַּל־תִּמּוֹט:

נָכוֹן כִּסְאֲךָ מֵאָז מֵעוֹלָם אָתָּה:

נָשְׂאוּ נְהָרוֹת יְהוָה נָשְׂאוּ נְהָרוֹת קוֹלָם יִשְׂאוּ נְהָרוֹת דָּכְיָם:

מִקֹּלוֹת מַיִם רַבִּים אַדִּירִים מִשְׁבְּרֵי־יָם אַדִּיר בַּמָּרוֹם יְהוָה:

עֵדֹתֶיךָ נֶאֶמְנוּ מְאֹד לְבֵיתְךָ נַאֲוָה־קֹדֶשׁ יְהוָה לְאֹרֶךְ יָמִים:

For see Your enemies, Lord!
   see how Your enemies shall perish,
   all who do evil shall scatter.
But You exalted my strength like an ox,
   anointed me with fresh oil.
My eyes saw the fate of my enemies;
   and those who rose up to harm me,
   my ears have heard their end.
The righteous shall flourish like the palm tree
   grow tall like a cedar in Lebanon.
Planted in the house of the Lord
   they shall flourish in the courts of our God,
bearing new fruit in old age
   still full of sap and still green,
to declare that the Lord is upright
   my rock in whom there is no wrong.

93

The Lord is king.
   He puts on the robes of pride.
He puts on the robes of power,
   strength surrounds Him.

So the world was set firm
   and cannot be shaken,
Your throne was set firm long ago,
   from eternity You are.

Lord, the floods may storm,
   the floods may storm aloud,
   the floods may storm and thunder.
But even above the roar of great waves,
   mighty breakers of the ocean,
   the might of the Lord is supreme.

The proofs You give are very sure,
   holiness is the mark of Your house,
   Lord, as long as time endures.

צה (א‎-ז)

לְכוּ נְרַנְּנָה לַיהוָה נָרִיעָה לְצוּר יִשְׁעֵנוּ:

נְקַדְּמָה פָנָיו בְּתוֹדָה בִּזְמִרוֹת נָרִיעַ לוֹ:

כִּי אֵל גָּדוֹל יְהוָה וּמֶלֶךְ גָּדוֹל עַל‎-כָּל‎-אֱלֹהִים:

אֲשֶׁר בְּיָדוֹ מֶחְקְרֵי‎-אָרֶץ וְתוֹעֲפוֹת הָרִים לוֹ:

אֲשֶׁר‎-לוֹ הַיָּם וְהוּא עָשָׂהוּ וְיַבֶּשֶׁת יָדָיו יָצָרוּ:

בֹּאוּ נִשְׁתַּחֲוֶה וְנִכְרָעָה נִבְרְכָה לִפְנֵי‎-יְהוָה עֹשֵׂנוּ:

כִּי הוּא אֱלֹהֵינוּ וַאֲנַחְנוּ עַם מַרְעִיתוֹ וְצֹאן יָדוֹ
הַיּוֹם אִם‎-בְּקֹלוֹ תִשְׁמָעוּ:

צו

שִׁירוּ לַיהוָה שִׁיר חָדָשׁ שִׁירוּ לַיהוָה כָּל‎-הָאָרֶץ:

שִׁירוּ לַיהוָה בָּרְכוּ שְׁמוֹ בַּשְּׂרוּ מִיּוֹם‎-לְיוֹם יְשׁוּעָתוֹ:

סַפְּרוּ בַגּוֹיִם כְּבוֹדוֹ בְּכָל‎-הָעַמִּים נִפְלְאוֹתָיו:

כִּי גָדוֹל יְהוָה וּמְהֻלָּל מְאֹד נוֹרָא הוּא עַל‎-כָּל‎-אֱלֹהִים:

כִּי כָּל‎-אֱלֹהֵי הָעַמִּים אֱלִילִים וַיהוָה שָׁמַיִם עָשָׂה:

הוֹד‎-וְהָדָר לְפָנָיו עֹז וְתִפְאֶרֶת בְּמִקְדָּשׁוֹ:

הָבוּ לַיהוָה מִשְׁפְּחוֹת עַמִּים הָבוּ לַיהוָה כָּבוֹד וָעֹז:

הָבוּ לַיהוָה כְּבוֹד שְׁמוֹ שְׂאוּ‎-מִנְחָה וּבֹאוּ לְחַצְרוֹתָיו:

95: 1–7

Come let us sing out to the Lord,
   call out to the rock of our safety.
Let us come before Him with thanks,
   call out to Him with psalms.
For the Lord is almighty God,
   mighty ruler beyond all gods.
The depths of the earth are in His hand
   and His are the mountain peaks.
The sea is His, it is He who made it,
   the land His hands have shaped.
Come in, let us worship and bend low,
   humble before the Lord who made us.
For He is our God
   and we are a people He pastures,
   a flock in His hand.
Today, if you would only hear His voice!

96

Sing to the Lord a new song,
   sing to the Lord all the earth,
   sing to the Lord, bless His name.
Proclaim His salvation day after day,
   describe His glory among the nations
   and His wonders among all peoples.
For great is the Lord and praised aloud.
   He is awesome beyond all gods
   for all the peoples' gods are false gods,
but the Lord has made the heavens.
   Splendour and radiance are in His presence,
   strength and beauty in His holy place.
Give to the Lord, you races and peoples,
   give the Lord glory and strength,
   give the Lord the glory due to His name.
Bear an offering and enter His courts

הִשְׁתַּחֲווּ לַיהוָה בְּהַדְרַת־קֹדֶשׁ חִילוּ מִפָּנָיו כָּל־הָאָרֶץ：

אִמְרוּ בַגּוֹיִם יְהוָה מָלָךְ אַף־תִּכּוֹן תֵּבֵל בַּל־תִּמּוֹט

יָדִין עַמִּים בְּמֵישָׁרִים ：

יִשְׂמְחוּ הַשָּׁמַיִם וְתָגֵל הָאָרֶץ יִרְעַם הַיָּם וּמְלֹאוֹ：

יַעֲלֹז שָׂדַי וְכָל־אֲשֶׁר־בּוֹ אָז יְרַנְּנוּ כָּל־עֲצֵי־יָעַר：

לִפְנֵי יְהוָה כִּי בָא כִּי בָא לִשְׁפֹּט הָאָרֶץ יִשְׁפֹּט־תֵּבֵל בְּצֶדֶק

וְעַמִּים בֶּאֱמוּנָתוֹ ：

צז

יְהוָה מָלָךְ תָּגֵל הָאָרֶץ יִשְׂמְחוּ אִיִּים רַבִּים：

עָנָן וַעֲרָפֶל סְבִיבָיו צֶדֶק וּמִשְׁפָּט מְכוֹן כִּסְאוֹ：

אֵשׁ לְפָנָיו תֵּלֵךְ וּתְלַהֵט סָבִיב צָרָיו：

הֵאִירוּ בְרָקָיו תֵּבֵל רָאֲתָה וַתָּחֵל הָאָרֶץ：

הָרִים כַּדּוֹנַג נָמַסּוּ מִלִּפְנֵי יְהוָה מִלִּפְנֵי אֲדוֹן כָּל־הָאָרֶץ：

הִגִּידוּ הַשָּׁמַיִם צִדְקוֹ וְרָאוּ כָל־הָעַמִּים כְּבוֹדוֹ：

יֵבֹשׁוּ כָּל־עֹבְדֵי פֶסֶל הַמִּתְהַלְלִים בָּאֱלִילִים

הִשְׁתַּחֲווּ־לוֹ כָּל־אֱלֹהִים：

שָׁמְעָה וַתִּשְׂמַח צִיּוֹן וַתָּגֵלְנָה בְּנוֹת יְהוּדָה

לְמַעַן מִשְׁפָּטֶיךָ יְהוָה：

כִּי־אַתָּה יְהוָה עֶלְיוֹן עַל־כָּל־הָאָרֶץ

מְאֹד נַעֲלֵיתָ עַל־כָּל־אֱלֹהִים：

אֹהֲבֵי יְהוָה שִׂנְאוּ רָע שֹׁמֵר נַפְשׁוֹת חֲסִידָיו

מִיַּד רְשָׁעִים יַצִּילֵם：

worship the Lord in the radiance of holiness,
tremble before Him all the earth.
Say among the nations: 'The Lord rules!'
The world too is set firm and cannot be shaken.
He will judge the peoples with justice.
Let the heavens rejoice and the earth delight,
let the sea thunder in its fullness.
Let the field be glad and all within it,
let all trees of the forest sing out
at the presence of the Lord who comes,
for He comes to judge the earth.
He will judge the world with righteousness
and the peoples with His truth.

97

The Lord is king, let the earth be glad,
let the many isles rejoice!
A cloud and darkness surround Him
but righteousness and justice
are the foundations of His throne.
Fire strides before Him
blazing round His foes.
His lightning lights up the world,
the earth sees and trembles.
Mountains melt like wax before the Lord,
before the master of all the earth.
The heavens declare His righteousness,
all peoples see His glory.
Shame on all those who are slaves to an image,
who puff up their pride with hollow gods.
False gods, bow down before Him!
Zion heard and rejoiced, the daughters of Judah were glad
because of Your judgments, O Lord.
Because You are the Lord, supreme over all the earth.
You are supreme beyond all gods.
Those who love the Lord, hate evil.
He guards the souls devoted to Him.
He saves them from the hand of the wicked.

אוֹר זָרֻעַ לַצַּדִּיק וּלְיִשְׁרֵי־לֵב שִׂמְחָה:
שִׂמְחוּ צַדִּיקִים בַּיהֹוָה וְהוֹדוּ לְזֵכֶר קָדְשׁוֹ:

צח

מִזְמוֹר

שִׁירוּ לַיהֹוָה שִׁיר חָדָשׁ כִּי־נִפְלָאוֹת עָשָׂה
הוֹשִׁיעָה־לּוֹ יְמִינוֹ וּזְרוֹעַ קָדְשׁוֹ:
הוֹדִיעַ יְהֹוָה יְשׁוּעָתוֹ לְעֵינֵי הַגּוֹיִם גִּלָּה צִדְקָתוֹ:
זָכַר חַסְדּוֹ וֶאֱמוּנָתוֹ לְבֵית יִשְׂרָאֵל
רָאוּ כָל־אַפְסֵי־אָרֶץ אֵת יְשׁוּעַת אֱלֹהֵינוּ:
הָרִיעוּ לַיהֹוָה כָּל־הָאָרֶץ פִּצְחוּ וְרַנְּנוּ וְזַמֵּרוּ:
זַמְּרוּ לַיהֹוָה בְּכִנּוֹר בְּכִנּוֹר וְקוֹל זִמְרָה:
בַּחֲצֹצְרוֹת וְקוֹל שׁוֹפָר הָרִיעוּ לִפְנֵי הַמֶּלֶךְ יְהֹוָה:
יִרְעַם הַיָּם וּמְלֹאוֹ תֵּבֵל וְיֹשְׁבֵי בָהּ:
נְהָרוֹת יִמְחֲאוּ־כָף יַחַד הָרִים יְרַנֵּנוּ:
לִפְנֵי־יְהֹוָה כִּי בָא לִשְׁפֹּט הָאָרֶץ
יִשְׁפֹּט־תֵּבֵל בְּצֶדֶק וְעַמִּים בְּמֵישָׁרִים:

צט

יְהֹוָה מָלָךְ יִרְגְּזוּ עַמִּים יֹשֵׁב כְּרוּבִים תָּנוּט הָאָרֶץ:
יְהֹוָה בְּצִיּוֹן גָּדוֹל וְרָם הוּא עַל־כָּל־הָעַמִּים:
יוֹדוּ שִׁמְךָ גָּדוֹל וְנוֹרָא קָדוֹשׁ הוּא:

A harvest of light is sown for the righteous,
and joy for the constant heart.
You who are righteous, rejoice in the Lord,
call His holiness to mind and praise Him!

98

A psalm.

Sing to the Lord a new song
for the wonders He has done.
He has saved through His right hand
and the power of His holiness.
The Lord has made known His power to save,
shown His righteousness in the sight of the nations.
He remembers His love,
keeping faith with the family of Israel.
All the ends of the earth have seen
the power of our God to save.
Call out to the Lord all the earth,
cheer and sing and play!
Play to the Lord with the harp,
with the harp and the voice of music.
With trumpets and the sound of the horn
call out before the king, the Lord.
Let the sea thunder in its fullness,
the world and all who live in it.
Let the rivers clap their hands,
let the mountains sing out as one
at the presence of the Lord
for He comes to judge the earth.
He will judge the world with righteousness
and the peoples with justice.

99

The Lord is king, let the nations tremble!
He is enthroned in judgment on the *cherubim*, let the earth shake!
The Lord is great in Zion.
He is high above all the peoples.
They shall praise Your name, great and awesome.
'Holy is He!'

וְעֹז מֶלֶךְ מִשְׁפָּט אָהֵב אַתָּה כּוֹנַנְתָּ מֵישָׁרִים מִשְׁפָּט וּצְדָקָה
בְּיַעֲקֹב אַתָּה עָשִׂיתָ׃

רוֹמְמוּ יְהֹוָה אֱלֹהֵינוּ וְהִשְׁתַּחֲווּ לַהֲדֹם רַגְלָיו קָדוֹשׁ הוּא׃

מֹשֶׁה וְאַהֲרֹן בְּכֹהֲנָיו וּשְׁמוּאֵל בְּקֹרְאֵי שְׁמוֹ
קֹרִאים אֶל־יְהֹוָה וְהוּא יַעֲנֵם׃

בְּעַמּוּד עָנָן יְדַבֵּר אֲלֵיהֶם שָׁמְרוּ עֵדֹתָיו וְחֹק נָתַן־לָמוֹ׃

יְהֹוָה אֱלֹהֵינוּ אַתָּה עֲנִיתָם אֵל נֹשֵׂא הָיִיתָ לָהֶם
וְנֹקֵם עַל־עֲלִילוֹתָם׃

רוֹמְמוּ יְהֹוָה אֱלֹהֵינוּ וְהִשְׁתַּחֲווּ לְהַר קָדְשׁוֹ
כִּי־קָדוֹשׁ יְהֹוָה אֱלֹהֵינוּ׃

ק

מִזְמוֹר לְתוֹדָה

הָרִיעוּ לַיהֹוָה כָּל־הָאָרֶץ׃

עִבְדוּ אֶת־יְהֹוָה בְּשִׂמְחָה בֹּאוּ לְפָנָיו בִּרְנָנָה׃

דְּעוּ כִּי־יְהֹוָה הוּא אֱלֹהִים הוּא־עָשָׂנוּ וְלוֹ אֲנַחְנוּ
עַמּוֹ וְצֹאן מַרְעִיתוֹ׃

בֹּאוּ שְׁעָרָיו בְּתוֹדָה חֲצֵרֹתָיו בִּתְהִלָּה הוֹדוּ־לוֹ בָּרְכוּ שְׁמוֹ׃

כִּי־טוֹב יְהֹוָה לְעוֹלָם חַסְדּוֹ וְעַד־דֹּר וָדֹר אֱמוּנָתוֹ׃

He is strong, a king who loves justice.
  It is You who established honesty, justice and righteousness.
  It is You who formed them in Jacob.
Exalt the Lord our God,
  bow down before His footstool.
  'Holy is He!'

Moses and Aaron were among His priests,
  and Samuel among those who called on His name.
  They called to the Lord and He answered them.

In a pillar of cloud He spoke to them.
  They kept His teaching
  and the law He gave them.

Lord our God, You answered them.
  To them You were a forgiving God,
  though You punished their wrongdoing.

Exalt the Lord our God,
  bow down before His holy mountain,
  for holy is the Lord our God.

100

A psalm of thanksgiving.

Shout to the Lord all the earth,
  serve the Lord with joy,
  come before Him with singing.

Know that the Lord is God.
  It is He who made us and we are His,
  His own people and the flock of His pasture.

Come into His gates with thanks,
  into His courts with praise,
  thank Him, bless His name.

For the Lord is good,
  His love is everlasting
  and His faithfulness for all generations.

קג

לְדָוִד

בָּרְכִי נַפְשִׁי אֶת־יְהֹוָה וְכָל־קְרָבַי אֶת־שֵׁם קָדְשׁוֹ:

בָּרְכִי נַפְשִׁי אֶת־יְהֹוָה וְאַל־תִּשְׁכְּחִי כָּל־גְּמוּלָיו:

הַסֹּלֵחַ לְכָל־עֲוֹנֵכִי הָרֹפֵא לְכָל־תַּחֲלוּאָיְכִי:

הַגּוֹאֵל מִשַּׁחַת חַיָּיְכִי הַמְעַטְּרֵכִי חֶסֶד וְרַחֲמִים:

הַמַּשְׂבִּיעַ בַּטּוֹב עֶדְיֵךְ תִּתְחַדֵּשׁ כַּנֶּשֶׁר נְעוּרָיְכִי:

עֹשֵׂה צְדָקוֹת יְהֹוָה וּמִשְׁפָּטִים לְכָל־עֲשׁוּקִים:

יוֹדִיעַ דְּרָכָיו לְמֹשֶׁה לִבְנֵי יִשְׂרָאֵל עֲלִילוֹתָיו:

רַחוּם וְחַנּוּן יְהֹוָה אֶרֶךְ אַפַּיִם וְרַב־חָסֶד:

לֹא־לָנֶצַח יָרִיב וְלֹא לְעוֹלָם יִטּוֹר:

לֹא כַחֲטָאֵינוּ עָשָׂה לָנוּ וְלֹא כַעֲוֹנֹתֵינוּ גָּמַל עָלֵינוּ:

כִּי כִגְבֹהַּ שָׁמַיִם עַל־הָאָרֶץ גָּבַר חַסְדּוֹ עַל־יְרֵאָיו:

כִּרְחֹק מִזְרָח מִמַּעֲרָב הִרְחִיק מִמֶּנּוּ אֶת־פְּשָׁעֵינוּ:

כְּרַחֵם אָב עַל־בָּנִים רִחַם יְהֹוָה עַל־יְרֵאָיו:

כִּי־הוּא יָדַע יִצְרֵנוּ זָכוּר כִּי־עָפָר אֲנָחְנוּ:

אֱנוֹשׁ כֶּחָצִיר יָמָיו כְּצִיץ הַשָּׂדֶה כֵּן יָצִיץ:

כִּי רוּחַ עָבְרָה־בּוֹ וְאֵינֶנּוּ וְלֹא־יַכִּירֶנּוּ עוֹד מְקוֹמוֹ:

103

David's.

Bless the Lord, my soul,
all that is in me, bless His holy name!
Bless the Lord, my soul,
and forget none of His kind deeds.

He who pardons all your deceit,
who heals all your suffering,
who redeems your life from the pit of death,
who surrounds you with love and compassion,
who fills your old age with goodness,
renewing your youth like an eagle.

The Lord does what is right,
does justice to all the oppressed.
He made His ways known to Moses,
His great acts to the children of Israel.

Tender and compassionate is the Lord,
slow to anger and full of love.
Not for all time does He accuse,
not forever does He keep His anger,
not according to our failings has He dealt with us,
not according to our deceit has He treated us.

As high as the sky over the earth,
so great is His love over those who fear Him;
as far as the east from the west,
so far has He taken our misdeeds from us.

As a father is tender to his children,
so the Lord is tender to those who fear Him;
for it is He who knows our nature,
remembers that we are dust.

Frail man, his days are like the grass,
he blossoms like a flower in the field;
but the breeze passes over it and it is gone
and its place knows it no more.

וְחֶסֶד יְהֹוָה מֵעוֹלָם וְעַד־עוֹלָם עַל־יְרֵאָיו וְצִדְקָתוֹ לִבְנֵי בָנִים:

לְשֹׁמְרֵי בְרִיתוֹ וּלְזֹכְרֵי פִקֻּדָיו לַעֲשׂוֹתָם:

יְהֹוָה בַּשָּׁמַיִם הֵכִין כִּסְאוֹ וּמַלְכוּתוֹ בַּכֹּל מָשָׁלָה:

בָּרְכוּ יְהֹוָה מַלְאָכָיו גִּבֹּרֵי כֹחַ עֹשֵׂי דְבָרוֹ לִשְׁמֹעַ בְּקוֹל דְּבָרוֹ:

בָּרְכוּ יְהֹוָה כָּל־צְבָאָיו מְשָׁרְתָיו עֹשֵׂי רְצוֹנוֹ:

בָּרְכוּ יְהֹוָה כָּל־מַעֲשָׂיו בְּכָל־מְקֹמוֹת מֶמְשַׁלְתּוֹ

בָּרְכִי נַפְשִׁי אֶת־יְהֹוָה:

קד

בָּרְכִי נַפְשִׁי אֶת־יְהֹוָה יְהֹוָה אֱלֹהַי גָּדַלְתָּ מְּאֹד הוֹד וְהָדָר לָבָשְׁתָּ:

עֹטֶה־אוֹר כַּשַּׂלְמָה נוֹטֶה שָׁמַיִם כַּיְרִיעָה:

הַמְקָרֶה בַמַּיִם עֲלִיּוֹתָיו הַשָּׂם־עָבִים רְכוּבוֹ

הַמְהַלֵּךְ עַל־כַּנְפֵי־רוּחַ:

עֹשֶׂה מַלְאָכָיו רוּחוֹת מְשָׁרְתָיו אֵשׁ לֹהֵט:

יָסַד־אֶרֶץ עַל־מְכוֹנֶיהָ בַּל־תִּמּוֹט עוֹלָם וָעֶד:

תְּהוֹם כַּלְּבוּשׁ כִּסִּיתוֹ עַל־הָרִים יַעַמְדוּ־מָיִם:

מִן־גַּעֲרָתְךָ יְנוּסוּן מִן־קוֹל רַעַמְךָ יֵחָפֵזוּן:

יַעֲלוּ הָרִים יֵרְדוּ בְקָעוֹת אֶל־מְקוֹם זֶה יָסַדְתָּ לָהֶם:

גְּבוּל־שַׂמְתָּ בַּל־יַעֲבֹרוּן בַּל־יְשֻׁבוּן לְכַסּוֹת הָאָרֶץ:

But the love of the Lord lasts forever and ever
for those who fear Him,
and His loyalty to the children's children
of those who keep His covenant,
bearing His precepts in their mind, to do them.
The Lord has set firm His throne in heaven
and His kingdom rules over all.
Bless the Lord, His messengers,
the mighty in strength who perform His word,
who obey the voice of His command!
Bless the Lord, all His creation,
His ministers who do His will!
Bless the Lord, all His works,
in all the places of His dominion!
Bless the Lord, my soul!

104

Bless the Lord, my soul!
Lord my God, how great You are,
clothed in majesty and glory,
wrapped in light like a robe.
You spread out the heavens like a tent,
building on the waters Your place on high,
using the clouds as a chariot,
moving on the wings of the wind.
You make the winds Your messengers,
flashing fire Your servant.

You set the earth on its foundations,
unshakeable forever.
You covered it with the ocean like a robe,
the waters overflowing the mountains.
At Your rebuke the waters fled,
at the sound of Your thunder they rushed away.
The mountains rose, the valleys sank
to the very place You fixed for them.
You set a boundary they should not cross,
nor return to cover the earth.

הַמְשַׁלֵּחַ מַעְיָנִים בַּנְּחָלִים בֵּין הָרִים יְהַלֵּכוּן:

יַשְׁקוּ כָּל־חַיְתוֹ שָׂדָי יִשְׁבְּרוּ פְרָאִים צְמָאָם:

עֲלֵיהֶם עוֹף־הַשָּׁמַיִם יִשְׁכּוֹן מִבֵּין עֳפָאיִם יִתְּנוּ־קוֹל:

מַשְׁקֶה הָרִים מֵעֲלִיּוֹתָיו מִפְּרִי מַעֲשֶׂיךָ תִּשְׂבַּע הָאָרֶץ:

מַצְמִיחַ חָצִיר לַבְּהֵמָה וְעֵשֶׂב לַעֲבֹדַת הָאָדָם

לְהוֹצִיא לֶחֶם מִן־הָאָרֶץ:

וְיַיִן יְשַׂמַּח לְבַב־אֱנוֹשׁ לְהַצְהִיל פָּנִים מִשָּׁמֶן

וְלֶחֶם לְבַב־אֱנוֹשׁ יִסְעָד:

יִשְׂבְּעוּ עֲצֵי יְהוָֹה אַרְזֵי לְבָנוֹן אֲשֶׁר נָטָע:

אֲשֶׁר־שָׁם צִפֳּרִים יְקַנֵּנוּ חֲסִידָה בְּרוֹשִׁים בֵּיתָהּ:

הָרִים הַגְּבֹהִים לַיְּעֵלִים סְלָעִים מַחְסֶה לַשְׁפַנִּים:

עָשָׂה יָרֵחַ לְמוֹעֲדִים שֶׁמֶשׁ יָדַע מְבוֹאוֹ:

תָּשֶׁת־חֹשֶׁךְ וִיהִי לָיְלָה בּוֹ־תִרְמֹשׂ כָּל־חַיְתוֹ־יָעַר:

הַכְּפִירִים שֹׁאֲגִים לַטָּרֶף וּלְבַקֵּשׁ מֵאֵל אָכְלָם:

תִּזְרַח הַשֶּׁמֶשׁ יֵאָסֵפוּן וְאֶל־מְעוֹנֹתָם יִרְבָּצוּן:

יֵצֵא אָדָם לְפָעֳלוֹ וְלַעֲבֹדָתוֹ עֲדֵי־עָרֶב:

מָה־רַבּוּ מַעֲשֶׂיךָ יְהוָֹה כֻּלָּם בְּחָכְמָה עָשִׂיתָ

מָלְאָה הָאָרֶץ קִנְיָנֶךָ:

זֶה הַיָּם גָּדוֹל וּרְחַב יָדָיִם שָׁם־רֶמֶשׂ וְאֵין מִסְפָּר

חַיּוֹת קְטַנּוֹת עִם־גְּדֹלוֹת:

You make springs flow in the valleys,
   running between the hills.
They give water to the beasts of the field,
   the wild asses quench their thirst.
Birds of the air nest beside them,
   singing among the branches.

You send rain on the mountains from above,
   the earth is full of the fruit of Your works.
You make grass grow for the cattle,
   plants for the labour of man
   to bring forth bread from the earth;
and wine to gladden man's heart,
   oil to freshen his face,
   bread to sustain his heart.

The trees of the Lord drink their fill,
   the cedars of Lebanon which He planted.
The birds build their nest in them
   and storks make the fir trees their home.
The high mountains are for the wild goats,
   badgers hide in the rocks.

You make the moon mark the seasons,
   the sun knows where to set.
You make the darkness and it is night,
   in it all forest beasts come out.
The young lions roar for their prey,
   seeking their food from God.
The sun rises, they steal away,
   returning to rest in their dens.
Man goes out to his work
   and to his labour until evening.

Lord, how great are Your works,
   You made them all in wisdom;
   the earth is full of Your creatures.
This vast expanse of ocean!
   There go swarms of creeping creatures,
   all forms of life, great and small!

שָׁם אֳנִיּוֹת יְהַלֵּכוּן לִוְיָתָן זֶה־יָצַרְתָּ לְשַׂחֶק־בּוֹ:

כֻּלָּם אֵלֶיךָ יְשַׂבֵּרוּן לָתֵת אָכְלָם בְּעִתּוֹ:

תִּתֵּן לָהֶם יִלְקֹטוּן תִּפְתַּח יָדְךָ יִשְׂבְּעוּן טוֹב:

תַּסְתִּיר פָּנֶיךָ יִבָּהֵלוּן תֹּסֵף רוּחָם יִגְוָעוּן וְאֶל־עֲפָרָם יְשׁוּבוּן:

תְּשַׁלַּח רוּחֲךָ יִבָּרֵאוּן וּתְחַדֵּשׁ פְּנֵי אֲדָמָה:

יְהִי כְבוֹד יְהוָה לְעוֹלָם יִשְׂמַח יְהוָה בְּמַעֲשָׂיו:

הַמַּבִּיט לָאָרֶץ וַתִּרְעָד יִגַּע בֶּהָרִים וְיֶעֱשָׁנוּ:

אָשִׁירָה לַיהוָה בְּחַיָּי אֲזַמְּרָה לֵאלֹהַי בְּעוֹדִי:

יֶעֱרַב עָלָיו שִׂיחִי אָנֹכִי אֶשְׂמַח בַּיהוָה:

יִתַּמּוּ חַטָּאִים מִן־הָאָרֶץ וּרְשָׁעִים עוֹד אֵינָם בָּרְכִי נַפְשִׁי אֶת־יְהוָה הַלְלוּ־יָהּ:

קה

הוֹדוּ לַיהוָה קִרְאוּ בִשְׁמוֹ הוֹדִיעוּ בָעַמִּים עֲלִילוֹתָיו:

שִׁירוּ־לוֹ זַמְּרוּ־לוֹ שִׂיחוּ בְּכָל־נִפְלְאוֹתָיו:

הִתְהַלְלוּ בְּשֵׁם קָדְשׁוֹ יִשְׂמַח לֵב מְבַקְשֵׁי יְהוָה:

דִּרְשׁוּ יְהוָה וְעֻזּוֹ בַּקְּשׁוּ פָנָיו תָּמִיד:

זִכְרוּ נִפְלְאוֹתָיו אֲשֶׁר־עָשָׂה מֹפְתָיו וּמִשְׁפְּטֵי־פִיו:

There go the ships,
    the sea monsters You formed to play with—
all of them depend on You
    to give them food when it is needed.
You give it to them—they gather it.
You open Your hand—they eat their fill.
You hide Your face—they vanish.
You take back Your spirit—they die
    and return to their dust.
You give breath—they are created,
    and You renew the face of the earth.

May the glory of the Lord endure forever.
    May the Lord rejoice in His works.
He scans the earth and it trembles.
    He touches the mountains and they pour out
        smoke.

I will sing to the Lord as long as I live.
    I will sing my God's praises as long as I exist.
May my thoughts give Him pleasure.
    I rejoice in the Lord.
May sinners vanish from the earth
    and the wicked be no more.
Bless the Lord, my soul!
    Praise the Lord!

105

Give thanks to the Lord, call on His name,
    make His deeds known among the peoples.

Sing to Him, sing praises to Him,
    think about all His wonders.
Glory in His holy name,
    let the hearts rejoice of those who seek the Lord.

Seek out the Lord and His strength.
    Seek always; look for His presence.
Remember the wonders He has done,
    His marvels, the judgments of His mouth.

זֶ֫רַע אַבְרָהָם עַבְדּוֹ בְּנֵי יַעֲקֹב בְּחִירָיו:

הוּא יְהוָֹה אֱלֹהֵינוּ בְּכָל־הָאָרֶץ מִשְׁפָּטָיו:

זָכַר לְעוֹלָם בְּרִיתוֹ דָּבָר צִוָּה לְאֶלֶף דּוֹר:

אֲשֶׁר כָּרַת אֶת־אַבְרָהָם וּשְׁבוּעָתוֹ לְיִשְׂחָק:

וַיַּעֲמִידֶהָ לְיַעֲקֹב לְחֹק לְיִשְׂרָאֵל בְּרִית עוֹלָם:

לֵאמֹר לְךָ אֶתֵּן אֶת־אֶרֶץ־כְּנָעַן חֶבֶל נַחֲלַתְכֶם:

בִּהְיוֹתָם מְתֵי מִסְפָּר כִּמְעַט וְגָרִים בָּהּ:

וַיִּתְהַלְּכוּ מִגּוֹי אֶל־גּוֹי מִמַּמְלָכָה אֶל־עַם אַחֵר:

לֹא־הִנִּיחַ אָדָם לְעָשְׁקָם וַיּוֹכַח עֲלֵיהֶם מְלָכִים:

אַל־תִּגְּעוּ בִמְשִׁיחָי וְלִנְבִיאַי אַל־תָּרֵעוּ:

וַיִּקְרָא רָעָב עַל־הָאָרֶץ כָּל־מַטֵּה־לֶחֶם שָׁבָר:

שָׁלַח לִפְנֵיהֶם אִישׁ לְעֶבֶד נִמְכַּר יוֹסֵף:

עִנּוּ בַכֶּבֶל רַגְלוֹ בַּרְזֶל בָּאָה נַפְשׁוֹ:

עַד־עֵת בֹּא־דְבָרוֹ אִמְרַת יְהוָֹה צְרָפָתְהוּ:

שָׁלַח מֶלֶךְ וַיַּתִּירֵהוּ מֹשֵׁל עַמִּים וַיְפַתְּחֵהוּ:

שָׂמוֹ אָדוֹן לְבֵיתוֹ וּמֹשֵׁל בְּכָל־קִנְיָנוֹ:

לֶאְסֹר שָׂרָיו בְּנַפְשׁוֹ וּזְקֵנָיו יְחַכֵּם:

וַיָּבֹא יִשְׂרָאֵל מִצְרָיִם וְיַעֲקֹב גָּר בְּאֶרֶץ־חָם:

Seed of Abraham, His servant!
  Son of Jacob, His chosen!
He is the Lord our God,
  His judgments fill all the earth.

He remembers His covenant forever,
  the promise He made for a thousand generations,
the covenant made with Abraham
  and His oath to Isaac.

He made it stand as a statute for Jacob,
  for Israel as a covenant forever,
saying: 'To you I shall give the land of Canaan,
  the portion of your heritage.'

When they were only few in number,
  just a few, and only strangers in the land,
straying from nation to nation,
  from one kingdom to another people.

He let no man illtreat them,
  warning kings on their behalf:
'Do not touch My anointed ones,
  do no harm to My prophets.'

He called a famine down, a famine on the land,
  and broke their staff of life, all their bread.
He had sent a man before them,
  Joseph sold as a slave.

They hurt his foot with fetters,
  the iron entered his soul.
Until the time his saying came to pass
  and the word of the Lord proved him true.

The king sent orders to release him,
  the ruler of peoples set him free.
He made him master of his household,
  the ruler of all he possessed.

To correct princes at will
  and teach his elders wisdom.
So Israel came to Egypt
  and Jacob settled in the land of Ham.

וַיֶּפֶר אֶת־עַמּוֹ מְאֹד וַיַּעֲצִמֵהוּ מִצָּרָיו׃

הָפַךְ לִבָּם לִשְׂנֹא עַמּוֹ לְהִתְנַכֵּל בַּעֲבָדָיו׃

שָׁלַח מֹשֶׁה עַבְדּוֹ אַהֲרֹן אֲשֶׁר בָּחַר־בּוֹ׃

שָׂמוּ־בָם דִּבְרֵי אֹתוֹתָיו וּמֹפְתִים בְּאֶרֶץ חָם׃

שָׁלַח חֹשֶׁךְ וַיַּחְשִׁךְ וְלֹא־מָרוּ אֶת־דְּבָרוֹ׃

הָפַךְ אֶת־מֵימֵיהֶם לְדָם וַיָּמֶת אֶת־דְּגָתָם׃

שָׁרַץ אַרְצָם צְפַרְדְּעִים בְּחַדְרֵי מַלְכֵיהֶם׃

אָמַר וַיָּבֹא עָרֹב כִּנִּים בְּכָל־גְּבוּלָם׃

נָתַן גִּשְׁמֵיהֶם בָּרָד אֵשׁ לֶהָבוֹת בְּאַרְצָם׃

וַיַּךְ גַּפְנָם וּתְאֵנָתָם וַיְשַׁבֵּר עֵץ גְּבוּלָם׃

אָמַר וַיָּבֹא אַרְבֶּה וְיֶלֶק וְאֵין מִסְפָּר׃

וַיֹּאכַל כָּל־עֵשֶׂב בְּאַרְצָם וַיֹּאכַל פְּרִי אַדְמָתָם׃

וַיַּךְ כָּל־בְּכוֹר בְּאַרְצָם רֵאשִׁית לְכָל־אוֹנָם׃

וַיּוֹצִיאֵם בְּכֶסֶף וְזָהָב וְאֵין בִּשְׁבָטָיו כּוֹשֵׁל׃

שָׂמַח מִצְרַיִם בְּצֵאתָם כִּי־נָפַל פַּחְדָּם עֲלֵיהֶם׃

פָּרַשׂ עָנָן לְמָסָךְ וְאֵשׁ לְהָאִיר לָיְלָה׃

שָׁאַל וַיָּבֵא שְׂלָו וְלֶחֶם שָׁמַיִם יַשְׂבִּיעֵם׃

פָּתַח צוּר וַיָּזוּבוּ מָיִם הָלְכוּ בַּצִּיּוֹת נָהָר׃

He made His people very fertile
and stronger than their enemies.
He turned the Egyptians to hate His people
and deal deceitfully with His servants.

He sent His servant Moses,
Aaron the man of His choice.
Through them He showed His signs
and wonders in the land of Ham.

He sent darkness, and it grew dark,
and they resisted His word no more.
He turned their waters into blood
and caused their fish to die.

Their land teemed with frogs,
even in the royal chambers.
He spoke, and swarms of insects came
and gnats in all their hordes.

He gave them hail in place of rain
and flashing fire in their land.
He struck their vines and fig trees,
and shattered the trees through their country.

He spoke, and the locust came,
grasshoppers, too many to count;
eating every blade in the land,
eating up all the fruit of their soil.

He struck down all the firstborn in their land,
the finest flower of their manhood.
He led Israel out with silver and gold,
in His tribes there were none who fell behind.

Egypt rejoiced when they left,
for dread had fallen upon them.
He spread a cloud to cover them
and fire to light up the night.

They asked for food and He brought quails,
food from heaven to satisfy them.
He pierced the rock and water gushed out,
to run like a river in the dry land.

כִּי זָכַר אֶת־דְּבַר קָדְשׁוֹ אֶת־אַבְרָהָם עַבְדּוֹ׃

וַיּוֹצִא עַמּוֹ בְשָׂשׂוֹן בְּרִנָּה אֶת־בְּחִירָיו׃

וַיִּתֵּן לָהֶם אַרְצוֹת גּוֹיִם וַעֲמַל לְאֻמִּים יִירָשׁוּ׃

בַּעֲבוּר יִשְׁמְרוּ חֻקָּיו וְתוֹרֹתָיו יִנְצֹרוּ הַלְלוּ־יָהּ׃

קיא

הַלְלוּ־יָהּ

אוֹדֶה יְהֹוָה בְּכָל־לֵבָב   בְּסוֹד יְשָׁרִים וְעֵדָה׃

גְּדֹלִים מַעֲשֵׂי יְהֹוָה   דְּרוּשִׁים לְכָל־חֶפְצֵיהֶם׃

הוֹד־וְהָדָר פָּעֳלוֹ   וְצִדְקָתוֹ עֹמֶדֶת לָעַד׃

זֵכֶר עָשָׂה לְנִפְלְאֹתָיו   חַנּוּן וְרַחוּם יְהֹוָה׃

טֶרֶף נָתַן לִירֵאָיו   יִזְכֹּר לְעוֹלָם בְּרִיתוֹ׃

כֹּחַ מַעֲשָׂיו הִגִּיד לְעַמּוֹ   לָתֵת לָהֶם נַחֲלַת גּוֹיִם׃

מַעֲשֵׂי יָדָיו אֱמֶת וּמִשְׁפָּט   נֶאֱמָנִים כָּל־פִּקּוּדָיו׃

סְמוּכִים לָעַד לְעוֹלָם   עֲשׂוּיִם בֶּאֱמֶת וְיָשָׁר׃

פְּדוּת שָׁלַח לְעַמּוֹ   צִוָּה־לְעוֹלָם בְּרִיתוֹ׃

קָדוֹשׁ וְנוֹרָא שְׁמוֹ׃   רֵאשִׁית חָכְמָה יִרְאַת יְהֹוָה

שֵׂכֶל טוֹב לְכָל־עֹשֵׂיהֶם   תְּהִלָּתוֹ עֹמֶדֶת לָעַד׃

He remembered His sacred promise
to Abraham His servant.
So He brought out His people with joy,
His chosen people with singing.

He gave them the lands of nations,
they inherited the labour of other peoples,
so that they might keep His laws
and obey His teachings.
Praise the Lord!

111

Praise the Lord!
I will thank the Lord with all my heart
in the meeting of honest men in the congregation.
Great are the works of the Lord,
studied by all who desire them.
Majestic and splendid is His work,
His righteousness stands forever.
He made His wonders famous,
generous and merciful is the Lord.
He gave food to those who fear Him.
He remembers His covenant forever.
The power of His works He made known to His people,
He gave them the heritage of nations.
The works of His hands are truth and justice,
all His precepts can be trusted.
Raised up to last forever and ever,
they are made of truth and integrity.
He came to His people's rescue,
commanding His covenant forever.
Holy and awesome is His name.
The fear of the Lord is the beginning of wisdom;
those who practise it grow in understanding.
His praise shall last forever!

קיב

הַלְלוּ־יָהּ

אַשְׁרֵי־אִישׁ יָרֵא אֶת־יְהֹוָה   בְּמִצְוֹתָיו חָפֵץ מְאֹד׃

גִּבּוֹר בָּאָרֶץ יִהְיֶה זַרְעוֹ   דּוֹר יְשָׁרִים יְבֹרָךְ׃

הוֹן־וָעֹשֶׁר בְּבֵיתוֹ   וְצִדְקָתוֹ עֹמֶדֶת לָעַד׃

זָרַח בַּחֹשֶׁךְ אוֹר לַיְשָׁרִים   חַנּוּן וְרַחוּם וְצַדִּיק׃

טוֹב־אִישׁ חוֹנֵן וּמַלְוֶה   יְכַלְכֵּל דְּבָרָיו בְּמִשְׁפָּט׃

כִּי־לְעוֹלָם לֹא־יִמּוֹט   לְזֵכֶר עוֹלָם יִהְיֶה צַדִּיק׃

מִשְּׁמוּעָה רָעָה לֹא יִירָא   נָכוֹן לִבּוֹ בָּטֻחַ בַּיהֹוָה׃

סָמוּךְ לִבּוֹ לֹא יִירָא   עַד אֲשֶׁר־יִרְאֶה בְצָרָיו׃

פִּזַּר נָתַן לָאֶבְיוֹנִים   צִדְקָתוֹ עֹמֶדֶת לָעַד

קַרְנוֹ תָּרוּם בְּכָבוֹד׃   רָשָׁע יִרְאֶה וְכָעָס

שִׁנָּיו יַחֲרֹק וְנָמָס   תַּאֲוַת רְשָׁעִים תֹּאבֵד׃

112

Praise the Lord!
Happy the man who fears the Lord,
who takes great joy in His commands.
His children will be powerful on earth,
an upright generation are well blessed.
Wealth and prosperity are in his house,
his righteous deeds stand firm forever.
He is a light in darkness for the upright,
he is generous, merciful and just.
It is good when a man is generous and lends
and conducts his affairs with honour.
For a righteous man will never waver
and he will be remembered forever.
He does not fear bad news,
his heart is firm, he trusts in the Lord.
His heart is steadfast, he does not fear,
he will see the downfall of his foes.
He is open-hearted, he gives to the poor;
his righteousness stands firm forever,
his head held high with honour.
The evil man sees and his anger rises,
he grinds his teeth and melts away;
the desire of the wicked leads to doom.

סדר הלל

בָּרוּךְ אַתָּה יְיָ אֱלֹהֵינוּ מֶלֶךְ הָעוֹלָם· אֲשֶׁר קִדְּשָׁנוּ בְּמִצְוֹתָיו
וְצִוָּנוּ לִקְרוֹא אֶת־הַהַלֵּל:

קיג

הַלְלוּ־יָהּ

הַלְלוּ עַבְדֵי יְהֹוָה הַלְלוּ אֶת־שֵׁם יְהֹוָה:

יְהִי שֵׁם יְהֹוָה מְבֹרָךְ מֵעַתָּה וְעַד־עוֹלָם:

מִמִּזְרַח־שֶׁמֶשׁ עַד־מְבוֹאוֹ מְהֻלָּל שֵׁם יְהֹוָה:

רָם עַל־כָּל־גּוֹיִם יְהֹוָה עַל הַשָּׁמַיִם כְּבוֹדוֹ:

מִי כַּיהֹוָה אֱלֹהֵינוּ הַמַּגְבִּיהִי לָשָׁבֶת:

הַמַּשְׁפִּילִי לִרְאוֹת בַּשָּׁמַיִם וּבָאָרֶץ:

מְקִימִי מֵעָפָר דָּל מֵאַשְׁפֹּת יָרִים אֶבְיוֹן:

לְהוֹשִׁיבִי עִם־נְדִיבִים עִם נְדִיבֵי עַמּוֹ:

מוֹשִׁיבִי עֲקֶרֶת הַבַּיִת אֵם־הַבָּנִים שְׂמֵחָה
הַלְלוּ־יָהּ:

קיד

בְּצֵאת יִשְׂרָאֵל מִמִּצְרָיִם בֵּית יַעֲקֹב מֵעַם לֹעֵז:

הָיְתָה יְהוּדָה לְקָדְשׁוֹ יִשְׂרָאֵל מַמְשְׁלוֹתָיו:

HALLEL

Blessed are You, Lord our God, king of the universe, who makes us holy through His commands and commands us to read the Hallel, the psalms of joy.

113

Praise the Lord!

Servants of the Lord,
    praise the name of the Lord!
May the name of the Lord be blessed
    now and evermore.
From the rising of the sun to its setting
    praised be the name of the Lord.

High above all nations is the Lord,
    beyond the heavens is His glory.
Who is like the Lord our God,
    who lives so far beyond,
    who dwells so close within,
    to watch the heavens and the earth?

He raises the weak from the dust,
    lifts the poor from the dirt,
to set them with the noble,
    with the noble of His people.
He gives the childless wife a home
    as the happy mother of children.

Praise the Lord!

114

When Israel came out of Egypt,
    the family of Jacob from a people of foreign tongue,
then Judah became His holy place,
    Israel were those He ruled.

הַיָּם רָאָה וַיָּנֹס הַיַּרְדֵּן יִסֹּב לְאָחוֹר׃
הֶהָרִים רָקְדוּ כְאֵילִים גְּבָעוֹת כִּבְנֵי־צֹאן׃

מַה־לְּךָ הַיָּם כִּי תָנוּס הַיַּרְדֵּן תִּסֹּב לְאָחוֹר׃
הֶהָרִים תִּרְקְדוּ כְאֵילִים גְּבָעוֹת כִּבְנֵי־צֹאן׃

מִלִּפְנֵי אָדוֹן חוּלִי אָרֶץ מִלִּפְנֵי אֱלוֹהַּ יַעֲקֹב׃
הַהֹפְכִי הַצּוּר אֲגַם־מָיִם חַלָּמִישׁ לְמַעְיְנוֹ־מָיִם׃

קטו

לֹא לָנוּ יְהוָה לֹא לָנוּ כִּי־לְשִׁמְךָ תֵּן כָּבוֹד
עַל־חַסְדְּךָ עַל־אֲמִתֶּךָ׃
לָמָּה יֹאמְרוּ הַגּוֹיִם אַיֵּה־נָא אֱלֹהֵיהֶם׃

וֵאלֹהֵינוּ בַשָּׁמָיִם כֹּל אֲשֶׁר־חָפֵץ עָשָׂה׃
עֲצַבֵּיהֶם כֶּסֶף וְזָהָב מַעֲשֵׂה יְדֵי אָדָם׃

פֶּה־לָהֶם וְלֹא יְדַבֵּרוּ עֵינַיִם לָהֶם וְלֹא יִרְאוּ׃
אָזְנַיִם לָהֶם וְלֹא יִשְׁמָעוּ אַף לָהֶם וְלֹא יְרִיחוּן׃

יְדֵיהֶם וְלֹא יְמִישׁוּן רַגְלֵיהֶם וְלֹא יְהַלֵּכוּ לֹא־יֶהְגּוּ בִּגְרוֹנָם׃
כְּמוֹהֶם יִהְיוּ עֹשֵׂיהֶם כֹּל אֲשֶׁר־בֹּטֵחַ בָּהֶם׃

יִשְׂרָאֵל בְּטַח בַּיהוָה עֶזְרָם וּמָגִנָּם הוּא׃
בֵּית אַהֲרֹן בִּטְחוּ בַיהוָה עֶזְרָם וּמָגִנָּם הוּא׃
יִרְאֵי יְהוָה בִּטְחוּ בַיהוָה עֶזְרָם וּמָגִנָּם הוּא׃

The sea saw it and ran away,
    Jordan turned back its course,
the mountains skipped like rams,
    the hills like young lambs.

Sea! why do you run away,
    Jordan! why turn back your course,
mountains, why do you skip like rams,
    hills like young lambs?

Earth, tremble before the Lord,
    before the God of Jacob,
who turns the rock into a pool,
    the flint into a spring of water.

Psalms 115 and 116 are not read on the New Moon and on the middle days of
Pesach.

115

Not to us, Lord, not to us,
    but to Your name give glory,
    for the sake of Your love and Your truth.
Why do the nations ask:
    'Where is their God?'

Our God is in heaven,
    all that pleases Him, He does.
But their idols are silver and gold,
    the work of human hands.

They have a mouth, but do not speak,
    they have eyes, but do not see.
They have ears, but do not hear,
    they have a nose, but do not smell.

With their hands they do not feel,
    with their feet they do not walk,
    they make no sound in their throat.
Their makers shall become like them,
    so do all who trust in them.

Israel, trust in the Lord—
    'He is their help and their shield'.
House of Aaron, trust in the Lord—
    'He is their help and their shield'.
All who fear the Lord, trust in the Lord—
    'He is their help and their shield'.

יְהוָֹה זְכָרָנוּ יְבָרֵךְ יְבָרֵךְ אֶת־בֵּית יִשְׂרָאֵל
יְבָרֵךְ אֶת־בֵּית אַהֲרֹן:

יְבָרֵךְ יִרְאֵי יְהוָֹה הַקְּטַנִּים עִם־הַגְּדֹלִים:

יֹסֵף יְהוָֹה עֲלֵיכֶם עֲלֵיכֶם וְעַל־בְּנֵיכֶם:

בְּרוּכִים אַתֶּם לַיהוָֹה עֹשֵׂה שָׁמַיִם וָאָרֶץ:

הַשָּׁמַיִם שָׁמַיִם לַיהוָֹה וְהָאָרֶץ נָתַן לִבְנֵי־אָדָם:

לֹא הַמֵּתִים יְהַלְלוּ־יָהּ וְלֹא כָּל־יֹרְדֵי דוּמָה:

וַאֲנַחְנוּ נְבָרֵךְ יָהּ מֵעַתָּה וְעַד־עוֹלָם

הַלְלוּ־יָהּ:

קטז

אָהַבְתִּי כִּי־יִשְׁמַע יְהוָֹה אֶת־קוֹלִי תַּחֲנוּנָי:

כִּי־הִטָּה אָזְנוֹ לִי וּבְיָמַי אֶקְרָא:

אֲפָפוּנִי חֶבְלֵי־מָוֶת וּמְצָרֵי שְׁאוֹל מְצָאוּנִי צָרָה וְיָגוֹן אֶמְצָא:

וּבְשֵׁם־יְהוָֹה אֶקְרָא אָנָּה יְהוָֹה מַלְּטָה נַפְשִׁי:

חַנּוּן יְהוָֹה וְצַדִּיק וֵאלֹהֵינוּ מְרַחֵם:

שֹׁמֵר פְּתָאיִם יְהוָֹה דַּלּוֹתִי וְלִי יְהוֹשִׁיעַ:

שׁוּבִי נַפְשִׁי לִמְנוּחָיְכִי כִּי־יְהוָֹה גָּמַל עָלָיְכִי:

כִּי חִלַּצְתָּ נַפְשִׁי מִמָּוֶת אֶת־עֵינִי מִן־דִּמְעָה אֶת־רַגְלִי מִדֶּחִי:

The Lord remembers us! May He bless us!
　　May He bless the house of Israel!
　　May He bless the house of Aaron!
May He bless all those who fear the Lord,
　　the small and great alike!

May the Lord increase you,
　　you and your children.
You are blessed by the Lord
　　maker of heaven and earth—
Heaven is the heaven of the Lord
　　but the earth He gave to the sons of man.

The dead do not praise the Lord,
　　nor all who go down into silence,
but we bless the Lord
　　now and evermore.

Praise the Lord!

116

I love the Lord for He hears
　　my voice, my pleading.
Because He turned His ear to me
　　throughout my days I will call Him.

The pangs of death drew tight around me,
　　the horrors of the grave took hold of me,
　　sorrow and grief I found,
then I called on the name of the Lord:
　　'Lord, rescue my spirit!'

Merciful is the Lord and just,
　　and our God has compassion.
The Lord protects simple people,
　　I was weak and He saved me.

Return, my soul, to your rest,
　　for the Lord has been generous to you.
You rescued my spirit from death,
　　my eye from tears
　　and my foot from stumbling.

אֶתְהַלֵּךְ לִפְנֵי יְהֹוָה בְּאַרְצוֹת הַחַיִּים:

הֶאֱמַנְתִּי כִּי אֲדַבֵּר אֲנִי עָנִיתִי מְאֹד:

אֲנִי אָמַרְתִּי בְחָפְזִי כָּל־הָאָדָם כֹּזֵב:

מָה־אָשִׁיב לַיהֹוָה כָּל־תַּגְמוּלוֹהִי עָלָי:

כּוֹס־יְשׁוּעוֹת אֶשָּׂא וּבְשֵׁם יְהֹוָה אֶקְרָא:

נְדָרַי לַיהֹוָה אֲשַׁלֵּם נֶגְדָה־נָּא לְכָל־עַמּוֹ:

יָקָר בְּעֵינֵי יְהֹוָה הַמָּוְתָה לַחֲסִידָיו:

אָנָּה יְהֹוָה כִּי־אֲנִי עַבְדֶּךָ אֲנִי־עַבְדְּךָ בֶּן־אֲמָתֶךָ
פִּתַּחְתָּ לְמוֹסֵרָי:

לְךָ־אֶזְבַּח זֶבַח תּוֹדָה וּבְשֵׁם יְהֹוָה אֶקְרָא:

נְדָרַי לַיהֹוָה אֲשַׁלֵּם נֶגְדָה־נָּא לְכָל־עַמּוֹ:

בְּחַצְרוֹת בֵּית יְהֹוָה בְּתוֹכֵכִי יְרוּשָׁלָיִם

הַלְלוּ־יָהּ:

קיז

הַלְלוּ אֶת־יְהֹוָה כָּל־גּוֹיִם שַׁבְּחוּהוּ כָּל־הָאֻמִּים:

כִּי גָבַר עָלֵינוּ חַסְדּוֹ וֶאֱמֶת־יְהֹוָה לְעוֹלָם

הַלְלוּ־יָהּ:

I shall journey in the presence of the Lord
    through the lands of the living.
I trust, though when I spoke out,
    I was deeply depressed.
I said in my panic: 'All men deceive!'

What can I return to the Lord
    for all His generosity to me?
I will lift up the cup of salvation
    and call on the name of the Lord.
I will fulfil my promises to the Lord
    in the presence of all His people.

Precious in the sight of the Lord
    are those who die, devoted to Him.
I am Your servant, Lord, Your servant,
    the child of a woman who served You.
    You freed me from my bonds.
To You I offer the offering of gratitude
    and call on the name of the Lord.

I will fulfil my promises to the Lord
    in the presence of all His people.
In the courts of the house of the Lord,
    in your midst, Jerusalem!

Praise the Lord!

117

Praise the Lord, all nations,
    glorify Him, all peoples!
For His love for us is strong
    and the truth of the Lord is eternal.

Praise the Lord!

קיח

הוֹדוּ לַיהוָה כִּי־טוֹב   כִּי לְעוֹלָם חַסְדּוֹ:

יֹאמַר־נָא יִשְׂרָאֵל   כִּי לְעוֹלָם חַסְדּוֹ:

יֹאמְרוּ־נָא בֵית־אַהֲרֹן   כִּי לְעוֹלָם חַסְדּוֹ:

יֹאמְרוּ־נָא יִרְאֵי יְהוָה   כִּי לְעוֹלָם חַסְדּוֹ:

מִן־הַמֵּצַר קָרָאתִי יָּהּ עָנָנִי בַמֶּרְחָב יָהּ:

יְהוָה לִי לֹא אִירָא מַה־יַּעֲשֶׂה לִי אָדָם:

יְהוָה לִי בְּעֹזְרָי וַאֲנִי אֶרְאֶה בְשֹׂנְאָי:

טוֹב לַחֲסוֹת בַּיהוָה מִבְּטֹחַ בָּאָדָם:

טוֹב לַחֲסוֹת בַּיהוָה מִבְּטֹחַ בִּנְדִיבִים:

כָּל־גּוֹיִם סְבָבוּנִי בְּשֵׁם יְהוָה כִּי אֲמִילַם:

סַבּוּנִי גַם־סְבָבוּנִי בְּשֵׁם יְהוָה כִּי אֲמִילַם:

סַבּוּנִי כִדְבוֹרִים דֹּעֲכוּ כְּאֵשׁ קוֹצִים בְּשֵׁם יְהוָה כִּי אֲמִילַם:

דָּחֹה דְחִיתַנִי לִנְפֹּל וַיהוָה עֲזָרָנִי:

עָזִּי וְזִמְרָת יָהּ וַיְהִי־לִי לִישׁוּעָה:

קוֹל רִנָּה וִישׁוּעָה בְּאָהֳלֵי צַדִּיקִים יְמִין יְהוָה עֹשָׂה חָיִל:

יְמִין יְהוָה רוֹמֵמָה יְמִין יְהוָה עֹשָׂה חָיִל:

118

Thank the Lord, for He is good,
    for His love is everlasting.
Let Israel now say:
    'For His love is everlasting.'

Let the house of Aaron now say:
    'For His love is everlasting.'
Let all who fear the Lord now say:
    'For His love is everlasting.'

Closed in by troubles I called on the Lord.
    The Lord answered me and set me free.
The Lord is for me, I shall not fear.
    What can men do to me?
The Lord is for me, my source of help,
    so I face up to those who hate me!

It is better to trust in the Lord
    than to rely on man.
It is better to trust in the Lord
    than to rely on leaders.

All nations surrounded me—
    but by the name of the Lord I cut them down.
They swarmed and surrounded me—
    but by the name of the Lord I cut them down.
They swarmed around me like bees,
    they were quenched like a fire among thorns—
    but by the name of the Lord I cut them down.

You pressed me so that I nearly fell,
    but the Lord helped me.
God is my strength and song
    and He is there to save me.

Shouts of joy and triumph
    are in the tents of the just:
'The Lord's right hand works mightily!
    The Lord's right hand is raised!
The Lord's right hand works mightily!'

לֹא־אָמוּת כִּי־אֶחְיֶה וַאֲסַפֵּר מַעֲשֵׂי יָהּ:

יַסֹּר יִסְּרַנִּי יָּהּ וְלַמָּוֶת לֹא נְתָנָנִי:

פִּתְחוּ־לִי שַׁעֲרֵי־צֶדֶק אָבֹא־בָם אוֹדֶה יָהּ:

זֶה־הַשַּׁעַר לַיהֹוָה צַדִּיקִים יָבֹאוּ בוֹ:

אוֹדְךָ כִּי עֲנִיתָנִי וַתְּהִי־לִי לִישׁוּעָה:

אֶבֶן מָאֲסוּ הַבּוֹנִים הָיְתָה לְרֹאשׁ פִּנָּה:

מֵאֵת יְהֹוָה הָיְתָה זֹּאת הִיא נִפְלָאת בְּעֵינֵינוּ:

זֶה־הַיּוֹם עָשָׂה יְהֹוָה נָגִילָה וְנִשְׂמְחָה בוֹ:

אָנָּא יְהֹוָה הוֹשִׁיעָה נָּא אָנָּא יְהֹוָה הַצְלִיחָה נָּא:

בָּרוּךְ הַבָּא בְּשֵׁם יְהֹוָה בֵּרַכְנוּכֶם מִבֵּית יְהֹוָה:

אֵל יְהֹוָה וַיָּאֶר לָנוּ אִסְרוּ־חַג בַּעֲבֹתִים עַד־קַרְנוֹת הַמִּזְבֵּחַ:

אֵלִי אַתָּה וְאוֹדֶךָּ אֱלֹהַי אֲרוֹמְמֶךָּ:

הוֹדוּ לַיהֹוָה כִּי־טוֹב כִּי לְעוֹלָם חַסְדּוֹ:

יְהַלְלוּךָ יְיָ אֱלֹהֵינוּ כָּל־מַעֲשֶׂיךָ · וַחֲסִידֶיךָ צַדִּיקִים עוֹשֵׂי רְצוֹנֶךָ וְכָל־עַמְּךָ בֵּית יִשְׂרָאֵל בְּרִנָּה יוֹדוּ וִיבָרְכוּ וִישַׁבְּחוּ וִיפָאֲרוּ וִירוֹמְמוּ וְיַעֲרִיצוּ וְיַקְדִּישׁוּ וְיַמְלִיכוּ אֶת־שִׁמְךָ מַלְכֵּנוּ · כִּי לְךָ טוֹב לְהֹדוֹת וּלְשִׁמְךָ נָאֶה לְזַמֵּר כִּי מֵעוֹלָם וְעַד עוֹלָם אַתָּה אֵל : בָּרוּךְ אַתָּה יְיָ מֶלֶךְ מְהֻלָּל בַּתִּשְׁבָּחוֹת:

I shall not die, but live
    and declare the acts of God.
God has taught me sharply
    but He has not surrendered me to death.

Open the gates of justice for me,
    I shall enter them and thank the Lord.
This is the gate of the Lord,
    the just may enter in.

I thank You, for You answered me,
    it was You who saved me.
A stone the builders rejected
    has become the corner-stone itself.
Through the Lord this came about,
    this wonder to our eyes.
This is the day the Lord has made,
    let us be glad and rejoice on it.

Lord, we pray You, save us now!
    Lord, we pray You, let us prosper now!

Blessed is he who comes in the name of the Lord,
    we bless you from the house of the Lord.

The Lord is God who gives us light.
    (Form the procession with the branches
    up to the horns of the altar.)

You are my God and I thank You.
    My God, I praise You!

Thank the Lord, for He is good,
    for His love is everlasting.

O Lord our God, all Your works shall praise You; and all who love You, the righteous who do Your will, and all Your people, the family of Israel, shall thank You with joyful song; and bless and praise and sanctify You, accepting You as our king. It is good to thank You and it is right to sing to Your name, for You are God from everlasting to everlasting. Blessed are You Lord, the king praised in all worship.

קכא

שִׁיר לַמַּעֲלוֹת

אֶשָּׂא עֵינַי אֶל־הֶהָרִים מֵאַיִן יָבֹא עֶזְרִי:

עֶזְרִי מֵעִם יְהוָה עֹשֵׂה שָׁמַיִם וָאָרֶץ:

אַל־יִתֵּן לַמּוֹט רַגְלֶךָ אַל־יָנוּם שֹׁמְרֶךָ:

הִנֵּה לֹא־יָנוּם וְלֹא יִישָׁן שׁוֹמֵר יִשְׂרָאֵל:

יְהוָה שֹׁמְרֶךָ יְהוָה צִלְּךָ עַל־יַד יְמִינֶךָ:

יוֹמָם הַשֶּׁמֶשׁ לֹא־יַכֶּכָּה וְיָרֵחַ בַּלָּיְלָה:

יְהוָה יִשְׁמָרְךָ מִכָּל־רָע יִשְׁמֹר אֶת־נַפְשֶׁךָ:

יְהוָה יִשְׁמָר־צֵאתְךָ וּבוֹאֶךָ מֵעַתָּה וְעַד־עוֹלָם:

קכב

שִׁיר הַמַּעֲלוֹת לְדָוִד

שָׂמַחְתִּי בְּאֹמְרִים לִי בֵּית יְהוָה נֵלֵךְ:

עֹמְדוֹת הָיוּ רַגְלֵינוּ בִּשְׁעָרַיִךְ יְרוּשָׁלָיִם:

יְרוּשָׁלַיִם הַבְּנוּיָה כְּעִיר שֶׁחֻבְּרָה־לָּהּ יַחְדָּו:

שֶׁשָּׁם עָלוּ שְׁבָטִים שִׁבְטֵי־יָהּ

עֵדוּת לְיִשְׂרָאֵל לְהֹדוֹת לְשֵׁם יְהוָה:

כִּי שָׁמָּה יָשְׁבוּ כִסְאוֹת לְמִשְׁפָּט כִּסְאוֹת לְבֵית דָּוִד:

שַׁאֲלוּ שְׁלוֹם יְרוּשָׁלָיִם יִשְׁלָיוּ אֹהֲבָיִךְ:

יְהִי־שָׁלוֹם בְּחֵילֵךְ שַׁלְוָה בְּאַרְמְנוֹתָיִךְ:

לְמַעַן אַחַי וְרֵעָי אֲדַבְּרָה־נָּא שָׁלוֹם בָּךְ:

לְמַעַן בֵּית־יְהוָה אֱלֹהֵינוּ אֲבַקְשָׁה טוֹב לָךְ:

121

A pilgrim song.

I lift up my eyes to the hills;
  where shall I find my help?
My help is from the Lord alone,
  maker of heaven and earth.
He will not allow your foot to slip,
  for your guardian does not slumber.
Know that the guardian of Israel
  never slumbers and never sleeps.
The Lord is your guardian,
  the Lord is your shade at your right hand.
The sun will not strike you by day
  nor the moon by night.
The Lord will guard you from all evil,
  He will guard your soul.
The Lord will guard your going out and your coming in
  now and for evermore.

122

A pilgrim song.   David's.

I rejoiced when they said to me:
  'Let us go to the house of the Lord!'
And now our feet are standing
  inside your gates, O Jerusalem!

Jerusalem rebuilt! As a city
  where all are united together.
Here the tribes came up,
  the tribes of the Lord
—for it is the mark of Israel
  to thank the name of the Lord.
There were the seats of justice,
  the thrones of the house of David.

Pray for the peace of Jerusalem,
  may those who love you prosper.
Peace be within your walls,
  tranquillity inside your homes.

For the sake of my brothers and friends
  I call out, 'Peace be with you!'
For the sake of the house of the Lord our God,
  I will seek your good.

קכד

שִׁיר הַמַּעֲלוֹת לְדָוִד

לוּלֵי יְהֹוָה שֶׁהָיָה לָנוּ יֹאמַר־נָא יִשְׂרָאֵל:

לוּלֵי יְהֹוָה שֶׁהָיָה לָנוּ בְּקוּם עָלֵינוּ אָדָם:

אֲזַי חַיִּים בְּלָעוּנוּ בַּחֲרוֹת אַפָּם בָּנוּ:

אֲזַי הַמַּיִם שְׁטָפוּנוּ נַחְלָה עָבַר עַל־נַפְשֵׁנוּ:

אֲזַי עָבַר עַל־נַפְשֵׁנוּ הַמַּיִם הַזֵּידוֹנִים:

בָּרוּךְ יְהֹוָה שֶׁלֹּא נְתָנָנוּ טֶרֶף לְשִׁנֵּיהֶם:

נַפְשֵׁנוּ כְּצִפּוֹר נִמְלְטָה מִפַּח יוֹקְשִׁים

הַפַּח נִשְׁבָּר וַאֲנַחְנוּ נִמְלָטְנוּ:

עֶזְרֵנוּ בְּשֵׁם יְהֹוָה עֹשֵׂה שָׁמַיִם וָאָרֶץ:

קכה

שִׁיר הַמַּעֲלוֹת

הַבֹּטְחִים בַּיהֹוָה כְּהַר־צִיּוֹן לֹא־יִמּוֹט לְעוֹלָם יֵשֵׁב:

יְרוּשָׁלַיִם הָרִים סָבִיב לָהּ וַיהֹוָה סָבִיב לְעַמּוֹ

מֵעַתָּה וְעַד־עוֹלָם:

כִּי לֹא יָנוּחַ שֵׁבֶט הָרֶשַׁע עַל גּוֹרַל הַצַּדִּיקִים

לְמַעַן לֹא־יִשְׁלְחוּ הַצַּדִּיקִים בְּעַוְלָתָה יְדֵיהֶם:

הֵיטִיבָה יְהֹוָה לַטּוֹבִים וְלִישָׁרִים בְּלִבּוֹתָם:

וְהַמַּטִּים עֲקַלְקַלּוֹתָם יוֹלִיכֵם יְהֹוָה אֶת־פֹּעֲלֵי הָאָוֶן

שָׁלוֹם עַל־יִשְׂרָאֵל:

124

A pilgrim song. David's.

'If the Lord had not been for us,'
  —let Israel repeat it,
'If the Lord had not been for us,
  when men rose up against us,
they would have swallowed us up alive
  in their burning rage at us;
the waters would have overwhelmed us,
  a torrent sweeping over our souls;
they would have swept away our lives,
  the high and mighty waters!'
Blessed is the Lord
  who did not make us a prey to their teeth.
Our soul is like a bird
  that escaped from the fowlers' trap.
The trap itself is smashed
  and we have escaped.
Our help is in the name of the Lord,
  maker of heaven and earth.

125

A pilgrim song.

Those who trust in the Lord are like Mount Zion,
  unshakeable, enduring forever.
Jerusalem! surrounded by mountains,
  as the Lord surrounds His people
  now and forever.
For the rod of the wicked shall not rest
  on the heritage of the righteous.
So the righteous shall not put
  their hand to injustice.
Lord, do good to the good,
  to those with honest hearts.
But the opportunists who turn to crooked ways,
  the Lord will send them away
  with those who do evil.
Peace upon Israel!

קכו

שִׁיר הַמַּעֲלוֹת

בְּשׁוּב יְהֹוָה אֶת־שִׁיבַת צִיּוֹן הָיִינוּ כְּחֹלְמִים׃

אָז יִמָּלֵא שְׂחוֹק פִּינוּ וּלְשׁוֹנֵנוּ רִנָּה

אָז יֹאמְרוּ בַגּוֹיִם הִגְדִּיל יְהֹוָה לַעֲשׂוֹת עִם־אֵלֶּה׃

הִגְדִּיל יְהֹוָה לַעֲשׂוֹת עִמָּנוּ הָיִינוּ שְׂמֵחִים׃

שׁוּבָה יְהֹוָה אֶת־שְׁבִיתֵנוּ כַּאֲפִיקִים בַּנֶּגֶב׃

הַזֹּרְעִים בְּדִמְעָה בְּרִנָּה יִקְצֹרוּ׃

הָלוֹךְ יֵלֵךְ וּבָכֹה נֹשֵׂא מֶשֶׁךְ־הַזָּרַע

בֹּא־יָבֹא בְרִנָּה נֹשֵׂא אֲלֻמֹּתָיו׃

קכז

שִׁיר הַמַּעֲלוֹת לִשְׁלֹמֹה

אִם־יְהֹוָה לֹא־יִבְנֶה בַיִת שָׁוְא עָמְלוּ בוֹנָיו בּוֹ

אִם־יְהֹוָה לֹא־יִשְׁמָר־עִיר שָׁוְא שָׁקַד שׁוֹמֵר׃

שָׁוְא לָכֶם מַשְׁכִּימֵי קוּם מְאַחֲרֵי־שֶׁבֶת

אֹכְלֵי לֶחֶם הָעֲצָבִים כֵּן יִתֵּן לִידִידוֹ שֵׁנָא׃

הִנֵּה נַחֲלַת יְהֹוָה בָּנִים שָׂכָר פְּרִי הַבָּטֶן׃

כְּחִצִּים בְּיַד־גִּבּוֹר כֵּן בְּנֵי הַנְּעוּרִים׃

אַשְׁרֵי הַגֶּבֶר אֲשֶׁר מִלֵּא אֶת־אַשְׁפָּתוֹ מֵהֶם

לֹא־יֵבֹשׁוּ כִּי־יְדַבְּרוּ אֶת־אוֹיְבִים בַּשָּׁעַר׃

126

A pilgrim song.

When the Lord brought back the captives to Zion
   we felt as if in a dream.
Then our mouths were filled with laughter,
   and our tongues with song.
Even among the nations they said:
   'What great things the Lord has done for them!'
Indeed the Lord has done great things with us!
   How we rejoiced!

Lord, bring back those who cannot return,
   like streams in a dry land;
that those who sow in tears
   may reap in joy.
Though a man goes out weeping
   carrying seed to sow;
he shall come back singing
   carrying his sheaves.

127

A pilgrim song.   Solomon's.

Unless the Lord builds the house,
   its builders toil in vain.
Unless the Lord guards the city
   the sentry keeps watch in vain.
It is vain for you to rise up early,
   or to sit up late,
toiling for the bread you eat,
   since He provides for His beloved while they sleep.

Children are a gift of the Lord,
   a reward, the fruit of the womb.
Like arrows in the hand of a fighter
   are the children of one's youth.
Happy is the man
   who has filled his quiver with them.
Such men shall not be put to shame
   when they confront their enemies at the gate.

קכח

שִׁיר הַמַּעֲלוֹת

אַשְׁרֵי כָּל־יְרֵא יְהֹוָה הַהֹלֵךְ בִּדְרָכָיו:

יְגִיעַ כַּפֶּיךָ כִּי תֹאכֵל אַשְׁרֶיךָ וְטוֹב לָךְ:

אֶשְׁתְּךָ כְּגֶפֶן פֹּרִיָּה בְּיַרְכְּתֵי בֵיתֶךָ

בָּנֶיךָ כִּשְׁתִלֵי זֵיתִים סָבִיב לְשֻׁלְחָנֶךָ:

הִנֵּה כִי־כֵן יְבֹרַךְ גָּבֶר יְרֵא יְהֹוָה:

יְבָרֶכְךָ יְהֹוָה מִצִּיּוֹן וּרְאֵה בְּטוּב יְרוּשָׁלָיִם

כֹּל יְמֵי חַיֶּיךָ:

וּרְאֵה־בָנִים לְבָנֶיךָ שָׁלוֹם עַל־יִשְׂרָאֵל:

קל

שִׁיר הַמַּעֲלוֹת

מִמַּעֲמַקִּים קְרָאתִיךָ יְהֹוָה:

אֲדֹנָי שִׁמְעָה בְקוֹלִי תִּהְיֶינָה אָזְנֶיךָ קַשֻּׁבוֹת לְקוֹל תַּחֲנוּנָי:

אִם־עֲוֹנוֹת תִּשְׁמָר־יָהּ אֲדֹנָי מִי יַעֲמֹד:

כִּי־עִמְּךָ הַסְּלִיחָה לְמַעַן תִּוָּרֵא:

קִוִּיתִי יְהֹוָה קִוְּתָה נַפְשִׁי וְלִדְבָרוֹ הוֹחָלְתִּי:

נַפְשִׁי לַאדֹנָי מִשֹּׁמְרִים לַבֹּקֶר שֹׁמְרִים לַבֹּקֶר:

128

A pilgrim song.

Happy is everyone who fears the Lord,
  who walks in His ways.
When you eat the work of your hands,
  happy shall you be and it shall go well with you:
your wife, like a fruitful vine,
  in the heart of your house;
your children, like shoots of the olive tree,
  around your table.
Surely this is how a man is blessed
  who fears the Lord!
The Lord bless you from Zion!
May you see the good of Jerusalem
  all the days of your life,
    and see your children's children!
Peace upon Israel!

130

A pilgrim song.

Out of the depths I called to You, Lord,
  Lord, hear my voice.
Let Your ears listen
  to the voice of my pleading.

Lord, if You should mark sins,
  O Lord, who could stand?
But with You there is forgiveness,
  for this You are held in awe.

I hope in the Lord,
  my soul has hope,
  and for His word I wait.

My soul waits for the Lord
  more than watchmen for the morning,
  watching for the morning.

יַחֵל יִשְׂרָאֵל אֶל־יְהֹוָה כִּי־עִם־יְהֹוָה הַחֶסֶד
וְהַרְבֵּה עִמּוֹ פְדוּת:

וְהוּא יִפְדֶּה אֶת־יִשְׂרָאֵל מִכֹּל עֲוֹנוֹתָיו:

קלא

שִׁיר הַמַּעֲלוֹת לְדָוִד

יְהֹוָה לֹא־גָבַהּ לִבִּי וְלֹא־רָמוּ עֵינַי וְלֹא־הִלַּכְתִּי בִּגְדֹלוֹת
וּבְנִפְלָאוֹת מִמֶּנִּי:

אִם־לֹא שִׁוִּיתִי וְדוֹמַמְתִּי נַפְשִׁי כְּגָמֻל עֲלֵי אִמּוֹ
כַּגָּמֻל עָלַי נַפְשִׁי:

יַחֵל יִשְׂרָאֵל אֶל־יְהֹוָה מֵעַתָּה וְעַד־עוֹלָם:

קלג

שִׁיר הַמַּעֲלוֹת לְדָוִד

הִנֵּה מַה־טּוֹב וּמַה־נָּעִים שֶׁבֶת אַחִים גַּם־יָחַד:

כַּשֶּׁמֶן הַטּוֹב עַל־הָרֹאשׁ יֹרֵד עַל־הַזָּקָן זְקַן־אַהֲרֹן
שֶׁיֹּרֵד עַל־פִּי מִדּוֹתָיו:

כְּטַל־חֶרְמוֹן שֶׁיֹּרֵד עַל־הַרְרֵי צִיּוֹן כִּי שָׁם צִוָּה יְהֹוָה
אֶת־הַבְּרָכָה חַיִּים עַד־הָעוֹלָם:

Israel, hope in the Lord,
   for with the Lord is constant love,
   and with Him great power to redeem.
It is He who redeems Israel
   from all their sins.

131

A pilgrim song.   David's.

O Lord, my heart is not proud,
   my eyes are not ambitious.
I am not busy with things too great
   or too wonderful for me.

Have I not set my soul
   in quietness and peace;
like a child at its mother's breast,
   my soul is like a weaned child.

O Israel, hope in the Lord
   now and forever!

133

A pilgrim song.   David's.

How good it is and how pleasant
   when brothers live in unity together.

It is like precious oil on the head,
   running down upon the beard,
running down from Aaron's beard
   upon the collar of his robes.

It is like the dew of Hermon,
   falling on the hills of Zion
where the Lord proclaimed His blessing,
   life forever!

קלד

שִׁיר הַמַּעֲלוֹת

הִנֵּה בָּרְכוּ אֶת־יְהֹוָה כָּל־עַבְדֵי יְהֹוָה
הָעֹמְדִים בְּבֵית־יְהֹוָה בַּלֵּילוֹת:
שְׂאוּ־יְדֵכֶם קֹדֶשׁ וּבָרְכוּ אֶת־יְהֹוָה:
יְבָרֶכְךָ יְהֹוָה מִצִּיּוֹן עֹשֵׂה שָׁמַיִם וָאָרֶץ:

קלז (א־ו)

עַל נַהֲרוֹת בָּבֶל שָׁם יָשַׁבְנוּ גַּם־בָּכִינוּ בְּזָכְרֵנוּ אֶת־צִיּוֹן:
עַל־עֲרָבִים בְּתוֹכָהּ תָּלִינוּ כִּנֹּרוֹתֵינוּ:
כִּי שָׁם שְׁאֵלוּנוּ שׁוֹבֵינוּ דִּבְרֵי־שִׁיר וְתוֹלָלֵינוּ שִׂמְחָה
שִׁירוּ לָנוּ מִשִּׁיר צִיּוֹן:
אֵיךְ נָשִׁיר אֶת־שִׁיר־יְהֹוָה עַל אַדְמַת נֵכָר:
אִם־אֶשְׁכָּחֵךְ יְרוּשָׁלָיִם תִּשְׁכַּח יְמִינִי:
תִּדְבַּק לְשׁוֹנִי לְחִכִּי אִם־לֹא אֶזְכְּרֵכִי אִם־לֹא אַעֲלֶה
אֶת־יְרוּשָׁלַיִם עַל רֹאשׁ שִׂמְחָתִי:

קלח

לְדָוִד

אוֹדְךָ בְכָל־לִבִּי נֶגֶד אֱלֹהִים אֲזַמְּרֶךָּ:
אֶשְׁתַּחֲוֶה אֶל־הֵיכַל קָדְשְׁךָ
וְאוֹדֶה אֶת־שְׁמֶךָ עַל־חַסְדְּךָ וְעַל־אֲמִתֶּךָ
כִּי־הִגְדַּלְתָּ עַל־כָּל־שִׁמְךָ אִמְרָתֶךָ:

134

A pilgrim song.

Come, bless the Lord,
 all who serve the Lord,
who stand night after night
 in the house of the Lord.
Raise your hands to the holy place
 and bless the Lord.
May the Lord bless you from Zion,
 the maker of heaven and earth.

137: 1–6

By the rivers of Babylon
 there we sat, yes, we wept
 as we remembered Zion.
There upon the willows
 we hung up our harps.
For it was there our captors asked for songs,
 our tormentors for joy:
 'Sing us one of the songs of Zion!'
How could we sing the Lord's song
 in a strange land!

If I forget you, O Jerusalem,
 let my right hand forget its cunning.
Let my tongue stick to the roof of my mouth,
 if I do not remember you,
 if I do not put Jerusalem
 above my highest joy.

138

David's.

I thank You, Lord, with all my heart.
 In the presence of the mighty I sing Your praise.

I bow down towards the temple of Your holiness,
 I give thanks to Your name for Your loyalty and love
 because it is Your nature to exceed Your promise.

בְּיוֹם קָרָאתִי וַתַּעֲנֵנִי תַּרְהִבֵנִי בְנַפְשִׁי עֹז׃

יוֹדוּךָ יְהֹוָה כָּל־מַלְכֵי־אָרֶץ כִּי־שָׁמְעוּ אִמְרֵי־פִיךָ׃

וְיָשִׁירוּ בְּדַרְכֵי יְהֹוָה כִּי גָדוֹל כְּבוֹד יְהֹוָה׃

כִּי־רָם יְהֹוָה וְשָׁפָל יִרְאֶה וְגָבֹהַּ מִמֶּרְחָק יְיֵדָע׃

אִם־אֵלֵךְ בְּקֶרֶב צָרָה תְּחַיֵּנִי עַל אַף אֹיְבַי תִּשְׁלַח יָדֶךָ
וְתוֹשִׁיעֵנִי יְמִינֶךָ׃

יְהֹוָה יִגְמֹר בַּעֲדִי יְהֹוָה חַסְדְּךָ לְעוֹלָם מַעֲשֵׂי יָדֶיךָ אַל־תֶּרֶף׃

קלט (א־יח, כג, כד)
לַמְנַצֵּחַ לְדָוִד מִזְמוֹר

יְהֹוָה חֲקַרְתַּנִי וַתֵּדָע׃

אַתָּה יָדַעְתָּ שִׁבְתִּי וְקוּמִי בַּנְתָּה לְרֵעִי מֵרָחוֹק׃

אָרְחִי וְרִבְעִי זֵרִיתָ וְכָל־דְּרָכַי הִסְכַּנְתָּה׃

כִּי אֵין מִלָּה בִּלְשׁוֹנִי הֵן יְהֹוָה יָדַעְתָּ כֻלָּהּ׃

אָחוֹר וָקֶדֶם צַרְתָּנִי וַתָּשֶׁת עָלַי כַּפֶּכָה׃

פְּלִיאָה דַעַת מִמֶּנִּי נִשְׂגְּבָה לֹא־אוּכַל לָהּ׃

אָנָה אֵלֵךְ מֵרוּחֶךָ וְאָנָה מִפָּנֶיךָ אֶבְרָח׃

אִם־אֶסַּק שָׁמַיִם שָׁם אָתָּה וְאַצִּיעָה שְּׁאוֹל הִנֶּךָ׃

אֶשָּׂא כַנְפֵי־שָׁחַר אֶשְׁכְּנָה בְּאַחֲרִית יָם׃

גַּם־שָׁם יָדְךָ תַנְחֵנִי וְתֹאחֲזֵנִי יְמִינֶךָ׃

In the day I called, You answered me
and increased the strength of my soul.

All the kings on earth give thanks to You
for they have heard the words of Your mouth.

They sing of the ways of the Lord:
'Great is the glory of the Lord!'

Though the Lord is high, He regards the lowly,
but He marks the haughty from afar.

Though I walk in the midst of sorrow
You keep me alive.

You stretch out Your hand against the wrath of my enemies
and Your right hand saves me.

The Lord will fulfil His purpose for me.
Lord, Your love endures forever,
do not abandon the work of Your hands!

139 : 1–18, 23, 24

For the choirmaster.   David's psalm.

Lord, You searched me, and You know me.
You know all—whether I sit or stand,
reading my thoughts from far away.

You watched my journey and my resting-place,
familiar with all my ways.

For there is not a word on my tongue
but You know it already, through and through.

You closed me in, behind me and before me,
laying Your hand upon me.

Such knowledge is too wonderful for me,
too high, beyond my reach.

Where could I go from Your spirit,
or where could I flee from Your presence?

If I climb to heaven, You are there,
there too, if I lie in the depths.

If I fly on wings to the dawn
and dwell at the sea's horizon,

even there Your hand would lead me,
Your right hand would hold me.

וָאֹמַר אַךְ־חֹשֶׁךְ יְשׁוּפֵנִי וְלַיְלָה אוֹר בַּעֲדֵנִי:

גַּם־חֹשֶׁךְ לֹא־יַחְשִׁיךְ מִמֶּךָ וְלַיְלָה כַּיּוֹם יָאִיר

כַּחֲשֵׁיכָה כָּאוֹרָה:

כִּי־אַתָּה קָנִיתָ כִלְיֹתָי תְּסֻכֵּנִי בְּבֶטֶן אִמִּי:

אוֹדְךָ עַל כִּי נוֹרָאוֹת נִפְלֵיתִי נִפְלָאִים מַעֲשֶׂיךָ

וְנַפְשִׁי יֹדַעַת מְאֹד:

לֹא־נִכְחַד עָצְמִי מִמֶּךָ אֲשֶׁר־עֻשֵּׂיתִי בַסֵּתֶר

רֻקַּמְתִּי בְּתַחְתִּיּוֹת אָרֶץ:

גָּלְמִי רָאוּ עֵינֶיךָ וְעַל־סִפְרְךָ כֻּלָּם יִכָּתֵבוּ

יָמִים יֻצָּרוּ וְלֹא אֶחָד בָּהֶם:

וְלִי מַה־יָּקְרוּ רֵעֶיךָ אֵל מֶה עָצְמוּ רָאשֵׁיהֶם:

אֶסְפְּרֵם מֵחוֹל יִרְבּוּן הֱקִיצֹתִי וְעוֹדִי עִמָּךְ:

חָקְרֵנִי אֵל וְדַע לְבָבִי בְּחָנֵנִי וְדַע שַׂרְעַפָּי:

וּרְאֵה אִם־דֶּרֶךְ־עֹצֶב בִּי וּנְחֵנִי בְּדֶרֶךְ עוֹלָם:

קמג

מִזְמוֹר לְדָוִד

יְהוָה שְׁמַע תְּפִלָּתִי הַאֲזִינָה אֶל־תַּחֲנוּנַי

בֶּאֱמֻנָתְךָ עֲנֵנִי בְּצִדְקָתֶךָ:

וְאַל־תָּבוֹא בְמִשְׁפָּט אֶת־עַבְדֶּךָ כִּי לֹא־יִצְדַּק לְפָנֶיךָ כָל־חָי:

כִּי רָדַף אוֹיֵב נַפְשִׁי דִּכָּא לָאָרֶץ חַיָּתִי

הוֹשִׁיבַנִי בְמַחֲשַׁכִּים כְּמֵתֵי עוֹלָם:

וַתִּתְעַטֵּף עָלַי רוּחִי בְּתוֹכִי יִשְׁתּוֹמֵם לִבִּי:

If I ask darkness to cover me
   and light to be night around me,
that darkness would not be dark to You,
    but night as bright as day
    and darkness like the light.
For it is You who created my innermost being,
   knit me together in my mother's womb.
I thank You for the awesome wonder that I am,
   for the wonder of Your works.
   How well my soul knows it!
My body was no mystery to You
   when I was made in secret,
   deep in the womb.
Your eyes saw my unformed substance,
   all my actions were written down in Your book.
The days were determined
   even before they had yet occurred.
God, how precious are Your thoughts to me,
   how vast the sum of them.
If I try to count them, they are more than the sand
   and even if I reach the end, You would still be with me.
Search me, God, and know my heart,
   test me, and know my thoughts.
See if the path to despair is within me,
   and lead me in the path of eternity.

143

A psalm of David.

Lord, hear my prayer,
   listen to my pleading.
In Your faithfulness and justice answer me
   and let not Your servant be tried,
   for no man is truly just in Your sight.

For the enemy persecutes me
   to crush my life into the ground.
He made me dwell in darkness
   like the dead of long ago,
and my spirit was faint within me,
   great fear inside my heart.

זָכַרְתִּי יָמִים מִקֶּדֶם הָגִיתִי בְכָל־פָּעֳלֶךָ

בְּמַעֲשֵׂה יָדֶיךָ אֲשׂוֹחֵחַ:

פֵּרַשְׂתִּי יָדַי אֵלֶיךָ נַפְשִׁי כְּאֶרֶץ־עֲיֵפָה לְךָ סֶלָה:

מַהֵר עֲנֵנִי יְהוָה כָּלְתָה רוּחִי

אַל־תַּסְתֵּר פָּנֶיךָ מִמֶּנִּי וְנִמְשַׁלְתִּי עִם־יֹרְדֵי בוֹר:

הַשְׁמִיעֵנִי בַבֹּקֶר חַסְדֶּךָ כִּי־בְךָ בָטָחְתִּי

הוֹדִיעֵנִי דֶּרֶךְ־זוּ אֵלֵךְ כִּי־אֵלֶיךָ נָשָׂאתִי נַפְשִׁי:

הַצִּילֵנִי מֵאֹיְבַי יְהוָה אֵלֶיךָ כִסִּתִי:

לַמְּדֵנִי לַעֲשׂוֹת רְצוֹנֶךָ כִּי־אַתָּה אֱלוֹהָי

רוּחֲךָ טוֹבָה תַּנְחֵנִי בְּאֶרֶץ מִישׁוֹר:

לְמַעַן־שִׁמְךָ יְהוָה תְּחַיֵּנִי בְּצִדְקָתְךָ תּוֹצִיא מִצָּרָה נַפְשִׁי:

וּבְחַסְדְּךָ תַּצְמִית אֹיְבָי וְהַאֲבַדְתָּ כָּל־צֹרְרֵי נַפְשִׁי

כִּי אֲנִי עַבְדֶּךָ:

קמה

תְּהִלָּה לְדָוִד

אֲרוֹמִמְךָ אֱלוֹהַי הַמֶּלֶךְ וַאֲבָרְכָה שִׁמְךָ לְעוֹלָם וָעֶד:

בְּכָל־יוֹם אֲבָרְכֶךָ וַאֲהַלְלָה שִׁמְךָ לְעוֹלָם וָעֶד:

גָּדוֹל יְהוָה וּמְהֻלָּל מְאֹד וְלִגְדֻלָּתוֹ אֵין חֵקֶר:

דּוֹר לְדוֹר יְשַׁבַּח מַעֲשֶׂיךָ וּגְבוּרֹתֶיךָ יַגִּידוּ:

I remember the days that are past,
  I meditate on all You did,
  I muse on the work of Your hands.
I stretch out my hands to You.
  My soul thirsts for You like parched land.

Make haste to answer me, Lord!
  My spirit fails.
Do not hide Your face from me
  lest I go down to the grave like the rest.

In the morning bring tidings of Your love,
  for in You I trust.
Show me the way that I should walk,
  for I put my hope in You.

Deliver me from my enemies, Lord.
  I take shelter in You.

Teach me to do Your will,
  for You are my God.
Let Your good spirit guide me
  on to gentle ground.

Lord, for Your name's sake save my life.
  In Your justice bring my soul from trouble.
In Your love cut off my enemies
  and destroy my oppressors,
    for I am Your servant.

145

A psalm of praise. David's.

I will glorify You, God my king,
  and bless Your name forever and ever.
Every day I will bless You
  and praise Your name forever and ever.

Great is the Lord and praised aloud
  and His greatness is beyond understanding.
One generation shall praise Your deeds to the next
  and tell of Your mighty acts.

הֲדַר כְּבוֹד הוֹדֶךָ וְדִבְרֵי נִפְלְאֹתֶיךָ אָשִׂיחָה׃

וֶעֱזוּז נוֹרְאוֹתֶיךָ יֹאמֵרוּ וּגְדוּלָּתְךָ אֲסַפְּרֶנָּה׃

זֵכֶר רַב־טוּבְךָ יַבִּיעוּ וְצִדְקָתְךָ יְרַנֵּנוּ׃

חַנּוּן וְרַחוּם יְהֹוָה אֶרֶךְ אַפַּיִם וּגְדָל־חָסֶד׃

טוֹב־יְהֹוָה לַכֹּל וְרַחֲמָיו עַל־כָּל־מַעֲשָׂיו׃

יוֹדוּךָ יְהֹוָה כָּל־מַעֲשֶׂיךָ וַחֲסִידֶיךָ יְבָרְכוּכָה׃

כְּבוֹד מַלְכוּתְךָ יֹאמֵרוּ וּגְבוּרָתְךָ יְדַבֵּרוּ׃

לְהוֹדִיעַ לִבְנֵי הָאָדָם גְּבוּרֹתָיו וּכְבוֹד הֲדַר מַלְכוּתוֹ׃

מַלְכוּתְךָ מַלְכוּת כָּל־עֹלָמִים וּמֶמְשַׁלְתְּךָ בְּכָל־דּוֹר וָדֹר׃

סוֹמֵךְ יְהֹוָה לְכָל־הַנֹּפְלִים וְזוֹקֵף לְכָל־הַכְּפוּפִים׃

עֵינֵי־כֹל אֵלֶיךָ יְשַׂבֵּרוּ וְאַתָּה נוֹתֵן־לָהֶם אֶת־אָכְלָם בְּעִתּוֹ׃

פּוֹתֵחַ אֶת־יָדֶךָ וּמַשְׂבִּיעַ לְכָל־חַי רָצוֹן׃

צַדִּיק יְהֹוָה בְּכָל־דְּרָכָיו וְחָסִיד בְּכָל־מַעֲשָׂיו׃

קָרוֹב יְהֹוָה לְכָל־קֹרְאָיו לְכֹל אֲשֶׁר יִקְרָאֻהוּ בֶאֱמֶת׃

רְצוֹן־יְרֵאָיו יַעֲשֶׂה וְאֶת־שַׁוְעָתָם יִשְׁמַע וְיוֹשִׁיעֵם׃

שׁוֹמֵר יְהֹוָה אֶת־כָּל־אֹהֲבָיו וְאֵת כָּל־הָרְשָׁעִים יַשְׁמִיד׃

תְּהִלַּת יְהֹוָה יְדַבֶּר־פִּי וִיבָרֵךְ כָּל־בָּשָׂר שֵׁם קָדְשׁוֹ לְעוֹלָם וָעֶד׃

וַאֲנַחְנוּ נְבָרֵךְ יָהּ מֵעַתָּה וְעַד־עוֹלָם · הַלְלוּיָהּ׃

The glorious splendour of Your majesty
and Your wonders will be my theme.
People will speak of the power of Your awesome deeds,
and I will describe Your greatness.

They will spread the fame of Your great goodness
and sing out loud Your righteousness.
Compassionate and merciful is the Lord,
slow to anger, and great in love.

The Lord is good to everyone,
His compassion is over all He made.
All You made shall praise You, Lord,
and those who love You will bless You.

They shall speak of the glory of Your kingdom
and talk about Your power,
to let mankind know of Your mighty acts
and the glorious splendour of Your kingdom.

Your kingdom is an everlasting kingdom,
Your authority for every generation.
The Lord supports the falling
and raises all those bent low.

The eyes of all look to You
and You give them food when it is time.
You open Your hand
and satisfy the needs of all living.

The Lord is just in all His ways
and loving in all He does.
The Lord is near to all who call Him,
to all who call Him sincerely.

He fulfils the needs of those who fear Him,
He hears their cry and saves them.
The Lord looks after those who love Him,
but all the wicked He destroys.
My mouth will speak the praise of the Lord
and let all flesh bless His holy name forever and ever!

But we bless the Lord now and evermore. Praise the Lord!

קמו

הַלְלוּ־יָהּ

הַלְלִי נַפְשִׁי אֶת־יְהוָֹה:

אֲהַלְלָה יְהוָֹה בְּחַיָּי אֲזַמְּרָה לֵאלֹהַי בְּעוֹדִי:

אַל־תִּבְטְחוּ בִנְדִיבִים בְּבֶן־אָדָם שֶׁאֵין לוֹ תְשׁוּעָה:

תֵּצֵא רוּחוֹ יָשֻׁב לְאַדְמָתוֹ בַּיּוֹם הַהוּא אָבְדוּ עֶשְׁתֹּנֹתָיו:

אַשְׁרֵי שֶׁאֵל יַעֲקֹב בְּעֶזְרוֹ שִׂבְרוֹ עַל־יְהוָֹה אֱלֹהָיו:

עֹשֶׂה שָׁמַיִם וָאָרֶץ אֶת־הַיָּם וְאֶת־כָּל־אֲשֶׁר־בָּם

הַשֹּׁמֵר אֱמֶת לְעוֹלָם:

עֹשֶׂה מִשְׁפָּט לַעֲשׁוּקִים נֹתֵן לֶחֶם לָרְעֵבִים יְהוָֹה מַתִּיר אֲסוּרִים:

יְהוָֹה פֹּקֵחַ עִוְרִים יְהוָֹה זֹקֵף כְּפוּפִים יְהוָֹה אֹהֵב צַדִּיקִים:

יְהוָֹה שֹׁמֵר אֶת־גֵּרִים יָתוֹם וְאַלְמָנָה יְעוֹדֵד

וְדֶרֶךְ רְשָׁעִים יְעַוֵּת:

יִמְלֹךְ יְהוָֹה לְעוֹלָם אֱלֹהַיִךְ צִיּוֹן לְדֹר וָדֹר

הַלְלוּ־יָהּ:

קמז

הַלְלוּ־יָהּ

כִּי־טוֹב זַמְּרָה אֱלֹהֵינוּ כִּי־נָעִים נָאוָה תְהִלָּה:

בּוֹנֵה יְרוּשָׁלַיִם יְהוָֹה נִדְחֵי יִשְׂרָאֵל יְכַנֵּס:

הָרוֹפֵא לִשְׁבוּרֵי לֵב וּמְחַבֵּשׁ לְעַצְּבוֹתָם:

146

Praise the Lord!

Praise the Lord, my soul!
  I will praise Him as long as I live.
  I will sing to the Lord as long as I exist.

Do not trust in human leaders,
  or any man—he cannot save you!
His breath departs, he returns to the clay.
  On that very day all his plans perish.

Happy the one whose help is the God of Jacob
  whose hope is in the Lord, his God;
the maker of heaven and earth,
  the sea and all that is in them.
It is He who keeps faith forever,
  who does justice for the oppressed,
who gives bread to the starving,
  the Lord who sets prisoners free.

The Lord who opens the eyes of the blind,
  the Lord who raises up those bent low.
The Lord who loves righteous people,
  the Lord who protects strangers,
who supports the orphan and the widow,
  who thwarts the way of the wicked.

The Lord will rule forever,
  your God, O Zion, for all generations.

Praise the Lord!

147

Praise the Lord!

It is good to sing praise to our God,
  it is pleasant, and praise is right.
The Lord builds up Jerusalem
  and gathers up the outcasts of Israel.
He heals the broken-hearted,
  He binds up all their wounds.

מוֹנֶה מִסְפָּר לַכּוֹכָבִים לְכֻלָּם שֵׁמוֹת יִקְרָא׃

גָּדוֹל אֲדוֹנֵינוּ וְרַב־כֹּחַ לִתְבוּנָתוֹ אֵין מִסְפָּר׃

מְעוֹדֵד עֲנָוִים יְהוָה מַשְׁפִּיל רְשָׁעִים עֲדֵי־אָרֶץ׃

עֱנוּ לַיהוָה בְּתוֹדָה זַמְּרוּ לֵאלֹהֵינוּ בְכִנּוֹר׃

הַמְכַסֶּה שָׁמַיִם בְּעָבִים הַמֵּכִין לָאָרֶץ מָטָר
הַמַּצְמִיחַ הָרִים חָצִיר׃

נוֹתֵן לִבְהֵמָה לַחְמָהּ לִבְנֵי עֹרֵב אֲשֶׁר יִקְרָאוּ׃

לֹא בִגְבוּרַת הַסּוּס יֶחְפָּץ לֹא־בְשׁוֹקֵי הָאִישׁ יִרְצֶה׃

רוֹצֶה יְהוָה אֶת־יְרֵאָיו אֶת־הַמְיַחֲלִים לְחַסְדּוֹ׃

שַׁבְּחִי יְרוּשָׁלַיִם אֶת־יְהוָה הַלְלִי אֱלֹהַיִךְ צִיּוֹן׃

כִּי־חִזַּק בְּרִיחֵי שְׁעָרָיִךְ בֵּרַךְ בָּנַיִךְ בְּקִרְבֵּךְ׃

הַשָּׂם־גְּבוּלֵךְ שָׁלוֹם חֵלֶב חִטִּים יַשְׂבִּיעֵךְ׃

הַשֹּׁלֵחַ אִמְרָתוֹ אָרֶץ עַד־מְהֵרָה יָרוּץ דְּבָרוֹ׃

הַנֹּתֵן שֶׁלֶג כַּצָּמֶר כְּפוֹר כָּאֵפֶר יְפַזֵּר׃

מַשְׁלִיךְ קַרְחוֹ כְפִתִּים לִפְנֵי קָרָתוֹ מִי יַעֲמֹד׃

יִשְׁלַח דְּבָרוֹ וְיַמְסֵם יַשֵּׁב רוּחוֹ יִזְּלוּ־מָיִם׃

מַגִּיד דְּבָרָיו לְיַעֲקֹב חֻקָּיו וּמִשְׁפָּטָיו לְיִשְׂרָאֵל׃

לֹא עָשָׂה כֵן לְכָל־גּוֹי וּמִשְׁפָּטִים בַּל־יְדָעוּם

הַלְלוּ־יָהּ׃

He determines the number of the stars,
He gives them all their names.
Great is our Lord and mighty in power,
His wisdom cannot be measured.
The Lord raises the lowly,
He humbles the wicked to the dust.
Sing to the Lord with thanksgiving,
sing psalms to our God on the harp.

He covers the heavens with clouds,
He prepares rain for the earth.
He makes grass grow on the mountains.
He gives the beasts their food,
and young ravens who cry to be fed.
He does not delight in the horse's strength
nor in a soldier's speed.
The Lord delights in those who fear Him,
in those who wait on His love.

Glorify the Lord, Jerusalem!
Zion, praise your God!
He has strengthened the bars of your gates.
He has blessed your children within you.
He makes peace in your borders.
He fills you with the finest wheat.
He sends out His command on earth,
His word runs very swiftly.
He sends snow like wool,
He creates frost like ashes.
He hurls His ice like crumbs.
Who can stand before His cold?
He sends out His word and it melts them,
He makes the wind blow and the waters flow.

He declares His word to Jacob,
His laws and decrees to Israel.
He has not treated any other nation like this.
They have not known His judgments.

Praise the Lord!

קמח

הַלְלוּ־יָהּ

הַלְלוּ אֶת־יְהוָה מִן־הַשָּׁמַיִם הַלְלוּהוּ בַּמְּרוֹמִים:
הַלְלוּהוּ כָל־מַלְאָכָיו הַלְלוּהוּ כָּל־צְבָאָיו:

הַלְלוּהוּ שֶׁמֶשׁ וְיָרֵחַ הַלְלוּהוּ כָּל־כּוֹכְבֵי אוֹר:
הַלְלוּהוּ שְׁמֵי הַשָּׁמָיִם וְהַמַּיִם אֲשֶׁר מֵעַל הַשָּׁמָיִם:

יְהַלְלוּ אֶת־שֵׁם יְהוָה כִּי הוּא צִוָּה וְנִבְרָאוּ:
וַיַּעֲמִידֵם לָעַד לְעוֹלָם חָק־נָתַן וְלֹא יַעֲבוֹר:

הַלְלוּ אֶת־יְהוָה מִן־הָאָרֶץ תַּנִּינִים וְכָל־תְּהֹמוֹת:
אֵשׁ וּבָרָד שֶׁלֶג וְקִיטוֹר רוּחַ סְעָרָה עֹשָׂה דְבָרוֹ:

הֶהָרִים וְכָל־גְּבָעוֹת עֵץ פְּרִי וְכָל־אֲרָזִים:
הַחַיָּה וְכָל־בְּהֵמָה רֶמֶשׂ וְצִפּוֹר כָּנָף:

מַלְכֵי־אֶרֶץ וְכָל־לְאֻמִּים שָׂרִים וְכָל־שֹׁפְטֵי אָרֶץ:
בַּחוּרִים וְגַם־בְּתוּלוֹת זְקֵנִים עִם־נְעָרִים:

יְהַלְלוּ אֶת־שֵׁם יְהוָה כִּי־נִשְׂגָּב שְׁמוֹ לְבַדּוֹ
הוֹדוֹ עַל־אֶרֶץ וְשָׁמָיִם:
וַיָּרֶם קֶרֶן לְעַמּוֹ תְּהִלָּה לְכָל־חֲסִידָיו
לִבְנֵי יִשְׂרָאֵל עַם קְרֹבוֹ

הַלְלוּ־יָהּ:

148

Praise the Lord!

Praise the Lord from heaven,
  praise Him in the heights.
Praise Him all His messengers,
  praise Him all His hosts.

Praise Him, sun and moon,
  praise Him, shining stars.
Praise Him, heaven of heavens,
  and waters above the sky.

Let them praise the name of the Lord,
  for He commanded, and they were created.
He established them for ever and ever
  by unchangeable decree.

Praise the Lord from the earth,
  sea creatures and all the deeps,
fire and hail, snow and mist,
  stormy winds that fulfil His word.

Mountains and all hills,
  fruit trees and all cedars,
wild animals and all tame ones,
  reptiles and winged birds.

Earthly rulers and all peoples,
  princes and all judges of the world,
both boys and girls,
  old people together with the young.

Let them praise the name of the Lord
  for His name alone is supreme,
  His majesty beyond earth and heaven.
He restored the honour of His people,
  the praise of those who love Him,
  the children of Israel,
  a people so close to Him.

Praise the Lord!

קנ

הַלְלוּ־יָהּ

הַלְלוּ־אֵל בְּקָדְשׁוֹ הַלְלוּהוּ בִּרְקִיעַ עֻזּוֹ׃
הַלְלוּהוּ בִגְבוּרֹתָיו הַלְלוּהוּ כְּרֹב גֻּדְלוֹ׃

הַלְלוּהוּ בְּתֵקַע שׁוֹפָר הַלְלוּהוּ בְּנֵבֶל וְכִנּוֹר׃
הַלְלוּהוּ בְּתֹף וּמָחוֹל הַלְלוּהוּ בְּמִנִּים וְעֻגָב׃

הַלְלוּהוּ בְצִלְצְלֵי־שָׁמַע הַלְלוּהוּ בְּצִלְצְלֵי תְרוּעָה׃
כֹּל הַנְּשָׁמָה תְּהַלֵּל יָהּ הַלְלוּ־יָהּ׃

שִׁירַת־הַיָּם

אָז יָשִׁיר מֹשֶׁה וּבְנֵי יִשְׂרָאֵל אֶת־הַשִּׁירָה הַזֹּאת לַיהוָה וַיֹּאמְרוּ
לֵאמֹר אָשִׁירָה לַיהוָה כִּי־גָאֹה גָּאָה סוּס
וְרֹכְבוֹ רָמָה בַיָּם׃ עָזִּי וְזִמְרָת יָהּ וַיְהִי־לִי
לִישׁוּעָה זֶה אֵלִי וְאַנְוֵהוּ אֱלֹהֵי
אָבִי וַאֲרֹמְמֶנְהוּ׃ יְהוָה אִישׁ מִלְחָמָה יְהוָה
שְׁמוֹ׃ מַרְכְּבֹת פַּרְעֹה וְחֵילוֹ יָרָה בַיָּם וּמִבְחַר
שָׁלִשָׁיו טֻבְּעוּ בְיַם־סוּף׃ תְּהֹמֹת יְכַסְיֻמוּ יָרְדוּ בִמְצוֹלֹת כְּמוֹ־
אָבֶן׃ יְמִינְךָ יְהוָה נֶאְדָּרִי בַּכֹּחַ יְמִינְךָ
יְהוָה תִּרְעַץ אוֹיֵב׃ וּבְרֹב גְּאוֹנְךָ תַּהֲרֹס
קָמֶיךָ תְּשַׁלַּח חֲרֹנְךָ יֹאכְלֵמוֹ כַּקַּשׁ׃ וּבְרוּחַ
אַפֶּיךָ נֶעֶרְמוּ־מַיִם נִצְּבוּ כְמוֹ־נֵד
נֹזְלִים קָפְאוּ תְהֹמֹת בְּלֶב־יָם׃ אָמַר

150

Praise the Lord!

Praise God in His holy place.
  Praise Him in His mighty heavens.
Praise Him for His powerful deeds.
  Praise Him for His surpassing greatness.

Praise Him with the *shofar* blast.
  Praise Him with the lyre and harp.
Praise Him with drums and dancing.
  Praise Him with the lute and pipe.

Praise Him with the clash of cymbals.
  Praise Him with the clanging cymbals.
Let everything that has breath
  praise the Lord.

Praise the Lord!

THE SONG AT THE SEA

Then sang Moses and the children of Israel this song to the Lord:

I will sing to the Lord for He has risen in triumph,
  horse and rider He hurled into the sea.
The Lord is my strength and song
  and He has become my salvation.
This is my God, I will praise Him,
  my father's God, I will exalt Him.
The Lord is a man of war,
  the Lord is His name.

Pharaoh's chariots and army He cast into the sea,
  the pick of his officers are sunk in the Red sea.
The depths cover them,
  they went down to the bottom like a stone.
Your right hand, O Lord, is majestic in power,
  Your right hand, O Lord, shatters the enemy.
In the fullness of Your triumph You throw down Your foes.
  You unleashed Your anger, it consumed them like chaff.
A blast of Your nostrils and the waters piled high,
  the waves stood up like a wall,
    in the heart of the sea the deeps congealed.

אוֹיֵב אֶרְדֹּף אַשִּׂיג אֲחַלֵּק שָׁלָל תִּמְלָאֵמוֹ

נַפְשִׁי אָרִיק חַרְבִּי תּוֹרִישֵׁמוֹ יָדִי: נָשַׁפְתָּ

בְרוּחֲךָ כִּסָּמוֹ יָם צָלֲלוּ כַּעוֹפֶרֶת בְּמַיִם

אַדִּירִים: מִי־כָמֹכָה בָּאֵלִם יְהֹוָה מִי

כָּמֹכָה נֶאְדָּר בַּקֹּדֶשׁ נוֹרָא תְהִלֹּת עֹשֵׂה־

פֶלֶא: נָטִיתָ יְמִינְךָ תִּבְלָעֵמוֹ אָרֶץ: נָחִיתָ

בְחַסְדְּךָ עַם־זוּ גָּאָלְתָּ נֵהַלְתָּ בְעָזְּךָ אֶל־נְוֵה

קָדְשֶׁךָ: שָׁמְעוּ עַמִּים יִרְגָּזוּן חִיל

אָחַז יֹשְׁבֵי פְּלָשֶׁת: אָז נִבְהֲלוּ אַלּוּפֵי

אֱדוֹם אֵילֵי מוֹאָב יֹאחֲזֵמוֹ רָעַד נָמֹגוּ

כֹּל יֹשְׁבֵי כְנָעַן: תִּפֹּל עֲלֵיהֶם אֵימָתָה

וָפַחַד בִּגְדֹל זְרוֹעֲךָ יִדְּמוּ כָּאָבֶן עַד־

יַעֲבֹר עַמְּךָ יְהֹוָה עַד־יַעֲבֹר עַם־זוּ

קָנִיתָ: תְּבִאֵמוֹ וְתִטָּעֵמוֹ בְּהַר נַחֲלָתְךָ מָכוֹן

לְשִׁבְתְּךָ פָּעַלְתָּ יְהֹוָה מִקְּדָשׁ אֲדֹנָי כּוֹנֲנוּ

יָדֶיךָ: יְהֹוָה יִמְלֹךְ לְעֹלָם וָעֶד:

Bradford Synagogue

The enemy said: "I will chase – overtake!
  Divide the spoil!
  Devour my fill!
  Draw my sword!
  My hand destroy them!"
One puff of Your breath and the waters covered them,
  they sank like lead in the terrible waters.
Who is like You, Lord, among the gods men worship?
  Who, like You, is majestic in holiness,
  awesome in praise, working wonders?

You stretched out Your right hand, the earth swallowed them.
  You led with constant love Your ransomed people.
  You guided them with Your strength to Your holy place of rest.
Peoples hear and tremble!
  Tremors grip the dwellers in Philistia.
Edom's chieftains are now dismayed.
  Shuddering grips Moab's leaders.
All dwellers in Canaan are in turmoil.
  Dread and terror fall upon them.
Through the power of Your arm they are still as stone,
  until Your people pass over, O Lord,
  till the people You have gained pass over.
You will bring them and plant them on the mountain that is Your own,
  the place You have made Your dwelling, Lord,
  the sanctuary, Lord, prepared by Your own hands.

The Lord alone shall rule forever and ever.

Exodus 15: 1–18

Bernard Baron St. George's Settlement

He whose voice is bad and unpleasant, and who cannot perform hymns and songs according to their tunes and who cannot remember melodies, even to a man like him it is allotted to raise his voice.

Menachem de Lonzano

SONG ANTHOLOGY

The Westminster Synagogue

SONGS FOR THE SABBATH

מְנוּחָה וְשִׂמְחָה

מְנוּחָה וְשִׂמְחָה אוֹר לַיְּהוּדִים · יוֹם שַׁבָּתוֹן יוֹם מַחֲמַדִּים :
שׁוֹמְרָיו וְזוֹכְרָיו הֵמָּה מְעִידִים · כִּי לְשִׁשָּׁה כֹּל בְּרוּאִים
וְעוֹמְדִים :

הוּא אֲשֶׁר דִּבֶּר לְעַם סְגֻלָּתוֹ · שָׁמוֹר לְקַדְּשׁוֹ מִבּוֹאוֹ וְעַד־
צֵאתוֹ ·

שַׁבַּת קֹדֶשׁ יוֹם חֶמְדָּתוֹ · כִּי שָׁבַת אֵל מִכָּל־מְלַאכְתּוֹ :

בְּמִשְׁנֶה לֶחֶם וְקִדּוּשׁ רַבָּה בְּרֹב מַטְעַמִּים וְרוּחַ נְדִיבָה ·
יִזְכּוּ לְרַב טוּב הַמִּתְעַנְּגִים בָּהּ · בְּבִיאַת גּוֹאֵל לְחַיֵּי הָעוֹלָם
הַבָּא :

לְכָה דוֹדִי

לְכָה דוֹדִי לִקְרַאת כַּלָּה · פְּנֵי שַׁבָּת נְקַבְּלָה :

שָׁמוֹר וְזָכוֹר בְּדִבּוּר אֶחָד · הִשְׁמִיעָנוּ אֵל הַמְיֻחָד ·
יְיָ אֶחָד וּשְׁמוֹ אֶחָד · לְשֵׁם וּלְתִפְאֶרֶת וְלִתְהִלָּה :
לְכָה דוֹדִי · · ·

לִקְרַאת שַׁבָּת לְכוּ וְנֵלְכָה · כִּי הִיא מְקוֹר הַבְּרָכָה ·
מֵרֹאשׁ מִקֶּדֶם נְסוּכָה · סוֹף מַעֲשֶׂה בְּמַחֲשָׁבָה תְּחִלָּה :
לְכָה דוֹדִי · · ·

SONGS FOR THE SABBATH

SABBATH EVE

Menuchah V'simchah

Rest and joy, a light for the Jews,
the Sabbath day is a day of delight.
Those who keep and remember it bear witness
that in six days all was created.

God proclaimed to His treasured people
to keep holy from sunset to sunset
the holy Sabbath in which He delighted,
for He rested from all His work.

With twin loaves of bread and kiddush wine,
plenteous food and a generous spirit,
those who delight in it usher in the goodness
when the redeemer will bring life evermore.

L'chah Dodi

Come, my friend, to greet the bride,
to welcome in the Sabbath eve.·

'Observe!', 'Remember!'—one command,
God made us hear a single phrase.
For He is one, His name is one,
in fame, in glory and in praise.

Come, my friend, to greet the bride,
to welcome in the Sabbath eve.

To greet the Sabbath let us join,
for from her endless blessings pour.
First of all creation willed,
the final act, thought long before.

Come, my friend, to greet the bride,
to welcome in the Sabbath eve.

מִקְדַּשׁ מֶלֶךְ עִיר מְלוּכָה · קוּמִי צְאִי מִתּוֹךְ הַהֲפֵכָה ·
רַב לָךְ שֶׁבֶת בְּעֵמֶק הַבָּכָא · וְהוּא יַחֲמֹל עָלַיִךְ חֶמְלָה :
לְכָה דוֹדִי · · ·

הִתְנַעֲרִי מֵעָפָר קוּמִי · לִבְשִׁי בִּגְדֵי תִפְאַרְתֵּךְ עַמִּי ·
עַל־יַד בֶּן־יִשַׁי בֵּית הַלַּחְמִי · קָרְבָה אֶל נַפְשִׁי גְאָלָהּ :
לְכָה דוֹדִי · · ·

הִתְעוֹרֲרִי הִתְעוֹרֲרִי · כִּי בָא אוֹרֵךְ קוּמִי אוֹרִי ·
עוּרִי עוּרִי שִׁיר דַּבֵּרִי · כְּבוֹד יְיָ עָלַיִךְ נִגְלָה :
לְכָה דוֹדִי · · ·

לֹא תֵבוֹשִׁי וְלֹא תִכָּלְמִי · מַה־תִּשְׁתּוֹחֲחִי וּמַה־תֶּהֱמִי ·
בָּךְ יֶחֱסוּ עֲנִיֵּי עַמִּי · וְנִבְנְתָה עִיר עַל־תִּלָּהּ :
לְכָה דוֹדִי · · ·

וְהָיוּ לִמְשִׁסָּה שֹׁאסָיִךְ · וְרָחֲקוּ כָּל־מְבַלְּעָיִךְ ·
יָשִׂישׂ עָלַיִךְ אֱלֹהָיִךְ · כִּמְשׂוֹשׂ חָתָן עַל כַּלָּה :
לְכָה דוֹדִי · · ·

יָמִין וּשְׂמֹאל תִּפְרוֹצִי · וְאֶת־יְיָ תַּעֲרִיצִי ·
עַל יַד אִישׁ בֶּן־פַּרְצִי · וְנִשְׂמְחָה וְנָגִילָה :
לְכָה דוֹדִי · · ·

You royal city, holy place,
rise from the ground where you have lain;
no more a valley washed by tears,
for He shall comfort you again.
   Come, my friend, to greet the bride,
   to welcome in the Sabbath eve.

Shake off the dust as you arise,
my people, don your finest dress!
Through Jesse's son, of Bethlehem,
release my soul from its distress.
   Come, my friend, to greet the bride,
   to welcome in the Sabbath eve.

Arouse yourself, arouse yourself,
your light is come, arise and shine!
Awake, awake and pour out song,
God's glory greets us at this time.
   Come, my friend, to greet the bride,
   to welcome in the Sabbath eve.

No more despised nor put to shame,
why are you bowed, why so cast down?
My humbled people wait for you,
rebuilt upon your ancient ground.
   Come, my friend, to greet the bride,
   to welcome in the Sabbath eve.

Those who would spoil you shall be spoil.
Your foes will scatter far and wide.
And God will share with you His joy
as does the bridegroom with the bride.
   Come, my friend, to greet the bride,
   to welcome in the Sabbath eve.

You shall spread out right and left
and worship there the Lord alone;
through one born out of Perez' seed,
with joy such as was never known.
   Come, my friend, to greet the bride,
   to welcome in the Sabbath eve.

בּוֹאִי בְשָׁלוֹם עֲטֶרֶת בַּעֲלָה · גַּם בְּשִׂמְחָה וּבְצָהֳלָה ·
תּוֹךְ אֱמוּנֵי עַם סְגֻלָּה · בּוֹאִי כַלָּה בּוֹאִי כַלָּה:
לְכָה דוֹדִי · · ·

מִפִּי אֵל

אֵין אַדִּיר כַּאדֹנָי וְאֵין בָּרוּךְ כְּבֶן עַמְרָם
אֵין גְּדוֹלָה כַּתּוֹרָה וְאֵין דּוֹרְשֶׁיהָ כְּיִשְׂרָאֵל:
מִפִּי אֵל · מִפִּי אֵל יְבֹרַךְ כָּל־יִשְׂרָאֵל:

אֵין הָדוּר כַּאדֹנָי וְאֵין וָתִיק כְּבֶן עַמְרָם
אֵין זַכָּה כַּתּוֹרָה וְאֵין חֲכָמֶיהָ כְּיִשְׂרָאֵל:
מִפִּי אֵל · · ·

אֵין טָהוֹר כַּאדֹנָי וְאֵין יָחִיד כְּבֶן עַמְרָם
אֵין כַּבִּירָה כַּתּוֹרָה וְאֵין לוֹמְדֶיהָ כְּיִשְׂרָאֵל:
מִפִּי אֵל · · ·

אֵין מֶלֶךְ כַּאדֹנָי וְאֵין נָבִיא כְּבֶן עַמְרָם
אֵין סְגוּלָה כַּתּוֹרָה וְאֵין עוֹסְקֶיהָ כְּיִשְׂרָאֵל:
מִפִּי אֵל · · ·

אֵין פּוֹדֶה כַּאדֹנָי וְאֵין צַדִּיק כְּבֶן עַמְרָם
אֵין קְדוֹשָׁה כַּתּוֹרָה וְאֵין רוֹמְמֶיהָ כְּיִשְׂרָאֵל:
מִפִּי אֵל · · ·

Come in peace and come in joy,
God, your husband; you, His pride;
among the faithful chosen people,
come my bride, come my bride!

Come, my friend, to greet the bride,
to welcome in the Sabbath eve.

Alkabetz

Mipi El

None so mighty as our Lord
and none so blessed as Amram's son;
nothing noble like Torah;
none seek its ways like Israel.

From the mouth of God,
from the mouth of God blessing for all Israel.

None so splendid as our Lord
and none esteemed like Amram's son;
nothing faultless like Torah;
none know its ways like Israel.

From the mouth of God . . .

None so perfect as our Lord
and none unique like Amram's son;
nothing awesome like Torah;
none learn its ways like Israel.

From the mouth of God . . .

None so regal as our Lord;
none prophesied like Amram's son;
nothing treasured like Torah;
none use its ways like Israel.

From the mouth of God . . .

None redeems us as our Lord
and none is just like Amram's son;
nothing holy like Torah;
none praise its ways like Israel.

From the mouth of God . . .

אֵין קָדוֹשׁ כַּאדֹנָי וְאֵין רַבִּי כְּבֶן עַמְרָם
אֵין שְׁמִירָה כַּתּוֹרָה וְאֵין תּוֹמְכֶיהָ כְּיִשְׂרָאֵל:
מִפִּי אֵל ···

צָמְאָה נַפְשִׁי

צָמְאָה נַפְשִׁי לֵאלֹהִים לְאֵל חָי ·
לִבִּי וּבְשָׂרִי יְרַנְּנוּ לְאֵל חָי:
אֵל אֶחָד בְּרָאָנִי · וְאָמַר חַי אָנִי ·
כִּי לֹא יִרְאָנִי · הָאָדָם וָחָי:
לִבִּי וּבְשָׂרִי יְרַנְּנוּ לְאֵל חָי:

בָּרָא כֹל בְּחָכְמָה · בְּעֵצָה וּבִמְזִמָּה ·
מְאֹד נֶעְלָמָה · מֵעֵינֵי כָל־חָי ·
לִבִּי וּבְשָׂרִי יְרַנְּנוּ לְאֵל חָי:

מִי זֶה יִצְטַדָּק · נִמְשַׁל לְאָבָק דָּק ·
אֱמֶת כִּי לֹא יִצְדַּק · לְפָנֶיךָ כָל־חָי:
לִבִּי וּבְשָׂרִי יְרַנְּנוּ לְאֵל חָי:

עַל כֹּל אֲהוֹדֶךָ · כָּל פֶּה תְּיַחֲדֶךָ ·
פּוֹתֵחַ אֶת־יָדֶךָ · וּמַשְׂבִּיעַ לְכָל־חָי:
לִבִּי וּבְשָׂרִי יְרַנְּנוּ לְאֵל חָי:

בָּרוּךְ אֲדֹנָי יוֹם יוֹם

בָּרוּךְ אֲדֹנָי יוֹם יוֹם ·
יַעֲמָס־לָנוּ יֶשַׁע וּפִדְיוֹם ·
וּבִשְׁמוֹ נָגִיל כָּל־הַיּוֹם ·
וּבִישׁוּעָתוֹ נָרִים רֹאשׁ עֶלְיוֹן ·
כִּי הוּא מָעוֹז לַדָּל וּמַחְסֶה לָאֶבְיוֹן:

None so holy as our Lord
and none can teach like Amram's son;
nothing shelters like Torah;
none keep its ways like Israel.

From the mouth of God . . .

Tsam'ah Nafshi

My soul thirsts for God, the living God.
My heart and flesh sing praise to the God ever living.
Our creator is One, He who said: 'As I live,
none can behold Me and remain among the living.'
    My heart and flesh sing praise to the God ever living.

All is made by His plan, by His wisdom and thought,
deeply hidden from the eyes of all living.
    My heart and flesh sing praise to the God ever living.

How can man who is likened to dust plead his cause?
Truly none can be just in the world of the living.
    My heart and flesh sing praise to the God ever living.

I thank and praise You, together with all who acclaim You,
for Your hand is ever open to satisfy all living.
    My heart and flesh sing praise to the God ever living.

Abraham Ibn Ezra

SABBATH NOON

Baruch Adonai Yom Yom

Blessed be the Lord who every day
sets on us salvation and redemption.
In His glorious name we delight at all times;
through His salvation we hold our head high.
A stronghold is He for the poor, for the needy a refuge.

בָּרוּךְ הוּא אֱלֹהֵינוּ שֶׁבְּרָאָנוּ לִכְבוֹדוֹ ·
לְהַלְלוֹ וּלְשַׁבְּחוֹ וּלְסַפֵּר הוֹדוֹ ·
מִכָּל־אֹם גָּבַר עָלֵינוּ חַסְדוֹ ·
לָכֵן בְּכָל־לֵב וּבְכָל־נֶפֶשׁ וּבְכָל־מְאֹד
נַמְלִיכוֹ וּנְיַחֲדוֹ :

שֶׁהַשָּׁלוֹם שֶׁלּוֹ יָשִׂים עָלֵינוּ בְּרָכָה וְשָׁלוֹם ·
מִשְּׂמֹאל וּמִיָּמִין עַל יִשְׂרָאֵל שָׁלוֹם ·
הָרַחֲמָן הוּא יְבָרֵךְ אֶת־עַמּוֹ בַשָּׁלוֹם ·
וְיִזְכּוּ לִרְאוֹת בָּנִים וּבְנֵי בָנִים
עוֹסְקִים בַּתּוֹרָה וּבְמִצְוֹת :
עַל יִשְׂרָאֵל שָׁלוֹם · פֶּלֶא יוֹעֵץ
אֵל גִּבּוֹר אֲבִי־עַד שַׂר־שָׁלוֹם :

יוֹם זֶה מְכֻבָּד

יוֹם זֶה מְכֻבָּד מִכָּל יָמִים ·
כִּי בוֹ שָׁבַת צוּר עוֹלָמִים :

שֵׁשֶׁת יָמִים תַּעֲשֶׂה מְלַאכְתֶּךְ
וְיוֹם הַשְּׁבִיעִי לֵאלֹהֶיךָ :
שַׁבָּת לֹא תַעֲשֶׂה בוֹ מְלָאכָה ·
כִּי כֹל עָשָׂה שֵׁשֶׁת יָמִים :
יוֹם זֶה מְכֻבָּד · · ·

רִאשׁוֹן הוּא לְמִקְרָאֵי קֹדֶשׁ ·
יוֹם שַׁבָּתוֹן יוֹם שַׁבַּת קֹדֶשׁ :
עַל־כֵּן כָּל־אִישׁ בְּיֵינוֹ יְקַדֵּשׁ ·
עַל־שְׁתֵּי־לֶחֶם יִבְצְעוּ תְמִימִים :
יוֹם זֶה מְכֻבָּד · · ·

Blessed be our God who for His glory created us
to praise and exalt Him and declare His majesty.
He has shown us above others His grace and His kindness.
So with all our heart, soul and might
we proclaim Him the king in His unity.

May He, source of peace, give us blessing and peace.
From all sides may peace come unto Israel.
All-merciful, bless Your people with peace,
that they may see their children, and their children's children,
busy with Torah, fulfilling its commands.
May Israel know peace from Him who is 'wonderful in counsel,
God the mighty, the eternal father, prince of peace'.

Simon bar Isaac bar Abun

Yom Zeh Mechubad

More than all other days the Sabbath is blessed;
for the Rock of all time made it His day of rest.

For completing your work He has given six days;
but the seventh belongs to your God.
On that day no work should be done,
for in six days He completed the work of creation.
　　More than all other days the Sabbath is blessed;
　　for the Rock of all time made it His day of rest.

The Sabbath is the first of all the year's holy days,
a day of pure rest, a day for holiness.
So each man should say *kiddush* upon the wine
and recite the blessing on the two loaves of bread.
　　More than all other days the Sabbath is blessed;
　　for the Rock of all time made it His day of rest.

הַשָּׁמַיִם מְסַפְּרִים כְּבוֹדוֹ ·
וְגַם־הָאָרֶץ מָלְאָה חַסְדוֹ ·
רְאוּ כִּי כָל־אֵלֶּה עָשְׂתָה יָדוֹ ·
כִּי הוּא הַצּוּר פָּעֳלוֹ תָמִים :
יוֹם זֶה מְכֻבָּד · · ·

אֵל אָדוֹן

אֵל אָדוֹן עַל כָּל־הַמַּעֲשִׂים ·
בָּרוּךְ וּמְבֹרָךְ בְּפִי כָּל־נְשָׁמָה ·
גָּדְלוֹ וְטוּבוֹ מָלֵא עוֹלָם ·
דַּעַת וּתְבוּנָה סוֹבְבִים אוֹתוֹ :
הַמִּתְגָּאֶה עַל חַיּוֹת הַקֹּדֶשׁ ·
וְנֶהְדָּר בְּכָבוֹד עַל הַמֶּרְכָּבָה ·
זְכוּת וּמִישׁוֹר לִפְנֵי כִסְאוֹ ·
חֶסֶד וְרַחֲמִים לִפְנֵי כְבוֹדוֹ :
טוֹבִים מְאוֹרוֹת שֶׁבָּרָא אֱלֹהֵינוּ ·
יְצָרָם בְּדַעַת בְּבִינָה וּבְהַשְׂכֵּל ·
כֹּחַ וּגְבוּרָה נָתַן בָּהֶם ·
לִהְיוֹת מוֹשְׁלִים בְּקֶרֶב תֵּבֵל :
מְלֵאִים זִיו וּמְפִיקִים נֹגַהּ ·
נָאֶה זִיוָם בְּכָל־הָעוֹלָם ·
שְׂמֵחִים בְּצֵאתָם וְשָׂשִׂים בְּבוֹאָם ·
עוֹשִׂים בְּאֵימָה רְצוֹן קוֹנָם :
פְּאֵר וְכָבוֹד נוֹתְנִים לִשְׁמוֹ ·
צָהֳלָה וְרִנָּה לְזֵכֶר מַלְכוּתוֹ ·
קָרָא לַשֶּׁמֶשׁ וַיִּזְרַח אוֹר ·
רָאָה וְהִתְקִין צוּרַת הַלְּבָנָה :
שֶׁבַח נוֹתְנִים לוֹ כָּל־צְבָא מָרוֹם ·
תִּפְאֶרֶת וּגְדֻלָּה שְׂרָפִים וְאוֹפַנִּים וְחַיּוֹת הַקֹּדֶשׁ :

The heavens tell of His glory,
the earth is full of His loving care.
See how all these things are the work of His hands,
for He is the Rock and His way is perfect.
  More than all other days the Sabbath is blessed;
  for the Rock of all time made it His day of rest.

Israel Najara

El Adon

God, the Lord of all creation,
blessed is He by all that draws breath.
His greatness and goodness fill the universe,
knowledge and wisdom surround Him.
Holy is He above all the forces of life,
glorious beyond every mystic vision.
Purity and integrity stand before His throne,
love and mercy in the presence of His glory.
Splendid are the lights created by our God,
fashioned with knowledge, wisdom and reason.
Strength and power He set within them
to govern in the world of man.
Full of radiance, glowing with light,
their beauty transforms the world.
They rejoice in their rising, are glad in their setting,
fulfilling in awe the will of their maker.
Honour and glory they bring to His name,
with joy and exultation acclaim His rule.
He called to the sun and it sent out light.
He looked and fashioned the cycle of the moon.
All hosts on high sing praise to Him.
Worlds unseen give Him glory and greatness.

יוֹם שַׁבָּתוֹן

יוֹם שַׁבָּתוֹן אֵין לִשְׁכּוֹחַ ·
זִכְרוֹ כְּרֵיחַ הַנִּיחוֹחַ ·
יוֹנָה מָצְאָה בוֹ מָנוֹחַ ·
וְשָׁם יָנוּחוּ יְגִיעֵי כֹחַ :

וּבָאוּ כֻלָּם בִּבְרִית יַחַד ·
נַעֲשֶׂה וְנִשְׁמַע אָמְרוּ כְּאֶחָד ·
וּפָתְחוּ וְעָנוּ יְיָ אֶחָד ·
בָּרוּךְ הַנּוֹתֵן לַיָּעֵף כֹּחַ :
יוֹנָה מָצְאָה · · ·

הָעָם אֲשֶׁר נָע כַּצֹּאן תָּעָה ·
יִזְכּוֹר לְפָקְדוֹ בְּרִית וּשְׁבוּעָה ·
לְבַל יַעֲבָר־בָּם מִקְרֶה רָעָה ·
כַּאֲשֶׁר נִשְׁבַּעְתָּ עַל מֵי נֹחַ :
יוֹנָה מָצְאָה · · ·

דְּרוֹר יִקְרָא

דְּרוֹר יִקְרָא לְבֵן עִם בַּת ·
וְיִנְצָרְכֶם כְּמוֹ בָבַת ·
נְעִים שִׁמְכֶם וְלֹא יֻשְׁבַּת ·
שְׁבוּ וְנוּחוּ בְּיוֹם שַׁבָּת :

דְּעֵה חָכְמָה לְנַפְשֶׁךָ ·
וְהִיא כֶתֶר לְרֹאשֶׁךָ ·
נְצוֹר מִצְוַת קְדוֹשֶׁךָ ·
שְׁמוֹר שַׁבָּת קָדְשֶׁךָ :

Yom Shabbaton

Let the Sabbath day never be forgotten,
but remembered as a taste of eternal peace.
  Just as Noah's dove found its rest on this day,
  let all who are weary be refreshed.

At Mount Sinai the covenant was affirmed,
when they said with one voice: 'Let us do and obey.'
For the Lord is our God, the Lord is One,
blessed is He who gives rest to the weary.
  Just as Noah's dove found its rest on this day,
  let all who are weary be refreshed.

This people has journeyed like a wandering flock.
Remember the covenant and the promise You gave
that no evil should ever befall them,
just as You promised Noah that the flood would come no more.
  Just as Noah's dove found its rest on this day,
  let all who are weary be refreshed.

Judah Halevi

D'ror Yikra

He declares freedom to boy and girl
and guards you like the apple of His eye.
Your name is pleasant and will never be destroyed.
Sit down and rest on the Sabbath day.

Know what is wisdom for your soul,
what is a crown for your head:
to guard the command of your Holy One,
to keep your holy Sabbath.

Dunash ben Labrat

כִּי אֶשְׁמְרָה שַׁבָּת

כִּי אֶשְׁמְרָה שַׁבָּת אֵל יִשְׁמְרֵנִי · אוֹת הִיא לְעוֹלְמֵי עַד · בֵּינוֹ
וּבֵינִי :

אָסוּר מְצֹא חֵפֶץ מֵעֲשׂוֹת דְּרָכִים · גַּם מִלְּדַבֵּר בּוֹ דִּבְרֵי
צְרָכִים · דִּבְרֵי סְחוֹרָה אַף דִּבְרֵי מְלָכִים · אֶהְגֶּה בְּתוֹרַת
אֵל וּתְחַכְּמֵנִי :

כִּי אֶשְׁמְרָה שַׁבָּת · · ·

הוּא יוֹם מְכֻבָּד הוּא יוֹם תַּעֲנוּגִים · לֶחֶם וְיַיִן טוֹב בָּשָׂר
וְדָגִים · מִתְאַבְּלִים בּוֹ הֵם אָחוֹר נְסוֹגִים · כִּי יוֹם שְׂמָחוֹת
הוּא וִישַׂמְּחֵנִי :

כִּי אֶשְׁמְרָה שַׁבָּת · · ·

יִשְׂמְחוּ בְּמַלְכוּתְךָ

יִשְׂמְחוּ בְמַלְכוּתְךָ שֹׁמְרֵי שַׁבָּת וְקוֹרְאֵי עֹנֶג · עַם מְקַדְּשֵׁי
שְׁבִיעִי · כֻּלָּם יִשְׂבְּעוּ וְיִתְעַנְּגוּ מִטּוּבֶךָ · וְהַשְּׁבִיעִי רָצִיתָ בּוֹ
וְקִדַּשְׁתּוֹ · חֶמְדַּת יָמִים אוֹתוֹ קָרָאתָ זֵכֶר לְמַעֲשֵׂה בְרֵאשִׁית :

יְדִיד נֶפֶשׁ

יְדִיד נֶפֶשׁ אָב הָרַחֲמָן מְשֹׁךְ עַבְדְּךָ אֶל רְצוֹנָךְ ·
יָרוּץ עַבְדְּךָ כְּמוֹ אַיָּל יִשְׁתַּחֲוֶה אֶל מוּל הֲדָרְךָ ·
יֶעֱרַב לוֹ יְדִידוֹתֶיךָ מִנֹּפֶת צוּף וְכָל־טָעַם :

Ki Eshmerah Shabbat

If I keep the Sabbath, God will keep me
for it is an eternal sign between Him and me.

Forbidden are business and practical tasks
even speaking of the things we need,
or of matters of money and matters of state;
let me study Torah and grow wise.
If I keep the Sabbath, God will keep me
for it is an eternal sign between Him and me.

A day to be honoured, a day for gladness,
bread and wine, the best of all food.
Even the saddest find their mood is changed
for this day is for joy and makes me rejoice.
If I keep the Sabbath, God will keep me
for it is an eternal sign between Him and me.

Abraham Ibn Ezra

Yismechu B'malchut'chah

May all who keep the Sabbath and call it a delight rejoice in Your
rule. May all the people who make it holy find serenity and delight in
Your goodness. For You Yourself desired the seventh day and made
it holy, proclaiming it the most precious of days, recalling the work
of creation.

Siddur

SONGS FOR THE THIRD MEAL—SE'UDAH SHELISHIT

Psalm 23   page 430

Yedid Nefesh

Beloved of the soul, merciful father,
    draw Your servant unto Your will,
that swift as a hart he may run
    to prostrate himself before Your majesty,
finding Your love sweeter than the honeycomb
    and every tempting savour.

הָדוּר נָאֶה זִיו הָעוֹלָם נַפְשִׁי חוֹלַת אַהֲבָתְךָ ·

אָנָּא אֵל נָא רְפָא נָא לָהּ בְּהֵרָאוֹת לָהּ נֹעַם זִיוְךָ ·

אָז תִּתְחַזֵּק וְתִתְרַפֵּא וְהָיְתָה לָהּ שִׂמְחַת עוֹלָם :

וָתִיק יֶהֱמוּ נָא רַחֲמֶיךָ וְחוּסָה נָא עַל בֵּן אֲהוּבְךָ ·

כִּי זֶה כַּמָּה נִכְסֹף נִכְסַפְתִּי לִרְאוֹת בְּתִפְאֶרֶת עֻזְּךָ ·

אֵלֶּה חָמְדָה לִבִּי וְחוּסָה נָא וְאַל תִּתְעַלֵּם :

הִגָּלֶה נָא וּפְרוֹס חֲבִיבִי עָלַי אֶת־סֻכַּת שְׁלוֹמֶךָ ·

תָּאִיר אֶרֶץ מִכְּבוֹדֶךָ נָגִילָה וְנִשְׂמְחָה בָּךְ ·

מַהֵר אֱהוֹב כִּי בָא מוֹעֵד וְחָנֵּנוּ כִּימֵי עוֹלָם :

אַל־תִּירָא עַבְדִּי יַעֲקֹב

אָמַר יְיָ לְיַעֲקֹב ·	אַל־תִּירָא עַבְדִּי יַעֲקֹב :
בָּחַר יְיָ בְּיַעֲקֹב ·	אַל־תִּירָא עַבְדִּי יַעֲקֹב :
גָּאַל יְיָ אֶת־יַעֲקֹב ·	אַל־תִּירָא עַבְדִּי יַעֲקֹב :
דָּרַךְ כּוֹכָב מִיַּעֲקֹב ·	אַל־תִּירָא עַבְדִּי יַעֲקֹב :
הַבָּאִים יַשְׁרֵשׁ יַעֲקֹב ·	אַל־תִּירָא עַבְדִּי יַעֲקֹב :
וְיֵרְדְ מִיַּעֲקֹב ·	אַל־תִּירָא עַבְדִּי יַעֲקֹב :
זְכָר־אֵלֶּה לְיַעֲקֹב ·	אַל־תִּירָא עַבְדִּי יַעֲקֹב :
חֶדְוַת יְשׁוּעוֹת יַעֲקֹב ·	אַל־תִּירָא עַבְדִּי יַעֲקֹב :
טֹבוּ אֹהָלֶיךָ יַעֲקֹב ·	אַל־תִּירָא עַבְדִּי יַעֲקֹב :

Exquisitely beautiful is the splendour of the world.
My soul pines for Your love.
O God, heal it, I pray You, by showing unto it
the delight of Your splendour,
then will it grow strong and be healed
and rejoice evermore.

O mighty One! manifest Your mercies
and have compassion upon Your beloved son.
For oh how long have I been consumed with longing
to behold the triumph of Your might!
These things my heart desires;
take pity and hide not Yourself.

Reveal Yourself, O adored One, and spread
over me the tent of Your peace.
May the earth be illumined with Your glory
and let us be glad and rejoice in You.
Hasten to show Your love; and be gracious
unto us as in the days of yore.

Eliezer Azkari

CONCLUSION OF THE SABBATH

Al Tirah, Avdi Ya'akov

The Lord has said to the house of Jacob	Fear not, My servant Jacob
The Lord has chosen Jacob	Fear not, My servant Jacob
The Lord has redeemed Jacob	Fear not, My servant Jacob
There has stepped forth a star from Jacob	Fear not, My servant Jacob
In days to come rooted will be Jacob	Fear not, My servant Jacob
Dominion shall be exercised by Jacob	Fear not, My servant Jacob
Remember these things, O Jacob	Fear not, My servant Jacob
There will be joy in the redemption of Jacob	Fear not, My servant Jacob
Goodly are your tents, O Jacob	Fear not, My servant Jacob

אַל־תִּירָא עַבְדִּי יַעֲקֹב: יוֹרוּ מִשְׁפָּטֶיךָ לְיַעֲקֹב ·

אַל־תִּירָא עַבְדִּי יַעֲקֹב: כִּי לֹא נַחַשׁ בְּיַעֲקֹב ·

אַל־תִּירָא עַבְדִּי יַעֲקֹב: לֹא־הִבִּיט אָוֶן בְּיַעֲקֹב ·

אַל־תִּירָא עַבְדִּי יַעֲקֹב: מִי מָנָה עֲפַר יַעֲקֹב ·

אַל־תִּירָא עַבְדִּי יַעֲקֹב: נִשְׁבַּע יְיָ לְיַעֲקֹב ·

אַל־תִּירָא עַבְדִּי יַעֲקֹב: סְלַח־נָא לַעֲוֹן יַעֲקֹב ·

אַל־תִּירָא עַבְדִּי יַעֲקֹב: עַתָּה הָשֵׁב שְׁבוּת יַעֲקֹב ·

אַל־תִּירָא עַבְדִּי יַעֲקֹב: פָּדָה יְיָ אֶת־יַעֲקֹב ·

אַל־תִּירָא עַבְדִּי יַעֲקֹב: צַוֵּה יְשׁוּעוֹת יַעֲקֹב ·

אַל־תִּירָא עַבְדִּי יַעֲקֹב: קוֹל קוֹל יַעֲקֹב ·

אַל־תִּירָא עַבְדִּי יַעֲקֹב: רָנּוּ שִׂמְחָה לְיַעֲקֹב ·

אַל־תִּירָא עַבְדִּי יַעֲקֹב: שָׁב יְיָ אֶת־גְּאוֹן יַעֲקֹב ·

אַל־תִּירָא עַבְדִּי יַעֲקֹב: תִּתֵּן אֱמֶת לְיַעֲקֹב ·

SONGS FOR CHANUKAH

מִי יְמַלֵּל

מִי יְמַלֵּל גְּבוּרוֹת יִשְׂרָאֵל אוֹתָן מִי יִמְנֶה

הֵן בְּכָל־דּוֹר יָקוּם הַגִּבּוֹר גּוֹאֵל הָעָם:

שְׁמַע · בַּיָּמִים הָהֵם בַּזְּמַן הַזֶּה מַכַּבִּי מוֹשִׁיעַ וּפוֹדֶה:

וּבְיָמֵינוּ כָּל־עַם יִשְׂרָאֵל יִתְאַחֵד יָקוּם לְהִגָּאֵל:

They shall teach Your judgments to Jacob	Fear not, My servant Jacob
For there is no enchantment with Jacob	Fear not, My servant Jacob
None has beheld iniquity in Jacob	Fear not, My servant Jacob
Who can count the dust of Jacob?	Fear not, My servant Jacob
The Lord has sworn by the pride of Jacob	Fear not, My servant Jacob
Forgive, we pray, the sin of Jacob	Fear not, My servant Jacob
Now God will turn back the captivity of Jacob	Fear not, My servant Jacob
The Lord will indeed redeem Jacob	Fear not, My servant Jacob
Ordain salvation for Jacob	Fear not, My servant Jacob
The voice is the voice of Jacob	Fear not, My servant Jacob
Sing with gladness for Jacob	Fear not, My servant Jacob
The Lord will surely restore the majesty of Jacob	Fear not, My servant Jacob
You will show truth to Jacob	Fear not, My servant Jacob.

SONGS FOR CHANUKAH

Mi Yemalel

Who can relate the heroic deeds of Israel,
who can count them?
Behold, in every generation a hero has arisen,
a saviour of the people.

Listen! in those days at this season
the Maccabi saved and rescued.
And in our days all the people of Israel
will unite, arise and be redeemed.

Menashe Rabina

חֲנוּכָּה

בָּאנוּ חֹשֶׁךְ לְגָרֵשׁ · בְּיָדֵינוּ אוֹר וָאֵשׁ :
כָּל־אֶחָד הוּא אוֹר קָטָן · וְכֻלָּנוּ אוֹר אֵיתָן :
סוּרָה חֹשֶׁךְ הָלְאָה שְׁחוֹר · סוּרָה מִפְּנֵי הָאוֹר :

SONGS FOR PURIM

חַג פּוּרִים

חַג פּוּרִים · חַג גָּדוֹל הוּא לַיְהוּדִים :
מַסֵּכוֹת רַעֲשָׁנִים זְמִירוֹת וְרִקוּדִים :
הָבָה נַרְעִישָׁה רַשׁ רַשׁ רַשׁ ·
בָּרַעֲשָׁנִים :

אֲנִי פּוּרִים

אֲנִי פּוּרִים שָׂמֵחַ וּמְבַדֵּחַ
הֲלֹא רַק פַּעַם בַּשָּׁנָה אָבוֹא לְהִתְאָרֵחַ :
הֵידָד פּוּרִים הַכּוּ בְּתֹף וּמְצִלְתַּיִם
הוֹי מִי יִתֵּן וּבָא פּוּרִים לְחֹדֶשׁ לְחָדְשַׁיִם :
רַב פּוּרִים אֱמֹר נָא לִי מַדּוּעַ
מַדּוּעַ לֹא יָחוּל פּוּרִים פַּעֲמַיִם בְּשָׁבוּעַ :

זֶה הַיּוֹם יוֹם פּוּרִים

זֶה הַיּוֹם יוֹם פּוּרִים מַה נָּעִים וּמַה טּוֹב ·
זְמִירוֹת נְזַמֵּרָה וְנִשְׂמַח עַד אֵין סוֹף :
שְׂמַח מָרְדְּכַי שְׂמַח הַצָּרוֹת נָא שְׁכַח :
לָנֶצַח לֹא נִשְׁכַּח הַנֵּס :
הוֹי שִׁירוּ נָא שִׁיר · כִּי בְּשׁוּשַׁן הָעִיר
הָמָן הָאֲגָגִי אָז מֵת :

Chanukah

We come to drive away darkness,
in our hands are light and fire.
Each one is a small light,
and all of us are a mighty light.
Away with darkness, away with blackness!
Away before the light.

Sarah Levy

SONGS FOR PURIM

Shoshanat Ya'akov   page 265

Chag Purim

The festival of Purim is a great festival for the Jews.
Masks, rattles, songs and dances.
Come let us make a noise: Rash, rash, rash,
with rattles.

Chasidic

Ani Purim

I am Purim happy and joking
I only come once a year to be your guest.

Hurrah Purim, beat drum and cymbal.
I wish Purim would come for a month or two.

Rabbi Purim, tell me why.
Why doesn't Purim come twice a week?

Zeh Hayom Yom Purim

Today is Purim, how fine and how good.
Let us sing songs and rejoice without end.
Rejoice, Mordecai, rejoice.
Please forget the troubles.
We will never forget this wonder.
Let us sing a song, for in the city of Shushan
Haman the Agagite is dead.

SONG FOR TU BISH'VAT

ט״ו בִּשְׁבָט

הַשְׁקֵדִיָּה פּוֹרַחַת · וְשֶׁמֶשׁ פָּז זוֹרַחַת:

צִפֳּרִים מֵרֹאשׁ כָּל־גָּג מְבַשְּׂרוֹת אֶת־בֹּא הֶחָג:

ט״ו בִּשְׁבָט הִגִּיעַ חַג הָאִילָנוֹת:

הָאָרֶץ מְשַׁוַּעַת · הִגִּיעָה עֵת לָטַעַת:

כָּל־אֶחָד יִקַּח לוֹ עֵץ בְּאֵתִּים נֵצֵא חוֹצֵץ:

ט״ו בִּשְׁבָט הִגִּיעַ חַג הָאִילָנוֹת:

נִטַּע כָּל־הַר וָגֶבַע · מִדָּן וְעַד בְּאֵר־שֶׁבַע:

וְאַרְצֵנוּ שׁוּב נִירַשׁ אֶרֶץ זֵית יִצְהָר וּדְבַשׁ:

ט״ו בִּשְׁבָט הִגִּיעַ חַג הָאִילָנוֹת:

SONGS FOR THE INTRODUCTION TO, OR CLOSING OF, THE SERVICE

הִנְנִי מוּכָן וּמְזוּמָן

הִנְנִי מוּכָן וּמְזוּמָן · לְקַיֵּם אֶת־מִצְוַת בּוֹרְאִי:

כְּמוֹ שֶׁכָּתוּב בַּתּוֹרָה · הִנְנִי מוּכָן וּמְזוּמָן ·

וְקִדַּשְׁתֶּם אֶת־יוֹם הַשַּׁבָּת · הִנְנִי מוּכָן וּמְזוּמָן:

SONG FOR TU BISH'VAT

Tu BiSh'vat

The almond tree blossoms
and a golden sun does shine.
Birds from every rooftop
announce the festive time:
Tu BiSh'vat is here—
The festival of trees!

The land cries out:
the planting time has come!
Let everyone take a sapling.
Let us go to dig and plant.
Tu BiSh'vat is here—
The festival of trees!

Let us plant every mountain and hill
from Dan to Be'er Sheva
and we shall again possess our land—
the land of olives, oil and honey.
Tu BiSh'vat is here—
The festival of trees!

Israel Dushman

SONGS FOR THE INTRODUCTION TO, OR
CLOSING OF, THE SERVICE

Hineni Muchan Um'zuman

Behold, I am prepared,
ready to fulfil the commandments of my creator,
as it is written in the Torah: Sanctify the Sabbath Day!

צַדִּיק כַּתָּמָר

צַדִּיק כַּתָּמָר יִפְרָח כְּאֶרֶז בַּלְּבָנוֹן יִשְׂגֶּה:
שְׁתוּלִים בְּבֵית יְהֹוָה בְּחַצְרוֹת אֱלֹהֵינוּ יַפְרִיחוּ:
עוֹד יְנוּבוּן בְּשֵׂיבָה דְּשֵׁנִים וְרַעֲנַנִּים יִהְיוּ:
לְהַגִּיד כִּי־יָשָׁר יְהֹוָה צוּרִי וְלֹא־עַוְלָתָה בּוֹ:

כִּי־בְשִׂמְחָה תֵצֵאוּ

כִּי־בְשִׂמְחָה תֵצֵאוּ וּבְשָׁלוֹם תּוּבָלוּן ·
הֶהָרִים וְהַגְּבָעוֹת יִפְצְחוּ רִנָּה:
וּשְׁאַבְתֶּם־מַיִם בְּשָׂשׂוֹן מִמַּעַיְנֵי הַיְשׁוּעָה:
צַהֲלִי וָרֹנִּי יוֹשֶׁבֶת צִיּוֹן:
הַלְלוּיָהּ:

מִי כָמוֹךָ

מִי כָמוֹךָ עֲמֻקּוֹת גְּלֵה
נוֹרָא תְהִלֹּת עֹשֵׂה־פֶלֶא:

יוֹצֵר הַמְצִיא כֹּל מֵאַיִן נִגְלָה לְלֵבָב לֹא לָעַיִן
כֵּן אַל־תִּשְׁאַל אֵיךְ וָאַיִן כִּי שָׁמַיִם וָאָרֶץ מָלֵא:

הָסֵר תַּאֲוָה מִקִּרְבְּךָ תִּמְצָא צוּרְךָ תּוֹךְ חֵכְּךָ
מִתְהַלֵּךְ לָאַט בִּלְבָבְךָ הוּא הַמּוֹרִיד וְהוּא הַמַּעֲלֶה:

וּרְאֵה דֶרֶךְ סוֹד הַנֶּפֶשׁ וַחֲקֹר אֹתָהּ וּבָהּ תְּנַפֵּשׁ
הוּא יַשְׂכִּילְךָ וְתִמְצָא חֵפֶשׁ כִּי אַתְּ אָסִיר וְעוֹלָם כֶּלֶא:

Tzadik Katamar

The righteous shall flourish like the palm tree,
  grow tall like a cedar in Lebanon.
Planted in the house of the Lord
  they shall flourish in the courts of our God,
bearing new fruit in old age
  still full of sap and still green,
to declare that the Lord is upright,
  my rock in whom there is no wrong.

From Psalm 92

Ki V'simchah Tetzeyu

For you shall go out with joy
and be led forth with peace.
The mountains and the hills
shall break forth into singing.
Therefore with joy shall you draw water
from the wells of salvation.
Cry aloud and shout, O inhabitant of Zion.
Hallelujah!

Isaiah 55: 12; 12: 3, 6

Mi Chamochah

Who is like You, revealing the deeps,
  fearful in praises, doing wonders?

The creator who discovers all from nothing
is revealed to the heart, but not to the eye;
therefore ask not how nor where—
  for He fills heaven and earth.

Remove lust from the midst of you;
you will find your God within you,
walking gently in your heart.
  He who brings low and lifts up.

And see the way of the soul's secret,
search it out and refresh yourself.
He will make you wise, and you will find freedom,
  for you are a captive and the world is a prison.

דַּעַת שִׂים צִיר בֵּינְךָ וּבֵינוֹ וּבַטֵּל רְצוֹנְךָ וַעֲשֵׂה רְצוֹנוֹ
וְדַע כִּי בַּאֲשֶׁר תַּסְתִּיר עֵינוֹ וְדָבָר מְנוּ לֹא־יִפָּלֵא:

הוּא הַחַי בְּאֵין עַפְרוֹת תֵּבֵל וְהוּא הָעֹשֶׂה וְהוּא הַסֹּבֵל
וְאָדָם נֶחְשָׁב כְּצִיצַת נֹבֵל מַהֵר יִבּוֹל כְּנֹבֵל עָלֶה:

אַגָּדָה

עַל שְׂפַת יָם כִּנֶּרֶת אַרְמוֹן רַב תִּפְאֶרֶת
גַּן־אֵל שָׁם נָטוּעַ • בּוֹ עֵץ לֹא יָנוּעַ:

מִי גָר שָׁם • רַק נַעַר כְּעוֹף בִּדְמִי יַעַר:
לוֹמֵד שָׁם תּוֹרָה הוּא מִפִּי אֵלִיָּהוּ:

הַס···גַּל לֹא קוֹלֵחַ: כָּל־עוֹף הַפּוֹרֵחַ
עוֹמֵד וְשׁוֹמֵעַ תּוֹרַת־אֵל בּוֹלֵעַ:

אַתָּה אֶחָד

אַתָּה אֶחָד וְשִׁמְךָ אֶחָד
וּמִי כְּעַמְּךָ יִשְׂרָאֵל
גּוֹי אֶחָד בָּאָרֶץ:
תִּפְאֶרֶת גְּדֻלָּה וַעֲטֶרֶת יְשׁוּעָה
יוֹם מְנוּחָה וּקְדֻשָּׁה לְעַמְּךָ נָתַתָּ:
אַבְרָהָם יָגֵל יִצְחָק יְרַנֵּן • יַעֲקֹב וּבָנָיו יָנוּחוּ בוֹ:

Make knowledge the envoy between yourself and Him.
Annul your will and do His will,
and know that wherever you hide, there is His eye,
   and nothing is too hard for Him.

He was the Living One, while there was yet no dust of the world,
and He is the maker and He the bearer,
and man is counted as a fading flower—
   soon to fade, as fades a leaf.

Judah Halevi

Agadah

On the shores of Lake Kinneret
there is a most glorious palace,
a garden of God is planted there,
in which no tree moves.

Who dwells there? Only a boy
like a bird in the silence of the forest!
There he learns the Torah
from the mouth of Elijah.

Hush! . . . Not a wave breaks.
Every bird that flies
stands and listens—
absorbing God's Torah.

Ya'akov Fishman

Atah Echad

You are One and Your name is One,
and who is like Your people Israel,
a nation unique on the earth?
A splendid greatness, a crown of salvation,
is the day of rest and holiness
You gave to Your people.
Abraham was glad, Isaac rejoiced,
Jacob and his sons rest on it.

שִׂמְחוּ בִירוּשָׁלַיִם

שִׂמְחוּ בִירוּשָׁלַיִם וְגִילוּ · רִינוּ אֶת־הַמָּשׂוֹשׂ ·
שִׂישׂוּ אֶת־הַמָּשׂוֹשׂ כָּל־הַמִּתְאַבְּלִים עָלֶיהָ:

מֵעַל פִּסְגַּת הַר הַצּוֹפִים

מֵעַל פִּסְגַּת הַר הַצּוֹפִים אֶשְׁתַּחֲוֶה לָךְ אַפַּיִם ·
מֵעַל פִּסְגַּת הַר הַצּוֹפִים שָׁלוֹם לָךְ יְרוּשָׁלַיִם ·
מֵאָה דוֹרוֹת חָלַמְתִּי עָלַיִךְ · לִזְכּוֹת לִרְאוֹת בְּאוֹר פָּנַיִךְ ·
יְרוּשָׁלַיִם יְרוּשָׁלַיִם · הָאִירִי פָּנַיִךְ לִבְנֵךְ :
יְרוּשָׁלַיִם יְרוּשָׁלַיִם · מֵחָרְבוֹתַיִךְ אֶבְנֵךְ :

מֵעַל פִּסְגַּת הַר הַצּוֹפִים שָׁלוֹם לָךְ יְרוּשָׁלַיִם ·
אַלְפֵי גוֹלִים מִקְצוֹת כָּל־תֵּבֵל נוֹשְׂאִים אֵלַיִךְ עֵינַיִם:
בְּאַלְפֵי בִּרְכוֹת חֲיִי בְּרוּכָה · מִקְדָּשׁ מֶלֶךְ עִיר מְלוּכָה ·
יְרוּשָׁלַיִם יְרוּשָׁלַיִם · אֲנִי לֹא אָזוּז מִפֹּה :
יְרוּשָׁלַיִם יְרוּשָׁלַיִם · יָבֹא הַמָּשִׁיחַ יָבֹא :

יְרוּשָׁלַיִם שֶׁל זָהָב

אַוִיר הָרִים צָלוּל כַּיַּיִן וְרֵיחַ אֳרָנִים :
נִשָּׂא בְּרוּחַ הָעַרְבַּיִם עִם קוֹל פַּעֲמוֹנִים :
וּבְתַרְדֵּמַת אִילָן וָאֶבֶן שְׁבוּיָה בַּחֲלוֹמָהּ ·
הָעִיר אֲשֶׁר בָּדָד יוֹשֶׁבֶת וּבְלִבָּהּ חוֹמָה :
יְרוּשָׁלַיִם שֶׁל זָהָב וְשֶׁל נְחוֹשֶׁת וְשֶׁל אוֹר
הֲלֹא לְכָל־שִׁירַיִךְ אֲנִי כִּנּוֹר :

Simchu Virushalayim

Rejoice in Jerusalem and be glad.
Sing its joy,
be glad of its joy
all who mourn for her.

Ta'anit

Me'al Pisgat Har Hatsofim

From the top of Mount Scopus I bow low to you,
from the top of Mount Scopus: Peace to you, Jerusalem!
A hundred generations I have dreamed of you
to be allowed to see the light of your face.
Jerusalem, Jerusalem, shine your face upon your son,
Jerusalem, Jerusalem, I will build you from your ruins.

From the top of Mount Scopus, Peace to you Jerusalem!
Thousands of exiles from the ends of the earth lift their eyes to you.
With a thousand blessings be blessed,
sanctuary of kings, royal city.
Jerusalem, Jerusalem, I will not move from here.
Jerusalem, Jerusalem, let the messiah come!

Avigdor Hameiri

Yerushalayim Shel Zahav

The mountain air is as clear as wine, and the smell of the pine tree
is carried on the evening breeze with the sound of bells.
The city is imprisoned in a sleep of tree and stone,
the city which dwells alone and in its heart a wall.
Jerusalem of gold, of copper and of light,
I am a harp for all your songs.

חָזַרְנוּ אֶל בּוֹרוֹת הַמַּיִם לַשּׁוּק וְלַכִּכָּר :

שׁוֹפָר קוֹרֵא בְּהַר הַבַּיִת בָּעִיר הָעַתִּיקָה :

וּבַמְּעָרוֹת אֲשֶׁר בַּסֶּלַע אַלְפֵי שְׁמָשׁוֹת זוֹרְחוֹת :

נָשׁוּב נֵרֵד אֶל יַם הַמֶּלַח בְּדֶרֶךְ יְרִיחוֹ :

יְרוּשָׁלַיִם שֶׁל זָהָב · · ·

אַךְ בְּבוֹאִי הַיּוֹם לָשִׁיר לָךְ וְלָךְ לִקְשׁוֹר כְּתָרִים ·

קָטֹנְתִּי מִצְּעִיר בָּנַיִךְ וּמֵאַחֲרוֹן הַמְּשׁוֹרְרִים ·

כִּי שְׁמֵךְ צוֹרֵב אֶת־הַשְּׂפָתַיִם כִּנְשִׁיקַת שָׂרָף :

אִם אֶשְׁכָּחֵךְ יְרוּשָׁלַיִם אֲשֶׁר כֻּלָּהּ זָהָב :

יְרוּשָׁלַיִם שֶׁל זָהָב וְשֶׁל נְחֹשֶׁת וְשֶׁל אוֹר

הֲלֹא לְכָל־שִׁירַיִךְ אֲנִי כִּנּוֹר :

הוֹדוּ

הוֹדוּ לַיהוָה קִרְאוּ בִשְׁמוֹ הוֹדִיעוּ בָעַמִּים עֲלִילֹתָיו :

שִׁירוּ לוֹ זַמְּרוּ־לוֹ שִׂיחוּ בְּכָל־נִפְלְאֹתָיו :

הִתְהַלְלוּ בְּשֵׁם קָדְשׁוֹ יִשְׂמַח לֵב מְבַקְשֵׁי יְהוָה :

זִכְרוּ נִפְלְאֹתָיו אֲשֶׁר עָשָׂה מֹפְתָיו וּמִשְׁפְּטֵי־פִיהוּ :

הוּא יְהוָה אֱלֹהֵינוּ בְּכָל־הָאָרֶץ מִשְׁפָּטָיו :

זִכְרוּ לְעוֹלָם בְּרִיתוֹ · דָּבָר צִוָּה לְאֶלֶף דּוֹר :

שִׁירוּ לַיהוָה כָּל־הָאָרֶץ בַּשְּׂרוּ מִיּוֹם־אֶל־יוֹם יְשׁוּעָתוֹ :

סַפְּרוּ בַגּוֹיִם אֶת־כְּבוֹדוֹ בְּכָל־הָעַמִּים נִפְלְאֹתָיו :

כִּי גָדוֹל יְהוָה וּמְהֻלָּל מְאֹד וְנוֹרָא הוּא עַל־כָּל־אֱלֹהִים :

הוֹד וְהָדָר לְפָנָיו עֹז וְחֶדְוָה בִּמְקֹמוֹ :

We have returned to the water cisterns, to the market and the squares.
A *shofar* is heard on the Temple Mount in the Old City.
In the caves in the rocks a thousand windows gleam.
Let us once again descend to the Dead Sea by way of Jericho.
Jerusalem of gold, of copper and of light,
I am a harp for all your songs.

But when I come today to sing to you and to crown you,
I am less than the least of your children and the last of your poets,
for your name burns the lips like the kiss of a seraph.
If I forget you, O Jerusalem, which is all gold.
Jerusalem of gold, of copper and of light,
I am a harp for all your songs.

Naomi Shemer

Hodu

Honour the Lord, call out in His name,
    teach His deeds among the peoples.
Sing to Him, play to Him,
    consider all His wonders.
Glory in His holy name,
    let those that seek the Lord be glad.
Remember the wonders He has done,
    His signs and the judgments of His mouth.
He is the Lord our God,
    His judgments are for all the earth.
Remember His covenant forever,
    the word He commanded to a thousand generations.
Sing to the Lord all the earth,
    tell day by day how He saves.
Describe His glory among the nations,
    His wonders among all peoples.
For great is the Lord and praised aloud,
    He is awesome beyond all gods.
Splendour and radiance are in His presence,
    strength and gladness with Him.

From I Chronicles 16

SUNG TEXTS

אִם אֵין אֲנִי לִי מִי לִי ·

וּכְשֶׁאֲנִי לְעַצְמִי מָה אֲנִי ·

וְאִם לֹא עַכְשָׁיו אֵימָתָי :

וְטַהֵר לִבֵּנוּ לְעָבְדְּךָ בֶּאֱמֶת :

מַה־טֹּבוּ אֹהָלֶיךָ יַעֲקֹב

מִשְׁכְּנֹתֶיךָ יִשְׂרָאֵל :

הִנֵּה מַה־טּוֹב וּמַה־נָּעִים

שֶׁבֶת אַחִים גַּם־יָחַד :

יְשֻׂשׂוּם מִדְבָּר וְצִיָּה וְתָגֵל עֲרָבָה

וְתִפְרַח כַּחֲבַצָּלֶת ·

כִּי־נִבְקְעוּ בַמִּדְבָּר מַיִם

וּנְחָלִים בָּעֲרָבָה :

בְּצֵאת יִשְׂרָאֵל מִמִּצְרָיִם

בֵּית יַעֲקֹב מֵעַם לֹעֵז :

הָיְתָה יְהוּדָה לְקָדְשׁוֹ

יִשְׂרָאֵל מַמְשְׁלוֹתָיו :

מַעֲשֵׂי יָדַי טוֹבְעִים בַּיָּם

וְאַתֶּם אוֹמְרִים שִׁירָה לְפָנָי :

SUNG TEXTS

Im Eyn Ani Li, Mi Li

If I am not for myself, who is for me?
But if I am only for myself, what am I?
And if not now, when?

Hillel

V'taheyr Libeynu

Cleanse our hearts, that we may serve You in truth.

Siddur

Mah Tovu

How good are your tents, O Jacob, and your homes, O Israel.

Numbers 24: 5

Hiney Mah Tov

How good it is and how pleasant
when brothers live in unity together.

Psalm 133: 1

Y'susum

The wilderness and the parched land shall be glad;
and the desert shall rejoice,
and blossom as the rose.
For in the wilderness shall waters break out,
and streams in the desert.

Isaiah 35: 1, 6

B'tzeyt Yisrael

When Israel came out of Egypt,
the family of Jacob from a people of foreign tongue,
then Judah became His holy place,
Israel were those He ruled.

Psalm 114: 1–2

Ma'asey Yadai

The creations of My hands are drowning in the sea—
yet you sing praises before Me!

Midrash

אָמַר רַבִּי עֲקִיבָא ·
וְאָהַבְתָּ לְרֵעֲךָ כָּמוֹךָ ·
זֶה כְּלָל גָּדוֹל בַּתּוֹרָה:

יִשְׂמְחוּ הַשָּׁמַיִם וְתָגֵל הָאָרֶץ
יִרְעַם הַיָּם וּמְלֹאוֹ:

מַה נָּאווּ עַל הֶהָרִים
רַגְלֵי הַמְבַשֵּׂר הוּ:
מַשְׁמִיעַ יְשׁוּעָה ·
מַשְׁמִיעַ שָׁלוֹם:

עֹשֶׂה שָׁלוֹם בִּמְרוֹמָיו הוּא יַעֲשֶׂה שָׁלוֹם
עָלֵינוּ וְעַל כָּל־יִשְׂרָאֵל · וְאִמְרוּ אָמֵן:

אֵלֶּה חָמְדָה לִבִּי
חוּסָה נָא וְאַל נָא תִתְעַלֵּם:

קוֹל דּוֹדִי הִנֵּה־זֶה בָּא ·
מְדַלֵּג עַל־הֶהָרִים
מְקַפֵּץ עַל־הַגְּבָעוֹת:

הַלְלוּהוּ בְּצִלְצְלֵי שָׁמַע ·
הַלְלוּהוּ בְּצִלְצְלֵי תְרוּעָה ·
כֹּל הַנְּשָׁמָה תְּהַלֵּל יָהּ הַלְלוּיָהּ:

לֹא־יִשָּׂא גוֹי אֶל־גּוֹי חֶרֶב
וְלֹא־יִלְמְדוּ עוֹד מִלְחָמָה:

Amar Rabbi Akiva

Rabbi Akiba said:
'You shall love your neighbour as yourself.'
This is the great rule of the Torah.

Midrash

Yismechu Hashamayim

Let the heavens rejoice and the earth delight,
let the sea thunder in its fullness.

Psalm 96: 11

Mah Navu

How beautiful upon the hills are the feet of the herald.
He speaks of salvation,
he speaks of peace.

Isaiah 52: 7

Osey Shalom

May He who makes peace in the highest bring this peace upon us
and upon all Israel. Amen.

Siddur

Eyleh Chamdah Libi

These my heart desires,
take pity and hide not Yourself.

From Yedid Nefesh

Kol Dodi

The voice of my beloved! Behold, he comes,
leaping upon the mountains,
skipping upon the hills.

Song of Songs 2: 8

Hal'luhu

Praise Him with the clash of cymbals.
Praise Him with the clanging cymbals.
Let everything that has breath
praise the Lord.

Praise the Lord!

Psalm 150: 6

Lo Yisa Goy

Nation shall not lift up sword against nation.
Never again shall they train for war.

Isaiah 2: 4

YIDDISH SONGS

Royz, royz

Royz, royz, vi vayt biz tu?
Vald, vald, vi groys biz tu?
Volt di royz nisht azoy vayt geven,
Volt der vald nisht azoy groys geven.

Sh'chine, sh'chine, vi vayt biz tu?
Golus, golus, vi lang biz tu?
Volt di sh'chine nisht azoy vayt geven,
Volt der golus nisht azoy lang geven.

Zog Nit Keynmol!

Zog nit keynmol az du geyst dem letstn veg,
Chotsh himlen blayene farshteln bloye teg,
Kumen vet noch undzer oysgebenkte sho,
S'vet a poyk ton undzer trot — mir zenen do!

Fun grinem palmen-land biz vaytn land fun shney,
Mir kumen on mit undzer payn, mit undzer vey,
Un vu gefaln s'iz a shprits fun undzer blut,
Shprotsn vet dort undzer gvure, undzer mut.

S'vet di morgn-zun bagildn undz dem haynt,
Un der nechtn vet farshvindn mitn faynt,
Nor oyb farzamen vet di zun un der kayor —
Vi a parol zol geyn des lid fun dor tsu dor.

Dos lid geshribn iz mit blut un nit mit blay,
S'iz nit kayn lidl fun a foygl oyf der fray,
Dos hot a folk tsvishn falndike vent,
Dos lid gezungen mit naganes in di hent.

So zog nit keynmol az du geyst dem letstn veg,
Chotsh himlen blayene farshteln bloye teg,
Kumen vet noch undzer oysgebenkte sho,
S'vet a poyk ton undzer trot — mir zenen do!

YIDDISH SONGS

Royz, royz

Rose, rose, how far are you?
Forest, forest, how vast are you?
If the rose were not so far away,
the forest would not seem so vast.

Holy Spirit, how far are You?
Exile, exile, how long are you?
If the Holy Spirit were not so distant,
then the exile would not seem so long.

Zog Nit Keynmol!

We must never lose our courage in the fight,
Though skies of lead turn days of sunshine into night.
Because the hour for which we've yearned will yet arrive,
And our marching steps will thunder: we survive!

From land of palm trees to the land of distant snow,
We have come with our deep sorrow and our woe.
And everywhere our blood was innocently shed,
Our fighting spirits will again avenge our dead.

The golden rays of morning sun will dry our tears,
Dispelling bitter agony of yesteryears.
But if the sun and dawn with us will be delayed—
Then let this song ring out the call to you instead.

Not lead, but blood inscribed this song which now we sing,
It's not a carolling of birds upon the wing,
But a people midst the crashing fires of hell,
Sang this song and fought courageous till it fell!

So we must never lose our courage in the fight,
Though skies of lead turn days of sunshine into night.
Because the hour for which we've yearned will yet arrive,
And our marching steps will thunder: we survive!

Hirsch Glick

HATIKVAH

As long as a Jewish soul
still yearns in the innermost heart,
and eyes turn eastward
gazing towards Zion,
then our hope is not lost,
the hope of two thousand years,
—to be a free people in our land,
the land of Zion and Jerusalem.

התקוה

כָּל־עוֹד בַּלֵּבָב פְּנִימָה

נֶפֶשׁ יְהוּדִי הוֹמִיָּה.

וּלְפַאֲתֵי מִזְרָח קָדִימָה

עַיִן לְצִיּוֹן צוֹפִיָּה.

עוֹד לֹא אָבְדָה תִקְוָתֵנוּ.

הַתִּקְוָה שְׁנוֹת אַלְפַּיִם.

לִהְיוֹת עַם חָפְשִׁי בְּאַרְצֵנוּ

בְּאֶרֶץ צִיּוֹן וִירוּשָׁלַיִם:

God save our gracious Queen,
Long live our noble Queen.
God save the Queen.
Send her victorious,
Happy and glorious,
Long to reign over us,
God save the Queen.

GLOSSARY

ABRAVANEL, ISAAC BEN JUDAH. Born 1437 in Lisbon, died 1508 in Venice. Statesman, Bible exegete, and religious philosopher.

ACHAD HA-AM. 'One of the people'. Pen name of Asher Hirsch Ginsberg, 1856–1927. Emphasised the spiritual and cultural aspects of Zionism.

ADON OLAM. Rhymed hymn in ten verses. The Sephardi rite has 12 verses. Author unknown. Describes God both as transcendent and immanent.

AGGADAH. see *Midrash.

ALAMOT. Heading of Psalm 46. Possibly a small flute, pipe, or high-pitched voice.

ALBO, JOSEPH. (c. 1360–c. 1445). Author of Sepher HaIkkarim (Book of Dogmas). Philosopher and apologist.

ALEXANDERER, THE. See *Chenoch of Alexander.

ALEYNU. Originally in Rosh Hashanah service, then a conclusion to daily services. First paragraph emphasises chosenness and task of Israel, and second paragraph the universal hope.

ALKABETZ, SOLOMON HALEVI. (c. 1505–76). Kabbalist and mystical poet, composer of *Lechah Dodi.

AMIDAH. Literally 'standing'. Also known as the Shemoneh Esreh ('eighteen') from the number of blessings it originally contained. From its central position in the service it also became known as HaTefillah ('the prayer'). First sections proclaim the continuity of the generations, God's power to redeem from death and God's holiness. On the Sabbath the middle benedictions (4–16) are replaced by one specific to the day.

AMMI BEN NATHAN. Palestinian teacher of the third century.

AMOS. Prophet, eighth century B.C.E. Spoke out against immorality and injustice in a time of power and prosperity.

ASAPH. Twelve psalms are associated with Asaph (50, 73–83) and may refer to the Temple musician in the time of David.

ASCH, SHOLEM. (1881–1957). Yiddish novelist and dramatist, born in Poland. Wrote about eastern Europe and Biblical subjects, also Christian themes.

AVOT D'RABBI NATAN. A small tractate, usually printed with the Babylonian *Talmud. Midrashic commentaries to the *Sayings of the Fathers.

AZKARI (AZIKRI), ELIEZER BEN MOSES. (1533–1600.) Kabbalist in Safed.

BAAL SHEM TOV. (The Besht.) 'Master of the Good Name'. (Israel ben Eliezer. c. 1700–60). Founder of *Chasidism. Stressed the joyful observance of commandments and popularised Kabbalistic teachings.

BABA BATRA. (Last gate) of the third tractate of the *Mishnah, order Nezikin (damages). Deals mainly with real estate, inheritance, and legal documents.

BABA METZIA. (Middle gate)—see *Baba Batra. Deals mainly with chattels lost property, embezzlement, fraud, etc.

BACHYA IBN PAKUDA. (c. 1050–1120). Religious philosopher. His Duties of the Heart speaks of trust in God, humility, and asceticism. Strong affinity with Arab mystics.

BAECK, LEO. (1873–1956.) Rabbi, teacher of Midrash and Homiletics in Berlin (Hochschule für die Wissenschaft des Judentums). Elected head of the representative council of the Jews in Germany in 1933, and stayed with his congregation until he was sent to Theresienstadt in 1943. Survived

* Indicates reference to a further entry.

the war and settled in London. Books include *The Essence of Judaism* and *This People Israel.*

BELLOW, SAUL. (1915– .) American novelist whose characters, many of them Jewish, search for ultimate reality in the modern world. Nobel prize.

BEN GURION, DAVID. (1886–1973.) From Poland emigrated to Palestine in 1906. Zionist and Trade Union leader. Served as first Prime Minister of the State of Israel.

BENJAMIN, WALTER. (1892–1940.) German philosopher and literary critic. Collaborated with the writer Berthold Brecht.

BERACHOT. First tractate of the *Mishnah, order *Zeraim* (seeds). Deals with the recitation of the Shema and blessings and prayers in general.

BERGMAN, S. HUGO. (1883–1975.) Czech Zionist and philosopher (Hebrew University). Influenced by *Achad Ha-am and *Buber. Friend of *Kafka.

BERLIN LIBERAL SYNAGOGUE, PRAYER BOOK OF. A radical prayer book published in 1848.

BERSHIDER REBBE. (d. 1816.) Chasidic disciple of Pinchas of *Koretz.

BESHT. See *Baal Shem Tov.

BIALIK, CHAIM NACHMAN. (1873–1934.) Hebrew poet, essayist, story writer. Born in Russia, settled in Palestine in 1924. Probably the greatest modern Hebrew poet.

BOERNE, LUDWIG. (1786–1837.) German political essayist and champion of Jewish emancipation. Criticised by *Heine.

BOMZE, NACHUM. (1906–54.) Yiddish poet. Served with the Red Army. Emigrated to U.S.A.

BUBER, MARTIN. (1878–1965.) Writer and philosopher from Vienna. In *I and Thou* saw faith as dialogue between man and God. Explored and popularised *Chasidism. Zionist and passionate advocate of Jewish–Arab understanding.

BUNAM OF PZHYSHA, SIMCHA. (1765–1827.) Chasidic Rebbe with intellectual approach who taught inwardness.

CELAN PAUL. (1920–70.) Rumanian born writer in the German language. His visionary poems confronted the Nazi horrors.

CHAFETZ CHAIM. (Israel Meir Ha-Kohen, 1838–1933.) Known after the name of his first book, *Chafetz Chaim*, an exposition of the laws on gossip, talebearing, and slander. His best known work is a commentary on part of the *Shulchan Aruch.

CHASIDISM. (See also *Baal Shem Tov.) A religious and social movement which developed quickly in depressed eastern Europe following the Chmielnicki massacre and persecution. It has parallels with other popular religious movements of the same period. Opposed by the '*Mitnagdim*' (Elijah, Gaon of Vilna).

CHENOCH OF ALEXANDER. (The Alexanderer.) (1798–1870.) Chasidic disciple of *Bunam of Pzhysha and *Mendel of Kotzk. Continued tradition of emphasising the importance of inwardness.

CHIYYA RABBAH. Collection of material not found in Mishnah. Second century C.E.

CHRONICLES. Late Biblical book in two parts which parallels some of the stories in *Samuel and *Kings about the reigns of *David and *Solomon, but differs by excluding David's misdeeds.

CHULLIN. (Profane matters.) Third tractate of the *Mishnah, order *Kodashim* (Holy things), dealing primarily with the laws of animal slaughter.

COHEN, ARTHUR A. (1928– .) American publisher and author (*The Natural and the Supernatural Jew*).

CORDOVERO, MOSES BEN JACOB. (Safed, 1522–70.) Kabbalist. Wrote *Pardes Rimonim* which discusses creation, the *Sephirot* and the human soul.

DAVID. King of Israel. (*c.* 1000–960 B.C.E.) Traditionally accepted as author of many of the psalms.

DAYS OF REPENTANCE. The ten days which include *Rosh Hashanah* (the New Year) and *Yom Kippur* (the Day of Atonement). Special penitential prayers are said on those days.

DE LONZANO, MENACHEM BEN JUDAH. (1550–*c.* 1624.) Linguist, poet, kabbalist. Probably born in Constantinople, emigrated to Jerusalem aged 25. Author of linguistic commentary on the Pentateuch and original works on Kabbalah which raised bitter opposition.

DERECH ERETZ ZUTA. Tractate appended to the Babylonian *Talmud which contains moral sayings.

DEUTERONOMY. See *Torah.

DUBNER MAGGID. (Jacob b. Wolf Kranz. 1741–1804.) Popular preacher famous for his parables.

DUBNOW, SIMON. (1860–1941.) Historian. Dealt particularly with the development of Jewish life in eastern Europe.

DUNASH BEN LABRAT. (*c.* 920–90.) Hebrew poet and grammarian from Baghdad. Introduced Arabic metre to Hebrew poetry.

DUSHMAN, ISRAEL. Prominent in modern Hebrew revival. Writer for children.

ECCLESIASTES. Late Biblical book with unique outlook concerned with triviality and transience of life.

ECCLESIASTES RABBAH. See *Midrash Rabbah.

ECCLESIASTICUS. Apocryphal book. Author Ben Sira, *c.* 170 B.C.E. Its moral teachings quoted in *Talmud.

EICHHORN, DAVID MAX. Contemporary American Reform Rabbi. Military chaplain. Author of midrashic study, *Cain, Son of the serpent*.

EINSTEIN, ALBERT. (1879–1955.) Physicist, Nobel Prize winner. Refugee from Nazism. Troubled by the use of the atomic bomb.

ELEAZAR BEN ARAK. Mishnaic Rabbi, mentioned in *Sayings of the Fathers.

ELEAZAR BEN JUDAH OF WORMS. (*c.* 1170–1238.) Known as the *Rokeach* after the name of his book (*Of the Spice-Dealer*) which embodies his ethical teaching and practical Kabbalah. Wife and daughters killed by Crusaders in Mainz. From 1201 Rabbi of Worms. Best known for his liturgical poetry.

ELIEZER BEN ISAAC. Rabbi of Worms. Eleventh century. Talmudic scholar mentioned by *Rashi.

EMDEN, JACOB. (1697–1776.) Halachist. Opponent of the Sabbateans. Published an edition of the prayerbook with his own commentary.

ERUBIN. Second tractate of the *Mishnah, order *Moed* (Seasons), dealing with restrictions on carrying, walking, and cooking on Sabbath and festivals.

ESTHER RABBAH. See *Midrash Rabbah.

EXODUS. See *Torah.

EXODUS RABBAH. See *Midrash Rabbah.

EYDOUX, EMMANUEL. (1917– .) Pen name of Roger Eisinger. French postwar author on Jewish themes.

EZEKIEL. Prophet and visionary of the Babylonian exile.

FARHI, DANIEL. Contemporary Rabbi in Paris.

FEUCHTWANGER, LION. (1884–1958.) German historical novelist. Most famous novel *Jud Suess* ('Jew Suess').

FISHMAN, YA'AKOV. (1878–1946.) Yiddish journalist in U.S.A.

FLANAGAN, BUD. (1896–1968.) (Born Robert Winthrop.) Anglo-Jewish comedian.

FLEG, EDMOND. (1874–1963.) French poet, playwright, and essayist who returned to Judaism after the Dreyfus affair.

FRANK, ANNE. (1929–45.) Born in Germany, grew up in Holland, and died in Belsen. Her diaries record her life during the German occupation of Amsterdam.

FRANKL, VIKTOR. (1905–   .) Psychiatrist, born in Austria. His ideas concerning purpose and meaning in life developed out of his experiences in Auschwitz and other concentration camps.

FREUD, SIGMUND. (1856–1939.) Founder of psychoanalysis, born in Vienna. Refugee in London in 1938.

FRIEDLANDER, ALBERT H. (1927–   .) Contemporary Rabbi. Director of Studies at the Leo Baeck College. Works include *Out of the Whirlwind* and a study of *Leo Baeck.

FROMM, ERICH. (1900–   .) U.S. psychoanalyst. Concerned with Biblical ideas and contemporary problems.

GENESIS. See *Torah.

GENESIS RABBAH. See *Midrash Rabbah.

GITTIN. Sixth tractate of the *Mishnah, order *Nashim* (Women), dealing with laws of divorce.

GITTIT. Heading for some psalms. Possibly from *Gat*, a 'winepress', or from the town of Gat.

GLATSTEIN, JACOB. (1896–1971.) U.S. poet who tried to revive the Yiddish language.

GLICK, HIRSCH. (1922–44.) Partisan fighter under Nazi occupation. His song 'Zog Nit Keynmol' became the battle song of the Vilna partisans.

GLUECKEL OF HAMELN. (1646–1724.) German diarist, living mainly in Hamburg. She provides a vivid picture of contemporary German Jewish life.

GOLD, WOLF H. (1889–1956.) Rabbi and leader of religious Zionism in the U.S.A.

GREENBERG, CHAIM. (1889–1953.) Labour Zionist theoretician. Born in Russia, worked in America.

HAFTARAH. The reading from the prophets which follows the Torah reading on the Sabbath. It is selected so as to have some connection with the portion read from the *Torah.

HAKOTUN, RABBI MOSHE. A legendary chasidic figure to whom many sayings are ascribed.

HALACHAH. See *Midrash*.

HALLEL. Psalms 113–18, sung on festivals and the New Moon.

HAMEIRI, AVIGDOR. (1890–1970.) Hebrew poet, novelist and translator.

HAVDALAH. The service at the end of the Sabbath.

HEINE, HEINRICH. (1797–1856.) German poet and writer, born Jewish but baptised in 1825. After a serious illness in 1847 he increasingly returned to Jewish themes, particularly the Bible.

HERZL, THEODOR. (1860–1904.) Journalist. Founder of political Zionism after observing the Dreyfus trial. Wrote *The Jewish State* and *Altneuland* (Oldnewland).

HESCHEL, ABRAHAM JOSHUA. (1907–72.) U.S.A. Conservative Rabbi, philosopher and theologian. His works include *God in Search of Man*, *The Sabbath*, and *The Prophets*.

HILLEL. (First century B.C.E.) Born in Babylon, studied in Jerusalem. Became a leading authority in Oral Law. Developed principles of Biblical interpretation, renowned for his humanity and ethical teachings.

HIRSCH, SAMSON RAPHAEL. (1808–88.) Leader of 'orthodoxy' in Frankfurt. Tried to fuse Western culture with orthodox Judaism.

HIRSCH, SAMUEL. (1815–1889.) Pioneer Reform Rabbi in Germany and U.S.A.

HOFSHI, NATHAN. Israeli pacifist, twentieth century.

HOLDHEIM, SAMUEL. (1806–60.) Radical leader of progressive Judaism. From 1847 led the Berlin Reform Congregation.

HOSEA. Eighth century B.C.E. Biblical prophet of the kingdom of Israel in the last years before the exile. He likened the bond between God and Israel to the stormy relationship between himself and his wife.

IBN EZRA, ABRAHAM. (1093–1167.) Spanish thinker, poet and Biblical commentator. From 1140 he spent much time wandering, visiting among other places London and Oxford.

IBN GABIROL, SOLOMON. (c. 1021–56.) Spanish poet and philosopher. His *Keter Malchut* (Crown of Kingship) is read during the *Days of Repentance.

IBN VERGA, SOLOMON. (Fifteenth–sixteenth centuries.) Historian and Marrano. Wrote on persecution and disputation (*Rod of Judah*).

IGGERET HAMUSAR. Probably by R. Solomon Alami, written after the disputation of Tortosa (1413–14).

ISAIAH. There are probably three sections in the Biblical book of Isaiah, chapters 1–39, 40–54, 55–66. The first is pre-exilic, the latter two post-exilic. The first Isaiah was probably a wealthy priest from Jerusalem eighth century B.C.E. The second Isaiah belonged to the Babylonian period and is the great emphasiser of monotheism—one God, creator of all.

ISSERLES, MOSES BEN ISRAEL. (The ReMA) (c. 1525–72.) Polish Rabbi and codifier. Composed glosses on the *Shulchan Aruch* which brought it in line with Ashkenazi practices.

JABÈS, EDMOND. (1912– .) Poet, born in Egypt, lives in Paris.

JACOBS, LOUIS. (1920– .) English Rabbi and theologian. Lecturer in Talmud at Leo Baeck College. Works include *We Have Reason to Believe*, *Chasidic Prayer*, *Principles of the Jewish Faith*, etc.

JEREMIAH. Born c. 645 B.C.E. and died after the fall of Jerusalem. Biblical prophet who warned of the destruction of Judah and the temple, but subsequently offered a message of hope.

JOEL. Biblical prophet of unknown date. The book includes an appeal to repentance and a vision of the end of days.

JOEL BEN ABRAHAM SHEMARIAH. Rabbi of Vilna. (Eighteenth century). His ethical will is an example of common and popular literature of the Jewish Middle Ages.

JOSE BEN ABIN. (Fourth century.) Palestinian Rabbi, a late Talmudic authority and possibly one of the redactors.

JOSEPH, MORRIS. (1848–1930.) English theologian and Rabbi of the *West London Synagogue from 1893. His *Judaism as Creed and Life*, emphasising the ethical basis of Jewish observance, is still a standard work.

JOSEPHUS, FLAVIUS. (Hebrew name, Joseph b. Mattityahu Hakohen, c. 38–100). Politician, soldier, and historian. Jewish apologist to the Roman world.

JUDAH BAR ILAI. (Second century.) Palestinian, pupil of Akiba.

JUDAH HALEVI. (c. 1075–1141.) Spanish Hebrew poet and philosopher. A physician who in old age left Spain to settle in Palestine during the period of the second crusade. His *The Kuzari* is an exposition of Jewish

life and thought in the form of a disputation before the king of the Khazars.

JUDAH HECHASID. (1150–1217.) Of Regensburg. Reputed to be a mystic. Little is known of him. Associated with *Sefer Chasidim.

KADDISH. (Aramaic for 'holy'.) Originally recited at the end of a course of study, and later incorporated into the service. It was recited in memory of a great scholar, following the principle that one should praise God in sorrow as well as joy. As the definition of a scholar became difficult, it was recited in memory of all who died. Written in Aramaic so that everyone could understand. A Hebrew version is also included in this prayer book.

KADDISH D'RABANAN. Special version of the *Kaddish used at the end of a session of study.

KAFKA, FRANZ. (1883–1924.) Czech author whose works depict the fear and despair of western man. Works include *The Trial*, *The Castle*, and many aphorisms.

KETUBOT. Second tractate of the *Mishnah, order *Nashim* (women), dealing mainly with widowhood, divorce and the mutual rights of husband and wife.

KIDDUSH. (Sanctification.) A blessing over wine (symbol of joy) and a prayer of thanksgiving for the Sabbath, referring to the creation and exodus.

KIDDUSHIN. Seventh tractate of the *Mishnah, order *Nashim* (women), dealing with betrothal and prohibited marriages.

KINGS, BOOK OF. Biblical book in two parts relating the history of Israel and Judah from the death of David to the releasing of Jehoiachin in the Babylonian captivity.

KITZUR SHULCHAN ARUCH. See *Shulchan Aruch.

KOOK, RAV ABRAHAM ISAAC. (1865–1935.) Chief Rabbi of Palestine, concerned with the religious problems of the new settlement. A poet and mystic.

KORACH. Heading to some psalms. The Sons of Korach are recorded as being a guild of Temple singers.

KORETZER, PINCHAS SHAPIRO. (1726–91.) Early chasidic Rabbi, opposed to Dov Baer and contemplative prayer, asserting that man should pray explicitly for human needs.

KRAUS, KARL. (1874–1936.) Austrian satirist and poet.

LAMENTATIONS. Third of the five *megillot* (scrolls) which consists of five chapters of eulogies and mourning over the destruction of Judah, Jerusalem and the Temple. Traditionally ascribed to *Jeremiah, it is read on the 9th of Av.

LAZARE, BERNARD. (1865–1903.) French author and poet. Concerned with antisemitism. After the Dreyfus affair favoured national home for the Jews.

LAZARUS, EMMA. (1849–87.) American poetess, whose sonnet is inscribed upon the Statue of Liberty.

LECHAH DODI. A poem composed by Solomon Halevi *Alkabetz, as the full version (an acrostic on his name on page 572) shows.

LEVITICUS. See *Torah.

LEVITICUS RABBAH. See *Midrash Rabbah.

LEVI YITZCHAK OF BERDITCHEV. (c. 1740–1810.) Chasidic leader, pupil of Dov Baer. Central doctrine was 'love for Israel'.

LEVY, SARAH. Contemporary Israeli teacher and composer of children's songs.

LITTMANN, ELLEN. (1900–75.) First lecturer in Bible at Leo Baeck College. Has written on *Mendelssohn and translated Elbogen.

LOEWE, HERBERT. (1882–1940). English orientalist. Collaborated with *C. G. Montefiore on *A Rabbinic Anthology*.

LURIA, ISAAC. (1534–72.) Kabbalist and mystic who settled in Safed. His great contribution to Jewish thought is his amplification of the idea of *Kavanah* (intention).

MAGNES, JUDAH LEON. (1877–1948.) American Reform Rabbi and first president of the Hebrew University of Jerusalem. Devoted to spiritual Zionism, he advocated a bi-national Jewish and Arab Commonwealth.

MAHARAL OF PRAGUE. (JUDAH LOEW BEN BEZALEL). (*c.* 1525–1609.) Kabbalist and leader of Ashkenazi Jewry, particularly interested in education. Associated with the legend of the Golem.

MAILER, NORMAN. (1923– .) U.S. Novelist and essayist.

MAIMONIDES, MOSES. (MOSES BEN MAIMON, RaMBaM). (1135–1204.) Philosopher, halachist, medical writer. Born Cordova, finally settled in Cairo where he became spiritual head of the community. Wrote the *Mishneh Torah*—a code covering all halachic subjects discussed in the *Talmud, and *Guide for the Perplexed*, an exposition of Judaism's basic teachings, influenced by Aristotelian thought.

MAKKOT. (Stripes.) Fifth tractate of the *Mishnah, order *Nezikin* (damages), dealing with punishments administered by the court, false witnesses and cities of refuge.

MALACHI. (*c.* 450 B.C.E.) Proper name or 'my messenger'. Biblical prophet. Protested against laxity in ritual and social obligations, and prophesied the coming day of judgment.

MARCUS, JACOB RADER. (1896– .) American historian and Rabbi, teacher at the Hebrew Union College, Cincinnati.

MARRANO. Spanish word meaning 'swine': a term applied in Spain and Portugal to descendants of baptised Jews suspected of secret adherence to Judaism. The group became numerous after the 1391 massacres. The Inquisition was partly an attempt to search them out.

MARX, KARL HEINRICH. (1818–83.) Philosopher and economist, theorist of socialist and communist movements. His parents were Jewish but converted before his birth, and he was baptised at the age of six.

MAYBAUM, IGNAZ. (1897–1976.) Rabbi. Refugee from Nazis. First lecturer in Theology and Comparative Religion at the Leo Baeck College. Author of several books including *The Synagogue and Society*, *Trialogue between Jew, Christian and Muslim*, *The Face of God after Auschwitz*.

MECHILTA. Second-century halachic *Midrash organised around the Book of Exodus and attributed to Rabbi Ishmael.

MENDEL OF KOTZK, MENACHEM. (1787–1859.) Chasidic leader, opposed to nationalism. His slogan was 'truth', which involved abandonment of self, and Torah study.

MENDELSSOHN, MOSES. (1729–86.) Philosopher, writer of the Enlightenment. Born in Dessau, studied in Berlin. Tried to combine Judaism with modern cultural and scientific approach. Translated the Pentateuch into German. Friend of Lessing, whose *Nathan the Wise* is based on him.

MICAH. (Eighth century B.C.E.) Prophet in Judah, apparently from a peasant family, who spoke for the people against the ruling classes. Foresaw the destruction of the country, the exile to Babylon, but also the future restoration.

MICHTAM. Heading used for some of the Psalms. Possibly means an inscription on a stone slab.

MIDRASH. The finding of new meaning, in addition to the literal one, of Biblical texts. Sometimes midrash teaches law (*halachah*), at other times myths, legends, ethics, parables, etc. (*aggadah*).

MIDRASH RABBAH. A collection of midrashim on the Pentateuch and the five

Megillot (Scrolls). The books stem from different periods and differ among themselves in their general character.

MIDRASH TEHILLIM. A midrashic collection on the Psalms.

MISHNAH. Legal codification of the Oral Law, compiled by Rabbi Judah HaNasi, second century. It is divided into six orders—(*a*) *Zeraim* (Seeds) dealing primarily with agricultural laws, but also containing the rules of prayer; (*b*) *Moed* (Seasons) dealing with the Sabbath, Festivals, etc.; (*c*) *Nashim* (Women) dealing with marriage and divorce and vows; (*d*) *Nezikin* (Damages) dealing with civil and criminal legislation; (*e*) *Kodashim* (Holy things) dealing with the laws of slaughter, sacrifice, and consecrated objects; (*f*) *Taharot* (Purities) dealing with laws of ritual purity. Each order is then subdivided, forming a total of 63 tractates, which are then further treated in the *Gemara*. Mishnah and *Gemara* together make up the *Talmud.

MITZVAH. 'Commandment' or 'precept'. A legal or social obligation incumbent on all Jews. From this it acquires the more general meaning of 'good deed'.

MONTAGU, THE HON. LILY HELEN. (1873–1963.) Social reformer and a founder of the Liberal Jewish movement in England.

MONTEFIORE, CLAUDE GOLDSMID. (1858–1938.) Anglo-Jewish scholar, concerned with New Testament period, and a founder of the Liberal Jewish movement in England. With Herbert *Loewe produced *A Rabbinic Anthology*.

MOSES CHASID. Chasidic leader. d. 1927.

NACHMAN OF BRATZLAV. (1772–1811.) Chasidic Rabbi and ascetic. His parables and stories exalt the importance of the *zaddik* (lit: 'Righteous man', coming to mean charismatic leader).

NACHMAN OF KOSOV. (d. 1746.) An early chasidic leader who emphasised constant contemplation of God.

NAJARA, ISRAEL. (*c.* 1555–1625.) Hebrew poet born in Damascus, moved to Palestine. Frequently refers to Jewish suffering and redemption.

NIDDAH. Seventh tractate of the *Mishnah, order *Taharot* (Purities), dealing with ritual impurity.

NUMBERS. See *Torah.

NUMBERS RABBAH. See *Midrash Rabbah.

ORCHOT ZADDIKIM. (The Paths of the Righteous.) A book of morals. Fifteenth century.

PEAH. (Corner.) Second tractate of the *Mishnah, order *Zeraim* (seeds), dealing mainly with setting aside corners of fields for the poor, and general dues.

PELZ, WERNER and LOTTE. (Born *c.* 1920.) As Jewish refugee children settled in England. Concerned with Judaism, Bible and modern thought. Co-authors of *God is No More*, *True Deceivers*, etc.

PESIKTA D'RAV KAHANA. Collection of midrashic sermons for the holydays and special Sabbaths of the year. Probably fifth century.

PESIKTA RABBATI. Collection of midrashic sermons for the holydays and special Sabbaths of the year. Probably seventh century.

PHILO. (*c.* 20 B.C.E.–50 C.E.) Alexandrian philosopher who combined Judaism with Greek philosophy by using allegory.

PROVERBS. Late Biblical book, an example with *Ecclesiastes and Job of wisdom literature. Includes aphorisms, exhortations to seek wisdom, etc. Also includes *Eshet Chayil*, the praise of a good wife.

PSALMS. (Hebrew: *Tehillim*.) Biblical collection of 150 poems, some anonymous but many attributed to authors. From different periods, some may go

back to the time of King *David, to whom authorship of the collection is traditionally attributed. Some were probably recited by the congregation, others by individuals. There are thanksgiving psalms, songs of praise, songs in honour of kings, war songs, songs connected with festivals and individual events, etc.

RABA. Early post-talmudic authority. Gaon of Pumbedita (651).

RABINA, MENASHE. Contemporary Israeli composer.

RASHI. (RABBI SHLOMO YITZCHAKI.) (1040–1105). French scholar, whose commentaries on Bible and *Talmud are still indispensable.

RATHENAU, WALTER. (1867–1922.) Writer and statesman. Minister during the Weimar Republic. Assassinated by antisemites.

RAV. (ABBA ARIKA.) Leading Babylonian teacher, 3rd century. Known as Rav because he was the 'teacher' (rav) of the entire diaspora.

REINHART, HAROLD F. (1891–1968.) American Reform Rabbi. Senior Minister of the *West London Synagogue and founder Rabbi of Westminster Synagogue. Responsible for the Association of Synagogues of Great Britain and the Forms of Prayer (1931 ed.).

ROPSHITZER, NAPHTALI ZVI. (1760–1827.) Chasidic leader in Galicia. His teachings preserved in numerous folk tales and stories.

ROSENZWEIG, FRANZ. (1886–1929.) German philosopher, born of an assimilated family, who came close to converting to Christianity, but then rediscovered Judaism and spent the rest of his life in Jewish education. Translated large part of the Bible into German together with *Buber. His principal philosophic work is the Star of Redemption.

ROTH, LEON. (1896–1963.) Philosopher. Professor at the Hebrew University 1928–1953. Influential in starting and endowing the Leo Baeck College.

RUDIN, JACOB. (1902– .) U.S.A. Rabbi. Former president of the Central Conference of American Rabbis.

SALZBERGER, GEORG. (1882–1975.) German-born Rabbi, came to England as refugee in 1939. For many years served the New Liberal Synagogue in London.

SAMUEL, BOOK OF. The two volumes give a history of Israel from the settlement in Canaan to just before the death of King *David, where it connects with the Book of *Kings. Jewish tradition ascribes the major part of its composition to the prophet Samuel.

SANHEDRIN. Fourth tractate of the *Mishnah, order Nezikin (damages), dealing with courts of justice and judicial procedures, particularly criminal law and punishments.

SAYINGS OF THE FATHERS. (Pirkeh Avot.) Tractate of the *Mishnah with no talmudic commentary. Contains sayings of Rabbis and teachers from the third century B.C.E. to the third century C.E. It is read in Ashkenazi communities on Sabbath afternoons.

SCHECHTER, SOLOMON. (1847–1915.) Founder of Conservative Judaism, lecturer in Talmud at Cambridge, discoverer of a genizah (store) of ancient Hebrew literature in Egypt. President of the Jewish Theological Seminary in New York.

SCHNITZLER, ARTHUR. (1862–1931.) Austrian dramatist and novelist. Interested in psychology and antisemitism.

SCHOENBERG, ARNOLD. (1874–1951.) Composer, who was a protégé of Mahler. He returned to Judaism and wrote the opera Moses and Aaron, music to the psalms and a setting of Kol Nidre.

SEDER ELIYAHU RABBAH. (Tanna d'veh Eliyahu.) *Midrash in two parts, probably ninth-century Italy, but perhaps earlier.

SEFER CHASIDIM. (Book of the Pious.) Ethical teachings of the *Chasideh Ashkenaz*, a German mystical movement of the twelfth and early thirteenth centuries.

SELA. A term which occurs seventy-one times in psalms and may have indicated a pause or some other musical instruction.

SEMACHOT. (*Evel Rabbati*). 'Great mourning', euphemistically called 'Joyful occasions'. Minor tractate dealing with death, mourning customs. Included in the *Talmud, though it is late.

SHABBAT. First tractate of the *Mishnah, order *Moed* (seasons), dealing with the rules of the Sabbath and its observance, including thirty-nine categories of prohibited work.

SHALOM, SHIN. (SHALOM JOSEPH SHAPIRA.) (1904–   .) Hebrew poet and author, born in Poland but emigrated to Palestine.

SHEMA. Three Biblical passages (Deuteronomy 6: 4–9; 11: 13–21; Numbers 15: 37–41). The use of the first paragraph at least in services is very old. It is a recitation, not a prayer, and stands as the central declaration of Judaism.

SHEMER, NAOMI. (1933–   .) Contemporary Israeli composer.

SHEMINIT. Term used in the heading to some psalms, meaning literally 'on the eighth'. May have referred to an eight-stringed instrument or to an 'octave'.

SHMUEL HANAGID. (993–1055.) Vizier of Granada, statesman, chief of muslim army, leader of the Jewish community and a poet.

SHNEUR ZALMAN BEN BARUCH OF LADI. (1747–1813.) Founder of the Chabad movement in *chasidism, which stresses an intellectual approach. Chabad stands for <u>Ch</u>ochmah (wisdom), <u>B</u>inah (understanding), and <u>D</u>a'at (knowledge). Author of the *Tanya*, the foundation book of Chabad.

SHULCHAN ARUCH. (The Prepared Table) by Joseph Caro (1488–1575.) Spanish scholar and mystic. An authoritative code of Jewish law and practice. The *Kitzur Shulchan Aruch* is a simplified and much later edition.

SIFRA. (The Book.) Halachic midrash on Leviticus.

SIFRE. (The Books.) Midrash on Numbers and Deuteronomy, mainly halachic.

SILVER, ABBA HILLEL. (1893–1963.) U.S.A. Rabbi and Zionist. Books include *Where Judaism Differed*.

SIMEON BEN GAMLIEL. Second century. After hiding during the Bar Kochba revolt, set up an academy in Usha, Galilee.

SIMON BAR ISAAC. Eleventh century, Mayence (Mainz). One of the earliest German liturgical poets. Many of his *piyyutim* (poetic prayers) are in German and French prayer books.

SIMON, OSWALD J. (1855–1932.) English author, *Faith and Experience*.

SLONIMSKY, HENRY. (1884–1970.) Born in Russia. Professor of Ethics and Philosophy of Religion, and Dean at the Jewish Institute of Religion, New York.

SOLOMON. King of Israel. (Tenth century B.C.E.) Son of *David and Bathsheba.

SOLOVEITCHIK, JOSEPH DOW. (1903– .) Polish-born, U.S.A. Talmudic scholar and religious philosopher. Leader of enlightened orthodoxy.

SONG OF SONGS. A Biblical collection of love songs. From its language a late book, though attributed traditionally to King *Solomon.

SPERBER, SHMUEL. Czech Rabbi, refugee in England. Jewish educationalist.

SPINOZA, BARUCH. (1632–77.) Dutch philosopher from a *Marrano family. Excommunicated by the Sephardi community in 1656 for unorthodox religious views.

STEINBERG, MILTON. (1903–50.) American Conservative Rabbi. Books include *The Making of the Modern Jew.*

SUKKAH. Sixth tractate of the *Mishnah, order *Moed* (seasons), dealing with the festival of *Sukkot* (Tabernacles).

SYRKIN, NACHMAN. (1868–1924.) Zionist socialist leader, born Russia.

SZOLD, HENRIETTA. (1860–1945.) Zionist leader and organiser of Youth Aliyah.

TA'ANIT. (Fast). Ninth tractate of the *Mishnah, order *Moed* (seasons), dealing with special fasts, for example at a time of drought.

TALMUD. (Teaching.) Name applied to the *Mishnah with its *Gemara* (later commentary and supplement). Most of the tractates of the Mishnah have this commentary. Two versions of Talmud: one compiled in Palestine (the *Yerushalmi*) completed about 400 C.E. and the other in Babylon (the *Bavli*) completed between 100–300 years later.

TAMARET, AARON SAMUEL. (1869–1931.) Rabbi, writer and philosopher from Grodno. Early supporter of Zionism, but became disillusioned and led a pacifist group in the First World War.

TAMID. (Perpetual offering.) Ninth tractate of the *Mishnah, order *Kodashim* (holy things), dealing with the daily burnt offerings and the Temple organisation.

TANCHUMA. *Midrash ascribed to R. Tanchuma bar Abba and based upon the portions read from the Torah each week, usually upon the opening verse.

TCHERNIKOWSKY, SAUL. (1875–1943.) Hebrew poet, born in Russia but emigrated to Palestine in 1931. Reacted against diaspora Judaism, radical influence on modern Hebrew poetry.

TORAH. (Teaching.) Usually considered as Written Torah and Oral Torah. The Written Torah consists of the five books of Moses (the Pentateuch), and the Oral Torah the totality of Jewish tradition. The Pentateuch (*Chumash*) contains Genesis, Exodus, Leviticus, Numbers and Deuteronomy—which deal with the period from the creation of the world until the death of Moses, and include social and criminal legislation and details of the priestly functions and the Tabernacle.

TUWIM, JULJAN. (1894–1953.) Polish poet and satirist. Returned to Poland after the Second World War.

TZUR, MUKI. Israeli kibbutznik, contributor to *The Seventh Day*, conversations that followed the Six Day War.

UNION PRAYER BOOK. Prayer book of the American Reform movement.

WEIZMANN, CHAIM. (1874–1952.) Chemist, Zionist leader and first president of the State of Israel.

WEST LONDON SYNAGOGUE OF BRITISH JEWS. The first Reform synagogue in Britain, founded in 1840.

WIESEL, ELIE. (1928–   .) Writer. Born in Transylvania and interned in Auschwitz and Buchenwald. His books concentrate on Jewish themes, his wartime experiences and *Chasidism.

WISDOM OF SOLOMON. Post-biblical Apocryphal work in praise of wisdom and the wise. Originally written in Greek, possibly by an Alexandrian Jew. Date uncertain.

WOUK, HERMAN. (1915–   .) U.S.A. novelist and playwright. Orthodox Jew, author of *This is my God*.

YANCHIKER, RABBI NACHUM. *Musar* Rabbi. Head of Slobodka Yeshivah, Lithuania.

YEBAMOT. (Levirates). First tractate of the *Mishnah, order *Nashim* (women), dealing with status of childless widow.

YEDUTUN. The name of a Levitical choir-leader in the Solomonic period. The relationship between his name and the usage in the heading of some psalms is not clear.

YERUSHALMI. See *Talmud.

YIDDISH. A language derived principally from Middle High German and Hebrew, written in Hebrew characters. It assimilated elements from the various countries in which it was the *lingua franca* of the Jewish population, principally eastern Europe.

YIGDAL. A brief summary of the thirteen principles of the Jewish faith as expounded by *Maimonides. Believed to have been composed in the fourteenth century by Daniel b. Judah.

YOCHANAN BEN ZAKKAI. Rabbi. First century C.E. Pupil of Hillel and a leader of the Pharisees. During the rebellion against Rome (66–70) he was among the peace party and was conveyed by his pupils from Jerusalem in a coffin. He was allowed to open a teaching centre at Yavneh and this became the new heart of Judaism.

ZADDIK. Leader of a chasidic community.

ZEPHANIAH. (seventh century B.C.E.) Biblical prophet, member of a noble family. His prophecies concerned mainly the end of time.

ZIV, SIMCHAH ZISSEL (BROIDA). (1824–98.) A leader of the *Musar* (ethical social) movement in Lithuania and Russia. Founded schools; emphasized the need for self-improvement, humility and making allowance for others.

ZOHAR. (Brightness.) Main work of Spanish Kabbalah in four parts, mainly as a commentary on the Pentateuch and *Song of Songs, Ruth and *Lamentations. There were probably two authors. End of the thirteenth century.

ZUNZ, LEOPOLD. (1794–1886.) Founder of the 'scientific study of Judaism', which researched fundamental questions such as the history of liturgy, *midrash and the details of the lives of Jewish leaders.

NOTES ON USE OF THE PRAYER BOOK

SABBATH EVE

Within this service there are four selections of opening readings, of songs for the Sabbath and of psalms. They can be used for the four weeks of the Hebrew month.

SABBATH MORNING

There are six different introductory sections to this service, each with a general theme:

1. Tradition
2. Life and Death
3. The Future
4. The Just Society
5. The Community
6. The Family of Israel.

The thematic prayer, the song of praise, the responsive readings and the study passages can be replaced by other suitable material which may be found in the Anthology sections. Suggestions concerning some particular services will be found below.

The readings (pages 148–154) in the Torah service are numbered to correspond with the thematic introductions to the services.

NEW MOON AND THE MIDDLE DAYS OF FESTIVALS

Daily services: The prayer 'Our God and God of our fathers, . . .' (page 246) is included before the final blessing in the prayer 'Lord our God, . . .' in the daily Amidah.

After the Amidah the half *hallel* (Psalms 113, 114, 117, 118) (during Succot the full *hallel*) is included.

Sabbath services: The Amidah on pages 240–248 is substituted for that on pages 36–40 (evening), 142–148 (morning), 174–178 (afternoon). After the Amidah the half *hallel* (during Succot the full *hallel*) is included.

DAYS OF REPENTANCE

The Amidah (pages 240–248) is substituted. Rubrics indicate where the appropriate regular Amidah can be followed.

On the Sabbath of Repentance the introductory prayer (page 250) is substituted for the thematic reading.

PURIM

The prayer 'We thank You . . .' (page 264) is inserted after '. . . our hope in You' page 236.

After the Amidah the Scroll of Esther is read. The blessings are on page 264. For a closing song that on page 265 or one of those on pages 592–8 is used.

CHANUKAH

For the lighting of the *Chanukiah* see page 266.

The prayer 'We thank You . . .' (page 267) is inserted after '. . . our hope in You' page 236 (daily), page 40 (Sabbath eve), and page 146 (Sabbath morning).

On Sabbath eve Psalm 30 (page 442) is sung instead of Psalm 92 (page 30).

After the Amidah the *hallel*, pages 528–538 is inserted.

The *Maoz Tzur* (page 268) is sung either following the lighting of the *Chanukiah* or in place of the final hymn.

ISRAEL INDEPENDENCE DAY

The passages on pages 260–262 may be used.

On the Sabbath preceding, the service on page 128 is read.

The prayer on page 259 is substituted for that on page 128.

One of the study passages on pages 260–262 is used in place of those on pages 134 and 135.

Psalm 122 is substituted for the Song of Praise.

Before the Kaddish the Memorial prayer (page 263) is read.

MEMORIAL SERVICE FOR THE SIX MILLION

The prayer on page 256 is substituted for the opening prayer. One of the study passages on pages 256–258 is used. Before the Kaddish the Memorial prayer (page 258) is read.

ACKNOWLEDGEMENTS

The publishers are indebted to the following for their kind permission to reproduce copyright material in this book:

George Allen & Unwin Ltd. for an extract from *God and Man* by Leon Roth, and for extracts from *The Art of Loving* by Erich Fromm; W. H. Allen & Co. Ltd. for an extract from *This People Israel* by Rabbi Leo Baeck; Beacon Press for extracts from *The Judaic Tradition* edited by Nahum N. Glatzer; Behrman House Inc. for extracts from The Chain of Tradition series, *Jewish Law; Jewish Ethics, Philosophy and Mysticism*, © 1968 and 1969 respectively, by Louis Jacobs; and from *The Talmudic Anthology: Tales and Teaching of the Rabbis* edited by Louis J. Newman with Samuel Spitz, © 1945; Jonathan Cape Ltd. for an extract from *Illuminations* by Walter Benjamin, and from *This is My God* by Herman Wouk (now published by Collins); The Central Conference of American Rabbis for an extract from *The Union Prayer Book II*; Chappell & Co. Ltd. for the song *Yerushalayim shel Zahav* by Naomi Shemer; Collins Publishers for an extract from *True Deceivers* by Lotte and Werner Pelz; Crown Publishers, Inc. for extracts from *A Treasury of Jewish Poetry* edited by Nathan and Marynn Ausubel, © 1957 by Nathan and Marynn Ausubel; André Deutsch for an extract from *The Presidential Papers* by Norman Mailer, and from *The Seventh Day* edited by Henry Near and the Editorial Board; Doubleday & Company Inc. for an extract from *The Treasury of Jewish Humour* edited by N. Ausubel, © 1951; Rabbi Max Eichhorn for an extract from his book *Cain, Son of the Serpent*, © 1957; M. Emmanuel Eydoux for an extract from *La Tour de Feu*, No. 103, September 1969, translated by Rabbi J. Magonet; Rabbi Daniel Farhi for a prayer, translated by Rabbi J. Magonet; Farrar, Straus & Giroux, Inc. for an extract from *The Sabbath* by A. J. Heschel, © 1951; Philipp Feldheim Inc. for an extract from *Ahavas Chesed* by the Chofetz Chaim, and for an extract from *The Nineteen Letters of Ben Uziel* by Rabbi Samson Raphael Hirsch; Rabbi Albert Friedlander for an extract from the essay *Humanity and Apocalypse: Confronting the Holocaust*, Autumn 1972; Habonim for songs from *Shiron Habonim*; Harper's Magazine for an extract from *Why I Choose to be a Jew* by Arthur Cohen; Mr. Samuel Hertz for extracts from *The Authorised Daily Prayer Book* with commentary by the late Dr. J. H. Hertz; Rabbi Arthur Hertzberg for extracts from *The Zionist Reader*, and from *The Zionist Idea*; Hodder & Stoughton Ltd. for an extract from *Man's Search for Meaning* by Viktor Frankl; Holt, Rinehart & Winston for an extract from *The Gates of the Forest* by Elie Wiesel, translated by Frances Frenaye; Edmond Jabès for a poem printed in *European Judaism* 1972, 2, translated by Anthony Rudolf; The Jewish Agency for Israel for extracts from *The Quality of Faith* by S. H. Bergman; The Jewish National Fund, Youth and Education Department, for songs from *Shiron—a Book of Hebrew Songs*; The Jewish Publication Society of America for an extract from *Post-Biblical Hebrew Literature* edited by B. Halper, and for a song from *Selected Poems of Jehudah Halevi*; Mr. J. Sonntag for an extract from *Shtralendike Yidn*, 1946, by Jacob Glatstein, published in *The Jewish Quarterly*, vol. 9, no. 4, winter 1971/2,

625   ACKNOWLEDGEMENTS

translated by Mr. J. Sonntag; *Judaism* for an extract from an article by Aaron Samuel Tamaret, and an extract from a speech delivered by Rabbi Nachum Yanchiker; Dr. E. Littmann ל"ז for an extract from *Ways to Religious Education*; Macmillan London and Basingstoke for extracts from *The Reform Movement in Judaism* edited by D. Philipson; *The Bible for Home Reading part 1* by C. G. Montefiore; *A Rabbinic Anthology* edited by Montefiore and Loewe; Frederick Muller Ltd. for an extract from *My Crazy Life* by Bud Flanagan; The National Jewish Welfare Board for a song from *The Jewish Center Songster*; Oxford University Press for extracts from *A Book of Jewish Thoughts* selected and arranged by the Very Reverend J. H. Hertz; The Rabbinical Assembly and the United Synagogue of America for an extract and for songs from *The Sabbath and Festival Prayer Book*; The Rabbinical Council of America for an extract from an essay *The Lonely Man of Faith* by Rabbi Joseph B. Soloveitchik published in *Tradition*, edited by Rabbi Walter S. Wurzburger, vol. vii, no. 2, Summer 1965; Robinson & Watkins Books Ltd. for an extract from *The Way of Man* by Martin Buber; Routledge & Kegan Paul Ltd. for an extract from *Trialogue between Jew, Christian and Muslim*, © 1973, by Rabbi I. Maybaum ל"ז, for extracts from *Star of Redemption* by Franz Rosenzweig, and for an extract from *Judaism as Creed and Life* by the Revd. Morris Joseph; Russell & Volkening Inc. for an extract from *Basic Judaism* by Rabbi Milton Steinberg, © 1947; Schocken Books Inc. for extracts from the following: *The Essence of Judaism* by Leo Baeck, © 1948; *Ten Rungs: Hasidic Sayings* by Martin Buber, © 1947; *Language of Faith* by Nahum N. Glatzer, © 1947, 1967; *The Hasidic Anthology* by Louis I. Newman, © 1934 by Charles Scribner's Sons, © 1963 Schocken Books Inc.; *A Jewish Reader* edited by Nahum N. Glatzer, © 1946, 1961; *Hammer on the Rock: A Midrash Reader* edited by Nahum N. Glatzer, © 1948, 1962; *Aspects of Rabbinic Theology* by Solomon Schechter; Search Press Ltd. for extracts from *Springs of Jewish Wisdom*, © 1969; Martin Secker & Warburg Ltd. for extracts from *Parables and Paradoxes* and *The Country Doctor* by Franz Kafka; Taplinger Publishing Co. Inc. for extracts from *The Jewish Heritage Reader* by Rabbi Morris Adler, edited by Lily Edelman, © 1965 by B'nai B'rith Adult Jewish Education; Thames & Hudson Ltd. for extracts from *Tales of the Hasidim* by Martin Buber; Twayne Publishers, Inc. for an extract from *Reform Movements in Judaism* by J. R. Marcus; Union of American Hebrew Congregations for an extract from *Giants of Justice* by Rabbi Albert Vorspan; The University of Alabama Press for an extract from *Paganism, Christianity, Judaism* by Max Brod, © 1970; Vallentine, Mitchell & Co. Ltd. for extracts from: *Creation and Guilt* by Rabbi I. Maybaum ל"ז, London, © 1969; *Faith* by Rabbi L. Jacobs, London, © 1968; *The Diary of Anne Frank*, 1952; *God and Man in Judaism* by Rabbi Leo Baeck, 1958; Rabbi Herbert Weiner for an extract from *9½ Mystics* published by Holt, Rinehart & Winston Inc., and for an extract from Dr. Slonimsky's address on *Prayer*; Wilshire Book Company for extracts from *A Treasury of Comfort* by Rabbi Sidney Greenberg; World Union for Progressive Judaism for an extract from *The Growth of Reform Judaism* by W. Gunther Plaut, and for an extract from *The Problem of Evil* by G. Salzberger ל"ז; Thomas Yoseloff Ltd. for extracts from *The Treasury of Jewish Quotations* by Joseph L. Baron, and for extracts from *A Modern Treasury of Jewish Thoughts* edited by Rabbi F. Greenburgh.

ILLUSTRATIONS

W. H. Allen & Co. Ltd. for the illustration of the Synagogue in Pesht from *Jewish Art: An Illustrated History* edited by Cecil Roth; Rabbi Hillel Avidan for the drawings of the Hochschule für die Wissenschaft des Judentums, the Leo Baeck College and 'The Reader' from the Birds' Head Haggadah; Alexander Bogen for the drawing 'Little Girl with Doll'; Thomas Y. Crowell Co. Inc. for the illustrations of Synagogues in Berdychev, Berlin, Budweis, Leghorn, Nuremberg, Pesaro, Prague Altneuschul, Zolkiev and Wilkowiszki, Toledo, Warsaw, and Worms from *The Jewish Encyclopedia*, © Funk and Wagnalls Co. 1916; Deutscher Koordinierungsrat der Gesellschaften für Christlich-Jüdische Zusammenarbeit for the illustration of the Synagogue in Bamberg from *Die Juden in Bamberg* by Heide Friedrich-Brettinger; East and West Library for the illustration of the Synagogue in Fürth from *Glückel of Hameln* by Beth-Zion Abrahams; Zena Flax for the illustrations of Synagogues in Berlin and Florence; Hutchinson Publishing Group Ltd. for the illustration of the Synagogue in Nasielsk from *Jewish Art in European Synagogues* by George Loukomski; The Jewish Publication Society of America for the illustrations of Synagogues in Woerlitz, Dresden, and Berlin from *The Architecture of the European Synagogue* by Rachel Wischnitzer; Miss M. E. Koelman for the illustration of the Amsterdam Liberal Synagogue; Ktav Publishing House, Inc. for the illustrations of Synagogues in Berdychev, Berlin, Budweis, Leghorn, Nuremberg, Pesaro, Prague Altneuschul, Zolkiev and Wilkowiszki, Toledo, Warsaw, and Worms from *The Jewish Encyclopedia*; Middlesex New Synagogue for the drawing of its Synagogue; Orstadius Boktryckeri AB for the illustration of the Synagogue in Goteborg from *Goteborgs Mosaiska Forsamling 1780–1955*; Oxford University Press for the illustration of the Synagogue in Trani from *Legacy of Israel* edited by Bevan and Singer (original illustration supplied by the Gesellschaft zur Erforschung jüdischer Kunstdenkmäler); Dr. Hannah Peters for the illustration 'If I forget thee, O Jerusalem' by Ephraim Moses Lilien; Portugees-Israelietische Gemeente Te Amsterdam for the illustration of the Amsterdam Sephardi Synagogue from *Synagogen in Amsterdam* by J. F. van Agt, Staatsiotgeverok -'sGravenhage 1974. Rijksdienst voor de Monumentenzog; Mr. Alfred Rubens for the illustrations of Synagogues in Ukraine and Mannheim; Rabbi A. Soetendorp for the illustration of the Liberal Synagogue of The Hague, formerly The Hague Sephardi Synagogue; James Clarke & Co. Ltd. for the illustrations by Beatrice Hirschfeld from *Mediaeval Hebrew Minstrelsy* by Herbert Loewe, 1926; Brenda Rudolph for the drawing of the wooden case for a *Mezuzah*; Zena Flax for the drawings of St. George's Settlement and the Bradford Synagogue and Rabbi Dr. Albert H. Friedlander for the illustration of the Westminster Synagogue.

Whilst every effort has been made to trace copyright owners of the material used, the publishers take this opportunity of tendering apologies to any owners whose rights may have been unwittingly infringed.

Throughout the book the illustrations of synagogues and institutions of learning pay tribute to the past, present and future of communities which bear witness to the human aspirations of our prayers. Some of them commemorate simply a few of the myriad European communities tragically destroyed in the Holocaust. By including them we symbolise our aim to keep alive their traditions of piety, learning and faith.

———————

Space for recording family events has been provided before pages 256 and 276.

תם ונשלם שבח לאל בורא עולם